Medieval to Modern

EARLY MODERN EUROPE

Mark Konnert

OXFORD

UNIVERSITY PRESS

OXFORD
UNIVERSITY PRESS

Oxford University Press is a department of the University of Oxford.
It furthers the University's objective of excellence in research, scholarship,
and education by publishing worldwide. Oxford is a registered trade mark of
Oxford University Press in the UK and in certain other countries.

Published in Canada by
Oxford University Press
8 Sampson Mews, Suite 204,
Don Mills, Ontario M3C 0H5 Canada

www.oupcanada.com

Library and Archives Canada Cataloguing in Publication
Konnert, Mark, 1957–, author
Medieval to modern : early modern Europe / Mark Konnert.

Includes bibliographical references and index.
ISBN 978-0-19-901848-2 (paperback)

1. Renaissance—Textbooks. 2. Reformation—Europe—Textbooks.
3. Europe—History—1492–1648—Textbooks. 4. Europe—History—1648–
1789—Textbooks. 5. Textbooks. I. Title.

CB359.K66 2017   940.2   C2016-907310-6

Cover image:
David Teniers (II), 1610–1690
Peasant Kermis, c.1665
Oil on canvas, 75 x 106.5 cm
On loan from the City of Amsterdam (A. van der Hoop Bequest)
Rijksmuseum, Amsterdam

Oxford University Press is committed to our environment.
This book is printed on Forest Stewardship Council® certified paper
and comes from responsible sources.

MIX
Paper from
responsible sources
FSC
www.fsc.org   FSC® C014174

Printed and bound in the United States of America

1 2 3 4 — 20 19 18 17

Contents

2 ⁜ Europe in the Age of the Renaissance 48

3 ⁜ The Reformations 92

4 ∞ The Age of Religious War 136

7 ∞ Diplomacy and Warfare in the Age of Absolutism   265

8 ∞ Economy and Society Transformed: The Eighteenth Century   284

List of Maps, Figures, and Illustrations

Maps

Figures

Illustrations

Preface

A century ago, it was generally assumed that the history of Europe—and by extension the world, since European civilization and its offshoots were self-evidently paramount—was divided into three great phases: ancient (the Greeks and Romans); modern (from the Renaissance to the present); and the Middle Ages (the interval between the first two).[1] Over time, however, this grand tripartite scheme became increasingly untenable. For one thing, as European empires dissolved and other regions of the world became more prominent, historians came to understand that it took no account of the history of other civilizations. In fact, it was increasingly inadequate even for European history, as historians began to discover that the civilization of the Middle Ages was nothing like the barbaric wasteland imagined by the writers of the Renaissance.

At the same time it was becoming clear that our world is more different from the world of 1500 than that world was from the Middle Ages. In the last sixty years or so, therefore, historians have developed the concept of early modern Europe: a period that was neither fully medieval nor truly modern, in which the basic elements of medieval civilization were fading, but were still present. It is a central contention of this book that the crucial phase in the transformation from medieval to modern occurred around the middle of the seventeenth century, when certain key elements of medieval civilization had disappeared and the outlines of the new were beginning to form, although they would not become distinct for some time yet.

If one of the goals of history is to discover the origins of the present, then early modern Europe is a good place to look. Modern western civilization, in Europe, the Americas, and elsewhere, is in many ways the direct descendant of early modern Europe. Moreover, since modern western civilization has dominated the globe for roughly the last two centuries, its influence on other civilizations has been profound, if only in prompting them to react against it.

Many aspects of life today are legacies of early modern Europe, but three in particular will stand out in this book. These three elements of modern western civilization are so pervasive that we often forget they are products of history and assume they are simply natural, although this is certainly not the case. One of these legacies is the concept of the nation-state. Modern states are sovereign, meaning that they have no responsibility to any person or institution outside themselves, and within their boundaries inhabitants share a common identity, often defined by language and culture, and a common allegiance to an abstract entity called "the nation." Their governments possess a monopoly on the legitimate use of violence (enforcing laws, apprehending and punishing criminals), as well as the maintenance of armed forces to keep order and defend the state against foreign enemies. Not every state necessarily matches this description in every detail, of course, but in our world these features are considered normal, if not natural.

Yet this has not always been the case. For most of human history, allegiances were much more local: one was loyal to one's family, clan, tribe, village, or city. This was certainly the case in Europe at the point where this book begins. In the late Middle Ages, local communities taxed themselves, provided for their own defence, policed themselves, and had legal jurisdiction over their inhabitants in most matters. The royal government was a distant presence, and its agents were usually perceived as hostile outsiders whose primary purpose was to extract tax revenue, though on occasion they might provide justice when local arrangements proved inadequate. Some people *may* have felt a certain loyalty to a king or dynasty, but this was not the same thing as allegiance to a nation.

These circumstances changed over the course of the early modern centuries, as governments began to consolidate their control over their territories and subjects. The project did not proceed in a linear fashion, and it often encountered obstacles, but by the eighteenth century it had been largely accomplished. As for allegiance to a "nation," national feeling may not have been completely absent in the Middle Ages, but it tended to be episodic, prompted by "us-against-them" situations; there was no sense that national allegiance ought to go hand in hand with political units, or that a "nation" ought to consist of the inhabitants of a single territory governed by members of their own nationality. It was not until the French Revolution that nationalism began to emerge as a major force and the national state became the norm of political organization.

Accordingly, this book will pay a great deal of attention to politics and government. In some quarters this approach may seem old-fashioned, a throwback to the bad old days of narrative political history recounting the accomplishments of dead white males. However, any history of early modern Europe that does not address those subjects fails to recognize their importance for the world as we know it today. They are certainly not the only issues to be considered, but they are vital.

The second of the three major legacies of early modern Europe is the concept of the individual as the primary building block of society. For most societies in the past (and many even today) what was important was not the individual but the group—the family, the guild, the tribe, and so on. In these acutely status-conscious societies, the rights and duties of individual members depended on their rank in the pecking order. The idea that individual identities come first, and by extension that people have certain rights simply by virtue of their humanity, was unknown before the early modern period, and (as with the nation-state) its development was neither uniform nor linear. Women, of course, continued to be seen as inferior to men throughout the period. And as Europeans moved into the non-European world, they rarely accorded indigenous peoples the same rights as themselves. Nevertheless, despite its imperfect application and uneven progress, the recognition of the importance of the individual and his or (less frequently) her rights was a major legacy of early modern Europe.

The third major legacy is the modern notion of progress: the idea that things not only can get better with time, but that they usually do. With very few exceptions, most past societies (including Europe's) believed that time brought decay and corruption rather than improvement. The ideal life was virtually always assumed to be in the past, whether in the Garden of Eden before the fall or in a mythical golden age. Although a notion of progress towards the Last Judgment is central to Christianity, this has not usually translated into a belief that conditions on earth will improve as history progresses towards its ultimate goal. Even in the Renaissance—the period often seen as the beginning of the modern era—the greatest progress that could be imagined was to revive the glories of classical antiquity. It was really not until the "Scientific Revolution" of the sixteenth and seventeenth centuries that Europeans began to think that they could surpass the ancients, that progress in human knowledge of nature was possible, and that scientific knowledge could be deployed to increase human happiness.

These three elements of the modern world, of course, are not the only legacies of early modern Europe to be discussed in this book. Among the others are the changing nature of warfare and diplomacy, changes in religious belief and practice, the evolution of gender roles and perceptions of gender, the commercialization of agriculture, the beginnings of what we now call the Industrial Revolution, Europe's increasing awareness of the rest of the world, and its changing role in that world.

Not all parts of Europe receive equal attention in what follows. The focus will be on western Europe: France, Spain, Italy, the Low Countries, Great Britain, and the western parts of Germany. Although in part this focus reflects my own training and research as a historian, it also reflects the fact these were the dominant areas of Europe. When appropriate, however, we will look farther afield, to Scandinavia, central Europe (including Poland, Hungary, and Bohemia), Russia, and the Ottoman Empire.

To write any work of history is to walk several tightropes. One is between coherence and comprehensiveness: to give a meaningful account of the past, a great deal must be omitted. Historians must also find a balance between understanding the past on its own terms and drawing connections to the present: although we must be wary of imposing modern standards and values on the past, the study of history would have no contemporary relevance if we did not try to understand how the past led to the present. To look at history this way, of course, is not to see it as a "march of progress" whose main purpose was to produce us and our world.

There is also a tightrope to walk between narrative and analysis. Although academic history in recent decades has tended to favour longer-term structural analysis over mere "history of events" narrative, the past did take place in a temporal sequence, and certain facets of the past are best presented that way. Thus I have taken a narrative approach when it is best suited to the material: primarily in the areas of politics and warfare, and to a lesser extent in religion and intellectual life. Even here, however, analytical sections will be included where appropriate. Other aspects of the past that do not lend themselves so well to a narrative presentation, such as demographics, social history, and economics, will be presented in a mainly analytical framework. One of my goals is to tell a story, or rather a series of interconnected stories, that are as true to our understanding of the past as I can make them, but that also help us to understand ourselves and our world.

An integral part of historical analysis is historiography: that is, the study of how historians' interpretations of the past have changed over time. The chapters that follow will draw attention to a number of historiographical debates, but these are only a small sample of the rich variety of interpretations that the study of early modern Europe has produced.

Readers who are interested in pursuing these debates will find some suggestions for further reading at the end of each chapter.

Historians are both guided and limited by the sources available to them. In a work such as this, it is literally impossible to acknowledge all the primary sources that have contributed to our current knowledge of the past. Nevertheless, each chapter includes a few excerpts from primary sources. Some of these are well known, others less so, but the purpose in each case is the same: to point readers towards the sources that have contributed to our understanding of early modern Europe.

Throughout, I have been very conscious of walking the various tightropes mentioned above. If the balance sometimes seems off, I can only observe that no work of history can be all things to all people. As Jacob Burckhardt, the great historian of the Renaissance, wrote: "History is . . . the record of what one age finds worthy of note in another."[2] I make no claim to speak for "History"; however, this book is, among other things, the record of what I find most worthy of note in early modern Europe.

Notes

1. The adjective "medieval" to describe the Middle Ages is derived from the Latin *medium ævum* ("middle age").
2. Jacob Burckhardt, *Judgements on History and Historians*, trans. Harry Zohn (London: Allen and Unwin, 1958), p. 158.

Timeline

1566	Iconoclastic preaching in the Netherlands
1568	Revolt of the Moriscos in Granada
1571	Battle of Lepanto
1572	St. Bartholomew's Day Massacres in France
	"Sea Beggars" capture Brill and Flushing
1576	"Spanish Fury" in Antwerp
1579	Union of Utrecht
1581	Philip II deposed as ruler of 13 of the 17 provinces in the Netherlands
1584	William the Silent assassinated
1587	Mary Stuart beheaded
1588	Spanish Armada
1589	Henry III of France assassinated
1598	Edict of Nantes
1600	Foundation of English East India Company
1602	Foundation of Dutch East India Company (VOC)
1609	Kepler publishes *New Astronomy*
	Expulsion of the *moriscos* from Spain
1609–21	Twelve-year truce in the Netherlands
1610	Galileo publishes *The Starry Messenger*
	Henry IV of France assassinated
1618	Defenestration of Prague; Bohemian revolt begins Thirty Years War
1618–19	Synod of Dordt
1619	Kepler publishes *The Harmony of the World*
1620	Battle of White Mountain
1628	Fall of La Rochelle
1629	Edict of Restitution
1629–40	Personal rule of Charles I
1631	Treaty of Bärwalde
	Battle of Breitenfeld
1632	Galileo publishes *Dialogue Concerning the Two Chief World Systems*
	Death of Gustavus Adolphus
1633	Trial of Galileo
1634	Battle of Nördlingen
1637	Descartes publishes *Discourse on Method*
1638	Galileo publishes *Discourses on Two New Sciences*
1640	Long Parliament begins
	Revolts against Castilian rule in Catalonia and Portugal
1643	Battle of Rocroi
1648	Peace of Westphalia
1648–53	The Fronde
1649	Execution of Charles I
1651	Thomas Hobbes publishes *Leviathan*

1652–54	First Anglo–Dutch War
1658	Death of Oliver Cromwell
1659	Peace of the Pyrenees
1660	Restoration of the monarchy in England
1661	Personal reign of Louis XIV begins
1664	Foundation of French East India Company
1664–67	Second Anglo–Dutch War
1667–68	War of Devolution; Treaty of Aix-la-Chapelle
1672–78	Dutch War; Treaty of Nijmegen
1672	Death of de Witt; William III takes power in the Dutch Republic
1672–74	Third Anglo–Dutch War
1681	French seizure of Strasbourg
1683	Ottoman siege of Vienna
1685	Edict of Fontainebleau revokes Edict of Nantes
1687	Newton publishes *Principia*
1688–89	Glorious Revolution in England; accession of William and Mary
1688–97	War of the League of Augsburg (Nine Years War); Treaty of Ryswick
1689	John Locke publishes *Two Treatises of Civil Government*
1699	Treaty of Karlowitz
1700–21	Great Northern War
1700	Death of Charles II of Spain
	Battle of Narva
1701	Elector Frederick III of Brandenburg crowned "King in Prussia"
1702–13	War of the Spanish Succession; Peace of Utrecht
1709	Battle of Poltava
1713	*Unigenitus* condemns Jansenism
	Emperor Charles VI issues the Pragmatic Sanction
1718	Treaty of Passarowitz
1721	Treaty of Nystad
	Montesquieu publishes *Persian Letters*
1726	Jonathan Swift publishes *Gulliver's Travels*
1733	John Kay patents the flying shuttle
	Voltaire publishes *Philosophical Letters*
1733–38	War of the Polish Succession; Treaty of Vienna
1740	Frederick the Great seizes Silesia
1740–48	War of the Austrian Succession; Treaty of Aix-la-Chapelle
1748	Montesquieu publishes *The Spirit of the Laws*
1750	Rousseau publishes *A Discourse on the Moral Effects of the Arts and Sciences*
1751–72	Publication of the *Encylopaedia*
1754	Rousseau publishes *Discourse on the Origins of Inequality Among Men*
1756	"Diplomatic Revolution"

1756–63	Seven Years War; Treaty of Paris, Treaty of Hubertusburg
1759	Voltaire publishes *Candide*
1761	Rousseau publishes *Julie, or the New Heloïse*
1762	Rousseau publishes *Emile*
	Rousseau publishes *The Social Contract*
1763	Voltaire publishes *The Treatise on Toleration on the Occasion of the Death of Jean Calas*
1764	James Hargreaves patents the spinning jenny
	Beccaria publishes *On Crimes and Punishments*
1766–9	Bougainville circumnavigates the globe
1768–71	Cook's first voyage
1769	Richard Arkwright patents the water frame
1771	Maupeou dissolves the Parlements in France
1772	First partition of Poland
1772–75	Cook's second voyage
1773	Suppression of the Society of Jesus
	Pugachev's Rebellion in Russia
1776	Adam Smith publishes *The Wealth of Nations*
	Edward Gibbon publishes *The Decline and Fall of the Roman Empire*
	US Declaration of Independence
1776–79	Cook's third voyage
1779	Samuel Crompton invents the spinning mule
1783	Treaty of Paris recognizes US independence
1785	Edmund Cartwright patents the power loom
1785–89	Voyage of Lapérouse
1789	French Estates-General meet; beginning of the French Revolution
1793	Second partition of Poland
1795	Posthumous publication of Condorcet's *Sketch for a Historical Picture of the Progress of the Human Spirit*
	Third partition of Poland
1798	Thomas Malthus publishes *Essay on Population*
1799	Dutch East India Company dissolved

Introduction

Europe at the End of the Middle Ages

Historians are usually more interested in change than continuity, and the more dramatic the change, the more attention they pay to it. The traditional interpretation of the cultural movement known as the Renaissance and its role in European history fits this pattern well: a dramatic break with the medieval world and the beginning of modern European civilization. It cannot be denied that the Renaissance brought some important changes. Yet not all the changes associated with the transition from medieval to early modern period can be attributed to it, even if they coincided in time; when it came to change, the Renaissance was not the only show in town. Equally, if we focus only on the elements that were new and different, we run the risk of obscuring equally important aspects of European civilization that did not change perceptibly until the eighteenth century. Specifically, there was a great deal of continuity in demography, patterns of social life and structure, and economic life. Important changes were taking place beneath the surface, but they were incremental and in many cases became identifiable only in hindsight. First, though, this introduction will sketch the general outlines of the political, religious, and intellectual landscape within which they occurred.

Christendom

A distinguishing feature of the Middle Ages was the concept that all Christian Europeans were part of a single entity called Christendom. This entity had three dimensions: religious, political, and intellectual.

In religion, Christendom was united by the Church of Rome: that is, the western (Latin or Roman) part of the Christian tradition. Although this church and its eastern (Greek or Orthodox) counterpart had originally formed a single institution, contact between them diminished after the collapse of the western Roman Empire in the fifth century. In the ninth century, a theological dispute over the use of icons further distanced them, and the separation became official in 1054. In a sense, however, that schism was only an official acknowledgement of a division that in practice was already clearly established.

The political dimension of Christendom was more problematic. Since the fall of the Roman Empire, actual political power had been exercised at a very local level, within the framework that we have come to know as feudalism. Nevertheless, the idea that all of Christendom was essentially part of a single Empire proved remarkably durable, and various rulers throughout the Middle Ages sought to restore the imperial unity that was widely considered the "normal" state of affairs.

Finally, the cultural and intellectual unity of Christendom—at least among members of the elite—was provided by the Latin language and the intellectual heritage of classical Greco-Roman civilization, along with an approach to philosophical inquiry known as scholasticism.

Christianity and the Church

Throughout the Middle Ages, almost all the inhabitants of Christendom were by definition members of the institution that eventually became known as the Roman Catholic Church ("catholic" means "universal"). The only exceptions were scattered communities of Jews, who were treated with grudging toleration at best, and often faced outright hostility.

In the course of the Middle Ages, Christianity had become closely woven into the fabric of everyday life. The village church was both the physical and the symbolic centre of community life, its yearly cycle of rituals marking both the passage of the agricultural seasons and the milestones of an individual's life from cradle to grave. By the thirteenth century, seven rituals had achieved special status as "sacraments": vehicles or channels of the divine grace (God's unmerited favour towards humans) without which salvation was impossible. The first sacrament, baptism, initiated newborns into the Christian community, cleansing them of the "original sin" attached to all descendants of Adam and Eve. Confirmation marked the passage into adulthood, while marriage marked the formation of a new family and a three-way partnership between husband, wife, and God. For those who chose to serve God as monks or priests, however, marriage was replaced by the sacrament of ordination, which set them apart as members of a priestly caste with special status and powers. Finally, just before death, extreme unction (the "last rites") prepared the Christian to meet his or her God. Ideally, each of these sacraments would be performed only once in a person's life.

By contrast, the two remaining sacraments—confession (or penance) and Mass (also known as the Eucharist or Lord's Supper)—were repeated throughout life. Although baptism had cleansed them of original sin, people would continue to sin as long as they lived, and confession addressed this reality. Although it later became an intensely private practice, in the Middle Ages it was usually a communal rite that served as a way of regulating social relations and restoring communal harmony when it had been ruptured.

In the sacrament of Mass, the priest consecrated bread and wine and used them to commemorate the Last Supper of Christ and his disciples. By the thirteenth century, the Church had developed the view that the bread and wine were miraculously transformed into the body and blood of Christ by virtue of the special powers of the priest granted through the sacrament of holy orders. In this view, known as transubstantiation, the bread and wine maintained their outward appearance (their "accidents," in the language of medieval philosophy), but their inner essence (or "substance") was transformed. Although laypeople were expected to attend Mass weekly, they typically participated only once a year, usually at Easter.

Beyond those seven sacraments, religious festivals marked the passage of the seasons, and a host of rituals could be performed to ensure the fertility of fields (or marriages), to prevent plague, to bring rain (or stop it), and so on. These lesser celebrations and rituals probably played a much larger role in most people's lives than any of the sacraments did. In short, the village church was well adapted to a society made up largely of illiterate subsistence farmers.

As an institution, however, the Roman Church followed a different path, which led many at the upper levels of the organization to put worldly interests ahead of moral and spiritual concerns. After Christianity was made the official (and only legal) religion of the Roman Empire in the fourth century, the Church began to amass wealth and political power. Its leader, the bishop of Rome or pope (from the Latin for "father"), ruled a significant portion of central Italy, later known as the Papal States. Other leadership positions in the Church—cardinal, archbishop, bishop, even abbot, in many cases—conferred significant wealth and power, and over time they came to be occupied predominantly by members of the nobility. The Church became the largest single landowner in Europe, and as such collected a tax called the tithe, a tax on agricultural production that was paid in kind. As one might expect, the institution became an avenue for ambitious men to pursue their own ends, at the expense of its spiritual ideals.

These problems did not go unnoticed, especially in the monastic orders where the spiritual and moral elite of the Church were concentrated. By the later Middle Ages there were two types of monastic orders in western Europe. In the majority of orders, monks or nuns devoted their lives to worship, prayer, and contemplation, and lived communally in monasteries set apart from the secular world. The second type of order, which developed in part in response to the growth of urban populations, were the friars (from *fratre* or brother), who lived and worked among laypeople, preaching, hearing confessions, and caring for the sick and poor. Committed to communal as well as individual poverty, they lived not on the endowments of their monasteries, but by begging for alms, and therefore were also known as mendicants (from the Latin for "beggar"). The two main orders of friars were the Franciscans, founded by St. Francis of Assisi (1182–1226), and the Dominicans, founded by St. Dominic de Guzman (1170–1221).

Rigorous reform movements developed at French monasteries such as Cluny in the tenth century and Cîteaux in the twelfth, for example, both of which gave rise to influential leaders and theologians. The Cluniac reform movement inspired Pope Gregory VII (r. 1073–1085), one of the great reforming popes of the Middle Ages, and the Cistercian movement (from "Cîteaux") furnished St. Bernard of Clairvaux (1090–1153), one of the outstanding preachers, philosophers, and theologians of the medieval period. And in the sixteenth century an Augustinian monk, Martin Luther, would launch the Protestant Reformation.

By the later Middle Ages, changes were under way in the political world that would only intensify the papacy's involvement in secular affairs. The growth of powerful feudal monarchies (see below) posed a challenge to the pre-eminence claimed by the popes, and in the late thirteenth century King Philip IV of France (r. 1285–1314) and Pope Boniface VIII (r. 1294–1303) came into conflict over taxation of the Church's lands and wealth. When the pope refused to back down, Philip had him taken prisoner, and Boniface died shortly thereafter. His successor, Pope Clement V (r. 1305–14)—a Frenchman—relocated the papacy to Avignon (now part of France, but at the time a papal possession), where it would remain for the next seventy years, through the reigns of seven popes, all of them French.

In leaving Rome and the Papal States, the papacy and curia (its central bureaucracy) lost a major source of revenue. To make up for the loss, they not only found ways to exploit other sources more effectively, but devised new ones. For example, much greater use was made of "papal reservations and provisions": the right of the pope to overrule the choices of local priests or monks and decide who would occupy important positions. These positions were then sold to (frequently unqualified) candidates who wanted the wealth and power they conferred. In the process, although the papacy became much more efficient at finance and administration, the spiritual prestige of the institution was further diminished. In 1377 Pope Gregory XI (r. 1370–8) made the move back to Rome, but he died shortly thereafter, and his successor, the Italian Urban VI (r. 1378–89), quickly alienated a majority of cardinals with his high-handed ways. Accordingly, many cardinals left Rome, declared Urban's election invalid, and elected a new pope, a Frenchman who took the name Clement VII (r. 1378–94). Clement and his supporters then returned to Avignon, leaving Urban in Rome. The Great Schism would continue until 1414, at which point no fewer than three popes claimed to be the only rightful Bishop of Rome.

The schism was finally ended by the Council of Constance, which deposed two popes, dismissed the claim of the third, and elected a single successor. It also attempted a fundamental shift in Church governance, declaring that the ultimate power lay not with the pope but with the Church's General Council: in other words, that the Church was an aristocracy governed by its leading men, rather than a papal monarchy. The restored popes of the fifteenth century, however, strove mightily against this principle, known as conciliarism, and did not hesitate to bargain away the powers of the Church to secular rulers in return for their diplomatic support. By 1460 conciliarism had been condemned as heretical and papal supremacy restored.

Meanwhile, growing numbers of people were becoming aware of the Church's failings, and the evidence of corruption was not the only problem. For centuries, the vast majority of the faithful had been illiterate peasants, but by the late fifteenth century there was a substantial urban population of literate middle-class people who longed for a deeper spiritual engagement and were not satisfied by the limited, mediated experience offered by the Church. Their "immense appetite for the divine"[1] found expression in a wide variety of devotional practices.

Some critics came to reject the authority of the Church altogether. Among them was John Wycliffe (c. 1330–84), a theologian at Oxford University who anticipated the

Protestant reformers of the sixteenth century in rejecting its authority in favour of reliance on Scripture alone and was the driving force behind the first English translation of the Latin Bible. Although a number of Wycliffe's English followers, known as Lollards, were executed as heretics, the movement would survive into the sixteenth century.

Wycliffe's work inspired a similar movement on the continent, led by the Czech theologian and preacher Jan Hus (c. 1370–1415), but his followers, the Hussites, were much more numerous, and the movement assumed the proportions of Czech national movement against the German ruling class in Bohemia. Hus was burned at the stake during the Council of Constance, setting off a decades-long religious and nationalist rebellion in Bohemia.

By 1450, the Great Schism had ended and the Church's leaders had defeated the conciliarists. Yet their political triumph obscured the increasing fragility of their authority not only over movements such as the Lollards and Hussites, but also over the literate middle class. Meanwhile, secular rulers were steadily chipping away at the power of the Church in their territories.

Politics: Feudalism and Feudal Monarchy

FEUDALISM

Following the disintegration of the western Roman Empire in the fifth century, political power was exercised on a very local level. There were kings, but their power was circumscribed by that of regional and local strongmen or warlords. "Feudalism" is the general term applied to the varied arrangements used to regulate these power relations.[2] To secure the military support of the strongmen, kings granted them lands and certain powers, and over time the strongmen began to form alliances among themselves, much as modern criminal gangs and organizations do. Weaker individuals needing protection turned to the strongmen, who in return for their loyalty granted them assistance. This was the essence of feudalism: a contractual arrangement between two men in which the weaker (the vassal) swore loyalty to the stronger (the lord). The contract was sealed when the lord granted the vassal a fief: a piece of land that would give him the means to support his family and equip himself to fight for the lord. Feudalism thus represented a kind of privatization of the king's function as defender of the realm, in which the powers to raise an army and wage war were delegated to those who could actually exercise them. Similarly, feudal lords were empowered to enforce laws and administer justice on their lands.

Over time, networks of feudal relationships were established that stretched from the humble local squire through more powerful regional figures such as counts and barons, all the way up to the king. In theory, feudal political society was a pyramid whose component parts were connected in a vast web of reciprocal relations of hierarchy and obedience. In practice, however, feudalism was characterized by constant, often violent jostling for power and resources. Royal authority was largely a fiction, as some of the king's vassals actually surpassed him in their lands and power.

THE ENDURING IMPERIAL IDEAL

Although the political reality of the Roman Empire vanished in the fifth century, it lived on in the minds of rulers, and over the course of the Middle Ages was revived on several occasions. The first revival took place under Charlemagne (Charles the Great; 764–814), the king of the Franks in what is now northeastern France and northwestern Germany. He expanded his kingdom until it included all of western Europe except for the Iberian peninsula and the British Isles. So powerful did Charlemagne become that contemporaries believed he had restored the rule of Rome. Accordingly, on Christmas Day 800, he was crowned Roman Emperor by the pope.

After Charlemagne's death in 814, his empire began to disintegrate under the pressure of competition among his successors and invasion by the Norsemen or Vikings. By the tenth century, what had been a single empire under Charlemagne had split into two major sections: the kingdoms of the West Franks and the East Franks were the embryos of France and Germany respectively.

In the kingdom of the East Franks, Charlemagne's dynasty had died out by the early tenth century, but before long the imperial title was revived, and for several centuries, successive German Holy Roman Emperors laid claim to an imperial status that in theory elevated them above mere kings.[3] Although their "empire" stretched from Denmark south across the Alps to Tuscany, from Bohemia west to Burgundy and the Low Countries, their power diminished steadily through the Middle Ages as they dissipated the empire's resources in the effort to establish effective control over the semi-autonomous cities and princes of northern Italy, with no lasting success. In the late eleventh century, the emperor entered into a bitter and protracted conflict with the pope over control of important Church positions. That struggle ended around 1200 in the triumph of the papacy, which then pronounced itself the supreme authority not only over the Church, but over secular governments as well. Successive imperial dynasties failed to firmly establish a hereditary right to the imperial title, and although reigning emperors tried to have their successors confirmed during their lifetimes, elections were sometimes required. In such cases, rival candidates would seek to buy the votes of the electors (regional lords and princes) by promising them rewards such as judicial powers, and as a result the power of the emperors themselves was gradually reduced over the generations.

FEUDAL MONARCHY

Feudalism was an unwieldy and chaotic system, and beginning in the eleventh century, many rulers tried to tame it. The result was the development of what some historians have labelled feudal monarchy. Although the centripetal forces of feudalism were not eliminated, rulers became more effective at enforcing their authority. This transition was most evident in what had been the western part of Charlemagne's empire. In the tenth century, the king of France controlled only a small area around Paris, and was actually weaker than a number of his theoretical vassals. Yet by 1300 the king governed a far larger area and was the most powerful ruler in Europe. One factor in the French kings' favour was sheer genealogical luck. For two centuries, not one of them had died without an adult son to take his place; none of them were imbeciles or idiots (always a risk in a hereditary system); and they included several rulers of real genius. More deliberate policies also played a role, however. For example, kings and their officials were able to use royal powers of justice to reward friends and punish enemies, and to expand the royal domain (the area under the effective direct control of the king) through means including conquest, purchase, inheritance, and escheatment (reversion of land to the Crown when its holder died without heirs).

Rulers were also aided by an economic revival that began about the year 1000 and was characterized by an expansion of commerce and the growth of towns. Urban merchants and craftsmen wanted the stability and security of a strong royal government and were willing to pay for it through taxation. The kings of France thus had greater resources at their disposal than did their feudal rivals. By the thirteenth century, the kingdom of

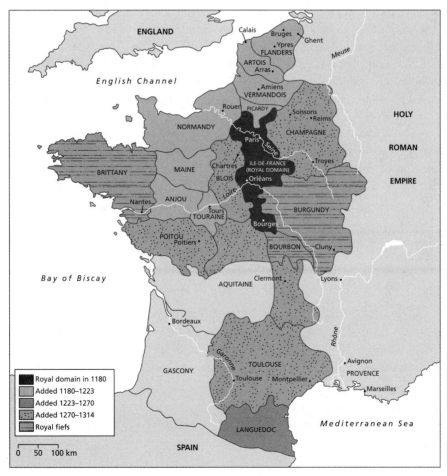

Map 0.1 The growth of the kingdom of France

France was both large and prosperous, and the royal government had gradually, if somewhat erratically, grown more powerful.

France provides the clearest example of the growth of strong feudal monarchy, but the same processes were at work elsewhere. In England, Roman rule had given way to an assortment of kingdoms established by Germanic invaders (among them Angles and Saxons—hence "Anglo-Saxon"), which by the ninth century were themselves under assault by Viking invaders. It was in the course of fighting off the latter that Alfred the Great (r. 871–899) and his successors united most of the territory we know as England. It was thus a single kingdom that Duke William of Normandy (himself the descendant of Viking settlers in northern France) conquered in 1066. William imposed feudalism on England and incorporated it into a dynastic state that spanned the Channel. His successors would add to their French possessions, so that in some ways it makes more sense to think of the medieval kings of England as continental rulers who also happened to rule England, than as English kings. This fact, and the complex feudal and dynastic ties between the ruling families of England and of France would in the fourteenth and fifteenth centuries produce the protracted conflict known to historians as the Hundred Years War (c. 1337–1453).

In the Iberian peninsula, the separate kingdoms of Castile, Aragon, and Portugal grew out of the *Reconquista*, the long process of recapturing the territory from the Moors: the Arab Muslims who in the early eighth century had conquered most of it, displacing the Visigoths who had taken it over in the fifth and sixth centuries. By 1264, Moorish holdings

Map 0.2 Spain in the Middle Ages

had been reduced to the kingdom of Granada in southeast corner of the peninsula. Over the course of the Middle Ages, the kings of Aragon incorporated the Balearic Islands into their territory, and by the fifteenth century they had also gained control of the southern Italian territories of Sicily and Naples, constituting an important commercial and maritime presence in the western Mediterranean. By 1250, the kings of Portugal had expelled the Moors and established the boundaries of modern Portugal. The spirit of the *Reconquista* lived on, however, as Portuguese sailors and soldiers carried the fight across the Straits of Gibraltar into Africa, and Castile remained in the forefront of efforts to expel the Moors, which would finally be completed in 1492 with the conquest of Granada.

Governance in northern and eastern Europe was generally less advanced and complex than in the west. In Scandinavia, the outlines of the modern states of Denmark, Sweden, and Norway began to emerge around 1000, when a number of warrior chieftains established themselves as kings and the people were converted to Christianity—another important element in the formation of monarchical states. For a long time, however, the power of these rulers was limited by their small populations, the strength of their nobles, and the fact that serfdom had never been imposed on the peasants, who remained freemen. The Union of Kalmar of 1397 brought the three kingdoms together under the Danish monarch, but in practice the regions retained a good deal of autonomy, and the union was fraught with tension. Denmark and Norway would remain united until 1814, but in the early sixteenth century the Swedish nobles broke away and chose one of their own as king of an independent Sweden.

In the west, as we have seen, the Roman Empire had disappeared in the fifth century, but it lived on in the east. Centred in Constantinople (modern Istanbul), it controlled not only Asia Minor (modern Turkey) and Greece, but parcels of territory in Italy, North Africa, and Spain. Although attempts were made to reconquer the lost western provinces, notably under Justinian (r. 527–565), over time the eastern Roman Empire lost touch with the west. This separation is reflected in the fact that historians often refer to the eastern section as the Byzantine Empire (from Byzantium—the ancient Greek name of Constantinople). Primarily Greek in language and culture, after Justinian (the last emperor to speak Latin as his native language) it became increasingly concerned with the threats posed by its neighbours to the east: the Sassanid Empire of Persia and, after the seventh century, the Muslim caliphate. Throughout the Middle Ages, the Empire waxed and waned (mostly the latter), but Constantinople remained one of the great cities of the world—densely populated, prosperous, and well-fortified against its enemies. Increasingly, east and west went their separate ways and the coherence of the Roman world was lost. In the fourteenth century, a new power arose in Asia Minor to threaten and eventually erase the last traces of the Byzantine Empire. This was the empire of the Ottoman Turks, who had originated in central Asia and took advantage of the weakness of both the Byzantine Empire and the Muslim caliphate to establish their rule over Asia Minor and most of southeastern Europe. Finally, in 1453 Ottoman armies overcame Constantinople's defences, bringing to an end the last vestiges of the Roman Empire.

Meanwhile, to the northeast, the Mongol invasions of the twelfth and thirteenth centuries had destroyed the medieval Russian state based in the city of Kiev. It was succeeded by a series of regional states under the thumb of the Mongol khans. One of these, the Grand Duchy of Muscovy, acquired pre-eminence in the fifteenth century, when Grand Duke Ivan III (r. 1462–1505) established the territory's independence from the Mongols and assumed the title of Tsar (derived from Caesar, or emperor). Nevertheless, for centuries Russia would remain isolated from the rest of Europe—religiously (it followed the eastern Orthodox version of Christianity), culturally, economically, and politically.

THE DISORDER OF THE LATER MIDDLE AGES

In the realm of politics, as in so much else, the later Middle Ages were a time of disorder and confusion. Feudalism had always entailed a moderate level of violence as the various players jostled for power, but the fourteenth and fifteenth centuries saw much of Europe engulfed in war. Originating in the complex feudal and dynastic relations between England and France, the conflict known as the Hundred Years War raged off and on from

Map 0.3 Europe in 1453

1337 to 1453. It was fought almost entirely in France, which suffered greatly: even when the fighting died down, large parts of the country were essentially lawless, the population terrorized by roving bands of criminals and soldiers who had deserted. After France finally expelled the English invaders, England became embroiled in a series of civil wars between rival factions of the royal family. Meanwhile, competition for the imperial crown was reflected in disputed elections and civil wars across the Holy Roman Empire.

This period of disorder had coincided with the Black Death, which devastated Europe from 1348 to 1350, and its aftermath. The peasants and workers who survived the plague should have benefited from increased demand for their labour, but landlords and employers used their political power to artificially inflate rents and control wages, and as a consequence the later fourteenth century was marked by peasant and urban revolts across Europe. Nevertheless, by the mid-1400s rulers began to reassert their control and the period of crisis receded.

Throughout this period, relatively large monarchies had been slowly consolidated out of earlier tribal or feudal entities in France, England, Castile, Aragon, Portugal, Poland, Muscovy (Russia), and the Scandinavian kingdoms. By contrast, in central Europe the Holy Roman Empire was becoming increasingly fragmented: Greece and the Balkans were under the control of the Ottomans; the Low Countries (the modern kingdoms of Belgium and the Netherlands), though technically part of the Holy Roman Empire, were an amalgam of wealthy autonomous territories and cities; and in Italy various regional rulers had taken advantage of the conflicts between pope and emperor to establish de facto independence from both. Indeed, self-governing city-states such as Florence, Milan, and Venice in many ways constituted a different political and social universe from the rest of Europe, one that is essential to understanding the Renaissance.

Culture and Intellectual Life

The cultural and intellectual life of the Middle Ages was heavily influenced by the Church. For several centuries following the collapse of the Roman Empire, the Church was virtually the only institution with the interest and ability to preserve learning and literature, and its clergy were virtually the only literate people. This began to change around the year 1000, with the growth of an urban middle class and a more complex society that required trained professionals—as did royal governments. The schools that had survived the previous centuries of disorder, almost all of them attached to cathedrals or monasteries and intended to train future priests and monks, began to expand, and new ones were established. Over time, a handful of these schools—in Paris, Oxford, Salerno, and Bologna—came to be known for the breadth and depth of their scholarship; these were the first universities. The university curriculum was based on the seven liberal arts of the later Roman Empire: grammar, rhetoric (basically the study of Latin language and literature), dialectic or logic (the rules governing inquiry and argumentation), arithmetic, geometry, astronomy, and music.

Another very important development was the rediscovery of crucial ancient texts that had been lost, among them the works of Aristotle. Until this point, medieval scholars had known the name Aristotle, and even a little about his thought, based on other writers' commentaries, but they had no first-hand knowledge of his work. This began to change, as did so much else, around the year 1000. Aristotle's works were actively sought out, and became available once again from a variety of sources.

In Aristotle medieval scholars discovered works of great subtlety and complexity, far more advanced and difficult than anything they had inherited from either the Romans or earlier medieval scholars. They were especially taken with Aristotelean dialectic or logic, which soon became the foundations of the standard undergraduate education.

Nevertheless, the fact that Aristotle was a pagan meant that Christian scholars had to undertake the difficult project of reconciling his work with Christianity. In their efforts, medieval scholars benefited from the work of Muslim scholars who had faced similar problems in reconciling pagan Greek philosophy with monotheistic Islam, primarily Avicenna (Ibn Sina, 980–1037) and Averroës (Ibn Rushd, 1126–1198).

The method they developed for this purpose, following Aristotle's own logical procedures, was called scholasticism, from the Latin *schola* (school): that is, the method employed in the "schools" or universities. Scholasticism was not so much a philosophy or body of thought as it was a way of approaching problems. It was based on the logical procedure known as a syllogism, in which you use something you already know to discover something you wish to know. For example, if A=B, and B=C; therefore, A=C; or (to use a classic example) Socrates is a man; all men are mortal; therefore, Socrates is mortal. This way of thinking put a premium on precise definitions and careful delineation of terms, since a small error at the beginning of a long chain of syllogisms could result in drastic error by the end. It also allowed no room for independent thought, but attributed the highest value to authorities such as Scripture, a Church Father such as St. Augustine, or Aristotle himself. Thus to prove your point, you would find an appropriate proposition in one of these sources and cite it as if it were true in all times and circumstances, without regard for historical or cultural context—let alone the author's intentions or audience. As we will see in Chapter 2, humanist thinkers would bring greater historical and cultural awareness to these ancient works. Although Latin remained the language of the universities and serious literature, as well as of the Church and governments, vernacular languages and literatures developed significantly in the later Middle Ages. Among the first great vernacular works was Dante's *Divine Comedy*, completed around 1320, which helped to cement his Tuscan dialect as the root of modern Italian. Although many or even most early vernacular works were religious in nature (lives of saints, devotional works, and so on), they included a growing variety of adventure tales, romances, and satires. The main audience for this literature was not the clergy, the nobility, or the intelligentsia, but the urban bourgeoisie: merchants, artisans, and professionals such as lawyers, notaries, and civil servants.

THE PRINTING PRESS

The growth in demand for vernacular literature was among the factors that led to the most important contribution to cultural and intellectual life in the later Middle Ages: the development of movable type and the printing press. Before these technological innovations, books were rare and precious, produced on demand for a particular monastery, nobleman,

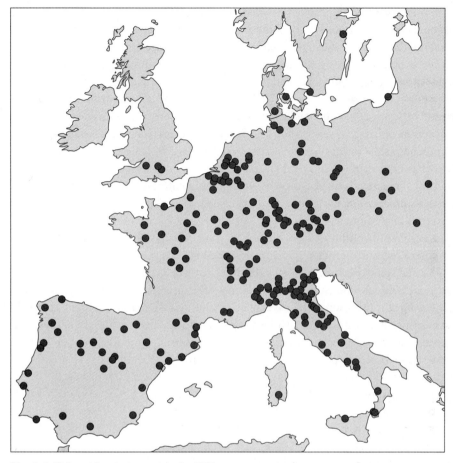

Map 0.4 Cities with printing presses by 1500

or scholar. Similar processes had already been developed in Asia, but in the 1450s a group of craftsmen in the German city of Mainz developed the technology of movable type, in which letters stamped on metal dies could be rearranged to print any text on two sides of a page. Johannes Gutenberg (c. 1397–1468) was clearly one of the central figures in these developments, but he was not the sole "inventor" of the printing press.

By 1500, some two hundred presses were in operation across Europe, not only in Germany, but in Italy, Switzerland, France, England, Spain, Poland, and Hungary, and approximately 40,000 titles had been printed, amounting to between eight and ten million copies.

Almost as important as the technology of printing itself was the availability of an inexpensive medium on which to print. Most medieval manuscripts were written on parchment (sheepskin) or vellum (calfskin), both of which were quite costly: to produce enough skin for one Bible would require roughly 30 calves or 170 sheep. Paper, originally made from cloth rags, was a Chinese invention in general use there by the second century. It spread to the Arab Middle East and from there to Italy, where it was first used around 1300. Printing a Bible on paper cost about one-sixth as much as printing it on parchment.

The printing revolution both responded to changing circumstances and helped to bring about further change. Although only a small minority of people were literate, the growing middle class represented a vital market, without which printing would not have been a viable business. Even those who were illiterate benefited from the new technology, since books were often read aloud, and many came with extensive illustrations.

The first work printed was the Bible, and religious works remained the single most important category of printed books: lives of the saints, devotional works, sermons, and biblical commentaries. However, a huge market for other sorts of material soon developed: works of scholarship, including the classics of ancient civilization, as well as practical volumes such as travel guides for merchants, almanacs, cookbooks, and technical manuals. In addition, there proved to be a huge market for commentaries on current events, as well as stories of romance and adventure, often published in very cheap and (unfortunately for historians) flimsy editions.

The advent of printing was a media revolution at least as far-reaching as the advent of computers and the internet in our time. It made knowledge much more affordable and accessible, and standardized information in a way never before possible. At the same time, it created a brand new industry and new sources of wealth, not only for the printers and publishers, but for their suppliers: papermakers, cloth workers, miners, and refiners. In the sixteenth century, Protestant religious reformers would make widespread use of the press to advance their cause; indeed, it is probably not too much to say that the press made the Protestant Reformation possible.

Conclusion

By the later Middle Ages, the various facets of Christendom were still present, but under increasing challenge from various quarters. Imperial political unity still existed as an ideal, but had never been further from reality. The Church continued to act as the intermediary between people and their God, but its leaders appeared to be more interested in shoring up their political power and wealth than in realizing Christianity's spiritual ideals. At the same time, the world around the Church was changing, and new realities were challenging a religious system designed for illiterate peasants. Finally, although scholasticism still dominated intellectual life, and questions of philosophy and theology were heatedly debated, the value of those debates was increasingly questioned. This system too would face serious challenges in the early modern period, first in Renaissance humanism and then in new approaches to the study of nature.

Further Reading

Eisenstein, Elizabeth. *The Printing Press as an Agent of Change: Communications and Cultural Transformations in Early Modern Europe*. Cambridge: Cambridge University Press, 1980. Still the single most important study of the impact of printing.

Hay, Denys. *Europe in the Fourteenth and Fifteenth Centuries*, 2nd ed. London: Longman, 1989. A useful survey of the later Middle Ages, by a leading historian of the period.

Ozment, Steven. *The Age of Reform, 1250–1550: An Intellectual and Religious History of Late Medieval and Reformation Europe*. New Haven: Yale University Press, 1980. A wide-ranging and relatively positive assessment of late medieval thought, emphasizing the roots of the Protestant Reformation.

Rosenwein, Barbara H. *A Short History of the Middle Ages*, 2nd ed. Peterborough, ON: Broadview Press, 2004. An accessible survey, especially strong on culture and the arts.

Notes

1. The phrase comes from Lucien Febvre, "Une question mal posée: les origines de la Réforme française et le problème générale des causes de la Réforme," *Revue historique*, vol. 1, no. 1 (1929), p. 39.
2. It must be stressed that since feudalism was essentially a local response to local conditions, it varied widely with time and place. What follows is a greatly simplified overview.
3. Although the term "Holy Roman Empire" did not come into general use until the thirteenth century, I will use it here for the sake of simplicity.

1

Continuities in Society and Economy

In recent decades many historians have turned their attention away from the history of events (*histoire événementielle*) towards the more slowly changing structures of environment, economy, and society (the *longue durée*). This chapter will examine areas of life in which change came over generations or centuries rather than days and years. In these areas the continuities with the Middle Ages were very strong. In addition to population and demography, including typical patterns of birth, marriage, and death, we will look at economic life, social structure and relations, and the roles and status of women, as well as one of the most striking phenomena in early modern Europe: the great wave of witch hunts.

Population and Demography

Between 1348 and 1350, the plague known as the Black Death killed up to half of Europe's population; however, this staggering total obscures regional variation. In general, mortality was highest in the crowded and dirty cities, especially the Mediterranean seaports of France and Italy where the plague struck first. The countryside suffered later and less, especially in Scandinavia and northeastern Europe, and some isolated areas managed to avoid it altogether. Nevertheless, the Black Death had significant repercussions across European societies and economies for centuries afterwards.

Following the Black Death, the overall European population remained at a relatively depressed level for several generations.[1] From a pre-plague high of perhaps 80 million people, it declined to somewhere around 40 million. But a powerful demographic revival began to take shape in the mid-fifteenth century, and by about 1600 Europe as a whole had recovered its pre-plague population, although some areas would take another three centuries to recover fully. Thereafter, overall population numbers remained relatively stagnant, albeit with significant regional variations, until the mid-1700s, when they began to expand at an unprecedented rate. The causes and consequences of this demographic revolution will be discussed in Chapter 8.

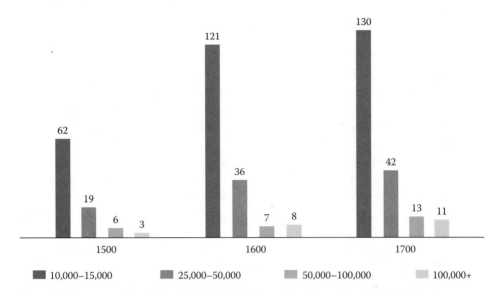

Figure 1.1 European urbanization 1500–1700: Number of European cities of different sizes

Source: Data compiled from Jan de Vries, *European Urbanization, 1500–1800* (Cambridge Mass: Harvard University Press, 1984), pp. 269–7.

While the population of England and Wales grew from about 2 million to almost 6 million between 1500 and 1750, France hovered between 18 and 20 million. The Holy Roman Empire lost approximately one-third of its 20 million people as a result of the Thirty Years War (1618–48) and would not recover until the nineteenth century. Meanwhile, Italy lost 15 per cent of its population between 1600 and 1750, and Spain 25 per cent.

The vast majority of people in early modern Europe lived in rural villages of several dozen to, in rare cases, a thousand people. Large cities were few: in 1500 only Paris, Naples, Milan, and Venice had more than 100,000 inhabitants. However, cities grew at a rate disproportionate to the overall population, especially the largest ones. By 1600 Antwerp, Seville, Rome, Lisbon, Palermo, and Amsterdam had also exceeded 100,000 mark. Naples, Paris, and London had over 200,000 residents by then, and a century later these three had exceeded 500,000. By 1700 Madrid, Vienna, and Moscow had also grown to more than 100,000.

Several regions had significant concentrations of large and mid-sized cities. Most notable was northern Italy, which in addition to the urban giants of Milan and Venice had such important cities as Florence, Genoa, and Bologna. In the Low Countries, Brussels, Antwerp, Ghent, and Bruges were also of significant size, although outside these centres, which had been the heartland of the medieval woollen industry, the size of cities dropped off quite rapidly. In 1700, when Paris had more than half a million people, the next largest cities in France were Rouen and Lyon, with only 60 to 70 thousand people each. The discrepancy was even more striking in England: whereas London had reached half a million before the rapid urbanization associated with the Industrial Revolution, Bristol—the second largest city—had only 20,000 inhabitants.

Birth, Marriage, and Death

FAMILY FORMATION

The demographic order that developed in the wake of the Black Death would remain in place at least until the eighteenth century. Contrary to the pattern in most pre-modern societies (and to popular misconceptions), early modern Europeans did not generally marry very young, nor did they live in extended households. In most of western Europe, the average age of first marriage was not dramatically different from what it is today: 25 or 26 for women and a few years older for men. In addition, most households consisted of nuclear families: mother, father, and children. These two phenomena—late age of marriage and nuclear households—were closely linked. Because most young couples had to save for several years before they could establish their own households, marriage was generally postponed for a decade or more past the age of physical and sexual maturity.

There were exceptions to this general pattern, of course. Among the wealthy elite, marriages were generally arranged by parents for social and economic benefit, and since there was no need to save in order to establish a new household, age at marriage could be quite low. Among the vast majority without wealth to manage, parental consent was not formally necessary, although it was usually sought. Even among ordinary peasant and working families, marriage was a more calculated matter than it is today. Economic security and social prestige were the primary considerations in choosing a spouse. As long as the young people were compatible, it was assumed that love would develop over time.

The exceptions to these patterns were parts of southern and eastern Europe. Here extended households made up of two or more married couples were more common. So was marriage between teenagers, or between older men and much younger women. Even in areas where the nuclear family was the general rule, the composition of a household tended to vary over time. To a much greater extent than today, widowed or elderly parents would move in with an adult child (usually the oldest son). Sometimes these arrangements were spelled out in contracts obliging the child to provide the parent with a living space and a stipulated amount of commodities such as firewood and wine. At any given time, therefore, a majority of households would be nuclear, but any given household might be multigenerational at various stages.

Perhaps 15 per cent of people in early modern Europe never married at all. Before the Protestant Reformation of the sixteenth century, most of these people were members of religious communities. Although this pattern would continue in Catholic areas, in Protestant lands the closure of monastic institutions denied these opportunities to the unmarried. The evidence is sparse and difficult to interpret, but it seems likely that the proportion of people who never married remained relatively constant until the late eighteenth century, when it began to increase.

Birth rates in early modern Europe remained fairly constant: for every thousand people, about 35 babies were born each year. This rate is about the natural maximum, and the developing countries where it prevails today are experiencing population explosions. In early modern Europe, however, population growth was limited by two major factors.

One was the relatively late age of marriage, which restricted women's child-bearing years. The other was an extremely high rate of infant mortality. The fact that approximately 50 per cent of children would die before reaching puberty meant that average life expectancy was very low. On the other hand, among those who survived childhood, lifespans of 65 or 70 years were not uncommon.

Once married, a woman would typically become pregnant no more than once every two years. Artificial contraception was rare or unknown, although various writers referred obliquely to various ways of preventing or terminating a pregnancy. It is likely that abstinence, careful timing, and *coitus interruptus* were the primary means of birth control. When these practices failed, the unwanted infants were sometimes abandoned, either to the elements, which meant certain death, or on the steps of a church or hospital, where death was only marginally less certain. Such cases were rare, however.

Most abandoned infants were probably born outside marriage. Yet until the eighteenth century, illegitimate births likely accounted for no more than 5 per cent of the total. Although premarital sex appears to have been fairly common (understandably, in a time of relatively late marriage), most of the couples involved likely intended to marry in any case: if a pregnancy resulted, the wedding date would simply have been moved up.

Childbirth was a dangerous business for both mother and infant. Between 6 and 7 per cent of births would result in the mother's death, often from puerperal fever contracted during the birth through the use of unwashed hands and instruments. Among ordinary people, childbirth was usually attended by a midwife who was also often the village healer or "wise woman." Although the wealthy could call on university-trained physicians, there was no appreciable decrease in mortality, as they knew no more than midwives did about the role of germs in infection.

If all went well, a woman who married at twenty-four could expect to become pregnant every two years until about the age of forty (menopause came earlier in the past). Assuming that some of her pregnancies would end in miscarriage or stillbirth, she would bear six or seven children, of whom three or four might survive beyond puberty. Thus even though the average family was larger than it is in industrial societies today, the difference was not dramatic.

These demographic factors had a direct influence on family life. Given the late age of marriage and lower life expectancy for both men and women, living grandparents were rarer than today, and widows and widowers were much more common. Remarriage was common, especially among men whose wives had died in childbirth. As a result, what we call blended families were very common, with all the conflict and tension that such situations can entail. The cruel stepmothers and wicked stepsisters who are stock figures in fairy tales were firmly rooted in social reality.

In his book *Centuries of Childhood* (1963), the French historian Philippe Ariès argued that the modern understanding of childhood as a time of careful nurture is a relatively recent development: in medieval Europe, children were seen as miniature adults and were often treated callously. In his view, the rate of child mortality was too high for parents to invest themselves emotionally in their offspring.

Ariès was the first to grapple with childhood as a serious historical issue. Nevertheless, most historians would now disagree with his thesis. No doubt some children did suffer neglect and abuse, but the same is true today. This does not mean that the majority of parents did not care deeply for their children and feel acute grief at their loss. Even the act of abandoning a child can be seen as evidence of parental love, and many parents attempted to reclaim abandoned children once their fortunes had improved. This note was pinned to an abandoned child in the French city of Rouen in 1789:

> I was born today, January 7, of a legal marriage. My father and mother are suffering extreme poverty and do not have it in their power to have me christened or to render me the services my tender youth requires them to give me. It is only with the most mortifying distress and acute sorrow that they abandon me.[2]

It may be that expressions of love and concern for children took different forms in the past than they do today. Before the eighteenth century, when Rousseau argued that children are born innocent and corrupted by society, corporal punishment was seen as essential, to teach the child the humility and obedience commanded by God: as the Bible said, "He who spareth the rod, hateth the child." Infants were tightly swaddled to keep them safe while their mothers were busy with older children or household chores. While formal education did become more common in the early modern period, most children were expected to work by the age of seven or so: for most families, daily life allowed very little leisure. Typically, the tasks given to children were appropriate to their age and strength: tending animals or sweeping floors, for instance. There is little evidence in the early modern period of the systematic economic exploitation of children that would characterize the Industrial Revolution and that still occurs today in the sweatshops of some developing countries.

Early modern society did not share the current idea that adolescents should be encouraged to explore their identities and question existing norms. Nevertheless, they did make allowances for the stage of life between childhood and full maturity. It was recognized that "youths," especially males, could be disorderly and rambunctious, and that a certain amount of mischief had to be tolerated, especially given the decade or more that separated sexual maturity and marriage. Young males were frequently organized in quasi-official gangs or clubs sometimes known as "abbeys of misrule." These groups often played a prominent role in Carnival festivities, in which role reversal, "the world turned upside down," was a major theme. They would often take the lead in the public humiliation of cuckolded husbands, men who were beaten by their wives, or older men who married much younger women, serenading them with raucous music, chants, and taunts. This custom, known in France as *charivari*, in Germany as *Katzenmusik*, and in England as "rough music," at once allowed young men to blow off steam and helped to reinforce communal norms by shaming those who deviated from them. Gangs of youths who roamed the streets drinking, carousing, and brawling were usually tolerated, within limits, the authorities recognizing with Aristotle that youths "are heated by Nature as drunken men are by wine." Most towns also accepted the existence of brothels, believing that they pro-tected "respectable" women from the unwanted attention of young men; in fact, many brothels were officially sponsored and run by the town, although this practice vanished with the advent of stricter moral codes during the Protestant and Catholic Reformations of the sixteenth century.

Our knowledge of same-sex relationships in early modern Europe is limited, as it is only in recent decades that historians have begun to explore the subject. The term "homo-sexuality" was not coined until 1868, and "sex" itself was not used in English before about 1800. Same-sex relations between males were understood in terms of a specific activity ("sodomy") rather than a sexual orientation or identity. There were severe punishments for sodomy, but the laws forbidding it were not uniformly enforced, at least in cases involv-ing members of the elite. Many same-sex relationships involved people who were socially unequal: older men and younger ones, or masters and servants—and did not preclude heterosexual relationships with wives or mistresses. In other words, although sodomy was not uncommon, the fact that some men were attracted exclusively to other men was not recognized before about 1700. It was only in the century that followed, as homosexual sub-cultures began to develop in larger cities such as Paris and London, that a "homosexual" orientation came to be understood as an identity.

Same-sex relations between women attracted less attention from authorities, as sodomy was generally thought to require penile penetration. When lesbian relationships did draw censure, it was directed not so much to the homosexual nature of the relationship as to the usurpation of male roles, whether through cross dressing or the use of dildos.

MORTALITY

Famine

The three principal causes of mortality were famine, disease, and war. Even in "normal" times, the vast majority of people in early modern Europe lived hand-to-mouth. The single most important determinant of human welfare was the harvest, and its bounty depended almost entirely on the weather. In a good year, just one hailstorm at the wrong time could ruin a crop. A cool, wet summer would result in widespread famine, and two or more in succession meant calamity. There is evidence of cooler and wetter conditions in the late sixteenth century—a "little ice age"—and there were several sustained periods of bad weather and poor harvests in many areas, most notably in the 1590s, 1620s, 1660s, and 1690s. The fact that this period of decreased agricultural fertility coincided with the popu-lation's recovery from the demographic catastrophes of the later Middle Ages only exacer-bated the resulting famines. In some cases, a neighbouring region might have provided relief for a localized famine, but primitive infrastructure made it prohibitively expensive to transport large quantities of grain any distance, and on the continent the movement of commodities was further hampered by complicated systems of tolls and duties.

It was taken for granted that for most people hunger was a basic fact of life, and that the poor would bear the brunt of famine. A report from Rome in 1558 made the point matter-of-factly: "Nothing new here, except that people are dying of hunger."[3] Although one might think that the people who grew the grain would have been slightly better off than the urban poor, this was not the case. At least in most cities there were stockpiles of grain that could be used in times of need, charitable institutions such as hospitals and monasteries, and wealthy people to beg or steal from. Rural people had none of these resources, and as a consequence were more likely to starve than their counterparts in the cities.

Disease

The most dramatic instance of epidemic disease and death in the early modern period was undoubtedly the Black Death of 1348–50. Originating in central Asia, the disease is thought to have entered Europe in the Crimea, been carried from there to the

VOICES

The Impact of War on Civilians

The Thirty Years War was the most destructive of all European conflicts prior to the twentieth century (see Chapter 4). In 1631, after a months-long siege, the wealthy Lutheran city of Magdeburg in north-central Germany was conquered by the army of the Catholic League, which destroyed most of the city, including approximately 80 per cent of its 25,000 people. Johan Adler Salvius, a Swedish diplomat, described the rampage:

> Whoever they [the invading soldiers] encountered, they slew. They raped wives and virgins, tyrannized young and old . . . and spared no one. . . . The clergy was most terribly treated. They were first massacred in their library and then burnt along with their books. Their wives and daughters were tied behind the horses, dragged into camp, raped, and terribly molested. The church of St. John was full of womenfolk, whom they locked in from the outside, thereafter throwing burning torches through the windows. The Croats and Walloons [French-speaking Netherlanders] behaved mercilessly, throwing children into the fire and tying the more beautiful and well-off women to their stirrups, made off with them behind their horses out of town. They spiked small children onto their lances, waved them around and cast them into the flames. Turks, Tartars, and heathens could not have been more cruel.

Linda S. Frey and Marsha L. Frey (eds.), *Civilians in Wartime Europe, 1618–1900* (Westport CT: Greenwood Press, 2007), p. 34.

At least town walls offered some protection. Peasant villages were completely at the mercy of soldiers. Martin Mallinger, a priest in Freiburg, in southwest Germany, described the impact of armies on the countryside in 1634:

Mediterranean, and then swept north at remarkable speed. In fact, its spread was so rapid that some modern historians have questioned the nineteenth–century theory that the disease in question was bubonic plague. The bacterium that causes plague, *Yersinia pestis*, is carried by a particular species of flea that is endemic in certain rodent populations in the Middle East and central Asia, and the Black Death spread more quickly than can be easily explained through transmission from fleas to rats to people. However, DNA testing on the remains of medieval plague victims has recently confirmed that the Black Death was indeed *Yersinia pestis*. Although the bubonic form of the disease (carried by fleas) is fatal in "only" 40 to 60 per cent of cases, once the infection reaches the lungs it can spread through the vapour in exhaled breath, and in this pneumonic form it is virtually 100 per cent lethal. Contemporary accounts clearly point to both bubonic and pneumonic forms of the disease.[4]

> They [the soldiers] sallied out every day, several companies strong, to seek out and plunder all the nearby valleys in the Black Forest. They not only drove off all the livestock—cows, oxen, calves, geese, horses—many hundred head, but they took all the grain and oats as well, many hundred quarters, not just as food for themselves and their horses but also large quantities to sell in the city.

Geoff Mortimer, *Eyewitness Accounts of the Thirty Years War 1616–48* (Basingstoke: Palgrave, 2002), p. 52

Peasants did not always meekly accept their fate. Here is a Swedish account of Bavarian peasants' resistance and the subsequent reprisals of the Swedish army:

> Although the land was in a pretty bad way, we could easily have got a lot more from it if the people had not brought a great misfortune down upon their necks. Wherever they were strong and encountered small numbers of Royal Swedish cavalry and soldiers, some of whom had been sent to protect them as Salvaguardien ["safeguards"], they set upon them terribly and most cruelly executed them, cut off their hands and feet, poked out their eyes, cut off their noses and ears, and (pardon the liberty) private parts, and otherwise martyred them inhumanly. These evil deeds and murders provoked such bitterness on the Royal Swedish side . . . that they returned and took their revenge most grimly with fire and sword. Thereby, not a few were cut down and several hundred villages burnt to the ground. . . .

Peter H. Wilson, *The Thirty Years War: A Sourcebook* (Basingstoke: Palgrave Macmillan, 2010), p. 255.

The symptoms of plague included fever, chills, headache, fatigue, and painful swellings ("buboes") in the lymph glands of the groin and neck. People understood that proximity to victims was dangerous and would flee at the first sign of the plague. However, because the period before symptoms appeared could be as long as six days, those who fled would often unwittingly spread the infection. Although quarantines were occasionally successful, there was no effective treatment for the disease.

Like hunger, the plague took its greatest toll on the poor. In this case, though, urban populations were at greater risk than peasants, partly because their crowded, unhygienic living conditions were rife with rats and fleas, and partly because the cities were where merchants travelled to do their business. The wealthy, by contrast, were often able to take refuge at country estates before they were infected. The massive scale of the fourteenth-century pandemic was unique, since those who survived it acquired some degree of immunity; yet every new generation would provide a new pool of potential victims. Thus London experienced additional outbreaks in 1563 (which killed one-quarter of the population), 1603, 1625, and 1665, when it killed approximately 90,000 people out of a total population of perhaps 500,000. And roughly 1 million people on the Atlantic coasts of France and Spain died in the "Great Atlantic Plague" of 1596–1603. However, these later epidemics were limited to a local or regional scale. Local recurrences of the plague could be expected on average about once a decade, and it remained a basic fact of life in early modern Europe until the eighteenth century. The last major European outbreak is generally said to have occurred in Marseilles in 1720–1, and although occasional recurrences continued into the nineteenth century, they were mostly confined to the southern and eastern fringes of Europe, and were contained relatively quickly.

Of course, the plague was not the only disease to afflict early modern Europe. Every year, tens of thousands succumbed to smallpox, which had become endemic by the sixteenth century. Highly contagious, it had a mortality rate of between 30 and 50 per cent and left its survivors permanently scarred, but completely immune. Other deadly diseases included dysentery, diphtheria, influenza, typhus, and typhoid. In the weak and malnourished, especially children and the elderly, even a common cold could lead to a deadly bout of pneumonia.

Warfare

The third great cause of mortality in early modern Europe was war, which was nearly continual from the sixteenth century through the eighteenth. Although few civilians died as a direct result of battle, warfare had the effect of worsening famine and disease, and even soldiers were more likely to die from disease than in battle. Most armies had little or no loyalty to the kings they were officially fighting for, were poorly and intermittently paid, and lacked any regular access to provisions. As a result, they preyed on civilian populations, robbing them and denuding the countryside of crops and animals to feed not only themselves but the wives, mistresses, children, prostitutes, and pawnbrokers (among others) who accompanied them; on average, there were five hangers-on for every soldier. Fear of approaching armies frequently drove peasants to flee, leaving their crops unsown or unharvested, while siege warfare exposed urban populations to deliberate starvation.

When armies established winter quarters, dysentery and typhoid often spread to the local people through unsanitary disposal of human waste.

Society and Social Relations

Early modern Europeans thought about the structure of society in terms of "orders" or "estates" rather than socio-economic classes defined primarily by income and wealth. An estate was a group whose existence was recognized by law or custom, and whose members had distinct "liberties" (i.e., rights and privileges). Medieval society had been understood to consist of three estates, defined by their functions: the function of the first estate, the clergy, was to pray; of the second, the nobility, to fight; and of the third, the peasantry, to work. These estates were hierarchical, with every gradation of clergy, nobility, and peasantry having its own rights and privileges. Although this simple theoretical scheme had never fully reflected the complex reality of their society, and was clearly outdated by the later Middle Ages, the assumptions behind it were still current among Europeans. Thus it is worth noting the elements of this social structure that differentiate it from modern western societies. First, it was collective or corporate in nature. Rights and privileges belonged to groups rather than individuals. Your rights, the taxes you would pay, the laws you would be judged by: all depended on the group (or groups) you belonged to. Each order had its own marks of prestige and status, and they were jealously guarded. This often made for in-fighting about who had the right to do (or not to do) what. Ceremonial occasions were frequently marked by conflict over who should precede whom, who should be received first, and so on. One of the most prized privileges was the right not to pay certain kinds of taxes, or any taxes at all.

It was also a social scheme that enshrined legal and social inequality. Not all were subject to the same laws and legal procedures. In Catholic lands, clergy were governed by canon law rather than the law of the ruler or land. Nobles could be judged only by other nobles, and when sentenced to capital punishment they were beheaded rather than hanged, since this was usually (though not always) a swifter form of death. Craft guilds had the legal right to regulate their trade and punish members for infractions. And since students typically came under the legal jurisdiction of their universities rather than that of local governments, the latter were frequently powerless to deal with rowdy or criminal types who continued to claim student status long after their studies were completed.

Social inequalities were visibly expressed in patterns of consumption, especially relating to dress. To limit the consumption of gold and furs, for example, sumptuary laws attempted to restrict their use to the nobility, and governments attempted to regulate spending on events such as weddings and baptisms according to social status. Jews and other outsiders were often required to identify themselves by wearing specific items of clothing. Inequality was also expressed in complex codes of protocol and deference designed to ensure that social inferiors treated their betters with due respect. Failure to use the proper form of address to a social superior was a serious offence, often punishable by law, as was any attempt to claim a status to which one was not entitled.

Some rights and privileges were based on social status, as in the case of the nobility. Some were occupational in nature, as in the case of craft guilds, universities, and law courts. Others were determined by geographic location: inhabitants of a certain province or town were entitled to specific rights and privileges. Within the Catholic Church were many groups with their own corporate identities, including not only orders such as the Benedictines, Franciscans, and Dominicans, but various lay religious organizations known as confraternities. Many people belonged to multiple orders. A craftsman, for instance, might be a member of a religious confraternity as well as his guild, and might enjoy additional privileges as a resident of a particular province, region, and urban commune. In time, however, this society of orders came under increasing pressure. When central governments, faced with paying the increasing costs of waging war, tried to roll back the privileges of various groups, they frequently met with resistance, if not outright rebellion.

At the same time, social organization was evolving towards a more modern class structure in which the primary determinant of class identity was wealth. For example, wealthy nobles might find that in many respects they had more in common with wealthy clergymen and wealthy merchants than they did with poorer nobles. Well-to-do master craftsmen of various guilds increasingly identified with one another rather than with the poorer members of their own guilds. By the same token, journeymen of various trades who increasingly found common cause with each other in their struggles against the bosses began to form organizations that in many ways resembled labour unions.

There was a great deal of social mobility in early modern Europe, even if people still thought of the social order as fixed and static. However, whereas today the self-made entrepreneur boasts of his humble roots, people on the way up in early modern Europe went to great lengths to obscure where they came from. In the words of the seventeenth-century German novelist H.J.C. von Grimmelshausen:

> In recent years . . . there has arisen a disease among humble folk which makes them claim noble birth and ancient lineage as soon as they have scraped together a little money to buy themselves fine clothes. . . . More often than not, their fathers were chimney sweeps, day labourers, card sharpers, or mountebanks; their brothers jailers and executioners; their sisters sempstresses, washerwomen, and whores; their mothers bawds or even witches; and in a word, their whole pedigree of thirty-two ancestors as soiled and stained as ever was the pastry-cooks' guild in Prague. . . . [5]

Von Grimmelshausen exaggerated the rapidity of social mobility for literary effect; in reality, intergenerational social mobility (across several generations) was much more the norm in early modern Europe than intragenerational (within one generation). It is often very difficult to track a family's mobility, precisely because they were so concerned with obscuring their origins. Significant wealth was the essential precondition of social mobility, not so much because people admired wealth for its own sake, but because social status depended on lifestyle, and wealth was required in order to live the life of a gentleman. To give a hypothetical example, a relatively successful peasant might send one of his sons to live in a nearby town and sell the products of the family's farm. That young man, or perhaps his son, might invest some of the profits in trade or finance, becoming a banker or an entrepreneur. In the next generation, the son might be sent first to grammar school and then to university to prepare for a career as a lawyer or civil servant. The daughters would be married to the sons of similarly upwardly mobile families, in order to cement alliances and advance business and professional interests. In this way, the peasant's great-grandson might be able to accumulate enough wealth to retire from business, purchase a country estate, and live the life of a leisured gentleman on the income from his investments. After a few more generations, the family might even acquire noble status, and by that time its peasant origins would have been forgotten.

In an age of economic and social turbulence, the newly wealthy wanted the status and power to which they now felt entitled, while those who already enjoyed status and power sought to keep them undiluted. Much of the unrest that characterized the early modern period can be traced to these social tensions.

NOBLES

In an agricultural society, wealth and power belonged to those who controlled the land. In early modern Europe this meant primarily the nobility, who controlled a proportion of the land that far exceeded their proportion in society at large.[6] Nobles claimed to be descended from an ancient caste or "race" whose privileges were justified by their inherent superiority. In fact, however, their ranks were continually replenished from below.

What made a nobleman? In theory, a noble was a member of a warrior caste whose superior status had been established by his ancestors, vassals of the king, who by virtue of the feudal contract had served him on the battlefield. By the sixteenth century, this type of army had been rendered obsolete and the armies of most rulers consisted of paid mercenaries; however, many nobles continued to serve as officers and commanders in the royal armies. Thus warfare continued to be an essential component of noble identity, and the culture of the nobility remained martial in nature. The sons of nobles were taught the skills of war—to use swords, ride, and shoot—and to practise those skills regularly by participating in sports such as fencing and hunting (still the pre-eminent noble pastime).

In fact, the right to bear arms was among the privileges that only nobles possessed. The most valuable noble privilege, however, was exemption from many forms of taxation: in Castile, for example, nobles were exempt from all royal taxation, while in France they were exempt from the *taille*, the most important royal direct tax, although they did pay a variety of indirect taxes.[7] Nobles justified these exemptions on the grounds that, as members of the warrior class, they paid their taxes "in blood."

Members of the nobility were also distinguished by a certain way of life. "Living nobly" meant above all not demeaning themselves by engaging in manual labour. Nobles were expected to live exclusively on the revenue from their estates and investments, together with their pensions and rewards from the king. Although they could invest in commercial or industrial enterprises, in France and Spain they risked losing their noble status if they took any active role in the management of those concerns; in England, however, the restrictions on noble activity were never as severe, and some English nobles were active in finance and commerce. While estate management and selective breeding of plants and animals were permitted, hands-on agricultural work was forbidden. Beginning in the seventeenth century, royal governments would attempt to loosen these restrictions in order to encourage noble participation in commerce and industry, but with limited success, as nobles sought to maintain their distinct and superior status

To live as a noble also required conspicuous consumption. Nobles were expected to maintain large households with numerous servants, and to distinguish themselves from lowly merchants by entertaining on a grand scale, without concern for the cost. As a result, there can be no doubt that for many people "living nobly" meant crushing debt and declining wealth.

Of course, status and wealth varied within the nobility. At the top were the magnates or grandees, the intimates and counsellors of kings, who had enough influence at court that at times they were able to challenge the ruler. At the other end of the spectrum were the lowly country squires, whose minimal holdings left them barely distinguishable from the peasants around them. The majority fell somewhere in the middle range. They had no pretensions to great wealth or power, but at least they were the big fish in their small local ponds. However poor or obscure they might be, they still considered themselves socially superior to even the wealthiest commoners.

European nobles faced a number of challenges in the early modern period. As market forces became more important in agriculture, the economics of estate management changed. Rising prices in the sixteenth century were followed by economic stagnation in the seventeenth. While some nobles were able to adapt to changing circumstances, those who were not faced indebtedness, foreclosure, and even the loss of their noble status.

Nobles also faced challenges to their political power. Throughout the Middle Ages, rulers had sought to curb the independent political power of the great noble families. In the process, they had begun to choose as ministers and advisers men who came from outside the traditional feudal nobility and had no power base of their own. Now, in the sixteenth and seventeenth centuries, the growing royal bureaucracies were staffed largely by newly ennobled and socially ambitious middle-class men. Thus nobles found their political power challenged and reduced not only at court but in local government as well.

THE MIDDLE CLASSES OR BOURGEOISIE

In the social world of the Middle Ages, the middle classes consisted of those who belonged to neither the peasantry, the nobility, nor the clergy. The alternative term for these people, "the bourgeoisie," reflects the fact that, unlike both peasants and nobles, they lived in the towns (*bourgs* in French). Among them were entrepreneurs, doctors and lawyers, civil servants, and master craftsmen who owned their own shops. Thus the bourgeoisie spanned a broad range of incomes and lifestyles, from the richest international financier down to the small business owner with a handful of employees.

The ultimate goal of the ambitious bourgeois was to enter the ranks of the nobility, both for the social prestige and for the privileges, in particular the tax exemptions. This required a significant amount of wealth, since the aspiring noble would have to leave his business behind in order to reach his goal. By the sixteenth century the primary route to ennoblement lay in appointment to government bureaucracy. Most governments, starved as they were for revenue, engaged in venality (the sale of government positions for cash), but the practice was most systematic in France. Some of the positions available, such as judge in a Parlement (sovereign court) in France, conferred a noble title on their holders automatically. Others might lead to noble status under certain conditions: for example, if a certain position had been held in the family for several generations, and its holders lived nobly through that period, then the family might eventually be recognized as part of the nobility.

While some socially ambitious bourgeois bought government positions for themselves or their sons, others, known as *rentiers*, lived on the revenue from their investments (*rentes*). Legally, the new nobles were equal to the oldest and grandest noble families. In practice, however, they were looked down on as "parvenus" not only by nobles who could trace their lineage back many generations, but by families that had been noble for only a few generations themselves. In time the grandchildren of these "parvenus" in turn would look down on more recent newcomers.

Social stratification marked the bourgeoisie as well. Wealthy businessmen and professionals increasingly formed an urban elite or patriciate that dominated the economic, social, and political life of the towns, while their less affluent counterparts were left on the outside looking in. Whereas in the past they had been members of the same social order, the same guilds and religious confraternities, now they were increasingly separated by distinctions based on wealth. In other words, they were beginning to behave as members of horizontal socio-economic classes rather than vertical orders.

Urban Workers: Skilled and Unskilled

Below the bourgeoisie were the working men—skilled journeymen and unskilled labourers—who were employed by middle-class business owners. Skilled workers were usually organized in guilds, which set prices and controlled quality, telling members what sorts of goods or services they could provide and how much they could charge for them. A guild was also a brotherhood, a benevolent association and a social club, providing assistance for widows and orphans of members, or lending a hand when required. In these respects, guilds resembled modern labour unions; however, the guild system did not differentiate between employers and employees. All practitioners of a particular trade or skill, bosses and employees alike, belonged to the same guild.

Admission to the various guilds was strictly controlled. An aspiring member first had to serve an apprenticeship in a master's shop, usually starting around the age of twelve or thirteen. After several years of training he would become a journeyman, leaving his home town to travel and develop his skills by working for different masters. Here again, we may be reminded of a stock character in fairy tales: the young man who sets out to seek his fortune. Ideally, once he had received letters from a variety of masters attesting to his skill and character, the journeyman would then return home, marry, and establish himself as a master in his own right—a process that required him to post a bond (pay a fee to the guild) and prove his proficiency at his trade by producing a "masterpiece."

In the sixteenth and seventeenth centuries, however, just as the urban elite were separating themselves from the ordinary bourgeois, so the masters of various trades themselves were taking steps to distinguish themselves from the journeymen. To protect their privileged positions and maintain their monopoly, they began making it more difficult for journeymen to join their ranks, often by demanding higher bonds or more difficult and costly masterpieces. Journeymen responded by forming their own associations with their own oaths, rituals, and networks—in other words, behaving as members of a distinct socio-economic class. They were being transformed into a permanent class of wage labourers, excluded from full participation both in the guilds and in civic life (in many towns, political participation was limited to masters). As a consequence of their exclusion from the guilds, journeymen developed not only organizational skills, but a strong understanding of their interests and a certain hostility to the establishment, and were typically at the forefront of urban protests. Just as we saw with the masters above them, journeymen were starting to behave and identify as a socio-economic class that cut across orders.

Below the journeymen on the social ladder were large numbers of unskilled labourers, who typically were not organized in guilds and had no job security, since they were usually hired by the day. If they were fortunate, they eked out a living as physical labourers, digging ditches, hauling water, or disposing of waste.

Most households of the middle class and higher had at least one servant, and many had several. Thus a large proportion of the inhabitants of early modern cities were cooks, maids, footmen, and so on. Although those who were able to maintain a good relationship with their employers could be economically quite secure, their status was very low. In the view of contemporaries, the fact that servants lived in their employers' household meant that they were consigned to a kind of perpetual childhood.

Peasants

The vast majority of people were peasants, subsistence farmers, living in rural villages. Although rural society was much more equal than urban society, there were significant variations in living standards, depending on factors such as geographical location, soil quality, and proximity to a town with a market. The prospects of most peasant families were determined by two variables: the size of their landholdings and the nature of their tenancy (for example, whether it was unwritten and "customary," or supported by documentation).

Few peasants could claim outright ownership of their land in our understanding of the term; ownership was "shared" between the peasant and a lord, usually the local nobleman, but in some cases a monastery or even a wealthy bourgeois who had bought an estate as an investment in social mobility. Each peasant family had strips of land scattered through the village fields, in patterns determined through generations of marriage and inheritance. Common lands such as meadows and forests were integral to the village community. Peasant families could supplement their diet by grazing a cow or a goat on common pastures, fishing in the lakes and streams, or hunting small game and gathering berries in the forest, which also served as a source of firewood.

The peasants who survived the demographic devastation of the Black Death were in a relatively advantageous position, despite landlords' efforts to restrain wages and maintain rents, since a reduced population meant that land was relatively plentiful and inexpensive compared to the labour required to farm it. In most of western Europe, landlords now had to compete for labour, and in time this competition led to the gradual elimination of serfdom. As population recovered and especially as cities grew, peasants were increasingly able to sell any surplus crops at local markets. For most peasants, the period around the turn of the sixteenth century was a relatively good time.

As the century progressed, however, circumstances shifted again, to the detriment of the peasants. Population growth meant that less land was available, and as labour was now more plentiful, wages stagnated or declined in real terms. Peasants were caught between what one leading historian has called "the twin processes of pauperization."[8]

The other major determinant of peasants' security was the nature of their tenancy. Since most peasants did not own their land outright but shared ownership with a lord, they could not sell it, which effectively limited their mobility. In addition, they were usually required pay various fees to the landlord (in cash or in produce) and to perform certain services for him, such as building or repairing roads, or cultivating the lands under the lord's direct control (his *demesne*). They might also be obligated to grind their grain in his mill, press their grapes in his winepress, or bake their bread in his oven, for all of which they would pay additional fees. Sometimes these obligations were spelled out in a written document, but in many cases they customary.

As the sixteenth century was a period of general inflation, money lost value over time, so that peasants who paid their fees in cash benefited, while those who paid in produce did not. At the same time, the growing commercial opportunities in the cities tempted landlords everywhere to make more profitable use of their lands: for example, by devoting more of it to commercial crops, or by converting farmland to pasture in order to raise sheep and sell their wool. In order to do so, they needed to alter their relationships with the peasants who farmed the lands. Peasants who had written records of their obligations to their lords generally fared better than those who did not. The subdivision of peasant landholdings through generations of inheritance meant that more and more peasants could not feed their families and were forced to find paid work as labourers on the lord's *demesne* lands. As we will see, this increase in production for sale in the market rather than for subsistence would be the most significant development in agriculture in the sixteenth and seventeenth centuries.

In central and eastern Europe (from central Germany east), rural society developed differently. During the economic and demographic expansion of the Middle Ages, landlords in these regions actively sought peasants to farm their underpopulated lands, and therefore offered more favourable terms. Thus peasants in the eastern half of Europe had generally been freer than those in the west. After the Black Death, however, eastern land-lords began reducing the freedom of peasants. The owners of the typically vast estates in eastern Germany, Poland, and elsewhere had discovered that there were huge profits to be made selling grain to the expanding cities of western Europe. In order to exploit their farm operations as commercial enterprises, they imposed serfdom on the peasants who until then had been freer than those in the west.

Like its urban counterpart, rural society became increasingly stratified in the six-teenth and seventeenth centuries. At the top were the large-scale farmers for whom agri-culture was a business, known in England as yeomen and in France as *fermiers*, who either owned their land outright or rented it as a commercial transaction. Below these rural cap-italists were relatively prosperous peasants who were able not only to feed their families but to produce surpluses to sell in the marketplace. Most peasant families, however, found themselves increasingly squeezed in the early modern period. Because their landholdings were not large enough to provide an adequate livelihood, they were forced to work either as sharecroppers or as labourers on someone else's land, even as wages were declining.

Rural society was generally more fluid than urban society, since wealth rather than ancestry was the primary determinant of status. In England particularly, smart or lucky peasants quite often rose up the ranks to become yeomen. On the other hand, even the luckiest peasant family was only a couple of bad harvests away from destitution.

ON THE MARGINS

At the bottom of early modern society was a marginal population of paupers that moved between town and countryside in search of sustenance. Although most of these nomads had genuinely fallen on hard times, some were part of a semi-criminal underworld, and were willing to steal if begging proved inadequate. Political and religious authorities were alarmed by the sheer numbers of the rootless poor, which threatened to overwhelm the es-tablished order. They always tried to distinguish, however, between the "deserving poor" and the "sturdy beggars" who were capable of working but preferred to beg or steal.

To cope with the deserving poor, they set up systems of poor relief, workhouses, or-phanages, and hospitals, but the supply never met the demand. In the Middle Ages, poor relief had consisted primarily of one-to-one almsgiving, a practice that benefited not only the recipient but also the donor, whose chances of salvation were improved both by per-forming a good deed and by the grateful recipient's prayers for his or her soul. By the sixteenth century, however, there was a growing awareness that this haphazard system of personal charity was inadequate to the task. This awareness was not limited to Protest-ants, who rejected any suggestion that salvation could be earned by good works. Many Catholics, especially humanists such as the Spaniard Juan Luis Vives, also argued that it was Christians' duty to relieve their fellow humans of suffering in the most effective way possible, and that self-interested gestures of charity were not enough to fulfill this civic obligation.

Systematic efforts at poor relief were almost always the responsibility of city governments, operated and paid for by taxpayers rather than religious organizations. Begging was regulated or outlawed altogether. Needy children were placed in orphanages and workhouses, while those who were capable of physical labour were put to work, and the ill and mentally incompetent were sent to hospitals, which could provide little in the way of treatment, but did offer some minimal care for those who were near death.

Some historians have argued that this system of poor relief was primarily a means of social control, designed to get the poor, the ill, and the mad off the streets and force them to conform to the norms of "respectable" society. The French philosopher and historian Michel Foucault (1926–84) was a pioneer in this way of thinking, although his work focused on the eighteenth century (see also Chapter 8). In books such as *Madness and Civilization* (1960), *The Birth of the Clinic* (1963), and *Discipline and Punish* (1975), Foucault described the institutionalization of marginalized groups as a movement towards a "great confinement" (*grand renfermement*) in which people who had formerly been tolerated in society were reclassified as fundamentally "other" or sub-human and subjected to discipline, surveillance, and regulation. There is no doubt that people in authority recognized the dangers posed by the marginalized. There is also little doubt, however, that many of them were motivated by a sense of religious and civic duty, and did the best they could to deal with complex problems. In any event, their efforts were hopelessly inadequate.

For "sturdy beggars" there was no sympathy at all. Without established police forces, legal authorities relied on the principle that punishment would deter other potential offenders. The penalties imposed on vagrants and petty thieves were savage: whipping, branding, amputation of hands or feet; some had their noses cut off, or holes drilled through their tongues. In France, a man who stole a loaf of bread could be sent to row in the royal galleys for three years—an almost certain death sentence. In England, vagrants could be executed for a third offence.

Early modern Europe differed from most other traditional societies in that it did not rely heavily on slave labour. This was not a reflection of moral scruples: Christian Europeans were enthusiastic participants in the African slave trade from the sixteenth century through the nineteenth. Rather, the nature of the European economy was such that it had no real use for slavery. Geography may also have played a part: the few places where slaves (mostly female domestic servants) were found in any numbers were Portugal, Spain, and Italy—places with relatively easy access to the traditional slave markets of the Middle East and North Africa. Unlike the ancient world and the plantation economies that were then being established in the New World, early modern Europe was a society with some slaves, rather than a slave society.

Another group on the margins of mainstream Christian society were Europe's Jews. In the later Middle Ages, Jews had been expelled from many countries, including England and France, but some had eventually been able to return. In 1492 they were expelled from Spain and in 1496 from Portugal, where many Spanish Jews had recently found refuge. Many of these Sephardic Jews found their way to the Netherlands and the Ottoman Empire, where their medical and financial expertise was highly sought after.

In most places Jews were forbidden to own land; therefore they almost always lived in urban centres. Since they were also barred from guild membership, they tended to specialize in commerce, including the new trades in tobacco and sugar, or occupations that Christians were barred from, such as moneylending. A handful of Jews became lenders to rulers; although these "court Jews" could become extremely wealthy, they often became lightning rods for dissent, and their positions were always vulnerable. Most Jews, however, kept a low profile, living in their own tightly knit communities and practising their religion as best they could.

Throughout the Middle Ages, periods of violent persecution of Jews had usually been associated either with large-scale religious movements such as the Crusades, or with disasters such as the Black Death. This pattern continued into the early modern period. In many places, Jews were required to wear distinctive clothing, or to live in a restricted area known as a ghetto (the term used in Venice, which established Europe's first ghetto in 1516). Although ghettoes served to segregate Jews from the rest of the population, at least they gave their residents a measure of self-government and protection. Jews' position in European society would not change appreciably until the later eighteenth century (Chapter 9).

If Jews lived on the margins of European society, Muslims occupied no physical space at all outside Spain. Christian Europe had, of course, had hostile relations with Islam at least since the eleventh century, when the first crusaders set out to take back the Holy Land from Muslim control. This hostility was compounded by the fact that since 1453, when the Ottomans took Constantinople, their empire extended not only over Asia Minor, much of the Middle East, and North Africa, but even into southeastern Europe as far north and west as Hungary, and posed a severe threat at sea in the Mediterranean. Nevertheless, for most Christian Europeans Islam was a distant threat rather than a presence in their midst. In Spain, on the other hand, the situation was very different. The conquest of Granada posed the problem of what to do with the Muslims who made up the majority of its population. Efforts to convert them to Christianity would produce a violent rebellion (1568–71), and in the early seventeenth century all remaining Muslims were expelled from the Spanish kingdoms, just as the Jews had been a century earlier.

UNREST, REVOLT, AND REBELLION

Popular uprisings were very common in early modern Europe, both in towns and in the countryside. Although those in positions of power saw the participants as a mindless rabble, striking out in primitive fury against their betters, this was rarely the case. In fact, unrest was almost always a reflection of fear that whatever security or social standing the people had was under threat. Far from seeking to overturn the traditional order of things, they sought to preserve or restore it.

In other words, most revolts were not inspired by revolutionary ideals. Rather, they were provoked from above, whether by landlords seeking to raise rents, by landowners attempting to restrict peasants' freedom, or by tax collectors abusing their authority. The rebels usually had a very clear agenda, and in their statements of grievances, they almost always insisted on their loyalty to the king, urging him not to be deceived by evil advisers.

Rebels often adopted elements from the culture that surrounded them. Often there would be an oath to the cause that resembled the oaths of guilds and religious confraternities. Another prominent theme, adopted from the celebration of Carnival or Mardi Gras, was the reversal of everyday norms and expectations, the "world turned upside down." At least in part, Carnival served as a safety valve: social norms were overturned for a time, but were reinforced when Carnival ended and authorities could in effect say: "You've had your fun: now it's back to the real world, where *we* run things." For them, an upside-down world that stayed that way was precisely what a popular rebellion represented.[9]

Another common form of popular violence was the bread riot. Since bread was the staple food for most people, city governments usually tried to prevent price increases in times of scarcity by stockpiling grain for use in emergencies, and sometimes providing subsidies from city funds. Quite frequently, however, prices escaped their control, and the result was public unrest. While of course bakeries were often looted, there were also many cases in which crowds seized them and sold the bread for what they considered a "just price." Those cases reflected what has been called a "moral economy,"[10] according to which something as necessary as bread was not just a commodity to be sold for whatever price the market would bear: if governments could not guarantee access to it at a just price, then the people were fully within their rights to set the price themselves.

THE ROLES AND STATUS OF WOMEN

Women in early modern Europe were legally inferior to men, under the legal control of their fathers before marriage and of their husbands thereafter. This legal inequality was justified by the traditional belief that women were less rational than men, more susceptible to the influence of bodily humours (the word "hysteria" comes from the Greek for "uterus"), and prone to unconstrained lust. Beyond that, it is extremely difficult to arrive at useful generalizations.

For the vast majority of families who lived on the edge of survival, women's labour was essential. On the farm, in addition to cooking, cleaning, and taking care of the children, women often helped in the fields by sheaving crops or gleaning the grain that had fallen to the ground during the harvest. Peasant wives might also tend small animals such as chickens and goats, and cultivate a vegetable garden. The processing of agricultural products, whether for home use or sale, usually fell to the woman as well: churning butter and making cheese, for example.

Some women, especially before marriage, worked as servants in households of wealthier people, to save for a dowry that would enable them to marry and establish households of their own. Of course, this kind of work made them vulnerable to sexual advances from male members of the household, and sexual abuse of all sorts was not uncommon. A pregnancy in these circumstances almost inevitably consigned the woman to a life of prostitution or begging and/or crime.

The economic roles of urban women were more varied. The wife of a master craftsman often played a crucial role in his business, serving customers, keeping the books, and in some cases even supervising employees. If her husband were to die, she might manage the shop herself, at least until she remarried (often to another master of the same craft). A guild might allow a widow to continue running her husband's business, but she could never participate in guild decisions.

The wives and daughters of urban wage labourers were not so fortunate. Many young women found employment as domestic servants, or at inns or taverns. Others worked in the marketplace, perhaps selling goods such as pies and sausages that they made themselves. The textile industry also provided employment for women, although they were almost never paid the same as men, as it was universally assumed that their earnings were supplementary to those of their husbands or fathers.

Among the very few occupations that were exclusively female was that of midwife. In the course of the seventeenth century, however, this role was increasingly taken over by male physicians, especially in the cities. Although midwives who were familiar with folk remedies and herbal medicines often acted as healers as well, especially in rural areas, this role too began to be filled by male barber-surgeons, who performed blood-letting (the most common medical procedure in the early modern era).

Women of the elite had an easier life in some ways than those of the lower classes. They were better nourished, their children were more likely to live, they had better access to medical care (for what it was worth), and were not subject to the endless drudgery that characterized the lives of the vast majority of women. In addition, to the extent that their fathers or husbands permitted, they also had greater access to education. On the other hand, as we have seen, their marriages were more likely to be arranged, without regard to their wishes, and the more significant the property at stake, the more likely they were to be treated as chattel.

All women were expected to bring a dowry with them to their married life. Among poorer women it consisted mainly of clothes and household items such as dishes and pots. Among the elite, however, the dowries required to attract a socially prestigious match could reach staggering amounts. Thus an elite family with several daughters might send the younger ones to become nuns, to avoid the cost of providing dowries for them. (Convents also required a dowry of sorts, known as an endowment, but it was typically smaller than a marital dowry.) However much those who had not chosen the religious life might have resented their fate, at least it gave them security and a measure of respect. After the Reformations of the sixteenth century, when the convent was no longer an option in Protestant lands, it could be difficult for unmarried women ("spinsters") to find any meaningful place in society.

The spread of education and literacy in the sixteenth and seventeenth centuries was dramatic. As we will see in Chapter 9, however, here too there was a striking divergence between the fortunes of males and females. In the past very few people had received any kind of formal schooling, but from the sixteenth century on, most boys did receive at least a rudimentary education: the catechism (basic religious instruction), and basic literacy and numeracy. By contrast, most girls were still denied the opportunity to learn even those basic skills: all they were taught was the catechism and the skills they would need as wives and mothers. While the sons of the elite attended grammar schools, where they learned Latin in preparation for university, the daughters were taught "womanly" skills such as music, dancing, and needlepoint. The very few girls who did receive a classical education were usually daughters of highly educated men, and even they were excluded from universities until the late nineteenth century.

WITCH HUNTS

In the sixteenth and seventeenth centuries, much of central Europe, as well as England and Scotland, was convulsed by fear of witchcraft. Although the precise numbers are unknown, one historian has estimated that approximately 110,000 witch trials were conducted, of which some 60,000 ended in the death of the accused.[11] During the Middle Ages, people had certainly believed in witches and witchcraft, but trials and executions were relatively rare. What accounted for the change? The answer appears to lie in a confluence of religious, social, legal, and economic factors.

In the Middle Ages, the only crime associated with witchcraft was the use of supernatural means to inflict harm on another (*maleficium*). In 1484, however, Pope Innocent VIII authorized two Dominican friars, Jakob Sprenger and Heinrich Kramer (also known as Institoris) to seek out and punish witches. Two years later, they published a manual for witch-hunters called the *Malleus Maleficarum*, or *Hammer of Witches*. It became the foundation of an elaborate ideology according to which witchcraft was a vast Satanic cult whose members (male as well as female) made a pact with the devil and sealed it by engaging in blasphemous sexual intercourse with him. Witches' gatherings, called "Black Sabbaths," were described as sacrilegious parodies of Christian worship, often including ritual cannibalism and perverted orgies. This ideology did not reflect popular traditions, but was constructed and spread by the religious and political elite.

The prosecution of witches was the business of secular governments, which (except in England) followed Roman law in permitting the use of torture to elicit confessions. In theory, the use of torture was to be carefully restricted to prevent abuse, but the gravity of the threat meant that in practice these safeguards were frequently ignored. To put an end to their torment, accused witches would often not only confess but name "accomplices," who would then be tortured in their turn. The result was a cascade of accusations, and increasing paranoia.

It is likely that many accusations of witchcraft were prompted by social and economic misfortunes such as the death of a child or the failure of a crop, but that without the religious and legal developments described above, they would not have grown into mass panic and paranoia. No doubt religious tensions also played some role in the persecution, but it began before the Protestant Reformation, and eventually Protestant as well as Catholic authorities hunted witches enthusiastically. The most likely scenario is that religious tensions helped to create the atmosphere of hostility in which suspicions led to accusations, which then set the official machinery into motion. It is probably not coincidental that the areas where witches were most actively pursued were those in which the confrontation between Protestants and Catholics was most intense: Switzerland, eastern France, southern and western Germany, Poland, and Scotland. Areas that were solidly Catholic (Spain, Italy) or Protestant (Scandinavia) saw relatively few prosecutions of witches.

The areas where witch hunts were common also tended to be ones where local political and legal authorities had considerable autonomy. In general, regions with stronger central authorities were more resistant. In Spain, for example, the fact that the Spanish Inquisition held the monopoly on the investigation of religious nonconformity acted as a restraint on local authorities who might have been inclined to pursue witches more vigorously. England was also highly centralized, politically and legally, and because it did not follow Roman law, it did not use torture to elicit confessions. Although it did enact laws against acts of *maleficium* in the sixteenth century, only those acts were illegal: simply being a witch was not. As a result, historians have observed that England did not experience the mass witch panics that were so widespread on the continent.

The vast majority of people accused of witchcraft were women, partly because they were believed to be morally weaker and more enslaved to their sexual appetites than men (hence more susceptible to Satan's temptations), and partly because they were believed to be less capable than men of achieving their goals without resorting to supernatural means. No doubt some accused witches actually did mix potions and cast spells, even if they did not fly on broomsticks or have sex with the devil.

Some women's occupations made them more likely than others to attract accusations of witchcraft. A cook was in an ideal position to slip a potion into an enemy's food; a "wise woman" could use her knowledge of herbs to harm as well as to heal; and a midwife made a convenient scapegoat for the grieving relatives of a mother or infant who died in childbirth. Early modern European society was clearly misogynistic by our standards, and this misogyny undoubtedly played a role in both accusations and prosecutions of witchcraft. Nevertheless, to portray the witch hunts as part of a concerted, deliberate campaign against women, as some popular writers have done, would be inaccurate, if only because men were also accused.

In most places, the witch hunts reached their peak around 1600, and by the mid-eighteenth were a thing of the past. There were isolated trials and executions as late as 1782 in Switzerland, but these were relics of a bygone era. The reasons behind the decline in witch hunting were as complex as those behind its rise. The gradual abating of religious tension, and the general improvement in economic conditions in the eighteenth century likely both played a role, if only by reducing the occasions for accusations of witchcraft. Meanwhile, increasing political and legal centralization served to limit the opportunities for overzealous local authorities to prosecute supposed witches. Most important, however, members of the various elites lost their faith in the diabolic conception of witchcraft as they adopted the rationalistic world view associated with developments in science and philosophy in the seventeenth and eighteenth centuries. Ordinary people continued to believe in the reality of witches, and to level accusations, though perhaps less frequently, but the authorities who had prosecuted and executed witches no longer took them seriously. What had been seen a real and present danger was increasingly dismissed as superstition and humbug.

Economic Life

The economic continuities between the Middle Ages and the early modern period were very strong. Although industry and commerce were growing, agriculture remained the central pursuit for the vast majority of people. Changes were under way, but they were incremental, and their cumulative impact would not be felt in any dramatic way until the eighteenth century, when (as we will see in Chapter 8) they amounted to a transformation of the European economy.

AGRICULTURE

The most important development in agriculture in this period was the gradual shift from subsistence to commercial farming: that is, the growth of agrarian capitalism. This transition had begun in the Middle Ages and would not be really complete until the nineteenth or even the twentieth century in some regions. Nevertheless, it made substantial progress in the sixteenth and seventeenth centuries.

Historians have detected three major patterns in this evolution. It was most complete in England and the Netherlands, where serfdom and the restrictions of the medieval village-based system were eliminated, and peasants were transformed from semi-independent subsistence farmers into agrarian wage labourers. Landholdings and common lands were consolidated and enclosed with fences, hedges, or ditches. While peasant families would receive an equivalent amount of land, they would be responsible for paying the costs associated with enclosure, such as surveying and fencing—costs more easily borne by larger landowners.

The beneficiaries of enclosure were the large landowners, yeomen or gentry, who were now able to farm substantial holdings as commercial enterprises. Some, especially in the densely populated Netherlands, focused on growing food for sale in the burgeoning cities, hiring former peasants to work the land as wage labourers. In England, however, many owners decided to profit from the booming demand for wool by devoting their newly enclosed lands to sheep grazing rather than crops—a use that required very little labour. In these cases, as the English statesman Sir Thomas More pointed out, sheep devoured men.

The transition to agrarian capitalism was slower and less complete in the rest of western Europe, where the traditional village system proved more resistant to landowners' efforts to assert their property rights at the expense of peasants. As population continued to grow through the sixteenth century, average landholdings decreased in size and real wages declined, with the result that many peasant families were no longer able to support themselves on the produce of their own lands. Some peasants were able to benefit from these circumstances by purchasing or leasing land, where they would often employ the less fortunate as wage labourers.

There was also an important difference in social structure on the continent that helps to explain its divergence from the English pattern. In England the titled nobility was very small and difficult to penetrate, and the rule of primogeniture was strictly enforced: only the eldest son inherited his father's noble status. In most of continental Europe, however, all the sons of a nobleman inherited noble status. In England, the younger brothers of the titled nobles, known as gentry, might still have been wealthy, but since they had little or no chance of ever attaining noble status, they were free of the obligation to "live nobly." Instead, they had to make their own way in the world, and many of them led the way in the transition to agrarian capitalism. On the continent, by contrast, the fact that younger brothers also carried noble status meant that they too were expected to "live nobly," and as a consequence they did not throw themselves into agrarian capitalism. In addition, because it was easier for middle-class people to gain noble status on the continent than in England, many of those who aspired to nobility were less likely to treat their landholdings purely as commercial enterprises. In most of western Europe, therefore, the traditional village system endured longer than it did in England.

The situation in large parts of central and eastern Europe was different again. Here the restrictions of serfdom actually increased in the sixteenth and seventeenth centuries, even though the transition to agrarian capitalism was already fairly complete. As we have seen, in the Middle Ages peasants in eastern Europe were more free than their counterparts to the west, but this pattern was reversed following the Black Death. Whereas in western Europe landlords competed for tenants and labourers by granting them greater freedom and more favourable terms, in the east landlords responded to the shortage of labour by turning free peasants into serfs. The most important reason for this difference had to do with the strength of royal governments. In western Europe, as we will see, royal governments were growing steadily stronger, partly at the expense of noble landowners, and therefore tended to look unfavourably on developments that would increase noble wealth and power. Central governments in eastern Europe, however, tended to be less powerful, and were either unwilling or unable to prevent noble landlords from imposing serfdom. Noble landlords in eastern Germany, Poland, the Baltic region, and elsewhere realized that there were huge profits to be made selling their grain on the open market in the growing cities of western Europe. They cultivated their large estates as commercial enterprises, and serfdom was their solution to the problem of controlling labour costs.

While the framework of the medieval agrarian system remained in place in most of Europe, then, and land continued to be cultivated much as it had been for centuries, the increasing prevalence of market relations and the growth of agrarian capitalism meant that important changes were under way. They would not pick up steam until the eighteenth century (at the earliest), but when they did, they would transform agriculture across Europe.

INDUSTRY

Industry and manufacturing played relatively minor roles in early modern economies. Most goods were still produced within the household, and those that were not were manufactured in small craft shops catering only to local markets. Among the few enterprises that operated on anything like a modern industrial scale was shipbuilding. Venice's famed Arsenal, which employed up to 16,000 workers and was said to be capable of producing a ship in one day, was the largest industrial site in Europe prior to the Industrial Revolution, but shipyards in seaports from Italy and Spain to England and Netherlands bustled to keep up with the demand for both trading vessels and warships. Mines and foundries as well could employ many hundreds of workers, supplying the iron and copper used largely in warfare, though demand for the silver mined in central Europe was also high.

Even so, by far the largest industrial sector in early modern Europe—the equivalent of the automobile industry today—was textiles (primarily woollens), and in this case the majority of operations were small-scale. Although a few large textile enterprises in places such as northern Italy and the Netherlands did produce for a broader market, most textiles were produced for local consumption, in local shops that were strictly controlled by guild regulations. By the later Middle Ages, however, textile entrepreneurs seeking to escape the regulations imposed by guilds began moving production out of the cities and into peasant households. In this new rural or "cottage" industry model, an agent would deliver raw wool to one household for spinning, then pick up the thread produced there and deliver it to another household for weaving into cloth.

This system was ideally suited to textiles, since the materials were light and easy to transport, no power source was required other than human muscles, and many peasant households already had both the skills (spinning and weaving) and the equipment (spinning wheels and hand looms) required. Women and children could do the work in their spare time, and the money they earned would be a welcome addition to the family's income. However, the rural industry model was suitable for only a limited number of products.

Industrial development faced some significant obstacles before the eighteenth century. First, not enough people had the purchasing power to spur large-scale manufacturing (the needs of the wealthy few could be met by luxury handicraft manufacturing). Second, successful entrepreneurs often turned their backs on industrial development, preferring to cultivate their social prestige by investing their capital in unproductive but safe vehicles such as government bonds, country estates, and royal offices. Third, power and fuel remained quite primitive. Although a few industries could use wind or water power, most relied on human or animal muscle. Wood and charcoal were by far the most commonly used fuels, but increased demand led to deforestation, scarcity, and higher prices. Some areas were able to use cheap and plentiful peat moss as fuel, but its weight and bulk made it difficult and expensive to transport. The same was true of coal, although mining operations in areas such as the southern Netherlands and northern England were expanding. Moreover, coal was used primarily for heating rather than metallurgy, as it imparted too many impurities to the refined product. Not until the eighteenth century would these obstacles begin to be overcome.

TRADE AND COMMERCE

One of the notable economic developments in early modern Europe was the growth in both the scale and the scope of trade and commerce. While the high Middle Ages (c. 1000–c. 1300) had seen significant expansion in trade, that growth would be dwarfed in the sixteenth and seventeenth centuries, when European powers began establishing global trade networks in the wake of the great voyages of exploration (see Chapter 5). Less glamorous but probably more important was the growth of the inter-European trade conducted via the seaports of northern and western Europe.

The importance of maritime trade reflected the primitive nature of overland transportation: most roads were barely more than dirt paths, and mud made them impassible to wheeled vehicles for much of the year. Although rivers and especially canals were important commercial arteries, they too were subject to seasonal disruptions that impeded commerce: winter ice, spring floods, and low water levels in the summer.

Other obstacles to commerce were man-made. Most states were neither legally nor economically unified, although England was an exception. This meant that merchants in different regions of the same country were often governed by different legal codes. Furthermore, within most states there were complex systems of internal tolls. In 1567 cargo travelling via the Loire River and its tributaries, all within France, was subject to some 200 tolls in 120 locations. A merchant calculating the cost of that shipment would have to take into account not only the tolls themselves, but the time and labour involved in docking at each tolling point. And of course the obstacles multiplied on rivers that passed through more than state, such as the Rhine, Danube, and Meuse. The fact that systems of weights and measures varied widely presented additional challenges: was a given bushel of wheat the bushel of Paris, or Lyon, or Florence, or Madrid?

Money was even more complicated. Although rulers claimed control over their currencies, many mints were privately owned, and the composition of the coins they produced could not always be trusted to contain the correct amount of gold or silver. Furthermore, because those metals are relatively soft, it was easy for thieves to trim the edges of coins and keep the "clippings" for themselves. (This is why many coins, even today, have serrated or "reeded" edges.) Governments would also periodically recall coins, melt them down, and then reissue them with the same face value, but a lower content of precious metal. Of course, merchants were well aware of these practices: when coins had obviously been clipped, they would demand more of them, and in many cases would weigh rather than count them. All these complications added to the cost of doing business and had the effect of restricting trade. Coins that acquired a reputation for integrity were used far beyond their issuing jurisdiction. Among the reliable gold coins were Florentine florins, Venetian ducats, English sovereigns, and Spanish doubloons; reliable silver coins included English crowns and Spanish "pieces of eight." For accounting purposes, most governments and large businesses used fictional "monies of account" that did not correspond to any physical coin.

Developments in banking helped to grease the wheels of commerce. The establishment of networks of banks in the Middle Ages allowed merchants to travel without carrying large quantities of coin. Now, in the sixteenth century, further advances in credit mechanisms meant that a letter of credit drawn on a particular bank was no longer tied to the original parties, but could be bought and sold over and over. These advances made it easier for merchants to undertake new operations without waiting for shipments in transit to arrive. The development of maritime insurance in the sixteenth century spread risk among a number of parties, so that the loss of a single ship to pirates or a storm did not spell total ruin.

In the Middle Ages, the Mediterranean had been the powerhouse of Europe's maritime trade. The great commercial expansion of the sixteenth and seventeenth centuries, however, involved mainly the Baltic and North Seas and the Atlantic Ocean. This change was driven in part by the fact that by 1500 much of the Mediterranean was controlled by the Ottoman Empire, and in part by population growth in northern and western Europe, but above all by the new opportunities for commerce offered by contact with the New World and Asia.

The merchants and sailors of the Dutch Republic—the seven northern provinces of the Netherlands that began establishing their independence from Philip II of Spain in the late 1500s (see Chapter 4)—would dominate European commerce for the next century. By the early 1600s the Republic's principal city, Amsterdam, not only had replaced Antwerp as the financial centre of European commerce and become a hub for shipbuilders, but was also the headquarters of the famed East India Company, or VOC (*Vereinigde Oostindische Compagnie*). Formed in 1602 as a private company, the VOC was granted a government monopoly on the spice trade with Asia, and soon became the dominant player in all the commerce between Europe and the Far East, ruthlessly defending its position against would-be competitors in England, France, and elsewhere. (There was also a Dutch West India Company, although it never enjoyed the same degree of success.)

More important, though less glamorous, was the Republic's leadership in inter-European trade. In the mid-seventeenth century, the tonnage (cargo-carrying capacity) of the Dutch merchant fleet was greater than that of all other European merchant fleets combined. Crucial to this achievement was the introduction of the *fluytschip*. Until then, almost all merchant ships had been expected to do double duty as warships, but this new vessel was designed specifically for use as a freighter, with a long, shallow hull and a flatter bottom that allowed more room for cargo. It was also significantly less expensive than other ships both to build and to sail, built of pine and fir rather than oak, and with simple rigging that required only half as many crew members. As a result, the Dutch could ship cargo more cheaply than any of their competitors.

The foundation of the Netherlands' prosperity in the seventeenth century was its dominance in shipping on the North and Baltic Seas. Grain grown on noble estates in eastern Germany and Poland would be shipped down river barges to Baltic ports such as Riga, Danzig (modern Gdansk), and Königsberg (modern Kaliningrad), where it would most often be loaded onto Dutch ships for transport to the cities of western Europe. Other commodities shipped from northern and eastern Europe included fish, iron ore, and lumber. On the return trips, Dutch freighters would carry processed and manufactured goods such as wine and textiles. Most of this trade was headquartered in the ports of the Dutch Republic, and Amsterdam became the financial and commercial nerve centre of seventeenth-century Europe.

Nevertheless, the Netherlands' trading and financial operations were essentially traditional. The Dutch enhanced and refined traditional commercial practices, and were better at them than anyone else, but there was nothing revolutionary about Dutch commercial capitalism. Dutch merchants and sailors shipped more goods, and a greater variety of them than ever before, but the basic trading patterns and methods had changed little since the later Middle Ages.

THE PRICE REVOLUTION

Over the course of the sixteenth century, the prices of most goods doubled in real terms; historians have called this period of inflation "the Price Revolution." Increases in grain prices were especially dramatic: in England wheat cost four times as much in 1600 as it had a century earlier, and in France the increase was six-fold. The prices of most manufactured goods rose as well, although these increases were less dramatic.

From our perspective, of course, the inflation of the sixteenth century was insignificant: even if everything had doubled in price over the century, the annual inflation rate would have averaged out to less than 1 per cent. But in an age when the economic order, like the social order, was assumed to be fixed, these changes were alarming, and neither individuals nor governments had the knowledge to understand them—let alone the tools to deal with them.

One factor that contributed to inflation in the 1600s was the flood of gold and silver arriving from the New World, which increased demand for the limited supply of goods available. The fundamental reason for the Price Revolution, however, was the strong population growth that began around the middle of the fifteenth century. Some blamed rising grain prices on hoarding, but that explanation mistook the symptom for the cause, since there would be no reason to hoard unless the price were already rising. Others recognized the impact of American silver, but had no idea of what to do about it. Although prices levelled off after 1600, there were significant variations by commodity and region. Even if workers were able to secure wage increases, they seldom kept up with rising prices. Governments also struggled, as the price increases hit consumers just as rulers were demanding more tax revenue in order to pay for their ongoing wars.

MERCANTILISM

Economic life in the early modern period was governed by a set of assumptions that had no name at the time, but that have been known since the late eighteenth century (when they were rejected) as mercantilism. Three ideas were fundamental to the mercantilist mindset:

1. That wealth consisted of precious metals—silver and gold—and therefore was finite;
2. That the only way to enrich oneself (short of striking silver or gold) was to make someone else poorer; and
3. That the purpose of economic activity was to strengthen the state and its ruler.

Given these assumptions, governments made it a priority to maintain a favourable balance of trade: that is, to maximize the amount of bullion coming into the state's coffers from other states, and minimize the amount going out. One way of doing this was to impose tariffs on imports; another was to subsidize domestic industries. Yet another was to acquire colonial possessions and rely on them for raw materials rather than foreign sources. In this way international trade became a sort of warfare by other means.

Governments did not begin to impose mercantilist principles until about 1650. This was not because the ideas were new, but rather because until then they had not had the power to override the objections of vested interests such as guilds, which sought to maintain their own privileged positions and monopolies. By the later seventeenth century, however, the processes of state-building were far enough advanced that governments were able to implement mercantilist policies even without the consent of those interests. The greatest exponent of mercantilism was Jean-Baptiste Colbert, the finance minister of Louis XIV of France (see Chapter 6), but virtually all European states agreed on the principles.

Chapter Conclusion

From the later Middle Ages until the eighteenth century, the aspects of life covered in this chapter appeared to change very little: demographic patterns, social relations, and economic life all continued much as they had for centuries. Beneath the surface, however, significant changes were under way. Village life was being transformed by the rise of commercial agriculture, while the members of the nobility were facing challenges to their political roles from increasingly powerful monarchs, and to their social pre-eminence from ambitious bourgeois. Increasingly, European society was dominated by an elite, made up of important nobles and affluent bourgeois, in which membership was determined primarily by wealth rather than birth or family. This highlights another important shift that was transforming European society: while privileged orders continued to exist, economic class was becoming more prominent as a category of social organization. As we will see in Chapter 8, the cumulative impact of these changes would become clear in the eighteenth century.

Questions for Critical Thought

1. Early modern Europeans tended to marry several years later than people in other pre-modern societies. How do you think this pattern might have affected European society? How might European society have differed from other pre-modern societies as a result?
2. In early modern Europe, rights or "liberties" generally belonged to groups ("orders" or "estates") rather than individuals. How might this have affected relations between people, and between people and governments?
3. How did popular conceptions of women and femininity contribute to the witch hunts of the sixteenth and seventeenth centuries?
4. A basic assumption of mercantilism was that wealth was determined by ownership of precious metal and was therefore finite. How might this assumption have affected economic activity? How did this view differ from current thinking about economic activity?

Weblink

An excerpt from the *Malleus Maleficarum*:
https://history.hanover.edu/texts/mm.html

Further Reading

Burke, Peter. *Popular Culture in Early Modern Europe*. London: Temple Smith, 1978. A wide-ranging and still useful synthesis, especially strong on Carnival traditions and attempts by political and religious authorities to reform popular culture.

Davis, Natalie Zemon. *Society and Culture in Early Modern France*. Stanford: Stanford University Press, 1975. A collection of classic essays from a pioneering historian of early modern social and cultural history.

DeVries, Jan. *The Economy of Europe in an Age of Crisis*. Cambridge: Cambridge University Press, 1976. Focuses on the economic crises of the "long" seventeenth century.

DuPlessis, Robert S. *Transitions to Capitalism in Early Modern Europe*. Cambridge: Cambridge University Press, 1997. A concise survey of early modern economic history.

Fairchilds, Cissy. *Women in Early Modern Europe, 1500–1700*. London: Longman, 2007. A comprehensive and generally positive overview.

Herlihy, David. *The Black Death and the Transformation of the West*. Cambridge, MA: Harvard University Press, 1997. A brilliant analysis by a leading medieval historian.

Huppert, George. *After the Black Death: A Social History of Early Modern Europe*, 2nd ed. Bloomington: Indiana University Press, 1998. Less comprehensive and more thematic than Kamen, but especially good on social structure and mobility.

Kamen, Henry. *Early Modern European Society*. London: Routledge, 2000. A revised and updated version of a classic and comprehensive work.

Levack, Brian. *The Witch-Hunt in Early Modern Europe*, 2nd ed. London: Longman, 1994. A balanced and comprehensive overview of witch crazes and conceptions of witchcraft.

Notes

1. There are no census figures for European populations before the late eighteenth century. These are very rough estimates based on average household size in the few areas for which documentation has survived.
2. Quoted in Linda A. Pollock, "Parent–Child Relations," in David I. Kertzer and Marzio Barbagli, *The History of the European Family*, vol. 1: *Family Life in Early Modern Times*, 217.
3. Quoted in Henry Kamen, *Early Modern European Society* (London: Routledge, 2000), 28.
4. For discussions of the evidence, see Samuel K. Cohn, *The Black Death Transformed: Disease and Culture in Early Modern Europe* (London: Arnold, 2002); V. Nutton (ed.) *Pestilential Complexities. Understanding Medieval Plague*, London: The Welcome Trust Centre for the History of Medicine at UCL, 2008 (Medicine History, Supplement, no 27); V.J. Schuenemann et al., "Targeted enrichment of ancient pathogens yielding the pPCP1 plasmid of *Yersinia pestis* from victims of the Black Death," *Proceedings of the National Academy of Sciences,* Sept. 2011, vol. 108:38. See also Rosemary Horrox (ed.), *The Black Death* (Manchester: Manchester University Press, 1994); Joseph P. Byrne, *Encyclopedia of the Black Death* (Santa Barbara CA: ABC-Clio, 2012).
5. H.J.C. von Grimmelshausen, *The Adventures of a Simpleton*, trans. Walter Wallich (New York: Continuum, 1962), 1.
6. The proportion of nobles in society varied widely across Europe. In France, Germany, and northern Italy, nobles made up only 1 to 1.5 per cent of the population, but in Poland, Hungary, and Castile, they accounted for as much as 10 per cent. In the Basque country of northern Spain, technically everyone was noble, which in effect meant that no one was.
7. There were some exceptions. In some parts of France, primarily in the south, the tax exemption belonged to the land, not the person. Thus if a noble acquired non-noble land, he would pay the *taille* on it.
8. Emmanuel Le Roy Ladurie, *The Peasants of Languedoc*, trans. John Day (Urbana: University of Illinois Press, 1974).
9. See, for example, E. Le Roy Ladurie, *Carnival in Romans*, trans. Mary Feeney (New York: George Braziller, 1979).
10. For the classic study, see the English historian E.P. Thompson, "The Moral Economy of the Crowd in the Eighteenth Century," *Past and Present*, 50 (1971), pp. 76–136.
11. Brian P. Levack, *The Witch-Hunt in Early Modern Europe* (London and New York: Longman, 1987), 19–22.

2

Europe in the Age of the Renaissance

In 1860 the Swiss historian Jacob Burckhardt proposed that the cultural movement known as the Renaissance marked a radical break with the Middle Ages and the beginning of modern European civilization. Today few historians subscribe to that view, and many would gladly discard both the term and the concept of the Renaissance altogether. Medieval historians long ago put to rest the idea of the Middle Ages as a wasteland separating the civilization of the Renaissance from ancient Greece and Rome, while specialists in economic and social history emphasize the continuities between the late Middle Ages and early modern Europe; they also point out that if there was anything distinct about the Renaissance period, it had nothing to do with a rebirth in literature and the arts. A large part of the problem stems from the fact that the scholars and artists of the Renaissance who praised their own time as one of rebirth and renewal really did believe that they were living at the dawn of a new age.[1]

Even if the Renaissance was not the pivotal movement identified by Burckhardt, there is no doubt that it was an important historical phenomenon: a broad intellectual and cultural movement characterized by rebellion against certain aspects of medieval civilization. Nevertheless, its influence was limited to the domain of arts and letters, and even there, older ideas continued to exist alongside those of the Renaissance. It is also important to recognize that the Renaissance was relevant to very few people: the vast majority continued to live as their ancestors had for generations, entirely untouched by it. In short, although the term "Renaissance" is often applied to everything that took place between the mid-fourteenth century and the mid-sixteenth, very few of those developments had anything to do with the Renaissance movement.

The first part of this chapter will look at the cultural, literary, and artistic movement of the Renaissance in the context that gave rise to it: that of late medieval Italian urban society. The second will examine the political world of the Italian city-states and compare it with the development of the "medieval" kingdoms of Europe outside Italy. The collision of these two political universes in 1494, when King Charles VIII of France invaded Italy, would transform both the politics and the culture of the Italian Renaissance.

The Italian Renaissance

SOCIAL AND POLITICAL CONTEXT

By the middle of the sixteenth century, the Renaissance would have spread across Northern Europe, but it originated in the early fourteenth century in a particular social, cultural, and political setting: the city states of central and northern Italy. It is worth considering how this setting might have contributed to the feeling, among the early Renaissance thinkers and artists, that they were living in a better world than the one their ancestors had inhabited.

Throughout the Middle Ages, northern and central Italy had been the most highly urbanized area of Europe. Its cities—Milan, Venice, Florence, and Bologna, to name only a few—were home to a large and prosperous middle class, people who earned their livings as master craftsmen, or merchants, or professionals dealing with an increasingly complex society. The same was true to some degree across western Europe, of course, but nowhere were such cities more concentrated than in Italy. In the later Middle Ages, almost all these cities had established some form of self-government, while north of the Alps political power remained in the hands of monarchs and feudal lords.

A social order that recognized only three kinds of people—clergy, nobles, and peasants—did not reflect the experience of the educated, ambitious citizens of Italy's self-governing urban republics. Such men no longer felt attuned to the feudal values that continued to govern societies north of the Alps—obedience, respect for hierarchy, deference to authority. And although they continued to be faithful Christians, they wanted more from the Church than exhortations to put eternal life in paradise above the transitory life of this sinful world. As a consequence, many of these people began to develop new values more relevant to their lives. They found a more congenial model in ancient Rome—like theirs, an urban, commercial society, governed by its leading men—and their window on this lost ideal world was ancient literature.

RENAISSANCE HUMANISM

Renaissance humanism originated in the world of business and government, among the notaries who drafted wills and contracts and the civil servants who drew up memoranda for city governments, drafted instructions for ambassadors, diplomatic treaties, and so on. To make their documents more elegant and persuasive, they looked for models in the literature of ancient Rome. They became known as humanists because of their practical focus on grammar and especially rhetoric, the *studia humanitatis* (humane studies, or humane letters) of the university curriculum, as opposed to the abstract dialectical reasoning that dominated scholastic thought. Over time, they discovered previously unknown texts and became aware of a decline in the Latin language over the centuries. Through their study of ancient Roman texts, they became conscious of the cultural gulf that separated their world from that of the ancients.

HISTORICAL DEBATE

Burckhardt's Renaissance and Its Critics

Jacob Burckhardt published *The Civilization of the Renaissance in Italy* in 1860, and for generations his argument that the Renaissance marked the beginning of modern European civilization was widely accepted. Although this view is still influential in popular culture, historians have largely rejected it as exaggerating both the originality and the importance of the Renaissance.

> In the Middle Ages both sides of human consciousness—that which was turned within as well as that which was turned without—lay dreaming or half awake beneath a common veil. The veil was woven of faith, illusion, and childish prepossession, through which the world and history were seen clad in strange hues. Man was conscious of himself only as member of a race, people, party, family, or corporation—only through some general category. In Italy this veil first melted into air; an *objective* treatment and consideration of the State and of all things of this world became possible. The *subjective* side at the same time asserted itself with corresponding emphasis; man became a spiritual individual and recognized himself as such. . . .
>
> To the discovery of the outward world the Renaissance added a still greater achievement by first discerning and bringing to light the full, whole nature of man.
>
> This period . . . first gave the highest development to individuality, and then led the individual to the most zealous and thorough study of himself in all forms and under all conditions.
>
> Jacob Burckhardt, *The Civilization of the Renaissance in Italy*, trans. S.G.C. Middlemore (New York: Harper Torchbooks, 1958), 143–44, 279, 303.

Renaissance humanism, conceived of as "a new philosophy of life" or a glorification of human nature in secular terms, melts away into vagueness as soon as the

Humanists were therefore concerned with reviving the study of ancient texts not only as an intellectual pursuit, but as a way of recovering the values of a civilization with which they felt a deep affinity. It would be incorrect to say that they rediscovered ancient literature itself, for medieval scholars had had access to a great deal of it. Unlike the latter, however, the humanists became conscious of the need for a fresh and historically more accurate understanding of this literature.

Humanism was not a discrete and coherent philosophy. Nevertheless, humanists did share a number of attitudes and aspirations, beginning with the desire to give new life to the values of antiquity. In this quest, many of them found a role model in Cicero: the Roman critical historian tries to define the terms of that philosophy or that glorification. . . . Likewise the central attribute of Burckhardt's interpretation, a new spirit of individualism, proves to be so nebulous that it threatens to become a universal human tendency that finds expression in all historical periods. Burckhardt made the mistake of putting a secondary characteristic, a heightened sense of individualism, in place of the truly primary characteristic, the new historical consciousness that emerged in the thought of Petrarch. This sense of being engaged in the restoration of true civilization after many centuries of barbarian darkness finds its first clear statement in the works of Petrarch, and some such claim is common to virtually all . . . the crucial figures in the history of humanism. The claim is of course wholly unfair to the cultural achievements of the Middle Ages, but it . . . was the defining characteristic of Renaissance humanism, and anyone who wants to understand humanism must take it into account.

Charles G. Nauert, *Humanism and the Culture of Renaissance Europe*, 2nd ed. (New York: Cambridge University Press, 2006), 21.

Like all self-images, that of the scholars and artists of the Renaissance was both revealing and misleading. Like other sons rebelling against their fathers' generation, these men owed more than they knew to the "Middle Ages" they so frequently denounced. If they overestimated their distance from the recent past, they underestimated their distance from the remote past, the antiquity that they admired so much. Their account of their rebirth was a myth in the sense that it presented a misleading account of the past; that it was a dream, a wish-fulfilment. . . .

    Burckhardt's mistake was to accept the scholars and artists of the Renaissance at their own valuation, to take this story of rebirth at its face value. . . .

Peter Burke, *The Renaissance*, 2nd ed. (New York: St. Martin's Press, 1997), pp. 1–4.

statesman, philosopher, and orator who was held to be the most eloquent of all Latin stylists, and was equally admired for his private virtue and his engagement in the civic life of Rome.

    Also central to humanism was the belief in that it was appropriate for humans to pay attention to this life and this world. This is in part what Burckhardt was referring to when he wrote of the Renaissance thinkers' discovery of both "the outward world" and "the full, whole nature of man." Burckhardt overestimated the secular nature of this discovery, for the humanists remained devoutly Christian in a solidly Christian society. Nevertheless, they did insist that the things of this world had value in themselves, alongside the eternal values of the Church and Christianity.

Humanism began outside the universities, in opposition to the world of the medieval scholastics, with what humanists considered their useless speculations, debased Latin, stultifying preoccupation with logic, and unthinking, ahistoric reliance on authorities. Humanist education was therefore designed to equip young men with the skills they would need to prosper in the real world of merchants, lawyers, and citizens: the ability to judge what was good and right, and to use elegant, compelling language to persuade others of their convictions.

HUMANIST PROFILES

Humanism found expression in a variety of ways and forms. Petrarch (Francesco Petrarca, 1304–74) is widely considered the first humanist. Born in Tuscany to a Florentine family in exile, he spent much of his youth in southern France during the Avignon papacy. Although obliged to study law by his father, after the latter's death in 1326 he abandoned his studies to devote himself to poetry. Soon after, he saw and—though he never met her—fell deeply in love with the young woman he called Laura. Thereafter he alternated between serious works in Latin (including an epic modelled on Virgil's *Aeneid* and numerous literary and scholarly works), and lyrical sonnets to Laura, written in Italian rather than Latin. It was through his letters, however, that he became a guiding figure for the humanists. One of the most famous, describing his ascent of Mount Ventoux, near Avignon, reveals both an appreciation of the natural world and a profoundly Christian conscience.

In the early fifteenth century, a number of humanists in Florence responded to a military threat from the powerful Duke of Milan with what some historians have called "civic humanism," condemning tyranny and extolling the virtues of republican liberty. Key to this circle was Coluccio Salutati (1330–1406) who served as Chancellor of Florence from 1375 until his death. His student and successor as Chancellor was Leonardo Bruni (1374–44), who wrote a *History of Florence* modelled explicitly on the Roman historian Livy's history of Rome, and a famous *Panegyric to the City of Florence*, in which he contrasted Florence's republican virtue, devotion to liberty, and accomplishments in the arts to Milan's suffering under the yoke of a tyrant. Poggio Bracciolini (1380–1459), like Bruni, was a protégé of Salutati and Chancellor of Florence from 1453 to 1459, but he was also a scholar, and as a delegate to the Council of Constance from 1414 to 1417, he spent his spare time hunting through the churches and monasteries of southern Germany and Switzerland for lost or little-known manuscripts of ancient works. Among other works, he rediscovered a complete text of Quintilian's work on rhetoric *De institutione oratore* (*On the Education of the Orator*), which became one of the major Renaissance textbooks on rhetoric.

The most prominent Latin scholar of the fifteenth century was a student of Bruni and associate of Bracciolini named Lorenzo Valla (1407–57). A secretary at the papal court and cultural adviser to King Alfonso of Naples, in 1444 he published *The Elegancies of the Latin Language*, with examples of correct and incorrect usage. He was most famous, however, for using his knowledge of Latin to prove that a document known as the *Donation of*

VOICES

Petrarch

About 500 of Petrarch's letters have survived; probably as many have been lost. In the first excerpt below, he responds to accusations that his literary efforts detract from his piety. In the second, he details his objections to the scholastic preoccupation with logic (dialectic).

Neither exhortations to virtue nor the argument of approaching death should divert us from literature; for in a good mind it excites the love of virtue and dissipates, or at least diminishes, the fear of death. To desert our studies shows want of confidence rather than wisdom, for letters do not hinder but aid the properly constituted mind which possesses them; they facilitate our life, they do not retard it. . . .

While I know that many have become famous for piety without learning, . . . I know of no one has been prevented by literature from following the path of holiness. . . .

Letter to Boccaccio, quoted in James H. Robinson, *Petrarch: The First Modern Man of Letters* (New York: G.P. Putnam's Son, 1914), pp. 391–4.

There is one thing which I myself long ago observed, and of which you now warn me anew. These logicians seek to cover their teachings with the splendour of Aristotle's name; they claim that Aristotle was wont to argue in the same way. . . . Why is not the name of Aristotelians a source of shame to them rather than of satisfaction, for no one could be more utterly different from that great philosopher than a man who writes nothing, knows little, and constantly indulges in much vain declamation? . . . Not only are they good for nothing else, but their perverted activity renders them actually harmful. . . . I know that it [logic] is one of the liberal studies, a ladder for those of us who are striving upwards, and by no means a useless protection to those who are forcing their way through the thorny thickets of philosophy. It stimulates the intellect, points out the way of truth, shows us how to avoid fallacies, and finally, if it accomplishes nothing else, makes us ready and quick-witted.

All this I readily admit, but because a road is proper for us to traverse, it does not immediately follow that we should linger on it forever. . . . Dialectics may form a portion of our road, but certainly not its end; it belongs to the morning of life, not to its evening.

Letter to Tomasso da Messina, in Robinson, *Petrarch*, pp. 219–22.

Constantine was a forgery. Supposedly written in the fourth century as a record of an edict by the Emperor Constantine ceding large portions of central Italy to the pope, it had long been used by the Church to justify its sovereignty over the Papal States. Based on the document's Latin, however, Valla proved that it could not possibly have been written before the eighth century and was therefore a fake.

At first, humanists concentrated their efforts on Latin language and literature. Western European scholars had lost virtually all knowledge of Greek during the Middle Ages, but in the course of the fifteenth century it was revived. In 1397 Coluccio Salutati had invited a famed Greek scholar from Constantinople named Manuel Chrysoloras to Florence, where he trained an entire generation of humanists in Greek language and literature. Diplomatic negotiations with the Byzantine Empire brought many Greek scholars to Italy, and many more came after the Ottoman conquest of Constantinople in 1453. From the middle of the fifteenth century, a basic knowledge of Greek was considered an essential part of a complete education.

For long time, humanism remained a strictly Italian phenomenon, so closely tied to the Italian context that it would have made little sense anywhere else. In the course of the fifteenth century, however, humanist ideas did begin to appear north of the Alps. Among the early German humanists were Peter Luder (1414–74), Rudolf Agricola (1444–85), and Conrad Celtis (1459–1508), all of whom had travelled to Italy as students. No doubt the presence of displaced Italians, such as Aeneas Sylvius Piccolimini (1405–64, later Pope Pius II), who served as a diplomat for Holy Roman Emperor Frederick III, also helped in the northward spread of humanism. Although it would be premature at this point to identify a distinctive "northern" humanism, such a movement would be taking shape by 1500 (Chapter 3).

Renaissance Neoplatonism

As we have seen, the humanists rejected the abstract and speculative philosophy that had so entranced scholastic thinkers, and were less concerned with ultimate questions of existence than with how to live in the here and now—that is, moral philosophy or ethics. Nevertheless, with the renewal of the study of Greek came a revival of interest in the philosophy of Plato, and in 1462 Cosimo de Medici established a Platonic Academy outside Florence, under the direction of Marsilio Ficino (1433–99). One of the leading Greek scholars of his time, Ficino had been groomed for this position from his youth, when he was adopted by Cosimo and raised in the Medici household. In addition to translating all of Plato's *Dialogues* into Latin, making them accessible to a wider audience, he wrote a massive *Platonic Theology* designed to harmonize Plato and Christianity. He also translated a series of writings known as the Hermetic corpus, attributed to the ancient sage that the Greeks knew as Hermes Trismegestus ("thrice-great Hermes") and to the Egyptians as the god Thoth. They were believed to contain esoteric knowledge from the very remote past, and proper understanding of them was thought to be a key to unifying all religions and philosophies, a goal central to Neoplatonism. In fact, these works were products of late antiquity, and rather than influencing Plato, they were influenced by Platonic thought.

One of the most famous writers to emerge from the Platonic Academy was Giovanni Pico della Mirandola (1463–94). The brilliant son of a noble family, he was fluent in Latin and Greek by the age of sixteen, and went on to learn both Hebrew and Arabic in order to read philosophical works in those languages, particularly the Hebrew mystical works known as Kabala. In 1486, after completing his studies with Ficino, he went to Rome and published his *900 Theses*: a collection of statements that he proposed to debate with leading scholars and philosophers. Although Pico's goal was to reconcile all religions and philosophies with Christianity, several of his theses were condemned as heretical, and he was forced to flee to France.

Pico's most famous work, *The Oration of the Dignity of Man*, was composed as an introduction to the *900 Theses*. In it he argued that God had assigned humanity no fixed place in the hierarchy of Creation, that man was free to cultivate all the facets of his nature, and that the highest form of existence was that of the "pure contemplator, unmindful of the body, [who] wholly withdraws into the inner chambers of the mind . . . [and] is neither a creature of earth nor a heavenly creature, but some higher divinity, clothed in human flesh."

Clearly, Neoplatonists such as Ficino and Pico employed the tools of humanism in understanding and translating Platonic literature. Yet there is a persuasive case to be made that their ultimate goal was something different than humanism as we have defined it. Humanism originated in the desire to equip men with the knowledge to live good lives here and now, to make practical contributions to society and governance of their time. Renaissance Neoplatonists had something very different in mind. Their vision was an otherworldly one, in which the goal was union with the divine, achieved through mystical contemplation. While its roots were in humanism, in many ways Renaissance Neoplatonism represented a retreat from the principles that had driven earlier humanists. It was at least in part a response to a changing world, one in which the urban republics that had given birth to humanism had fallen into the hands of powerful lords or oligarchs.

RENAISSANCE ART

Alongside the literary culture of humanism, what defined the Renaissance as a movement were achievements in painting, sculpture, and architecture. As a rule it is hazardous to generalize about a period or society on the basis of something so individual and idiosyncratic as its art. In this case, however, developments in art dovetail with the larger movement. Indeed, the world of art furnished a kind of template for Burkhardt's conception of the Renaissance; among his section titles, for example, was "The State as a work of art." It is in the world of the arts that we see most clearly the Renaissance's discovery of both the world and man. Paralleling the evolution of Renaissance art was an evolution in the status of the artist, from simple artisan to, at the highest level, divinely inspired genius. This development can be seen as a kind of complement to humanism's emphasis on individuality and the dignity of man.

Characteristics of Renaissance Art

Among the defining characteristics of Renaissance art is what we might call its naturalism. The idea that the real world was a suitable subject for the artist had a clear parallel in humanist thought (not surprisingly, since the people who commissioned or bought such work were, if not humanists themselves, influenced by humanist ideals). Part of the new naturalism can be attributed to the discovery of the rules of perspective, which enabled artists to create the illusion of three-dimensional space on a flat surface. Although landscapes remained relatively rare, increasingly realistic depictions of the natural world began to appear in the backgrounds of paintings in many genres.

The new emphasis on realism was even more evident in depictions of the human figure. Most medieval art had given no sense of a human body beneath the clothes. Now, Renaissance artists worked from human models, and some, like Leonardo da Vinci, actually dissected cadavers in order to understand anatomy. In the Middle Ages, actual portraits of people were so rare as to be virtually unknown. Paintings that purported to depict individuals—whether rulers, saints, or biblical figures—in fact portrayed ideal types designed to evoke emotions such as reverence, awe, sorrow, or pity. In the Renaissance, however, realistic individual portraiture—unseen since antiquity—once again became central, a concrete expression of Burckhardt's "discovery of man." Not only did wealthy patrons pay for portraits of themselves and their families, but artists themselves began to produce self-portraits (completely unknown in the Middle Ages).

In addition, whereas medieval artists had focused almost exclusively on religious subjects, those of the Renaissance sometimes addressed classical themes, as in Botticelli's *Birth of Venus* (p. 61) and often incorporated classical elements into depictions of religious subjects, as in Massacio's *Trinity* (p. 58) or Piero della Francesca's *Flagellation of Christ* (p. 60). Michelangelo's *David* (p. 61) depicts a biblical figure in a style that strongly suggests a Greco-Roman god.

It is in architecture that we see the classical influence most clearly. Italians were surrounded by the architectural remnants of Roman civilization, and Renaissance architects studied them closely. The simplicity, clarity, and balanced proportions of the style they derived from those classical models stood in sharp contrast to the "Gothic" style of the Middle Ages.[2]

Finally, there is a general sense of harmony and balance in Renaissance art that distinguishes it from both the heavy ornamentation of the late Gothic period and the drama of the seventeenth-century Baroque period. Among the elements that Renaissance artists discovered in Greco-Roman models was the relaxed, informal pose known as *contrapposto*, in which most of the figure's weight is carried on one leg, leaving the other free; the result is a sense of natural movement, caught in a moment of repose.

The Development of Art in the Renaissance

The sixteenth-century artist and art historian Giorgio Vasari believed that the revival in art began with Giotto di Bondone (c. 1267–1337). Although most art historians today would classify Giotto as a late medieval painter, there is no doubt that he pointed the way to the future. In his work, human figures are clearly distinct individuals, portrayed with a solidity and depth that were lacking among his contemporaries, and they are placed in natural settings (below).

Alfredo Dagli Orti / The Art Archive at Art Resource, NY

Giotto, *The Flight into Egypt*

Masaccio, *Holy Trinity with the Virgin and St. John*

It would be almost a century before anyone took up the path that Giotto had opened. No doubt the Black Death was largely responsible for this hiatus: not only did it kill many artists (and patrons) outright, but it cast a pall over the confidence of those who survived. The result was a period of conservatism that lasted for several generations. Not until the early fifteenth century did a new generation of artists once again begin to expand the boundaries of possibility in art. Three major figures heralded the arrival of the new Renaissance style.

Although Masaccio (1401–28) died very young, before he could train any students, his works announce the arrival of the new style almost fully developed. In addition to showing his mastery of perspective, his *Holy Trinity with the Virgin and St. John* (above)

Masaccio, *The Expulsion from the Garden of Eden*

Donatello, *David* (c. 1430)

Filippo Brunelleschi, the Pazzi Chapel

Piero della Francesca, *The Flagellation of Christ*

Sandro Botticelli, *The Birth of Venus*

Michelangelo, *David*

Michelangelo, *The Creation*, from the Sistine Chapel

Raphael, *Madonna and Child with St. John the Baptist*

incorporates fully realistic human figures in classical architectural setting, and his *Expulsion from the Garden of Eden* (p. 59) is surely one of the most vivid expositions of grief and despair in all of art.

Donatello (c. 1386–1466) was the first sculptor to produce free-standing human figures since antiquity. His bronze David shows the biblical hero as a young boy, standing (in classical *contrapposto*) over the head of the slain Goliath (p. 59). Later works, such as his reliefs of *St. George and the Dragon* and the *Feast of Herod*, show his increasing mastery of perspective.

Donatello's friend Filippo Brunelleschi (1377–1456) also began as a sculptor, but became known above all as the architect of the dome that crowns the cathedral in Florence—the first dome to be constructed since antiquity. The two friends had travelled to Rome to learn from the achievements of ancients, and it seems likely that Brunelleschi's work on the dome owed something to his study of Rome's Pantheon (c. 120 CE). Among the other buildings in Florence that reflect his classically simple style is the Pazzi Chapel (p. 60).

Both Donatello and Brunelleschi lived long enough not only to teach and inspire others, but to witness a virtual explosion of artistic genius in the fifteenth century. The worldly monk Filippo Lippi (c. 1406–69) became known for his beautiful and sensitive Madonnas, while Paolo Uccello (c. 1397–1475) applied his skills most famously to the battlefield. Giovanni Bellini (c. 1431–1516) and Giorgione (1478–1510) developed a distinctive Venetian style, with sumptuous colours. Andrea Mantegna (c. 1431–1506) was court painter to the Gonzaga rulers of Mantua. Sandro Botticelli (1444–1510) was a favourite of Lorenzo de Medici; several of his works, including *La Primavera* (*Allegory of Spring*) and *The Birth of Venus* (p. 61), are rich in Neoplatonic imagery, evoking the beauty both of nature and of the human body.

Most art historians would agree that three artists represent the pinnacle of Renaissance art: Leonardo (1452–1519), Michelangelo (1475–1564), and Raphael (1483–1520). Leonardo was a true genius and polymath, an engineer as well as a painter and architect. His *Last Supper* and *Mona Lisa* are surely two of the most famous paintings ever executed. Michelangelo thought of himself primarily as a sculptor, but he also worked as a painter and architect. The Florentines adopted his *David* as a symbol of their city, and Pope Julius II commissioned him to carve statues for his tomb, before insisting that he abandon that work to paint the ceiling of the Sistine Chapel (p. 62). Raphael was so highly regarded for his subtle and peaceful Madonnas (p. 62) that he consorted with popes and cardinals, and, according to Vasari "lived more like a prince than a painter."

That Raphael, who died at 37, enjoyed such lofty standing in his own lifetime is a measure of how dramatically the social status of the artist changed in the Renaissance. Medieval artists had been skilled journeymen who, like any craftsmen, laboured in anonymity and were governed by the rules of their guilds. This system continued through the Renaissance, with apprentices and lesser artists working in the studios of the famous painters, preparing materials and filling in background according to the directions of the master. Yet by the peak of the Renaissance, the great artists of the age were revered as uniquely talented geniuses. Giorgio Vasari, an eminent Renaissance artist in his own right, wrote of Leonardo:

> In the normal course of events many men and women are born with various remarkable qualities and talents; but occasionally, in a way that transcends nature, a single person is marvellously endowed by heaven with beauty, grace, and talent in such abundance that he leaves other men far behind, all his actions seem inspired, and indeed everything he does clearly comes from God rather than from human art.[3]

As was the case with humanism, much of the artistic life of Renaissance Italy was centred in Florence, especially under the patronage of Cosimo and Lorenzo de Medici. As we will see in the next section, however, in 1494 France invaded Italy, plunging Florence into the first in a series of political crises. As a consequence, many artists relocated either to Rome or to Venice, where they continued developing in new directions.

Politics and Governance in the Renaissance

In Burckhardt's view, modern political history began in Renaissance Italy, where he saw exhibited for the first time "the State as the outcome of reflection, the State as a work of art"[4]—as the product of human agency, rather than something natural or divinely ordained. In this section we will examine the evolution of the Italian states from their emergence as self-governing entities in the later Middle Ages until 1494, when the Italian political universe was transformed by the French invasion. Then we will look at the development of the supposedly backward and medieval monarchies to the north and west. In the process we will put to the test Burckhardt's view of the Renaissance Italy as the birthplace of the modern state.

In order to do that, however, we need a standard of modernity. Among the markers of political modernity that have been proposed are these:

1. a common allegiance among the people, a sense of the nation as an "imagined community";[5]
2. generally recognized territorial boundaries;
3. general stability of institutions and constitutional arrangements; and
4. sovereignty: that is, the state recognizes no obligation or allegiance to any power outside itself.

THE ITALIAN STATES OF THE RENAISSANCE

Although Renaissance cities such as Florence, Milan, and Venice are often called "city-states," it would be a mistake to think of them as either small versions of modern states, or the capital cities of small states. A city like Florence or Venice extended its control over the neighbouring countryside or *contado*, as well as over neighbouring towns, but the residents of those towns and villages did not have the right to call themselves Florentines or Venetians: only inhabitants of Florence or Venice identified themselves as such, and even among those people, only a select few (generally guild masters) were citizens. The fact that Florence conquered Pisa, for example, did not make Pisans into Florentines: they remained Pisans, and would rebel at the first opportunity.

While it is true that modern states have not always respected the boundaries of other states, in general territorial integrity is recognized today. By contrast, the city-states of Renaissance Italy were inherently expansionistic. Thus when Duke Giangaleazzo Visconti of Milan conquered large parts of northern Italy and threatened the independence of Florence in the late fourteenth century (inadvertently lighting the spark of civic humanism), he had no concept either of Florence as a sovereign entity or of Milan as a state whose boundaries he wanted to expand: he was simply conquering as much territory as he could.

Similarly, whereas today political institutions and constitutions are generally stable, a notable feature of the Italian states was the instability of their institutions and constitutions. From the later Middle Ages through the Renaissance, despots overthrew republics

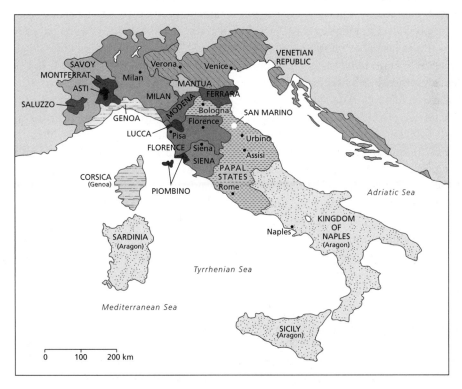

Map 2.1 The states of Renaissance Italy, 1453

and were overthrown in their turn, and powerful families constantly vied for control. There was no concept of a loyal opposition, or of a state as an abstract entity that commanded the loyalty even of those who considered the people in power their enemies. Often, those who lost power faced exile, confiscation of property, and even death. Italian politics was a cutthroat business, played for the highest stakes: the winner took all the spoils, and kept them until he in turn was overthrown.

The Renaissance city-states sometimes behaved as if they were sovereign, owing no allegiance to any higher authority. Yet officially most of Italy north of Rome was part of the Holy Roman Empire, while much of central Italy was officially subordinate to the pope, and those higher authorities were still capable of taking action for or against the city-states under their jurisdiction.

It was in their relations with each other that the Italian states look the most like modern sovereign states, pursuing their own interests, independent of any outside power, and competing for land and resources. It was the fact that relations among them were almost inevitably hostile that led them to invent much of the machinery of modern diplomacy: permanent embassies and ambassadors, diplomatic immunity, and intelligence services.

In 1454 the five major Italian states signed the Peace of Lodi, which ushered in forty years of relative peace. The treaty recognized the relatively recent power of Cosimo de Medici in Florence and Francesco Sforza in Milan, and guaranteed the security of Venice's mainland possessions, which had been under threat from Milan. It also established a balance of power among the states, and bound them together to defend Italy against foreign attack. From 1454 until the French invasion of 1494, relations among the Italian states became more tranquil, as their conflicts were carried out mainly in the realm of diplomacy rather than on the battlefield.

Warfare among the Italian states was generally conducted by independent military contractors or *condotierri*, who put their mercenary armies at the disposal of their employers. This contributed to the general instability of relations among the states, as rivals would try to bribe or intimidate their enemies' generals into changing sides or simply quitting. The interests of the *condotierri* often ran counter to those of their employers, as they had no interest in a war to the death; they wanted to preserve their investment in their armies, to live and fight again another day. Thus much Italian warfare of the Renaissance has an air of display and ritual about it: armies would manoeuvre, seeking to gain a tactical advantage, and when one of them succeeded, the other would agree to an honourable retreat and everybody would go home happy. Their familiarity with this "phony war" pattern would place the Italians at a distinct disadvantage after the French invasion of 1494, when they would face the much larger and more ruthless military machines of the "feudal" monarchies.

Most Italian cities had established themselves as self-governing urban republics in the Middle Ages. Although none of them were democratic in the modern sense, they had at least granted a degree of political participation to the men recognized as citizens. By the fifteenth century, however, there were few truly republican regimes left. Instead, most had evolved in one of two directions, becoming either despotisms under the rule of a single lord and his family, or oligarchies, controlled by a handful of powerful families.

By the fifteenth century, warfare, expansion, and consolidation among the Italian states had produced five major states and a few smaller ones. The five major ones were, from north to south: Milan, Venice, Florence, the Papal States, and the Kingdom of Naples. Among the smaller and less powerful states were Mantua, Ferrara, Urbino, and Genoa. What follows is a brief introduction to the Italian city-states as they existed on the eve of the French invasion of 1494. We will examine the consequences of that ground-changing event later in the chapter.

Milan

The large and wealthy city of Milan dominated the fertile Lombard plain of northern Italy, and its geographic position gave it control over several important passes through the Alps into northern Europe. Originally a self-governing commune, by about 1200 it had fallen under the rule of the Visconti family. In 1395 Giangaleazzo Visconti (1352–1402) purchased the title of Duke of Milan from the Holy Roman Emperor. Although Giangaleazzo was in many ways an enlightened and cultured ruler, his successors reverted to the cruel and capricious tyranny of earlier Visconti rulers. Duke Filippo Maria (1392–1447) was so hated that he shut himself up in his fortified palace for fear of assassination. To defend his empire in northern Italy, he employed the leading *condotierre* of the time, Francesco Sforza, husband of his illegitimate daughter Bianca. When Filippo Maria died without a male heir in 1447, the citizens of Milan enlisted Sforza's aid in restoring a republican regime, but Sforza then turned his army on the infant republic and had himself installed as the new duke. Like Giangaleazzo Visconti, Sforza was an able and effective ruler. He was also an enlightened and cultured patron of the Renaissance arts. He played an influential role in the Peace of Lodi of 1454, which not only recognized him as Duke of Milan, but also brought a measure of peace and stability to Italy.

On Francesco's death in 1466, however, a prolonged period of feuding began among his prospective successors. His immediate heir, Galeazzo Maria—a vicious tyrant who preyed on the property and wives of his nobles—was assassinated in 1476 and succeeded by his young son Giangaleazzo Sforza (1469–94), but the real power lay with the boy's uncle Lodovico, who governed for him as regent. A younger son of Francesco, called *il Moro* (the Moor) because of his swarthy complexion, Lodovico was an able and cultured man, and for the most part a master diplomat. Nevertheless, it would be Lodovico who, as we will see, unwittingly set off the chain of events that led to the French invasion of Italy in 1494 and the end of Milan's independence, as well as his own imprisonment and death.

Venice

Venice was known as *la serenissima* (the "most serene one"), and its political history was much the same. Sheltered by its lagoons and marshes, it was able to avoid much of the turmoil that characterized medieval Italy. Because of its dependence on the sea, it became the leading naval and commercial power in the Mediterranean, profiting especially from the Crusades, and becoming fabulously wealthy. In order to protect and promote the trade that was its lifeblood, Venice established an empire of territorial possessions throughout the Adriatic and eastern Mediterranean. It enjoyed privileged relations first with the Byzantine Empire and then with the Ottomans, and exercised a practical monopoly on all the Asian trade travelling through Asia Minor and the Black Sea.

Until the time of the Renaissance, Venice remained largely isolated from the rest of Italy. In the fourteenth century, however, it was compelled to acquire territory on the mainland, both to feed its growing population and to prevent the expansion of Milan from cutting off its merchants' access to markets both in Italy and north of the Alps. Therefore Venice set out to conquer an "empire" in northeastern Italy.

In theory Venice was a republic, but in practice it was a tightly controlled oligarchy. There was a nominal chief executive known as the doge, who was usually elected from among the senior statesmen as a kind of capstone on a distinguished career in public life, but over the Middle Ages his power had become mostly ceremonial. The real source of political power was the Great Council, which for centuries had consisted of all male Venetians entitled to political participation. In 1297, however, membership in the Great Council was restricted to those families who had already been represented on it. They numbered about 250, and would maintain a tight grip on the republic for the next five hundred years. All important offices were held by members of these families. There was the Senate, the legislative arm, elected by the Great Council from among its members. The Great Council also elected the *collegio* or cabinet, whose members ran the various branches of the government. On top of this, there was the secretive Council of Ten, elected annually by the Great Council from among its own members. Its mandate was the security of the state, and it was empowered take over various governmental functions whenever that was thought necessary.

The complex Venetian system worked in ways that those of other Italian city-states did not, partly because there were no competing interests: every Venetian's livelihood depended on the city's trade. It also worked because the Council of Ten maintained a network of informers and spies throughout the city, and a network of boxes throughout the city, the infamous *bocche del leone* (lions' mouths), invited individual Venetians to submit anonymous denunciations (on the other hand, false accusations were severely punished).

Venice's most frequent opponent in Italian diplomacy was Milan, whose expansion threatened the ability of Venetian merchants to gain access to markets on the mainland. The two cities were at war for most of the early fifteenth century, and Venice strongly objected to Francesco Sforza's seizure of power in Milan. Although the 1454 Peace of Lodi recognized Sforza's grip on Milan, it also guaranteed the integrity of Venice's mainland territories.

Despite its conquest of Padua, an important university town full of scholars and libraries, acquired in 1405, Venice remained largely aloof from the culture of the Renaissance until the later fifteenth century. In particular, its history, economy, and political culture meant that humanist ideals found little resonance there. After the

French invasion of 1494, however, it was the only city-state other than Rome that remained independent of outside control, and it soon became a focal point of Renaissance literature and art.

Florence

The city of Florence is inextricably associated with the Renaissance. Nevertheless, in many ways it is the poster child for both the prosperity and the political instability of medieval Italian cities. The foundation of its economy was the woollen industry, which provided profits that led families such as the Medicis to expand into banking. Yet despite, or perhaps because, of its prosperity, the city was rent by economic and social strife. In 1378 a group known as the *Ciompi* (workers in the woollen trade) led a popular revolt that resulted in the installation of a more democratic regime, but in 1381 that regime in turn was overthrown by a coalition of artisans and merchants in support of the leading aristocratic families. The pendulum then swung to the other extreme, and although formally Florence remained a republic, it was controlled by a handful of leading families, most notably the Albizzi, in their own interests.

Opponents of this aristocratic oligarchy, the Medici family rose to power in the fifteenth century. Cosimo de Medici (1389–1464), the founder of the family's political fortunes, became the spokesman of the lesser craftsmen who had been excluded from a political role in the reaction to the revolt of the *Ciompi*. In 1434 Cosimo gained control of the governing council, the *Signoria*, and his family would be the dominant political force in Florence for the next sixty years.

Cosimo maintained Florence's republican constitution, exercising control subtly, from behind the scenes. In order to prevent empire-building, most offices were held for very short terms, and their occupants were selected by drawing lots from among eligible citizens. The Medici political machine operated primarily by manipulating the lists of those eligible for office in favour of its supporters. Cosimo himself lived a relatively modest life, held formal office only when his name was drawn, did not flaunt his power, and assiduously maintained a wide circle of friends and clients. He was also extremely adept in the complex and dangerous world of Renaissance diplomacy. He was the moving spirit behind the Peace of Lodi in 1454, which brought a measure of peace and stability to the fractious and violent relations among Italian states. He was also an important patron of scholarship and the arts. It was Cosimo who founded the Platonic Academy. It was also Cosimo who sponsored the competition to complete Florence's still unfinished cathedral (a lingering civic embarrassment), and it was under his influence that the commission was won by Brunelleschi. When Cosimo died in 1464, the mourning was genuine, and he was granted the title *pater patriae*, or "father of the fatherland."

Power passed without incident to his son Piero (1416–69), under whom the first cracks in Medici power began to appear. Educated as a humanist and raised like a nobleman, he was aloof and haughty, in distinct contrast to his accessible father. When Piero died in 1469, power passed to his eldest son Lorenzo (1449–92), later known as *il Magnifico*. It was under Lorenzo that the Renaissance in Florence reached its peak. Highly educated himself, he was a talented poet and amateur artist, and the leading artistic patron of the fifteenth century, sponsoring not only Michelangelo, but Fra Filippo Lippi and Sandro Botticelli as well. From the point of view of high culture, his Florence does indeed appear as a golden age. Yet Lorenzo also neglected the foundations of his family's power. He had little interest in the Medici bank, and its prosperity waned. Over time, he neglected the networks of clients and "friends of friends" that Cosimo had cultivated, taking their support for granted rather than continuing to nurture it.

In 1478 his family's bitterest rivals, the Pazzi family, entered a conspiracy with Pope Sixtus IV (r. 1471–84), whom Lorenzo had angered by refusing his request for a loan. On Easter Day 1478, Lorenzo and his brother Giuliano were attacked while attending Mass in the cathedral. Giuliano was killed and Lorenzo seriously wounded. The sacrilege of the attack, along with genuine support for the Medici, roused the public against the conspirators, and Medici control lived on. Nevertheless, the experience changed Lorenzo. He began to travel with armed guards, and in 1480 he altered the constitution in ways that made his family's formerly subtle control of the city more overt.

Disenchantment with the Medicis is most clearly seen in the career of Girolamo Savonarola (1452–98), a Dominican friar, apocalyptic preacher, and self-appointed guardian of public morality. Inveighing tirelessly against the wickedness of the age, condemning its arts and literature as pagan and sinful, he attracted a significant following. His influence reminds us that the culture of the Renaissance was not all-pervasive, that traditional Christianity and "medieval" values still exerted a strong hold on large numbers of people. In fact, the list of Savonarola's supporters came to include the Neoplatonist Pico della Mirandola, the painter Botticelli, and even the sick and dying Lorenzo, who summoned the friar to his bedside.

When Lorenzo himself died in 1492, the reins of power passed to his son Piero (1472–1503), who proved incapable of maintaining his family's political power and was equally out of his depth in the dangerous waters of late-fifteenth century diplomacy. In particular, he neglected the balance of power implicit in the Peace of Lodi of 1454, which Cosimo and Lorenzo had carefully nurtured. When the French army arrived in 1494, Florence was the first domino to fall. The Medici were ousted and exiled from the city, the republic was restored, and Savonarola became its leading figure.

Rome and the Papal States

Together, Rome and its surrounding area constituted the Papal States, or States of the Church. Their history in the Middle Ages was closely tied to the nature and concerns of individual popes. Some were saintly and took seriously their duties as successors of St. Peter. Others were scholars and patrons of the arts. Still others saw the papacy as a vehicle to be used for the benefit of themselves and their families. We will discuss their characters and failings as the leaders of Christendom when we examine the origins of the Protestant Reformation. In this chapter, we will focus on the popes' roles as Italian rulers.

For most of the Middle Ages the popes' control over the Papal States was more theoretical than real, even in Rome itself. One of the motivations behind the papacy's move to

Avignon in 1309 was the fact that Rome itself had been made unsafe by ongoing feuding among the Roman noble clans. During the seventy years that the popes resided in Avignon, cities such as Bologna, Ancona, and Rimini established a practical independence from Rome, and lawless nobles did whatever they could get away with.

With the end of the Great Schism, the restored Pope Martin V (r. 1417–31) returned to Rome in 1420, only to find the city in ruins and its population reduced to some 20,000 from a medieval peak of perhaps 50,000. Rebuilding Rome thus became a priority for Martin and his successors, and in this they were very successful. Martin himself was an important patron of scholarship and the arts, as was Nicholas V (r. 1447–55), who founded the Vatican Library, and Pius II (r. 1458–64) was himself an important humanist.

Another major concern of the restored papacy was to eliminate the threat that conciliarism posed to its control of the Church. In order to gain a secure base of revenue and power that would insulate them from challenges to their position, the popes needed to establish real control over Rome and the Papal States. And to that end the popes of the Renaissance played the game of Italian politics by the same cutthroat rules as everyone else. As we shall see, the Pazzi conspiracy was just one example.

The most venal and corrupt of all the popes of the period was unquestionably the Spaniard Rodrigo Borgia, who reigned from 1492 to 1503 as Pope Alexander VI. Not only did he live openly with his mistresses (one, the married noblewoman Giulia Farnese, was the virtual Queen of Rome), but whereas most previous popes had at least pretended that their offspring were "nieces" and "nephews," he openly acknowledged his children Cesare, Juan, and Lucrezia. He was also open in his practice of nepotism, placing both sons in important Church positions (Cesare was made a cardinal at a very young age, while Juan was given command of the papal armies). Meanwhile, he used Lucrezia as a pawn for political advantage. When her first marriage was no longer politically expedient, he had it annulled through perjury, and after her second husband was murdered by her brother Cesare, married her off to the powerful Duke of Ferrara.

After Juan was murdered, Cesare (the prime suspect) quickly stepped into his shoes, working with his father to carve out a Borgia principality in the Romagna (a particularly lawless and chaotic part of the Papal States). Cesare was well on his way to achieving this goal when his father died suddenly in 1503 and was succeeded by his bitterest enemy, now Pope Julius II (1503–13). Although Cesare fled to Naples, he was captured and imprisoned there for two years before being sent to Spain, where he died in 1507.

It was under Julius II that the papacy's control of the Papal States was firmly established. A huge and terrifying figure, known as *papa terribile*, he strapped himself into his papal armour and personally led the army that subdued the wealthy and important city of Bologna. He was also extremely adept at manipulating the complex and shifting alliances of the period following the French invasion of 1494, and became one of the most important artistic patrons of the Renaissance.

From one point of view the popes of the Renaissance were successful rulers, rebuilding Rome, taking control of the Papal States, and in the process defeating the threat of conciliarism. In terms of their roles as the spiritual leaders of Christendom, however, those worldly victories were pyrrhic at best. As we will see in the next chapter, the very qualities that allowed them to succeed in politics and diplomacy undermined their authority as the spiritual leaders of Christendom.

The Kingdom of Naples

The Kingdom of Naples occupied the entire southern half of the Italian peninsula and, at times, the island of Sicily. The only kingdom in Italy, it was a land of impoverished peasants and autonomous barons that in many ways had more in common with the feudal world north of the Alps than with the prosperous, highly urbanized Italian city-states that gave rise to humanism and the Renaissance.

If the kingdom itself was unaffected by those movements, however, its tangled political and dynastic history had a profound, if indirect, effect on them. During the later Middle Ages it was claimed by two rival dynasties: a branch of the French royal dynasty known as the Angevins, and the ruling family of the Spanish Kingdom of Aragon. After decades of disorder, the dispute was finally settled in the late fourteenth century in favour of the Aragonese, who had the support of the pope. As a consequence, the papacy continued to regard the Kingdom of Naples as a papal fief and its crown the pope's to bestow.

From 1416 to 1458, Naples and Sicily were united under the rule of the Aragonese king Alfonso the Magnanimous, and on his death in 1458 Sicily remained under the rule of Aragon. The mainland, however, passed into the hands of Alfonso's illegitimate son Ferrante (r. 1458–94), whose hold on power depended on the support of Florence and the Medici, for whom Naples represented an important ally against Rome. Meanwhile, the Angevin claim to Naples had been inherited by the kings of France, and when Ferrante died in 1494, King Charles VIII of France decided that the time was right to press that claim, with disastrous consequences not only for Italy but for the Renaissance movement itself.

Minor Italian States

Italian politics and diplomacy were dominated by the "Big Five," but other rulers and states survived the political struggles and consolidation of the later Middle Ages. The port city of Genoa, on the Ligurian Sea in northwestern Italy, became Venice's great rival for Mediterranean commercial and naval dominance. Unlike its rival, however, the Genoese republic was very violent and unstable, with frequent coups, dictatorships, and foreign interventions, and in the end, Venice gained the upper hand. Although Genoa remained nominally independent after the French invasion and the beginning of the Italian wars, in reality it was closely tied to Spain, diplomatically, militarily, and financially. Politically, after much internal disorder, it became an oligarchy of its noble mercantile families.

Three other small states were of negligible importance in terms of the larger Italian political scene, but nevertheless played major roles in the cultural movement of the Renaissance. Sandwiched between Venice, Milan, and the Papal States, Mantua was ruled by the Gonzaga family, and its court became a showplace of Renaissance culture after Francesco II Gonzaga, marquis of Mantua, married Isabella d'Este (1474–1539). The daughter of the duke of the neighbouring city of Ferrara, Isabella was among the most important art patrons of the time. She was also known for her learning and intellect. Ruling as regent after her husband's death, she proved to be an able diplomat, managing to negotiate the dangerous shoals of Italian diplomacy and preserve Mantua's independence.

Isabella's native Ferrara had flourished under the enlightened and cultured leadership of her grandfather, Duke Borso d'Este (1413–71), and father, Ercole I (1413–1505), both of whom were active patrons of the arts. In addition to establishing Ferrara as a leading musical centre, Ercole rebuilt much of the city in elegant Renaissance style.

The third small city-state, Urbino, became renowned as the home of Duke Federigo da Montefeltro (1422–82), a skilled general and *condotierre* who was universally respected for his honour and trustworthiness. An accomplished humanist scholar, he employed a

Federigo da Montefeltro and his son Guidobaldo, by Pedro Berruguete (c. 1450–1504) or Justus van Ghent (c. 1410–c. 1480). Considered the model prince of the Renaissance, Federigo was first Count and then Duke of Urbino. His armour indicates his military prowess, while the book he is reading points to his scholarship and patronage of scholars. The pearl-encrusted mitre in the upper left was a gift from the Ottoman sultan.

staff of scribes to copy classical texts from his impressive library, and filled his palace with works by the leading artists of the time. When the soldier, diplomat, and writer Baldessare Castiglione wrote his famous treatise on the qualities of an ideal Renaissance courtier (see below), he set it at the court of Urbino, where he had spent years in the service of Federigo's son Guidobaldo and his wife, Elisabetta Gonzaga.

THE FEUDAL MONARCHIES

As we have seen, the fourteenth century in northern Europe was marked by multiple crises: political fragmentation and violence, the Black Death, peasant and urban revolts, the Avignon Papacy. Once the worst of the crises had passed, however, most of the rulers involved were able to resume the centuries-long process of centralizing their power. Indeed, the recovery was so swift and dramatic in these kingdoms (at least in hindsight) that some historians have proposed that their rulers represent what they call "New Monarchy."

None of these rulers saw themselves as doing anything new or revolutionary. They were always careful to justify their actions as traditional and customary, and their goal was identical to the goal of their ancestors: to enhance their control of their territory and their subjects. On the other hand, it is possible to argue that fifteenth-century monarchs attained a level of success that had eluded their medieval predecessors. At the same time, one can see in the late fifteenth century the beginnings of an institutional structure and professional bureaucracy, separate from the person and household of the king.

All these monarchies faced similar obstacles to the expansion of their power. One was the independent political power of the nobility, derived from feudalism. The age of the great feudal magnates who were capable of challenging their kings was coming to an end. But every ruler had to deal with hundreds or thousands of nobles who exercised virtually independent political, judicial, and military power. In the eyes of the nobles, the king was only the first among equals, and they were his natural partners in governing. They believed that they owed him obedience when he was right, but that when he was wrong, it was their duty to rebel.

The second obstacle concerned money, or rather the lack of it. Then as now, governments were chronically short of revenue, especially in wartime. Ideally, a medieval king was supposed to be able "live of his own": to administer the country's affairs using nothing more than the revenue from his own lands and certain customary fees, without imposing taxes. Taxation was considered an extraordinary measure, reserved for emergencies only. In practice, however, by the later Middle Ages most kingdoms had established institutions whereby rulers could legitimize taxation by consulting their leading subjects and gaining their approval. The precise composition of these consultative bodies varied from country to country, as did the terms they were known by—the Estates-General in France, Parliament in England, *Landtags* in the German states, *Cortes* in the Spanish kingdoms—but their purpose was the same: to represent the wealthy and powerful, whose consent and cooperation the king required. Of course, these assemblies were not in any sense democratic.

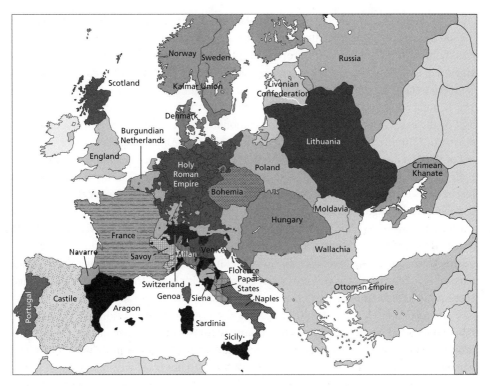

Map 2.2 Europe c. 1500

The Church was another obstacle to the expansion of royal power. Its influence had declined in the later Middle Ages, but was still substantial, and its wealth was largely immune to taxation. Many functions that we associate with the state, such as laws governing marriage and inheritance, were handled by the Church; every penny paid in tithes was a penny that escaped the royal treasury; clergy were subject to canon law and largely immune to royal law. Although the popes had bargained away some of the Church's power in the fight against conciliarism, it was still very real.

None of these obstacles was completely overcome by any ruler in this period. Nevertheless, substantial progress was made, and the ability of the barons to limit royal power was clearly on the wane.

The Recovery of France

For more than a century, the kings of France had been fighting the kings of England in the Hundred Years War. Although the earlier stages of the conflict had been disastrous for France, the tide turned in the 1430s, and by 1453 the only remaining English foothold in France was the Channel port of Calais. Over the next four decades France's situation would improve to the point that its king would be able to invade Italy and contend for European supremacy.

Although most of this recovery took place under King Charles VII (r. 1422–61) and his son Louis XI (r. 1461–83), the reasons for it go beyond individual personalities. France was the wealthiest kingdom in Europe, in resources and population. In the course of the Hundred Years War, several institutional changes were made that allowed the royal government to tap into this potential in ways that few other rulers could.

Among the most important was the eclipse of the Estates-General, which had first met in the early fourteenth century, as a national representative body. At several points during the Hundred Years War, the institution might have become a permanent component of the royal government, but this did not happen, partly because many provinces had their own assemblies and therefore saw no need for a national one. The main reason for the institution's eclipse, however, was that during the 1430s, when the danger of travel made it difficult to arrange meetings, the Estates-General empowered the king to collect taxes without its consent. Although this measure was intended only as a temporary response to a wartime emergency, it would remain in place until the French Revolution. As a consequence, the royal government was able to collect its most important tax (the *taille*) in large parts of France without the consent of any representative body. Thus the French kings had access to revenue that none of their rivals could match.

The *taille* was a kind of primitive income tax that—once exemptions for the Church, most nobles, and many individuals, towns, and regions were taken into account—fell disproportionately on the peasants. Imperfect and inefficient as the *taille* was, it was unmatched as a source of revenue. In addition, a host of sales taxes were assessed on goods such as wine, wheat, and salt.

Charles VII was able to use this tax revenue to establish the embryo of a permanent royal army. The earlier stages of the Hundred Years War had been fought, with disastrous results, by an army that was essentially feudal in nature, composed of soldiers provided by the king's noble vassals for a specified period of time. Although knights were usually well trained and equipped, foot soldiers often were not, and disagreements among the nobles meant that their forces were plagued by factionalism. Between 1445 and 1448, however, Charles VII established the core of a professional royal army: 15 mounted *compagnies d'ordonnance* commanded by officers named by and responsible to the king, and a parallel infantry force known as the *francs-archeurs*.

At the same time, Charles VII was enhancing his control over the Church in France. In 1438, as the restored papacy was in the midst of its struggle with the conciliarists, he issued a document known as the Pragmatic Sanction of Bourges, which threw the weight of his crown behind the conciliarists. Although the document was never fully enforced, it cast a long shadow, serving France as a kind of blackmail against the papacy. This was the beginning of what would become known as Gallicanism, or the Gallican liberties of the French Church: the principle that for certain purposes of finance, personnel, and administration, the Catholic Church in France was autonomous from Rome.

Charles VII and Louis XI also made significant progress in reducing or eliminating the power of the feudal magnates who had so troubled their predecessors. In particular, Louis XI was successful in countering the Duke of Burgundy. The title was inherited from a younger son of an earlier king, who had been given the province (north of the Alps) to govern as a kind of branch office of the monarchy. Over several generations, successive dukes had expanded their territory into the Netherlands, and by the early fifteenth century they were acting as independent rulers, outshining their cousins and supposed feudal superiors, the kings of France, both in wealth and in power. Louis XI, who was famous for his intricate plotting, outwitted Duke Charles the Bold, and after the latter was killed in battle in 1477, he seized the Duchy of Burgundy and the County of Artois, while Charles's sole heir, his daughter Mary, managed to retain the neighbouring Free County of Burgundy (Franche-Comté) and the rest of her father's lands in the Netherlands. This made the youthful Mary one of the wealthiest rulers in Europe, and the chief prize in dynastic diplomacy. Louis also strengthened the ties between the French crown and the largely independent Duchy of Brittany by marrying his son and heir to the daughter and heir of the Breton duke.

In addition to dealing with these magnates, both Charles and Louis also had to face a number of noble revolts against their centralizing policies. In the end, however, the nobles were undone by their self-interest, which made them susceptible to divide-and-conquer tactics. Louis XI was especially adept at out-manoeuvring his opponents.

Louis XI was succeeded on the throne by his young son Charles VIII (r. 1483–98), who did nothing to undo the gains made by his father and grandfather. His reign was most notable for the invasion of Italy in 1494 to gain control of the Kingdom of Naples, which he believed to be rightfully his by virtue of dynastic inheritance. This watershed event was made possible only by the dramatic recovery that France had experienced in the previous seventy years, a recovery in which we can see the faint outlines of a modern state.

England after the Hundred Years War

Following its virtual expulsion from France at the end of the Hundred Years War, England became embroiled in a series of civil conflicts known as the Wars of the Roses. Henry VI (r. 1422–61), who had been king since infancy and suffered from intermittent bouts of mental illness, was a weak and ineffectual ruler. Two factions of the royal family sought to control him before he was deposed, and after his death they fought for the crown itself. These were the houses of York and Lancaster.[6] The great nobles who contended for power recruited their own private armies, and without an able king to rein them in, they drove England towards anarchy.

After a lengthy series of coups, counter-coups, and palace revolutions, the Wars of the Roses came to an end in 1485. It was at the Battle of Bosworth Field that the Yorkist King Richard III (r. 1483–85) was defeated and killed, leaving the victor—Henry Tudor, who had inherited the Lancastrian claim to the throne—to claim the throne as King Henry VII (r. 1485–1509) by virtue of heredity and right of conquest in a just war.

Henry's genealogical claim to the throne was tenuous, as he was descended from an illegitimate child of a younger son of King Edward III (r. 1327–77). And even though he married the foremost Yorkist heiress soon after taking the crown, ensuring that their children would be descendants of both houses, there were still plenty of Yorkists around who had stronger claims. Several times during his reign, Henry VII had to suppress rebellions in the name of Yorkist pretenders. But he proved to be a very effective ruler, and overcame or weakened a number of obstacles to royal power.

There was very little "new" about what the way Henry VII ruled. The laws he decreed against the raising of private armies by nobles were difficult to enforce, and the practice lived on for some time. But he turned the practice to his own benefit by requiring nobles to furnish a certain number of armed men for his own use. Those who resisted faced trial in Parliament, which Henry ensured was packed with loyal supporters. Some of those found guilty were indeed executed or had their property confiscated, or both. More commonly, however, Henry exacted bonds from the guilty party, or confiscated part of their property, and then held out the hope of restitution on condition of good behaviour and future service. This policy killed a number of birds with one stone: reducing a noble's wealth not only reduced his ability to resist the king but enriched the royal treasury, and gained the king a useful servant tied to the Crown by material interest.

Henry was very conscious of the fact that in order to be respected, a king needed wealth. He directed Parliament to pass an act that restored to the Crown all lands alienated under previous kings. He enforced a host of fees and dues that had been allowed to lapse uncollected. Peace and the demographic and economic recoveries of the later fifteenth century brought increased royal revenue through customs and excise taxes, especially on the woollen trade, which Henry took steps to encourage. Over the course of his reign, his annual revenue almost tripled.

Henry was also cautious on the expenditure side of the budget. Because he avoided expensive entanglements in foreign affairs, keeping England mostly on the sidelines of the period's tumultuous diplomacy, he avoided the necessity of building and maintaining a costly army. As a result, for the most part he was able to "live of his own" and rarely had to rely on Parliament for grants of taxation. Although he called Parliament ten times between 1485 and 1497, as he consolidated his grip on England, from 1498 until his death in 1507 it met only once, and it was always under firm royal control. His good management of Parliament strengthened the king, not only by ensuring that it would grant taxation when necessary, but by demonstrating to the kingdom and the world that he had the support of his most important subjects.

As in France, then, royal authority in England was significantly strengthened in the later fifteenth century. However, whereas in France this revival required the eclipse of the Estates-General, the ability to tax without consent, and the creation of a permanent royal army, Henry VII was able to accomplish it almost entirely with the traditional tools at hand. On his death, he left his successor a peaceful and well-ordered kingdom, a nobility with a weakened capacity to challenge the throne, and a full treasury.

The Iberian Kingdoms

In the later Middle Ages there was no such thing as a kingdom of "Spain." Rather, the Iberian peninsula was home to four distinct political, cultural, and linguistic entities: Granada to the south; Castile in the centre, Aragon to the northeast, and Portugal to the west.

Granada was the last outpost of the Muslim power that in the eighth century had occupied most of the peninsula, but had been gradually driven back by the forces of the

Christian *Reconquista*. Castile, whose military nobility had been in the forefront of that campaign, was the largest and most populous kingdom, and was expanding economically as demand for its merino wool increased in the industrial centres of Flanders and Italy. Aragon, a federation of three smaller territories (Valencia, Catalonia, and Aragon proper), was more urban and commercial, although its economy was stagnating. Finally, Portugal, facing the Atlantic, was busy exploring the west coast of Africa (see Chapter 5).

In 1469 the heirs to the thrones of Aragon and Castile, Ferdinand and Isabella respectively, married. Isabella inherited the Castilian crown in 1474 and Ferdinand that of Aragon in 1479. Although the couple ruled jointly, the two kingdoms would remain institutionally and politically separate until the early eighteenth century.

Royal power in Aragon was constrained by the fact that, in addition to the *Cortes* (representative assembly) for the entire kingdom, there were separate *Cortes* for each of the three territories, which jealously guarded their rights and privileges. In Castile, by contrast, royal power was in theory much greater: although there was a Castilian *Cortes*, it met only when summoned by the monarch, and its membership was determined by royal invitation. Yet in practice the power of the Castilian monarchy was constrained by a handful of powerful nobles or grandees who ruled their vast estates almost as independent fiefdoms. To make their theoretical power real, therefore, Isabella and Ferdinand needed to curb the power of the grandees.

To this end, they cultivated the support of the Castilian towns through frequent meetings of the Cortes, which of course was packed with their supporters. Both the rulers and the towns had a direct interest in suppressing noble power and the lawlessness that it often gave rise to. At a meeting of the Cortes in 1476, they established a combination police force and judicial tribunal known as the *Santa Hermandad* (Holy Brotherhood) to keep order in the countryside. At the same time, the rulers relied increasingly on professional administrators rather than the grandees in their government. While careful to preserve the grandees' social status and avoid any direct attack on their wealth, the rulers marginalized them from the centres of power. The grandees were also excluded from the royal council, whose membership was limited to commoners from the 1480s on.

Isabella and Ferdinand also took steps to address Castile's debt, reforming the coinage and forcing nobles to return vast amounts of land that had been alienated from the Crown during the reigns of her predecessors. The real boost to Castile's fiscal fortunes, however, lay in the future, when gold and silver would begin to flow into its coffers from the New World.

The most important achievement of Isabella and Ferdinand's reign came in 1492, when the last Muslim forces were driven out of Granada. In recognition of their devotion to the Church, the pope awarded them the honorific title "Most Catholic Monarchs." In the aftermath of the conquest of Granada, Ferdinand and Isabella took what they believed to be the glorious final act in the restoration of religious unity to Castile when they expelled all practising Jews. Of approximately 80,000 Jews, about half converted and stayed; the other half took what they could carry and fled; many of the latter met their death through starvation, disease, and exposure.

Medieval Spain had had a long history of tolerance and coexistence among Christians, Muslims, and Jews. As the *Reconquista* advanced, however, Jews faced increasing suspicion and persecution, and this led many to convert to Christianity. A considerable number of these New Christians, or *conversos,* rose to prominence in Castilian society, but the sincerity of their Christian faith was often questioned, especially since many retained their Jewish names, dress, and cuisine. Many Old Christians wrongly came to believe that there was a widespread conspiracy of *conversos* who were only pretending to be Christians.

It was to address this "problem" that the Spanish Inquisition was created in 1478. Although it was established with the permission of the pope, its operations were completely outside papal control, and its members were named by the rulers alone. Its original mandate was specifically to root out the secretly practising Jews among the *conversos,* not to deal with Jews or Muslims or Christian heretics as such, although it would later be deployed against all these groups. Significantly, the Inquisition was the one institution common to both Castile and Aragon; one of its purposes was to strengthen religious uniformity in a land that lacked other sources of unity. Ironically, the expulsion of the Jews in 1492 only exacerbated the problem that the Inquisition had been created to solve, creating a whole new class of people whose Christianity was open to question in that (unlike that of the original *conversos*) it was forced on pain of exile.

Today, of course, the Spanish Inquisition is a byword for fanaticism and cruelty. Yet without whitewashing the historical record, it must be said that both the reach and the cruelty of the Inquisition pale in comparison with the more recent horrors of the Nazi Holocaust, Stalinism, or the Khmer Rouge. Torture was used not to punish, but to elicit confessions, and was tightly regulated. By the time the institution was abolished in 1834, it had been responsible for perhaps 5000 deaths: not an insignificant number, but far fewer than the estimated 60,000 executed as witches in the same period. Much more frequent than execution was public humiliation and confiscation of property.

Spanish rulers exerted influence over the Church in other ways as well. One-third of all tithes paid in Castile went to the royal treasury, which also collected the proceeds from the *cruzada,* an indulgence that had been introduced to pay for the *Reconquista,* but was continued after 1492.[7] In the newly conquered Granada, the pope awarded to the Crown the right to appoint church officials, and this right was eventually extended to Castile's overseas possessions. Although the Crown never achieved the same degree of control outside Granada and the colonies, in 1523 Ferdinand and Isabella's grandson would obtain the right to choose his candidates for bishop throughout his Iberian territories. Unlike many other rulers of the period, Isabella was personally very devout, and she took a sincere interest in the welfare of both the Church and the souls of her subjects. As we will see in Chapter 3, her support of the reform-minded Cardinal Ximenez de Cisneros, the Archbishop of Toledo, would render the Protestant Reformation largely irrelevant in Castile.

Ferdinand and Isabella were less successful at consolidating and expanding the monarchy's power in Aragon. After 1494, Ferdinand's Aragonese interests would lead him, and inevitably Castile, into the maelstrom of Italian warfare and diplomacy. Since Ferdinand and Isabella's only surviving son had died in 1497, on her death in 1504 the crown of Castile passed to their daughter Juana, but she was incapacitated by mental illness, and therefore Ferdinand served as regent until his death in 1516. At that point Juana's son Charles, born in 1500, became king of Aragon and co-ruler of Castile as Charles I. As unexpected as this turn of events might have been a decade earlier, it would soon be followed by two equally unforeseen developments that would change the future of European diplomacy. The first was the fact that in 1519 Charles would be elected Holy Roman Emperor. The second was the discovery of fabulously productive gold and silver deposits in Mexico and Peru, which would give Charles and his successors vast resources to use in the pursuit of their foreign policy.

The Holy Roman Empire

By the late fifteenth century France, England, and the Spanish kingdoms were all developing into centralized monarchies, but this was not the case for the Holy Roman Empire. Although formally its territory included northern Italy, the Low Countries, and Switzerland, even the emperors acknowledged that, for all practical purposes, it did not extend beyond Bohemia and Germany; and in reality their power had been greatly diminished even in Germany. In the fourteenth century, Emperor Charles IV had decided to focus on expanding and consolidating his own dynasty's hereditary lands in Luxemburg, Bohemia, and Brandenburg, rather than seeking to restore imperial power *per se*. Accordingly, in 1356 he issued a document known as the Golden Bull, which regularized imperial elections. It defined as imperial electors the rulers of seven principalities: the Duke of Saxony, the Margrave of Brandenburg, the King of Bohemia, the Count Palatine of the Rhine, and the Archbishops of Mainz, Trier, and Cologne (the last three not only were important church offices, but also controlled significant German territories). These seven princes would hold a special rank within the empire as Electors and be recognized as sovereign within their own lands; the Emperor would have no rights in those territories. Charles was in fact gambling that a majority of the Electors would continue electing his own Luxembourg dynasty to the imperial throne. This was not an unreasonable gamble, since he himself was King of Bohemia, his son was Elector of Brandenburg, and he had the support of the ecclesiastical Electors.[8] What Charles could not have foreseen was that neither of his two sons would have male heirs to continue the dynasty.

In 1438 the Electors chose Albert of Habsburg, Archduke of Austria, as Holy Roman Emperor. From then until the end of the Empire in 1806, all emperors but one would come from the Habsburg dynasty. Albert was chosen primarily because he was not a powerful prince and posed little threat to German rulers. Here again, however, unforeseeable events intervened to vastly enlarge the Habsburg lands and give future emperors enough resources to make many attempts to restore imperial power in Germany.

A few months before Albert's grandson Maximilian married Mary of Burgundy, in 1477, her father, Duke Charles the Bold, had died in battle. As we have seen, Louis XI of France managed to seize the Duchy of Burgundy, but the adjacent Free County of Burgundy (Franche-Comté) and most of the Netherlands remained under the control of Mary and her husband. When the latter became Emperor Maximilian I in 1493, therefore,

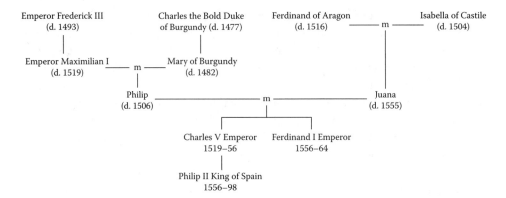

Figure 2.1 The Habsburg inheritance

Map 2.3 The empire of Charles V

he had not only the resources of the Habsburg hereditary lands of Austria, but also the wealth of the Netherlands to devote to his plans for reform, which included a single supreme court for the Empire, a common tax, and a common army.

In the end, though, none of these plans amounted to much. They were hampered by Maximilian's absorption in the Italian wars after 1494, a lack of sustained attention, the hostility of German rulers, and a lack of funds. Thus the Empire remained a loose conglomeration of roughly 150 imperial cities, several hundred princes, and several thousand imperial knights held together by virtually nothing apart from the Emperor himself and a periodic assembly called the Diet, or Reichstag.

It was to strengthen his dynasty that Maximilian arranged the marriage of his son Philip to Juana of Spain. Quite unintentionally, then, a scenario was taking shape in which Philip's oldest son, the young Charles of Habsburg, would become the heir to a vast multinational empire. From his maternal grandparents he would inherit the Spanish kingdoms of Castile and Aragon, along with Castile's nascent colonial empire and Aragon's Italian claims. From his paternal grandmother, Mary of Burgundy, he would inherit the Franche-Comté and the Netherlands. And from his paternal grandfather, Maximilian I, he would eventually inherit the Austrian lands and the title of Holy Roman Emperor. In time, the future Emperor Charles V would not only disrupt the balance of power among Europe rulers, but bring his enormous resources to bear on restoring imperial power in Germany.

THE FRENCH INVASION AND THE ITALIAN WARS

In 1494 King Charles VIII of France launched an invasion that was to have enormous consequences for the Renaissance, for Italy, and for Europe as a whole. The reason for the invasion was to take possession of the Kingdom of Naples, to which the ruling French Valois dynasty had inherited a claim. This in itself tells us something about the importance of dynastic relations in European politics and diplomacy: who ruled what was determined largely by relations among ruling families. It did not occur to anyone to ask the Neapolitans whether they wanted to be ruled by France. Nor did it matter to Charles that the poor and remote Kingdom of Naples brought no real advantage to France, strategic or otherwise.

It was Lodovico Sforza who set the wheels in motion. He governed Milan in the name of his nephew, but desperately wanted the title of Duke for himself. He enlisted France's support and offered its armies free passage across his territory. From there the French marched south virtually unopposed and easily took Naples.

France's success not only demonstrated how vulnerable Italy was, but cast a long shadow over European diplomacy. Since no other ruler wanted to see France add to its power by expanding into Italy, in 1495 Pope Alexander VI, Ferdinand of Aragon, Emperor Maximilian, and Lodovico Sforza formed an alliance that succeeded in driving the French back across the Alps. Although Charles VIII intended to try again, he died in 1498 before he was able.

The French invasion set off more than sixty years of war among European rulers. The great prize was control of Italy, which would guarantee European hegemony for whichever foreign monarch could take it. The victories of foreign powers such as France and Spain demonstrated the vulnerability of the Italian states to "barbarians" with greater resources and the tools to access them relatively efficiently. It is unnecessary to recount the course of these wars in any detail, but several important developments deserve mention.

Since Charles VIII had died childless, he was succeeded on the French throne by his cousin Louis XII (r. 1498–1515), who in addition to the claim to Naples had inherited a claim to the Duchy of Milan, which was economically and strategically much more important. Thus in 1499 Louis marched into Italy with the goal not only of retaking Naples, but of taking Milan as well, in both of which he succeeded. In 1503, however, the accession of the warlike Pope Julius II led to the formation of an anti-French alliance among the Italian states, Ferdinand of Aragon, and Maximilian. By 1504 the French had been driven from Naples by Ferdinand, and by 1513 the latter had expelled them from Milan as well, causing Louis to renounce any claim to it. On his death two years later, however, the throne passed to his cousin Francis I (r. 1515–47). Young and vigorous, the new king was anxious to win military glory, and in 1515 he led yet another French army across the Alps. Following a huge victory at Marignano, just outside Milan, Francis had himself installed as Duke of Milan.

In 1516, therefore, the French dominated the north of Italy, while the Spanish dominated the south, leaving Venice and Rome the only major Italian states not under foreign control. It was at this point that young Charles of Habsburg reached the age of majority and began to govern his vast empire.[9] From then on, the Italian war would be a duel for European supremacy between the Spanish/Imperial Habsburg dynasty and the Valois kings of France.

In Florence, Savonarola had hailed Charles VIII and his army as God's avengers, sent to punish the Florentines for their sins. The Medici fled for their lives and the citizens then restored a republican regime along pre-Medicean lines, but stability remained elusive. Savonarola appeared to be the only figure who could restore order, and he was brought into the government, where he remained the leading figure for several years. He put into action his puritanical vision for Florence, outlawing gambling, swearing, horse races, and profane songs. He organized gangs of youths to roam the streets, searching out and punishing offenders, and sponsored "bonfires of the vanities" in which people could publicly demonstrate their repentance by burning such frivolities as books, jewellery, makeup, and works of art. By 1498, however, his puritanical regime was wearing thin, and he had proven to be at least as politically inept as Piero de Medici. These factors, combined with the hostility of Pope Alexander VI, whom Savonarola condemned in the harshest terms, and the resentment of the aristocratic families who believed that they should have been running Florence, eventually led to the friar's overthrow. Excommunicated by the pope and abandoned by his supporters, he was arrested, and on May 23, 1498, he was hanged and his body burned in the Piazza della Signoria. The citizens of Florence then installed a moderate republican regime, but it was unable either to end the factional strife or to defend the city militarily. In 1512 a Spanish army allied with the pope took Florence and restored Medici rule.

The Later Renaissance

Renaissance humanism was closely linked to the social and political context of the republican city-states in which it developed. By the middle of the fifteenth century, however, as we have seen, most of those republics had succumbed to either despotism or oligarchy. In such a world, what place did the values of Salutati and Bruni have? Where was the scope for virtuous and eloquent statesmen in the Ciceronian tradition to steer the fortunes of their fellow citizens?

Worse, by the early sixteenth century Italy was facing foreign invasion, nearly continual warfare, and the loss of political control to foreign "barbarians." Italians were keenly aware that a catastrophe had befallen them, and it was natural that they sought to understand what had gone wrong and how to fix it. These transformed circumstances can be seen in some of the most influential literature of the later Renaissance.

LITERARY RESPONSES

Niccolò Machiavelli

The fact that Niccolò Machiavelli (1469–1527) wrote primarily in Italian was in part an indication of how urgent he felt that his message to be: he sought to address not a limited circle of humanist scholars who would appreciate elegant classical Latin, but as broad an audience as possible. Machiavelli was a Florentine diplomat and civil servant who rose to great prominence in the republican regime that followed the expulsion of the Medici in 1494. When Medici power was restored in 1512, however, he left political life and devoted himself to writing.

Unfortunately, his most famous work, *The Prince*, is usually read in isolation, and this often leads readers to think of its author as an amoral apologist for tyrants. When *The Prince* is read in conjunction with his *Discourses on the First Ten Books of Titus Livius* (reflections on the history of Rome written by the ancient Roman historian Livy), it becomes clear that Machiavelli did not support authoritarian rule on principle. Rather, he was a confirmed republican who recognized with regret that a republican government was incapable of dealing with the disorders of the time: what was needed was a single ruler, a prince, strong enough to fight back against the evils of the age. It was important, therefore, that this ruler be adept at gaining and maintaining power. Nevertheless, he believed that the support of the people was the surest guarantee of the prince's power, and the ultimate goal was always the welfare of the state.

Machiavelli recognized that times change, and that men must change their methods and outlooks to suit the circumstances. The quality that allowed successful men and rulers to do this he called *virtù*. Although the term is often translated as "prowess," it also connotes foresight, bravery, strength, and manliness. It was *virtù* that sometimes allowed men to rise above the vicissitudes of fortune, just as building dikes and canals can allow a city to withstand a flood. *Virtù* would not always be enough; just as some floods can overwhelm the best preparations, so the force of events could still overcome it, but sometimes it would enable men to transcend the dire circumstances of their time. *The Prince* ends with an exhortation to free Italy from its "barbarian" invaders and an excerpt from Petrarch's poem *Italia mia* ("My Italy"):

Then virtue boldly shall engage
And swiftly vanquish barbarous rage,
Proving that ancient and heroic pride
In true Italian hearts has never died.

VOICES

Machiavelli:
From *The Prince* and *The Discourses*

From *The Prince*, Chapter 15: Of the means by which men, and especially princes, win applause, or incur censure.

It remains now to be seen in what manner a prince should conduct himself towards his subjects and his allies. . . . as my aim is to write something that may be useful to him for whom it is intended, it seems to me proper to pursue the real truth of the matter, rather than to indulge in mere speculation on the same; for many have imagined republics and principalities such as have never been known to exist in reality. For the manner in which men live is so different from the way in which they ought to live, that he who leaves the common course for that which he ought to follow will find that it leads him to ruin rather than to safety. For a man who, in all respects, will carry out only his professions of good, will be apt to be ruined amongst so many who are evil. A prince therefore who desires to maintain himself must learn to be not always good, but to be so or not as necessity may require.

Chapter 17: Of cruelty and clemency, and whether it is better to be loved than feared.

. . . every prince ought to desire the reputation of being merciful, and not cruel; at the same time, he should be careful not to misuse that mercy. . . . A prince, therefore, should not mind the ill repute of cruelty, when he can thereby keep his subjects united and loyal; for a few displays of severity will really be more merciful than to allow, by an excess of clemency, disorders to occur, which are apt to result in rapine and murder; for these injure a whole community, whilst the executions ordered by the prince fall only upon a few individuals.

Francesco Guicciardini

While Machiavelli used history to support his ideas, the approach of his contemporary Francesco Guicciardini was more nuanced and profound, at least in the eyes of modern historians. Machiavelli saw the ancient world as a storehouse of examples and cautionary tales from which concrete lessons could be extrapolated. Guicciardini, by contrast, made extensive use both of primary sources, such as diplomatic correspondence, and of his own experience.

From an aristocratic Florentine family, Guicciardini achieved significant wealth and success as a politician and diplomat in the service of both Florence and the pope.

From *The Discourses*: Book I, Chapter 58: The people are wiser and more constant than princes.

And finally . . . both governments of princes and of the people have lasted a long time, but both are required to be regulated by laws. For a prince who knows no other control but his own will is like a madman, and a people that can do as it pleases will hardly be wise. If now we compare a prince who is controlled by laws, and a people that is untrammelled by them, we shall find more virtue in the people than in the prince; and if we compare them when both are freed from such control, we shall see that the people are guilty of fewer excesses than the prince, and that the errors of the people are of less importance, and therefore more easily remedied. For a licentious and mutinous people may easily be brought back to good conduct by the influence and persuasion of a good man, but an evil-minded prince is not amenable to such influences, and therefore there is no other remedy against him but cold steel.

Book III, Chapter 9: Who desires constant success must change his conduct with the times.

I have often reflected that the causes of the success or failure of men depend upon their manner of suiting their conduct to the times. . . . But he errs least and will be most favored by fortune who suits his proceedings to the times, . . . and always follows the impulses of his nature. . . .

It is this which assures to republics greater vitality and more enduring success than monarchies have; for the diversity of the genius of her citizens enables the republic better to accommodate herself to the changes of the times than can be done by a prince. For any man accustomed to a certain mode of proceeding will never change it, as we have said, and consequently when time and circumstances change, so that his ways are no longer in harmony with them, he must of necessity succumb.

Niccolò Machiavelli, *The Prince* and *The Discourses on the First Ten Books of Titus Livius*, from vol. II of *The Historical, Political, and Diplomatic Writings of Niccolò Machiavelli*, trans. Christian E. Detmold (Boston, 1882).

He wrote several important works, including a collection of personal observations and maxims (*Ricordi*), and a history of Florence from the revolt of the *Ciompi* (1378) to his own times. His most important work was his *History of Italy*, an unflinching examination of current events from 1490 to 1534. Like Machiavelli, he contrasts fortune and *virtù*, but comes to very different conclusions: in his view, people are helpless in the face of their selfishness, shortsightedness, and weakness. The French invasion was not foreordained, but was brought about by accident (the death of Lorenzo de Medici), and stupidity (the actions of Lodovico Sforza). History can be read as a cautionary tale, but the lesson it teaches is how circumstances can run roughshod over the most carefully laid plans.

Castiglione and The Courtier

The Book of the Courtier (1528) by Baldessare Castiglione (1478–1529) became an international bestseller. The fact that, like Machiavelli, Castiglione wrote in Italian rather than Latin was a measure of how the culture was changing. The book is a fictional dialogue among real historical individuals set in 1507 at the refined court of the Duke of Urbino, where his Duchess, Elisabetta Gonzaga (1471–1526)—the sister-in-law and close friend of Isabella d'Este—presides over an illustrious salon. Over four successive evenings, the Duchess leads her highly cultured guests, female as well as male, in a lively discussion of questions such as the attributes of the ideal courtier.

It is worth noting that the man they are discussing is not a citizen of a self-governing city, but a noble servant of a princely ruler. This is a reflection of a different political universe from the one that gave birth to humanism. Although different opinions are expressed, Count Ludovico insists that the ideal courtier must be of noble birth, and his main profession, apart from that of his prince's servant, must be that of a soldier (which Castiglione himself had been). When not at war, he should be modest and gentle, handsome, graceful, athletic, and adept at music, all without appearing to try. The term used for this latter quality is *sprezzatura*, defined as

> a certain nonchalance which conceals all artistry and makes whatever one says or does seem uncontrived and effortless. . . . So we can truthfully say that true art is what does not seem to be art; and the most important thing is to conceal it, because if it is revealed this discredits a man completely and ruins his reputation.[10]

The ideal courtier should be

> a more than average scholar, at least in those studies we call the humanities; and he should have a knowledge of Greek as well as Latin, because of the many different things that are so beautifully written in that language. He should be very well acquainted with the poets . . . orators and historians, and also skilled at writing both verse and prose . . . for in addition to the satisfaction this will give him personally, it will enable him to provide constant entertainment for the ladies, who are usually very fond of such things.[11]

Thus the study of rhetoric—the art, so central to Renaissance humanism, of persuasive writing, appropriate to expressing the highest values of the citizens of self-governing republics—has become a mere ornament, something to please the ladies at the court of the prince. This too was a reflection of an Italian reality that was fundamentally transformed by foreign invasion, warfare, and loss of political and cultural control.

Chapter Conclusion

Although the cultural movement of the Renaissance directly involved very few people, humanism profoundly affected the education and outlook of European elites for centuries through works such as *The Courtier*. The renewed historical approach to Greco-Roman literature and culture profoundly influenced the nature of historical studies, helping to bring about greater historical consciousness. The philological research of the humanists, when applied to sacred literature—both the Bible itself and the writings of the Church Fathers—would play an important role in both the Protestant and Catholic Reformations, as we will see in Chapter 3. And the sublime achievements of the great Renaissance artists not only reflected but helped to bring about a renewed appreciation both of the individual and of the natural world.

In other areas, however, the Renaissance produced no dramatically new ways of thinking. The society of Renaissance Italy was no less conservative and "medieval" than that of Europe beyond the Alps. Although there were significant social differences between Italy and the rest of Europe, these were more a cause of the Renaissance than a result. Even among "advanced" Renaissance thinkers, social attitudes were far from modern.

Leon Battista Alberti (1404–72), for example, was an esteemed humanist, painter, art theorist, architect, and priest—a man of such broad learning that he has often been called the original "Renaissance man." In the 1430s he wrote a four-volume work called *On the Family*. It takes the form of a dialogue in which various participants express their views on subjects such as the differences between men and women and the duties of wives. For example:

> The character of men is stronger than that of women and can bear the attacks of enemies, can stand strain longer, is more constant under stress. . . . Women, on the other hand, are almost all timid by nature, soft, slow, and therefore more useful when they sit still and watch over our things. . . .

The work is considered a faithful portrait of attitudes among well-to-do Florentines of the period. In general, the opportunities for women were greater among the aristocracy and in princely courts than in the urban republics that had given birth to humanism. Educated noblewomen such as Isabella d'Este and Elisabetta Gonzaga were not only the guiding lights of important salons: both also served as regents in the absence of their husbands. Another noblewoman, Vittoria Colonna (c. 1490–1547), the Marchesa of Pescara, was a poet, an advocate of religious reform, and a close friend of Michelangelo; Castiglione wrote that "Her divine intellect explores regions of the mind still unknown to others."

The artist Sofonisba Anguissola (1532–1625) became the official court painter to Philip II of Spain, and opened the way for other women to study art, although they were typically forbidden to work from nude models. There were also a few well-known women humanists, among them Isotta Nogarola (1418–66) and Laura Cereta (1469–99). Nevertheless, humanism was almost entirely a male affair, and no woman could gain recognition for her intellect without the support of an important man.

Burckhardt may have unjustly disparaged medieval civilization in his presentation of the Renaissance as a new and better age, but no one can deny that the Renaissance helped to shape the modern world. The humanist emphasis on living an active and committed life, as well as its critical approach to received wisdom, survived well beyond the period of the Renaissance itself. If, by our standards, the humanists' idealization of Greco-Roman civilization suggests a limited notion of human potential, in the end their studies opened the way for unprecedented discoveries in the centuries to come. The more they studied the ancient world, the more they learned that the ancients did not speak with one voice, that they themselves had disagreed, often vehemently, on some of life's most essential questions. In that case, what recourse did people have but to begin thinking for themselves? It may be that, quite contrary to their intentions, one important contribution of the Renaissance humanists to the modern world was the notion that it is more important to build the future than to rebuild the past.

Questions for Critical Thought

1. In what ways was humanism a product of its social and political environment?
2. How did changes in political and social circumstances affect the character and development of the Renaissance as a cultural and artistic movement?
3. In their confrontation with northern monarchies after 1494, what handicaps did the Italian states face?
4. In what ways does the Renaissance movement represent a break with the past, with medieval civilization? What were the continuities with the world of the Middle Ages? Which seem more significant to you?

Weblink

Giovanni Pico della Mirandola, *Oration on the Dignity of Man:*
http://bactra.org/Mirandola/

Further Reading

Allmand, Christopher. *The Hundred Years War: England and France at War, c. 1300–c. 1450.* Cambridge: Cambridge University Press, 1989. Especially useful on the institutional development of the French and English monarchies.

Bartlett, Kenneth R. *A Short History of the Italian Renaissance*. Toronto: University of Toronto Press, 2013. Comprehensive and lavishly illustrated.

Cunningham, Sean. *Henry VII*. London: Routledge, 2007. The most recent biography of the first Tudor.

Elliott, J.H. *Imperial Spain, 1469–1716*. A classic work by a pre-eminent historian.

Kamen, Henry. *The Spanish Inquisition: A Historical Revision*. 4th ed. New Haven: Yale University Press, 2014. The predominant revisionist interpretation.

King, Margaret L. *The Renaissance in Europe*. Boston: McGraw-Hill, 2005. A useful recent survey, which, despite its title, focuses predominantly on Italy.

Martines, Lauro. *Power and Imagination: City-States in Renaissance Italy*. Baltimore: Johns Hopkins University Press, 1979. Especially useful on the political context and the impact of political changes on the Renaissance movement.

Nauert, Charles G. *Humanism and the Culture of Renaissance Italy*. 2nd ed. Cambridge: Cambridge University Press, 2006. An important and accessible interpretation of humanism and its context.

Potter, David. *A History of France, 1460–1560: The Emergence of a Nation State*. London: Macmillan, 1995. Stresses the continuities between the later Middle Ages and the sixteenth century.

Notes

1. The term "Renaissance" was not used until the nineteenth century. Burckhardt took it from the French historian Jules Michelet, along with the idea that the essence of the Renaissance was "the discovery of the world and of man."
2. In fact, it was the artists and architects of the Renaissance who first characterized the style of the Middle Ages as "gothic." This was not a compliment: they considered it barbaric.
3. Giorgio Vasari, *Lives of the Artists*, trans. George Bull (Harmondsworth: Penguin, 1965).
4. Jacob Burckhardt, *The Civilization of the Renaissance in Italy*, trans. S.G.C. Middlemore (New York: Harper Torchbooks, 1958), pp. 22.
5. Benedict Anderson, *Imagined Communities: Reflections on the Origin and Spread of Nationalism* (London: Verso, 1983).
6. This conflict came to be known as the Wars of the Roses because (according to Shakespeare in *Henry VI*) the House of York had as its emblem a white rose and the House of Lancaster a red rose.
7. An indulgence was a release from acts of penance imposed by the church in return for some other service, such as going on a crusade or, as in this case, making a financial contribution to a cause. The Church's abuse of indulgences would be among the primary targets of reformers such as Martin Luther (see Chapter 3).
8. The normal practice was for the reigning emperor to secure the election of his heir during his lifetime. The heir to the imperial throne carried the title "King of the Romans."
9. He had been Duke of Burgundy since the age of six, when his father Philip the Handsome died. On the death of his grandfather Ferdinand of Aragon, in 1516 he became King of Aragon and co-ruler of Castile with his mother, Juana. On the death of his other grandfather, Emperor Maximilian I, in 1519, Charles would become Archduke of Austria, and later that year he would be elected Holy Roman Emperor Charles V.
10. Baldesar[re] Castiglione, *The Book of the Courtier*, trans. George Bull (Harmondsworth: Penguin, 1967), p. 67.
11. Castiglione, p. 90.

3

The Reformations

In the course of the sixteenth century, the religious unity that had been the most essential feature of Christendom disappeared forever.[1] Political unity had already given way to the challenges posed by regional and national monarchies, while the intellectual unity of scholastic thought had been powerfully challenged by Renaissance humanism, and was about to be further undermined by developments in scientific thought in the sixteenth and seventeenth centuries. Now, the religious tradition that had put the "Christ" in "Christendom" was forever fragmented.

Although the movement responsible for that fragmentation is usually referred to as "the Reformation," this term needs to be qualified. First, there was not a single reformation. At the most basic level there were at least two: the Protestant Reformation, in which large numbers of Europeans rejected the single church that had dominated the Middle Ages; and a Catholic or Counter-Reformation (the terminology and its implications will be examined later in this chapter), in which the organization that we know as the Roman Catholic Church both cleaned up many abuses, and (partly in response to the Protestant Reformation) altered and more clearly articulated some of its theological positions and liturgical practices.

Even this two-fold approach, however, does not do justice to the historical reality. In fact, Europe became divided not between two forms of Christianity—Catholic and Protestant—but among many. To group all forms of non-Catholic Christianity into one category called "Protestant" with no further distinction would be misleading, for they differed among themselves in important ways.

Furthermore, the very term "reformation" implies the transformation of a flawed form of Christianity into something more perfect. Certainly many people, especially Protestants, believed their new faith to be superior, but that was a moral or religious judgment, not a historical one. It would be equally inaccurate to suppose that medieval or "traditional" Christianity continued unaltered alongside, or in opposition to, a reformed Protestant Christianity. Rather, what we see in the sixteenth century is the division of "traditional" Christianity into two new streams, one labelled "Protestant" but containing several variants, and the other labelled "Roman Catholic." The fact that there were significant continuities between the medieval church and the early modern Roman Catholic Church does not mean that it was identical to "traditional" pre-Reformation Christianity.

There is also an understandable tendency, because we know what happened next, to interpret earlier history in the light of that knowledge. In the case of the Reformation(s), reading history backwards in that way might lead us to conclude that there must have been something so profoundly wrong with the previous state of affairs that the Reformations were inevitable. Although some sort of upheaval might have seemed likely by the early sixteenth century, it was certainly not foreordained that the Catholic Church would fragment. After all, it had managed to preserve its unity through several cycles of reform in the Middle Ages. That this did not happen in the sixteenth century can be attributed to three factors. First, powerful secular rulers, for a variety of reasons, were willing and able to defy Rome in order to enhance their own power; even Catholic rulers used the threat of breaking with Rome for their own purposes, and continued to whittle away at the power of the Church in their territories. Second, whereas in the Middle Ages the upper hierarchy of the Church had responded to calls for reform (for example, in what are known as the Gregorian reforms of the eleventh century), by the late fifteenth century its priorities had changed radically. Finally, growing numbers of influential people—humanists, religious leaders, and the literate urban middle class—found traditional Christianity lacking in the spiritual fulfillment they craved.

Traditional Christianity and Its Challenges

It is not always appreciated that medieval Christianity in practice encompassed a good deal of variety and diversity. The medieval church, although in theory a single hierarchical organization, did not enforce the kind of theological and liturgical uniformity that the behaviour of its early modern successor might lead one to expect. In fact, it was only after, and partly in reaction to, Protestant challenges that the Catholic Church began to insist on the uniformity and conformity that characterized the early modern period; as long as there was no alternative for people to turn to, the institution in place could tolerate some diversity. It was only when the "other" challenged the status quo that it became important to define more precisely what "we" believed and who "we" were.

In the course of the Middle Ages, Christianity as it was practised at the popular level had developed in ways particularly suited to an agrarian society made up largely of illiterate peasants. Historians have debated how much ordinary people actually understood of Church teachings, some suggesting that, especially in the countryside, Christianity was at best a thin veneer on top of pre-Christian beliefs. In this view, many saints were actually pre-Christian figures or gods that had been "baptized" and incorporated into Christianity, the sacraments were understood as a form of magic, and the priest was a kind of shaman. Others suggest that what was important was not people's grasp of theology, but their understanding that they stood before the priest—God's intermediary—as a member of a community. One was a Christian by virtue of belonging to a Christian community, and membership in that community was defined primarily by what one did rather than by what one believed: baptizing one's children, attending Mass every week, confessing one's sins and receiving communion once a year, and otherwise behaving as the Church prescribed.

The realms of the sacred and profane, the physical and the spiritual, were inextricably intertwined. The saints played an important role here, offering to intercede with God on behalf of those who requested their help. Every community and occupation had its own patron saint, on whom it relied for assistance. Saints had certain specialties as well: St. Roch helped against the plague, St. Christopher (who appears to have been a Christianized version of a pagan figure, and was never officially canonized) protected travellers, and so on. Certain places—churches, saints' shrines, and wells, for example—were held to be holy. So were certain times of year, notably Lent, the forty days preceding Easter, which was a period of sombre reflection and self-denial.

As well adapted as medieval Christianity was to the peasant farmers who made up the majority of the population, they were not the only group in society who found a place in it. The Crusades gave nobles—the warrior class—the opportunity to channel their violence in the service of the Church. For the intellectual elite, there was the world of scholastic thought. Finally, men who sought to devote their lives to the faith could enter the priesthood, and women as well as men could join religious orders.

There was one element of society, however, that was an uneasy fit in this traditional Christianity: the literate urban middle class. Although they were active participants in the economic, political, and social life of their cities, when it came to spiritual life the Church allowed them no relationship with God except through the mediation of a priest. Although laypeople did form their own religious organizations, called confraternities or brotherhoods, their only role in the institutional church was that of passive, obedient spectators. Their dissatisfaction with the traditional Church grew rapidly as the exchange of information and ideas accelerated in the years that followed the development of the printing press. In Germany and Switzerland in particular, many cities paid for endowed preacherships to provide the spiritual meat that was lacking in their parish churches. It was no accident that the Protestant Reformation found its earliest and most fervent supporters among the educated middle classes of these regions.

The Institutional Church and Anticlericalism

The popes of the later fifteenth and early sixteenth century were less concerned with spiritual leadership than with power politics and artistic patronage. It is therefore not surprising that they initially failed to meet the challenges of protest and reform. The first pope to confront the challenge of the Protestant Reformation was Leo X (r. 1513–21). A son of Lorenzo de Medici, and an avid patron of the arts, on his election as pope he was reported to have said, "As God has given us the papacy, let us enjoy it."

Among those challenges was the corruption attracted by the wealth and power that came with positions of the leadership in the Church. Rules against nepotism, simony (purchase of Church positions), absenteeism, and pluralism (holding more than one office at a time) were routinely violated, often with the connivance of the popes, who were more than willing to grant a dispensation (permission to violate the rules) for a price. Bishops, archbishops, and abbots collected the revenue their positions provided, but often left the actual work in the hands of underpaid and frequently unsuitable substitutes.

Not all powerful clergymen were corrupt, and many spoke out about the abuses they observed. Many monastic orders established Observantine branches, with stricter rules than those of the regular Conventual houses. Other bishops and abbots did what they could within their own jurisdictions. Nevertheless, reform remained a piecemeal, haphazard enterprise, without institutional support.

One important reason for this lack of support was the papacy's opposition to conciliarism. Fifteenth-century popes fought long and hard against the movement, and in 1460 Pius II had effectively crushed it. Although he had been an ardent conciliarist earlier in his career, as pope he issued the bull *Execrabilis*, which condemned as heresy any attempt to convene a council without permission from the pope.

By 1500 anticlericalism was common at all levels of European society, inspired not only by Church corruption, but by the discrepancy between the humility of Christ, who had lived to serve others, and the vast entitlements claimed by his representatives on earth. What is surprising to modern eyes is that virtually no one rejected the Church altogether: despite everything that was wrong with the Church, the religious life of the period was remarkable in its fervour.

Some Christians found solace in mysticism: direct, unmediated communion with God. While most mystics remained orthodox in their beliefs, mysticism was always a potential threat to the Church, as it was by definition beyond Church control. Others found fulfillment in the so-called "new devotion," living communal lives of monastic simplicity without taking formal vows. Perhaps the best known of these communities were the Brethren of the Common Life, who flourished in the Low Countries and northwest Germany in the fifteenth century. The Brethren also ran a number of schools that helped to spread their message of poverty and simplicity to students such as Thomas à Kempis (1380–1471), author of the influential devotional work entitled *The Imitation of Christ*.

"Christian" Humanism

Many supporters of Church reform were influenced by humanism. As we saw in the last chapter, humanism began to spread outside Italy in the later fifteenth century, but did not attract significant interest in the north until about 1500. Although northern humanism is sometimes called Christian humanism, this term should not be taken to imply that the Italian humanists were not Christian: this was definitely not the case. On the other hand, the label can be useful in that the northern humanists were more explicitly Christian, putting their humanism in the service of their faith. They shared with humanists more broadly a "back to the sources" (*ad fontes*) mentality; however, whereas earlier humanists had sought to revive classical Greco-Roman civilization, Christian humanists also sought

VOICES

Anticlericalism in Germany

Jakob Wimpheling (1450–1528) was a German humanist and defender of German interests against what he saw as a grasping, corrupt, and Italian-dominated hierarchy. In 1515 he published a response to Cardinal Aeneas Sylvius Piccolimini (later Pope Pius II), who decades earlier, in 1457, had written in praise of Germany.

Rightly does Enea Silvio [Piccolimini] praise Germany. . . . Because he is an Italian, however, and loves the land of his birth, he would not enjoy seeing the flow of money from our country to his own slowed to a trickle. . . . Enea speaks with lavish praise of our fatherland, of our cities and buildings. For what purpose? For one only: to make our ears more receptive to the demands coming from Rome dressed in Christian garb, but serving Italian interests; in other words, to put us in the mood for wasting our fortunes on foreigners. . . .

Is there a nation more patient and willing to receive indulgences, though we well know that the income from them is divided between the Holy See and its officialdom? Have we not paid dearly for the confirmation of every bishop and abbot? . . .

Thus we are done out of fortune, and for no purpose other than to support the innumerable retainers and hangers-on that populate the papal court. . . .

. . . the sums of money our prelates must send to Rome are taken from the pockets of poor burghers, rural clerics, and impoverished peasants, and many a husband and father cannot nourish his family for the taxes he must pay. Such a reduction of our tribute might well prevent the outbreak of a violent insurrection of our people against the Church. My own ears, God be my witness, have overheard the grumbling, muttering, and threats of popular discontent. It would not take much for the Bohemian poison [the teachings of the Hussites] to penetrate our German lands. . . .

Gerald Strauss, ed. and trans. *Manifestations of Discontent in Germany on the Eve of the Reformation* (Bloomington: Indiana University Press, 1971), pp. 41–6.

to revive the purity of primitive Christianity, applying the techniques developed by humanist scholars both to Scripture and to the writings of Church fathers such as St. Jerome (c. 347–420) and St. Augustine (354–430).

Queen Isabella's confessor, Cardinal Ximenes de Cisneros (1437–1517), was in many ways a transitional figure, bridging the worlds of the traditional Church and the "new learning." The Archbishop of Toledo and Grand Inquisitor, he was second only to the Catholic monarchs in power. Unlike other powerful clergymen, however, he used his influence to press for reform, and some of the means he adopted were influenced by humanism.

For example, he believed that the best way to produce better Christians was to produce better priests. Accordingly, in 1499 he established the University of Alcalà to train priests. From the beginning, the curriculum at Alcalà emphasized the study of Hebrew and Greek, the original languages of the Bible, and in 1520 scholars there would produce one of the most important works of the period. This was the Complutensian Polyglot, an edition of the Old and New Testaments that made it possible to read and compare the same passage in four languages—the official Latin Vulgate version, Greek, Hebrew, and Aramaic—on a single page.

Without a doubt, the most prominent Christian humanist, and the most famous scholar of the time, was Erasmus of Rotterdam (1466–1536). The illegitimate son of a priest, as a child Erasmus attended a school (possibly run by the Brethren of the Common Life) that was renowned for its teaching of Latin. Although he was then packed off to an Augustinian monastery, where he became a monk, he did not have a deep religious vocation, and in later years he was officially relieved of the restrictions of monastic life. As a young man, he studied at one of the most prestigious colleges at the University of Paris, but was repulsed by both its arcane scholastic theology and the inferior Latin used there. In 1499 he travelled to England, where he met his lifelong friend and correspondent Thomas More.

© PRISMA ARCHIVO / Alamy Stock Photo

A page from the Complutensian Polyglot. The upper portion contains, from left to right, the Septuagint or Greek version of the Old Testament, with the Latin translation between the lines, the Latin Vulgate Bible in the middle, and on the right, the original Hebrew. The lower portion contains the same passage in Aramaic with a Latin translation, and in the margin, the Hebrew roots (above) and the Aramaic roots (below).

Erasmus' literary output was large and varied, but all of it reflected his "philosophy of Christ," according to which true Christianity consisted not in rituals or theological knowledge, but in fidelity to the inner spirit of Christ and the apostles. One of his most popular works was *The Colloquies* (1496–1526), a series of dialogues, many humorous and satirical, designed not only to teach proper Latin, but also to reform and instruct. In *The Handbook of a Christian Knight* (1501) Erasmus expresses two ideas central to his philosophy of Christ: that knowledge of Scripture is essential, and that true religion is not to be found in institutions, theology, or sacraments, but in the love of God and one's neighbours. In a more purely scholarly vein, and in the best humanist tradition, he assembled new editions of the works of many early Christian writers, including St. Jerome. Although he denied it, he was also almost certainly the author of *Julius Excluded from Heaven* (1517), in which St. Peter pointedly excludes from heaven Julius II, the recently deceased warrior pope:

> I see the man who wants to be regarded as next to Christ and, in fact, equal to Him, submerged in the filthiest of all things by far: money, power, armies, wars, alliances—not to say anything at this point about his vices. But then, although you are as remote as possible from Christ, nevertheless you misuse the name of Christ for your own arrogant purposes; and under the pretext of Him who despised the world, you act the part of a tyrant of the world.[2]

Erasmus published his most important work, a new edition of the New Testament, based on the earliest Greek manuscripts available, in 1516. (A later edition included an annotated Latin translation, which varied in some details from the traditional Vulgate New Testament used by the Church.) It was a triumph of humanist and biblical scholarship, and would remain the gold standard in New Testament scholarship until the nineteenth century. In the introduction to this work, he justified his labours in a famous passage:

> I absolutely dissent from those people who don't want the holy scriptures to be read in translation by the unlearned—as if, forsooth, Christ taught such complex doctrine that hardly anyone outside a handful of theologians could understand it, or as if the chief strength of the Christian religion lay in people's ignorance of it. . . . I wish these writings were translated into all the languages of the human race, so that they could be read and studied, not just by the Irish and the Scots, but by the Turks as well, and the Saracens. . . . I would hope that the farmer might chant a holy text at his plow, the spinner sing it as she sits at her wheel, the traveler ease the tedium of his journey with tales from the scripture.[3]

Unlike Erasmus and Cisneros, the Englishman Thomas More (1478–1535) was a layman, a lawyer and politician who served King Henry VIII (r. 1509–47) as Speaker of the House of Commons and Chancellor. Deeply devoted to the traditional Church, he adamantly opposed what he considered the heresy of the Protestant reformers, and would play a central role in the pursuit of several dissidents who were eventually burned at the

VOICES

The Praise of Folly

The Praise of Folly is Erasmus's most famous and enduring work. Its Latin title, *Enconium moriæ*, is a pun on the name of his friend Sir Thomas More, to whom the work was dedicated. In it, Folly is personified as a woman who describes all the ways in which people worship her. The first excerpt refers to people's enthusiasm for indulgences, while the second displays Erasmus's contempt for scholastic theologians.

What's to be said of those who happily delude themselves with forged pardons for real sins, measuring out time to be spent in purgatory as if on a chronometer, calculating the centuries, years, months, days, and hours as if on a mathematical table so as not to make the slightest error . . .

Here I think I see some businessman or soldier or judge putting down one solitary coin out of the great pile that he has successfully stolen, and expecting that that will atone for the whole pestilent swamp of his life; all his perjuries, lusts, drunken brawls, murders, deceits, treacheries, and double crossings will, he thinks, be redeemed as if by purchase. . . . These things are so stupid that I myself am almost ashamed of them, yet they are accepted and approved, not just by the uneducated, but even by the teachers of religion . . . (p. 42).

For the whole life of Christians everywhere is infected with idiocies of this sort; yet priests tolerate them without misgivings, and even encourage them, being well aware how much money can be coined out of them . . . (pp. 43–4).

[Theologians] are a class of men so arrogant and irritable that they're likely to attack me by squadrons with their six hundred conclusions and force me into a recantation. . . .

. . . They all boast such mighty erudition and write such tortured prose that I should think the apostles themselves must have had a very different spirit if they were discuss topics like these with our new breed of theologians. Paul could display faith; but when he said "Faith is the substance of things hoped for, the evidence of things not seen," that was a very unacademic definition. In I Corinthians 13, he wrote a wonderful exhortation to charity, but he altogether failed to divide charity into its component parts or define it in the proper dialectical way. . . .

. . . Of course it would be unfair to expect academic correctness of the apostles, because they never heard so much as a word on the matter from their master . . . (pp. 57–8).

Desiderius Erasmus, *The Praise of Folly and Other Writings*, ed. and trans. Robert M. Adams (New York: Norton, 1989). Copyright © 1989 by W.W. Norton & Company, inc. Used by permission of W.W. Norton & Company, Inc.

stake (among them William Tyndale, whose English translation of the Bible would be a major influence on the King James Bible). In the end, as we will see, More himself paid the ultimate price for his defence of the Church against his own king.

Today, however, More is probably best known for his *Utopia* (1516): a fictional account of a voyage (at the time when European sailors were just beginning to explore other continents) to the land of Utopia (from the Greek for "nowhere"). Although it is often taken to be his blueprint for an ideal society, this seems unlikely, for the very devout More makes it clear that the Utopians are not Christian, and the work appears to be at least in part satirical mirror held up to his own society. To criticize avarice, for example, More has the Utopians hold gold and silver in contempt, using them to make chamber pots and the chains that bind prisoners. To criticize gross inequality, he has all Utopians work equal (hence shorter) hours. Excessive display and ostentation in Europe are contrasted with the simplicity and purity of the Utopians' diet and lifestyle. In making the Utopians non-Christian, although they are extremely moral and come to realize the truth of Christianity, More is in fact holding supposedly Christian Europeans up to shame: what does it say about us if the pagan Utopians, purely through the light of reason, live a more Christian life than we do? What can our excuse be?

A much sharper satire of the traditional Church was published by two German humanists, Ulrich von Hutten and Johannes Jäger, writing as Crotus Rubeanus, in 1515–17. The *Letters of Obscure Men* was written in support of the leading Christian Hebrew scholar of the time, Johannes Reuchlin (1455–1522), after a converted Jew named Johannes Pfefferkorn called for the destruction of all Hebrew literature on the grounds that it was anti-Christian. The result was a bitter pamphlet war in which liberal-minded humanists (including Erasmus) lined up behind Reuchlin, and conservative monks (Dominicans in particular) and scholastics behind Pfefferkorn. In the end, Reuchlin and the humanists prevailed. Before long, many of the same people would be among the earliest supporters of Martin Luther.

The relationship between Christian humanism and the Protestant Reformation has been the subject of debate ever since the sixteenth century, when Erasmus was often charged with having "laid the egg that Luther hatched." There can be no doubt that, although his work was intended to argue for reform, for many people it had the effect of undermining the Church's authority and prestige. His "philosophy of Christ" often conveyed the unintended message that the rituals and sacraments of the Church were superfluous. His scholarly work could also bring Church teaching into question. For example, when he translated his Greek New Testament into Latin, he made a seemingly minor change in the wording of Romans 2:4, from the Latin equivalent of "do penance" to "be penitent." This small shift implied that what was important was repentance, an inner attitude, rather than penance, a sacrament of the Church.

Martin Luther (1483–1546)

Sometime before 1517, an obscure German monk and professor of biblical studies named Martin Luther had a theological insight that would lead to the fragmentation of

European Christianity. Two points here require special emphasis. The first is that, as a monk, Luther's relationship with the Church was that of an insider, and he originally had no intention of breaking the unity of Christendom. The second is that, although Luther, like many others, was disturbed by the moral and ethical failings of the Church, what drove him to take action was theology: specifically, an understanding of salvation that differed from the one taught by the Church. As he would write:

> Someone said to me: "What a sin and scandal all these clerical vices are, the fornication, the drunkenness, the unbridled passion for sport!" Yes, I must confess that these are dreadful scandals indeed, and they should be denounced and corrected. But the vices to which you refer are plain for all to see; they are grossly material, everyone perceives them, and so everyone is stirred to anger by them. Alas, the real evil, the incomparably more baneful and cruel canker, is the deliberate silence regarding the word of Truth . . . [4]

The Church taught that salvation required both good works and divine grace (the unmerited favour of God). Since no human could ever meet God's standard of perfection, no works could ever be good enough to merit salvation: divine grace was essential, and the vehicles of that grace were the sacraments of Mass and Confession provided by the

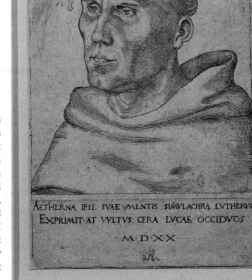

Luther as an Augustinian monk by Lucas Cranach the Elder. Luther would write of his time as a monk: "I was indeed pious and kept the rules of my order so strictly that I can say: If ever a monk gained heaven through monkery, it should have been I. . . . I would have martyred myself to death with fasting, praying, reading, and other good works had I remained a monk much longer." "Though I lived as a monk without reproach, I felt that I was a sinner before God with an extremely disturbed conscience. I could not believe that he was placated by my satisfaction."

AETHERNA IPSE SVAE MENTIS SIMVLACHRA LVTHERVS
EXPRIMIT·AT VVLTVS CERA LVCAE OCCIDVOS·
·M·D·XX·

Church. Nevertheless, good works were also required: one had to meet God halfway. The question then became "How much is enough?" How could one know if one had performed enough good works? The Church's answer to this question was *facere quod in se est*, "do what is within you." Do your best, and a loving and merciful God will take pity on you and bestow the grace required for salvation.

Martin Luther was tormented by his own unworthiness. How could he know if he had confessed all his sins, or if his repentance was truly sincere? It had been his anxiety on this point that had driven him to become a monk. Yet still he had found no solace. To occupy his mind, his superiors encouraged him to study for a doctorate in theology, which he received in 1512. He then became a professor at the recently established (1502) University of Wittenberg in Saxony. It was in the course of preparing lectures for his students that he had the theological insight that would lead him to reject the Catholic Church.

While preparing lectures on St Paul's letter to the Christians in Rome, he was struck in a new way by Romans 1:17: "For [in the gospel] is the righteousness of God revealed from faith to faith: as it is written, 'The just shall live by faith'" (KJV). Until then, Luther had understood the phrase "the righteousness of God" to mean His standard of perfection, the standard that he, Luther, could never meet. Now he understood it to mean that he no longer had to struggle to achieve the impossible. Christians were saved (justified, or made righteous in God's eyes) not through their own efforts, but entirely through God's unmerited favour or grace. Supposedly, in his own Bible, Luther added the word *sola* to the text: "The just shall live by faith *alone*." All that was required was faith in divine grace. As Luther himself would later write: "Here I felt that I was altogether born again and had entered paradise through open gates."[5] The point was not that he was now free to sin as he wished, but that he was now free to perform good works willingly, out of gratitude and love of his neighbour, rather than under compulsion or for fear of hell.

Thus far, Luther had solved the personal problem of his torment over his unworthiness of salvation. Neither he nor anyone else could have anticipated that this would lead to a religious revolution. What would thrust him into the limelight was a controversy regarding the use and abuse of indulgences. The first indulgences had been granted during the Crusades, as a reward for those who went to the Holy Land, but over time both the practice and the theory behind it had been greatly expanded. By Luther's time, indulgences could be acquired not only on behalf of the living, but on behalf of the dead, whose time in Purgatory could thereby be reduced or eliminated altogether. In theory, indulgences were not available for purchase: rather, one who had been granted an indulgence would then make an offering in gratitude. And in theory, an indulgence did not remit guilt for sins: it simply remitted the penance imposed by the Church. In practice, however, both distinctions were routinely glossed over, and many people came to believe that indulgences could be purchased as "tickets to heaven." Officially such notions were condemned, but in practice they were tolerated because, together, they represented an astonishingly rich source of income.

The particular indulgence that bothered Luther had been proclaimed to finance the rebuilding of St. Peter's Basilica in Rome. The official in charge of the indulgence in that part of Germany was a Dominican named Johann Tetzel, an accomplished indulgence salesman.

VOICES

From Tetzel's Preaching on Indulgences

What are you thinking about? Why do you hesitate to convert yourself? Why don't you have fears about your sins? Why don't you confess now to the vicars of our Most Holy Pope? . . .

JOHANNES · TECELIUS PIRNENSIS
Dominicanus, Nundinator Romani Pontificis, anno
1517. à μικαλαίσδεκ LUTHERO territus & in fugam versus,
uti talis ejus effigies visitur in templo Pirnensi.

You should know that all who confess and in penance put alms into the coffer according to the counsel of the confessor, will obtain complete remission of all their sins. . . . Why are you then standing there? Run for the salvation of your souls! Be as careful and concerned for the salvation of your souls as you are for your temporal goods, which you seek day and night. Seek the Lord while he may be found and while he is near. Work, as St. John says, while it is yet day, for the night comes when no man can work.

Tetzel selling indulgences. The last two lines of the poem on the upper left contain Tetzel's famous sales pitch: "As soon as the coin in the coffer rings, the soul into heaven springs."

Don't you hear the voices of your wailing dead parents and others who say, "Have mercy upon me, have mercy upon me, because we are in severe punishment and pain. From this you could redeem us with a small alms and yet you do not want to do so." Open your ears as the father says to the son and the mother to the daughter . . . , "We have created you, fed you, cared for you, and left you our temporal goods. Why then are you so cruel and harsh that you do not want to save us, though it only takes a little? You let us lie in flames so that we only slowly come into the promised glory." You may have letters which let you have, once in life and in the hour of death . . . full remission of the punishment which belongs to sin.

Hans J. Hillerbrand, *The Reformation: A Narrative History Related by Contemporary Observers and Participants* (New York: Harper and Row, 1964), pp. 41–3.

Luther was outraged by Tetzel's tall tales of the power of his indulgence. Having struggled for years with his own fear of unworthiness, and having relieved his burden through his new understanding of salvation, Luther feared not only that his students, neighbours, and friends were being cheated, but that their immortal souls were being endangered by this chicanery. As a professor, he responded in the way he knew best: by making a formal statement of his objections. This was the genesis of his famous *Disputation on the Power and Efficacy of Indulgences*, or "Ninety-Five Theses."

Whether or not Luther actually posted his theses on the door of Wittenberg's Castle Church on October 31, 1517, is unclear, but it hardly matters. The document was not by any means the revolutionary manifesto that is often imagined: Luther did not deny the efficacy of indulgences in remitting penances imposed by the Church, or challenge the power of the pope, let alone declare independence from Rome. Rather, in good academic Latin, he simply presented a series of propositions regarding the theory and practice of selling indulgences and offered to debate them.

Without Luther's consent or knowledge, his theses were translated into German, printed, and sold all over Germany. Luther quickly became famous, quite against his will, as the monk who challenged Rome. The Church's response was to condemn Luther and summon him to Augsburg to explain himself to the papal legate there. Although Luther complied, he went into hiding before the legate could arrest him.

While outraged Dominicans defended Tetzel, Luther had the support of many humanists, including Erasmus, who argued that he should at the very least be given an impartial hearing. Although the humanists did not necessarily grasp Luther's fundamental theological motivation, they were outraged by what they perceived as an attack on academic freedom by the scholastic theologians. Luther's objections to indulgences also struck a chord deep within many people, not because they had doubted indulgences, but precisely because they had so fervently believed in them. Luther had relieved them of the burden of having to perform good works and purchasing indulgences by rendering them irrelevant to salvation. Above all, Luther had the support of his own ruler, Frederick the Wise, the Elector of Saxony. Frederick was very proud of his new university, and protective of its faculty, especially one who had become as prominent as Luther. He was also reluctant to turn over one of his subjects to a foreign jurisdiction without a proper hearing; at the very least, he insisted that Luther should have a fair hearing in Germany, rather than in Rome. He was also genuinely perplexed; he wanted to do the right thing, but was receiving conflicting advice, and so he delayed taking any decisive action.[6]

Political circumstances also conspired in Luther's favour. Emperor Maximilian was attempting to secure the Imperial throne for his grandson, the young King Charles I of Spain. Pope Leo X was desperate to prevent this, as it threatened the independence of the Papal States, and was casting about for alternative candidates. Among the prospects was Elector Frederick, and if he could not be persuaded to be a candidate, he was nevertheless one of the seven men who would choose the next Emperor. So the pope had political reasons not to press Frederick too hard when it came to Luther.

Luther himself had not set out to break away from the Catholic Church; all he had wanted was a debate about some of the more dubious practices surrounding indulgences. Nor did he realize all the implications of his new understanding of salvation. Nevertheless, the Church was determined to defend its authority, and to that end it spent several years attempting to pressure Luther into submission. In the process, it ultimately drove him to reject its authority altogether. But the final break did not come immediately.

Although Luther was formally excommunicated in 1520, the protection of Frederick the Wise kept him beyond the reach of the Church. In the meantime he published three of his most important works. First, in *The Address to the Christian Nobility of the German Nation*, he argued that God had put secular rulers in place to restrain evil-doers, no matter who they might be, and called on the Emperor and the German ruling class to reform the German church themselves, since the pope and the Roman hierarchy were unwilling. Second, in *The Babylonian Captivity of the Church*, he rejected not only scholastic theology but five of the seven sacraments, retaining only Baptism and the Eucharist or Lord's Supper.[7] Finally, in *The Freedom of a Christian*, a devotional work intended for ordinary people, he argued that Christian freedom consisted of trying to please God freely and out of a gratitude for grace already received rather than out of fear and compulsion.

In 1521 Luther was summoned to appear before the princes of the Holy Roman Empire and Emperor Charles V in the Imperial Diet or Reichstag meeting in the city of Worms. There, when told to recant his views, he refused, uttering the famous words:

> Unless I am convicted by Scripture and plain reason—I do not accept the authority of popes and councils, for they have contradicted each other—my conscience is captive to the Word of God. I cannot and I will not recant anything, for to go against conscience is neither right nor safe. [Here I stand. I cannot do otherwise.[8]] God help me. Amen.

Charles responded by placing Luther under the Ban of the Empire, meaning not only that he was now an outlaw, but that anyone who was able to apprehend him, alive or dead, was authorized to do so. Luther spent most of the next year in hiding before re-emerging in Wittenberg.

THE APPEAL AND SPREAD OF LUTHER'S REVOLT

Soon Luther's religious revolt began to take tangible form, spreading from Wittenberg to Saxony and then beyond, to large parts of Germany and northern Europe. First, church services were conducted in the local vernacular rather than Latin. Clergy became pastors rather than priests, occupying no special place in society, and having no special powers or special relationship with God differentiating them from the laity. A corollary of this principle was "the priesthood of all believers": if all Christians were equal before God, then all had equal access to the divine, without the mediation of a priest. Accordingly, there was no longer any reason for clergy to remain celibate, and pastors were encouraged to marry. (Luther himself married Katherina von Bora, a former nun, and they had a large and loving family.)

In the traditional sacrament of Eucharist, lay people received only the bread; the wine was reserved for the priest, as a sign of his superior spiritual status. By contrast, in the Protestant sacrament lay people received both the bread and wine ("communion in both kinds"). Furthermore, whereas the traditional Church maintained that its laws, rulings, and interpretations were equal to the Scriptures in authority, for the Protestants Scripture was the only authority. Accordingly, Protestants were not only allowed but encouraged to read the Bible for themselves.

By the time of Luther's death in 1546, large parts of Europe had officially severed their ties with Rome and established their own churches based on Luther's teachings. Why was this so? Some historians have emphasized the political advantages that Protestantism offered to rulers, the opportunity to expel a foreign authority, confiscate its lands, and enhance their own control over their territories and subjects. As we will see in Chapter 6, this was certainly the case in Denmark and Sweden, but it was not the whole story. In other places, while support of the ruler was essential, that support was often driven by popular demand. That is, large segments of society agitated for religious change, and this agitation prodded rulers into action. The Protestant Reformation was thus at the same time driven from below and implemented from above.

Why were so many people prepared to reject the church of their ancestors? Many were no doubt driven by opposition to abuses such as the sale of indulgences, and perhaps by a nationalistic desire to free their homelands of a corrupt foreign institution. Many people also shared in the feeling of liberation that Luther experienced at the separation of salvation from the performance of good works. Some people expressed this sense of liberation through iconoclasm, destroying the images in churches as symbols of the spiritual burden that the Church had imposed on them. No longer were lay people made to feel inferior by the special status of the clergy. The idea of the "priesthood of all believers" was music to the ears of the literate middle class who had longed for a more direct relationship with God, free of priestly intermediaries. Peasants and workers too, heard (or thought they did) in Luther's teaching a promise of liberation not only from the spiritual burdens of traditional religion, but also from the social and economic burdens imposed by bosses and landlords.

VIOLENCE AND DISORDER

Catholics had predicted chaos if the Church's authority was challenged, and the predictions seemed to be coming true. In 1522, a group of German nobles led by Ulrich von Hutten (one of the authors of the *Letters of Obscure Men*) and Franz von Sickengen formed a "fraternal union of the nobility" to defend the new religion and the German nation against a corrupt foreign Church. But when they attacked the territory of the Archbishop/Elector of Trier, one of the leading ecclesiastical princes in Germany, their "Knights' Revolt" was easily crushed. More seriously, in 1524 revolts broke out in a number of peasant villages in southwestern and central Germany. The rebels drew up lists of grievances (for example, the "Twelve Articles of the Swabian Peasants"; see Weblinks). Although most of the grievances concerned the same issues that had sparked peasant revolts in the Middle Ages—the tithe, labour services and serfdom, the enclosure of common lands, and so on—some of their demands were clearly inspired by Luther's calls for "freedom" and "equality."

Luther was horrified, for despite his own revolt against the Roman Church, his temperament remained deeply conservative. For him, freedom and equality were spiritual qualities, not earthly ones, and since rulers were put in place by God, to rebel against them was not only a crime but a sin. In *Against the Murderous and Thieving Hordes of Peasants* (1525) he wrote:

> If the peasant is in open rebellion, then he is outside the law of God, for rebellion is not simply murder, but it is like a great fire which attacks and lays waste a whole land. Thus, rebellion brings with it a land full of murders and bloodshed, makes widows and orphans, and turns everything upside down like a great disaster. Therefore, let everyone who can, smite, slay, and stab, secretly or openly, remembering that nothing can be more poisonous, hurtful or devilish than a rebel. It is just as when one must kill a mad dog: if you don't strike him, he will strike you and the whole land with you.[9]

One factor that predisposed Luther against the peasants was the role that Thomas Müntzer (1489–1525) played in the insurgency. As a colleague of Luther's in Wittenberg, Müntzer had argued that Luther's reforms were not radical enough, and that Luther himself was too cowardly to see through the true reformation that was needed. As a consequence, Luther had had him expelled from Wittenberg. In 1524, however, Müntzer saw in the peasants' revolt an ideal opportunity to bring that true reformation about by force of arms. Thus he assumed a position of leadership in the uprising, and in May of 1525 led a ragtag army of peasants to Frankenhausen, where they were massacred by the thousands and Müntzer himself was captured, tortured, and executed. After Frankenhausen, the rebels ran out of steam, and rulers and landlords exacted severe retribution: as many as 100,000 peasants were put to death for their roles in the rebellion.

Other Visions of Reform

ULRICH ZWINGLI AND SWITZERLAND

Almost simultaneously with Luther, other reformers began to express their own visions. It was as if discontent had been seething beneath the surface, waiting for someone to take the first step. Once it had been taken, all hell broke loose, figuratively and (in the view of many Catholics) literally. Among the earliest and most influential voices was that of the Swiss priest Ulrich Zwingli (1484–1531). Zwingli had arrived at many of Luther's positions independently, and by 1518 was already preaching his new ideas in Zürich's main church. Over the next several years, he and his associates slowly but surely guided Zürich away from the Catholic Church. To minimize turmoil, each step was carefully considered and approved by the city council, and the Catholic Mass was not fully abolished until 1525. This approach would serve as a kind of template for other Swiss and German cities seeking to break with Rome.

In most respects, Zwingli's beliefs were similar to Luther's, especially regarding salvation by faith alone. What differences there were can be largely ascribed to their educational backgrounds and political contexts. Whereas Luther was a subject of a powerful prince, Zwingli was a citizen of a self-governing town within the Swiss Confederation, a loose alliance of thirteen districts or cantons. Zwingli was also more of a humanist than Luther, and retained greater faith in human potential and the possibility of constructing a Christian commonwealth on earth.

Another very important difference between the two men concerned the sacraments. Like Luther, and indeed all Protestants, and for the same reasons, Zwingli reduced the number of sacraments from seven to two: Baptism and the Lord's Supper. It was on the nature of the Lord's Supper that their views diverged. While both rejected the Catholic doctrine of transubstantiation, they disagreed vehemently on what happened to the bread and wine during the sacrament. Luther maintained that the elements were somehow transformed, that Christ's body and blood were somehow really present alongside the bread and wine. His belief has been characterized as "Real Presence," where the body and blood of Christ are present along with the bread and wine. Zwingli, by contrast, maintained that the bread and wine were simply symbols that represented the body and blood of Christ, and that Jesus had been speaking figuratively at the Last Supper when he said, "This is my body" and "This is my blood." Today this may seem a minor theological issue, but in the sixteenth century it was profoundly important, since one's position on this question was closely linked to other important considerations regarding the nature of the church and the Christian's place in society. Indeed, it was the single most important reason for division among Protestant movements in the Reformation, and it made any cooperation between Luther and Zwingli impossible.

In 1529 Landgrave Philip of Hesse sponsored a conference in his capital city of Marburg in the hope of uniting the various reform movements in Germany and Switzerland to counter growing Catholic antagonism. Luther and Zwingli were clearly the main actors: if they could agree, the others would fall into line. They agreed readily on all points except the question of what happened to the bread and wine, and this was sufficient to prevent any broad agreement. The consequences of this failure were enormous: not only did the Protestant movement fail to establish a common front, but the Lutheran princes of Germany lost the opportunity to form any alliance with the Swiss. Zwingli then focused his attention on Switzerland, but his efforts to convert his countrymen ended in civil war between Protestant and Catholic cantons, and in October 1531 Zwingli died while defending Zürich from a Catholic attack. The subsequent Peace of Kappel determined that henceforth each canton would be free to determine its own religion.

The importance of Zwingli and his movement went far beyond Zürich. His version of reform was in many ways more attuned than Luther's to the concerns and attitudes of the self-governing cities of Germany and Switzerland, and his faith in the possibility of positive human action was in harmony with the urban elites' views of their world. It gave city fathers another tool with which to reinforce communal bonds in defence of their autonomy. With his successor Heinrich Bullinger (1504–75), Zwingli also advised a number of city governments in Switzerland and Germany on managing the process of religious reformation. As a consequence, urban reformations in Switzerland and southern Germany looked more like Zwingli's than Luther's.

RADICAL VOICES

Virtually simultaneously with Luther's revolt, more radical visions had begun to emerge among a variety of groups dissatisfied with the slow and deliberate pace of reform promoted by rulers and city councils. They believed they knew the Truth, and would brook no further delay in casting off the errors of the past. As soon as Luther had returned to Wittenberg in 1522, he found that other reformers had already become too radical for his taste. The chief offenders were Thomas Müntzer, who would go on to play an important part in the peasant revolt of 1524–5, and Andreas von Karlstadt (1480–1541), a colleague of Luther's who was expelled from the University of Wittenberg and spent the rest of his life wandering from town to town and preaching his version of reform. Luther's condemnation of the peasant uprising led many to conclude that if true reform were to be achieved, they would have to take action themselves.

There was no overall organization or coherence to this radicalism: rather, disparate grassroots groups responded to similar conditions in similar ways. The three major areas of radical activity   the Netherlands and northwestern Germany (the Rhineland), Switzerland, and Moravia—were all characterized by decentralized political systems and a good deal of local autonomy, which allowed radical groups to flourish. Finally, a bewildering variety of lone individuals saw Christianity as a purely interior matter and founded no groups at all. Among the most prominent of these Spiritualists (as some historians have called them) was Sebastian Franck (1499–1552), who explained his position this way:

> There are already in our times three distinct Faiths, which have a large following, the Lutheran, Zwinglian, and Anabaptist; and a fourth is well on the way to birth, which will dispense with external preaching, ceremonies, sacraments, ban and office as unnecessary, and which seeks solely to gather among all peoples an invisible, spiritual Church in the unity of the Spirit and of faith, to be governed wholly by the eternal, invisible Word of God. . . . [10]

The Anabaptists

The most prominent elements of the radical reformation were an assortment of groups that their enemies called Anabaptists ("rebaptisers"), in reference to their practice of adult baptism. From their perspective this practice was not "rebaptism" at all, since they believed the baptism they had received as infants to be meaningless. However, from the perspective of political and religious authorities (Protestant as well as Catholic) to administer a second baptism was to threaten the very foundations of the existing order, which depended on the idea that all members of the society were members of the state church. By denying the validity of infant baptism, they were denying the validity of the mutually supportive relationship between the state and its official church. To call someone an Anabaptist in the sixteenth century, therefore, was the equivalent of calling someone a terrorist today, and to perform a second baptism was a crime punishable by death.

The first manifestation of what would become known as Anabaptism emerged in Zürich around 1525. Disappointed with the pace and direction of Zwingli's reforms, a small group began meeting and performing baptisms to mark their initiation into the true church. This posed a threat to Zwingli's vision of a Christian commonwealth in Zürich, and the leaders were either executed or exiled. Another Anabaptist leader, Jakob Hutter (c. 1500–36), led his flock from the Swiss Tyrol to Moravia and back, and although he too was put to death, his followers scattered throughout eastern Europe. In time the Hutterites established such a strong reputation as peaceful and productive farmers that rulers of underpopulated lands such as Moravia, Transylvania, and Ukraine sought them out as colonists. (In the late nineteenth and early twentieth centuries, Canada would follow their example and recruit Hutterite families to the western provinces, where they continue to operate communal farms today.)

Although there was never a single unified Anabaptist church or movement, most Anabaptist groups did share a number of beliefs. Foremost among them were the convictions that true Christians would never be more than a small minority, and that religion should be entirely separate from the state. Therefore they generally chose to live in closed communities, removed from the sinful world, and refused to serve the state in any capacity, including as soldiers, civil servants, judges, or tax collectors.

Most Anabaptists sought to model their conduct on the life and teachings of Jesus. If this recalls Erasmus's "Philosophy of Christ," it is worth noting that many Anabaptist leaders had at least some humanist education. Even their enemies acknowledged their upright morality; but that only made them more dangerous, as it could seduce the unwary into accepting their damnable heresies. They were often accused of Pelagianism, an ancient heresy according to which people could achieve salvation without the assistance of God's grace.[11]

As a consequence of their literal interpretation of Christian teachings such as "turn the other cheek" and "love your enemies," most Anabaptists were pacifists. Refusing to fight back against persecution, thousands of them calmly accepted martyrdom. The most notable episode in which this was not the case unfolded in the Rhineland city of Münster.

By 1534, Anabaptists had taken over its government and the town had become a magnet for fellow believers from the Netherlands, led by the charismatic Jan Matthys (c. 1500–34). Dutch Anabaptists were more likely than others to emphasize the coming Apocalypse (the Second Coming of Christ and the Last Judgment), and while most of them were willing to passively await Christ's return, Matthys believed that positive action was required to bring it about. Thus he expelled all non-believers and began to introduce radical reforms inspired by the primitive church, such as community of property. Meanwhile, however, the exiled Catholic Bishop of Münster, allied with the Lutheran ruler Philip of Hesse, had laid siege to the city, and Matthys was killed in battle with them. Power was then assumed by his disciple Jan van Leyden (1509?–36), who was not only more radical, but mentally unbalanced as well. He crowned himself "King of Righteousness Over All," decreed a new moral code under which capital offences included blasphemy, scolding one's parents, lewd conduct, gossiping, and complaining; in addition, after legalizing polygamy, he married some 16 women himself (among them Matthys's beautiful young widow). His reign ended in June 1535, when the besieging army entered the city and massacred virtually all its remaining inhabitants.

Münster proved to be a kind of catharsis for Anabaptism. Afterwards, most groups renounced the idea of imposing their vision on others and were content to live in their own communities, keeping a low profile and avoiding unwanted attention from outsiders. This was certainly true of the largest and most influential group after the Münster episode: the Mennonites, named after their founder, the former Dutch priest Menno Simons (1496–1561). Like the Hutterites, many Mennonites found their way to central and eastern Europe, and then to North America in the nineteenth and twentieth centuries. The general renunciation of violence in the aftermath of Münster did nothing to slacken their persecution. As Zwingli's successor in Zürich, Heinrich Bullinger, would write: "God opened the eyes of the governments by the revolt at Münster, and thereafter no one would trust even those Anabaptists who claimed to be innocent."[12]

JOHN CALVIN

From the middle of the sixteenth century on, the dominant Protestant movement in Europe was that founded by John Calvin (1509–64). Born in northern France and raised a Catholic, he received a first-class humanist and legal education. At some point in the early 1530s he experienced a conversion, and in late 1534 he fled France amid a sudden crackdown on Protestants that was sparked by an incident known as the "Affair of the Placards." Overnight on October 17, 1534, a series of placards denouncing the Catholic Mass had appeared throughout France—even on the door of the bedroom in the palace at Amboise where the king, Francis I, was staying. Fear of a widespread conspiracy led to a wave of persecution, and a number of Protestants were burned at the stake.

Until then, the king had been fairly tolerant of religious dissent. His own sister, Marguerite de Navarre, supported a group of reform-minded clergymen in Meaux, outside Paris, and as a patron of artists and scholars Francis himself was accustomed to associating with advocates of reform. He also needed the support of Protestant princes in Germany against Charles V. Nevertheless, the placards incident could not be ignored, and the government's response led Calvin to leave France.

In July 1536 Calvin was on his way to Strasbourg when he happened to stay overnight in Geneva, which was then in the midst of the struggle for religious and political reform. When the leader of the Protestants asked Calvin to stay and assist in the process, Calvin reluctantly agreed. He would spend most of the rest of his life in Geneva.

Geneva was not a theocracy, and Calvin was never a religious dictator. He never held political office; his only official positions were as a pastor and the Moderator of the Company of Pastors, but his influence and moral authority were very great. When John Knox, the leader of the Scottish Reformation, took refuge in Geneva in the 1550s, he described the city as "the most perfect school of Christ that ever was on earth since the time of the Apostles." Moral order was supervised through a body known as the Consistory, made up of the pastors of the city (including Calvin) and a group of elders chosen from among the ruling elite. The existence of such a body was not at all unusual: every early modern government attempted to regulate moral conduct. What did distinguish the Calvinist Consistory was its organization and thoroughness.

The usual punishment for most of the offenders who came before it, charged with transgressions such as failing to attend church, dancing on a Sunday, or saying that the pope was a good man, was suspension from communion. On the other hand, the case of Michael Servetus has attracted a lot of bad press over the centuries. Servetus (c. 1511–53) was a Spanish lawyer and physician who published several books condemning the doctrine of the Trinity. For two decades he lived under an assumed name in southern France, but in 1553 his true identity was revealed and he fled, steps ahead of the authorities. When he passed through Geneva on his way to Italy, he was recognized, put on trial for heresy with Calvin as his leading accuser, and in October burned at the stake.

Such treatment of a dissident is an affront to our ideas of religious liberty, tolerance, and freedom of speech. However, Servetus was a notorious heretic, already condemned *in absentia* in France, and politics alone demanded that Protestant authorities condemn him: otherwise their Catholic opponents would have had a field day. Moreover, while Calvin agreed that Servetus must die, he did plead for a less painful method than burning, but was overruled by the court. In the words of an eminent Reformation historian, "We are today horrified that Geneva should have burned a man for the glory of God, yet we incinerate whole cities for the saving of democracy."[13]

In 1559 Calvin became a citizen of his adopted city and published the fourth and final edition of his major theological work, *The Institutes of the Christian Religion*. In the same year, the Genevan Academy was established to train the pastors and missionaries who would make Calvinism an international movement. By 1564 the school had more than 300 students. Although 80 per cent were French refugees, others came from all over Europe, including England, Scotland, Germany, and the Netherlands. True to Calvin's humanist background, it emphasized studies in the original languages of the Bible, Greek and Hebrew.

Calvin had a great deal of respect for Luther, whose theological views he for the most part shared. Where he differed from other Protestant reformers and theologians was in his emphasis on the doctrine of election, or predestination:

> We call predestination God's eternal decree, by which he compacted with himself what he willed to become of each man. For all are not created in equal condition; rather, eternal life is foreordained for some, eternal damnation for others. . . . As Scripture, then, clearly shows, we say that God once established by his eternal and unchangeable plan those whom he long before determined once and for all to receive into salvation, and those whom, on the other hand, he devoted to destruction. We assert that, with respect to the elect, this plan was founded upon his freely given mercy, without regard to human worth, but by his just irreprehensible judgment he has barred the door of life to those whom he has given over to damnation.[14]

Although predestination has frequently been seen as the central tenet of Calvin's theology, in fact it was only a consequence of his emphasis on God's omnipotence and man's depravity and sinfulness. To have recognized any human contribution to salvation would have been to detract from God's essential attributes:

> We shall never be clearly persuaded, as we ought to be, that our salvation flows from the wellspring of God's free mercy until we come to know his eternal election [i.e., predestination], which illumines God's grace by this contrast: that he does not indiscriminately adopt all into the hope of salvation but gives to some what he denies to others.[15]

The actual mechanism of salvation or of justification was still faith, but since humans in themselves were incapable of it, that faith too had to be a gift that God gave to some and denied to others. God therefore actively chose some for salvation and others for damnation, which is all that humanity actually deserves. Calvin explicitly denied that this predestination was the result of God's foreknowledge, that He knew who would be good and chose them for salvation. Moreover, until the Last Judgment no one could know for certain whom God had chosen for salvation. Human conduct had nothing to do with it, nor could God's eternal judgment be changed.

In the early twentieth century the German sociologist Max Weber proposed that Calvinist theology contributed to the rise of modern capitalism by promoting frugality, sobriety, discipline, moderation, and hard work for its own sake rather than any rewards it might bring. According to the "Weber thesis," because Protestant capitalists could not rest on their laurels and enjoy the fruit of their success, they kept working and plowing their profits back into the business.

Weber located the origin of this work ethic in the anxieties produced by Calvin's insistence on the uncertainty of salvation: Calvinists' inability to affect their eternal destiny drove them to seek reassurance that they were indeed among the Elect. In this way worldly success became a self-fulfilling prophecy: the harder one worked and the more successful one was, the more certain one was of salvation. Why would God bless with material success someone He had condemned to eternal damnation, especially if He had given that person the grace to lead a virtuous life?

Over the last century, critics have pointed out that Weber cited little real evidence of what predestination meant to early Calvinists, and ignored significant evidence that what they felt was not deep anxiety, but rather the same freedom from anxiety concerning good works that Luther had felt. They did not have to worry about confessing sins, or performing penance, or even if their faith was strong enough; it was entirely out of their hands. This freed them to serve God on earth, which after all was the purpose of humanity. It is also unclear why evidence of salvation should have been sought in economic success rather than in charitable works, missionary activity, or personal morality. Finally, while there is certainly evidence of a "capitalist ethic" developing in early modern Europe, it was by no means limited to Calvinists: we can also find it among Catholics. Thus Weber appears to have erred in identifying it with Calvinist predestination.

Another area where Calvin differed from Luther was in regard to church organization and governance. Luther took no interest in how a church was governed or organized, as long as it taught correct doctrine; thus in states that adopted Lutheranism as their official religion (primarily in Scandinavia and northern Germany), the churches in effect became departments of the government. By contrast, Calvin prescribed a presbyterian model in which churches would be governed cooperatively by pastors and lay elders (presbyters). This gave laymen (but not laywomen) a voice in religious affairs that the Catholic Church had typically denied them.

In addition, local churches were connected on a national basis in a system of synods, or periodic assemblies. Each local church would send delegates, lay and clerical, to a regional or provincial synod. The regional and provincial synods would then send delegates to national synod, which would set policies and procedures for the church as a whole. This form of organization was crucial in at least two respects. First, it improved Calvinist churches' ability to survive in hostile environments by ensuring that even if the leadership were wiped out in one fell swoop, there were people throughout the structure with experience in governance. In addition, with input from below, national synods were unlikely to adopt positions that were out of step with local congregations.

Relatively few states adopted Calvinism as their official creed: Geneva and Protestant areas of Switzerland, Scotland, the Dutch Republic (the United Provinces of the Netherlands), and limited areas of Germany. These will be discussed in the next chapter. But the influence of Calvinism extended much farther. Calvinists became a significant and powerful minority in France. In England they agitated for more extensive reform of the Church of England. In Bohemia, Poland, Austria, Hungary, and elsewhere, Calvinism was widely adopted by nobles who opposed the centralizing agendas of their Catholic rulers. In the later sixteenth and seventeenth centuries, it was Calvinism that became the primary antagonist of a revived and resurgent Catholic Church.

THE REFORMATION IN ENGLAND

The Reformation in England took a fundamentally different form from its counterparts on the continent. Elsewhere, as we have seen, rejection of the Church's authority went together with the doctrinal change from Catholic to Protestant. The support of the ruler was essential, and rulers of course had various political motives, but in the end, the rejection of Rome's authority coincided with the adoption of Protestant doctrine. In England, however, the rejection of Rome's authority preceded by decades the introduction of Protestant doctrine, and was related to it only tangentially. Rome's authority was rejected for political and dynastic reasons, although it was encouraged and welcomed by advocates of religious reform.

The roots of the English Reformation lie in the desire of King Henry VIII (r. 1509–47) for a male heir. Since the Tudor dynasty was new on the throne and its claim to rule was relatively weak, Henry believed that, to avoid a disputed succession, he must have an adult son to succeed him. For the first twenty years of his reign, he was content to pursue war and diplomacy and leave the actual government of England in the hands of his chief adviser, Cardinal Thomas Wolsey (1473–1530). By the mid-1520s, however, his only living child was a daughter, Princess Mary, and his queen, Catharine of Aragon (a daughter of

Isabella and Ferdinand), was approaching the end of her child-bearing years. Desperate for a male heir, Henry put Wolsey in charge of securing an annulment of his marriage from Pope Clement VII (r. 1523–34).[16] When the pope refused, Wolsey was charged with treason, and he escaped execution only by dying in prison before his trial. It seemed the only way for Henry to end his marriage was to reject the authority of the pope.

In 1529, Henry called Parliament to consider the "King's Great Matter." The so-called "Reformation Parliament" would sit until 1536 (the longest session in English history to that point), and would pass a number of acts that legally severed the ties between England and Rome. Henry could have achieved the same result through royal decrees, but he chose to use Parliament because it showed the world, and especially Rome, that he was acting with the support of his subjects. In 1533 Parliament passed the Act in Restraint of Appeals, which prevented Queen Catharine from appealing her case to Rome, and Henry was granted his annulment. In 1534 the Act of Supremacy declared that the king was Supreme Head of the Church of England. The same year saw the Act of Succession, which declared that Henry's children by his subsequent marriage(s) were legal heirs, and that to say or think otherwise was high treason. It was his refusal to acknowledge this act that led to Thomas More's downfall. Although he had largely kept silent regarding the annulment and relations with Rome, in the end his refusal to support the king could not be tolerated. Before he was beheaded in 1535, he declared from the scaffold, "I die the King's good servant, but God's first." In the meantime, Henry had married his mistress, Anne Boleyn (1501–36), but although she bore a daughter, Princess Elizabeth in 1533, she too failed to produce a boy. After having her executed for treason, Henry married Jane Seymour, who finally gave birth to the long-sought son, Prince Edward, in 1537, but died of complications less than two weeks later.[17]

By this point Henry had established an independent Church of England, with himself rather than the pope at its head, but this was only a political and administrative revolution: nothing at all had changed with respect to theology or doctrine. Although the extent of popular demand for religious reform in England has been widely debated (see Debate box), there was significant support for Protestant ideas at court and among the elite. Among those with Protestant leanings was Thomas Cromwell (c. 1485–1540), Wolsey's replacement as Henry's chief adviser, who drafted the Reformation legislation and guided it through Parliament. Thomas Cranmer (1489–1556), who was made Archbishop of Canterbury in 1532, was also sympathetic to Protestant ideas. As long as Henry was king, however, supporters of reform had to tread very cautiously.

In the later 1530s, at the urging of Protestant sympathizers such as Cromwell and Cranmer, the government dissolved England's monasteries and confiscated their lands and property. This, more than anything else, guaranteed the permanence of England's break with Rome. It also provoked a serious opposition movement in the north of England, where attachment to the old ways was still strong and monasteries were closely integrated into local communities. This rebellion, known as the Pilgrimage of Grace, was brutally suppressed and its leaders tortured and executed. However, it was the only expression of mass resistance, and it was provoked by the dissolution of the monasteries, not the Royal Supremacy as such. On the whole, resistance to Henry's break with Rome was muted.

HISTORICAL DEBATE

The Appeal of Protestantism in England

Few areas of early modern historiography have produced more debate than the nature of the English Reformation. All historians agree that the process of Reformation was top-down, driven by the political and dynastic needs of the king. According to A.G. Dickens, *The English Reformation* (1964), Henry's changes were welcomed by a broad cross-section of English society that had become dissatisfied with the old faith. In the 1980s, however, a "revisionist" interpretation began to emerge as historians such as Christopher Haigh, Eamon Duffy, and J.J. Scarisbrick argued there was little popular demand for religious change. In their view, the process of making the English people into Protestants required all the coercive power of the state. An excerpt from Dickens, below, is followed by one from Haigh.

> Here we are confronted by one of the great formative factors in the origins of the Reformation. The gradual yet portentous growth of a literate laity . . . was far from being limited to the gentry and the richer merchant classes. In the long run it was bound to involve not merely critical attitudes toward the Church but also more constructive intellectual and religious ambitions which could not be excluded from the sphere of religion . . . (p. 9).
>
> In the field of religion many weaknesses of the late medieval Church were plainly apparent. . . . Scholastic religion, having overestimated its powers, had ended in disharmony, irrelevance and discredit. Beliefs of marginal authenticity, especially those relating to purgatory and saint-worship, had been suffered in everyday practice to occupy central places in the Christian life. The professional education of parish priests was criticised as quite inadequate . . . and its character reflected in the paucity of direct religious teaching outside the larger towns. With certain notable exceptions monasticism was uninspired . . . (pp. 326–7).
>
> A.G. Dickens, *The English Reformation* (New York: Schocken Books, 1964).

Only Thomas More, Bishop John Fisher of Rochester, and several London monks had paid with their lives to preserve the power of the pope; and only one important clergyman, Cardinal Reginald Pole, had gone into exile in protest. The relative ease of the transition can be explained by several factors. One was widespread anticlericalism, which the government was able to use to advance its agenda. Another was fear of renewed civil war if the king could not remarry and provide the kingdom with a male heir. Much of the credit must go to Cromwell, who organized and executed the Reformation with such efficiency that those who might have opposed it were simply overwhelmed.[18] Once the principle had been established that the proper form of religion was within the power of the monarch, without any changes so dramatic or wrenching that people felt compelled to resist, the vast majority of people were inclined to go along with later changes.

In some cities of Germany and Switzerland, Reformation came with enthusiasm and violence; altars and images were cast down and smashed by rioting mobs, eager to destroy the symbols with which priests had kept them in awe. In England (and especially away from London) it was different: altars and images were carefully removed on government orders, were often kept safe, in case of future need. On the continent, princes and city councils declared themselves for "the Reformation": they swept away papal power and clerical privilege, they seized Church property, they introduced vernacular services and Bibles, and they prescribed Protestant and proscribed Catholic beliefs—often in weeks, months, or a very few years. In England, it was different: change was piecemeal, and it took twenty years to get to the first Protestant church service in 1552 . . . (pp. 12–13).

Catholic Christianity before England's break with Rome was flourishing; we must not assume that the Reformations prove otherwise. For it was the break with Rome which was to cause the decline of Catholicism, not the decline of Catholicism which led to the break with Rome. Before the intrusion of political considerations which had little to do with religion, early Tudor England was not heading towards a Reformation. . . . In England, late medieval parish religion was not just a going concern, it was an expanding business with good prospects for the future. . . (pp. 28–9).

The political Reformations had succeeded in driving Catholic public worship from the churches; but the Protestant Reformation did not destroy essentially Catholic views of Christian life and eternal salvation. The political Reformations had succeeded in imposing more Protestant ways of worship; but the Protestant Reformation did not generate widespread attachment to Protestant doctrines of justification (p. 289).

Christopher Haigh, *English Reformations: Religion, Politics, and Society under the Tudors* (Oxford: Oxford University Press, 1993). Republished with permission of Oxford University Press; permission conveyed through Copyright Clearance Center, Inc.

When Henry VIII died in 1547, his nine-year-old son became King Edward VI (r. 1547–53) and his uncle Edward Seymour, Duke of Somerset, seized power as Lord Protector. It was under Somerset's regency that the first Protestant reforms were introduced in the Church of England. Since he needed to preserve stability and a national consensus, the changes were relatively modest: some English was introduced into the liturgy, and in the sacrament of communion, laypeople could receive not only the bread, but also the wine ("communion in both kinds"), though it was not yet required. The liturgy was set out in the Book of Common Prayer of 1549, which is thought to have been produced primarily by Cranmer. Widely considered a masterpiece of the English language, it attempted to appeal to moderate opinion through creative ambiguity. For example, while it provided for communion in both kinds, it maintained the basic form of a Catholic Mass, and never explicitly denied transubstantiation even while it hinted at a Protestant interpretation of the sacrament.

In 1549 Somerset was overthrown in a palace coup by John Dudley, Earl of Warwick, subsequently Duke of Northumberland. For political reasons, Dudley had aligned himself with more zealous Protestants, and his period in power saw more thoroughgoing Protestant reforms. In 1552 a new Prayer Book was issued that excluded any ambiguity or compromise with Catholic doctrine. Clergy were explicitly declared to be pastors rather than priests, and were instructed to wear plain robes rather than elaborate vestments. In an implicit rejection of the transubstantiation doctrine, the altars at which the sacrament of Mass had been performed were replaced with ordinary tables.

On Edward's death in 1553, the accession of his elder half-sister Mary (r. 1553–8) was greeted with tremendous wave of popular enthusiasm. Unfortunately, she interpreted the people's support for her and the Tudor dynasty as support for the restoration of her Catholic religion. In addition, unlike both her father and her half-sister Elizabeth, she was unwilling to compromise on religion, even when political circumstances seemed to demand it.

The daughter of Catharine of Aragon, she had seen her mother repudiated and expelled from court. In a moment of weakness as a young woman, she had signed the loyalty oath demanded by her father's legislation, and was now determined to make up for it by returning England to the Roman Catholic Church. Although she was unable to restore the confiscated monastic property, by the end of 1554 she had had Parliament repeal the legislation that had removed England from the Catholic Church. At first she was relatively lenient towards Protestants, giving them time to re-embrace the old ways. Even Thomas Cranmer, whom she had every reason to hate, was allowed to remain free, although he was replaced as Archbishop of Canterbury by Cardinal Reginald Pole.

To the surprise of Mary and her advisers, the public's reaction to the return of the old religion was lukewarm. This probably had less to do with deep-seated Protestant conviction than with the turmoil of the previous twenty years and uncertainty about what might happen next. However, Mary's decision to marry Prince Philip of Spain—the son of Emperor Charles V, and the most prominent Catholic prince in Europe—aroused not only loud objections but an uprising led by an important nobleman and general, Sir Thomas Wyatt. Although it was quickly suppressed, it was enough to persuade Mary and her advisers that their leniency had been mistaken, and they decided to pursue a harder line.

At first they made examples of an important few, including Thomas Cranmer. Even though he had recanted his Protestant beliefs under duress, he was sentenced to burning in 1556. At the stake, he held the hand that had signed his recantation into the fire and declared that it would be punished first, "for writing contrary to [his] heart." Also burned were Hugh Latimer, previously Bishop of Winchester, and Nicholas Ridley, previously Bishop of London. Far from deterring others, these executions transformed the victims into martyrs, inspiring further cycles of resistance and punishment. In the end, approximately 300 Protestants were burned at the stake during Mary's reign, and even though this persecution was comparatively mild by the standards of the time, it earned

The Burning of Thomas Cranmer, 1556, from *Foxe's Book of Martyrs*. Cranmer holds his offending right hand, with which he had recanted his Protestant faith, into the fire, while saying, "Lord, receive my spirit."

her the name "Bloody Mary." A Protestant named John Foxe recorded the deaths in a book that he called *Acts and Monuments* (1563), but that came to be better known as *The Book of Martyrs*, situating them in the line of all those who had died for their faith since the time of Christ. Apart from the English Bible, no other book did more to create a Protestant England.

Having restored England to the Church of Rome, it was Mary's fondest desire to guarantee a Catholic succession. Her marriage to Philip of Spain went ahead as planned, despite widespread fear that it would subordinate England to Habsburg interests, and Mary fell deeply in love with her young husband, though her feelings were not reciprocated. After a false pregnancy, she died of a tumour in 1558, childless, abandoned by her husband, and despised by a substantial portion of her subjects. When her younger half-sister Elizabeth, the daughter of Anne Boleyn, succeeded her as queen (Chapter 4), there were good reasons to fear for the future, given the turmoil and instability of the previous thirty years.

The Catholic Counter-Reformation

The term "Counter-Reformation" was coined by nineteenth-century German Protestant historians who believed that the reforms undertaken by the Church of Rome in the sixteenth century were attributable solely to the challenges posed by the Protestant Reformation: if the Catholic Church had done anything positive, it was only because the Protestant Reformation had forced it to take action. Catholic historians responded by identifying what they claimed was a genuine Catholic Reformation, prior to and independent of the Protestant challenges, which would have taken care of all the Church's problems, had ignorant and immoral heretics such as Luther and Calvin not derailed it.

While few historians today would defend either of these extreme positions, most agree that in fact both things were going on. There were reform movements underway within the Church, but the way the Church responded and promoted reforms was certainly influenced by the existence of the Protestant Reformation. The author of a classic text on the phenomenon would write:

> the Reformation on its religious side, and the Counter-Reformation on *its* religious side can reasonably be regarded as two different outcomes of the general aspiration towards religious regeneration which pervaded late fifteenth- and early sixteenth-century Europe. . . .[19]

It is probably reasonable to speculate that without the shock of the Protestant Reformation, the Catholic Church would have developed in ways that looked more "Protestant," rather than reject Protestant principles wholesale, as it eventually would do.

What to call this complex period of development and reform has proven a problem. One leading historian has suggested "early modern Catholicism," while others continue to use the terms "Counter" and/or "Catholic Reformation."[20] This is the approach adopted here: insofar as it is possible or useful to distinguish between Catholic and Counter Reformations, that will be done. In no case, however, does use of either term here carry with it any of the polemical overtones discussed above.

PRE-REFORMATION AND CATHOLIC REFORM

There is no doubt that sincere and effective reform efforts were undertaken prior to Luther's protest against indulgences. We have already mentioned the reforms of Ximenes de Cisneros and the establishment of Observantine wings of monastic orders. Savonarola's puritanical revival in Florence may also be seen in this light, as may Christian Humanism. Another clergyman who took it on himself to reform religious life in his diocese was Gian Matteo Giberti, Bishop of Verona from 1524 to 1543, who disciplined lax priests and monks, conducted tours of inspection and encouraged preaching (in the past, services had focused on the Mass, and sermons were not a regular feature). It is also true, however, that these reformers had no support from Rome or the papacy, and often faced active hostility from them.

To be fair, the popes of the period had a great deal to contend with besides the Protestant challenges, including bureaucratic opposition and political circumstances. We can see examples in the pontificates of Adrian VI (r. 1522–3) and Clement VII (r. 1523–34).

A Dutchman who had been tutor to Emperor Charles V, Adrian VI was the last non-Italian pope elected before the Polish John Paul II in 1978. Unlike the typical Renaissance pope, he was personally very devout and determined to reform the Church, beginning in Rome, but was frustrated by the "circle the wagons" mentality of the bureaucracy, which was determined to stifle any attempt at reform lest it appear to justify the Protestants' charges against the Church. His successor, Clement VII (a member of the Medici family) had to deal with the competition between France and the Habsburgs for European supremacy: although he tried desperately to preserve Rome's independence from both, in 1527 the army of Charles V captured and sacked the city, and Clement became a virtual prisoner.

At the same time, there were many influential Catholics who believed that although reformers like Luther went too far, they had some valid points. Many devout Catholics were troubled by the Church's overwhelming emphasis on the sacraments and good works in attaining salvation, not to mention the abuse of indulgences. These "Catholic Evangelicals" sought ways to repair the schism throughout the 1520s and 1530s. In the highly charged atmosphere of the times, however, moderates who tried to steer a middle course risked charges of heresy. Criticism was treason, and anyone who agreed with anything that Luther had said was suspected of being a heretic himself. The fate of Erasmus is instructive here. The great humanist had offered qualified support to Luther before his excommunication in 1520, saying that he deserved a fair hearing even if one could not agree with everything he said or wrote. After Luther's excommunication, Erasmus remained largely silent, but many within the Church blamed him for the schism. Finally, in 1524, under significant pressure to prove his Catholic loyalty, he wrote a book arguing against Luther in the one area in which he felt there was genuine and significant disagreement. In *On the Freedom of the Will*, Erasmus maintained, contrary to Luther, that humans were free to perform the good works necessary for salvation. In 1525, Luther responded with *On the Bondage of the Will*, in which he stated that, although humans might be free to act in their daily lives, when it came to questions of good and evil they were inevitably bound to sin, and could not freely choose to do good of their own will. Erasmus remained suspect in the eyes of both sides, however, and the moderate path he preferred was lost in the chaos.

PAUL III AND THE COUNCIL OF TRENT

It took more than a decade following Luther's initial protest for reform to become Church policy. The key figure was Pope Paul III (r. 1534–43). A Roman nobleman, he was an unlikely figure to launch a reform program, but in 1536 he appointed a commission called the *Consilium de emendanda ecclesium* (Council for improving the church) and stacked it with reformers. Its 1537 report was a sweeping and brutally frank indictment of the church hierarchy. Although it was supposed to be secret, it was soon leaked, and Luther gleefully republished it, along with his own sarcastic commentary.

Paul III understood that the best way to achieve meaningful reform was to convene a General Council with the moral authority to produce a consensus. After more than century without such a meeting, however, careful management would be required to ensure that the council followed the papacy's lead without appearing to do so. Timing was also tricky. Emperor Charles V, on the front lines of the religious conflict in Germany, had been pressing the Church for years to call a council, but the pope had to avoid any appearance of knuckling under to him, for fear of alienating the King of France, Europe's other major Catholic ruler, with whom the Emperor was at war for much of the period.

In 1545 Paul III finally succeeded in convening a council in the alpine town of Trent. The Council of Trent would meet in three sessions over a period of eighteen years: 1545–7, 1551–2, and 1562–3. Its stated aims were to reform the Church, restore Christian morality, and reunite Christendom.[21] It therefore took as its mandate issues of both institutional reform and doctrine. Although attendance was sometimes sparse and the agendas of secular rulers often hindered its deliberations, its achievements were immense. In fact, the reformed Roman Catholic Church as established at Trent has been called the Tridentine Church, after the Latin name for Trent. The Tridentine Church would persist almost unchanged for 400 years, until the reforms of the Second Vatican Council in the 1960s.

With the development of competing faiths, the kind of diversity that had been tolerated prior to the Reformation could no longer be allowed. Forced to define the core doctrines of the Church, the council chose confrontation over conciliation, directly repudiating the theological positions of the Protestants, but also dashing the hopes of the moderate Catholic Evangelicals. The necessity of all seven sacraments for salvation was reaffirmed, as was the necessity of good works. The doctrines of transubstantiation and communion in one kind only for the laity were also affirmed, and any other position was declared heretical. Church law and tradition were declared equal in authority to Scripture. The Latin Vulgate version of the Bible was affirmed to be the true word of God. The goal was not only to condemn and reject Protestant doctrine, but to clearly and carefully define what one must believe and do in order to achieve salvation, to draw a clear line between "us" and "them."

The Council of Trent firmly established that the Church was a papal monarchy rather than a conciliar aristocracy. While the doctrine of papal infallibility would not be officially proclaimed until the nineteenth century, it was implicit in the decrees of Trent. For example, while the position of bishops was strengthened with respect to their authority over clergy and laity, the declaration that they held their office not directly from God, but from the pope, clearly undermined their position in relation to the papacy.

In terms of reform, the Church finally acted on many of the issues that had driven people away in the first place. Indulgences were kept, but were more strictly defined and controlled. Pluralism (holding multiple offices) was strictly forbidden. Bishops were required both to reside in their dioceses and to establish seminaries, to ensure that priests were properly trained. This was clearly a huge undertaking, and it would take generations before full compliance was achieved (if it ever was).

The Council of Trent was not the totality of the Catholic Counter-Reformation, but in many ways it was the centrepiece. More than anything else, it represents the moment when the institutional momentum of the Church was turned towards reform and revival after decades of hesitation over how best to respond to the challenges of Protestantism.

It was nevertheless only the beginning of the process. Full implementation of the program of Catholic reform would take generations.

THE INQUISITION AND INDEX

The repressive reputation of the Counter-Reformation (as distinct from a broader Catholic Reformation) can be traced in part to the work of Cardinal Gian Pietro Caraffa (1476–1559), Archbishop of Naples and later Pope Paul IV (r. 1555–9). A rigid and severe character, in 1542 he persuaded Paul III to revive the Roman Inquisition to pursue and punish heresy and dissent throughout Catholic Europe. Most rulers refused it permission to operate in their territories, however, and as a result its activities were limited almost entirely to the parts of Italy under papal jurisdiction.

It was also Caraffa who in 1559, as Pope Paul IV, established the *Index librorum prohibitorum* (Index of Forbidden Books), a list of works that Catholics were forbidden to read without Church permission. The catalogue of banned books extended well beyond works by "heretical" authors such as Luther and Calvin: also included were many humanist works (especially those of Erasmus), books considered immoral or impious, or simply insufficiently Catholic. Whereas the Protestant reformers urged laypeople to study the Scriptures themselves, the Index went so far as to ban almost all editions of the Bible.

THE SOCIETY OF JESUS

Other than the Council of Trent, there is no more prominent feature of the Catholic Counter-Reformation than the Society of Jesus (the Jesuits). Indeed, in it we see elements of both the Catholic and the Counter-Reformation. Although the order might have existed without the impact of the Protestant Reformation, its nature was inevitably shaped by the fragmentation of Christendom.

The Society of Jesus was the creation of Ignatius Loyola (1491–1556), a Spanish Basque nobleman who was wounded in battle in 1521. During a long convalescence he began to read mystical and devotional

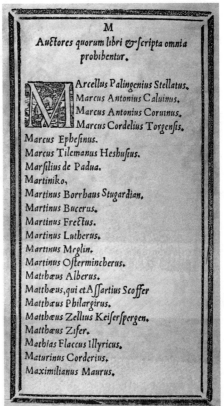

© INTERFOTO / Alamy Stock Photo

The Index of Forbidden Books. This page from the 1559 edition of the Index features the name of Martin Luther (Martinus Lutherus) as one of the authors whose works were forbidden.

VOICES

From the *Spiritual Exercises of St. Ignatius Loyola*

The Spiritual Exercises was a system of meditation and purification that had its roots in Loyola's own experience during his year-long period of retreat. Many people are disappointed when they read the text for the first time. Rather than a mystical or contemplative masterpiece, what they find is a set of instructions for the director of the exercises, rather than the participant; they are very concrete and practical. The exercises are divided into four "weeks," although they may take more or less than a week, if necessary. Following the exercises themselves are several sets of practical rules for the director and the participant, of which the most famous are "Rules for Thinking with the Church."

DIRECTIONS FOR ACQUIRING AN UNDERSTANDING OF THE SPIRITUAL EXERCISES THAT FOLLOW AND THUS ASSISTING BOTH THOSE WHO ARE TO GIVE THEM AND THOSE WHO MAKE THEM

1. The expression "Spiritual Exercises" embraces every method of examination, of meditation, of contemplation, or vocal and mental prayer, and of other spiritual activity that will be mentioned later. For just as strolling, walking, and running are bodily exercises, so spiritual exercises are methods of preparing and disposing the soul to free itself of all inordinate attachments, and after accomplishing this, of seeking and discovering the Divine Will regarding the disposition of one's life, thus insuring the salvation of his soul.

PURPOSE OF THE EXERCISES

The purpose of these Exercises is to help the exercitant to conquer himself, and to regulate his life so that he will not be influenced in his decisions by any inordinate attachment.

PRINCIPLE AND FOUNDATION

Man is created to praise, reverence, and serve God our Lord, and by this means to save his soul. All other things on the face of the earth are created for man to help him fulfill

literature, as a result of which he decided to devote his life to God. After spending almost a year as in contemplation as a hermit, he made a pilgrimage to Jerusalem, where he decided that his life's mission was to be the conversion of the Muslim world. It was during this period of retreat that he began to employ the meditative techniques that would form the basis of his *Spiritual Exercises.*

Loyola discovered, however, that his education was not equal to the task, and he spent the next decade remedying that defect, first at Alcalà and then in Paris, where he attracted a small group of followers who shared his devotion and goals. In 1534 they swore oaths of poverty, chastity, and obedience; although they hoped to go to the Holy Land as missionaries, they vowed to dedicate themselves to whatever work the pope assigned them. This was the end for which he is created. From this it follows that man is to use these things to the extent that they will help him attain his end. Likewise, he must rid himself of them in so far as they prevent him from attaining it.

RULES FOR THINKING WITH THE CHURCH

In order to have the proper attitude of mind in the Church Militant we should observe the following rules:

1. Putting aside all private judgment, we should keep our minds prepared and ready to obey promptly and in all things the true spouse of Christ our Lord, our Holy Mother, the hierarchical Church.

9. Finally, to praise all the precepts of the Church, holding ourselves to be ready at all times to find reasons for their defense, and never offending against them.

13. If we wish to be sure that we are right in all things, we should always be ready to accept this principle: I will believe that the white that I see is black, if the hierarchical Church so defines it. For, I believe that between the Bridegroom, Christ our Lord, and the Bride, His Church, there is but one spirit, which governs and directs us for the salvation our souls, for the same Spirit and Lord, who gave us the Ten Commandments, guides and governs our Holy Mother Church.

14. Although it be true that no one can be saved unless it be predestined and unless he have faith and grace, still we must be very careful of our manner of discussing and speaking of these matters.

16. In like manner, we must be careful lest by speaking too much and with too great emphasis on faith, without any distinction or explanation, we give occasion to the people to become indolent and lazy in the performance of good works, whether it be before or after their faith is grounded in charity.

The Spiritual Exercises of St. Ignatius, Anthony Mottola ed. and trans. (New York: Doubleday, 1964), pp. 37, 47, 139–41.

the nucleus of the Society of Jesus, and right from its beginning, it was an international movement: of Loyola's original nine followers, four were Spanish, one was Portuguese, two were from Savoy, and two were French.

They were prevented by war from going to Palestine, so they stayed in Rome, preaching and working among the poor and sick. They attracted a good deal of attention, not all of it favourable. Monastic orders saw in them upstart rivals, and Cardinal Caraffa was suspicious of the soldier turned would-be monk. While still a student in Spain, Loyola had been questioned by the Inquisition on several occasions because he discussed theology without holding any recognized credentials. Nevertheless, in 1540 Pope Paul III granted the Society of Jesus official Church sanction and recognition.

Several features distinguish the Jesuits from other religious orders and identify them as uniquely a product of the Catholic Counter-Reformation. Whereas traditional monks withdrew from society to live lives of contemplation and prayer, the Jesuits were emphatically oriented towards a life of action in the world. Following the founder's example, a Jesuit would study for more than a decade before taking his vows and formally joining the Society. This ensured that the leadership had extensive opportunity to weed out unsuitable candidates, and that only the truly committed were able to join the Society. Unlike traditional monastic orders, which usually featured an element of collective self-governance, the Society of Jesus was highly centralized and hierarchical. Although the idea that Loyola's model was the military has sometimes been overemphasized, the Jesuit emphasis on discipline was certainly related to his experience as a soldier. At the same time, initiative and spontaneity were rewarded and encouraged where appropriate.

From the Society's foundation it had three major goals: education, foreign missions, and the reconversion of Protestants. In order to influence future generations, the Jesuits founded and ran many secondary schools and universities, notable for their excellence and rigour. Before 1600, Jesuit missionaries were active in India, Japan, and China, and in Europe they succeeded in converting Poland from Protestantism back to the Catholic Church. They also established seminaries to train priests to minister to Catholic populations in Protestant lands; Peter Canisius (1521–97) came to be known as the apostle to Germany, and Edmund Campion (1540–81) and Robert Parsons (1546–1610) began the Jesuit mission to England in 1580.

Numbering about one thousand at the time of Loyola's death in 1556, by 1626 the order had 15,000 members and more than 400 colleges, and many Jesuits exercised influence as advisers and confessors to nobles and rulers. Not surprisingly, they were not without enemies even within the Catholic Church, especially among the Dominicans who had traditionally dominated university theology faculties. Throughout Catholic Europe, the Society was often suspected of being in the service of the King of Spain. The election of Gian Pietro Caraffa, who was fanatically anti-Spanish, as Pope Paul IV in 1555 caused Loyola to "shake in every bone in my body." Nevertheless, the Society became an integral part of the Catholic revival and resurgence in the sixteenth and seventeenth centuries.

Impact of the Reformations

The Reformations of the sixteenth century destroyed the religious unity of Christendom beyond any hope of recovery. They also had far-reaching effects in the religious lives of ordinary people, their relationships to their churches and governments, and the relations between rulers, as well as the relations between rulers and ruled.

RELIGION AND THE PEOPLE

The traditional practice of Christianity was transformed in the course of the sixteenth century. With the development of competing faiths, it became essential to distinguish clearly between Truth and Error. Thus Protestant and Catholic churches alike sought to ensure uniformity of belief among their followers and transform collective into individual Christians. As we have seen, in the world of traditional (pre-Reformation Christianity) one was a Christian by virtue of belonging to a Christian community, whose unity was both created and demonstrated in the performance of the sacraments. Now, however, Christianity (of whatever variety) became a matter of what one believed, rather than what one did. This process, which historians call "confessionalization," has been defined as "the internalization of church teaching, the drawing of sharp dichotomies, and the quest for 'holy uniformity.'"[22]

With the Protestant emphasis on the "priesthood of all believers," the individual stood alone before God, without a specially empowered priest to serve as intermediary. People therefore had to able to read the Bible for themselves and understand the basic elements of their faith. Education became essential, and Protestant authorities invested considerable resources in making it available. Pastors were instructed to hold catechism classes for children and adults, and commissions were regularly dispatched to gauge progress.

The Catholic Church too sought to internalize belief in its adherents. Not only did it begin teaching its own catechism, but it encouraged the faithful, who had once been expected to take part in confession just once a year, to do so more frequently. It also introduced the confessional box, which isolated the priest and the penitent, and in this way what had been a communal practice became more individual and interior. At the same time, the Church sought to establish a monopoly on religious activity by concentrating it in the parish church under the watchful eye of the parish priest. Thus confraternities, for example, were subordinated to the parochial structure of the church and put under the surveillance of the parish priest.

The clergy also saw significant changes as a result of the Reformations. Protestant clergy were of course pastors with no special status or powers, fully integrated into the community. Their job was to administer the sacraments and teach and preach to the faithful, but with the priesthood of all believers, they lost their role as intermediaries between humanity and God. The Catholic Church went in the opposite direction, imposing stricter controls on admission to the priesthood, and reinforcing the special status of the priest. The ideal priest of the reformed Catholic Church was a remote and austere figure, set apart from his flock by his education, who lived in the community but was not a part of it.

Both Protestant and Catholic churches sought to purify the religion of ordinary people, removing vestiges of pagan religion as well as practices deemed immoral or insufficiently pious. Protestants eliminated the cult of the saints altogether on the reasoning that their holiness was an unmerited gift of God's grace. Catholics had a more delicate task in retaining the concept of sainthood but removing unverified figures such as St. Christopher and transforming the remaining saints from helpful "friends in high places" to models of heroic faith or virtue.

Both Protestant and Catholic religious authorities attempted to draw stricter boundaries between the sacred and the profane. Here too, Protestants took the easier route of simply eliminating practices such as the riotous Carnival celebrations that had preceded the deprivations of Lent. Catholics, however, attempted to curb the excesses and turn the event into a more genuinely religious observance, with only mixed success.

RELIGIOUS VIOLENCE AND PEACEFUL COEXISTENCE

In a world where political authority was explicitly based on divine sanction, religious unity within the state became paramount. Rulers and governments therefore took a direct interest in the process of confessionalization and put their resources and authority behind it. Thus while the religious unity of Christendom was destroyed, the ideal of religious unity was reinforced on a smaller scale. Inevitably, some of the means used to this end involved coercion, from the Spanish Inquisition and the Index of Forbidden Books to the Calvinist consistory. Confessionalization also led to popular violence when believers of different faiths clashed over the "true" doctrine. Although much of this violence has been interpreted as essentially irrational, a frenzied mob blindly striking out against anything different, some researchers have found that in most cases religious violence was the outcome of deliberate consideration. If religion truly was collective, then toleration of heretics threatened the entire community with disaster in this life and damnation in the next, and if the authorities could not or would not do their job, ordinary people felt it was their duty to act.

On the other hand, a number of historians have found evidence throughout Europe of relatively peaceful coexistence between Protestants and Catholics, long before the spread of modern ideals of religious freedom. Even in places where the practice of another religion was officially forbidden, authorities would often turn a blind eye, as long as the minorities were not too obvious about their activities, and in some cases Protestant and Catholic communities even shared church buildings. Although this research is still under way, it may turn out that coexistence of different faiths was the norm and religious violence the exception.

WOMEN AND THE REFORMATIONS

Historians have disagreed, often loudly, on the impact of the Reformations on women. Those who think that Protestant reform brought women significant benefits emphasize that the "priesthood of all believers" applied to women as well as men, making them spiritually equal to clergy; that women as well as men were expected to read the Bible themselves; that the married state was no longer considered inferior to celibacy; and that the Protestant pastor's wife frequently became a model of piety. Once marriage was no longer a sacrament, divorce became possible, and either the husband or wife could initiate it. In many families, women were the first to convert, and then converted their husbands, sons, and brothers. Protestant women marched, demonstrated, sang hymns, and died as martyrs alongside Protestant men.

It will come as no surprise, however, that in reality women's circumstances did not change as much as Protestant apologists suggest. Although spiritually equal to men in theory, women were still effectively shut out of leadership roles in Protestant churches. In the early stages of reform, some women did in fact assume positions of leadership, praying in public, and even preaching, but male clergy quickly reasserted control. Surprisingly, there is little evidence of widespread female dissatisfaction with this state of affairs. However, Protestants not only invested family life with particular value, but emphasized women's responsibility for role-modelling and religious education in the household, and it may well be that the majority of women found fulfilment in these roles. It serves little purpose to impose modern notions of gender equality on the sixteenth century.

Protestant writers might praise the companionship of marriage, but civil laws still placed wives and daughters under the authority of their husbands and fathers. Although women could and did legally initiate divorce, usually for cruelty, abandonment, or adultery, the playing field was still clearly uneven. While the closure of convents in Protestant lands liberated some women who had been sent there by their families without a particular religious vocation, other women, especially from elite backgrounds, resisted fiercely. In Lutheran Nuremberg, the aristocratic abbess Caritas Pirckheimer defied the city government and kept her convent going until the last of her nuns died in 1536. Another German abbess, Mathilde Willen, managed to keep her convent in Protestant territory going for forty years.[23] The elimination of the saints and the veneration of the Virgin deprived many women of female role models and inspiration.

Meanwhile, Catholic women were further subordinated to the hierarchical authority of the Church. Maintaining that celibacy was a superior spiritual state, the Church de-emphasized the role of women as spiritual household role models, insisting that the place for religious instruction was the parish church, not the family home. Indeed, a leading historian of the sixteenth-century Catholic Church wrote that "the Counter-Reformation hierarchy seems to have taken it for granted that household religion was a seed-bed of subversion."[24] While convents, female saints, and the veneration of Mary of course continued, the hierarchy attempted to exert greater control over female spirituality. The Council of Trent insisted that female religious orders be strictly enclosed or cloistered, not only to protect the nuns against the evils of the outside world, but to protect the world from the influence of a community of unmarried women. Although women may have run the daily affairs of the convent, they were firmly subordinated to a male church official. There were attempts to found female religious orders along the same lines as the Jesuits, but they were eventually suppressed.

The model religious woman was St. Teresa of Avila (1515–82). From a noble Spanish family, she was put in the Carmelite convent in her hometown of Avila at a young age, but quickly discovered her religious vocation. Her visions attracted some unfavourable attention from the Spanish Inquisition, but she persisted and gained a number of supporters, notably among the Jesuits. She was terribly troubled by the problems in the Church and resolved to do whatever she could while obeying Church authority:

> And, seeing that I was a woman, and a sinner, and incapable of doing all I should
> like in the Lord's service, . . . I determined to do the little that was in me—namely,

to follow the evangelicals counsels as perfectly as I could, and to see that these few nuns who are here should do the same, confiding in the great goodness of God.[25]

What she did was resolve to be the best nun she could, according to the dictates of the reformed Catholic Church. She established a particularly austere wing of her order, the Discalced ("barefoot") Carmelites.

Some women's organizations did manage to live and work within the world, but only by carefully working within Church restrictions while subtly subverting them. The Daughters of Charity, founded by St. Vincent de Paul (1581–1660), were able to provide education and assistance to the poor by insisting that they were not a religious order and by working only in areas where they had the permission of a priest or bishop.

Neither Protestant nor Catholic churches established gender equality, but to condemn them for this would be an anachronism of the first order. Women remained subordinate to men, but in different ways. In Protestant areas, men and women shared a single religious sphere, and all were spiritually equal, but this spiritual equality did not mean equal power or participation. Catholic women, on the other hand, had a uniquely female religious sphere, but one that was firmly subordinate to the male Church hierarchy.

THE STATE AND THE REFORMATIONS

The religious fragmentation of the Reformations was a significant factor in the development of the state. In Protestant areas, rulers no longer had to contend with a foreign power that claimed jurisdiction over the lives, beliefs, and conduct of their subjects. Church wealth was confiscated, and the flow of revenue into Church coffers was either eliminated or, more often, redirected to the royal treasury. Clergy became subordinate to the secular law of the state rather than canon law. Many of the functions previously carried by the Catholic Church now fell to the government, especially matters of family law and inheritance. In the Lutheran states of northern Germany and Scandinavia the churches retained the episcopal structure of the Catholic Church; the main difference was that the bishops were now appointed not by the pope but by the ruler, and the churches became in essence government departments. This was also the case in England.

Catholic rulers too saw their authority strengthened. During the Middle Ages, as we have seen, most rulers had already established some control over the Catholic Church in their lands, and most did not allow the Roman Inquisition to operate inside their borders. Furthermore, the Protestant Reformation gave even Catholic rulers additional leverage to use against the Church if they wished: in France, for example, Francis I considered following the example of Henry VIII. Protestant reformers insisted that the power of the ruler came from God, and that he was responsible to God alone for its use. Luther especially extolled secular power, and condemned popular disobedience of the ruler as sinful. Calvin did as well, although he left open several loopholes that permitted political action. Thinking of France, his homeland, Calvin maintained that in certain states, there were "lesser magistrates" whose job it was to correct and guide the ruler. If these "lesser magistrates" (by which he meant the nobles) led the way, resistance to the ruler might not be sinful. Likewise, thinking of Old Testament prophets who defied kings of Israel, Calvin conceded that, from time to time, God might raise up "open avengers" to punish rulers for their wickedness. What distinguished an "open avenger" from a garden-variety rebel? Later Calvinists (though not Calvin himself) came to the conclusion that success in rebellion, as in commerce, was a sign of divine approval.

Wherever Calvinism was adopted as the official creed—most notably in Scotland and the Dutch Republic—the self-governing structure of Calvinist churches made for continual tension with the state. To maintain social order and stability, states sometimes had to make compromises that offended the sensibilities of devout Calvinists. For example, when the Dutch Republic gained independence from Spain (see Chapter 4) it was officially Calvinist, but many of its citizens were still Catholics. In most towns, the latter were allowed to worship as long they weren't too obvious about it; discretion made it possible for officials to "look through their fingers" and avoid seeing any illegal activity. A similar policy was used with the significant Jewish population in Amsterdam. However, this sort of practical toleration offended strict Calvinists who advocated stringent enforcement of religious uniformity. Governments resisted such demands, understanding that they would lead to nothing but turmoil, misery, and economic complications. Similarly with foreign policy, zealous Calvinists wanted to strike out at Catholicism whenever and wherever possible, while governments and rulers were prudently wary of arousing the hostility of countries such as France or Spain.

One result of the religious fragmentation of Christendom was a century or more of virtually continual warfare. In addition to vast human costs, waging war entailed vast expenditures, which meant that governments had to extract enormous amounts of revenue from their subjects in the form of taxation. This required the construction of elaborate apparatuses for assessment and collection of taxes, and the means to coerce payment from reluctant taxpayers. By the middle of the seventeenth century, most states in Europe had made such significant strides in this direction that many historians believe they passed over the threshold that qualified them as "absolute" monarchies. The next chapter will examine the warfare of the period, and later chapters the evolution of royal governments.

Chapter Conclusion

The Reformations brought significant change to European society. The fragmentation of Christendom enhanced the authority of rulers by reducing or eliminating the power of the papacy. The process of confessionalization further enhanced rulers' power over their subjects by putting the coercive power of the state behind religious uniformity. The religious warfare that followed the Reformations required states to enhance their bureaucratic and fiscal machinery.

The religious violence engendered by the Reformations serves to remind us that religious belief was a deadly serious business whose importance transcended the merely

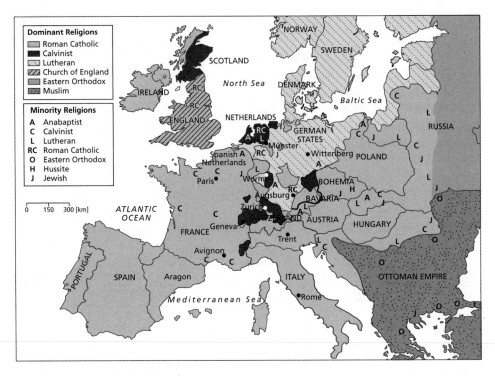

Map 3.1 The religious affiliations of Europe, c. 1560

individual. Yet it would be a mistake to assume that people of different faiths were inevitably at one another's throats. In the long run, recognition of the futility of coercion and religious violence may have helped to pave the way for modern notions of diversity and tolerance.

At the same time, radical movements such as the Anabaptists, who rejected the identification of church and state along with the authority of the latter, hinted at a future where religious belief was a private matter, between the individual and God alone. Likewise, the "priesthood of all believers" principle emphasized spiritual equality, even as Protestants such as Luther maintained the divine origins, and hence necessity, of earthly inequality. Although the people involved would have been horrified by it, the long-term consequences of the Reformations may be said to include religious liberty in our sense of the term, freedom of conscience, and greater equality among people.

Questions for Critical Thought

1. Why was the medieval Church unable to reform itself on the eve of the Reformation?
2. How did the protest of an obscure monk lead to the fragmentation of the Catholic Church?

3. Why were many people less than satisfied with Luther's vision of religious reform? Why was there no single Protestant Church?
4. How did the unique origins of the English Reformation influence the course of religious change in that country?
5. In what ways were Protestant and Catholic reform similar? How did they sometimes try to achieve the same ends by different means? Or different ends by the same means?

Weblinks

Luther's 95 Theses:
http://www.luther.de/en/95thesen.html

The Twelve Articles of the Swabian Peasants:
http://courses.washington.edu/hist112/Twelve%20Articles%20of%20the%20Swabian%20
Peasantry%201525.htm

Decrees of the Council of Trent:
http://history.hanover.edu/texts/trent.html

Further Reading

Benedict, Philip. *Christ's Churches Purely Reformed: A Social History of Calvinism*. New Haven: Yale University Press, 2004. The essential study of international Calvinism.

Bossy, John. *Christianity in the West, 1400–1700*. Oxford: Oxford University Press, 1985. A positive assessment of "traditional Christianity" accompanies a nuanced treatment of its transformation in the Reformations.

Duffy, Eamon. *Saints, Sacrilege and Sedition: Religion and Conflict in the Tudor Reformations*. London: Continuum, 2012. By a leading revisionist historian of the English Reformation, especially useful for its analysis of the historiography.

Evennett, H.O. *The Spirit of the Counter-Reformation*. Notre Dame: Notre Dame University Press, 1968. Still a classic and sensitive treatment of reformed Catholic spirituality.

Gordon, Bruce. *Calvin*. New Haven: Yale University Press, 2009. A recent and comprehensive biography.

Haigh, Christopher. *English Reformations: Religion, Politics, and Society under the Tudors*. Oxford: Clarendon, 1993. A nuanced assessment from a leading revisionist.

Hsia, R. Po-chia. *The World of Catholic Reform, 1540–1770*, 2nd ed. Cambridge: Cambridge University Press, 2005. A comprehensive recent survey that also examines worldwide Catholicism.

Kaplan, Benjamin J. *Divided by Faith: Religious Conflict and the Practice of Toleration in Early Modern Europe*. Cambridge MA: Belknap, 2007. A wide-ranging discussion of the forces that made for both religious violence and practical toleration.

Lindberg, Carter. *The European Reformations*. Oxford: Blackwell, 1996. A recent overview, especially strong on the thought of the reformers.

Oberman, Heiko A. *Luther: Man between God and the Devil*. New York: Doubleday, 1992. A classic biography by the leading Luther scholar of the past generation.

Ozment, Steven E. *The Reformation in the Cities: the Appeal of Protestantism to Sixteenth-Century Germany and Switzerland*. New Haven: Yale University Press, 1975. A pioneering work by an eminent historian, it casts early Protestant reforms in a positive light, emphasizing liberation from religious and social burdens.

Williams, G.H. *The Radical Reformation*, 3rd ed. Kirksville MO: Sixteenth Century Publishers, 1992. A monumental work on all aspects of the Radical Reformation.

Notes

1. I am referring here to western Europe, which came under the jurisdiction of the Roman Catholic Church, that is, of the universal ("catholic") church based in Rome. Large portions of southern and eastern Europe followed the Eastern Orthodox form of Christianity, which had earlier succumbed to regional or ethnic subdivision, so that we see a Greek Orthodox Church, a Russian Orthodox Church, and so on, even as they maintained a general liturgical and theological similarity.

2. J. Kelley Sowards, (ed.), Paul Pascal (trans.), *The Julius Exclusus of Erasmus* (Bloomington: Indiana University Press, 1968), pp. 87–8.

3. Desiderius Erasmus, *The Praise of Folly and Other Writings*, ed. and trans. Robert M. Adams (New York: Norton, 1989), p. 121.

4. Quoted in Henri Daniel-Rops, *The Protestant Reformation*, trans. Audrey Butler (London: J.M. Dent and Sons, 1961), p. 297.

5. Quoted from *Martin Luther: Selections from his Writings*, ed. John Dillenberger (New York: Anchor Doubleday, 1962), p. 11.

6. Frederick's attitude is especially noteworthy in that he was an avid collector of holy relics, the viewing of which, along with an appropriate contribution, conferred an indulgence reducing one's time in Purgatory by 1,902,202 years and 270 days. Frederick would not allow Tetzel's indulgence to be sold in Electoral Saxony, but Wittenbergers could easily cross the border and return in a day.

7. For Luther, in order to be a sacrament, the practice needed to be uniquely Christian, and instituted by Christ in Scripture. Thus, marriage, no matter how honourable, was not a sacrament. Luther was conflicted by Confession; he thought it a useful practice, but in the end denied its sacramental character.

8. The words in brackets do not appear in eyewitness accounts or in the earliest transcripts of the proceedings.

9. Quoted in Bainton, *Here I Stand*, pp. 216–17.

10. Quoted in A.G. Dickens, *Reformation and Society in Sixteenth-Century Europe* (London: Thames and Hudson, 1966), p. 146.

11. One consequence of this was that many Anabaptists refused to swear oaths of any kind, following Jesus' commandment in Matthew 5: 34–5. Persecuting authorities would frequently use the swearing of oaths (much more common then than now) as a handy means of identifying Anabaptists.

12. Quoted in A.G. Dickens, *Reformation and Society in Sixteenth-Century Europe* (London: Thames and Hudson, 1966), p. 134.

13. Roland H. Bainton, *The Travail of Religious Liberty: Nine Biographical Studies* (Philadelphia: Westminster, 1951), p. 94.

14. John Calvin, *Institutes of the Christian Religion*, III.xxi.5, III.xii.7, quoted in Hugh T. Kerr (ed.), *Calvin's Institutes: A New Compend* (Louisville: Westminster/John Knox Press), pp. 114–15.

15. Ibid, p. 113.

16. An annulment was required, as divorce (the dissolution of a valid marriage) was not possible in the Catholic Church. The marriage between Henry and Catharine had required a papal dispensation, as Catharine had married Henry's older brother Arthur five months before his death, and canon law forbade the marriage of brothers and sisters-in-law. Pope Julius II had granted the dispensation on the grounds that the

marriage between Catharine and Arthur had never been consummated, and was therefore not a valid marriage. Now, Wolsey and Henry needed Clement VII to declare that Julius's dispensation had been granted in error. This was unlikely, as the Reformation had made the papacy defensive about its power, and more importantly, Rome had been conquered by the army of Emperor Charles V, Catharine's nephew, and the pope was his virtual prisoner.

17. Henry would marry three more times. The German princess Anne of Cleves agreed to an annulment; Catherine Howard was beheaded for adultery; and Catherine Parr survived him.

18. It is a tragic irony, therefore, that Cromwell himself was executed at the behest of the king whom he had served so well. He had been the chief proponent of Henry's marriage to Anne of Cleves, in order to cement an alliance with German Lutheran states. When she arrived in England, Henry found her fat and ugly; he called her his "Rhenish mare." Cromwell's enemies at court used this against Cromwell, who was tried on trumped up charges of heresy and treason, and executed in 1540, an act which Henry regretted almost immediately.

19. H.O. Evennett, *The Spirit of the Counter-Reformation* (Notre Dame IN: Notre Dame University Press, 1968), p. 9.

20. John W. O'Malley, *Trent and All That: Renaming Catholicism in the Early Modern Era* (Cambridge MA: Harvard University Press, 2000).

21. Some Protestant delegates did in fact attend the sessions in 1551–2, but this really only drove home how irreconcilable the differences had become.

22. Benjamin J. Kaplan, *Divided by Faith: Religious Conflict and the Practice of Toleration in Early Modern Europe* (Cambridge MA: Belknap, 2007), p. 29.

23. Cissy Fairchilds, *Women in Early Modern Europe, 1500–1700* (Harlow: Longman, 2007), p. 217.

24. John Bossy, "The Counter-Reformation and the People of Catholic Europe", *Past and Present,* 47, 1 (1970), p. 68.

25. Teresa of Avila, *The Way of Perfection*, trans. and ed. E. Allison Peers (New York: Doubleday, 1964), pp. 36–7.

4

⚜

The Age of Religious War

Nearly continual warfare was a fact of life in early modern Europe. In addition to the succession of wars that began with the French invasion of Italy in 1494, which would continue until 1559, there was a series of wars provoked by the religious schism of the Protestant Reformation. Until about forty years ago, historians tended to downplay the role that religion played in these wars, believing that the "real" causes lay elsewhere: in geopolitics, in domestic power struggles, in class warfare, or in naked lust for power. Since then, however, the religious element has re-emerged as a serious factor in these wars, although certainly not the only one. The approach adopted here is based on several assumptions, all strongly supported by historical research. First, religious differences were real and important: as long as enough people were willing to kill and be killed in the name of the "true faith" (theirs), religious warfare was more or less inevitable. Second, while other factors—economic, political, and social—contributed to these conflicts, it is impossible to understand their length and brutality without the passions aroused by religion. Finally, the changing nature of warfare was an important element in the continuing evolution of the state.

Changes in Warfare

Some historians have maintained that the changes to warfare that took place in early modern Europe were so significant that they amounted to a "military revolution"; others disagree. There is no denying that the period saw far-reaching changes in the ways wars were fought, but they did not happen overnight. Although gunpowder had been introduced from China in the 1300s, it took more than a century to fundamentally alter the nature of warfare. The first cannons, for instance, were too large and heavy to be transported on the primitive road system of medieval Europe: the only way to deploy them was by water, and this limited their usefulness. They were also primitive and unreliable—as likely to explode and kill the gunners as they were to kill the enemy. At first they fired rocks that had been roughly shaped to fit the barrel, but by about 1500 they had become much more reliable and effective, firing iron cannonballs. France led the way, with the more modern military forces that it developed in the later stages of the Hundred Years War. When Charles VIII invaded Italy in 1494, the fortifications of Italian towns proved no match for French artillery.

Indeed, the evolution of artillery made most medieval fortifications obsolete. Built to repel human assaults, their walls were high but not particularly thick, and they were easily battered down by artillery. Francesco Guicciardini observed French cannons in operation:

> They were planted against the walls of a town with such speed, the space between the shots was so little, and the balls flew so quick and were impelled with such force, that as much execution was done in a few hours as formerly, in Italy, in the like number of days.[1]

In the later fifteenth and sixteenth centuries, therefore, a new style of fortification known as the *trace italienne* or star fort was introduced, mainly by Italian military engineers. Since great height was no longer essential, walls became lower and thicker. They were angled outward to deflect the force of cannonballs, and so that defenders could fire on enemies at the base of the wall. Straight walls were interspersed with angled bastions and outworks in order to provide crossfire against attackers. Walls were surrounded by ditches

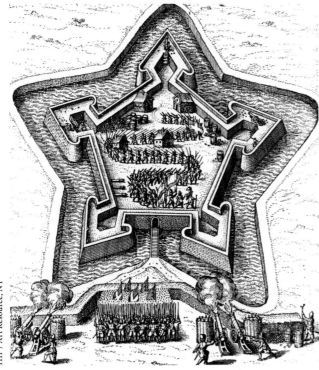

A star fort, or *trace italienne*

or moats, with or without water, so that defenders could have a clear field of fire to prevent the approach of enemy miners and sappers.

These fortifications were enormously expensive both to build and to maintain. In addition, they needed to be supplied with enough troops, food, and ammunition to survive sieges that might last years. It is no surprise, therefore, many towns and fortresses retained their medieval defences.

Of course, the star fort defence also increased the cost of offensive operations, since no attacking army would dare to leave a well-fortified enemy position in its rear. As a result siege warfare assumed a new importance, and this too was very expensive. To lay siege to a town or fortress required not only cannon, soldiers, and engineers, but also a line of fortifications to prevent relief forces from reaching the besieged site; the siegeworks at the Dutch siege of s'Hertogenbosch (Bois-le-Duc) in 1629 stretched for 40 kilometres. Thus even though lengthy sieges were not uncommon, the human and financial costs meant that no state could afford to conduct very many of them simultaneously. As a result, early modern warfare often took the form of relatively small-scale raids and harassment of the enemy's forces and positions. Although pitched battles were fought, and were occasionally decisive, the real value of a victory on the battlefield often lay in the fact that it prevented the defeated army from going to the rescue of a besieged city or fortress.

Gunpowder also had a profound effect on the battlefield. Although the longbow had given the English a series of decisive victories over the French during the Hundred Years War, more often medieval warfare had been centred on cavalry. Most battles consisted of simultaneous duels between mounted knights, with foot soldiers or infantry offering support and archers and crossbowmen deployed primarily in advance of cavalry charges.

Early handheld guns were quite primitive. The arquebus, for example, was notoriously inaccurate and unwieldy, with an effective range of only about 100 metres. It also took several minutes to reload, and required the use of a lighted match to ignite the powder that fired the ball. By the seventeenth century, however, it had been largely replaced by the flintlock musket, in which pulling the trigger caused a flint to produce a spark that ignited the gunpowder. A well-trained musketeer could reload in about 30 seconds, but the effective range remained relatively restricted until the introduction of rifled barrels in the eighteenth century.

The development of handheld gunpowder weapons made it possible for the lowliest infantryman to fell the noblest knight. The Italian poet Ludovico Ariosto (1474–1533) lamented this democratization of warfare in his epic poem *Orlando Furioso*, one of the bestsellers of the sixteenth century:

> How, foul and pestilent discovery,
> Didst thou find place within the human heart?
> Through thee is martial glory lost, through thee
> The trade of arms became a worthless art:
> And at such ebb are worth and chivalry,
> That the base often plays the better part.

Through thee no more shall gallantry, no more
Shall valour prove their prowess as of yore.

However primitive these early firearms may have been, they had two great advantages over bows and arrows. First, whereas an effective archer required years of training and constant practice, an effective arquebusier or musketeer could be trained in a matter of days. Second, whereas arrows could not usually penetrate plate armour, a ball fired from an arquebus or musket could.

It took some time to figure out how best to employ firearms on the battlefield. In the later fifteenth century, Swiss mercenaries had been the most effective soldiers, fighting as infantry in square formations of perhaps a thousand men armed with pikes. Such tightly packed formations were extremely vulnerable to firearms, however. In the course of the Italian wars, the Spanish added arquebusiers (and later musketeers) to the square of pikemen, who served to protect the gunmen from cavalry or infantry charges while they were reloading. Consisting of up to 3000 men, these Spanish *tercios* dominated the battlefields of sixteenth-century Europe. They relied on a core of well-trained professional soldiers, which made them difficult for other armies to duplicate.

The use of firearms continued to evolve through the later sixteenth and early seventeenth centuries. Two pioneers in this regard were Maurice of Nassau and King Gustavus Adolphus of Sweden. Maurice was the son of William of Orange, the leader of the Dutch rebels against Spain, and he took over the command of Dutch forces after his father was assassinated (see below). Inspired in part by his reading of Roman military theorists, he deployed his musketeers in narrow lines rather than large squares. Those in the front line would kneel, fire their weapons, and then move to the back of the formation to reload while the second line fired. This allowed for nearly constant rates of fire, even as the width of the formation increased, exposing the enemy to a broader attack. This evolution of tactics required greater discipline and training, and as a result units decreased in size while the number of officers increased. Under Maurice the Dutch also led the way in standardizing firearms and in training methods. There were numerous drill manuals complete with illustrations showing the various phases in loading a musket and different positions for the pike.

Dutch methods were widely imitated, but the Swedes under Gustavus Adolphus improved on them in the Thirty Years War (see below). With constant practice, the number of rows of musketeers required to maintain a continuous barrage was reduced from ten to six, and whereas the Dutch had employed these formations primarily for defence, the Swedes also used them to attack. In addition, Gustavus employed large numbers of standardized mobile field artillery. Pikemen remained essential to all these formations until the introduction of the bayonet in the 1690s.

Armies also increased dramatically in size during the sixteenth and seventeenth centuries. Whereas in 1494 Charles VIII invaded Italy with an army of 18,000 men, in 1552 Henry II used 36,000 men to capture Metz. Emperor Charles V commanded perhaps 100,000 against the Turks in Hungary. In the 1630s, during the Thirty Years War, Spain had as many as 300,000 men in arms, while France had 150,000 and Sweden 45,000.

The changing nature and growing scale of warfare imposed enormous burdens on societies. Until the later seventeenth century, underpaid and undersupplied armies would continue to take what they needed from civilian populations, at home as well as abroad. At the same time, governments needed to extract unprecedented amounts of tax revenue from their people to pay for all the innovations and improvements outlined above. Constructing the apparatus to assess and collect those taxes was the primary force that drove the strengthening of central governments in early modern Europe. We will return to the link between warfare and the development of the state in Chapter 6, when we consider the evolution of absolute monarchy.

VOICES

Mercurino di Gattinara on Universal Monarchy

Mercurino Arborio di Gattinara (1465–1530) was a native of Piedmont in northern Italy. Trained as a humanist, lawyer, and bureaucrat, in 1519 he became grand chancellor of the newly elected Holy Roman Emperor Charles V. Both before and after his appointment, he advocated for a "universal monarchy" that would restore peace and unity to the fractured and warring peoples of Europe. He based his views on an amalgam of ancient and medieval political theory, biblical prophecy, and mystical writings, which he interpreted to mean that Charles V had been appointed by God to restore the glory and power of the imperial title. In the first excerpt, from Gattinara's autobiography, he recounts his arguments against those who counselled the young Charles (already King of Spain) against seeking election as Holy Roman Emperor. This is followed by two excerpts from his *Oratio supplicatoria* (1516) in which he set out his vision for a glorious imperial future. The last excerpt is from a memorandum from Gattinara to Charles shortly after his election.

> [Gattinara] argued one point: that the title of empire legitimizes the acquisition of the entire globe, as was ordained by God himself, foreseen by the prophets, predicted by the apostles, and approved in word and deed by Christ our Saviour by his birth, life, and death. It is true that the empire had sometimes been given to weak princes and had been damaged by these. Nevertheless, it would be cause for hope if the title of emperor were joined to a powerful king, propped up with so many and so great kingdoms and dominions. Under the shadow of the imperial title, not only could he serve his own hereditary lands and kingdoms, but he could also gain greater ones, enlarging the empire until it encompassed the monarchy of the whole world.

From the autobiography of Mercurino Gattinara, quoted in Rebecca Ard Boone, *Mercurino di Gattinara and the Creation of the Spanish Empire* (London: Pickering and Chatto, 2014), p. 92.

> . . . it is fitting that one ruler ought to be appointed to all things on earth, a single supreme leader, a king of kings, a master of masters, whose command the masses obey,

Habsburg–Valois Wars to 1559

The wars that had begun in 1494 with the French invasion of Italy continued until the Treaty of Cateau-Cambrésis in 1559. What had started out as a multi-sided contest for dominance in Italy had, by 1520, been transformed into a duel between the two most powerful rulers in Europe. On one side was the vast multinational dynastic empire of the Habsburgs, led by Emperor Charles V. On the other was France, led first by the Valois king Francis I (r. 1515–47) and then by his son, Henry II (r. 1547–59). Other states and rulers of course played important roles, but the Habsburg–Valois contest was clearly the primary one.

follow, and submit to. One whom all respect, fear, heed, and cherish as an absolute monarch, without whom neither justice nor peace may be obtained in this world. In truth, without such a supreme leader . . . the poor are oppressed, abuses arise, lawsuits arise, wars are fought, the stronger suppress the weaker, and justice, who ought to watch over us, turns her back and departs. . . .

From *Oratio supplicatoria*, British Library, MS 18008, fols. 24, r. and v., trans. Laura Gauthier.[2]

I do not mean that Caesar [that is, the emperor, Charles V] should be given ownership of everything in particular, nor that each and every kingdom and domain be put into his hands, nor that kings and princes should be robbed of their kingdoms and domains. But I think that all kings and princes ought to recognize the superiority of the empire, and they should agree to it as they are legally bound. And their disputes, which are the cause of so many wars, will dissolve under the authority of the monarchy.

From *Oratio supplicatoria*, quoted in Rebecca Ard Boone, *Mercurino di Gattinara and the Creation of the Spanish Empire* (London: Pickering and Chatto, 2014), p. 29.

Sire, . . . it has pleased God the Creator in His grace to raise you in dignity above all kings and Christian princes in making you the greatest emperor and king there has been since the empire of Charlemagne your predecessor: and [He] has set you on the path towards a monarchy that will submit the whole world to a single shepherd. . . . This is the reason that your Imperial Majesty [ought]. . . to continually and sincerely pray to [God] to inspire you with His grace, and to illuminate and build you up . . . [so that] the exaltation of the Holy Catholic Faith, the increase of all Christendom, and the preservation of the Holy Apostolic See will achieve that universal peace that can be attained only by a monarchy. . . .

Cited in Carlo Bornate, *Historia vite et gestorum per dominum magnum cancellarium: (Mercurino Arborio di Gattinara): con note, aggiunte e documenti* (Torino: Artigianelli, 1914), pp. 405–6, trans. M. Konnert.

The abiding goal of Charles V, as of the medieval emperors who had preceded him, was to re-establish the significance of the imperial title. But two factors set Charles apart from his predecessors: the sheer extent of the territory he had inherited, and the wealth of the lands he controlled outside Germany: specifically, the Netherlands and Castile. Together, the commercial prosperity of the former and the New World possessions of the latter gave him unprecedented resources to use as he wished. His opponents feared, with reason, that his goal was the establishment of what they called a "universal monarchy"—in other words, the medieval ideal of a restored Roman empire, but on a global scale.

For all the resources that Charles V possessed, the obstacles to his project were significant. Foremost among them was France, which was already hemmed in by Habsburg lands on three sides—to the south in Spain and Italy, to the east in Franche-Comté, and to the north in the Netherlands. If Charles were to succeed in restoring Imperial power in Germany, the French would be trapped in the jaws of a Habsburg nutcracker. This situation also helps to explain why Italy was so important to France: if either side gained dominance there, it might be enough to tip the balance in one direction or the other. At the same time, the German Catholic princes understood that any revival of imperial power would diminish their own, and the popes feared that any extension of Habsburg power in Italy would threaten both their independence and their control of the Papal States.

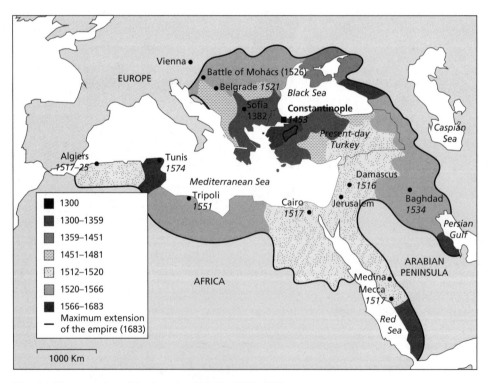

Map 4.1 The expansion of the Ottoman Empire, 1300–1683

Nor were these the only challenges that Charles faced. His was a purely dynastic empire, with no institutional or administrative unity, and each of his territories had its own problems, the solutions to which could cause difficulties elsewhere. Governing such a far-flung and diverse empire in peacetime would have been a monumental challenge; in the chaotic atmosphere of the early sixteenth century, it may well have been impossible. In Spain, for example, fear that the Flemish-born Charles and his foreign advisers would subordinate Spanish interests to their own sparked a rebellion in 1520–1, known as the revolt of the *comuneros* (townspeople, that is, members of urban communes).

Meanwhile, the danger posed to Christian Europe by the Muslim Ottoman Empire had only increased since the conquest of Constantinople in 1453. By 1500 the Ottomans controlled most of southeastern Europe, and their westward advance continued under Sultan Suleiman the Magnificent (r. 1520–66). Having conquered Belgrade in 1521, in 1526 they killed King Louis II of Hungary and Bohemia in battle and took over most of the Kingdom of Hungary. Louis's widowed queen, Mary, was a Habsburg, the sister of Charles V, and the Habsburg connection was reinforced when the Hungarian and Bohemian nobles elected Mary and Charles's brother Ferdinand, who was married to

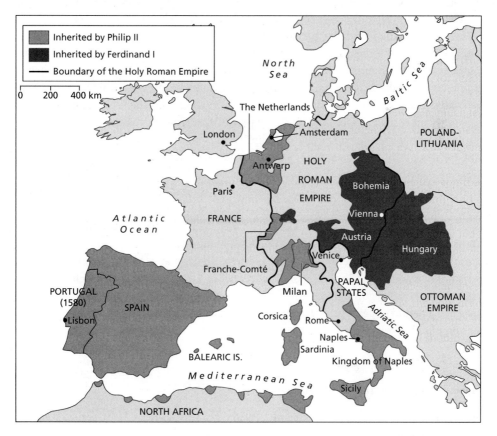

Map 4.2 The division of the Habsburg Empire

Louis's sister, to succeed him. The Ottoman threat to central Europe had a direct impact on Charles's efforts to restore religious unity in Germany, as he periodically had to appease German Protestant princes in order to gain their cooperation defending Germany against it.

Opponents of Charles V also combined against him in various ways, on the principle that "my enemy's enemy is my friend." The kings of France were not averse to forming alliances with German Lutheran princes; nor was Henry VIII of England, even though he was burning Protestants at home. Pope Clement VII allied himself with France in the 1520s in order to prevent Habsburg domination of Italy. In retaliation, in 1527 an imperial army sacked Rome and took the pope prisoner. In 1536, Francis I concluded an anti-Habsburg alliance with the Ottomans, and in 1541 allowed a Turkish fleet to spend the winter in the French port of Toulon.

By the mid-1550s, after decades of travel, war, and overindulgence, Charles was worn out and prematurely aged. He was also despondent, his grand vision apparently further from realization than ever. Accordingly, before retiring to a Spanish monastery (where he would die in 1558), in 1555 and 1556 he abdicated his various positions and titles. Recognizing that his empire was too large and diverse to be effectively ruled by any one man, he divided it in two. His eldest son Philip inherited the Spanish kingdoms as King Philip II (r. 1556–98), the Italian lands (primarily Naples and Milan, which had been taken from the French in 1525), and the Burgundian inheritance of Franche-Comté and the various provinces of the Netherlands. Charles's younger brother Ferdinand (already king of Bohemia and Hungary) inherited the imperial title as Holy Roman Emperor Ferdinand I (r. 1558–64) and the Austrian lands, which he had been ruling on his brother's behalf since 1521.

After more than six decades of war, all parties concerned were exhausted, both physically and economically. In 1557 both Philip II and Henry II of France defaulted on loans, and both were concerned that they could not address the threat posed by the spread of Calvinism in their lands (see below), while involved in a major international war. Accordingly, in 1559 they concluded the treaty of Cateau-Cambrésis, which confirmed Spain's dominance in Italy, making it the dominant power in Europe for the next century. While Spain retained control of Naples and Milan, France renounced almost all its claims in Italy, keeping only some fortresses in the Alps, along with Calais (which it had retaken from the English) and three towns on the border with Germany (Metz, Toul, and Verdun), which it had conquered in the 1550s. The treaty of Cateau-Cambrésis brought to an end the wars that had begun with Charles VIII's invasion of Italy in 1494; it did not, however, usher in a period of peace and recovery. Instead, for the next century or so Europe would be convulsed by a new series of wars originating in the religious schisms of the sixteenth century.

The French Wars of Religion, 1559–1598

For the last four decades of the sixteenth century, France was racked by a series of vicious civil wars, known in French history as the Wars of Religion, that would threaten its future as a single kingdom. Although other factors—political, economic, and social—were also in play, the principal cause of this prolonged period of violence and instability was the conflict between Catholics and Calvinists.

RELIGIOUS CRISIS: THE GROWTH OF CALVINISM

Calvin had always been concerned with his homeland, and he ensured that his followers directed much of their missionary activity there. As a result, by the early 1560s perhaps 10 per cent of the French people had converted to Calvinism, which was organized in about 2000 churches scattered across France. Known as Huguenots,[3] they were a wealthy and powerful group that included disproportionate numbers of the "lesser magistrates" who, as we have seen, Calvin believed to be justified in resisting a tyrannical king: that is, members of the nobility. Calvinist missionaries focused much of their effort on the aristocracy; by the early 1560s as many as half of the French nobility had converted, including members of the powerful Bourbon and Montmorency clans. The other segments of French society that were strongly represented among the Huguenots were the educated middle class and skilled craftsmen: people who welcomed the Calvinist emphasis on independent Bible study, the priesthood of all believers, and participation in church governance. Accordingly, French Calvinism was a distinctly urban movement, concentrated especially in the south and west of France, which were traditionally more autonomous than other regions of the kingdom. By the late 1550s Huguenots were holding worship services in the open and ostentatiously rejecting Catholic observances such as saints' days and fasting during Lent, sparking increasingly violent confrontations with Catholics, who feared that heretic "pollution" in their midst threatened not only God's wrath in this life, but eternal damnation in the next.

POLITICAL CRISIS

In itself, religious division might not have led to civil war, but an unforeseeable event made the religious crisis intractable. Henry II (r. 1547–59) was a strong and effective king, adept at balancing the great noble factions who schemed for power and influence at court. In 1559, however, he was killed in a jousting accident, leaving a widowed queen—the Italian princess Catherine de Medici—and four young sons, the eldest of whom was a sickly youth of fifteen. The accession of Francis II (r. 1559–60) destroyed the balance of the noble factions that his father had cultivated, for it brought to power the zealously anti-Protestant family of his mother-in-law, Marie de Guise. (His young wife, known to history as Mary, Queen of Scots, had inherited the Scottish crown as an infant, but had been raised at the French court while her mother ruled Scotland as regent.) During Francis's brief reign (July 1559 to December 1560), François, Duke of Guise, and his brother Charles, Cardinal of Lorraine, seized the levers of power and used them to enact more punitive legislation against the Huguenots, actively inflaming the religious tensions that were already raging across France.

Unlike Francis, who at least had been legally an adult, Charles IX was only ten when he became king. Thus the Queen Mother, Catherine de Medici, became regent, and she would continue to play a crucial role in French politics until her death in 1589. Although she herself was Catholic, her priority was to preserve royal power for her sons, and to that end she attempted to moderate the harsh legislation of the Guises by issuing a decree that established limited toleration of the Huguenots. But the effort proved futile: Huguenots ignored the limitations on their freedom of religious practice, and zealous Catholics ignored the (limited) Huguenot rights established by the edict.

CIVIL WAR

Civil war erupted in March 1562 when soldiers escorting the Duke of Guise broke into a Protestant service in the town of Vassy (modern Wassy) in eastern France and massacred dozens of worshippers. Protestant nobles led by a prince of the Bourbon family, Louis de Condé, took up arms, and Huguenot forces seized roughly thirty towns throughout France. After some minor skirmishing, the Peace of Amboise, signed in 1563, expanded the Huguenot right to worship, but (like earlier measures) proved impossible to enforce. Two more wars in the 1560s followed the same general pattern: an outrage would prompt either side to declare war, a bit of fighting would ensue, a few towns would change hands, and a peace treaty would be signed. The Huguenots were too strong to be decisively defeated, but not strong enough to convincingly defeat royal armies. Each peace treaty would tinker with the precise terms of toleration for the Huguenots, but it was always too little for them and too much for zealous Catholics, who looked to the Guises for leadership and inspiration.

The basic nature of Huguenot resistance to the government, and the nature of the wars themselves, would change in August 1572. Until then the Huguenots had always protested that they were the king's most loyal subjects, and that the only authority they rejected was that of his "evil advisers" (the Guises). As part of her overall agenda to reconcile religious factions and restore order to the kingdom, Catherine arranged for her daughter Marguerite to marry the Huguenot prince Henry of Navarre. A member of the Bourbon family, he was raised as a Huguenot by his devout mother, Jeanne d'Albret, Queen of Navarre, and was poised to become the next great Huguenot leader. On his mother's death in June 1572, he became King of Navarre, and was thus a suitable match for a royal princess. Catherine hoped that the symbolism of their marriage would help to reconcile the warring factions.

The wedding took place in Paris on August 18, 1572, and several dozen Huguenot leaders attended, including Gaspard de Coligny, a member of the powerful Montmorency clan and the military commander of the Huguenot forces. Four days later Coligny was wounded in an assassination attempt that was in all likelihood ordered by Duke Henry of Guise, who blamed Coligny for the 1563 murder of his father, Duke François. To pre-empt violent reprisals, Catherine and her son Charles IX agreed to have the Huguenot leaders killed. In the early morning of August 24, St. Bartholomew's day, the wounded Coligny was

© Classic Image / Alamy Stock Photo

The St. Bartholomew's Day massacre. This contemporary illustration shows various events as if they had occurred at the same time. In the upper left, an assassin fires the shot that wounds Admiral Coligny, seated on his horse. In the upper right, Coligny is murdered in his bed, and his body thrown out of the window to the street below. In the background are scenes of Huguenot men, women, and children being dragged from their houses and murdered.

murdered in his bed and perhaps another 50 Huguenot nobles were subsequently killed. In addition, although Henry of Navarre was too important to kill, he was taken prisoner, forced to abjure his Protestant faith, and kept under a kind of house arrest at court.

The plot was supposed to be limited to the Huguenot leaders, but in the confusion and panic that followed, militant Parisian Catholics attacked all the Huguenots they could lay their hands on. The city gates were closed, while Huguenots—men, women, and children—hid for their lives. Although Guise had been a moving force behind the strike on the Huguenot leadership, he played no part in the general massacre, and even sheltered Huguenots from the mob. Through September and October, similar massacres erupted in several provincial cities, and by the time the bloodshed ended, approximately 5000 people were dead.

Far from eliminating the Huguenot threat, however, the massacres led Huguenots throughout the south and west of France to form their own political federation, in essence an autonomous quasi-state within the Kingdom of France, complete with its own civil service, army, and fiscal and legal structures, as well as its own church. The permanent division of France along religious lines, as would happen in the Netherlands, was a real possibility.

VOICES

Theodore Beza on Legitimate Resistance

After the massacre, Huguenots could no longer tell themselves that they had only to free the king from evil advisers, for the king himself had ordered their deaths, or so they believed. Some examined the circumstances in which resistance to rulers might be justified, among them Theodore Beza (1519–1609). A French noble who had sought refuge in Geneva, where he succeeded Calvin as the Moderator of the Company of Pastors and unofficial leader of international Calvinism, like Calvin he retained a vital interest in his homeland, and his *Ecclesiastical History of the Reformed Churches in the Kingdom of France* (1580) is an essential, if biased, source for the history of the Huguenot movement. In 1574 he published anonymously *On the Rights of Magistrates over Their Subjects* in which he helped to redefine the nature of Huguenot resistance.

I come now to the lesser magistrates who hold a lower rank between the sovereign and the people. I do not mean officers of the king's household, who are devoted rather to the king than the kingdom, but those who have public or state responsibilities in either the administration of justice or in war. . . .

Now, although all these officers are beneath the sovereign in that they take commands from him and are installed in office and approved by him, they hold, properly speaking, not of the sovereign, but of the sovereignty. That is why, when the sovereign magistrate dies, they nonetheless remain in office, just as the sovereignty remains intact. . . .

It is thus apparent that . . . the government of the kingdom is not in the hands of the king in its entirety. . . . If the king, hereditary or elective, clearly goes back on the conditions without which he would not have been recognized and acknowledged, can

THE CATHOLIC LEAGUE AND DYNASTIC CRISIS

The civil war provoked by the massacres of 1572 ended in 1576 with the Edict of Beaulieu or Peace of Monsieur, so-called after the king's younger brother (known simply as "Monsieur"), who was instrumental in bringing it about. One more in a succession of peace settlements that promised different degrees of freedom for the Huguenots, this one was the most lenient yet—so lenient that it prompted a new level of reaction from their opponents. Throughout France, Catholic nobles ignored its provisions and formed a Catholic League to preserve their faith, vowing to extirpate the heretics themselves if the king would not. The Duke of Guise did not create the organization, but he quickly became its leading figure.

there be any doubt that the lesser magistrates of the kingdom . . . are entitled to resist flagrant oppression of the realm which they swore to defend and protect according to their office and their particular jurisdiction?

. . . Is it not then reasonable, by all law divine and human, that more should be permitted to these lesser magistrates, in view of their sworn duty to preserve the law, than to private persons without office? I say, therefore, that they are obliged, if reduced to that necessity, and by force of arms where that is possible, to offer resistance to flagrant tyranny . . . [To do so] is not to be seditious or disloyal towards one's sovereign, but to be fully loyal and to keep one's faith toward those from whom one's office was received against him who has broken his oath and oppressed the kingdom he ought to have protected. . . .

It remains only to resolve an issue of the greatest consequence. Where there is tyranny in matters of religion, may persecution be resisted by force of arms according to the above distinctions and conditions? . . .

I answer, to begin with, that it is utterly absurd and false to say that worldly methods of resistance, such as appeal to courts or resort to arms, are not only different from spiritual resistance, but are also so opposed and repugnant to it that they can have no place whatsoever in religious matters. On the contrary, the chief duty of a good magistrate is to employ all the means that God has given him to make sure that God is recognized and served as king of kings by the subjects whom God has committed to his care. To this end, accordingly, he should use the weapon of the law against disturbers of the true religion who will not listen to the admonitions and censures of the Church and his military arm against those who cannot otherwise be halted.

Julian H. Franklin, ed. and trans., *Constitutionalism and Resistance in the Sixteenth Century: Three Treatises by Hotman, Beza, and Mornay* (New York: Pegasus, 1969), pp. 110–12, 133.

At first the League had little effect. Henry III (r. 1574–89) had by now succeeded his brother Charles as king, and he managed to defuse much of the threat that it posed to royal authority by declaring himself its leader. In 1584, however, the League was revived in a much more potent form after the heir presumptive, François, Duke of Anjou—the only living brother of the childless Henry—unexpectedly died. The laws that governed succession to the French throne meant that the new heir presumptive was Henry of Navarre, who by now had renounced his forced conversion to Catholicism and assumed his position as leader of the Huguenot movement. The prospect of a heretic as king revived the Catholic League as nothing else could have, since many people who would not fight to the death to eliminate the Huguenots, or for the Guise family, or even for their Catholic faith, would fight to keep a heretic off the throne. Once again headed by the Duke of Guise, the revived League was bankrolled by King Philip II of Spain.

In 1588 a clandestine faction of Leaguers in Paris, known as the *Seize* or Sixteen (after the sixteen districts of Paris), took over the city, forcing Henry III to flee his own capital and decide on a bold gamble. On his orders, during a meeting of the Estates-General in Blois in December 1588, the Duke of Guise and his brother, the Cardinal of Guise, were murdered, and a number of prominent Leaguers were arrested. Rather than crippling the League, however, Henry's actions stirred up a hornet's nest. The pope excommunicated him, absolving his subjects of their duty to obey him. The University of Paris declared him a tyrant and no true king. With no alternative, Henry III made common cause with Henry of Navarre and the Huguenots.

A few months later, in August 1589, Henry III was himself assassinated by a zealous Catholic, making Henry of Navarre King Henry IV of France (r. 1589–1610) and the first king of the Bourbon dynasty. But the vast majority of his subjects refused to acknowledge him as the rightful king because of his religion. Henry had likely known for some time that he would have to convert if he were to rule France. It needed to be done properly, however: from a position of strength rather than weakness, and in a way that left no doubt as to its sincerity.

Command of the Catholic League was assumed by the Duke of Guise's younger brother, the Duke of Mayenne, who was supported by Spanish gold, and on occasion, by the Spanish army in the Netherlands. Mayenne, however, could not hold the League together, and he was further handicapped by the fact that the League had no acceptable alternative to propose as king. Philip II urged that his daughter Isabella be named Queen of France, but French law did not permit a woman to inherit the throne. Finally, in 1593, Henry IV announced his intention to convert. The decision was perfectly timed, coming at a point when internal divisions within the League were growing more intense. Although his conversion is often seen as a cynical ploy, based on reports that he commented "Paris is worth a Mass," enough of his Catholic subjects were apparently persuaded that they had a sincerely Catholic king—which, after all, was the whole point of the Catholic League.

THE EDICT OF NANTES

One by one, those who had previously declared their undying opposition to Henry made their peace with the new king. By 1598 order and obedience had been largely restored, but now the Huguenots were growing increasingly restless and dissatisfied. In order to preserve their loyalty, in 1598 Henry IV issued the Edict of Nantes. In a sense, it was just another in the long line of peace treaties that attempted find the exact right amount of freedom that would satisfy the Huguenots without outraging Catholics. Yet this one worked, at least for a time, where the others had failed miserably. One reason was surely war weariness. Increasing numbers of Catholics in particular were unwilling to prolong the chaos of civil war for the sake of a seemingly unattainable religious uniformity. This view was expressed by a group known as *Politiques*, who believed that while a Catholic France was still the ideal, belief could not be coerced, and that the costs of eliminating the heretics were simply too high to accept. Henry IV must also be crediting with a great deal of political savvy in gaining grudging acceptance of the edict.

The Edict of Nantes granted the Huguenots complete freedom of conscience and the limited freedom to continue Protestant worship wherever it had existed in August 1597. Catholic worship was to be permitted everywhere, even in Huguenot towns where it had not taken place in years. Huguenots were to suffer no legal discrimination: they had full civil rights, could serve in the military and the royal bureaucracy, go to university, and practise any profession. To judge legal cases involving parties of the two faiths, special sections were set up in the supreme law courts (Parlements) that had both Catholic and Huguenot judges. In a further series of secret articles, the king agreed to pay the salaries of Huguenot pastors and, as a guarantee of royal adherence to the terms of the Edict, granted the Huguenots approximately 200 fortified towns, which were to be garrisoned by Huguenot soldiers paid by the government.

The Edict of Nantes was not a blow for the modern ideal of religious liberty. It was a messy compromise that left everybody less than satisfied, but not unhappy enough to continue waging a vicious civil war. In fact, it was intended to remain in effect only until the Huguenots returned to the Catholic fold. Its stated goal was religious reunification, and the secret articles granted the Huguenots political and military powers for only eight years. On the other hand, could anyone really believe that the Huguenots would give up their "state within the state" without a fight? There was, then, a fundamental discrepancy between the edict's avowed aim (religious reunification) and the means it adopted to bring peace (acceptance of a Huguenot "state within the state"). This more or less guaranteed that the religious conflict would continue in churches, schools, courts of law, and the arena of public opinion. Furthermore, could any future King of France really claim to be sovereign as long as a substantial minority of his subjects had their own towns, army, and political structure, effectively beyond the reach of royal power?

Spain and the Netherlands

While the people of France were fighting one another in the Wars of Religion, those of the Netherlands were rebelling against their ruler, Philip II of Spain, who had inherited the territory when his father, Emperor Charles V, divided his empire in the 1550s. Today we might assume that the Dutch rebellion originated in the desire for national independence, but this was not the case, although that desire did take form in the course of the revolt. Nor was it sparked by religious differences in themselves. Rather, it was Philip's response to those differences that drove his Dutch subjects—Protestant and Catholic—to rebel against his authority.

PHILIP II, THE SPANISH KINGDOMS, AND THE SEVENTEEN PROVINCES

Like that of his father Charles V, the empire ruled by Philip II was purely dynastic. Each of his territories retained its own laws, customs, and government. Thus just as he was the king not of "Spain" but of Castile and Aragon, he was the ruler not of the "Netherlands," but rather of each of its seventeen provinces: Count of Flanders, Duke of Brabant, Count of Holland, and so on. "Netherlands" or "Low Countries" was simply a term of convenience to describe a region, much like "Maritime provinces" or "New England states." Although there was a rudimentary version of a central government based in Brussels, with a regent appointed by the king and a States-General made up of delegates from the provincial assemblies or States, the powers of the regent were severely limited by local independence, and all decisions of the States-General had to be unanimous.

Over the centuries, Protestant critics constructed a "Black Legend" according to which Catholic Spain under Philip's rule was a hotbed of ignorance, superstition, fanaticism, and intolerance (by contrast, the Protestant English and Dutch are presented as paragons of liberty, tolerance, and progress). For example, a nineteenth-century American Protestant historian of the Dutch Revolt wrote: "If there are vices . . . from which he [Philip] was exempt, it is because it is not permitted to human nature to attain perfection even in evil."[4]

It is true that Philip, unlike his cosmopolitan father, saw the world through distinctly Castilian eyes; in fact, after 1559 he never left the Iberian peninsula. He also saw himself

© Lukasz Janyst / Alamy Stock Photo

El Escorial. In 1563 Philip II, who was a keen and knowledgeable patron of the arts, began construction of a permanent royal palace at El Escorial, northwest of Madrid. It is an architectural statement of his guiding principles. Severe and restrained in ornamentation, the complex included a monastery and a church at its centre, and Philip could observe the monks at worship from his bedchamber. The palace also housed an extensive library, which he intended as a centre of learning to advance the Catholic cause.

as the champion of the Catholic cause. But he did not distinguish between the interests of Castile, the Habsburg dynasty, and the Catholic Church. As a consequence, his desire for religious purity led him to adopt policies that were counter-productive from a political point of view.

Governing such a diverse empire was extremely difficult, and the task was made all the more difficult by Philip's micromanaging style. Information was compartmentalized and only he had the full picture. He spent long hours in his office going over correspondence, even correcting the grammar and checking the arithmetic in the reports that crossed his desk. Often weeks or months would elapse before Philip responded to requests for instructions, leading one of his counsellors in the Netherlands to quip, "If death came from Spain, I should be immortal." Although some historians have seen Philip's foreign policy as incoherent and reactive, Geoffrey Parker has argued that he did have a "Grand Strategy" based on two overarching principles: preservation of Catholicism against the Protestant heretics and the Turks, and preservation of the Habsburg dynastic empire. Implementation of that strategy, however, was complicated by conflicting priorities. For example, in the case of the Netherlands, Philip's desire to preserve Catholicism ran counter to the preservation of the Habsburg empire, while suppressing the Dutch Revolt tied up resources that could have been used in Italy and the Mediterranean.

Furthermore, Philip's governments faced continual fiscal difficulty. Even though gold and silver from the New World made him the wealthiest ruler in Europe, his government defaulted on its loans three times during his reign. Nor was Castile able to support Philip's grand ambitions with its own resources. The handful of great nobles who controlled the majority of the land were more interested in the profits to be made by grazing sheep for the textile trade than they were in improving agricultural productivity. As a result, Castilian peasants were impoverished and incapable of paying much in the way of taxes.

Philip insisted on religious purity in his dominions, and under his rule Spain became a stronghold of reformed Catholicism. Thus a once heterogeneous society became obsessed with purity not only of belief but of blood, casting suspicion on families of Jewish or Muslim descent that had been Christian for generations. Philip's commitment to religious uniformity provoked the most serious crisis that Spain experienced during his reign: the revolt of the *moriscos* (Spanish Muslims) in 1568. After the conquest of Granada, the last Muslim outpost in Spain, in 1492, all Muslims had been ordered to convert to Christianity, but enforcement was haphazard. Thus in 1567 further restrictions were imposed on Muslim dress, surnames, and use of Arabic. When authorities failed to respond to their peaceful petitions and protests, the *moriscos* in the mountainous region of Alpujarras launched a rebellion. By 1570 the revolt had been bloodily suppressed and the surviving *moriscos* deported from Granada to Castile, where they were dispersed among the Christian population. The ultimate conclusion would come in 1609 during the reign of Philip's son, when the *moriscos* were expelled from Spain entirely.

The revolt of the Dutch provinces has tended to overshadow Philip's successes. Most notably, in October 1571 an allied fleet of Spanish, Venetian, and papal ships defeated the mighty Turkish navy at Lepanto, off the Greek coast. And in 1580, a disputed succession in Portugal led to a Spanish invasion that put Philip on the Portuguese throne. (Both his mother and his first wife were Portuguese princesses.)

DUTCH REVOLT, REPRESSION, INDEPENDENCE

In the course of his reign Philip's possessions in the Low Countries would split into two parts: those in the north forming an independent Protestant state known as the United Provinces or the Dutch Republic, and those in the south, in the Spanish Netherlands, remaining Catholic under Spanish rule. But this outcome had nothing to do with any inherent differences between north and south, religious or otherwise (in fact, there were fewer Protestants in the north than the south): it was merely the product of the fortunes of war.

The origins of the revolt lay in Philip's religious policies, but only indirectly. By sixteenth-century standards, the Dutch people were relatively tolerant when it came to religion, following what we might think of as a policy of "don't ask, don't tell." This was contrary to everything Philip held most dear, but when he formulated a plan to strengthen the Church's ability to repress heresy in the Netherlands, opposition was not limited to Calvinists: many Catholics also believed that it violated their rights and privileges. Noble opposition was led by William the Silent, Prince of Orange, and Counts Hoorn and Egmont, who forced the resignation of Philip's chief adviser in the Netherlands, Cardinal Granvelle.

In the summer of 1566, self-appointed Calvinist preachers delivered open-air sermons throughout the Netherlands, inciting crowds to harass Catholic priests, invade churches, and destroy the idolatrous images they found there. Many Catholics who had previously resisted Philip were very troubled by these developments. Had Philip taken a moderate course, he could well have divided his opponents and reconciled Catholics while marginalizing the Calvinists. Instead, he sent a Spanish army to the Netherlands under his leading general, the Duke of Alba, whose preferred solution to any problem was to apply maximum military force. Martial law was imposed and Alba ruled through a "Council of Troubles," or "Council of Blood" as it became known. Of the more than 12,000 people tried for their roles in the revolt, 9000 had their property confiscated and 1000 were executed, including Egmont and Hoorn. William of Orange escaped the same fate only by fleeing to Germany. The Netherlands were made to pay for the military occupation through a sales tax of 10 per cent, known as the Tenth Penny.

In 1572, a group of Calvinist sailors and raiders known as Sea Beggars, operating in the North Sea under the authority of William of Orange, captured the Zeeland ports of Brill and Flushing and, since they were not accessible over land, put them beyond the reach of Spanish armies. This fundamentally changed the nature of the resistance to Philip II. Zealous Calvinists, they imposed their religious views across the areas they now controlled. Whereas in the earlier stages of the revolt, Calvinists had formed just one part of the general opposition to Philip, their success now enabled them to take the lead. Realizing that their support would be crucial to the revolt's success, William of Orange, the leading figure in the opposition, reluctantly joined the Calvinist church.

Alba's approach having backfired, he was replaced in 1573 with the more moderate Don Luis de Requesens, a close friend of Philip since childhood. Requesens repealed most of Alba's repressive measures, but Philip again overlooked an opportunity to divide the rebels by refusing to compromise on religion. Meanwhile, his financial troubles were having a significant impact. The pay of Spanish soldiers was continually in arrears, and between 1573 and 1576, there were annual mutinies. In November 1576, with their pay two years in arrears, the soldiers mutinied once again, attacking the large and prosperous port of Antwerp. In the course of the "Spanish Fury" 8000 inhabitants were killed and about a third of the city destroyed. All seventeen provinces signed an agreement, the Pacification of Ghent, in which they agreed to cooperate in expelling the Spanish, and to put religious questions aside for the time being.

In 1578, a new commander arrived on the scene: Philip's nephew Alessandro Farnese, Duke of Parma, who was on his way to becoming the leading general of the later sixteenth century. Parma quickly put his political skills to work, playing on the rebels' divisions to persuade the French-speaking Walloon provinces of the south to desert the rebel cause in exchange for the withdrawal of Spanish troops. In response, the three northern provinces of Holland, Zeeland, and Utrecht, and a handful of southern cities signed the Union of Utrecht in 1579, agreeing to closer cooperation in the fight against Spain.

Although we can see here the origins of the eventual split between the Protestant Dutch Republic in the north and the Catholic Spanish Netherlands in the south, and indeed the origins of the modern kingdoms of the Netherlands and Belgium, this was not intentional, nor was it apparent at the time. Neither side foresaw or desired a permanent split, and both thought they could still prevail. In 1581 William of Orange persuaded thirteen of the seventeen provinces to depose Philip as their ruler. In 1584, however, he was assassinated by a Spanish agent, depriving the resistance of its most important figure. Meanwhile, the Spanish army under Parma was quite successful in the southern provinces, re-establishing control over the provinces of Brabant and Flanders, including the cities of Brussels, Ghent, and Antwerp. Parma was not as successful in the north, however, where the geographic barriers of the Rhine and other rivers divided north from south. As he established Spanish control over the south, more and more Calvinists fled north, and the rebel provinces steadily became more Protestant in character.

Parma's attention was also diverted at key points by Philip's other strategic imperatives. In 1588, for example, his army was to invade England, escorted across the Channel by the Spanish Armada (see below). It never happened, of course, but Parma's troops stood idle while waiting. On several other occasions, his army was diverted to France to assist the Catholic League in its struggle against Henry IV. Then Parma died unexpectedly in 1592.

The fighting continued, through the death of Philip II in 1598, until 1609. Then the parties signed a truce that was to last for twelve years, and during that time the northern provinces established de facto independence as the Dutch Republic. When the truce expired in 1621, however, Spain still refused to recognize the independence of the Dutch Republic, and so war resumed.

Map 4.3 The Netherlands divided, 1609

England under Elizabeth I

In France religious differences sparked decades of civil war, while in the Netherlands they contributed to the division of the country. By contrast, England under Queen Elizabeth I (r. 1558–1603) managed to find the elusive point of equilibrium between competing religions relatively quickly, and without civil war. Much of the credit for this was due to the queen's personality, policies, and ability to delegate to capable ministers and advisers. In addition, since the Middle Ages, England had been considerably more unified, legally and administratively, than France, and much more so than the Netherlands. Thus questions of religion did not become as intertwined with questions of local power and autonomy in England as they did on the continent. Since the reign of Henry VIII, the majority of the English people had apparently accepted the principle that religious matters were within the power of the government, and because the changes made under Henry were quite minor, few people had felt it necessary to oppose the king in order to preserve the power of the pope. Once the principle had been established that the proper form of religion was within the power of the monarch, it was easier for all but the most zealously Catholic to accommodate whatever further changes the government imposed than it was to resist them.

Today we know that Elizabeth would have a long and glorious reign. In 1558, however, there were many reasons to fear for the future. She came to the throne as a young and inexperienced woman in an age that thought women incapable of ruling, and at a time when England had been through thirty years of political and religious turmoil, with no end in sight. Yet Elizabeth was able to turn her disadvantages in her favour. She knew how to get her way with men by playing the fragile woman, but she also knew how to turn stereotypes on their heads. Before the arrival of the Spanish Armada, she famously told the army at Tilbury:

> Let tyrants fear, I have always so behaved myself that, under God, I have placed my chiefest strength and safeguard in the loyal hearts and goodwill of my subjects; and therefore I am come amongst you, as you see, at this time not for my recreation or disport, but being resolved, in the midst and heat of the battle, to live and die amongst you all; to lay down for my God, and for my kingdom, and for my people, my honour and my blood, even in the dust. I know I have the body but of a weak and feeble woman; but I have the heart and stomach of a king, and of a king of England too . . .

She was also able to turn her status as an unmarried woman to her advantage, using one potential marriage or another as a diplomatic ploy at various times throughout her reign. Despite her advisers' frequent pleas to marry and guarantee the succession, she was determined to remain single in order to preserve her power and freedom. She was also well aware of the public's response when her sister had chosen to marry Philip II of Spain. In addition, she knew both how to pick able advisers and how to allow them to do their jobs while maintaining ultimate control herself. Among the very capable ministers and advisers she employed were William Cecil (Lord Burghley) and his son Robert, Francis Walsingham, and Nicholas Throckmorton.

THE RELIGIOUS SETTLEMENT

Elizabeth's immediate priority was to settle the religious issue. Although she had conformed to Catholicism under Mary, she had been raised as a Protestant, and the fact that the papacy deemed her a bastard with no right to rule meant that England under her rule had to be independent of Rome. The only questions were what form the Church of England would take and what its core doctrines would be. Although she kept her own religious views well hidden, it seems likely that they would have been more or less Lutheran. But she was not completely free to impose her own preferences, as zealous Protestants, many of whom had either lived through the Marian persecutions or sought refuge in Geneva, would not have been satisfied with half-hearted reform. Elizabeth needed to find a way to keep the broad majority of people satisfied while still maintaining royal control over the Church.

She quickly had Parliament pass an Act of Supremacy making England once again independent of Rome. The restored Church of England was quite Catholic in its structure: although its head was the monarch rather than the pope, it was to be governed through bishops appointed by the head. It was moderately Protestant in doctrine, but not militantly so. As far as worship went, the more explicitly Protestant Prayer Book of 1552 was adopted rather than the conservative 1549 version. However, the language used for the sacrament of the Eucharist was adopted from the earlier version, and was ambiguous on the question of what happened to elements, paying homage to various doctrinal positions. The Thirty-Nine Articles, adopted by the Church of England in 1563, continued this practice of artful ambiguity (see the Weblink at the end of this chapter). Rather than call herself Supreme Head of the Church, as her father had done, Elizabeth chose the less provocative title of Supreme Governor.

On both sides, the most zealous believers rejected Elizabeth's "middle way." Thus Mary's Catholic bishops resigned in protest, while the more zealous Protestants, known as Puritans, condemned the new church's retention of "popish vestiges" such as bishops and elaborate clerical vestments. Even if a good many English people remained devoted to their traditional faith, however, very few were willing to fight or die for the pope. And the Puritans believed that in time they could nudge the queen towards more stringent reforms.

It was under Elizabeth that the real work of making the English people Protestant took place. Certainly there was a vocal minority firmly devoted to Protestant theology of one kind or another. Another, probably smaller, minority were devout Roman Catholics and would always refuse any compromise with what they considered heresy. After three decades of turmoil, however, the majority of people were unwilling to go out on a limb. Even if they would have been happy to go back to their traditional religion, they were content to accept changes as long as they were not too traumatic.

Unlike her sister Mary, Elizabeth was willing to tolerate a little inconsistency when it came to religion. For the most part she punished treason rather than heresy: that is, overt acts rather than inner beliefs. In one of her proclamations on religion, she famously asserted: "We do not wish to make windows into men's souls." In other words, you could believe what you wanted: you would be punished only if those beliefs led to actions against either the church or state.

DIPLOMACY AND WARFARE: SCOTLAND, SPAIN, AND THE SPANISH ARMADA

The significance of the Elizabethan religious settlement reached beyond England's borders. Relations with Spain—England's partner in a long-standing alliance against France—were not immediately affected, partly because Philip II had more pressing concerns in Italy and the Netherlands, but primarily because the next in line for the English throne, should Elizabeth die without heirs, was Mary Stuart, the French-raised Queen of Scotland, who happened to be the granddaughter of Henry VIII's elder sister Margaret. For the time being at least, Philip preferred a Protestant Elizabeth to a Catholic but French Mary Stuart on the English throne; in fact, he even proposed marriage to Elizabeth.

For Elizabeth, Scotland was a more immediate priority than Spain. On returning to Scotland after the death of Francis II, Mary had found her kingdom in both religious and political turmoil. The Protestant Reformation had made significant progress under the fiery leadership of John Knox, recently returned from Geneva. At the same time, the nobles and clan chiefs resented royal efforts to reduce their power and influence. Mary quickly poured gasoline on both fires. Her Catholic faith offended Protestants, her high-handed ways alienated nobles, and her personal behaviour (including affairs) offended all parties. She also alienated Elizabeth by marrying Henry Stuart, Lord Darnley, who like herself was a descendant of Henry VIII's sister, and thereby strengthening her claim to the English throne. Unhappy in her marriage, Mary had an affair with her private secretary, David Rizzio, whom Darnley had murdered before dying himself in circumstances that suggested Mary's knowledge, if not complicity. She had then married the Earl of Bothwell, the prime suspect in Darnley's death. By 1567 she had alienated any possible support in Scotland, and abdicated in favour of her infant son, who became King James VI of Scotland (r. 1567–1625), and who would eventually succeed Elizabeth as King James I of England (r. 1603–25).

Not truly grasping how dangerous she was to Elizabeth, Mary then sought refuge in England, where she became the focal point of numerous plots to remove Elizabeth and restore the Roman Catholic Church and therefore was kept under house arrest and close supervision for twenty years. (Although she did knowingly participate in some of those plots, she was ignorant of most of them.) Elizabeth's advisers begged her to arrange Mary's demise, but she resisted, not wanting to set a precedent by executing a lawful sovereign because of her religion, and no doubt recalling that her sister Mary Tudor had spared her own life when it was hanging by a thread.

Meanwhile, now that France was in chaos, the traditional alliance between England and Spain had lost much of its reason for being, and relations with Spain were deteriorating from cautious neutrality into a kind of cold war. Spain was irritated by English raids on Spanish commerce and provision of aid to the Dutch rebels. And when Jesuit priests began entering England in the early 1580s, the government took their presence as a sign that English Catholics ("recusants") had crossed the line from religious dissent into treason, and therefore subjected them to more stringent punishment. By the mid-1580s Philip II had decided that England would have to be punished and Elizabeth replaced, even if that meant putting Mary Stuart on the throne. (Through his bankrolling of the Catholic League in France, Philip no doubt believed that he would be in a position of influence in both France and England.) An invasion plan was put in place that called for the Spanish fleet to sail to the Netherlands, rendezvous with Parma's troops, load them onto barges, and escort them across the Channel.

Although Philip had devoted two years to his plan, it was badly flawed. Some problems were recognized from the start: the rendezvous with Parma would be difficult to coordinate; it would require sailing through hostile waters in the Channel; the Spanish Netherlands lacked a good deep-water port; and the army would be extremely vulnerable both while boarding the barges and while crossing the Channel.

Other problems developed along the way. The strategic purpose of the Armada was thrown into serious question in February 1587, when Elizabeth finally agreed to the execution of Mary Stuart. At that point Philip decided to put his daughter Isabella on the English throne instead, regardless of the opposition that a Spanish queen would have been sure to provoke. Furthermore, although preparations for the invasion were supposed to be secret, it was impossible to conceal such a massive undertaking (one historian called it "the worst-kept secret in Europe").[5] Thus in May 1587 Sir Francis Drake raided Cadiz and destroyed many of the supplies intended for the fleet, which were impossible to replace on such short notice.

There was also a major problem that could not have been foreseen. Early in 1588, the Armada's commander, the Marquis of Santa Cruz, unexpectedly died. His replacement, the Duke of Medina Sidonia, was an experienced general but had no naval experience, and in fact thought the whole scheme was dubious. Then there was the weather. The Armada set sail from Lisbon on May 28, 1588, with 130 ships and 30,000 men, but foul weather forced it to put into the northern Spanish port of Corunna for nearly a month before it could sail for England.

When the fleet arrived at the mouth of the Channel in late July, it was met by an English fleet of about the same size, but composed of smaller and quicker vessels, which harassed the Spanish as they sailed up the Channel to the Spanish Netherlands for their rendezvous with Parma. They arrived on August 6, only to find that the port was too shallow for the ships to dock and take on Parma's army. The next day, the English sent fireships adrift into the midst of the anchored Spanish vessels, many of which cut their anchor ropes to escape. Even then, the Spanish might have been able to regroup, but a violent gale blew them into the North Sea, making a return to the Channel impossible. Medina Sidonia then decided that the best course of action was to keep the fleet together and return to Spain via the North Atlantic. Once again, however, horrendous weather intervened, and many ships were wrecked on the Irish coast. Only 80 of the original 130 ships returned home, with significant loss of life.

The importance of the failure of the "enterprise of England" has often been overstated. It was not "the beginning of the end" for Spain's pre-eminence in Europe, nor did it represent the beginning of English naval dominance. Spain would retain its dominant position in Europe for more than half a century yet, while small and isolated England remained a bit player in European diplomacy. It was much more significant as a victory to England than as a defeat to Spain. The relief and joy at defeating the most powerful ruler in Europe helped to produce a golden age of confidence and creativity in England, the age of Shakespeare, Marlowe, Jonson, Spenser, and Bacon. In *Richard II*, Act II, Scene I, Shakespeare captured this sense of a special English destiny and divine favour:

> This royal throne of kings, this scepter'd isle,
> This earth of majesty, this seat of Mars,
> This other Eden, demi-paradise,
> This fortress built by Nature for herself
> Against infection and the hand of war,

This happy breed of men, this little world,
This precious stone set in the silver sea,
Which serves it in office of a wall,
Or as a moat defensive to a house,
Against the envy of less happier lands,
This blessed plot, this earth, this realm, this England.

POLITICS, PARLIAMENT, AND PURITANS

Yet with the defeat of the Armada, religious and political tensions that had been submerged while England was under dire threat came to the surface. The Puritans' opposition to the moderate nature of the Elizabethan religious settlement intensified. They objected

The Armada Portrait of Elizabeth I. Artist unknown (possibly George Gower). This portrait was painted in 1588 to celebrate the defeat of the Spanish Armada. The Queen's hand rests on a globe, symbolizing England's worldwide reach. More specifically, it rests on the New World, where England's colony in Virginia had just been established. Above the globe, an arched imperial crown emphasizes that Elizabeth has no earthly superior. The two pillars behind the queen to the left may allude to the Pillars of Hercules (the Straits of Gibraltar), the emblem of the Holy Roman Emperor Charles V, the father of Philip II. Through the arch on the left we see the arrival of the Armada, and on the right its destruction by the forces of providential nature. Elizabeth's dress is extravagantly decorated with pearls, symbols of purity and virginity. The mermaid carved on the chair to the lower right may represent the queen who lured the men of Philip's Armada to a watery doom.

to the ambiguities in doctrine, and were scandalized by the "popish vestiges" retained in the form of worship prescribed by the Book of Common Prayer. And rather than an epis- copal church (governed by bishops appointed by the ruler), they wanted a Calvinist pres- byterian system that would allow greater input from below. Once the immediate threat of the Armada had been eliminated, Elizabeth's Archbishop of Canterbury, John Whitgift, cracked down. Puritan cells were broken up, ministers dismissed, printing presses de- stroyed, and Puritans imprisoned. Some went into exile in Germany and the Netherlands, and eventually found their way to New England, where they would put into practice their vision of a Christian community, a "city on a hill."

At the same time, opposition to the Queen's policies in Parliament was becoming more overt. As far as Elizabeth was concerned, it was Parliament's job to approve her policies, not to question them. But during the war with Spain, Parliament had had to meet more frequently to approve taxation, and in the process many members of the House of Commons had become more conscious of their interests and identity. Now they began to voice their discontent with royal policies, insisting that, as the wealthy and powerful of the kingdom, those who paid most of the taxes, their views ought to be taken seriously.

When the government crushed debate on bills proposed by Puritan members, even non-Puritans objected to the infringement of their rights as MPs. A major clash occurred in 1601 over the Queen's power to grant and license monopolies, as many MPs objected to these infringements on their economic interests. Elizabeth appeased them by promising an inquiry, but Parliament increasingly became a forum for debating royal policy.

Despite these tensions, Elizabeth managed to avoid major confrontations on either religion or politics throughout her long reign. Her chief accomplishment was to bring re- ligious and political stability to England after decades of uncertainty and turmoil. Almost uniquely among sixteenth-century rulers, she succeeded in bringing religious peace to the vast majority of her subjects. The settlement she put in place was flexible enough to accommodate a range of opinions, and thus England was able to avoid both fratricidal civil war, as happened in France, and the division of the country along religious lines, as happened in the Netherlands. When she died in 1603, she was succeeded on the throne by King James VI of Scotland, the son of her old nemesis Mary Stuart, who then became King James I of England. Would he and his successors be able to maintain the stability that Elizabeth had brought to a troubled kingdom?

The Thirty Years War

RELIGIOUS CONFLICT IN GERMANY TO 1555

By 1530 most northern German rulers had rejected the Roman Catholic Church and im- posed a Lutheran Reformation on their subjects. Charles V was of course adamantly op- posed, but his hands were tied by a number of factors: war with France and the Turks, the revolt of the *comuneros* in Spain, and the difficulties in ruling an empire of such size and diversity. He had left Germany after the Diet of Worms in 1521 and was absent for the better part of a decade, leaving German affairs in the hands of his brother Ferdinand. On his return in 1530 he decided that the time for decisive action in Germany had arrived. In response, in 1531 Lutheran princes and self-governing Imperial cities formed an alliance, the Schmalkaldic League to protect themselves.

War between Charles V and the Schmalkaldic League would break out in 1546, and in April 1547 the Catholic imperial forces won a stunning victory at Mühlberg. From this position of strength, Charles imposed a compromise religious settlement on Protestant subjects of the Holy Roman Empire, pending the outcome of the Council of Trent. Known as the Augsburg Interim, it allowed for clerical marriage, communion in both kinds, and some latitude on salvation, but Protestants by and large rejected it as a coerced reversion to Catholicism.

By the early 1550s, even German Catholic rulers were becoming alarmed by the Emperor's growing power. King Henry II of France formed an alliance with the Lutheran princes of Germany, and in early 1552 they both attacked, while German Catholic rulers remained on the sidelines. Charles himself was almost captured in the city of Innsbruck. The sick emperor had to be carried on a litter out one city gate in a blinding snowstorm as his enemies entered the city by another gate.

Clearly, there was a stalemate. The Lutheran forces were too strong to be eliminated militarily, but not strong enough to overcome Catholic forces. Prematurely aged, ill, and despondent, in 1554 Charles V set the wheels into motion to abdicate his positions, and left the settlement of the situation in Germany to his brother Ferdinand.

In 1555 the Imperial Diet meeting in the city of Augsburg negotiated the Peace of Augsburg, which legitimized Lutheranism within the Holy Roman Empire, but stopped well short of granting religious liberty. Its guiding principle—that the religion of the territory was determined by the religion of the ruler—was expressed in the Latin phrase *cuius regio, eius religio*: "who rules, his religion." There were only two options: Lutheranism and the Roman Catholic Church. In Imperial cities where both faiths were practised, both would continue to be permitted, and people whose religion was at odds with that of their ruler were permitted to emigrate. Although Lutheran rulers who had taken over Church lands before 1552 were allowed to keep them, Ferdinand insisted on a clause called the ecclesiastical reservation, which prohibited any further secularization of Church lands. Ecclesiastical princes—bishops and archbishops who also ruled territories—were free to convert, but would have to resign their positions; their territory and subjects could not be converted with them.

The Peace of Augsburg was the result of political calculation and military stalemate, not a commitment to religious liberty. While it brought peace to the Holy Roman Empire for 60 years, its flaws are obvious in hindsight. In particular, it did not allow for the practice of Calvinism, which was to become the dominant form of Protestantism in the later sixteenth century. Nor, of course, did anyone in 1555 foresee that a revived and resurgent Catholic Church would attempt to roll back the Protestant tide. The Peace of Augsburg attempted to preserve a status quo that was the outcome of particular historical circumstances. When those circumstances changed, its inability to accommodate those changes would help to produce the bloodiest and most destructive war in European history prior to the twentieth century: the Thirty Years War (1618–48).

THE ORIGINS OF THE THIRTY YEARS WAR

Even though it was technically illegal, Calvinism continued to make important inroads into Germany in the later sixteenth century. In 1584 the Count Palatine of the Rhine, one of the seven Electors of the Holy Roman Empire, became a Calvinist. His capital city of Heidelberg became an important Calvinist centre, second only to Geneva, and he sent troops to assist Calvinists in France and the Netherlands. In 1613 the Elector of Brandenburg converted to Calvinism, although he continued to allow the practice of Lutheranism in his lands. At the same time, the Catholic Counter-Reformation was having an impact in Germany, particularly in Bavaria and Austria. In the latter, ruled by the Habsburg dynasty, Protestantism had become very prominent at all levels of society. From the 1580s on, however, guarantees of freedom of worship were withdrawn, and privileges were granted to the Jesuits, who led the way in the re-Catholicization of these lands. In a number of Imperial cities where the Peace of Augsburg had permitted both creeds, Catholics took over and outlawed Protestant worship.

When Emperor Ferdinand I had died in 1562, he was succeeded by his son Maximilian II (r. 1562–76), who had no desire to rock the boat. In addition to needing the cooperation of German Lutheran princes to resist the Ottoman Turks, he was personally sympathetic to Lutheranism. However, his son and successor, Emperor Rudolf II (r. 1576–1612), was a committed Catholic, and instrumental in supporting the Jesuits in Austria. By the time of his death the religious tensions in Germany had become militarized, as we can see in the formation of two rival alliances. In 1609 the Protestant Union was formed under the leadership of the Calvinist Elector Palatine, and in response German Catholic rulers formed the Catholic League, led by the Duke of Bavaria, the following year.

What is more—and crucial to understanding the Thirty Years War—almost every other ruler in Europe had an interest in what happened in Germany. Not only were the Habsburg kings of Spain tied to their German cousins by blood and religion: in addition, they relied on Habsburg power in Germany to preserve the "Spanish Road," the network of routes than ran from northern Italy through Switzerland and eastern France to the Netherlands. This was the primary corridor through which Spanish communications, men, materiel, and money were conveyed to the Netherlands. Disrupting the Spanish Road was therefore crucial to both the Catholic King of France and the Protestant Dutch Republic.

THE BOHEMIAN CRISIS AND THE GERMAN WAR TO 1630

The spark that ignited the Thirty Years War was a rebellion in Bohemia, a region that was distinct within the Holy Roman Empire in several respects. Czech rather than German in language and culture, it had also been religiously distinct since the Hussite revolts of the fifteenth century, and by 1600 most of the Bohemian nobles had become Calvinist.[6]

In addition, the Bohemian monarchy was elective, and although the nobles had elected Habsburgs since 1526, there was no guarantee that they would continue to do so. By the early seventeenth century the Protestant nobles were reluctant to elect another member of the dynasty, which was becoming ever more zealously Catholic, and Habsburg successes in repressing Protestants in Austria only increased their anxiety. In 1609, therefore, in order to guarantee the future of Habsburg rule in Bohemia, Emperor Rudolf II issued the Letter of Majesty, in which he promised to abide by the religious and political liberties of the Bohemian nobles. In this way, the childless Rudolf secured the Bohemian succession for his nephew, Ferdinand, who was elected King in 1617.

Ferdinand, however, almost immediately violated the Bohemians' liberties by, among other things, appointing Catholics to powerful positions in the government and harassing Protestants. In May 1618, during a meeting of the Bohemian nobles in Prague, a group of Protestants seized Ferdinand's two chief advisers in Bohemia and threw them out a window in the royal palace.[7] Although they maintained the legal fiction that they were not rebelling against the king's authority, merely against his "evil advisers," they were in fact rejecting all that Ferdinand stood for. They established their own government and solicited support from Protestant rulers.

To make matters worse, in 1619 Ferdinand was elected Holy Roman Emperor Ferdinand II (r. 1619–37). In response, the Bohemian nobles deposed him as their king and chose the leading Calvinist in the Empire, the young Elector Palatine Frederick V, to replace him. This act of rebellion changed the electoral politics of the Empire, since if Frederick were allowed to keep the title of King of Bohemia, all four of the secular electors would be Protestant, posing a direct threat to the imperial future of the Habsburg dynasty. Furthermore, if the Bohemian rebellion succeeded, others could follow: already some Austrian Protestants had rebelled and, with the Bohemians, laid siege to Vienna in June 1619.

The Bohemian rebellion was likely doomed from the start. Frederick was young and inexperienced, and the support he had counted on from outside Bohemia did not materialize. Within Germany, most Protestant rulers were Lutheran and did not look kindly on the Calvinist Frederick; in fact, the Lutheran Elector of Saxony actually assisted the Emperor, hoping to gain the territory of Lusatia. Louis XIII of France was campaigning against the restive Huguenots, and the Dutch were preparing for the end of their truce with Spain. Although he was Frederick's father-in-law, James I of England remained neutral, largely because he did not want to ask Parliament for money.

Emperor Ferdinand lacked an army of his own capable of punishing the Bohemians, but Duke Maximilian of Bavaria put the army of the Catholic League at his disposal. With its help, he first subdued the rebellion in Austria and then turned towards Bohemia, where he crushed the rebels at the Battle of White Mountain in November 1620. Frederick fled into exile in the Netherlands, leaving the Bohemians to face the consequences. Twenty-seven leading rebels were executed; roughly half the land was confiscated and given to loyal nobles and officers; all Protestant pastors were expelled; any remaining Protestants were ordered to convert to Catholicism or go into exile; and the Bohemian crown was declared to be hereditary in the Habsburg dynasty. Thus the opening phase of the war enhanced Habsburg control of both Austria and Bohemia as well as the Emperor's power in the Holy Roman Empire as a whole.

That the war did not end here was due largely to the interests of foreign rulers. In 1625 Denmark's King Christian IV (r. 1588–1648), who possessed territories in northern Germany and felt threatened by the Emperor's growing power, went to the defence of the German Protestants against the possibility of further Catholic repression. In August of 1626, however, Ferdinand defeated the Danes at the Battle of Lutter and occupied large parts of northern Germany. The peace concluded in the Treaty of Lübeck in 1629 was again favourable to Ferdinand.

The most important factor in Ferdinand's triumph over the Danes was the fact that he now had an army at his disposal, which freed him from depending on the army of Catholic League. This army had been provided by Albrecht von Wallenstein (1583–1634), a Bohemian noble, born Protestant, who had converted to Catholicism and profited handsomely from the punishment of the Bohemian rebels. He married a wealthy widow and used her funds to build a fortune by speculating in the lands confiscated from Bohemian nobles. At one point he personally owned about one-quarter of Bohemia. Made Duke of Friedland by the Emperor, in 1625 he agreed to organize an army for Ferdinand on a contractual basis. Although this was standard procedure for military leaders at the time, what set Wallenstein apart were his efficiency and ruthlessness. War was his business, and business was good. In fact, his continued prosperity depended on the continuation of the war. Ferdinand paid him handsomely for the use of his army, but Wallenstein kept the money for himself and paid his troops through systematic extortion and pillage of civilian populations.

THE EDICT OF RESTITUTION AND THE EUROPEAN WAR TO 1648

By the late 1620s, after a decade of war, Ferdinand's position was very strong. His hold on Austria and Bohemia had been strengthened and Protestantism effectively outlawed there. His armies had occupied large patches of northern Germany, and the leading Calvinist prince in Germany had been sent into exile, his lands and titles confiscated. Now Ferdinand was in a position to impose his will on the Holy Roman Empire. Accordingly, in 1629 he issued the Edict of Restitution, which restored to the Catholic Church all the lands secularized since 1552. In a number of cities where the Peace of Augsburg had permitted Lutheran worship, it was now forbidden, and several of them were forcibly re-Catholicized.

In hindsight, we can see that Ferdinand overplayed his hand. Not only did the Edict of Restitution preclude any further cooperation with Lutheran princes: it also alienated German Catholic princes such as the Duke of Bavaria, who feared (with reason) that the Emperor's goal was to bring all of the Empire, including their territories, under his control. In addition, France and the Dutch republic were naturally disturbed by any expansion of Habsburg power, while Ferdinand's victories in northern Germany in particular alarmed the King of Sweden, Gustavus II Adolphus (r. 1611–32). A sincere and committed Lutheran, he was genuinely concerned for the fate of German Protestants. But he was also the ruler of the dominant power in northern Europe, and as such was aware of the threat that growing Habsburg power in northern Germany posed to his territories, which included Finland, large parts of modern Estonia and Latvia, and scattered pockets around the southern shore of the Baltic. An experienced commander, in June 1630 he led his large and effective army into northern Germany.

Within a few weeks of the Swedish army's arrival in Germany, Ferdinand dismissed Wallenstein in an effort to appease the German rulers who hated and feared him, and therefore was in a weakened position. Another factor that aided Gustavus was the formation of an alliance with King Louis XIII of France: under the secret Treaty of Bärwalde, signed in January 1631, France would subsidize the Swedish army to fight the Habsburg forces in Germany while France fought them in the Netherlands and Italy (see below). Gustavus and the Swedes won some enormous successes, beginning in September 1631, when their defeat of the Imperial army at Breitenfeld, which reversed all the gains that Ferdinand had made in northern Germany over the previous decade. A desperate Emperor

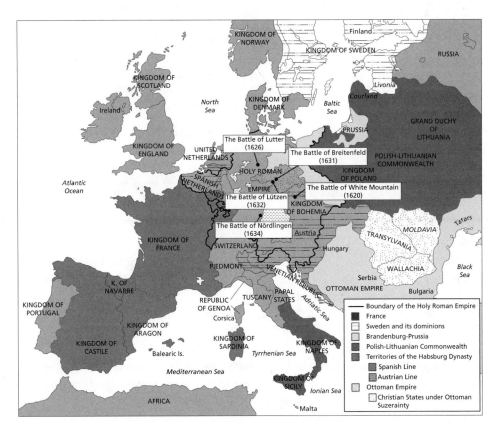

Map 4.4 Europe in 1648

HISTORICAL DEBATE

Interpreting the Thirty Years War

Possibly no European conflict before the twentieth century has sparked as much debate as the Thirty Years War. In the nineteenth century, German nationalists emphasized its destructiveness and blamed the Peace of Westphalia for retarding the development of a German national state. Following the First World War, C.V. Wedgwood saw it as foreshadowing what was then the great conflict of the twentieth century. More recently, local and regional studies have produced a more nuanced picture.

Gustav Freytag (1816–95) was a German novelist, playwright, and liberal journalist who focused on all that the war destroyed.

> . . . When the war ended, there was little remaining of the great nation. For yet a century to come, the successors of the survivors were deficient in that most manly of all feelings,—political enthusiasm.
>
> All this gives to the Thirty Years War the appearance of foredoomed annihilation. . . . Above the strife of parties a terrible fate spread its wings; it carried off the leaders and prostrated them in the dust, the greatest human strength became powerless under its hand; at last, satiated with death and devastation, it turned its face slowly from the country which had become a great charnel house. . . .

Gustav Freytag, *Pictures of German Life in the XVth, XVIth, and XVIIth Centuries*, trans. Georgiana Malcolm (London: 1862), quoted in Theodore K. Rabb (ed.) *The Thirty Years War: Problems of Motive, Extent, and Effect* (Boston: D.C. Heath, 1964) pp. 1–4.

In 1938 C.V. Wedgwood published what was the standard history of the Thirty Years War in English for many decades. As she noted, her approach was conditioned by her own times:

> Preoccupation with contemporary distress made the plight of the hungry and the desolate in the Thirty Years War exceptionally vivid to me . . . . Many of my generation who grew up under the shadow of the First World War had a sincere, if mistaken, conviction that all wars were unnecessary and useless . . . (pp. 7–8).
>
> In Germany the [Thirty Years War] was an unmitigated catastrophe. In Europe it was equally, although in a different way, catastrophic. The peace, which had settled the disputes of Germany with comparative success because passions had cooled, was totally ineffectual in settling the problems of Europe.
>
> After the expenditure of so much human life to so little purpose, men might have grasped the essential futility of putting the beliefs of the mind to the judgment of the sword. Instead, they rejected religion as an object to fight for and found others.
>
> . . . The war solved no problem. Its effects, both immediate and indirect, were either negative or disastrous. Morally subversive, economically destructive, socially degrading, confused in its causes, devious in its course, futile in its result, it is the outstanding example in European history of meaningless conflict . . . (pp. 505–6).

Cicely V. Wedgwood, *The Thirty Years War* (New York: Anchor Books, 1961).

In 1947, S.H. Steinberg (1899–1969) challenged Wedgwood's interpretation:

> . . . To Miss Wedgwood's version the following may be opposed. . . . [T]he final over-
> throw of the Hapsburg hegemony established the principle of the balance of power,
> which would henceforth militate against every attempt to set up a single-state rule
> over Europe. . . . It is the outstanding example in European history of an intrinsically
> successful settlement (pp. 89–90).
>   . . . Ignorance of scientific demography and inability to visualize large figures ac-
> count for the legend of the enormous loss of population. . . . All these figures are purely
> imaginary. . . [,] designed to support some special pleading: to obtain a grant in aid, a
> reduction of payments, or alleviation of services . . . (p. 99).
>   What actually happened was an extensive inner migration chiefly from the agrarian
> countryside into the industrial towns, and from the economically retrograde towns to the
> prosperous ones. . . . [I]t is more appropriate to speak of redistribution than of destruction.
>   . . . The legend of cultural exhaustion and desolation . . . is perhaps easiest to refute. It
> is solely due to the aesthetic standards of nineteenth-century criticism in literature, art,
> architecture and music. . . . The war itself had little, and certainly no detrimental effect
> upon the cultural life of Germany . . . (pp. 100–1).
>
> S.H. Steinberg. *The Thirty Years War and the Conflict for European Hegemony, 1600–1660.* (London: W. W. Norton and
> Company, 1967).

In 2009, Peter Wilson drew on an enormous amount of research on the impact of the war.

> Some historians started to question this Gothic atrocity narrative around 1900. The mil-
> itary historian Robert Hoeniger sparked controversy by arguing the German population
> declined by only an eighth. . . . This argument was pushed to its logical extreme . . . by
> Sigfrid Henry Steinberg [who] claimed that the Empire experienced some slackening of
> growth and redistribution of inhabitants, but overall both the economy and the popu-
> lation increased. Though he cited very little evidence, his interpretation rapidly gained
> acceptance. . . .
>   A major reason for this debate is that the war's impact varied across time and space,
> producing seemingly contradictory evidence. . . (pp. 780–1).
>   . . . The only comprehensive survey remains that by Günther Franz who concluded
> that urban areas fell by a third, while the population in the countryside fell by 40 per
> cent. Most other accounts broadly agree by putting the overall loss at a third. . . .
>   Even a 15 per cent decline would make the Thirty Years War the most destructive
> conflict in European history. By comparison the Soviet Union, which suffered the heavi-
> est casualties of the Second World War lost less than 12 per cent of its population. . . .
> Overall totals of course obscure wide regional variations (p. 787).
>
> Peter H. Wilson, *Europe's Tragedy: A History of the Thirty Years War* (London: Allen Lane, 2009).

recalled Wallenstein, and in November 1632 the two armies met at Lützen in Saxony. Again the Swedes prevailed, though at the cost of the king's life. Since Gustavus's heir, Queen Christina, was underage, his chancellor, Axel Oxenstierna, assumed control of the government and the war effort.

Meanwhile, Wallenstein had once again managed to alienate his employer by shopping his services to Sweden and France, among others, even while continuing to take the Emperor's money. In early 1634 Ferdinand once again dismissed him and ordered his arrest. When Wallenstein attempted to flee, he was murdered by a group of his own officers, whom the Emperor had bribed.

In September 1634, Imperial and Spanish forces together crushed the Swedes at the Battle of Nördlingen in southern Germany. Just as the Swedish victory at Breitenfeld had confirmed Protestant control of the north, so this victory confirmed the predominance of Catholicism in the south. Most of Sweden's German allies now made peace with the Emperor. The Edict of Restitution was repealed and the religious settlement of Augsburg reaffirmed. Religious boundaries were affirmed as they had been in 1627; thus Bohemia remained Catholic, but most of northern Germany was restored to Lutheranism. The religious settlement reflected the military stalemate, and what had begun as a religious and civil war within the Holy Roman Empire was effectively concluded. The war continued, however, for it had become inextricably linked with broader European conflicts.

France was concerned above all with preventing Habsburg encirclement. At war with Habsburg Spain since the late 1620s, in 1635 France entered the German war openly to assist its Swedish ally. The Swedes too had reasons to continue fighting: after investing so much, they wanted some north German territory in return. In addition, there was real concern that the "Swedish" army—by now mostly made up of mercenaries—might invade Swedish territory to extort payment if the fighting were to conclude before the soldiers had a chance to pay themselves by pillaging Germany. The Dutch too found the war in Germany a useful diversion for their Habsburg enemies. This last phase of the Thirty Years War was both the most pointless and the most destructive, marked by rival armies traipsing back and forth across Germany to no purpose, at great cost to loss of life and property.

THE PEACE OF WESTPHALIA, 1648

By 1644 general exhaustion had led to peace negotiations, but as they were not accompanied by a truce or ceasefire, hostilities only intensified as each party sought to improve its bargaining position. Nevertheless, by October 1648 all the warring parties signed the treaties of Münster and Osnabrück, collectively known as the Peace of Westphalia. This was a turning point in European history in several ways. For the Habsburg dynasty it marked the final defeat of its longstanding ambition to control the Holy Roman Empire. Emperor Ferdinand III (r. 1637–57) acknowledged that all the German princes were fully sovereign in internal affairs, and only slightly less so in external relations: a German prince could sign treaties and make alliances as he pleased, as long as they were not directed against the Emperor. In effect, the Peace of Westphalia was the final nail in the coffin of a unified Christian empire. The Augsburg principle—*cuius regio, eius religio*—was retained, but Calvinism was permitted alongside Lutheranism and Catholicism. Religiously, therefore, as well as politically, Germany remained disunited, with the north solidly Lutheran and the south solidly Catholic, and pockets of Calvinism along the Rhine and in the west. Although German historians of the nineteenth century would condemn Westphalia for its contribution to national disunity, to imagine that it could have imposed a nineteenth-century nationalism in 1648 was to ignore seventeenth-century realities.

France and Sweden both realized territorial gains from the Peace of Westphalia. Sweden's pre-eminence in the Baltic was confirmed by its gaining western Pomerania and the important port city of Stettin (modern Szcecin in Poland), as well as Bremen and Verden. These territories gave Sweden control of the mouths of the Oder, Elbe, and Wesel rivers, which were essential linchpins in the Baltic grain trade. France gained parts of Alsace and Lorraine, as well as some important fortresses along the Rhine that strengthened its eastern frontier and, most importantly, allowed it to obstruct the "Spanish Road." France also gained formal recognition of its possession of the border fortresses of Metz, Toul, and Verdun, which it had occupied for a century. France and Sweden were also named guarantors of the terms of the treaties, or "protectors of German liberties." This would give the kings of France a virtually free hand to intervene in German affairs: all they had to do was manufacture some violation of the treaty.

Chapter Conclusion

The Peace of Westphalia was the first entirely secular peace conference in European history, and it marked the end of the religious warfare that had begun with the Protestant Reformation. The papacy took no part in the negotiations; although Pope Pius X condemned the Peace as "null, void, invalid, iniquitous, unjust, damnable, reprobate, inane, empty of meaning and effect for all time," his invective fell on deaf ears. Indeed, by the later stages of the war religion had become largely irrelevant to the conflict; left on their own, Germans would likely have settled their religious issues in the 1630s. After Westphalia, religion would continue to complicate diplomacy, and would often be trotted out as a pretext, but no war would truly be motivated by the "true faith," even if rulers did continue to insist on religious uniformity among their subjects. Throughout the later seventeenth and eighteenth centuries, wars would be fought for more limited and therefore more attainable goals: territories, trade, resources, and so on. Not until the wars that followed the French Revolution at the end of the eighteenth century would ideology once again assume a primary role in European diplomacy.

At the same time, by the later seventeenth century, governments were increasingly successful at controlling their armed forces, taking steps, for example, to supply troops more regularly and punish lapses in discipline. Thus even though continuing developments in weapons and tactics were making combat more deadly, its impact on civilian populations was becoming less traumatic. In the end, a century of warfare driven largely by religious division produced a system of states and rulers in which religion was increasingly irrelevant. Meanwhile, the conduct and resolution of those conflicts furthered the evolution of the state, both in accelerating the development of its institutional framework and, through the weakening of the notion of Christendom, in enhancing its sovereign status.

Questions for Critical Thought

1. How did the evolution of technology affect the conduct of war? How did these changes influence the development of governments and states?
2. How did the dynastic nature of governments impact diplomacy and warfare?
3. How might changes in the nature of religious observance and belief ("confessionalization," discussed in Chapter 3) have influenced the nature of religious war?
4. What role(s) did religious division play in the French Wars of Religion, the Dutch Revolt, and the Thirty Years War? What differences and similarities do you see? How did the differences affect the outcomes of these conflicts?
5. Why did England not experience religious civil war in the sixteenth century? Did the nature of the Reformation in England play a role?

Weblinks

Edict of Nantes:
www.museeprotestant.org/en/notice/the-edict-of-nantes-1598/
www.stetson.edu/~psteeves/classes/edictnantes.html

The Thirty-Nine Articles:
www.churchofengland.org/prayer-worship/worship/book-of-common-prayer/articles-of-religion.aspx

Further Reading

Black, Jeremy. *European Warfare, 1494–1660*. New York: Routledge, 2002. A leading military historian qualifies the notion of "the Military Revolution" in this accessible overview.

Darby, Graham, ed. *Origins and Development of the Dutch Revolt*. London: Routledge, 2001. A useful collection of essays by some of the leading historians of the revolt.

Diefendorf, Barbara. *Beneath the Cross: Catholics and Huguenots in Sixteenth-Century Paris*. Oxford: Oxford University Press, 1991. The best recent account of the St. Bartholomew Massacre, putting it in its religious, political, and social context.

Elliott, J.H. *Europe Divided, 1559–1598*. Oxford: Blackwell, 2000. By one of the preeminent early modern historians of our time.

Fernandez-Armesto, Felipe. *The Spanish Armada: The Experience of War in 1588*. Oxford: Oxford University Press, 1988. A revision of the classic triumphalist view.

Holt, Mack P. *The French Wars of Religion, 1562–1629*, 2nd ed. Cambridge: Cambridge University Press, 2005. The definitive general treatment, putting the religion back into the Wars of Religion.

Konnert, Mark. *Early Modern Europe: The Age of Religious War, 1559–1715*. Toronto: University of Toronto Press, 2008. A comprehensive and accessible overview.

Levin, Carole. *The Reign of Elizabeth I*. New York: Palgrave, 2002.

Lynch, John. *Spain 1516–1598: From Nation State to World Empire*. Cambridge MA: Blackwell, 1992. A comprehensive survey with an extensive bibliography.

MacCaffrey, Wallace T. *Elizabeth I: War and Politics, 1588–1603*. Princeton: Princeton University Press, 1992.

MacCulloch, Diarmaid. *The Later Reformation in England, 1547–1603*. New York: St. Martin's Press, 1990. A succinct and balanced treatment of religious changes under Elizabeth I.

Parker, Geoffrey. *The Grand Strategy of Philip II*. New Haven: Yale University Press, 1998. Argues that Philip had coherent strategic objectives that were foiled by messy reality.

Parker, Geoffrey. *The Military Revolution: Military Innovation and the Rise of the West, 1500–1800*. Cambridge: Cambridge University Press, 1986. A leading military and political historian extends and refines the notion of a "military revolution."

Wilson, Peter H. *Europe's Tragedy: A History of the Thirty Years War*. London: Allen Lane, 2009. The most recent and complete treatment in English.

Notes

1. Quoted in Geoffrey Parker, *The Military Revolution: Military Innovation and the Rise of the West, 1500–1800* (Cambridge: Cambridge University Press, 1988), p. 10.
2. I am grateful to Professor Rebecca Ard Boone of Lamar University both for providing a copy of this manuscript and for her general assistance on the subject of Gattinara.
3. The name was likely a French corruption of the German name for the Swiss Confederation, *Eidgenossenschaft*, literally "those united by oath."
4. John Lothrop Motley, quoted in John C. Rule and John J. TePaske, *The Character of Philip II: The Problem of Moral Judgments in History* (Englewood NJ: D.C. Heath, 1966), p. 17.
5. De Lamar Jensen, "The Spanish Armada: The Worst-Kept Secret in Europe," *Sixteenth Century Journal*, 21, 4 (1988), pp. 621–41.
6. In the fifteenth century, one of the Hussite factions had gained de facto toleration within the Roman Catholic Church. It became known as the Utraquist Church, because its members were allowed to receive communion in both kinds (Latin: *sub utraque specie*): that is, both the bread and the wine.
7. This incident became known as the Defenestration of Prague. Catholics attributed the fact that both men survived the fall to divine protection, while Protestants pointed out that their landing was cushioned by a heap of manure and garbage.

5

"Discovering" New Worlds

In the course of the sixteenth and seventeenth centuries, two further elements of Christendom fell by the wayside. Neither was inherently "Christian" in the way that the unity of the Church of Rome had been, but both were prominent features of medieval European civilization. One was the insularity resulting from Europe's geographical location on the western fringe of the Eurasian landmass, which had hindered contact with the older, wealthier, and more advanced civilizations of the Middle East and Asia. Beginning in the late fifteenth century, European sailors, merchants, and explorers came into increasingly meaningful contact with a growing variety of other civilizations, not only in the previously recognized (if dimly known) regions of Asia and Africa, but in the previously unknown "New World." As a result, Europe began to participate in global networks of trade, people, and power—a process that by the end of the early modern period would see Europe assume the dominant position in global politics and the global economy.

The second element of Christendom that fell away in the sixteenth and seventeenth centuries was a view of the universe and humanity's place in it that had originated in ancient Greece and been transmitted to medieval Europeans partly through Roman literature and partly through the research of Muslim scholars. Gradually, as scientific "truths" that had been accepted for millennia were questioned, understanding of the physical universe was fundamentally transformed. What has become known as the "Scientific Revolution" played a crucial role in the formation of the modern world. Because religious establishments (both Catholic and Protestant) remained committed to increasingly discredited ancient views of the universe, an antagonism developed between science and Christianity that was neither intended nor foreseen by the scientists involved. By about the middle of seventeenth century, the point of no return had been reached in both processes of discovery. Although with hindsight we can see the end results, for contemporaries the consequences would become apparent only over the course of the next several centuries.

Europe "Discovers" the World

Over the last several decades, the idea that Europeans "discovered" the rest of the world has rightly been overturned. Certainly the civilizations concerned, whether in the New World, Africa, or Asia, had no need of a "discovery" that in most cases spelled nearly unmitigated catastrophe. On the other hand, from the perspective of early modern Europeans, the process of exploring the world beyond their borders was certainly one of discovery. Without ignoring the disastrous consequences of European contact for indigenous populations, especially in the Americas, this discussion will focus on the consequences for Europeans.

Throughout the Middle Ages, European civilization had been far less advanced than its counterparts in the Middle East, India, and East Asia. Those few hardy Europeans who found their way to Byzantium, Baghdad, or China ("Cathay") were continually astounded by the wealth and sophistication they encountered. In fact, when the most famous of them—the Venetian merchant Marco Polo (1254–1324)—wrote an account of his travels, the stories he told seemed so implausible that he was widely suspected of fabricating them. Medieval Europeans were certainly aware that other civilizations existed to the east, but much of what they thought they knew about them came from fanciful medieval treatises describing people with the heads of dogs, or with mouths in their abdomens.

The almost complete collapse of the Roman Empire in western Europe meant that, whereas other Eurasian civilizations had deep reservoirs of cultural, political, and economic knowledge available to them, medieval Europeans had very limited resources to draw on. Furthermore, the fragmentation of the classical civilizations in the early Middle Ages meant that travel along the network of overland routes connecting Europe and East Asia became more difficult and dangerous. Medieval Europe thus not only was poorer, more sparsely populated, and less advanced than its Eurasian counterparts, but was also in a geographical position that made contact with these more advanced civilizations problematic. How did this relatively poor backwater, in the space of several centuries, manage to become the world's dominant political and economic power?

"SEEKING CHRISTIANS AND SPICES"

When the Portuguese mariner Vasco da Gama landed in India in 1497, the inhabitants asked him why he was there. "We come," he said, "seeking Christians and spices." That brief statement summed up the two primary motivations behind the European voyages of exploration: religion (the desire to find fellow Christians and convert "heathens" to their faith) and profit (the quest for valuable commodities that could not be produced at home, such as spices and gold).

As a result of the Crusades, European elites had acquired a taste for luxury goods such as silk from China, cotton from India, incense from Arabia, but above all the spices (pepper, cloves, cinnamon, nutmeg, and so on) that made salted, dried, and often rancid food more palatable. These commodities—small, light, easy to transport, and with huge profit margins—found their way to Europe by two basic routes. One was overland via the network of routes known as the "Silk Road" to the Black Sea, from where they would be transshipped to Italy for distribution throughout Europe. In the classical period, this commerce had been facilitated by the political stability of the empires that straddled the Eurasian landmass: from the Han Empire in China to the Parthian and then the Sassanian Empires in Persia and the Middle East, to the Roman Empire itself. The disruptions of the post-Classical period, including the fall of the western Roman Empire and prolonged instability among the nomadic tribes in central Asia and Eastern Europe, made travel and commerce along the Silk Road much more dangerous and difficult. A period of stability under the Mongol Empire in the thirteenth and fourteenth centuries restored communication between Europe and Asia, making possible the travels of Marco Polo and others, and creating a new appetite for Asian luxuries in Europe. But with the fragmentation of the Mongol Empire and the rise of the Ottoman Empire, which controlled the Black Sea and the eastern Mediterranean or Levant, overland trade fell dramatically. Thus European commerce with the Ottomans was conducted largely through Venetian merchants, who enjoyed a privileged relationship with them, as they had with the Byzantines in earlier times.

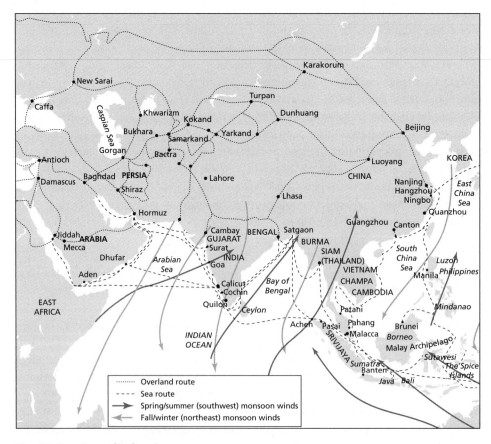

Map 5.1 Eurasian and Indian Ocean commerce

Goods also found their way to Europe from the Indian Ocean via the Red Sea and Persian Gulf. Regular commercial and cultural contact between the Middle East and East Africa, India, and China was encouraged by the seasonal monsoon winds, which blow from the southwest between April and September, facilitating voyages from East Africa to India and China, and in the opposite direction between October and March. From the Indian Ocean goods were shipped to Europe by way of the Red Sea and the Mediterranean, once more through lands controlled by the Ottomans. Since most of this trade was handled by the Venetians, there was a powerful economic incentive for other European merchants and sailors to find a different route to the riches of the east. It was no accident that many of the sailors who led the voyages of exploration, beginning in the late 1400s, were from Genoa, Venice's great rival in European commerce.

Another problem facing Europeans in their commerce with Asia was the fact that European economies produced nothing that Asians wanted. As a result, luxury imports had to be bought with gold and silver rather than exchanged for other commodities. Europeans knew that much of their gold came from mines in west Africa, in the powerful Kingdom of Mali, and passed through the fabled entrepôt of Timbuktu before making its way across the Sahara in caravans to the ports of North Africa and thence to Europe. By the fourteenth century, therefore, adventurous Europeans were attempting to reach the gold mines of west Africa by sea, though with little or no success.

Religious motivation came into play in several ways. European hostility to Islam had been more or less constant since the Crusades, and the militarism of the crusaders was still strong among European rulers and nobles. It was no accident that the pioneers in the European voyages of exploration were the Spanish and Portuguese, whose efforts to "reconquer" the Iberian peninsula put them in the front lines of the struggle against the Ottoman Empire, which by the late Middle Ages controlled the Black Sea and eastern Mediterranean.

The desire to outflank the Ottomans was heightened by the belief that somewhere to the east (possibly in Ethiopia or India, where Christian communities had existed since ancient times) was a powerful Christian empire ruled by "Prester John." If contact could be made with Prester John, European Christians could gain a powerful ally against the Muslim Ottomans. The desire to convert "heathens" to Christianity played a secondary role in the earliest voyages of exploration, but assumed greater importance later in the sixteenth century, in response to the spiritual revival of the Counter-Reformation and the new emphasis given to missionary work by orders such as the Jesuits.

Technology

If Europeans were to gain direct access to the lucrative Asian trade, their only real option was to sail west, via the Atlantic Ocean.[1] However, the winds in the European latitudes blow from the west, making sailing in that direction difficult and time-consuming. A series of technical improvements in shipbuilding and navigation in the later Middle Ages would facilitate the European voyages of exploration.

Many of these improvements were the work of anonymous craftsmen whose modifications in hull design and rigging made ships more manoeuvrable in the face of contrary winds. Because most medieval ships were rigged with square sails, they were quite efficient at sailing with the wind, but otherwise had to rely either on oars or on laborious tacking into the wind—activities that were manageable in the relatively protected waters of the Mediterranean, Baltic, or North Seas, but not in the rough waters and powerful winds of the open Atlantic. By the fifteenth century Portuguese sailors had begun rigging their ships with triangular lateen sails (adopted from the Arab *dhows* that plied the Indian Ocean) that were more effective for sailing into the wind. Likewise, the magnetic compass, developed first in China, made it easier for navigators to sail out of sight of land, while early versions of the sextant allowed sailors to calculate their latitude by plotting their position relative to the sun and the stars. (A reliable method of establishing longitude—the Holy Grail of navigation—had to await the development of an accurate chronometer in the eighteenth century.) The impact of these developments must not be overstated, however. They did not come into general use until the sixteenth century, by which time the European voyages of exploration were already well under way. Probably a more significant factor in the early Atlantic voyages was the steady accumulation of practical knowledge regarding winds and coastlines compiled by successive generations of sailors and navigators as they ventured ever farther from known waters.

Early Voyages

The first steps in Europe's "discovery" of the globe were undertaken by the Iberian kingdoms of Portugal and Castile, situated on the Atlantic coast that, since the Mediterranean was controlled by the Ottomans, represented Europe's only maritime access to the rest of the world. Well before the first voyages to the New World, Portugal and Castile had ventured westward into the Atlantic. The Canary Islands, vaguely known to the ancients but later forgotten, were rediscovered in the late Middle Ages, and after brutally subduing the islands' indigenous people, the Castilian crown asserted its authority over them in the late fifteenth century. The uninhabited island of Madeira was claimed by the Portuguese crown in the 1420s and colonized by Portuguese settlers who introduced sugarcane and imported slaves from west Africa to cultivate it. Two other uninhabited island groups, the Azores and the Cape Verde Islands, were claimed and colonized by the Portuguese in the fifteenth century. These islands served not only as forward bases for further Atlantic exploration but as training grounds for further overseas expansion. Madeira, for example, gave the Portuguese a template for using African slaves to grow sugarcane on large plantations, while the process of subjugating the Canary Islanders gave Castilian *conquistadors* experience that they would draw on when they encountered hostile populations in the New World.

The fact that the kingdoms of Portugal and Castile were on the front lines of the *Reconquista* meant that their ruling elites were steeped in the crusading mentality. Throughout the fifteenth century, Castile was in conflict with Granada, the last outpost of Muslim power in Iberia, and would finally defeat it in 1492, not coincidentally the year of Columbus's first voyage. Although Portugal's territorial reconquest had been completed centuries earlier, Muslim power in North Africa still remained a concern and a threat.

In 1415 a Portuguese force crossed the Straits of Gibraltar and captured the Muslim port of Ceuta, from which pirates had been raiding the Portuguese coast. Its commander was Prince Henry (1394–1460), a younger son of King John I (r. 1385–1438). This mission ignited a passion for exploration in the young prince, who went on to support a series of voyages into the Atlantic and along the coast of West Africa, for which he later became known as Henry the Navigator, although he personally did not go on these voyages. To assist his captains in navigation, he sponsored and supported cartographers, astronomers, and mathematicians. He also accelerated the adoption of the caravel, rigged with lateen sails for greater maneuverability into the wind. (Eventually they would be equipped with both square and lateen sails, the best of both worlds.) The driving force behind the colonization of Madeira, the Azores, and the Cape Verde Islands, Henry was motivated by religious zeal as well as thirst for the resources of Africa, primarily gold and slaves. In the course of these voyages, fortresses and trading posts were established at several strategic locations. At some point Henry realized that it might be possible to reach Asia by sailing south around Africa, and in 1488 (well after his death), Bartolomeu Dias did succeed in rounding the Cape of Good Hope before contrary winds and a fearful crew forced him to turn back.[2] In 1497, Vasco da Gama (c. 1460–1524) led a Portuguese expedition around the southern tip of Africa, up its eastern coast, and across the Arabian Sea to the southwestern coast of India.

The key figure in the Castilian voyages of exploration, of course, was Christopher Columbus (1450/51–1506). The son of a Genoese weaver, he went to sea as a young man and eventually became involved in the trade with the Portuguese Atlantic islands and West Africa. Based on his reading of various ancient geographical treatises and accounts of medieval travellers, he became convinced that it was possible to reach Asia by sailing

© INTERFOTO / Alamy Stock Photo

A Portuguese caravel

west across the Atlantic. Although he was unable to interest King John II of Portugal (r. 1481–95) in his scheme, he eventually gained the support of Isabella of Castile and Ferdinand of Aragon by emphasizing the opportunity such a voyage offered to further the cause of Christianity.

Two major miscalculations led Columbus to believe that the voyage to Asia would be relatively short. First, based on his reading of ancient geographers, primarily Ptolemy (whose *Geography* had been rediscovered by fifteenth-century humanists), he underestimated the circumference of the globe by about one-third. Second, his reading of medieval travellers such as Marco Polo led him to overestimate the eastward distance between Europe and Asia, and therefore to underestimate the westward distance he would have to sail to reach it.

Columbus left Castile with three small ships in August 1492. After provisioning in the Canary Islands, they sailed for five weeks before making their first landfall, probably in the Bahamas, on October 12. Believing that he had reached Asia, and that the riches of the east were just over the horizon, he called the islands he encountered the "Indies," and their inhabitants "Indians." He was to persist in that belief through three more voyages (1493, 1498, and 1502), in the course of which he explored the Caribbean and the northern coast of South America and claimed the lands he encountered for Ferdinand and Isabella.

In some ways, Columbus died a failure. Despite overwhelming evidence, he refused to acknowledge that he had not reached Asia. An attempted settlement on Hispaniola (the island currently shared by Haiti and the Dominican Republic) struggled mightily. The gold he hoped to find never materialized on any scale during his lifetime. He allowed his subordinates to massacre and enslave the people with whom they came into contact, even though Ferdinand and Isabella had decreed that they must be protected. He was not only replaced as governor of Hispaniola but briefly imprisoned, and his death in 1506, in the Spanish city of Valladolid, passed unnoticed by the civic chronicler. Yet the significance of his accomplishments was enormous. The establishment of the first known contact between the Old World and the New was a watershed in world history.[3] Columbus discovered and exploited the wind patterns and currents that governed most trans-Atlantic travel until the advent of steam power in the nineteenth century. Ships leaving Europe would sail southwest until they caught the prevailing northeasterly trade winds that would take them to the Caribbean. On the return journey, they would follow the Gulf Stream northeast until they caught the prevailing westerlies, which blew them eastwards back to Europe.

By the time Columbus had returned to Spain, Portugal was already disputing Spain's right to the lands he had claimed for Ferdinand and Isabella. Asked to mediate, the Spanish Pope Alexander VI ruled in 1493 that Castile had exclusive rights to land west of a line drawn in what was believed to be the middle of the Atlantic, and granted lands to the east of the line to Portugal. Before this arrangement was formalized in the Treaty of Tordesillas (1494), the line was moved a few degrees farther west, with the result that Portugal would be able to lay claim to Brazil in 1500, when a Portuguese expedition to the East Indies, led by Pedro Alvares Cabral, was blown off course and landed on the east coast of South

America. (Earlier generations of Portuguese sailors had discovered that rather than hug the coast of Africa in the face of contrary winds, it was more efficient to sail far to the southwest into the open Atlantic, from where westerly winds would eventually take them around the southern tip of Africa.)

Even though Portugal had a monopoly to the east of the line, the Portuguese captain Ferdinand Magellan (1480?–1521) shared Columbus's conviction that a westward route to Asia was more practical than da Gama's eastern route, and he managed to convince King Charles I of Spain (Holy Roman Emperor Charles V) to sponsor him. Setting sail in 1519, he travelled across the Atlantic and around South America into the Pacific Ocean (which he so named because it seemed more peaceful than the turbulent Atlantic). But Magellan himself was killed in a battle with the people of what we know as the Philippines, and by the time a handful of survivors finally returned to Spain in 1522, completing the first circumnavigation of the globe, it was clear that the westward route to Asia was not practical after all.

Mariners from other countries soon joined the quest for a westward route to Asia, and they found support at the courts of rulers eager to gain a slice of the potential riches for themselves, the Treaty of Tordesillas notwithstanding. In 1496, another Genoese captain named Giovanni Caboto, anglicized as John Cabot (c. 1450–c. 1499), obtained a commission from Henry VII of England to find a northwestern route to Asia. Instead, he found the island that we know as Newfoundland, and rather than spices or gold, he discovered the vast cod stocks of the Grand Banks, which would draw fishermen from France, Spain, and Portugal, as well as England.

Amerigo Vespucci (1454–1512) was a Florentine cartographer and explorer who participated in several Portuguese and Spanish voyages across the Atlantic. These expeditions established that South America extended much further south than Columbus had thought, and Vespucci was convinced that rather than outlying Asian islands, Europeans had discovered a heretofore unknown continent that lay between Asia and Europe. In a series of letters and accounts attributed to Vespucci, he claimed to have established the existence of a "New World" (Latin *Mundus Novus*). Whatever his actual accomplishments, the discovery of this New World was attributed to Vespucci, and in 1507 the German cartographer Martin Waldseemüller named this continent "America" after the Latin form of Vespucci's name, Americus.[4]

Yet another Italian captain in the service of a northern European monarch was Giovanni da Verrazzano (1485–1528), who obtained the backing of King Francis I of France to find a route to Asia. In 1524 he encountered the mainland of North America and established that the lands discovered by Columbus and the "new founde land" discovered by Cabot, were in fact contiguous. He was followed by Jacques Cartier, a Breton sailor who made three voyages between 1534 and 1542 to explore the Gulf of St. Lawrence and the St. Lawrence River as far upstream as Hochelaga (modern Montreal). That he was searching for a passage to Asia is borne out by the name he gave to a series of rapids near Montreal: "Lachine." However, further French exploration was forestalled by the Habsburg wars and religious conflict that preoccupied France for the rest of century.

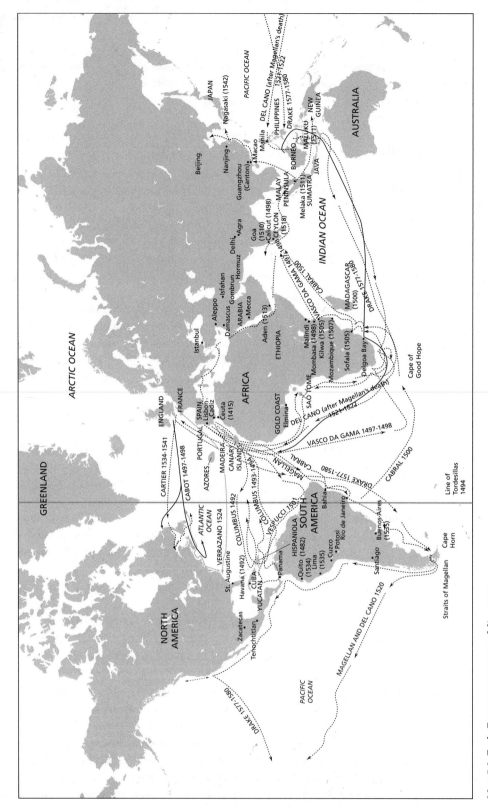

Map 5.2 Early European voyages of discovery

By about 1550 it was clear that what Columbus and his followers had discovered was in fact a previously unknown landmass, and that sailing around its southern perimeter to Asia, as Magellan had done, was impractical. Thus attention shifted to the search for a northwest passage, which was to preoccupy mariners for several centuries. Although the early voyages and discoveries were greeted with enthusiasm, their initial results must have disappointed sailors and rulers alike. Columbus's claims to have discovered vast gold deposits were not immediately borne out, and codfish, however abundant, were a poor substitute for the exotic riches that Europeans had dreamed of. There were a few attempts at settlement (see below), but almost all of them were defeated by eiher harsh living conditions or hostile indigenous people.

Consequences: Global Networks

With the early voyages to Asia and the New World, Europeans and the peoples they encountered began to form a global network that would be characterized by the exchange of goods, ideas, technologies, flora and fauna, diseases, and people. When Europeans established contact with the "New World," vast stretches of the Americas were inhabited by tribal groups living a "Stone Age" hunter-gatherer existence. While of course there were (and had been) sophisticated civilizations in the Americas, communication between them had been limited by geography. By contrast, in the Old World, the middle latitudes of North Africa and Eurasia had supported a variety of civilizations that had been in direct or indirect contact since antiquity. As a consequence, different societies had been able to learn from one another. Thus Europeans, as we have seen, were able to take advantage of Chinese inventions such as gunpowder, paper, and the magnetic compass, of Arabic scholarship, and so on. New World civilizations had not had the same opportunities to benefit from cultural cross-pollination. Consequently, although civilizations such as the Maya were very advanced in some areas, such as mathematics and astronomy, in others they were less advanced than Europeans. (For example, although the Mayans made wheeled toys or models, they did not have wheeled transportation.) As a result, the direction of the exchange that began when Columbus landed in the New World was largely from east to west, across the Atlantic from the Old World to the New.

The Columbian Exchange

The term "Columbian Exchange" was introduced in 1972, when the historian Alfred W. Crosby used it to refer to the profound biological and cultural consequences of the exchange between Europe and the Americas that began in 1492. The most tragic consequence was one of the earliest: the transfer of European diseases to American populations that had no immunity to them. By 1500, Eurasian societies had been living in close proximity both to one another and to domesticated animals such as cattle, pigs, and sheep for several millennia, and thus had acquired some immunity to a wide range of diseases. In the New World, however, the majority of people lived in relatively isolated conditions, either as nomadic hunter-gatherers or in small farming villages scattered across a vast landscape, and therefore had no experience of the kinds of diseases that were endemic to Europeans.

The most lethal and terrifying of those diseases was smallpox. Even in Europe, it killed between 30 and 50 per cent of its victims, but since 80 per cent of its victims were under the age of ten, immunity in adult populations was widespread. In the New World, however, all it took was one infected person to spread the disease to a virgin population. An incubation period of ten to fourteen days meant that a carrier could travel a long distance before becoming symptomatic, and thus smallpox easily reached populations that had never seen a European.

The results were catastrophic. The indigenous population of the West Indies was wiped out by the 1540s, and that of Mexico declined from an estimated 27 million to about 1 million in the course of the sixteenth century. Between 1500 and 1620, the population of Peru fell from roughly 7 million to about 500,000. As European explorers worked their way inland, therefore, they encountered vast spaces inhabited by very small numbers of people, which led them to the erroneous conclusion that the land was an unclaimed wilderness that was theirs for the taking. More than a few saw divine providence at work. John Winthrop, the first governor of the Massachusetts Bay Colony, would write: "For the natives, they are all neere dead of small Poxe, so as the Lord hathe cleared our title to what we possess."[5] Other pathogens that made voyage to the New World included measles, malaria, yellow fever, typhus, and influenza. The only disease that travelled in the other direction was syphilis, which attracted a good deal of attention in Europe, but was hardly a threat to entire populations.

The effects of such mass mortality were catastrophic. Indigenous populations were demoralized, and their will to resist shattered. Bewildered survivors often fled, inadvertently spreading disease. Social and economic networks were destroyed and religious beliefs were undermined. In short, European conquest was only partly a matter of warfare.

In addition to disease, Europeans introduced many new animals to the New World, some intentionally and some by accident. Among the former were cattle, horses, sheep, pigs, and chickens. Although most of these domestic species did not survive very long when they escaped captivity, pigs, cattle, and horses were able to establish breeding populations in the wild, with lasting consequences for the environment of the Americas. Foremost among the inadvertent introductions were black and brown rats, which reproduced at astonishing rates. In the other direction, the only notable introduction from the New World to the Old was the turkey, which has never established a wild population in either Eurasia or Africa.

The exchange was less one-sided in the case of plants. In addition to wheat, barley, rye, olives, wine grapes, and apples, Europeans introduced bananas, coffee, and coconuts from Africa and sugarcane, which had originated in south and southeast Asia. Among the American crops transplanted to Europe were corn (maize), potatoes, tomatoes (long thought to be poisonous), peppers, sweet potatoes, peanuts, manioc, chocolate, pineapples, and avocadoes. Tobacco too was an American plant that was to have an enormous impact on European culture.

EMPIRE AND TRADE, SETTLEMENT AND CONQUEST

Another consequence of the European voyages of exploration was the development of a global trade network. Whereas in Africa and Asia, Europeans reoriented trade patterns of very long standing, in the New World the process of establishing commercial networks involved conquest and settlement on a scale that was neither practical nor necessary elsewhere.

Within decades of reaching India, the Portuguese had established a network of fortresses and trading posts at strategic chokepoints around the Indian Ocean and in East Asia: Goa (1510), Malacca (1511), Hormuz (1515), as well as in Sri Lanka and Mozambique. Although they did establish a colonial presence in Brazil, where sugarcane would eventually be cultivated by African slaves on large plantations, that was the exception. The majority of Portugal's overseas possessions were intended not for settlement, or even to establish control of large territories, but to control the lucrative trade in Asian goods; theirs was a "trading-post empire." Even though Portugal was a small and poor country, it had an important advantage in its fleet of highly manoeuvrable caravels, heavily armed with cannon, which Asian states could not easily duplicate. In addition, the Portuguese were able to exploit rivalries between Asian rulers, and often used intimidation or violence to appropriate parts of the inter-Asian "country trade"; the proceeds from the latter were then used to purchase Asian goods for sale in Europe.

The wealth generated by Asian trade soon attracted other competitors, including the VOC (East India Company), which functioned as a semi-autonomous agent of the infant Dutch government. In the course of the seventeenth century, the Dutch eclipsed the Portuguese as the major European players in Asian trade. In time, the trading posts that the VOC established in the East Indies would become the foundations of the Dutch East Indies (roughly modern Indonesia). In order to resupply ships on the long voyage to the Indies, the Dutch also established a port near the Cape of Good Hope that would become the city of Cape Town in South Africa.

An English East India Company had been founded in 1600 and competed with the VOC for control of the East Indies trade, but it never successfully challenged Dutch supremacy in the East Indies. Therefore it turned its attention to China and, in particular, India, where it eventually prevailed over the French East India Company (founded in 1664) and became the dominant political force on the subcontinent, using its wealth and commercial influence to gain control not only of territory but of Indian rulers.

Although European merchants managed to insert themselves into Asian and Indian Ocean commerce, migration from Europe to Asia and Africa remained numerically insignificant. Tropical diseases took a large toll on newcomers who lacked immunity to them, and many overseas possessions were peopled by criminals and beggars who were forcibly relocated to them. Since few European women made the difficult voyage to the east, in time significant mixed-race populations developed in places such as Batavia (modern Jakarta), Goa in India, and Macao.

The situation was quite different in the New World, where most societies were at a less advanced stage of development and even the most sophisticated civilizations lacked any equivalent to European firearms and cavalry (the horse was unknown in the Americas). Very shortly after establishing themselves on Caribbean islands such as Cuba and Hispaniola, Spanish explorers and soldiers began to explore the mainland. These *conquistadors* were for the most part members of Castile's lower nobility who saw in the New World opportunities for wealth, status, and glory that they could never have achieved at home. In 1519 Hernán Cortés (1485–1547) led a small expedition (about 600 men) from Cuba to

Mexico, where by 1521 he had conquered the mighty Aztec empire. Among the factors that made this possible were the alliances he formed with the Aztecs' restive subject populations, without whom his tiny force could never have succeeded, and the rapid spread of diseases such as smallpox, whose victims included the last two Aztec rulers. In 1531, when Francisco Pizarro (1478?–1541) invaded the Incan Empire of the Andes, he too had the benefit of epidemic disease. In addition, Inca resistance was weakened by a disputed succession and civil war. Nevertheless, the imposition of Spanish power would not be complete until the 1570s.

In Mexico and Peru the conquerors found gold and especially silver beyond their imaginations. Productive sources of ore were found at Zacatecas in central Mexico and above all at Potosí in Peru. The quest for more led to further exploration into Central and South America, northern Mexico, and what is now the southwestern US as far north as Kansas.

Together, the decimation of indigenous populations and the lack of economic infrastructure in the Americas meant that the Europeans seeking to exploit their riches faced a fundamentally different situation from the one their counterparts faced in Africa or Asia. Since there were not enough indigenous people to work the mines and sugar plantations, manual labour would have to be imported from abroad, along with more skilled workers to supervise them and build and operate the infrastructure required to transport their products to Europe. All these people—slaves, supervisors, soldiers, sailors, workers—had to be fed, requiring farms and agricultural labour.

As a result, European migration to the New World was more extensive than to Africa or Asia. By the early seventeenth century, between 3000 and 4000 Spaniards left for the New World every year, while about 2000 Portuguese left for Brazil annually, out of a much smaller population than Spain. Most of these were young single men seeking either escape from unfortunate circumstances such as imprisonment or debt, or opportunities and status that were unavailable at home. Settlers of higher status, including the *conquistadors* and their relatives, were granted large estates through a system known as *encomienda*, which gave them rights not only to land but to the labour of indigenous people.

In the New World, the Spanish conquerors either founded new settlements or remade existing ones. Thus Tenochtitlan, the massive Aztec capital, was transformed into the Spanish colonial city of Mexico, while Lima, on the Peruvian coast, was established by Pizarro to replace the Incas' inland capital of Cuzco. On the island of Cuba, Havana became the principal port for trade with Spain and the transport hub of Spanish America. Once a year, the Spanish treasure fleet would assemble in Havana to transport each year's production of gold and silver to Spain. On Mexico's Pacific coast Acapulco was the departure point for a Pacific fleet that took bullion to the Philippines, where it was used to pay for Asian imports.

Efforts by other European countries to defy the Treaty of Tordesillas and share in the wealth of the New World almost all failed. A large part of the problem was that the wealthiest indigenous civilizations in Mexico and Peru had already been occupied by the Spanish. Although a French colony in Brazil, established in 1555, lasted more than a decade and attracted a number of Huguenots fleeing the religious turmoil in France, they were driven off by the Portuguese in 1567. Similarly, the Spanish scuttled a short-lived settlement attempt by Huguenots in Florida in 1565.

The lands to the north were free of Spanish and Portuguese settlers, but no more hospitable to newcomers. On his third voyage to North America, in 1541, Jacques Cartier carried 400 prospective colonists to the Iroquoian territory on the St. Lawrence, near modern Cap-Rouge, where they established a settlement named Charlesbourg-Royal. But in the face of a harsh climate, disease, hunger, and hostile relations with the indigenous people, the settlement was abandoned two years later.

French exploration was virtually halted by the religious wars of the later sixteenth century, but picked up once peace had been restored. Under the leadership of Samuel de Champlain (1574–1635) French settlements were established settlements at both Port-Royal (1605) in what is now Nova Scotia, and Quebec (1608), which became the centre of the lucrative fur trade. In addition, Champlain was the first European to explore the Great Lakes region, and he established alliances with several indigenous peoples against their Iroquoian enemies. Meanwhile, although the French had been active in the burgeoning seasonal fishery off Newfoundland since the early 1500s, they had not established any permanent settlement there: like all the European fishermen who worked the Grand Banks, they merely set up temporary camps on the shoreline to salt and dry their catch. Permanent European settlements were not necessary for either fisheries or the fur trade; indeed, they were in some ways detrimental, as they complicated relations with the indigenous populations whose knowledge and cooperation were essential. The colonies of New France would languish until the 1660s, when the mercantilist policies of Jean-Baptiste Colbert would place a greater value on exploitation of colonial raw materials for the benefit of the mother country rather than of individual explorers and merchants.

The English too sought a piece of New World wealth for themselves. War with Spain in the later sixteenth century legitimized privateering raids on Spanish shipping and settlements in the Caribbean, and Drake himself harried the Spanish in the Pacific while circumnavigating the globe in 1579. Establishing colonies was a more difficult proposition, however. Although Humphrey Gilbert claimed possession of Newfoundland for Elizabeth I in 1583, he made no attempt to found a settlement at the time, and was lost at sea a few weeks later. Gilbert had also been involved in organizing and financing the first English settlement in the New World: established in 1585, the Roanoke colony in what is now North Carolina received more than a hundred settlers in 1587, but by 1590 they had all disappeared, and their fate has remained a mystery. Thus England's first lasting settlement was the Virginia colony at Jamestown, established in 1607 by a private company with a royal charter. By 1624, however, inadequate resources and conflict with the local people threatened the colony's survival: thus the royal charter was revoked and Virginia became the first royal colony, under the direct control of the government. Meanwhile, various groups of Protestant dissenters or Puritans had begun establishing settlements in Massachusetts. By 1630, therefore, several English settlements had been established on the east coast of North America, although their continued existence was by no means guaranteed.

The Dutch too were establishing footholds in the New World in this period. The New Netherland colony began with a fort near what is now Albany, New York, established in 1615, and construction of New Amsterdam, on Manhattan Island, began ten years later.

The colony was something a of poor stepchild in the Dutch commercial empire, however, and its population never reached more than about 5000 before 1664, when it was captured by the English and renamed New York. In South America, the Dutch controlled much of northern Brazil from 1630 to 1654, when they were forced out by the Portuguese. In 1668, under the Treaty of Breda, they gave up their claim to New York in exchange for the colony of Suriname, on the northeast coast of South America.

No European ruler or country in the sixteenth or seventeenth century contemplated large-scale colonization of the New World, although that is what eventually occurred. Settlements might be necessary to extract the wealth and resources from overseas possessions, but they were always a means rather than an end: the interests of the homeland took priority. For example, Spain's trade with its American possessions was legally a monopoly in which all trade passed through the port of Seville. Colonists were legally forbidden to engage in any other trade, even with other Spanish colonies, let alone with French, English, Portuguese, or Dutch merchants. The same was generally true of other European colonies. Dutch settlers in New Amsterdam were excluded from the fur trade, in order to privilege the merchants of the mother country. These monopolies were routinely violated, however, and smuggling was widespread. That European settlements in the New World would eventually develop a sense of their own identity and interests was completely unanticipated and unwelcome. But these developments were still far in the future.

SUGAR AND SLAVERY

Probably no commodity had a more dramatic effect on European and American societies than sugar. It quickly became the most important product in trans-Atlantic trade, and its economic importance was comparable to that of the oil industry today. Its quasi-addictive nature remade European taste, and its ready availability and decreasing cost ensured continual demand. The practicalities of growing and processing sugar had a profound impact not only in the Americas, but worldwide.

Although sugarcane requires a hot and humid climate, by the later Middle Ages it was being cultivated in Sicily, Cyprus, and Crete as well as Madeira. But its limited supply and high cost made it a luxury commodity, and it was often seen more as a drug than as food. Columbus had immediately seen the New World's potential for sugar cultivation, which was introduced on Hispaniola by 1515. Although Portuguese Brazil soon became the epicentre of the industry, in time other European nations established their own plantations on islands such as Cuba, Jamaica, Barbados, and Martinique.

Growing and processing sugarcane was both capital- and labour-intensive, requiring economies of scale, as well as difficult and dangerous work that few Europeans would undertake voluntarily. Large plantations and slavery therefore became intimately associated with its cultivation from an early date. Since the decimation of indigenous populations in the Americas meant that they could not supply the required labour, and Spanish law in theory prohibited the enslavement of indigenous peoples, the demand was ultimately met with African slaves.

Well before the discovery of the New World, sub-Saharan slave traders, mainly Muslim Arabs, had been supplying black African slaves to places around the Indian Ocean and Mediterranean. But the extent of the demand from the Americas expanded the trade many times over, especially as the plantation model was extended to the cultivation of commodities such as coffee, cotton, and indigo: between 1450 and 1800, approximately 10 million Africans were enslaved for transport to the New World. The consequences for African society were devastating, including warfare and weakened political structures, in addition to the destruction of families.

Slavery in the New World bore little resemblance to slavery as it was known in Europe, where relatively small numbers of slaves were engaged mostly in household duties. Although black African slaves were not unknown in Europe, especially in Spain and Portugal, the overwhelming predominance of Africans in this new form of slavery helped to reinforce contemporary notions of their innate inferiority. The extensive commerce in slaves to the Americas was one leg of the triangular Atlantic trade network that would become so important in the development of the European economy in the eighteenth century (see Chapter 11).

NEW PEOPLES

Historians' understanding of the encounters between Europeans and the peoples of the New World have been revolutionized since the 1960s. Commemorations of the four hundredth anniversary of Columbus' voyage in 1892 hailed him as a hero who took the blessings of European civilization to the primitive inhabitants of the New World. A century later the explorer was condemned as the harbinger of imperialism and genocide.

In recent decades our understanding of Europeans' encounters with indigenous populations has been fundamentally reoriented by the development of what has been called "postcolonial" or "subaltern" history. The latter term, introduced by the Italian cultural theorist Antonio Gramsci (1891–1937), refers to groups excluded from the dominant group, and initially referred specifically to the subject peoples of European colonial powers; today, however, it is also applied to groups in the homeland or "metropole" who have been similarly marginalized because of their race, class, culture, or gender. Some historians have also been influenced by literary theories such as "deconstructionism" or "post structuralism." The "linguistic turn" in historiography draws attention to the unreliable nature of historical sources that in fact reveal only their creators' perceptions of historical reality. At the extreme, this approach can lead to the denial that there is any objective historical reality to be perceived.

Thus post-colonial theorists point out how often European explorers' accounts of indigenous peoples present them as fundamentally "other," emphasizing their strangeness and even inhumanity, and thereby justifying their subjugation.[6] Different cultural practices and religious beliefs raised questions that Europeans had not confronted before. Were these people truly human? Did they have souls? If they were unknown to the writers of the Bible, where did they fit into God's divine plan? On one hand, the accounts of Columbus and his successors praised the people of the New World as creatures of childlike innocence and purity. On the other, in many cases they also described practices such as cannibalism and human sacrifice. Some scholars have argued that these accounts were invented by Europeans to justify the theft of indigenous lands and the abrogation of indigenous people's rights. On the other hand, as David Abulafia puts it,

> [t]o argue that the American cannibals were a fiction, or indeed that all cannibalism is just an exercise in Western humiliation of subject peoples, is to ignore the detailed and persistent evidence from European visitors to South America, where

VOICES

The Valladolid Debate

In 1550, King Charles I of Spain (Holy Roman Emperor Charles V) ordered a debate to determine whether it was legal to make war on the people of the New World in order to convert them to Christianity. The principals in this debate, held in the city of Valladolid before a panel of judges, were Bartolomé de las Casas (1484–1566), and Juan Ginés de Sepúlveda (1489–1573). Las Casas was a priest, the first Bishop of Chiapas in Mexico, who had emerged as the chief defender of the indigenous people, whom he saw as childlike, innocent victims of Spanish rapacity. Sepúlveda was a humanist, lawyer, and theologian who had never been to the New World, but based his argument on the writings of Gonzalo Fernández de Oviedo (1478–1557), a colonial administrator whose *General History of the Indies* portrayed its people in a very unflattering light. Unfortunately, there is no record of the judges' decision on the debate.

From Sepúlveda:

> In prudence, talent, virtue, and humanity they [the Indians] are as inferior to the Spaniards as children are to adults, women to men, as the wild and cruel to the most meek, as the prodigiously intemperate to the continent and temperate . . . as monkeys to men. . . .
>
> [They] not only lack culture but do not even know how to write, . . . keep no records of their own history except certain obscure and vague reminiscences of some things put down in certain pictures, and . . . do not have written laws but only barbarous institutions and customs. . . . [W]hat can you expect from men who were involved in every kind of intemperance and wicked lust and who used to eat human flesh? . . .
>
> The greatest philosophers declare that such wars may be undertaken by a very civilized nation against uncivilized people who are more barbarous than can be imagined, for they are absolutely lacking in any knowledge of letters, do not know the use of money, generally go about naked, even the women, and carry burdens on their shoulders and backs just like beasts for great distances.
>
> The proof of their savage life, similar to that of beasts, may be seen in the execrable and prodigious sacrifices of human victims to their devils . . . and in other crimes condemned by natural law, whose description offends the ears and horrifies the spirit of civilized people. They on the contrary do these terrible things in public and consider

very similar practices were documented by independent observers throughout the sixteenth century and into modern times."[7]

Learned commentators also expressed a variety of opinions on these issues and how Europeans ought to address them. Some, echoing Aristotle, thought that peoples who did not possess the elements of a "civilized" society, such as cities, a recognizable political

---

them pious acts. The protection of innocent persons from such injurious acts may alone give us the right, already granted by God and nature, to wage war against these barbarians to submit them to Spanish rule.

From las Casas' response:

. . . the Creator of every being has not so despised these peoples of the New World that he willed them to lack reason and made them like brute animals, so that they should be called barbarians, savages, wild men, and brutes. . . . On the contrary, they are of such gentleness and decency that they are, more than the other nations of the entire world, supremely fitted and prepared to abandon the worship of idols and to accept . . . the word of God and the preaching of the truth.

The worshippers of idols . . . have never heard the teaching of the Christian truth even through hearsay; so they sin less than the Jews or Saracens [Muslims], for ignorance excuses to some small extent. . . .

Therefore, since the Church does not punish the unbelief of the Jews . . . , much less will it punish idolaters who inhabit an immense portion of the earth . . . who have never been subjects of either the Church or her members, and who have not even known what the Church is.

. . . those who willingly allow themselves to be sacrificed, and all the common people in general, and the ministers who sacrifice them to the gods by command of their rulers and priests labor under an excusable, invincible ignorance and . . . their error should be judged leniently, even if we were to suppose that there is some judge with authority to punish these sins. If they offend God by these sacrifices, he alone will punish this sin of human sacrifice.

Now if Christians unsettle everything by wars, burnings, fury, rashness, fierceness, sedition, plunder, and insurrection, where is meekness? . . . Where are the holy deeds that should move the hearts of the pagans to glorify God? . . . I cannot overcome my amazement that a learned man, a priest, an older person, and a theologian should offer deadly poisons of this type to the world from his unsettled mind.

From Lewis Hanke, *All Mankind is One: A Study of the Disputation Between Bartolomé de las Casas and Juan Ginés de Sepúlveda in 1550 on the Intellectual and Religious Capacity of the American Indians* (DeKalb: Northern Illinois University Press, 1974), pp. 82–97. With permission from Northern Illinois University Press. Copyright © 1974. Copyright Northern Illinois University Press.

structure, and a formal religion, with an organizational structure ("church" or "temple") and personnel ("clergy" or "priests") were "natural slaves," and that even if they were not actually enslaved, they could be treated as savages until they adopted "civilized" ways, including Christianity. Others believed that even "barbarians" had the right to govern themselves, as long as they observed the principles of natural law.

By what right did Europeans seize control of indigenous peoples' land? The rulers of Spain and Portugal pointed to the papal grant in the Treaty of Tordesillas, arguing that the pope's role as God's representative on earth put all peoples under his jurisdiction. Others pointed to the medieval principle of "just war," particularly in the case of groups that practised human sacrifice, such as the Aztecs. There was also a widespread sense that apparently unoccupied territory should be put to productive use.

Before her death in 1504, Queen Isabella had declared that the inhabitants of the lands claimed in her name were her subjects, and therefore not to be mistreated or enslaved unless they practised cannibalism or refused to convert to Christianity. This was one of the factors (along with the decimation of local populations) behind the reliance on African slaves in the New World. It will surprise no one, however, that such principles were frequently ignored.

These issues were confronted first and most squarely by the Spanish, as they were the first to acquire extensive territories in the Americas. Other Europeans in this early phase did not consider them so systematically. For one thing, many European settlement projects in the Caribbean and North America were private initiatives, and although they had government charters, they were not necessarily subject to government policy. For another, since most of these settlements were preoccupied above all with survival, they tended to treat the indigenous people around them as local circumstances dictated: sometimes as allies on whose assistance they depended (this was certainly the case in the fur trade), and sometimes as enemies from whom they could take whatever they wanted.

RELIGION

Although the captains who sailed for Portugal's Henry the Navigator were provided with letters of introduction to the legendary Christian ruler Prester John, missionary activity was not a major part of the early Portuguese voyages. By the later sixteenth century, however, the Catholic Reformation had sparked a new zeal for missionary work in Portugal and Spain. In contrast, Protestant powers had little interest in foreign missions, as they lacked the long proselytizing traditions of the Catholics as well as the religious orders that provided most of the impetus and personnel.

The religious order most interested in foreign missions was the Society of Jesus. By 1542, the Jesuit Francis Xavier had arrived in Goa in Portuguese India, and after three years there he travelled first to Indonesia and then to Japan by 1549. Japanese rulers initially supported the Jesuits' efforts, and by 1600 the country had as many as 300,000 Christians. In 1614, however, a new regime outlawed Christianity as part of a broader program to isolate Japan from the outside world. Missionaries were less successful in other parts of Asia, where converts came under suspicion as agents of foreign influence.

Jesuit missionaries were also present in China at an early date, but to reach the educated classes, they first had to master the language and the Confucian classics. As we will see in Chapter 9, the fact that Jesuit missionaries in China were willing to accommodate some Chinese beliefs and practices, such as ancestor veneration, attracted criticism from other orders.

In Africa Christian missions achieved only limited success. Portuguese missionaries did convert the ruler of the central African Kingdom of Kongo in the fifteenth century, and an indigenous church was established. But their lack of immunity to tropical diseases was a severe problem for European missionaries in Africa, many of whom lost their lives. In addition, large parts of sub-Saharan and especially East Africa were solidly Muslim, and the establishment of the transatlantic slave trade turned many Africans against Christianity.

In Spanish America, and to a lesser extent in Portuguese Brazil, the conversion of indigenous populations to Christianity was a declared aim of the royal government. In some cases the people voluntarily adopted the victorious religion of the conquerors. In others, however, conversion was more or less forced—an issue that caused considerable controversy within the Church and the orders who furnished most of the missionaries. From an institutional point of view, the Christianization project was a huge success: across Spanish America, indigenous religions were largely suppressed, along with human sacrifice, cannibalism, and polygamy, and their former practitioners brought into the Catholic fold. On the other hand, especially outside the major centres, Christianity was often a thin veneer over indigenous traditions. The Catholic Church had converted many "pagan" peoples in the course of the Middle Ages, and was well aware that incorporating some elements of native beliefs and culture could ease the transition.

In North America, the conversion project was later getting started and was never as systematic, partly because European settlements were much smaller and more vulnerable than their South American counterparts, and partly because religion was not a priority for the governments in question. Jesuit missionaries were active around the Great Lakes in the seventeenth century, but they never enjoyed the unalloyed support of the French government. Nor did England make conversion an official policy, although there were individual missionaries in its colonies.

SUMMARY

By the middle of the seventeenth century, Europe was no longer an isolated outpost on the western fringe of Eurasia, but was increasingly integrated into a global network of trade, commodities, ideas, and people. The flow of people from the Old World to the New, although it transformed the Americas, was insignificant in Europe, at least in numerical terms. By about 1700, when France alone had roughly 20 million people, the total population of European descent in the Americas amounted to no more than 2 million.[8] In Central and South America, increasingly distinct colonial Spanish and Portuguese societies were flourishing, while in North America the footholds established by England and France were still tenuous. Although the implications of these developments were barely beginning to be felt in Europe, that would change over the next 150 years. Through the military and economic dominance made possible largely by the transfer of wealth from the New World to the Old, Europe would become the centre of the emerging global network. These issues will be explored further in Chapter 11.

Discovering the World of Nature

At the same time that Europeans sailors, merchants, soldiers, and settlers were "discovering" the rest of the globe, European scholars were discovering new ways of understanding the natural world. Although not all historians of science agree that these discoveries amounted to a "Scientific Revolution" (see Debate box below), there can be no doubt that their impact was revolutionary.

Because science is such an integral part of the modern world, it can be hard to imagine any other state of affairs. For most of human history, however, most societies have had little interest in what we would call pure science: knowledge of the physical universe for its own sake. Naturally, people have taken a keen interest in applied science—learning how to predict the seasons for agricultural and ceremonial purposes, sail the oceans, mine ore, build houses, and so on. As long as the prevailing scientific theory was sufficient for the task at hand, however, there was little interest in questioning it.

The science of medieval Christendom was based on the views of the ancient Greeks as transmitted by Roman and Muslim scholars. In every field, from astronomy and mathematics to medicine, biology, and chemistry, ancient authority was understood to be virtually unquestionable. This began to change in the first half of the sixteenth century, however, and by the later seventeenth century there was very little left of the scientific theories that had been accepted for two thousand years. The changes were most dramatic in the realms of astronomy and physics, but there were also significant developments in medicine and chemistry.

To properly understand these phenomena, we need to rid ourselves of several misconceptions, beginning with the idea that we owe modern science to a brave handful of progressive scientists who triumphed over the forces of ignorance and superstition. Adherents of this view identify "good guys" and "bad guys," and ignore their heroes' many false leads and dead ends. They also ignore the fact that some of the heroes' views seem distinctly "unscientific" today.

Science and scientists must also be placed in their proper social and cultural context. Scientists have never been purely detached observers of nature, isolated in their laboratories, developing their hypotheses without reference to the rest of the world. Research into the history of science in the early modern period has revealed the complexity of the social, economic, religious, and cultural forces that influenced early modern science. In particular, it is important to recognize that scientists of the period saw no inherent conflict between their work and Christianity. Most, if not all, were sincere Christians, and many of them were notably devout. Many considered their scientific inquiries to be a form of worship, dedicated to deepening human understanding of divine creation and thus of the Creator. There were occasional clashes, most notably between Galileo and the Catholic Church, but they were not the norm, and more often than not were attributable to factors other than religion itself.

In addition, we should not assume that what emerged from the Scientific Revolution were "truths" that overturned the errors of the past. What emerged were better explanations, and the old explanations that they replaced were not necessarily stupid or flawed. They explained observable phenomena almost as well as the new ones did, and many of them were not only mathematically sophisticated and aesthetically pleasing, but consistent with observation and common sense. In fact, it was a rare scientist who deliberately set out to overturn accepted explanations. More often than not, they were trying to improve the old explanations, or to resolve inconsistencies.

THE REVOLUTION IN ASTRONOMY AND PHYSICS

The Universe According to Aristotle and Ptolemy

For at least 1500 years, Western concepts of the heavens and the laws of motion were those of the ancient Greeks, most notably Aristotle (384 BCE–322 BCE) and Ptolemy (90–168 CE). According to Aristotle, the cosmos was finite, spherical, and geocentric (i.e., centred on the earth), and the sun, moon, planets, and stars were embedded in crystalline spheres that revolved around the earth at uniform speeds. There was a fundamental distinction between earth and the heavens, or more precisely, between the sublunar sphere—that is, the sphere below the moon, encompassing earth and the space immediately surrounding it—and the celestial spheres. In the sublunar sphere, everything was imperfect, corrupt, and subject to change. Everything on earth was composed of some combination of the four elements: the two heavy elements of earth and water, and the two light elements of air and fire. Motion was explained by the composition of the moving thing. "Earthy" objects such as stones will seek their natural "home" at the centre of the earth, and thus, if dropped into a pond, will sink to the bottom. Lighter things, composed of air and/or fire, will seek their natural places at the circumference of the sublunar sphere.

This explained "natural motion," toward or away from the centre of the earth. Unnatural or "violent" motion (i.e., motion in any other direction), by contrast, Aristotle believed to be caused by some external mover: "everything that is moved, is moved by something else." The major shortcoming of Aristotelian physics was its failure to explain projectile motion: if an arrow (an "earthy" thing) followed Aristotle's principles, it should fall to the ground as soon as it leaves the bowstring propelling it. Over the centuries, a number of explanations were advanced for projectile motion, none of them completely satisfactory. Aristotle's explanation of motion worked well enough, however, to be accepted for many centuries.

In contrast to the imperfect, mutable sublunar sphere, the celestial spheres were perfect and unchanging. Whereas the sublunar sphere was composed of the four elements, the sun, planets, and stars were composed of a perfect fifth element, quintessence or *æther*. Motion in the heavens was also perfect, circular and uniform. Beyond the sphere of the stars was the domain of the *primum mobile*, the unmoving mover. Although medieval philosophers interpreted this prime mover as God, the creator and sustainer of the universe, for the ancient Greeks it too was part of the natural order, not external and prior to it.

HISTORICAL DEBATE

Was There a Scientific Revolution?

The concept of the "Scientific Revolution" is an invention of historians, among them Herbert Butterfield (1900–1979), who wrote that the Scientific Revolution "outshines everything since the rise of Christianity and reduces the Renaissance and Reformation to the rank of mere episodes." More recent historians, however, have debated both the concept's validity and its value.

Betty Jo Teeter Dobbs points out some of the problems with the revolutionary paradigm:

. . . It is a teleological story we tell: Newton is the hidden end toward which the whole narrative is inexorably drawn. . . . Had he not really existed at that time and in that place, perhaps we would have had to invent him. Perhaps in some sense we did invent him . . . one may reasonably argue that our "Newton as Final Cause" is a historical construct bearing little resemblance to the historical record. . . .

. . . we choose for praise the thinkers that seem to us to have contributed to modernity, but we unconsciously assume that their thought patterns were fundamentally like ours. Then we . . . discover to our astonishment that our intellectual ancestors are not like us at all: they do not see the full implications of their own work; they refuse to believe things that are now so obviously true; . . . horror of horrors, they take seriously such misbegotten ideas as astrology, alchemy, magic, the music of the spheres, divine providence, and salvation history. . . .

. . . How could Copernicus have taken just that one small step of transposing Sun and Earth and not have gone further . . . ? How could Galileo have ignored Kepler's ellipses even after he proclaimed the Book of Nature to be written in mathematical language? How could Descartes have persisted in believing deductive reasoning to be the way to true knowledge when all about him the experimental method was being pushed forward? . . .

But above all, how could Newton, the epitome of austere scientific mathematical rationality, have pursued alchemy as he did?

From B.J.T. Dobbs, "Newton as Final Cause and First Mover," in Margaret J. Osler (ed.), *Rethinking the Scientific Revolution* (Cambridge: Cambridge University Press, 2000), pp. 25–39.

Richard S. Westfall defends its value:

. . . Let me begin with an issue that Dobbs makes prominent, Whig historiography[9]. . . . Butterfield's assertion about the Scientific Revolution appears to me to fall into quite a different category. Merely describing the past in its own terms does not constitute the historian's function in my notion of it. We are not antiquarians. We are called to help the present understand the past by understanding how it came to be. We strive to find a meaningful order in the multifarious events of the past and thus, explicitly or implicitly, we pass judgments on the relative importance of events. . . .

. . . To me, it appears that the existence of modern science is the precondition for most of the central features of our society. . . .

. . . When I open the morning newspaper, almost every story either involves science directly or involves factors that depend on science. Very little has to do with religion. . . . Before the Scientific Revolution, theology was queen of the sciences. . . . Dispense with the concept of the Scientific Revolution? . . . How can we dream of it? . . .

In any event, with Newton the new science and the new philosophy of nature found their definitive form in which they shaped the scientific tradition in the West for the coming two centuries

The issues [Dobbs] has raised deserve the attention of all historians of science because the concept of the Scientific Revolution has been our central organizing idea. . . . without it our discipline will lose its coherence and, what is more, the cause of historical understanding will take a significant step backward.

From Richard S. Westfall, "The Scientific Revolution Reasserted," in Margaret J. Osler (ed.), *Rethinking the Scientific Revolution* (Cambridge: Cambridge University Press, 2000), pp. 25–39.

Steven Shapin provides a useful synthesis:

There was no such thing as the Scientific Revolution, and this is a book about it. Some time ago . . . historians announced the real existence of a coherent, cataclysmic, and climactic event that fundamentally and irrevocably changed what people know about the natural world and how they secure proper knowledge of that world. It was the moment at which the world became modern, it was a Good Thing, and it happened sometime during the period from the late sixteenth to the early eighteenth century.

. . . Many historians are now no longer satisfied that there was any singular and discrete event, localized in time and space, that can be pointed to as "the" Scientific Revolution. . . .

Yet . . . there remains a sense in which it is possible to write about the Scientific Revolution unapologetically and in good faith. . . . many key figures in the late sixteenth and seventeenth centuries vigorously expressed *their* view that they were proposing some very new and very important changes in knowledge of natural reality and in the practices by which legitimate knowledge was to secured, assessed, and communicated. They identified *themselves* as "moderns" set against "ancient" modes of thought and practice.

From Steven Shapin, *The Scientific Revolution* (Chicago: University of Chicago Press, 1996), pp. 1–7. Republished with permission of University of Chicago Press; permission conveyed through Copyright Clearance Center, Inc.

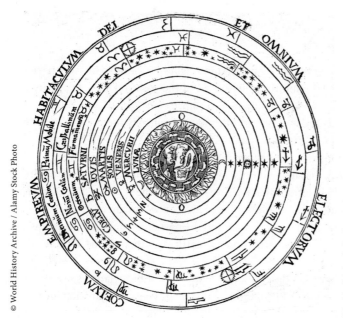

Aristotle's universe. From 1539, this woodcut shows an early modern conception of Aristotle's universe. The four sublunar elements of earth, water, air, and fire are represented in concentric rings in the centre, outside of which are the circular orbits of the moon (*Lunæ*), the sun (*Solis*), the planets, and the stars, represented by the astrological symbols of the zodiac. The outermost ring is that of the prime mover (*Primum Mobile*). Outside the final circle is "The Kingdom of Heaven, the dwelling place of God and the Elect."

According to Aristotle's view, the planets should move in perfect circles, but in fact, as the name "planet" ("wanderer") suggests, they appear to wander over the sky, stopping and backing up before resuming their original course. This phenomenon, known as the retrograde motion of the planets, is most pronounced in the case of Mars.

Almost five centuries after Aristotle's death, the Greek mathematician and astronomer Ptolemy found a way to refine his model of the cosmos in a way that accounted for retrograde motion. While preserving Aristotle's notions of geocentrism and uniform circular motion, Ptolemy proposed that the retrograde motion of the planets could be explained by a second set of circular motions, known as epicycles, operating within the larger circles (the deferents). This hypothesis described planetary motion as it appears from earth almost as well as the theory of elliptical orbits does today. It was also a mathematically sophisticated system, based on Ptolemy's calculations of how large the epicycles and deferents needed to be, as well as the speeds at which the planets moved. He did not believe that his system explained the actual cause of planetary motion. But that was not his goal. Rather, his goal was to "save the phenomena"—to make it possible to describe and predict planetary motion—and in that it succeeded.

Unraveling the Old System

Any account of the development of modern astronomy must begin with the Polish priest and mathematician Nicholas Copernicus (1473–1543). While studying in Italy, he was heavily influenced by Renaissance Neoplatonism, particularly the Hermetic writings (see Chapter 2) suggesting that the sun was the source of light and life, and that the key to controlling nature lay in discovering the mathematical harmonies of the universe.

Figure 5.1 Epicycle

During the same period he was exposed to a recently discovered ancient Greek work by Aristarchus of Samos (c. 310–c. 230 BCE), who had put the sun rather than the earth at the centre of the universe. Copernicus did the same in his most important work, *De revolutionibus cœlestium orbium* (*On the Revolution of Heavenly Bodies*, 1543).

In so doing, Copernicus was not boldly challenging the errors of the past. His intention was simply to remedy the weaknesses in Ptolemy's system. By putting the sun rather than the earth at the centre of the cosmos, he was able to dramatically reduce the number of epicycles required, while retaining the notion of uniform circular motion. To explain the cycle of day and night with the sun at the centre of the universe, he proposed that the earth rotated on its own axis as it revolved around the sun.

Copernicus was not an astronomer in the sense that he observed and recording celestial motion; rather he was a mathematician who appreciated the fact that placing the sun in the centre made the universe mathematically simpler. He was also aware that

The Copernican universe. A diagram from *De revolutionibus* (1543) showing the sun (*Sol*) in the centre and the earth (*Terra*) third from the centre.

a heliocentric universe was consistent with mystical Neoplatonic and Hermetic beliefs about the sun:

> In the middle of all sits the Sun enthroned. In this most beautiful temple could we place this luminary in any better position from which he can illuminate the whole at once? He is rightly calls the Lamp, the Mind, the Ruler of the Universe; Hermes Trismigestus names him the visible God, Sophocles Electra calls him the All-seeing. So the sun sits as upon a royal throne ruling his children the planets which circle around him.[10]

Copernicus expected strong resistance to his work, and therefore delayed publishing it until just before his death. He was not mistaken. Catholic and Protestant theologians alike denounced the book, which called into question not only the view of the cosmos that had been accepted for 1500 years, but also the literal interpretation of Scripture and humanity's central place in creation. One historian of science has identified only ten scholars before 1600 who accepted Copernicus's views, and he suggests that what persuaded them was not so much the science as their Hermetic and Neoplatonic convictions.[11]

Aristotle and Ptolemy believed there was a fundamental distinction between the corrupt and changing sublunar sphere and the perfect and unchanging celestial realm. When confronted with a change in the heavens—a comet or shooting star, for example—it was assumed to be taking place in the sublunar sphere. In the 1570s, however, the appearance of both a supernova and a comet piqued the curiosity of Tycho Brahe (1546–1601), a Danish astronomer and mathematician with a keen interest in astrology. He then built an advanced astronomical observatory and, after years of observation, used his data to show that such events were not sublunar but celestial. If the heavens were perfect and unchanging, how could there be a new star? How could a comet travel through Aristotle's crystalline spheres? Brahe posited a hybrid of the Ptolemaic and Copernican views in which the earth remained at the centre while the planets and stars revolved around the sun as the latter circled the earth. Brahe's chief motivation was not the advancement of science for its own sake, however: he wanted to cast more accurate horoscopes.

When Brahe died, his data were appropriated by his research assistant, Johannes Kepler (1571–1630), in whom we see the same combination of "scientific" and "mystical" thought. Kepler was among the still tiny minority of scholars who were dedicated Copernicans. He spent years manipulating Brahe's data, filling hundreds of pages with handwritten calculations, and in 1609 he published *Astronomia Nova* (*New Astronomy*), in which he stated what would become his first two laws of planetary motion. First, the orbits in which planets revolve around the sun are not circular but elliptical, and the sun is not in the centre of the ellipse but towards one end. Second, an imaginary line drawn between the planet and the sun would sweep equal areas in equal times (see illustration). This meant that the speed of the planet is not uniform: it moves faster when it is nearer the sun, and more slowly when it is farther away.

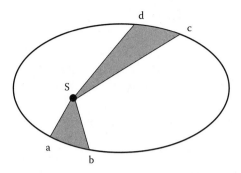

Figure 5.2 Kepler's first and second laws

Kepler's elliptical orbits with the sun (S) at one focus of the ellipse.
His second law states that the shaded areas (a-b-S and c-d-S) will
be equal where the time intervals a-b and c-d are equal.

In 1619 Kepler's *Harmonice Mundi* (*The Harmony of the World*) outlined his third law of planetary motion: there is a constant mathematical relationship between the planet's distance from the sun and the time it takes to complete its orbit. In addition, Kepler proposed that this mathematical relationship corresponds to the laws of musical harmony: as they revolve around the sun, the planets produce musical tones that together comprise the harmony of the spheres.

Kepler's work demolished the remaining assumptions of the Ptolemaic universe. Nevertheless, his laws did not explain the motion of the planets: they merely described it. He was still tied to Aristotle's physics, in which "everything that is moved is moved by something else": thus he understood the sun to be like a giant magnet whose force propelled the planets in their orbits, much like the spokes of a wheel. Kepler's argument for elliptical orbits was not widely accepted, and scholars such as Galileo and Descartes continued to support the idea of perfect circular motion. It was not until the time of Isaac Newton (1640–1727) that Kepler's views gained wide acceptance.

The Italian mathematician Galileo Galilei (1564–1642) was, like Kepler, one of the few who supported Copernican astronomy. He first became prominent in 1610 with the publication of *Siderius Nuncius* (*The Starry Messenger*). Having heard of a Dutchman who invented a telescope, he made one for himself and trained it on the night sky. He saw sunspots, as well as peaks and valleys on the moon, from which he concluded that the heavens were not perfect and unchanging, but rather made of the same sort of matter as the earth. He discovered four moons of Jupiter, which showed that the earth could not be the sole centre around which all else revolved. Ironically, logical reasoning led him to reject Kepler's elliptical orbits and maintain that the planets must revolve in circular orbits.

Kepler's music of the spheres. According to Kepler, the relations between the planets' speed of revolution around the sun corresponded to the ratios that govern musical harmony. Here we see in musical notation Kepler's assessment of the six known planets as well as the moon.

Galileo's conviction that the heavens were composed of the same matter as the earth led him to conclude that motion too must be the same throughout the universe. In his *Dialogue Concerning the Two Chief World Systems* (1632), and *Discourses on Two New Sciences* (1638), he established the basis of modern physics. In his view, motion was explained not by the composition of the moving object, as it had been for Aristotle, but by the forces acting upon it. Motion itself no longer required explanation: only changes in motion did. He came very close to proposing the law of inertia as it would later be expressed by René Descartes and Pierre Gassendi: a body in motion will remain in motion until acted on by other forces, and a body at rest will remain at rest until acted on by other forces. He discovered the law of uniform acceleration: that falling bodies accelerate at the same rate no matter their size or composition, and that this rate is governed by a mathematical formula. Projectile motion is parabolic in nature, as it is a continuous combination of forces.

It would be an exaggeration to see Galileo as the father of a radically new "experimental method." Although he did conduct experiments, much of his work relied more on "thought experiments" (it is highly unlikely that he actually dropped two objects of different weights from the leaning tower of Pisa). In some cases he arrived at his conclusion and only then conducted an experiment demonstrating it. In his *Dialogue*, for instance, he wrote of one conclusion: "I, without observation, know that the result must be as I say, because it is necessary."[12]

Today Galileo is best known for the clash with the Catholic Church that led to his trial for heresy, his recanting of his Copernican views, and the fact that he spent the last decade of his life under house arrest. These events were not the outcome of an inevitable conflict between science and religion, however. Galileo remained a devout Catholic, and protested that he was simply seeking to understand divine creation. As we see in his letter to the Grand Duchess Christina of Tuscany (see Weblink), he saw theology and science as different pursuits (although with the same goal), each with its own proper methods and procedures.

It was his support of Copernicus that brought Galileo to the attention of the Inquisition in 1616, but he also had supporters within the Church, one of whom noted that the Bible "teaches us how to go to heaven, not how the heavens go." Among his most influential supporters were Cardinal Robert Bellarmine, one of the most respected theologians of the day, and Cardinal Maffeo Barberini, later Pope Urban VIII (r. 1623–44). Although the Inquisition condemned heliocentrism as heresy, Galileo obtained a letter from Bellarmine stating that he was innocent of heretical thought; in return, he agreed to treat the Copernican cosmos as a mathematical hypothesis, rather than as a description of physical reality.

For more than a decade, the controversy lay dormant, but in 1632 Galileo published a book, in vernacular Italian rather than academic Latin, that came to be known as the *Dialogue Concerning the Two Chief World Systems*. In it a supporter of the Ptolemaic system, Simplicio, and an advocate of the Copernican, Salviati, discuss the two positions with a neutral third party, the intelligent layman, Sagredo. In the end, Sagredo embraces the Copernican view, and Simplicio—in whose mouth Galileo had, intentionally or not, put some words of his former supporter Cardinal Barberini, now Pope Urban VIII—is shown to be mistaken at best.[13]

The result is well known. The *Dialogue* was placed on the Index of Forbidden Books and Galileo tried for heresy by the Inquisition. At first he refused to acknowledge that he had held heretical views, but under threat of torture, Galileo, now aged and ill, confessed. Sentenced to house arrest, he would remain at home until his death in 1642. Nevertheless, he continued to research and write as his health allowed, and in 1638 he published *The Two New Sciences*, which in many ways did for physics what his *Dialogue* had done for astronomy, summing up his life's work.[14]

The conflict between Galileo and the Church was not a clash between science and religion: it was a political and philosophical conflict, part of which took place within the Church. In the Middle Ages, the philosophy of Aristotle had been integrated into Catholic theology, and it was that integration that Galileo challenged. In addition to upending the geocentric universe of Aristotle and Ptolemy, Galileo's work destroyed Aristotelian physics, in which motion was explained by the composition or essence of the moving body. For Galileo what counted were phenomena that could be measured—mass, speed, size, and direction—not the composition of the moving object with its "secondary" qualities such as colour, taste, and smell. It was this emphasis on objective measurement of impersonal forces that led Galileo's critics to fear that his universe was a gigantic machine operating according to mathematical laws, with no place for divine providence.

By the middle of the seventeenth century, views of the cosmos that had been almost universally accepted for millennia had been shown to be false, and the rough outlines of the new views were in place: a heliocentric universe, with elliptical orbits and uniform physical laws throughout. If this seems obvious today, it is important to recognize that at the time it left many people with a deep sense of dislocation, which the English poet John Donne (1572–1631) evoked in his poem *An Anatomy of the World* (1611):

> And new Philosophy calls all in doubt,
> The Element of fire is quite put out;
> The Sun is lost, and th'earth, and no man's wit
> Can well direct him where to look for it.
> And freely men confess that this world's spent,
> When in the Planets, and the Firmament
> They seek so many new; they see that this
> Is crumbled out again to his Atomies.
> Tis all in pieces, all coherence gone;
> All just supply, and all Relation.

Within half a century of Galileo's death, a new synthesis had emerged, one that not only combined the conclusions of Copernicus, Kepler, Galileo, and others into a harmonious and elegant system, but went beyond describing motion to explain it. This was the supreme achievement of Isaac Newton (1642–1727), the most brilliant mind of the early modern era. A mathematician of genius, he invented calculus more or less simultaneously with his bitter rival, the German Gottfried Wilhelm Leibniz. He also conducted research into optics, using a prism to demonstrate that white light is composed of a spectrum of colours, and invented the reflecting telescope. His historical importance, however, rests squarely on his master work, *Principia mathematica philosophiæ naturalis* (*Mathematical Principles of Natural Philosophy*, usually referred to as *Principia*; 1687), perhaps the most important scientific work ever written. (It was also among the last major scientific works to be written in Latin.) Newton combined the unified physics of Galileo with a heliocentric universe. Newton explained the elliptical orbits of the planets as the result of two forces. First, he adapted from Galileo the notion of inertia, according to which objects in motion will remain in motion until acted on by other forces. For Newton, however, inertial force was not circular (as it was for Galileo), but linear. That is, left unchecked, the inertial motion of the planets would carry them along a straight line into infinite space. This did not happen, however, because this inertial motion was counterbalanced by the force of gravity. According to Newton, every object in the universe exerts a gravitational attraction on every other object, and the force of this attraction is proportional to both the masses of the objects and the distance between them. Thus larger objects exerted a greater pull than smaller ones, and closer objects a greater pull than farther ones. He also discovered that Galileo's calculation of the rate of acceleration of falling bodies applies to the motion of the planets as well. Thus the same force that causes apples to fall to the ground also keeps the planets from flying off into infinite space.

Newton's synthesis was not immediately accepted. One problem was that very few could understand the advanced mathematics of the *Principia*. Another was the fact that Newton could not explain how gravity operated. To many, therefore, including Leibniz, Newton's hypothesis seemed to require a mysterious, unseen force that violated the mechanistic view of the universe. For many years, especially in continental Europe, the mechanistic ideas of René Descartes (1596–1650; see below) seemed more persuasive than an occult force such as gravity operating across the vast distances of empty space.

Newton also held many beliefs inconsistent with the image of the detached and rational scientist. Passionately, if unconventionally, religious, he believed that the doctrine of the Trinity had no basis in Scripture (a belief that he had to keep hidden to preserve both his freedom and his position at Cambridge), and spent years calculating biblical chronologies in an effort to determine the date of the Second Coming and Apocalypse, concluding that they will occur in 2060. He also devoted a great deal of time and money to alchemy, although to be fair, what he was doing was not very different from chemistry. An integral part of the Neoplatonic and Hermetic traditions, alchemy may seem farfetched today, but it was a respectable pursuit in the sixteenth and seventeenth centuries, and Newton was not its only prominent student (others included Francis Bacon and Tycho Brahe).

Although his scientific work would later be seen as the cornerstone of a mechanistic, "watchmaker" universe, Newton himself was horrified by the suggestion that the universe might not require God's oversight to function. To Newton, the creator was not just the supreme mechanic who constructed the universe according to mathematical principles:

he was also the supreme artist who endowed it with beauty and harmony, and the eternal presence who preserved it.

IMPACT OF THE NEW SCIENCE

From our vantage point it is hard to imagine the dislocation caused by the destruction of the old certainties. Many thinkers came to reject the possibility of any certainty at all. "I shall leave here [this life] ignorant of everything except my ignorance," wrote the French philosopher and essayist Michel de Montaigne (1533–92). Montaigne embraced scepticism:

> The sky and stars have been moving for three thousand years; everybody had so believed, until it occurred to Cleanthes of Samos; or (according to Theophrastus) to Nicetas of Syracuse, to maintain that it was the earth that moved, through the oblique circle of the Zodiac, turning about its axis; and in our day, Copernicus has grounded this doctrine so well that he uses it very systematically for all astronomical deductions. What are we to get out of that, unless that we should not bother which of the two is so? And who knows whether a third opinion, a thousand years from now, will overthrow the preceding two?[15]

Others sought refuge in philosophies. Some continued to explore Neoplatonism and the Hermetic tradition. Others looked to ancient moral philosophies such as Epicureanism and Stoicism, each of which had its own view of the physical universe. Epicurus (341–270 BCE), had postulated an infinite, uncreated universe composed of an infinite number of indivisible particles, or atoms, and reasoned that the proper response to this meaningless cosmos was to pursue pleasure and avoid pain. The French priest and philosopher Pierre Gassendi (1592–1655) made Epicureanism safe for Christianity by putting God outside the natural order, making Him the creator of a finite number of atoms, who continued to play a role in nature through divine providence.

Stoics, on the other hand, believed that the universe, including mankind, was pervaded and governed by a divine principle and was continually evolving towards a state of goodness. The vehicle of this purpose was *pneuma*, an all-pervading substance that filled the universe. The proper human response was to accept this purpose and work towards its fulfilment. This meant calmly accepting both the pains and pleasures of existence, as both were part of the universe's purpose and unfolding. Justus Lipsius (1547–1606) was a Flemish humanist and philosopher who identified Stoic fate with God's will and placed God outside and prior to the purpose of the universe that He had created. Kepler showed some Stoic influences when he hypothesized that the motion of the planets could be explained by something like *pneuma* that transmitted the sun's magnetic attraction. Newton too was influenced by Stoicism, believing both that the universe was filled with an invisible and insensible *æther*, and that it was through this medium that God sustained and preserved the universe.

VOICES

Blaise Pascal

Blaise Pascal (1623–62) was a mathematician and scientist who, as a young man, performed experiments on barometric pressure, further disproving Aristotelian physics, and invented a mechanical computer. In November of 1654, however, he underwent an ecstatic religious experience—he called it his "night of fire"—that was to change his life. Pascal was to devote the rest of his short life to his faith. Attracted to the austerity and morality of the Jansenists (see Chapter 6), he spent a good deal of time at Port-Royal and energetically defended them against their Jesuit critics.

Although Pascal never turned his back on science, maintaining that it was essential for knowledge of the universe, he believed that only the Christian faith could answer the important questions, and feared that the mechanistic view of the universe would lead people away from God. He began assembling notes for what he thought would his masterpiece, reconciling science and faith. Although he died before it could be written, about 1000 of these notes survived and were published posthumously under the title *Pensées* ("thoughts"):

206

The eternal silence of these infinite spaces frightens me.

273

If we submit everything to reason, our religion will have no mysterious and supernatural element. If we offend the principles of reason, our religion will be absurd and ridiculous.

277

The heart has its reasons, which reason does not know. We feel it in a thousand things. I say that the heart naturally loves the Universal Being, and also itself naturally, according as it gives itself to them . . .

278

It is the heart which experiences God, and not the reason. This, then, is faith: God felt by the heart, not by the reason.

526

The knowledge of God without that of man's misery causes pride. The knowledge of man's misery without that of God causes despair. The knowledge of Jesus Christ constitutes the middle course, because in Him we find both God and our misery.

From W.F. Trotter, trans., *Pascal's Pensées*, introduction by T.S. Eliot (New York: EP Dutton, 1958).

One of the most obvious consequences of the revolution in astronomy and physics was the dethroning of the ancient authorities that had been assumed for millennia to represent the pinnacle of human wisdom. If Aristotle and Ptolemy could not be trusted, where was certainty to be found? Increasingly, educated Europeans looked to experimentation. This approach was not new: medieval scientists had performed experiments, and the contribution of new methods to the breakthroughs examined above were slight. Copernicus employed no new method. Galileo has often been credited as the pioneer of an "experimental method," but although he certainly did experiment, measure, and record, this aspect of his career has been overemphasized and its novelty exaggerated. Newer views of how scientists ought to proceed emerged over time, as scientists sought to rationalize and explain their ideas. Second, there was never (nor is there now) a single "scientific method" that scientists in all fields follow. Over the course of the seventeenth century, there were substantial differences in opinion over how scientific certainty was to be ascertained.

One of the most important figures in the quest for knowledge of the natural world was the English politician, writer, and amateur scientist Sir Francis Bacon (1561–1626). In *Novum Organon* ("New Instrument"; 1620) he argued that Aristotle and the ancients had approached scientific research backwards, beginning with theories, deducing conclusions, and then searching for evidence to support them. This faulty method, he argued, must be replaced by an inductive, empirical method that would begin with observation, data collection, and experimentation, with general explanations and theories as the products of research rather than the starting points.

Bacon also believed that the increase in scientific knowledge would produce practical improvements in the human condition. In *New Atlantis* (1627) he described a fictional ideal land where teams of scientists worked together to discover nature's secrets. As modern as this may sound, Bacon had only a vague notion of how scientists actually worked, and in his overwhelming emphasis on observation and collection of facts, he underestimated the importance of forming hypotheses. He had an almost naïve faith that once enough facts were collected, the truth would somehow emerge on its own, almost independently of human agency. Nevertheless, his emphasis on collaboration was timely, for all over Europe scientists and interested laymen were forming organizations to further their research. Institutions such as the Royal Society in England, founded in 1662, and the Académie des sciences in France, founded in 1666, facilitated communication within the scientific community and helped to promote scientific ideas among the literate elite.

A generation after Bacon, the French mathematician and philosopher René Descartes (1596–1650) proposed a radically different method for reaching the truth, based not on induction from empirical observation but on a priori and deductive reasoning. In his famous *Discourse on Method* (1637), he outlined his approach to knowledge. Finding that received authorities frequently contradicted each other, he resolved to reject as false anything of which he could conceive the least doubt, and then see what would be left standing. Having rejected the experience of his senses as a source of certainty, since the senses can deceive us, in the end the only thing he could not doubt was that he was thinking, and—since thinking cannot be done by something that does not exist—from that certainty he deduced that he must exist. This was the source of his famous phrase *cogito ergo sum* ("I think, therefore I am"), and the foundation for all further investigation: now that he knew what certainty felt like, he could be confident that whatever he perceived with the same degree of certainty must also be true. From here he went on to deduce the existence of God: if he knew himself to be imperfect, then he must have an innate notion of perfection, which could have come only from a perfect Being. Further, since God is perfect, He does not deceive us: the world is orderly and rational, comprehensible through human understanding.

The same deductive method of reasoning led Descartes to a philosophical dualism in which mind was radically distinct from matter. Since he could imagine himself without a body, but could not imagine that he did not exist, he concluded that he was "a substance whose whole essence or nature resides only in thinking, and which, in order to exist, has no need of place and is not dependent on any material thing." It followed, then, that mind (or soul, or thinking substance) was entirely distinct from matter, or "extended substance."[16] In his view, the physical world was a giant machine that ran according to physical laws accessible to the human mind through deduction and describable in the language of mathematics. Descartes was not the only seventeenth-century thinker to espouse this "mechanical philosophy": another key proponent was Thomas Hobbes (1588–1679; see Chapter 6). Whereas Hobbes was a strict materialist, however, by embracing dualism Descartes was able to include a place for the Christian God and the human soul in his otherwise mechanistic universe. This was not enough for the Catholic Church, which objected that Descartes opened the door to atheism by reducing the Creator of the universe and Redeemer of mankind to a logical necessity, and after his death placed his work on the Index of Forbidden Books. Nevertheless, many of Descartes's contemporaries found both his mechanical view of the natural world and his theory of knowledge compelling.

It was only toward the end of the century that the English philosopher and political theorist John Locke (1632–1704) offered an alternative answer to the question of how we know what we know. Concerned that Descartes's reliance on innate knowledge provided no grounds for certainty, since ideas and perceptions clearly vary from one individual to another, in his *Essay Concerning Human Understanding* (1690) Locke argued that we are born without any innate ideas; rather, the mind at birth is a blank slate (*tabula rasa*). For Locke, all knowledge was the product of sensation and reflection, the experience of the senses as processed by the mind. He believed that there was "a common stock of reason" in all people and that, given the proper education and environment, reason would ultimately lead them to the truth. Aspects of Locke's philosophy may seem superficial; for example, what is this "reason" that governs reflection, if not an innate quality of the mind? Further, although he should logically exclude divine revelation as source of knowledge, he tried to maintain a role for it. Yet it was Locke's philosophy of human nature and knowledge that the literate elite of the eighteenth century would broadly embrace, and that, with Newton's views on the physical universe, would provide the foundation for the Enlightenment.

MEDICINE AND CHEMISTRY

Although the advances made in medicine and chemistry in the sixteenth and seventeenth centuries were less dramatic than the discoveries in astronomy and physics, they were also significant. In both cases, the authority of ancient writers was first questioned and then rejected.

All three of the leading authorities in medicine were Greek: the ancient physician Hippocrates (c. 460 BCE–c. 377 BCE), Aristotle (384 BCE–322 BCE), and the Roman-era physician and philosopher Galen (129–199 CE). For more than a thousand years, good health, both mental and physical, was thought to depend on the correct balance of four bodily "humours" (fluids): blood, phlegm, black bile, and yellow bile. So someone with an

The title page of Vesalius. The title page of the second edition (1555) of *De humani corporis fabrica* shows Vesalius himself dissecting a human cadaver for his students; the traditional practice was for the professor to read from a text while an assistant (usually a barber-surgeon) dissected an animal.

excess of blood (*sanguis*) was sanguine—excessively bold, confident, and optimistic. An excess of phlegm made one phlegmatic—apathetic and sluggish. Too much yellow bile (choler) made one angry or choleric, while too much black bile led to depression and sadness (melancholy). Restoring health was a matter of rebalancing humours through bleeding, purging, vomiting, sweating, and so on. Blood was thought to be generated by the liver, and to flow through two separate blood systems: arteries carried the bright red blood that nourished flesh and muscles, while the veins carried the dark red blood that governed digestion.

Among the first to question the received wisdom of the ancients was Andreas Vesalius (1514–64). Born in Brussels, he was not only the court physician to the Holy Roman Emperor Charles V, but the founder of modern anatomy. Whereas Galen had based his anatomy on the dissection of animals, Vesalius examined human cadavers at the University of Padua (which would later employ Galileo as well), and proved the error of many of Galen's claims. His master work was *De humani corporis fabrica* (*On the Fabric of the Human Body*; 1543), a meticulously detailed and illustrated record of his findings.

Ancient medical authority was further undermined by William Harvey (1587–1657). As a student at Padua, he was taught by students of Vesalius, and in his book *De motu cordis et sanguinis* (*On the Motion of the Heart and Blood*; 1628) he showed that there were not two separate blood systems, as Galen had taught: rather, the same system pumped the blood away from the heart through the arteries and returned it through the veins. Although he could not explain how blood got from the arteries to the veins, that mystery would be solved in 1661, when the Italian Marcello Malpighi (1628–95) used a microscope to identify the previously invisible capillaries.

More radical challenges to traditional medical wisdom were posed by the Swiss physician Theophrastus Bombastus von Hohenheim (1493?–1591), who called himself Paracelsus, "beyond Celsus" (an ancient Roman medical writer). Contemptuous of the authorities of the day, he rejected the theory of humours and anticipated germ theory in arguing that illness was caused by external agents. He also embraced the Neoplatonic and Hermetic belief that the body was a microcosm of the physical universe, and argued that the correct treatment for physical ailments could be determined by observing the movements of the stars and planets corresponding to various parts of the body and bodily functions. Believing that natural substances had secret properties that with the proper knowledge could be used to treat illness, he was especially intrigued by the element of mercury (which is liquid at room temperature), but also experimented with sulphur, salt, and antimony, hoping to discover the ultimate cure, the "elixir of life." He also maintained that if otherwise toxic substances were administered in the correct doses, they could cure disease—a principle not very different from the one behind the modern practice of chemotherapy. Although his arrogant personality prevented him from attracting many followers during his lifetime, in time his work gained a wider following.

If Paracelsus formed a bridge from alchemy to modern medicine, Robert Boyle (1627–91) bridged the transition from alchemy to modern chemistry. A wealthy gentleman of leisure, a friend and colleague of Newton's, Boyle was not only a founder of the

Royal Society (on which he imprinted his firm belief in empirical observation and ex-perimentation) but a pioneer of the experimental method. His own experiments with air and gasses led to the discovery of Boyle's law (roughly, that the pressure of a gas increases as its volume decreases), but he was also a confirmed believer in alchemy who claimed to have witnessed the transmutation of lead into gold. By his time scientific thinking was dominated by the "mechanical philosophy" expounded by Descartes, among others, according to which the only properties that mattered were those that could be measured and quantified, such as size, mass, and velocity, but Boyle argued for what he called a "corpuscular philosophy": that chemical processes were the product of particles ("cor-puscles") that reacted with one another in ways that could not be explained through strictly mechanical processes.

Chapter Conclusion

In his classic interpretation of the Renaissance as the beginning of modernity, Jacob Burckhardt emphasized its contributions to the "discovery of the world" and the role that Italians of the Renaissance period played in the exploration both of the globe and of the physical world. Both of these were certainly crucial to the formation of the modern world, but their connection to the cultural movement of the Renaissance was actually very slight. It takes serious twisting of historical reality to turn Columbus—a talented but entirely "medieval" Italian sailor—into a Renaissance figure. In fact, it was the supposedly "back-ward" and "medieval" Portuguese and Spanish who led the way in the age of European exploration.

The situation was similar with science. Renaissance humanists were not greatly interested in science, considering it an impractical pursuit inappropriate for real men living in a real world. Although scientists such as Copernicus were influenced by Neoplatonic thought, the main contribution of the Renaissance to the development of science was a function of the humanist passion for rediscovering forgotten ancient manuscripts. By showing that the supposedly authoritative ancients had often dis-agreed among themselves, the humanist discoveries forced early modern scholars to look beyond ancient authority and rely on their own understanding. In the words of Francis Bacon:

> men have been hindered from making progress in the sciences by the spell (I may say) of reverence for antiquity. . . . it is reasonable that greater things be expected from our age than from old times (if it only knew its strength and was willing to try it and exert it). . . . With regard to authors, it is a mark of supreme cowardice to give unlimited credit to authors and to deny its rights to Time, the author of authors and thus of all authority. For truth is rightly called the daughter of time and not of authority. Therefore it is no wonder if the spell of antiquity, of authors and of consent has so shackled men's courage that (as if bewitched) they have been unable to get close to things themselves.[17]

True progress is evolutionary in nature: we know more because we come later in time. Truth was no longer the exclusive province of ancient authority.

The discoveries outlined in this chapter were fundamental in shaping the world we know today. Europe's "discovery" of the globe in the early modern period would lead to roughly two centuries of European imperialism—a period that is now well in the past, but that continues to produce fallout. European geographic discoveries also contributed to the demolition of medieval Christendom: early modern Europeans surpassed the ancients in their knowledge of the globe, and the discovery of previously unknown civilizations led eventually led some European thinkers to question not only long-standing assumptions about the superiority of European civilization but, in some cases, even the truth of Christianity.

Christendom was further eroded by new ways of thinking about the natural world. Since the understanding of the cosmos associated with Aristotle and Ptolemy had been incorporated into Christian theology, and seemed to be consistent with a literal interpretation of Scripture, challenges to it were vigorously resisted (as Galileo discovered). None of the scientists involved intended to set science against Christianity. Yet by the later seventeenth century, the concept of a finite universe centred on the earth was no longer tenable. The outlines of a new worldview had been sketched by Newton and Locke, among others, but its full implications would not become clear until the eighteenth century (see Chapter 9). Although Bacon was confident that scientific inquiry would increase human happiness, this did not happen immediately. No one's health or happiness or standard of living was improved by the understanding that the earth orbited the sun, or that bodies in motion stay in motion unless acted upon by other forces. The application of scientific discoveries to the problems of humanity would not begin for some time yet.

Questions for Critical Thought

1. How did the twin motives of religion and profit ("Christians and spices") affect European voyages of exploration and Europeans' interactions with the populations they encountered? Did they work together or at cross-purposes?
2. In 1492 Columbus established what was thought to be the first contact between the Old World and the New. What consequences did this contact have for world civilizations? How did the two worlds influence each other?
3. To what extent is it useful to think in terms of a "Scientific Revolution?" What arguments can be advanced for and against such a concept?
4. What issues were at stake in the conflict between Galileo and the Catholic Church? Was it a conflict between "science" and "religion"?
5. How might developments in science have looked to an educated layperson in 1650? Would they have inspired doubt or insecurity, or confidence and boldness?
6. Imagine that you were an educated European who had somehow been transported from 1450 to 1650. What differences would you find most striking, both in Europe's relations with the rest of the world, and in the prevailing understanding of the physical universe?

Weblinks

Simon Schama on observing the quincentennial of Columbus's voyage:
https://newrepublic.com/article/70179/they-all-laughed-christopher-columbus

Galileo's letter to the Grand Duchess Christina of Tuscany:
www.inters.org/galilei-madame-christina-Lorraine

Further Reading

EUROPEAN EXPLORATION

Abulafia, David. *The Discovery of Mankind: Atlantic Encounters in the Age of Columbus*. New Haven: Yale University Press, 2008. A fascinating analysis of the cultural impact of the discovery of new worlds and their inhabitants.

Armesto-Fernandez, Felipe. *Columbus*. Oxford: Oxford University Press, 1992. An excellent biography, published for the quincentennial of Columbus's voyage.

Chaudhuri, K.N. *Trade and Civilization in the Indian Ocean: An Economic History from the Rise of Islam to 1750*. Cambridge: Cambridge University Press, 1989. The classic study of commerce in the Indian Ocean.

Crosby, Alfred W. *Ecological Imperialism: The Biological Expansion of Europe, 900–1900*. Cambridge: Cambridge University Press, 1986. An expansion and updating of the author's pioneering *The Columbian Exchange* (Westport, CT: Greenwood Press, 1972).

Scammell, G.V. *The First Imperial Age: European Overseas Expansion c. 1400–1715*. London: Unwin Hyman, 1989. An overview of the origins and development of European exploration and expansion, focusing primarily on the Portuguese and Spanish.

THE SCIENTIFIC REVOLUTION

Henry, John. *The Scientific Revolution and the Origins of Modern Science*. Basingstoke: Macmillan, 1997. A brief and accessible overview, with a useful historiographical introduction and a comprehensive bibliography.

Kuhn, Thomas. *The Structure of Scientific Revolutions*, 2nd ed. Chicago: University of Chicago Press, 1962. A classic by a pioneering historian of science.

Osler, Margaret J. (ed.). *Rethinking the Scientific Revolution*. Cambridge: Cambridge University Press, 2000. An important collection of essays challenging and refining the notion of a Scientific Revolution.

Shapin, Steven. *The Scientific Revolution*. Chicago: University of Chicago Press, 1996. An accessible account that refines the notion of a Scientific Revolution.

Westfall, Richard S. *Never at Rest: A Biography of Isaac Newton*. Cambridge: Cambridge University Press, 1980. A classic biography.

Notes

1. By this time, virtually no Europeans thought that sailors risked sailing off the edge of a flat earth; since ancient Greece, educated people had known that the earth was a sphere.
2. Dias believed he had rounded Africa and named the cape the Cape of Storms. King John II renamed it for the hope it promised of reaching India. In fact, however, the southernmost point of Africa is Cape Agulhas, 150 kilometres to the southeast.
3. The hypothesis that the Americas had been settled by migrants from Siberia during the last Ice Age was not widely accepted until the twentieth century, and the evidence of Viking exploration along the coast of Newfoundland, including a short-lived settlement at L'Anse-aux-Meadows around the year 1000, was not discovered until the 1960s.
4. Waldseemüller shortly thereafter realized that Columbus had been the first to arrive in the New World, but by then the name "America" was already in common use.
5. Quoted in Alfred W. Crosby, *Ecological Imperialism: the Biological Expansion of Europe, 900–1900* (Cambridge: Cambridge University Press, 1986), p. 208.
6. This insight is not limited to European encounters in the New World. One of the foundational works in the field of post-colonial studies was *Orientalism* (1978) by the Palestinian-American literary theorist Edward Said (1935–2003), who showed how European writers developed the concept of "orientalism," portraying Asian populations as fundamentally "other" and inferior.
7. David Abulafia, *The Discovery of Mankind: Atlantic Encounters in the Age of Columbus* (New Haven: Yale University Press, 2008), p. 126.
8. G.V. Scammell, *The First Imperial Age* (London: Unwin Hyman, 1989), p. 254.
9. This term comes from an approach to English history that was prominent in the nineteenth century. Whig historians interpreted English history as a long progression whose ultimate purpose was to produce a limited parliamentary monarchy of the kind that emerged in the eighteenth century. The term has since been applied to similar views of the past in other disciplines.
10. Quoted in Hugh Kearney, *Science and Change, 1500–1700* (New York: McGraw-Hill, 1971), pp. 99–100.
11. Robert S. Westman, "The Astronomer's Role in the Sixteenth Century: A Preliminary Assessment," *History of Science* 18, 2 (1980), p. 106. See also John Henry, *The Scientific Revolution and the Origins of Modern Science* (New York: St. Martin's, 1997), pp. 56–61.
12. Quoted in I. Bernard Cohen, *The Birth of a New Physics* (New York: Anchor Books, 1960), p. 94.
13. Although Galileo maintained that the name was a reference to a sixth-century scholar, Simplicius of Cilicia, its connotations were hard to ignore.
14. A popular legend maintains that, at the end of his trial and recantation, Galileo commented under his breath "And yet it [the earth] moves," but there is no contemporary evidence to support it.
15. Michel de Montaigne, "Apology for Raymond Sebond," in *The Complete Essays of Montaigne*, trans. Donald M. Frame. Stanford: Stanford University Press, 1958, p. 429.
16. René Descartes, *A Discourse on the Method of Correctly Conducting One's Reason and Seeking Truth in the Sciences*, trans. Ian Maclean (Oxford: Oxford University Press, 2006), p. 29.
17. Francis Bacon, *The New Organon*, ed. Lisa Jardine and Michael Silverthorne (Cambridge: Cambridge University Press) pp. 68–9.

6

Absolute and Limited Monarchies in the Seventeenth Century

In the course of the seventeenth century, most European rulers managed to strengthen their authority over their subjects. This development has usually been described as the rise of "absolutism" or "absolute monarchy." Although some historians have challenged that description as an anachronism (see Debate, below), there is no denying that by 1700 the power of most European rulers was greater than it had been a century earlier.

This development was not inevitable, nor was it smooth. Around the middle of the seventeenth century, many European states underwent a period of crisis in which the power of the state was profoundly challenged. Some historians have seen in this mid-century turmoil a "general crisis" that extended beyond politics and government. The economic and demographic expansion of the sixteenth century had petered out; European agricultural systems were likely at the limits of their productive capacity; and, as we have seen, there is evidence that food shortages were exacerbated by a general climatic cooling, a "little ice age," in the period. In addition, the nearly continual warfare of the time drove governments to extract ever-greater amounts of tax revenue from their subjects at a time when their ability to pay was already reduced. This spurred governments to roll back the privileges enjoyed by various orders in society—a move that those affected naturally resisted. Although circumstances varied from one country to another, in many cases this resistance was the underlying cause of the mid-century disturbances. In other words, there was a direct link between warfare, taxation, and the development of absolute monarchy; as the historian Perry Anderson put it, "absolutist states . . . were machines built overwhelmingly for the battlefield."[1]

Most rulers emerged from this period of crisis with their power significantly strengthened, and as a result absolute monarchy became the dominant political model of the later seventeenth century. The exceptions were places such as England, the Dutch Republic, and Poland, where the powers of rulers were constrained in important ways. In these cases, the rulers tried to enhance their power but failed, and the result was what we will call "limited monarchy."

It is important to distinguish centralization or state-building from absolutism. The former refers to the long-term development of institutions of the modern state, such as

VOICES

Theories of Absolute Monarchy

Most early modern political theorists emphasized that royal power not only came from God, but resembled divine power. One exception was Jean Bodin (1530–96), a French lawyer, judge, and politician who lived through his country's Wars of Religion. In his *Six Livres de la République* (*Six Books of the Commonwealth*) he dissects the origins and purposes of political power. Although he stresses the responsibility of the ruler to God, he argues that political power is secular and artificial in its origins. He is particularly concerned with the issue of sovereignty: that is, the locus and nature of the ultimate authority within a state.

> Let us now . . . consider the force of the word *absolute*. . . . [s]overeign power given to a prince charged with conditions is neither properly sovereign nor absolute, unless the conditions of appointment are only such as are inherent in the laws of God and of nature. . . .
>
> If we insist however that absolute power means exemption from all law whatsoever, there is no prince in the world who can be regarded as sovereign, since all the princes of the earth are subject to the laws of God and of nature, and even to certain human laws common to all nations.
>
> If the prince is not bound by the laws of his predecessors, still less can he be bound by his own laws. . . . It follows of necessity that the king cannot be subject to his own laws . . .
>
> It is far otherwise with divine and natural laws. All the princes of the earth are subject to them, and cannot contravene them without treason and rebellion against God. His yoke is upon them, and they must bow their heads in fear and reverence before His divine majesty.

From Jean Bodin, *Six Books of the Commonwealth*, trans. M.J. Tooley (Oxford: Blackwell, 1967), pp. 25–36, 56–69.

Jacques-Bénigne Bossuet (1627–1704) was a French bishop and court preacher to Louis XIV of France. He extolled the divine origin and nature of royal power, and the divine right of kings, in his *Politique tirée des propres paroles de l'Écriture Sainte* (*Politics Drawn from the Very Words of Holy Scripture*):

> Book III—*Where we begin to explain the nature and properties of royal authority*
> Article 2—*Royal authority is sacred*
> Proposition 1—*God established kings as His ministers, and through them reigns over the nations*

We have already seen that all power comes from God.

Princes therefore act as ministers of God, and as His lieutenants on earth. It is by them that He exercises His rule. . . .

It is for this reason that we have seen that the royal throne is not the throne of a man, but of God Himself. . . .

Proposition 2—*The person of kings is sacred*

It seems from all this that the person of kings is sacred, and that to attempt to kill them is sacrilege.

God has caused them to be anointed by the prophets with sacred oil, as he has anointed popes and altars.

It is necessary to keep kings as sacred things, and whoever neglects to do so is worthy of death.

Proposition 4—*Kings must respect their own power, and employ it only for the public good*

Their power coming from on high, kings must not believe that they are masters in order to use it according to their own will, but that they must dispose of it with fear and moderation, as a gift from God, and for which God will demand an accounting. . . . Kings must therefore tremble in using the power that God gives them, and ponder how horrible would be the sacrilege of using for evil the power that comes from God.

Book IV

Article 1—*Royal authority is absolute*

In order to render the term odious and insupportable, many seem to confuse absolute government and arbitrary government. But there is nothing more distinct than these, as we will see when we speak of justice.

Proposition 1—*The prince owes to no one an account of what he orders*

Without this absolute authority, he can neither do good nor punish evil. His power must be such that no one may hope to escape him, and finally, the only defence of individuals against the public power ought to be their innocence.

Proposition 2—*When the prince has judged, there is no other judgment*

It is therefore necessary to obey princes as it justice itself, without which there is no order. . . .

They are gods, and in some measure partake in divine independence . . .

God alone may judge their judgments and their person . . .

The prince may redress himself when he knows he has done badly, but against his authority, there can be no remedy outside his authority.

Jacques Bénigne Bossuet, *Politique tirée des propres paroles de l'Ecriture Sainte* (Paris: 1709), trans. M. Konnert.

legal and judicial systems, armed forces, and the tax system. The latter refers to the centre of power within the state: that is, who determines the policies these institutions will implement. Although it is often assumed that the two were inherently linked, this was not the case. In England, for example, the power of the monarch over the government—though still considerable—was limited in important ways in the later seventeenth century, but the government itself was very effective in enforcing its wishes throughout the kingdom. By contrast, in France—the usual exemplar of absolute monarchy—the ruler had much greater control of government policy, but the government's control of the kingdom was in some ways less than in England.

Although the concept of absolutism is useful for historical understanding, some qualifications are required. First, we must rid ourselves of any association with modern totalitarian regimes: no early modern monarchy attempted to control the lives of its subjects in the way that Nazi Germany or the Soviet Union under Stalin did. Nor was absolutism tyranny: no absolute ruler could deprive a subject of life, liberty, or property without cause. Subjects were not slaves; they had rights and privileges, and rulers were bound by natural law. They were also bound by certain fundamental laws of the kingdom, such as those governing succession to the throne, if only because no ruler, however powerful, could enforce his wishes from the grave. Nevertheless, during his lifetime all legitimate political power was in the hands of the ruler. He did not share it with any person, group, or institution (nobility, Church, Parliament, etc.), nor was he responsible to them for its exercise: his only responsibility was to God, and only God could judge him. To justify the king's power, royal lawyers turned to the principles of Roman law: like the Roman emperors, an absolute king had no earthly superior.

The word "absolute" has also misled students. In current usage it is a binary, all-or-nothing term: either something is absolute or it is not. When early modern writers used the term, however, they meant "pure" or "unmixed." Thus when they spoke of the king's absolute power, they did not mean that his power was unlimited or unrestrained: only that it was not shared with any other person or institution.

In the seventeenth century royal power was understood to exist in two modes or spheres. In one sphere, the ruler's power really was absolute, and it was exercised without constraint. This power, known as the "royal prerogative," covered such vital matters as the selection of ministers, the composition of the royal household, and the conduct of war and diplomacy. In the other sphere, the ruler's power was limited by the rights and liberties of his subjects, and its exercise required their consent in some form. The matters within this sphere included the exercise of justice, since it affected the lives and liberty of the subjects, and taxation, which affected their property. Since these two spheres often overlapped, their exact boundaries were subject to frequent debate and conflict. To give one very important example: while the conduct of war and diplomacy was clearly within the royal prerogative, exercising that prerogative required money, which was usually obtained through taxation of the ruler's subjects, which required their consent in some form.

It is also important to recognize whatever else absolutism was, it was definitely not revolutionary or innovative. Its roots were thoroughly historical. While nineteenth-century historians, seeking the origins of the national state as it existed in their time, focused on what was novel in the absolute monarchies of the seventeenth century, research over the past fifty years has revealed that those monarchies were highly traditional both in the way they exercised power and in their theoretical understanding of it. The growth of royal power was not accompanied by a revolution in the methods of government. It is true that seventeenth-century governments attempted to impose rational order and control on the unwieldy and cumbersome systems they had inherited, and sometimes even achieved a limited success, but on the whole the machinery of government laboured on as it had for centuries.

In an age without modern communications and transportation, when information could move no faster than a man on horseback, there were limits on the degree of control that any far-off monarch could exert. In practice, therefore, absolute monarchs and their governments had to appease local elites to gain their cooperation. Although the threat of force or coercion was always present, in most cases the government brought local elites into the system of absolute monarchy by promising them a share in the spoils of power, both tangible (a portion of tax revenue, for example) and intangible (social prestige).

As illogical as it may seem, absolute monarchies could be limited both in theory and in practice. Absolute and limited monarchies were not polar opposites, but different points along a spectrum. Towards one end royal powers were greater and the rights of subjects weaker, while towards the other the situation was reversed. However, to determine exactly where on this spectrum a monarchy went from being limited to absolute is impossible.

In some ways, absolutism was as much as response to vulnerability as it was an assertion of strength. The age of religious war was a dangerous time to be a ruler. We have already seen that Henry III was assassinated; his successor, Henry IV, would meet the same fate (see below); William of Orange was murdered by Spanish agents; there were numerous plots against Elizabeth I; and the target of the infamous Gunpowder Plot (1605) was her successor James I (r. 1603–25). It was in part to protect the king that apologists for royal power attempted to elevate his status above that of mere mortals by playing up the notion of "divine right": insisting that the king's power not only came from God, but resembled divine power in its nature and extent, and that to resist it was not only treason but heresy.

The ritual display that typically surrounded absolute rulers was a kind of propaganda. In addition to building the palace of Versailles as a showcase for his power, Louis XIV of France (r. 1643–1715; see below) instituted an elaborate court protocol that focused attention on himself as a divinely ordained ruler. In many ways, the rituals of the court were a kind of sleight-of-hand designed to distract attention from the reality that the king's power was not as great as he claimed. If Louis XIV actually did have the power he claimed over his most important subjects, would he have needed to manipulate them with flattery, honours, and monetary rewards? This is not to say that absolutism was not real; it simply means that the reality did not necessarily conform to the definitions of later historians.

From the vantage point of the present, the most important theorist of absolute monarchy was the Englishman Thomas Hobbes (1588–1679). Like Bodin, he lived through a period of disorder, turbulence and civil war, and he analyzed political power from a secular point of view. Unlike Bodin, however, he deduced the nature and purpose of political power from what he supposed to be its origins. Seeing humans as essentially selfish and power-hungry, in his *Leviathan* (1651) he concluded that the purpose of the state (the "commonwealth," as he called it) was to terrify people into obedience. Without an all-powerful sovereign, people had lived in a "State of Nature," which Hobbes character-ized as a "war of all against all." In order to escape this state of affairs, people had agreed with each other to put themselves under the rule of a sovereign. This grant was unlimited

---

HISTORICAL DEBATE

Absolute Monarchy

In the nineteenth century many observers interpreted the French Revolution as a reaction against "absolutism." In fact, it was then that the term was invented. According to the French writer and historian Alexis de Tocqueville (1805–59), the absolute monarchy of the seventeenth and eighteenth centuries paved the way for the modern bureaucratic national state by elimin-ating potential restraints on the monarch's power: among those elements were representative assemblies, provincial privileges, and the liberties of the society of orders in general. Absolute monarchy therefore represented not only a conscious departure from the medieval past, but a deliberate and coercive emasculation of rival sources of political authority. This view is now largely discredited, and some historians argue that the term "absolutism" should be discarded as an anachronism, an imposition on the past of later ideas and concerns. Thus in 1992 Nicholas Henshall published an article entitled "The Myth of Absolutism," in which he argued that the concept was misguided and anachronistic. His major points were as follows.

> Monarchy was absolute by definition. That was the point of it. Decisions were made by one man and not a committee. That at least is what Frenchmen of the *ancien régime* understood by absolute power. Not so their nineteenth-century historians, who turned absolute power into "absolutism." It was identified as the autocratic enemy of consent, the despotic foe of popular rights and liberties, the bureaucratic subverter of society's natural elites. It was also seen as alien to England. Her limited monarchy was saluted as the standard-bearer of liberty and government by consent: 1688 was the final breach between England and the Continent. . . .
>
> So how was the myth of "absolutism" created? It began with Fortescue in the fif-teenth century. He launched the attractive and indestructible notion that parliaments were uniquely English. It was inaccurate history but serviceable propaganda against the French national enemy. So was the deliberate blurring by English political theory, during the wars against Louis XIV, of the distinction between absolute and despotic power.
>
> By the 1850s "absolutism" had established itself in the history books. . . . It soon fused conveniently with another nineteenth-century experience—the rise of nation states

and irrevocable, because the only alternative was to return to the State of Nature, "which is the greatest evil that can happen in this life." Although Hobbes contributed in important ways to the development of political thought, his work was distinctly unpopular in his own day, as he stressed the artificial nature of political power, and his view of human nature left him open to charges of atheism.

with huge armies and modern bureaucracies. . . . Present preoccupations again defined perspectives on the past. Standing armies and bureaucratic devices, as they existed in the 1860s and 1870s, were now detected in the France of Louis XIV. They too became part of "absolutism."

Nicholas Henshall, "The Myth of Absolutism," *History Today*, 42, 6 (1992), pp. 40–7.

William Beik is a leading historian of early modern France, whose *Absolutism and Society in Seventeenth-Century France: State Power and Provincial Aristocracy in Languedoc* (Cambridge: Cambridge University Press, 1985) put forward what has become known as the "collaborationist thesis": that absolute monarchy was a cooperative venture between the king and local elites, in which both parties benefited at the expense of the ordinary peasants and workers who bore the brunt of the tax burden. The article excerpted here is a review of several more recent works on French absolutism.

French absolutism is . . . best conceptualized as a social compromise with the . . . nobility and other influential persons, but recent studies suggest corrections and additions. . . .

These studies thus reveal a basic contradiction between the king's primary efforts to maintain a traditional system by reinforcing hierarchical differences and defending property, and the same king's impulse to universalize and standardize procedures, which implied limiting the rights and privileges of those he wanted to defend. All the studies discussed here are saying, at least indirectly, that Louis XIV was a king with a traditional view of his power, not an avid state-builder. But to meet large objectives he stretched the old system to its limits, more so than any previous monarch had done, even introducing innovations which had the potential to undermine property and hierarchy. Absolute monarchy was not the centralizing leveller of intermediate bodies that Tocqueville imagined.[2] It was a backward-looking force that rebuilt an old system by adapting old practices to new uses. Louis [XIV] pushed the marketing of privilege to its limits, raised government through personal ties to a high art, redefined the relationship between the officer corps and the state, brought about a makeover of the provincial estates, and found ways to tax the privileged with abandoning the system of privilege.

William Beik, "The Absolutism of Louis XIV as Social Collaboration," *Past & Present*, 188 (2005), pp. 221–3.

Title page of *Leviathan* (1651). The figure of the sovereign wears an arched imperial crown, signifying that he has no superior on earth. In his hands he bears a sword and a bishop's crozier, indicating his supreme civil and ecclesiastical power. His body is made up of innumerable individual figures who together have agreed to grant him sovereign power. The Latin inscription is from Job 41:24: "There is no power on earth which can be compared to him."

France, 1589–1715: Royal Absolutism

The reign of Louis XIV (1643–1715) is often seen, with some justification, as the pinnacle of absolute monarchy not only in France but in Europe as a whole. This is certainly true in the sense that no French king before or after would reign in as absolute a fashion. However, he did not invent the system that allowed him to exercise such power. Rather, he built on the foundations established by his grandfather Henry IV (r. 1589–1610) and his father Louis XIII (r. 1610–43).

HENRY IV AND RECOVERY, 1598–1610

Having restored peace to France by 1598, Henry IV devoted the rest of his reign to allowing France to recover from decades of vicious civil war and restoring the royal authority that had been weakened during the Wars of Religion. In both these aims he succeeded. Religious peace was established through scrupulous adherence to the Edict of Nantes, even though, after converting, Henry himself sincerely embraced Catholicism. He was also personally very popular, deliberately earning a public image as the friend of the common man.

In re-establishing the royal finances he was more than ably assisted by his finance minister, the Huguenot Duke of Sully, an old comrade in arms. Wide-ranging reform of the fiscal system was impractical, given the vested interests involved, but Sully did manage to make the existing system work better. By the time of the king's death in 1610, the debt had been halved and a large cash reserve put aside, even as the burden of the *taille* had been reduced.

The most important innovation in finance was the introduction of the *droit annuel* or *paulette* (named after the official who proposed it). This was an annual fee charged to venal bureaucrats, which allowed them to pass their offices on to their heirs. Government office-holding was the main avenue of social mobility for ambitious bourgeois, and keeping an office in the same family across several generations was essential for attaining noble status. The *paulette* gave the government ongoing revenue from offices that had already been sold; over time, however, instead of securing the loyalty of venal officeholders, it created dynasties of office-holding families whose hold on their positions could not be easily challenged and whose interests were not necessarily those of the king and his ministers.

In foreign policy Henry IV was quite cautious, as he knew that France was in no condition to undertake a major war. Nevertheless, his chief concern was the same one that had preoccupied his predecessors: to prevent the encirclement of France by lands ruled by the Habsburg dynasty. By 1610 he felt secure enough to intervene in a German succession dispute in favour of the Protestant candidate, whose claim was disputed by a Habsburg-supported Catholic. In May 1610, while in Paris preparing to join his army, he was assassinated by a zealous Catholic determined to prevent the king from waging war on a fellow Catholic monarch.

LOUIS XIII AND CARDINAL RICHELIEU, 1610–1643

Henry IV was succeeded by his nine-year-old son Louis XIII (1610–43), with the Queen Mother, Marie de Medici, as regent.[3] As was often the case with a regency, however, especially when the regent was a woman and a foreigner, ambitious nobles seized the chance to cause trouble. Marie tried to buy their loyalty with generous grants and pensions, and by calling a meeting of the Estates-General where grievances could be aired. Although the Estates met for several months in 1614–15, the exercise proved futile, as the representatives of the three estates—clergy, nobles, and commoners (mostly venal officeholders)—blamed one another for the kingdom's problems. The Estates-General would not meet again until 1789, on the eve of the French Revolution.

In 1624 Louis XIII appointed to the royal council Armand Duplessis, Bishop of Luçon and Duke of Richelieu (1585–1642). Later named a cardinal of the Catholic Church, he was to serve as the king's primary adviser and chief minister for the rest of his life. Contrary to the view that Alexandre Dumas would popularize in *The Three Musketeers* (1844), the king and the cardinal formed a very effective partnership, and together they laid the foundations for the absolute monarchy of Louis XIV.

Towards the end of his life, Richelieu outlined the goals that had guided his advice to the king:

> to ruin the Huguenot party, to abase the pride of the nobles, to bring all your [the king's] subjects back to their duty, and to restore your reputation among foreign nations to the station it ought to occupy.[4]

On several occasions in the 1620s, the Huguenots had used their status as a "state within the state" to openly defy the king. Thus in 1627 the royal army laid siege to La Rochelle, the seaport that was the Huguenots' military stronghold. Finally surrendering after a year-long siege, the city was placed under direct royal control and its defences were demolished. Its people did retain their right to worship and their civil rights, however, and in 1629 the same settlement was imposed on the Huguenots throughout France.

Together, the king and cardinal also sought to turn the nobles from independent political players into obedient, though still socially dominant, subjects. Noble conspiracies against Richelieu, the "evil adviser" who supposedly held the king in his thrall, were ruthlessly suppressed. To undermine the independent military potential of the nobility, in 1626 a royal decree ordered the demolition of all the fortifications owned by nobles in the interior of France, and when the order was not universally obeyed, the royal army besieged and destroyed a number of castles. There were also attempts to crack down on the noble custom of duelling, which not only threatened the public order but symbolized nobles' exemption from royal justice. Draconian laws were enacted against the practice, but even though examples were made of several high-profile offenders, it was not eliminated.

When Richelieu wrote of bringing "your subjects back to their duty" he was thinking primarily of the duty of paying taxes. Taxes rose dramatically in the 1630s and 1640s, driven by incessant warfare (see below); by 1640 the amount collected in *taille* had doubled, and many other taxes were instituted or increased. Taxpayers rebelled, and in many cases the venal bureaucrats who were supposed to assess and collect the taxes refused to do so, whether because they sympathized with the taxpayers or because they feared for their lives. To overcome this resistance, Richelieu turned to a class of officials known as intendants, who did not own their positions and were therefore more direct and accountable instruments of the royal will. Such officials were not new, but the scope of their responsibilities was now greatly expanded. The new reliance on intendants was not part of a premeditated administrative revolution in government: it was an improvised solution to an immediate problem. They were intended to force the venal bureaucrats to do their jobs and, failing that, to collect the taxes themselves, with armed escorts if necessary.

Although they would later become a regular feature of the royal government, that was not the intent in the 1630s.

In foreign policy the chief aim of the king and his chief minister continued to be the prevention of Habsburg encirclement. As we have seen, France subsidized the Swedish army in the Thirty Years War and after 1635 entered the war openly. At the same time, from the late 1620s onwards, France was also battling Spain in a war that was fought in northern Italy, in western Germany, and along France's borders with both the Spanish Netherlands to the north and Spain itself to the south. In 1636 the Spanish army reached the town of Corbie, only 130 kilometres from Paris.

In the end, however, France prevailed, and in May 1643, at the battle of Rocroi, the famed *tercios* of the Spanish army suffered their worst defeat in over a century. More than any other event, this defeat heralded the end of Spanish military dominance. Neither Louis XIII nor Richelieu lived to see it, however, for the king had died a week earlier, and the cardinal in late 1642.

LOUIS XIV, THE REGENCY, AND THE FRONDE

Since the new king, Louis XIV (r. 1643–1715), was just four years old, once again a foreign Queen Mother—Anne of Austria—served as regent. She was assisted by Richelieu's protégé and handpicked successor, Cardinal Giulio Mazarini (1602–61), known in France as Jules Mazarin. As the wars in Germany and against Spain continued, so did the need for enormous amounts of revenue. But Anne and Mazarin insisted on governing as if they had the full authority of an adult king, and this further inflamed the resentments built up under Louis XIII and Richelieu.

By 1648 their high-handed ways had provoked serious resistance, leading the judges of the Parlement of Paris (effectively the Supreme Court of France) to draw up a list of demands that included reduction of the *taille*, abolition of the intendants, and an end to the creation and sale of new offices. The government agreed, in order to buy peace, but quickly reneged and tried to have several leading judges arrested. Widespread unrest followed, forcing the royal court to leave Paris. This insurrection became known as the Fronde ("sling"), after the slingshots used by the crowds to pelt the carriages of the high and mighty with stones and refuse.

A number of nobles announced their support for the Parlement and their willingness to defend it militarily if need be. They cared little for the legal principles espoused by the Parlement, but they did want for themselves the power that they charged Anne and Mazarin with abusing. Several years of political confusion and instability followed as various factions contended for power. By 1651 Mazarin had become the focal point of dissent, and to defuse the situation, he went into exile, although he remained in close contact with Anne and the royal government. The following year saw serious fighting around Paris as the royal government attempted to regain control. The judges of the Parlement were horrified by the chaos that their effort to restore a constitutional balance had unleashed; no doubt the English civil war and the execution of Charles I in 1649 (see below) also weighed on their minds. In any event, the appetite for resistance waned as increasing numbers of judges and their supporters were bribed or otherwise persuaded to abandon the cause, and once Louis XIV had been declared an adult in 1652, there was no longer any reason to fight back against the abuse of power by the regency. By 1653 the revolt had been extinguished.

The Fronde demonstrated that there was no real alternative to a strong royal government demonstrating both the weaknesses and strengths of absolute monarchy in France. Its major weakness was the fact that groups such as the Parlement, the nobles, and the venal bureaucrats represented separate centres of power, each with its own jealously guarded rights and privileges. Although for a time they were united by their hatred of Mazarin, in the end their individual interests made them susceptible to divide-and-conquer tactics, and this was the major strength of royal power. Under a capable adult king, the restrictions imposed on royal absolutism by the society of orders could be limited, but not entirely eliminated. The Fronde demonstrated to the royal government that the society of orders—in particular the nobles and venal bureaucrats—needed to be treated with kid gloves. Nothing was gained by running roughshod over their rights and privileges. At the same time, it revealed to the privileged orders that they had nothing to gain by attempting to limit royal power, since the resulting chaos would endanger their own wealth, power, and status.

LOUIS XIV AND THE ZENITH OF ROYAL ABSOLUTISM

Mazarin's last major accomplishment was the negotiation of the Peace of the Pyrenees (1659), which marked the beginning of France's ascendancy in Europe. Until his death in 1661, however, he continued to instruct the young Louis XIV in the art of governing. When the cardinal died, the twenty-three-year-old Louis took the reins of power himself, and until his own death in 1715 he would not only reign over France but govern it as well. Above all, he was guided by his own sense of what the French call *gloire*. Although often translated as "glory," this does not quite do the term justice, for it combines connotations of dignity, power, and reputation or renown. It was not enough for Louis to be the most powerful monarch in Europe: the rest of Europe had to acknowledge his dominance.

Nothing is more symbolic of Louis's reign than the palace he built outside Paris at what was then the village of Versailles (see Weblink). Begun in the 1670s and largely complete by the mid-1680s, Versailles became the new capital of France, and its significance was both political and symbolic. It was undefended, for Louis had no need of mere physical defences. Vast symmetrical gardens demonstrated the king's mastery over nature itself, while, throughout the palace, images of the sun—Louis's personal emblem, the centre of the cosmos, the source of light and power—reflected the Sun King's place at the centre of the political cosmos both in France and in Europe. The king was frequently portrayed as Apollo, the Greco-Roman god closely associated with the sun, as well as the bringer of peace and harmony.

Versailles was also a political tool that Louis used to tame the nobility, or at least the small portion of it with national political and social aspirations. Louis could not force nobles to live at court, but if they wanted to benefit from the king's largesse and bask in his prestige, they had to be physically present. Once there, they were caught up in a glittering whirlwind of court life, all of it focused on the person of the king. Meanwhile, the real business of government

Louis XIV as Apollo, by Joseph Werner (1637–1710). Louis XIV portrayed as Apollo, leaving the temple of the sun on his daily round to bring light to the world.

was conducted behind the scenes by Louis and his ministers, who, although most were noble themselves, had no power base independent of the king's favour (see Weblink: Versailles 3D).

Among the Sun King's most important ministers was Jean-Baptiste Colbert (1619–83), who served as kind of super-minister of trade, finance, industry, and infrastructure and, as was noted in Chapter 1, is closely associated with the concept of mercantilism. Colbert understood that the royal fiscal system was undermined by the numerous exemptions from the *taille*, widespread graft and corruption, and the sale of offices. Given the king's ambitious military agenda (see Chapter 7), however, he could not afford to arouse the opposition that a program of wholesale reform would arouse. Like Sully before him, Colbert had to be satisfied with cleaning the system up rather than fundamentally transforming it.

Colbert was the son of a merchant, and he understood that sustaining the king's power would require a prosperous kingdom. He took many measures to ensure general prosperity, all of them guided by mercantilistic assumptions. Tariff barriers were erected to discourage imports. New industries were founded and old ones were subsidized to enhance self-sufficiency and limit the flow of bullion out of the kingdom. French overseas colonies were developed as sources of raw materials and markets for French goods. New France, after languishing for decades, received more attention; French colonies were established in the Caribbean; and several companies were formed to compete with English and Dutch merchants in Asia and the Americas, among them the French East India Company (1662). To carry and protect this trade, both the navy and the merchant marine were enlarged.

The success of these efforts was mixed, however. The heavy regulation inherent in mercantilism tended to stifle initiative and innovation, and subsidies were directed to the production of luxury goods rather than sectors that would have had a more significant impact on productivity. The zero-sum assumptions of mercantilism would eventually lead France into a war with the Dutch Republic, which distracted attention from economic reform (see Chapter 7). Moreover, the later seventeenth century was a period of economic stagnation across Europe, and this made wholesale economic reform more challenging.

Louis deliberately encouraged rivalry among his ministers, and Colbert's great rivals were the father and son who together served as war ministers for the better part of Louis' reign: Michel le Tellier (1603–85) and his son, François-Michel le Tellier, Marquis of Louvois (1641–91). They built the largest and most formidable army in Europe, transforming an unwieldy conglomeration of mercenary units and semi-autonomous forces under the control of powerful nobles into a fighting force under strict royal control. In 1667, on the eve of Louis's first major war, the War of Devolution (1667–8; see Chapter 7), the army consisted of 72,000 soldiers; at its height in 1703, almost 400,000 men were under arms. To reduce the burden that the presence of the army imposed on civilians, storehouses and barracks were established throughout the kingdom, and training and discipline were regularized through often brutal military codes. Under the brilliant military engineer Sébastien le Prestre de Vauban, a network of fortresses was built along France's frontiers that reflected the latest developments in the science of fortification (see Chapter 4).

Governance during the Sun King's reign was firmly traditional. Intendants were widely used as inspectors and troubleshooters, but they were instructed to work in cooperation with the venal officeholders as far as possible, and they themselves worked in much the same way, by building local networks of allies and clients. Louis had little trouble with the Parlements, as the Fronde had demonstrated to all parties what happened when either one pushed the traditional boundaries too far. To raise money for his wars, Louis continued expanding the venal bureaucracy throughout his reign, even though Colbert advised against it and another minister is said to have told him that "every time Your Majesty creates an office, God creates a fool to buy it."[5] The royal government was usually able to achieve its goals without resorting to intimidation. Although the latter was not unknown, more often the king and local elites worked as partners, the king lending them his prestige and authority in return for their obedience. The oil that made the system work was the money that flowed to the government in the form of the fees charged for venal offices and tax revenue, and to office-holders in salaries and financial opportunities, legal (lending to government, for example) and otherwise.

A conventionally devout Catholic, Louis saw God as his more or less equal partner in the governance of France.[6] Nevertheless, his relations with the papacy were complicated by his support of Gallicanism (see Chapter 2). Louis had clashed with Rome on several issues pertaining to Church finance and administration, and his relations with Pope Innocent XI (r. 1676–89) were so poisonous that the latter refused to install French bishops and excommunicated the French ambassador to Rome.

Louis's relations with the Church, both in France and in Rome, were further complicated by his animosity towards Jansenism. Cornelius Jansen (1585–1635) was a Dutch Catholic theologian who believed that the Jesuits had led Rome to put too much emphasis on the role of human action in attaining salvation, thereby degrading the role of divine grace. Centred at the convent of Port-Royal, just outside Paris, the movement had attracted many followers in France, including Blaise Pascal (Chapter 5). The fact that the Jansenists were among the strongest proponents of Gallicanism should have recommended them to the King. However, a number of the judges involved in the Fronde had been Jansenists, and this predisposed him against them. No doubt the influence of his Jesuit confessors and his long-time mistress (later his wife), Madame de Maintenon was another factor. Finally, Louis believed that, as dissenters from officially approved orthodoxy, they stood in the way of the religious uniformity that was his goal, and thus detracted from his *gloire* as king.

Under normal circumstances, Rome would have supported the king in his desire to suppress the Jansenists. But relations between Louis and Innocent XI were already toxic, and as it happened, Innocent actually admired the Jansenists' strict morality. However, subsequent popes proved to be more cooperative, and Louis was finally able to crack down on the Jansenists. Port-Royal had been forbidden to receive new novices since 1661; in 1712 it was physically demolished and the twelve remaining nuns were dispersed at swordpoint. In 1713 Louis prevailed on Pope Clement XI (r. 1700–21) to issue the bull *Unigenitus*, condemning Jansenist teachings. But it overshot the mark and denounced a number of teachings that had long been accepted as orthodox Catholic doctrine. Many French clergy, including bishops, declared their support for the rejected teachings, and although the bull had the support of the government, their objections weakened its immediate force. As a consequence Jansenism retained its support in legal and academic circles, and it continued to be a divisive force in French religious and political life throughout the eighteenth century (see Chapter 10).

At the height of his conflict with Rome in 1685, Louis XIV issued the Edict of Fontainebleau, revoking the Edict of Nantes, in part to demonstrate his unimpeachable Catholic orthodoxy. For some time, the Edict of Nantes had been interpreted in the narrowest fashion possible. Soldiers were billeted with Huguenot families, and conversion to Catholicism was rewarded by payments from a slush fund as well as valuable tax exemptions. By 1685, Louis and his advisers were confident that there were not many Huguenots left. The Edict of Fontainebleau ordered Huguenot pastors to convert or leave the kingdom, and Huguenot churches and schools to be destroyed, outlawed Protestant worship, and declared any remaining Huguenots to be Catholic.

In reality, the Huguenot population still numbered approximately 1 million in 1685, of whom roughly 200,000 chose exile rather than conversion. They went to England and its colonies in the New World, Protestant areas of Germany, and the Dutch Republic and its colony at the Cape of Good Hope. Although the economic impact of the Revocation has been exaggerated, there can be no doubt that it cost France a number of educated and hard-working people. Nor did the revocation have the desired effect. Huguenot communities continued to worship illegally, and during Louis's last and most desperate war, a Huguenot revolt in the Cévennes mountains of central France would divert one of his armies from fighting his foreign enemies (see Chapter 7). The Revocation further complicated the Sun King's relations with Protestant states, and Protestant propaganda throughout Europe increasingly portrayed him as a political and religious tyrant.

From the perspective of the privileged classes the Sun King's reign appears as a golden age, "the Splendid Century" in which the language and culture of France displaced those of Italy as the models to be emulated throughout Europe.[7] In theatre it was the age of the tragedies of Pierre Corneille (1606–84) and Jean Racine (1639–99) as well as the comedies of Molière (1622–73). Musicians and composers such as Jean-Baptiste Lully (1632–87) and François Couperin (1668–1733) graced the court at Versailles. In painting, Nicolas Poussin (1594–1665) and Jean-Antoine Watteau (1684–1721) inherited the mantle of the Italian Renaissance masters. Yet from the point of view of workers and peasants, the age must have seemed anything but golden, especially in its later years. Louis's aggressive foreign policy led to nearly continual warfare with all the attendant misery, including sky-high taxation (see Chapter 7). By the 1690s the *taille* had reached the point of diminishing returns, as suppressing the resistance to new tax increases cost more revenue than they produced. Peasant debt, closely linked to taxation, resulted in widespread foreclosures that forced many peasant families to take to the road or seek charity in the towns. On top of this, poor harvests in 1693 and 1694 and again in 1709 led to massive famine and disease.

England: The Evolution of Limited Monarchy

By the end of the seventeenth century England had developed a political system that looked very different from its counterpart in France. Although the English themselves attributed this difference to their moral superiority (freeborn Englishmen would never have tolerated the kind of absolute monarchy that the servile French did), it was actually the result of historical circumstances: the ineptness of the English kings' efforts to enhance their power, the confluence of political and religious opposition, and institutional differences between the two kingdoms. England ended up with a monarchy whose still considerable power was limited by the parliamentary representatives of the monarch's most important subjects. Precisely because England's royal government incorporated those elites, it had greater power over the kingdom than the more absolute monarchy of Louis XIV had over France.

This state of affairs was not deliberately planned. It came about because English kings had tried and failed to render their power more absolute, provoking opposition, rebellion, and a revolution that resulted in the abolition of the monarchy. In the end, the ensuing instability and disorder persuaded the English elites that the only solution was to restore the monarchy, but in such a way that no monarch could never again attempt to govern England against their interests. Just as in France, therefore, king and elites reached an accommodation and understanding, although the precise nature of this accommodation was different. The monarchies of England and France were not polar opposites, one absolute and one "constitutional," one servile and one "free": they were merely situated at different points on the spectrum.

JAMES I AND THE PRESERVATION OF THE STATUS QUO

When Elizabeth I died without heirs in 1603, the kingdom passed to her Scottish cousin, the son of Mary Stuart, King James VI of Scotland (r. 1567–1625), who thus became King James I of England (r. 1603–25) as well. England and Scotland were united in the fact that they were ruled by the same man, but otherwise they remained separate kingdoms, each with its own legal, political, religious, and social systems, much like Castile and Aragon.

Elizabeth left some serious problems for her successor on both the religious and the political front: namely the grievances of Puritans and Parliament. When their new king arrived from Scotland, many hoped he would show more sympathy for their grievances than the late queen had. They were sorely disappointed. King of Scotland since the age of thirteen months, when his mother, Mary Queen of Scots, had abdicated, James had written a book on the divine right of kings and absolute monarchy, and he was a true believer. When MPs resisted his wishes, he would lecture them on the divine origins and nature of his power, and he was unwilling or unable to work within the system, to flatter and manipulate Parliament as Elizabeth had done. To avoid regular meetings of Parliament, he resorted to unsavoury measures such as forced loans (whereby certain people were compelled to lend the government money or face imprisonment), which further disillusioned many in the politically active classes. At the same time, he insisted on a lavish court, whose conduct gave rise to rumours of corruption and debauchery that were not unjustified. For advice and companionship, he relied on a series of handsome but disreputable playboys such as George Villiers (1592–1628), on whom he lavished money and titles including that of Duke of Buckingham.

English Puritans had hoped that James, coming from Presbyterian Scotland, would be sympathetic to their cause. But he was content with the episcopal structure of the Church of England, which firmly subjected the church to royal control. In a famous meeting with Puritan ministers within the Church of England, he informed them that "a Scottish Presbytery agreeth as well with a monarchy as with the devil. . . . No bishops, no king."[8] James also alienated Puritans in the area of foreign policy, making peace with Spain and failing to go to the aid of German Protestants in the early stages of the Thirty Years War, even though Frederick, the Elector Palatine and King of Bohemia, was his son-in-law (see Chapter 4). James died in 1625 without having resolved the tensions he inherited, but without actively inflaming them; he had largely maintained an increasingly unpopular status quo.

Charles I, Rebellion, Civil War, and Revolution

James I was succeeded by his eldest surviving son, who became King Charles I (r. 1625–49). Having inherited difficult circumstances, Charles made them infinitely worse through his stubborn self-righteousness and political ineptitude. Parliament displayed its mistrust of the king very early in his reign, when it refused to grant him the revenues from customs and excise taxes that were traditionally granted for life at the beginning of every reign. Charles simply ordered that the revenue be collected anyway, and resorted to a number of other shady fiscal practices, including a very controversial forced loan. He also continued to rely on his father's favourite, the unpopular Buckingham, for advice and support. Just three years into his reign, in 1628, both houses of Parliament approved a resolution called the Petition of Right, which catalogued the king's abuses of his power and set out what they considered to be the limits of the royal prerogative. Charles agreed to it, but once Parliament had been dismissed, he simply ignored its restrictions.

In 1629 Charles resolved to rule without Parliament. This was not illegal or unconstitutional, as Parliament did not meet unless summoned by the king. As long as the government needed no new sources of tax revenue, it could continue to function. Charles managed to rule without calling Parliament until 1640, a period known as either the "Personal Rule" or the "Eleven Years' Tyranny." To make ends meet, the government revived and expanded a host of half-forgotten practices, most of which were highly unpopular but not strictly illegal. Without Parliament as a forum to air their grievances, members of the political class could only seethe in private.

In religion, too, Charles actively alienated many of his subjects. His queen was a sister of Louis XIII of France, and with her household she openly practised her Catholic faith at court. Moreover, whereas his father had preserved the status quo, Charles sought to move the Church of England in a direction that the Puritans considered Catholic, downplaying the Calvinist doctrine of predestination and insisting on a rich and lavish liturgy, as well changes to the layout of churches.

To enforce his will, Charles relied primarily on two men: Thomas Wentworth, Earl of Strafford (1593–1641), the Lord Deputy of Ireland, and William Laud, the Archbishop of Canterbury (1573–1645). (Buckingham had been assassinated in 1628, for which the king blamed his enemies in Parliament, further poisoning their relations.) To punish their enemies, his advisers relied primarily on the Court of Star Chamber[9] and the Court of High Commission. Exempt from the rules of procedure that governed the common-law courts, such as respect for the rights of the accused to cross-examine witnesses and to examine the evidence against them, these "prerogative courts" were effective tools of royal power, but they further alienated Puritans and the king's political opponents, as well as ordinary people who increasingly came to see them as threats to their own perceived rights and liberties as "free-born Englishmen."

Even so, Charles might have been able to rule without Parliament indefinitely had he not made an enormous political blunder. In 1637 he attempted to bring the liturgy and doctrine of the Presbyterian Scottish Kirk into line with the Church of England, provoking widespread resistance in Scotland, and eventually an armed rebellion. This had to be punished, but Charles had no army capable of the task, and no money to acquire one. The only way to raise the funds was to call Parliament, which he did in the spring of 1640. Before they would consider the king's request, however, MPs insisted on redress of their grievances, which had been festering for eleven years. Charles angrily dissolved Parliament after three weeks, causing the session to become known as the Short Parliament. Almost immediately, the rebellious Scots invaded England and insisted they would negotiate only with Parliament, not with an untrustworthy king.

Thus Parliament was recalled for a sitting that in various permutations would continue on and off for twelve years. This Long Parliament quickly acted to restrict what it considered to be abuses of royal power. The Triennial Act of 1641 required that Parliament meet at least once every three years (no more "Eleven Years Tyranny"). Another act declared that Parliament could not be dissolved without its own consent (no more Short Parliaments). All taxation not explicitly granted by Parliament was declared illegal, and the prerogative courts were abolished. Archbishop Laud and Strafford were accused of treason, attainted (tried in Parliament), and eventually executed. It is important to note that members of Parliament did not think they were doing anything revolutionary. In resisting the king they were merely defending their traditional rights as Englishmen, not demanding any new civil or human rights. From their perspective it was the king who had violated the customary balance of the constitution: they were simply restoring the rightful political order against an abusive king.

At this point, a comparison with France may be instructive. The goals of Charles and his advisers were much the same as those of Louis XIII and Cardinal Richelieu: to make the king's will supreme throughout the kingdom, and to neuter any potential source of opposition. The English failure to achieve those goals can be attributed in part to personality and circumstance. Charles was rigid and self-righteous, equating disagreement and criticism with treason, and unlike Louis, was incapable of making a tactical retreat to achieve long-term objectives. Neither Strafford nor Laud was Richelieu's equal in political acumen or ruthlessness.

In addition, various structural elements made it more difficult to strengthen royal control in England than in France. The latter had a large and relatively well-trained salaried bureaucracy, whose members were for the most part effective agents of the royal will, although (as the Fronde demonstrated) they could be obstructive when crossed. In England, by contrast, the salaried bureaucracy was very small and confined mostly to London. Thus to enforce laws and govern the kingdom, the government relied on a network of volunteers: locally prominent men who served as judges, justices of the peace, and sheriffs. Yet these were the very people most alienated by Charles's policies and conduct. Without their cooperation, the government would have almost no one to do the work of governing. Furthermore, they were the men who elected the members of the House of Commons (membership in the upper House, the House of Lords, was defined by heredity and office.) Since the Reformation Parliament of the 1530s, they had acquired a sense of common purpose and identity as the political class of the kingdom, and they believed that they had a legitimate voice in the government of England. France, on the other hand, had no experience of a regular national assembly: the Estates-General met much less frequently than the English Parliament had before 1629, and the meetings that did take place were generally unproductive (at the most recent session, in 1614–15, the three estates had blamed one another for the kingdom's troubles). As a result, the Estates-General was useless either as a tool of royal government or as a constraint on royal power, and it never became a feature of the government in the way that the English Parliament did. In France, unlike England, there were numerous regional and provincial assemblies, but they were narrowly concerned with their own particular interests and were susceptible to divide-and-conquer tactics. The French monarchy also had a greater ability to tax without consent, and thus a freedom of action that English monarchs did not. Another important difference between the two states was the religious zeal that the Puritans brought to the opposition, an element that was lacking in France.

In the early 1640s the Long Parliament had sought to restore what its members believed to be the customary balance of the constitution. But as the attacks on royal power continued, increasing numbers of MPs felt uneasy, and a royalist party began to take shape in Parliament. Thus a "Root and Branch Bill" abolishing the episcopal structure of the Church of England was passed by the House of Commons in September 1641 by a margin of only eleven votes. In November the Grand Remonstrance listed all the king's abuses of power and proposed that he be required to select his advisers and ministers from among men approved by Parliament, even though the choice of ministers had always been an undoubted part of the royal prerogative. Although it was passed, the margin of victory was narrow, with 159 in favour and 148 opposed.

Meanwhile, a revolt that had broken out among Catholic peasants in Ireland needed to be suppressed, but Parliament was reluctant to give Charles an army that might be used against it. When the Militia Bill of 1642 stripped him of his control over the armed forces—another undoubted part of the royal prerogative—this was too much for Charles. He invaded Parliament with 400 soldiers, seeking to arrest his most vehement critics, only to find that they had been forewarned and had slipped away. [10] A few days later he set out for the north of England to gather support and form an army, leaving Parliament to declare him the aggressor and establish its own army and government. England had passed from political strife to civil war.

While Charles had the support of the relatively poor north and west of the country, Parliament controlled the wealthier and more populous south and east, including London. It moved quickly to take control of the navy, which it used to intercept shipments of supplies to the royalists. And though initially it relied on local militias, by 1645 it had formed a full-time, professional force known as the New Model Army. Promotion in this army was based on merit rather than family or political connections, and its most important commander was the MP for Cambridge, an obscure country gentleman named Oliver Cromwell (1599–1658). A deeply devout Puritan, convinced that God had chosen him for a special destiny, Cromwell proved to be a highly effective leader and an outstanding general—the only one who could reliably win battles. By 1646 the fighting was largely over: Parliament had prevailed over the royalists, and the king was its prisoner.

Why did some members of the English political class choose to support Parliament while others remained loyal to the king? Historians have debated this question without arriving at a satisfactory general answer. For most people it was an agonizing personal decision that required them to weigh many conflicting factors: traditional loyalty, personal belief, and political interest. Puritans, however, invariably supported Parliament, and they brought their religious zeal and conviction to the struggle. Ordinary people—farmers and workers—played little or no role in the origins of the civil war. It was not a conflict between the elites and the masses, but rather a conflict within the political and social elite of the kingdom.

THE INTERREGNUM, THE SEARCH FOR STABILITY, AND THE RESTORATION

Once it had won the war, Parliament faced the difficult question of what to do next. Charles might have been defeated, but he was still king, and he still had significant support. In Parliament two basic factions were forming. The Presbyterian faction consisted mainly of men of higher social standing who favoured a moderate settlement that would restrain royal power and retain a purified Church of England as the official national church. The other faction, the Independents, rejected the idea of any official national church and called for a congregational system of church government, in which each local church would

Visual Arts Library / Art Resource, NY

The execution of Charles I, by John Weesop. The painter John Weesop claimed to have witnessed the execution of Charles I. Those present were clearly aware of the enormity of the act. According to one observer, the crowd "let out such a groan as I never heard before, and I desire that I never hear again." In the foreground one woman is fainting, while in the lower right panel, a bystander catches the king's blood with a handkerchief.

govern itself. These were in general men of lesser wealth and social status, and their political goals ranged from Parliamentary supremacy to outright abolition of the monarchy in favour of a republic.

Many of the army commanders, including Cromwell, were Independents, and fear of Presbyterian collusion with the king led them to forcefully purge Parliament of its more conservative members, leaving behind a "Rump." Cromwell was now convinced that no possible accommodation with the king was possible and that not only must Charles face trial, but the monarchy must be abolished. As he put it in his characteristically blunt manner: "we will cut off his [the king's] head with the crown on it."[11] Brought to trial for treason before a special Parliamentary tribunal, Charles refused to acknowledge the court's legitimacy: how could he commit treason against himself? Nevertheless, he was found guilty and sentenced to death. His beheading, on January 30, 1649, was unprecedented in European history. Kings had certainly been murdered, but never before had a king been tried by his subjects and executed for treason.

Over the next decade Cromwell and his colleagues tried a variety of political systems, but none succeeded in restoring stability to England. In 1649 England was declared to be a Commonwealth under the supremacy of the Rump Parliament, and executive power was entrusted to a Council of State. Real power, however, lay with Cromwell and the army, which in 1653 dissolved the Rump Parliament at swordpoint and replaced it with a carefully chosen assembly of Puritans. But this "Barebones" Parliament, named after the Puritan preacher Praisegod Barebones, proved no more effective than the Rump, and it too was quickly dissolved. In late 1653 Cromwell was made "Lord Protector" of England, in essence an uncrowned king.[12] The Protectorate was in fact a military dictatorship, and just like Charles I, Cromwell was reduced to ruling England alone. Indeed, with the army to carry out his orders, Cromwell was able to impose absolute rule on England in a way that Charles never could.

Now English Puritans were in a position to carry out the godly reform of society. Taverns and alehouses were strictly regulated and theatres outlawed altogether. Observance of the Sabbath was strictly enforced. Popular practices considered immoral or pagan were outlawed. Village Mayday celebrations were forbidden, and in 1647 Christmas festivities were banned on the grounds that they were not only unseemly occasions for excess, but pagan in origin (there is no evidence that Christ was born on December 25, and Christmas was timed to coincide with the Roman pagan festival of Saturnalia). This agenda of godly reform was not unique to England, but only in England did the reformers gain the political power to implement it.

Political turmoil led to social and religious radicalism as the authority of monarchy and church were questioned. Religious groups such as the Muggletonians and Fifth Monarchy Men believed that the Last Judgment was approaching, while the Quakers, who literally shook with the Holy Spirit, rejected all outward forms of social distinction and religious organization. The Diggers (named for their practice of filling in the ditches and demolishing the walls that delineated property boundaries) advocated a kind of primitive communism. In politics, the Levellers pressed for universal male suffrage, annual Parliaments, and radical legal reforms that would end the social and political ascendancy of the elite. They were especially prominent in the army, whose leaders, with Cromwell, confronted the Leveller leaders in 1647 in a series of debates held at Putney (see Weblink). Colonel Rainsborough, the highest ranking Leveller in the army, famously declared:

> that the poorest he that is in England hath a life to live, as the greatest he; and therefore truly, Sir, I think it's clear, that every man that is to live under a government ought first by his own consent to put himself under that government; and I do think that the poorest man in England is not bound in a strict sense to that government that he hath not had a voice to put himself under.

Although Cromwell was unable to achieve political stability, his regime was successful in war. In 1649 he led the New Model Army to Ireland and brutally suppressed the Catholic rebellion that had begun in 1641. Irish Catholic peasants were displaced and their land was given to Protestant settlers from England and Scotland, sowing the seeds for centuries of sectarian conflict. Scotland chafed under Cromwell's rule, and when it recognized Charles I's son as king, Cromwell invaded in 1650 and subjected it to the same military dictatorship as England. In 1654, England triumphed in the first of several naval wars with the Dutch Republic (known as the Anglo–Dutch Wars), and after entering the war between France and Spain in 1654 on the French side, acquired Jamaica from Spain in the Peace of the Pyrenees (1659).

No amount of military success, however, could disguise the fact that Cromwell's regime lacked legitimacy and was increasingly dependent on military power alone to prop it up. On his death in 1658, his designated successor—his son Richard (1626–1712)—was unable to secure the loyalty of the army. While ambitious generals schemed to replace him, for roughly eighteen months there was no effective government. Finally, in early 1660 General Monck led his army to London and restored the Long Parliament, which then voted to restore the monarchy and invited the eldest son of Charles I to return from exile in the Netherlands as King Charles II.

Thus England's experiment in republicanism ended with the restoration of the monarchy. Like their French counterparts during the Fronde, English elites had seen what happened when the political order was overturned, and they did not like what they saw.

FROM RESTORATION TO OLIGARCHY

When Charles II (r. 1660–85) returned to England, the powers of the monarch that he took up were the ones that had existed in 1641, in the early days of the Long Parliament. The laws to which his father had assented were kept, but those he had rejected were declared null and void. Thus the prerogative courts were not revived, and the Triennial Act remained in force, as did the requirement that any new taxes be approved by Parliament. The episcopal structure of the Church of England was also restored. The monarch still had great power, including command of the armed forces and the right to choose his own ministers and advisers.

More importantly, no one wanted to repeat the experience of the preceding twenty years. Charles II was acutely conscious of his father's fate. Far from seeking vengeance, he was quite magnanimous to his father's enemies: only thirteen people were executed for the roles they had played in the civil war. An accomplished ladies' man (the original "good time Charlie"), he acknowledged fathering at least fourteen illegitimate children, and unlike his rigid father, Charles II had a sense of humour. This is not to say that he was uninterested in governing, or that he meekly accepted Parliamentary limitations. But he knew better than to overtly challenge Parliament and the general consensus that had brought him to power. The monarch and the representatives of his leading subjects had established a partnership, and although its exact nature was still being worked out, neither side was willing to pursue a confrontation to its ultimate conclusion.

In the years that followed the restoration, two loosely organized parties began to take shape in Parliament. The Tories, who tended to represent the landed gentry, believed in the divine right of kings but not absolute monarchy, which they called "arbitrary" and associated with the France of Louis XIV. They also believed that a just balance between Parliament and monarchy had been reached, and generally supported royal power. In religion they favoured the restored Church of England, and they opposed greater toleration for either Catholics or non-Anglican Protestants ("Dissenters" or "non-conformists"). The Whigs, on the other hand, tended to represent business and commercial interests. Although not republicans, they tended to be wary of "abuses" of royal power and to push for greater Parliamentary influence. They favoured greater toleration for Protestant Dissenters, but not for Catholics.

The king himself formally converted to Catholicism on his deathbed, and might have been Catholic at heart all along, but he knew that any attempt to restore the Catholic Church in England would be political (and perhaps literal) suicide. In the 1670 Treaty of Dover, he agreed to an alliance with France, and in a series of secret articles accepted a hefty pension from Louis XIV on the understanding that England would be restored to the Catholic Church when circumstances allowed (although he well knew that those circumstances would never exist). The most serious crisis of the reign concerned religion and the succession to the throne. Despite his numerous bastards, Charles and his queen had no children. Thus the heir presumptive was his younger brother, James, Duke of York, who had converted to Catholicism as an adult and was as rigid as his father had been. In 1678, however, a faction of Whigs led by the Earl of Shaftesbury either fabricated or capitalized on a supposed "popish plot" to murder Charles, place James on the throne, restore Catholicism, and eliminate Parliament. Shaftesbury took advantage of the resulting hysteria to introduce a bill excluding James from the succession. This was too much for Charles: he would not fight to the end for Catholicism, or for royal power, but he drew the line at the legitimate succession of the Stuart dynasty. From 1679 to 1681, three successive Parliaments attempted to pass the Exclusion Bill, only to be summarily dismissed by the king.

At the height of the crisis the king fell very ill, and the prospect of his imminent death and renewed civil war caused cooler heads to prevail. Shaftesbury was discredited and fled into exile rather than face arrest and trial. With the Whigs largely on the defensive,

Charles was able to rule from 1681 until his death in 1685 without Parliament, ignoring the Triennial Act with only the barest outcry. Booming traded filled the treasury with excise taxes, and he had no need to call Parliament to grant revenue. In some ways, he looks like an absolute monarch, but he was careful to limit his actions to what Tories would support. It was a tacit admission that the king in some sense exercised his power in conjunction with his powerful subjects.

When Charles died in 1685, his brother became King James II (r. 1685–8) with only minimal fuss.[13] With the zeal of an adult convert, he was determined to restore England to the Roman Catholic Church. He simply ignored or suspended the legislation that discriminated against Catholics, and appointed them to positions in the government, armed forces, and universities. Most of the movers and shakers in the kingdom were willing to tolerate this behaviour because the only potential heirs to the throne were James's two adult daughters from his first marriage, Mary and Anne. Both were Protestant, and the husband of the former—William of Orange, the de facto of ruler of the Dutch Republic (see below)—was not only a grandson of Charles I but among the leading Protestant princes in Europe. James's second marriage, to an Italian Catholic princess, was still childless, and since he was already 53 when he became king, it was expected to remain so. In June 1688, however, the queen gave birth to a baby boy. Since, as a male, the infant Prince James Francis Edward took precedence over his adult half-sisters, Protestant England thus faced the prospect of a Catholic dynasty into the indefinite future. This prompted the series of events known to historians as the "Glorious Revolution."

A self-selected group of politicians, both Whigs and Tories, wrote to William of Orange inviting him to England to protect the Protestant faith, secure a meeting of Parliament, and investigate the legitimacy of the newborn prince.[14] Landing in the southwest of England with a large fleet and an army of 40,000 men in November, William led his army to London virtually unopposed, as English commanders either joined him or refused to fight. James II panicked and fled into exile in France. This response was a huge miscalculation; if the king was unwilling to fight for his throne, why should anyone else?

In January 1689 William convened an irregular assembly called a Convention (legally it could not be called a Parliament, since it had not been summoned by the king), which declared the throne to be vacant, James II having abdicated by fleeing.[15] The Convention then declared William and Mary joint rulers of England by virtue of heredity and right of conquest in a just war. At their coronation they swore "to govern the people of this kingdom of England, and the dominions thereunto belonging, according to the statutes in Parliament agreed on, and the laws and customs of the same." Their power was further restrained by a Bill of Rights (1689) that forbade both the arbitrary use of power and the maintenance of a standing army during peacetime without Parliament's approval. Elections to Parliament and debate within it were both to be free. William and Mary were granted an annual income insufficient to govern the kingdom even in peacetime, ensuring frequent meetings of Parliament. Finally, Catholics were excluded from the royal succession, and if William and Mary were to remain childless (as indeed they did), Mary's younger sister Anne was to inherit the throne.

Mary died in 1694, and William reigned alone for the remaining eight years of his life. He saw England primarily as a source of revenue to finance his war against Louis XIV, which was his major concern (see Chapter 7). The actual government of England he left largely in the hands of his ministers and advisers. On his death in 1702 the throne passed to Anne. With her husband, a Danish prince, Anne had had at least seventeen pregnancies, but only one child had survived infancy, and he had died at the age of ten in 1700. To prevent the throne from passing back to the Catholic James II or his heirs, in 1701 Parliament passed the Act of Settlement, which excluded the first fifty-four potential claimants, all of whom were Catholic, and declared the first Protestant in the genetic line to be the heir presumptive. This was Electress Sophie of Hanover, a mid-sized north German state. But Sophie predeceased Anne, and thus on Anne's death in 1714 the throne passed to Sophie's son, Elector Georg Ludwig of Hanover, who became King George I of England (r. 1714–27).

By the end of the seventeenth century the power of the English monarch was constrained by the interests of the kingdom's elites as represented in Parliament. The evolution towards this limited monarchy was not the product of any forethought or deliberation. It was an accident, the result of miscalculation, stubbornness, and ineptitude on the part of English kings. Although the limitations imposed on the monarchy in England clearly did distinguish it from the absolute monarchy of France, this should not deceive us into seeing the two systems as polar opposites. In both England and France, rulers had to balance the interests of various elites, both local and national. The ways in which they did this, and the precise balances and distributions of powers, differed, of course, but these were differences of degree rather than of kind. The absolute monarchy of Louis XIV looks more powerful, and Louis did exercise greater authority over his government than his English counterparts did over theirs. On the other hand, precisely because the English government was a more explicit partnership between king and elites, it was able to exert greater control over the kingdom as a whole.

Spain in the Seventeenth Century

The Peace of the Pyrenees in 1659 marked the end of at least a century during which Spain dominated Europe, largely on the strength of American gold and silver. In hindsight it is tempting to see signs of a decline in Spanish power long before they became evident to contemporaries. In fact, Spain remained dominant until about 1640, when it began to decline quite quickly. Put another way, the inflow of gold and silver from the New World allowed Spain's rulers and governments to paper over some serious flaws in the Spanish economy, government, and society in general, even as it made some of these flaws worse. Many were aware of these flaws, but addressing them would have required brilliant leadership, and even that might not have sufficed. Although the parallels are not exact, Spanish rulers failed to enhance their powers at the same time that absolutism in France was reaching its peak.

Although we use "Spain" as a term of convenience, the empire ruled by the Habsburg monarchs was still a conglomerate of separate territories, each of which had its own government, laws, and institutions: Castile, Aragon, and Portugal on the Iberian peninsula; several significant territories in Italy, including Milan and Naples; the Free County (Franche-Comté) of Burgundy in western Germany; and the Spanish Netherlands. The core of the empire was Castile: the most populous territory, the wealthiest (thanks to its American colonies), and the one largely responsible for financing the rest. How much bullion was delivered to Castile is hard to tell, since smuggling, graft, and corruption were widespread. However, it is clear that shipments began to decline in the 1590s, and although occasional spikes may have occurred after 1600, the overall trend was downwards. By the 1660s, shipments of bullion had fallen to roughly one-tenth of their peak levels.

American gold and silver served to obscure some serious problems in the Castilian economy and society. While France had perhaps 16 million inhabitants in the early seventeenth century, Castile's population was about 6 million and declining. Its climate was relatively arid, its soil poor, and its agriculture unproductive; its towns were relatively small and poor; and its society was dominated by a handful of great nobles—the grandees—who lived on the income from royal pensions and government bonds, along with the revenue from sheep raising, and governed their vast estates almost as independent principalities. Since Spanish nobles were exempt from all taxation, the tax burden fell overwhelmingly on the poor peasants, whose poverty was exacerbated by the fact that so much land was devoted to raising sheep rather than crops. When they could no longer support themselves on the land, many peasants were forced to look for work or charity in the towns. But the only industrial work available was in the production of luxury goods: basic goods were imported, and had to be paid for with gold and silver. Nearly continual warfare meant that the government owed enormous debts, primarily to Italian bankers. Most American bullion therefore passed through Castile on its way to foreign merchants and bankers.

When Philip II died in 1598, his son became King Philip III (r. 1598–1621). Fundamentally lazy and uninterested in ruling, he left the work of government in the hands of his favourite minister, the Duke of Lerma, who used his power to enrich himself, his family, and his friends rather than to address the serious problems that Spain and its empire faced. This was doubly unfortunate because Lerma could have effected real reform between 1609 and 1621, during the truce in the war with the rebel forces in the Netherlands (see Chapter 4). Ironically, the one enterprise carried out with any efficiency in that period only made things worse. This was the expulsion of Spain's remaining Muslims— the *moriscos*—in 1609. Having been expelled from Granada in the 1570s and resettled elsewhere in Spain, they were numerically insignificant in most of Castile, but in Valencia (part of the Kingdom of Aragon) they made up one-third of the population and provided essential agricultural labour. Although they posed no threat, they made convenient scapegoats for a government anxious to deflect attention from its problems. It was no coincidence that the expulsion decree was issued on the very day that the truce was signed with the Dutch.

Philip III in turn was succeeded by his son Philip IV (r. 1621–65), then a boy of sixteen, who would prove to be more energetic and effective than his father. His chief minister for much of his reign was Gaspar de Guzman, Count–Duke of Olivares (1587–1645),

VOICES

Diagnosing a Society in Decline

The problems that confronted Spain in the seventeenth century did not go unperceived by contemporaries. Reformers, known as *arbitristas*, proposed a range of solutions from soundly practical to hopelessly utopian. One of the most prominent *arbitristas* was Martín González de Cellorigo, who in 1600 wrote the following:

> What is most certain is that our republic has declined so greatly from its former state because we have disregarded natural laws, which teach us to work, and because we have put wealth, which is acquired through natural and human industry, into gold and silver. . . .
>
> Spain has turned its eyes so completely towards the Indies, from which gold and silver is coming, that . . . if all the gold and silver that its natives have found and are finding in the New World were to enter here, it would not make Spain as rich and powerful as it would have been without it. . . . A lot of money in a kingdom perverts relations among men. . . .
>
> There is nothing worse than the excessive wealth of some and the extreme poverty of others, which has done so much to disorient our republic. . . . And though it would not be good to say that everyone must be equal, it would not be unreasonable to say that the two extreme situations are equally bad. . . .

who brimmed with ideas for reform. Politically, he advised the king that he must make himself King of Spain:

> By this I mean, Sir, that Your Majesty should not be content with being King of Portugal, Aragon, and Valencia, and Count of Barcelona, but should work and secretly scheme to reduce these kingdoms of which Spain is composed to the style and laws of Castile, with no differentiation. . . . [16]

He reduced grants and pensions to nobles, as well as the expenses of the royal court, which had reached 10 per cent of government expenditures under Philip III. He tried (with limited success) to restrain noble extravagance by, for example, forbidding the massive collars of ruffled lace that were then the height of fashion. He also tried to lessen the burden on Castile's poor and overtaxed peasants, but met enormous resistance from the privileged nobles and towns.

Olivares might have achieved some of his planned reforms had he kept Spain from resuming its war against the rebellious Dutch provinces in 1621. But he did not. Spanish armies also went to the aid of the Habsburg Holy Roman Emperor in the Thirty Years War,

It is fate that gold and silver be taken out of Spain, and that this kingdom only holds temporarily the wealth that it soon returns to other kingdoms. . . .

The merchant, for the sweetness of the fixed gain of *censos* [a kind of loan often made to farmers], sets aside his commerce, the official disdains his office, the farmer abandons his farming, the shepherd his flock, the noble sells his lands, exchanging the hundred they were worth for the five hundred he hopes to make in interest. . . .

Our republic has come to the extremes of rich and poor, without there being any middle to moderate them; so we are either rich people who do nothing, or poor people who ask for things; . . . as a result, . . . those who want to cannot, and those who can do not want to; and so the lands remain unworked, the crafts not pursued . . . and many projects necessary for the public good remain undone.

In Jon Cowans (ed.), *Early Modern Spain: A Documentary History* (Philadelphia: University of Pennsylvania Press, 2003), pp. 133–40.

[Wealth is] dissipated on thin air—on papers, contracts, *censos*, and letters of exchange, on cash, and silver, and gold—instead of being expended on things that yield profits and attract riches from outside to augment the wealth within. And thus there is no money, gold, or silver in Spain, because there is so much, and it is not rich, because of all its riches. . . .

In J.H. Elliott, *Imperial Spain, 1469–1716* (Harmondsworth: Penguin, 1970), p. 317.

and from the late 1620s Spain was also at war with France. Olivares saw no contradiction between the pursuit of a reform agenda at home and an aggressive foreign policy: what would be the point of reforming a kingdom and leaving it at the mercy of its enemies?

By 1640, all of Olivares's grand schemes were falling apart. Catalonia, part of the Kingdom of Aragon, revolted against royal rule and the Catalans placed themselves under French protection. In Portugal, long-standing resentment of Castile led the nobles to elect one of their own as king in 1640 and launch a war for independence. In light of these revolts, for which he was widely blamed by nobles, Olivares retired from royal service in defeat.

Olivares and Richelieu were almost exact contemporaries; their careers ran along parallel tracks, and in their time they were considered the dominant statesmen of the age. Yet historians have judged Richelieu largely successful and Olivares a failure. Richelieu was probably more clear-sighted and more ruthless than Olivares in pursuing his goals. France certainly enjoyed greater resources and a larger population than Spain, and despite its regional diversity, it was more unified, linguistically and culturally, than the Spanish kingdoms, let alone the Netherlands and Italy. In a conservative age that mistrusted innovation, Richelieu and Louis XIII were attempting to restore royal power and the greatness of

France after the Wars of Religion, whereas Olivares was attempting something unprecedented in Spanish history.

With the resignation of Olivares, Philip IV's government lost its direction, and plans for fundamental reform were abandoned. The Catalonian revolt had been subdued by 1652, but Philip swore to observe Catalonia's privileges and liberties, thereby killing Olivares's scheme to create a single Spanish kingdom. Portugal, on the other hand, managed to defend its independence with Dutch and English aid, and although Philip never acknowledged it, after his death in 1665 his widow, acting as regent for their young son, finally did.

Charles II (r. 1665–1700) was just three years old when Philip died. The unfortunate product of generations of Habsburg inbreeding, he was sickly and mentally challenged, did not speak until he was four, and did not walk until he was eight. Although he married twice, he fathered no children and was likely infertile. With an incompetent king, the government was for the most part a legal fiction, and Spain was dominated as never before by its most privileged groups, the nobles, who treated the royal treasury as their own piggybank, and the clergy, whose numbers increased even as the population continued to decline. Everyone knew that Charles II would be the last Habsburg ruler of Spain. What would become of the Spanish empire when he died was the most significant diplomatic issue in seventeenth-century Europe. As we will see in Chapter 7, when his death finally came, in 1700, it would precipitate worldwide conflict.

The Dutch Republic

The Dutch Republic, or United Provinces of the Netherlands, fits uneasily in any discussion of seventeenth-century government. Although formally a republic, it was dominated for long periods by the Princes of Orange, who exercised near-monarchical powers. It was riven by deep-seated political, social, and religious tensions that kept it perpetually on the brink of civil war. Nevertheless, the Dutch were able to preserve their independence when war with Spain resumed in 1621, to fight three naval wars against England in the seventeenth century, and to repel an invasion by the most powerful army in Europe, that of Louis XIV.

As we saw in Chapter 4, the republic had been born of the struggle to preserve local and provincial liberties against Philip II. But there was a fundamental ambiguity at the centre of its political life. The "regents"—members of the urban merchant class who dominated not only commerce but both urban and provincial governments—saw the republic as a vehicle to preserve those liberties. The Princes of Orange and their supporters, on the other hand, saw the republic as the expression of a nascent Protestant nationality, whose interests ought to supersede local and provincial privileges. The central government was the States-General, whose jurisdiction was limited to military and diplomatic matters; all other affairs—justice, taxation, economic regulation—were the responsibility of individual provinces and towns. The States-General was made up of delegates from each of the provincial States, who were selected by city governments. In the States-General, each province had a single vote, and in theory, all votes had to be unanimous, although some exceptions were made. The regents wanted to limit the authority of the States-General, thus preserving their own power, while the Orangists favoured an expanded role for the States and greater centralization of power.

The richest and most influential province by far was Holland, with its wealthy and populous capital of Amsterdam. Since virtually nothing could be done without Holland's money, the direction of national politics was largely determined by whoever controlled Holland. When the States-General was not in session, its business was carried out by a series of standing committees. Only Holland was entitled to a seat on all these committees, and during the periods when the regents dominated the central government, the leader of Holland's delegation acted as a de facto chief executive of the republic.

If the regents espoused a particularist vision of the republic, the Princes of Orange represented a centralizing vision. They had the prestige of William the Silent's crucial role in the revolt against Philip II and his position as father of the country. In times of war (most of the time), the leader of the House of Orange also held the titles of captain-general and admiral-general, or commander-in-chief of the army and the navy. The fact that the Prince of Orange at any time also held the position of *stadtholder* (provincial governor) in most of the seven provinces conferred not only prestige, but also significant powers of appointment and patronage.

These political cleavages were mirrored and intensified by religious divisions. Calvinism in the seventeenth century was divided by a doctrinal controversy that paralleled the Jansenist–Jesuit dispute within the Catholic Church. A Dutch Protestant theologian named Jacob Arminius (1560–1609) had downplayed Calvin's extreme concept of predestination, seeking greater scope for free will in accepting or rejecting divine grace. His views became popular in regent circles, and in many towns Arminian preachers were appointed to churches. They were opposed by strict Calvinists who upheld Calvin's views.[17] As late as 1600, Roman Catholics were a numerical majority in the supposedly Protestant Dutch Republic, and there were also substantial minority populations of Lutherans, Mennonites, and Jews. While the Calvinists wanted to enforce religious uniformity more stringently, forbidding other forms of worship, the regents foresaw the complications that would follow such a move, and therefore took a more relaxed view. Thus the Dutch Republic appears as a haven of relative religious tolerance in the seventeenth century, not so much as a matter of principle (although principle was certainly present), but because no one had sufficient authority to enforce uniformity and persecute minorities. The Arminian regents tended to favour peace with Spain, which would benefit their business, but for the strict Calvinists the only conscionable option was to continue the struggle against the popish forces of Spain. This naturally inclined them to support successive Princes of Orange, who also favoured continuing the war as it enhanced their authority through their military command. These political and religious divisions were also reflected in Dutch society. The urban working classes seized the opportunity to oppose their regent bosses and governors by adopting strict Calvinism and supporting the House of Orange in its push for centralization.

The signing of the twelve-year truce with Spain in 1609 was a triumph for the regents, led by Jan van Oldenbarneveld (1547–1619), Advocate of the States of Holland at the States-General, and a defeat for the Orangists led by Maurice of Nassau (1567–1625), the son of William the Silent. Maurice courted the support of the strict Calvinists against the largely Arminian regents, and in 1618 he led his army into Holland, where he purged Arminians and regents from positions of power in the church and state. He then marched to The Hague, the seat of the States-General, and arrested Oldenbarneveld and his chief supporters. The 72-year-old Advocate was beheaded the following year, and a number of his followers were imprisoned, including the famous scholar Hugo Grotius.

Maurice also used his influence to purge Arminianism from the Dutch Reformed Church. In 1618–19 a synod met in the city of Dordrecht (Dordt), which included not only Dutch theologians and ministers, but representatives from Calvinist churches in Germany, Scotland, England, and Switzerland. The Synod of Dordt decisively condemned Arminius's theology and deprived Arminian pastors of their positions. Henceforth, the strict Calvinists strove to implement an agenda of moral reform similar to the one that the Puritans would attempt in England when they seized power in the 1640s and 1650s. The Calvinists had only limited success, however, because of the decentralized nature of the Dutch political system.

From 1618 until 1650, the Orangists dominated Dutch politics. After Maurice's death in 1625, his half-brother Frederick Henry (1584–1647) cultivated a quasi-monarchical style, building palaces, patronizing artists, and arranging a marriage for his son William with a daughter of Charles I of England. The 1648 Treaty of Münster finally brought peace after decades of war, along with official Spanish recognition of the Republic's independence. By then Frederick Henry's son had succeeded his father as William II (1626–50), and he strongly opposed the peace because it meant the loss of the military command that was one of the pillars of his power. But he was powerless to prevent it, as a war-weary and fiscally exhausted Holland withdrew its contributions to the armed forces.

The years that followed were difficult for the republic. The "peace dividend" was slow to materialize, unemployment rose as soldiers were demobilized, and peace allowed the revival of the republic's commercial and industrial rivals in the Spanish Netherlands. Calvinists believed that these difficulties were the republic's punishment for having forsaken God's work and made peace with Spain. In July 1650 William staged a coup against the regents, but he died of smallpox before he could celebrate his victory. At the time of his death he was still childless, but barely a week later his wife gave birth to their son, who immediately became William III of Orange (1650–1702), the Prince who would eventually rule England with his wife, Mary Stuart.

Now that the Orangists were effectively leaderless, the regents once more seized control of the political machinery of the Dutch Republic. For the next two decades, the central government was dominated by the Grand Pensionary of Holland, Johan de Witt (1625–72). The titles of captain-general and *stadtholder* were abolished, and the powers of the latter given to the provincial States. The implementation of the regents' religious agenda introduced a policy of relative toleration for minorities such as Catholics and Jews, and the army was dismantled, removing a key component of Orangist power.

De Witt's foreign policy was based on friendship with France and hostility to England, increasingly the republic's most important commercial and maritime rival, against which it would fight two Anglo–Dutch naval wars (1652–4 and 1664–7). The friendship with France ended in 1672, however, when Louis XIV, egged on by Colbert, attacked the Republic (see Chapter 7). In the ensuing panic, the regents were discredited, de Witt and his brother were lynched by an angry mob, and William III, now grown to manhood, became the national saviour. William's first concern was to defend the republic against the aggression of Louis XIV. As we will see in the next chapter, he used diplomacy to turn Louis's allies against him—a project in which he was aided by the Sun King's own hubris and miscalculations. Sixteen years later, when William was invited to "rescue" the Protestant English from their Catholic king, he was reluctant to leave the Dutch Republic vulnerable to French aggression. But Louis, assuming that a Dutch invasion of England would produce another civil war there, launched a military campaign in Germany instead (see Chapter 7), giving William the window he needed to accept the English invitation. For the rest of his life, he was able to use the wealth and resources of England against France.

When William III died childless in 1702, the regents once again asserted their dominance in the Dutch Republic, and the position of *stadtholder* remained vacant. By this time, however, a century of war had drained the Dutch treasury, and the republic had passed its peak both economically and politically. Around the world, Dutch merchants and sailors came under increasing pressure from their French and English rivals in particular, who could now bring their greater populations and resources to bear on the struggle. Meanwhile, more and more of the merchants and entrepreneurs who had powered the Dutch rise to commercial pre-eminence were choosing to retire from the fray and live on the revenues from their investments, rather than continue as active managers of their businesses.

As in England, the forces that favoured enhanced executive power faced powerful resistance.[18] The Princes of Orange were handicapped by both the irregular and informal nature of their power and the ambiguity at the heart of the Dutch political system. Unlike the English, whose civil war and revolution in the end produced a stable system in which the powers of the monarch were constrained by Parliament, the Dutch never found a way to balance the interests of the rulers (the Princes of Orange) with those of their leading subjects (the regents) in a way that allowed the central government to operate effectively regardless of who was giving the orders.

Northern and Eastern Europe

Rulers in northern and eastern Europe also attempted to enhance their power over their kingdoms. Like their counterparts in western Europe, these regimes were not consciously innovative or revolutionary: they built on historical foundations, and their evolution was conditioned by local circumstances.

Map 6.1 The Baltic world in the seventeenth century

THE BALTIC WORLD

Sweden and Denmark

In 1397 the Union of Kalmar united the Scandinavian kingdoms of Denmark, Norway, and Sweden (including modern Finland) in a single kingdom under Danish rule in, but in 1520 Swedish nobles led by Gustav Vasa established an independent Swedish kingdom, and Vasa became King Gustav I (r. 1523–60). Compared to France, England, and Spain, Sweden in the sixteenth century was small, poor, and undeveloped. The middle class was small and weak, and Stockholm, by far the largest town, had a population of only about 7000. Most commerce was conducted by the German merchants of the Hanseatic League, who were effectively beyond the control of the royal government. Another significant difference from the lands to the south was that feudalism had never taken hold in Sweden. Thus Swedish peasant farmers were not burdened by feudal or manorial entanglements. They owned about half the farmland in the country, and sat in their own chamber in the national assembly or *Riksdag*, alongside the nobles, clergy, and representatives of the towns. As result, although Swedish nobles were politically powerful, as a group they were not extremely wealthy.

By 1530 Sweden had broken from Rome and the government had established Lutheranism as the official religion. Thus Sweden's was a top-down Reformation, driven mainly by the political and economic imperatives of the government rather than popular demand. The closest parallel to the Lutheran Church in Sweden was the Church of England under Henry VIII.

Vasa also sought to diminish the political power of the nobles who had dominated the Swedish government for two centuries through their control of the royal council and their right to elect the king. To achieve this, he cultivated the support of the non-noble chambers of the *Riksdag*. In a pattern that may look strange to us, but was repeated several times over the next century, the *Riksdag* insisted on the absolute nature of royal power, as a way of decreasing the political influence of self-interested nobles. In 1544 the *Riksdag* accepted the principle of hereditary monarchy, and when Gustav Vasa died in 1560, his eldest son inherited the throne without incident as King Erik XIV (r. 1560–69).

Despite the smooth transition, the turmoil that followed threatened to undo Gustav Vasa's achievements. Erik was mentally unbalanced, and his younger half-brothers vied for control while resentful nobles tried to recover their lost influence. Erik was deposed in 1569 in favour of his younger half-brother King John III (1569–92), whose son Sigismund was married to a daughter of the king of Poland. When Sigismund, who had converted to Catholicism, was elected King of Poland in 1587, he expected that when his father died and he became King of Sweden as well, the two countries would be united under the rule of the same dynasty. Sigismund was opposed, however, by his uncle Charles, Duke of Södermanland, who whipped up dissent and presented himself as the defender of Protestant Sweden and the protector of ordinary Swedes against a clique of selfish nobles. Sigismund was deposed and driven from Sweden in 1599, and in 1604 his uncle took the throne as Charles IX (r. 1604–11).

These conflicts did not prevent Swedish forces from extending their country's territory. By the 1590s Sweden was the dominant power in the eastern Baltic, having seized much of Livonia (modern Latvia), Estonia, including the port of Reval (modern Tallinn), as well as the Russian port of Narva. Control of these Baltic ports was important, as they were situated at the mouths of the rivers down which the grain grown in eastern Germany and Poland for export was shipped, and from them that it was loaded onto ships bound for western Europe.

Although Charles IX had come to throne with significant public support, he proved to be a divisive and unpopular ruler. He also lost a number of the territorial gains made by earlier Swedish kings, including both Estonia and Livonia. On his death, his son Gustav II Adolf (Gustavus Adophus, r. 1611–32), then sixteen years of age, thus faced some difficult circumstances, both domestically and internationally.

In order to accede to the throne, Gustavus had to agree to a number of conditions that restricted his power and increased the influence of the nobles in the government. Nevertheless, in time he was able to free himself from most of these restrictions. A genuinely attractive and popular character, Gustavus had the ability to work with people to achieve his aims. Thus even though his chancellor, Axel Oxenstierna (1583–1654), had drawn up the list of restrictions on royal power, the two men became close friends and formed a very effective partnership.

By 1629 Gustavus had recovered the territory lost by his father, but a new threat to Sweden's influence in the Baltic emerged when the forces of Holy Roman Emperor Ferdinand II and his general Albrecht von Wallenstein occupied large swaths of northern Germany (see Chapter 4). This prompted Sweden's entry into the Thirty Years War, to protect both German Protestants and Sweden's Baltic empire. Success in the war in Germany was made possible by wide-ranging civil and military reforms that rationalized previously haphazard "systems." In many ways, Sweden under Gustavus became the most efficiently governed state in Europe with a powerful navy and conscript army that enabled a small and relatively poor country to become the dominant power in northern Europe.

When Gustavus died in battle in 1632, he was succeeded by his young daughter Christina (r. 1632–54). Oxenstierna continued to serve as chancellor for the next twelve years. When Christina attained legal adulthood in 1644, however, she relegated him to the sidelines and decided to pay for the expenses of war by selling Crown land to nobles. This had the effect of simultaneously weakening the Crown and strengthening the nobles. Moreover, to make up for continuing shortfalls, taxation on the peasants was increased. Christina, who had converted to Catholicism, wanted to abdicate the throne in favour of her cousin Charles, but the nobles called for the restoration of an elective monarchy. In 1650, however, she threatened to confiscate the Crown lands, rights, and revenues that had been sold or given to the nobles. This was enough to persuade them to recognize Charles as heir. On the day of his coronation, Christina left for Rome.

When Charles X, who had acceded to the throne in 1654, died unexpectedly in 1660, his four-year-old son became King Charles XI (r. 1660–97). During his childhood, the nobles once more gained political ascendancy, but after assuming personal power in 1672 he fundamentally altered the nature of the Swedish monarchy. In its 1693 Declaration of Sovereignty, the *Riksdag* declared Charles to be

> an absolute and sovereign king, who is responsible for his actions to no one on earth, but has authority and power, according to his pleasure, and as a Christian ruler, to guide and direct his kingdom.[19]

Much more explicitly than in France, therefore, absolutism in Sweden was based on the consent and cooperation of the king's subjects. This strongly suggests that absolute monarchy was not an alien concept imposed on Swedish society against its will, but was a development in tune with the political culture of the time.

In Denmark, the dissolution of the Union of Kalmar in 1523 had resulted in the overthrow of King Christian II (r. 1513–23) and the election of his uncle as Frederick I (r. 1523–33). The Danish monarchy would remain theoretically elective until the mid-seventeenth century. Although the Oldenburg dynasty remained on the throne, each new king had to swear to uphold the privileges of the nobility.

For the next 150 years, Denmark would be Sweden's great rival for domination in the Baltic. In addition to modern Norway, its territory included a number of provinces in what is now southern Sweden, which gave the king control over the sound that linked the Baltic and North Seas. Tolls on shipping passing through the sound made up a large portion of royal revenue. Like Sweden, Denmark had become officially Lutheran, and in much the same ways and for the same reasons. During the long reign of Christian IV (1588–1648), the king and his nobles arrived at a mutual understanding that gave the latter a great deal of power domestically, but left Christian free to pursue his diplomatic agenda of territorial expansion, reunion with Sweden under the Danish crown, and protection of Danish territory and rights in the Baltic. By 1660, however, Sweden had established its pre-eminence in the region and taken over the Danish provinces in what is now southern Sweden. Although Denmark's military defeats were largely due to the miscalculations of King Frederick III (r. 1648–70), the aristocratic royal council became the scapegoat, while Frederick became a symbol of national resistance. Much like Charles XI in Sweden, Frederick was able to use the public's support for him and resentment of the nobles to fundamentally alter the political system. In 1660 the Danish Estates declared the monarchy to be hereditary, and the Royal Law of 1665 decreed that

> The absolute hereditary king of Denmark and Norway shall hereafter be, and by all subjects be held and honored as, the greatest and highest head on earth, above all human laws and knowing no other head or judge above him, either in spiritual or secular matters, except God alone. . . .
>
> . . . the king shall neither orally nor in writing subscribe to any oath or any obligation whatsoever, for he, as a free and unfettered absolute king, cannot be bound by his subjects to any oath or prescribed obligations.[20]

As in Sweden, therefore, absolute monarchy in Denmark was not arbitrarily imposed by the monarch, but was the product of cooperation with his subjects.

POLAND

Poland was the other power that contended for power in the Baltic, and its political evolution serves as a useful counter-example to the growth of absolute monarchy in the seventeenth century. In the later middle ages Poland was an elective monarchy, ruled by kings of the Jagiellonian dynasty, which also furnished the kings of Bohemia and Hungary until the Ottoman victory over Louis II in 1526 (Chapter 4). The King of Poland was also the Grand Duke of Lithuania, and the two territories were governed as part of a personal union similar to the one in Castile and Aragon. This Polish–Lithuanian commonwealth had a large population (second only to France), but was relatively poor in resources. Thus although this period is considered a golden age in Polish history, especially under King Casimir the Great (r. 1333–70), its apparent prosperity is somewhat misleading; if Poland seemed to be doing well, this impression was largely a matter of contrast to the disintegrating Union of Kalmar (see above), and the declining Holy Roman Empire.

Poland was also distinct in its social structure. It had an unusually large nobility (approaching ten per cent of the population), but few important towns, and its middle class was both small and weak. During the demographic expansion of the later fifteenth and sixteenth centuries, as we saw in Chapter 1, Polish nobles began growing grain for export to western Europe, and imposed serfdom on the peasants in order to secure a low-cost source of labour.

Both numerous and wealthy, Polish nobles also had enormous political power. Not only did they elect the king, but the assembly of nobles, or *Sejm*, required unanimity on most matters: thus each and every Polish noble held veto power over government policy. By the later seventeenth century, this *liberum veto* ("free veto") was being used not only to defeat individual proposals, but also to dissolve the assembly and nullify previous transactions of the *Sejm*. This not only hamstrung Polish kings, but made it easy for other rulers to meddle in Polish politics: all they had to do was bribe a single noble to exercise his veto. In the course of the Reformation, many Polish nobles had become Protestant as a way of reinforcing their independence from a Catholic king. Without a strong middle class to provide tax revenue, Polish rulers had great difficulty exercising their authority, let alone enhancing it. In many ways, the Kingdom of Poland was actually a republic of nobles rather than a monarchy.

The point of no return in the political (d)evolution of Poland occurred during the reign of Sigismund III (r. 1586–1632). The son of King John III of Sweden (r. 1569–92), he had married the daughter of Sigismund II of Poland (1548–72), the last king of the Jagiellonian dynasty. As we saw above, he inherited the Swedish throne in 1592, but was deposed in 1599, and Poland was no more receptive to his desire to impose royal absolutism and Roman Catholicism. His attempt to put his son on the Russian throne during that state's "Time of Troubles" (see below) was defeated, and unsuccessful wars against

VOICES

Religious Toleration in Poland

In the course of the Reformation, many Polish nobles had broken with Roman Catholic Church, and a variety of Protestant sects flourished there. In 1573, however, the most likely candidate for election as king was a Catholic: the future Henry III of France, then Duke of Anjou (see Chapter 4). To allay the fears of Polish Protestants, the lay members of the Sejm unanimously agreed to the Compact of Warsaw, in which Polish nobles swore to protect one another's religious freedom.

> And whereas in our Commonwealth there are considerable differences in the Christian religion, . . . we swear, that we who are divided by faith, will keep peace among ourselves, and not shed blood on account of differences in faith or church, nor will we allow punishment by the confiscation of goods, deprivation of honour, imprisonment or exile, nor will we in any fashion aid any sovereign or agency in such undertakings. . . .
>
> All these things we solemnly swear to uphold and maintain for ourselves and our descendants, by our faith, honour and consciences. And whosoever should wish to oppose this and damage the peace and order of the people we shall all rise up in condemnation against such action.

Henry of Anjou was in fact elected King of Poland in 1574, but only after extensive negotiations, whose restrictions were reflected in his coronation oath:

> I, Henry, . . . freely elected by common agreement of all the Orders of each people . . . I promise the Clergy, the Princes, the Barons, the Nobles, the citizens, the inhabitants and any person existing at any rank and condition that I shall guard, observe, protect and defend all rights, liberties, immunities, privileges public and private which are not contradictory to the common law and liberties of each state. . . . I shall protect and guard the peace and tranquility between the religious dissidents. Nor shall I permit them in any way to be broken or abolished by any jurisdiction of my own or by any authority of my officials or of the Ranks for the sake of religion. And I myself shall not break or abolish them.

M.B. Biskupski and James I. Pula, *Polish Democratic Thought from the Renaissance to the Great Emigration: Essays and Documents* (New York: Columbia University Press, 1990), pp. 132–3, 141–2.

Gustavus Adolphus of Sweden resulted in the loss of Poland's Baltic territories of Estonia and Livonia, cementing the kingdom's demise as Baltic power.

Sigismund III was succeeded by his sons Ladislas IV (r. 1632–48) and Johan Casimir (r. 1648–68), neither of whom had a legitimate male heir. From the point of view of Polish nobles, the mid-seventeenth century was a second golden age: the Baltic grain trade was at its height, and the nobles themselves had worked out a system of compromises that allowed religious minorities to coexist in relative peace. It could not last, however. A rebellion among the Cossacks in 1647, supported by Tsar Alexis of Russia, prompted Johan Casimir to attempt once more to strengthen royal authority. His plans elicited strong resistance among the nobles and eventually civil war, prompting him to abdicate and retire to France.

By the later seventeenth century, the balance of power between ruler and elites had tilted so far to the side of the latter that Poland was no longer able to function as an effective state. While in England the limitations on the monarchy made it possible for rulers and their powerful subjects to form an effective working partnership, in Poland we see limited monarchy (paradoxically) run amok. Eventually, Poland would be dismembered by neighbour states whose political evolution had run in the opposite direction.

Central and Eastern Europe

In the course of the seventeenth century, central and eastern Europe came to be dominated by three increasingly powerful states. All three had grown out of previous states, but had undergone such significant transformations that we may think of them as substantially renovated. These were Russia, Brandenburg–Prussia, and the Habsburg monarchy. All three developed absolute monarchies, but they varied among themselves, and were also different from the absolute monarchies of western Europe. One key factor that distinguished them from the absolute monarchy of Louis XIV, for instance, was their social structure. Societies east of central Germany were both more agrarian and more completely dominated by the nobility than those to the west, while their middle-class populations were considerably smaller and weaker. Thus the rulers of these lands could not use the support and resources of an ambitious bourgeoisie as a counterweight to the power of the nobility. At a time when nobles themselves were growing wealthier through their commercial grain operations, rulers needed the cooperation of their nobility if they were to enhance their power. Thus they struck deals with their respective nobilities—some formal, some tacit—agreeing to let them run their estates and govern their serfs as they saw fit. In return, nobles agreed to support the ruler by serving in his government and armed forces.

Brandenburg–Prussia

In the later seventeenth century, the north German state that historians call Brandenburg–Prussia rose to unexpected prominence. An unwieldy amalgam of poor, sparsely populated territories scattered across the north German plain, with no natural frontiers or defences, it had been formed through the vagaries of inheritance and war, and its only unifying feature was its ruling family: the Hohenzollern dynasty. The rise of Brandenburg–Prussia was due primarily to the single-minded devotion and ruthlessness of those rulers.

The Hohenzollern territories had three components: the Electorate of Brandenburg, with its capital at Berlin (then a small town of perhaps 10,000 people); the Duchy of Prussia to the east, along the southern shore of the Baltic; and the territories of Cleves, Mark, and Ravensburg along the Rhine River in northwestern Germany. In 1648 the total population of the region was approximately 1.5 million.

The ruler who put this unlikely constellation of territories on the path to prominence was Frederick William (r. 1640–88), known as the Great Elector. His lands had suffered terribly in the Thirty Years War, and Frederick William determined that in order to protect them from future invasion, he needed a powerful army. Thus he increased its size from 2000 men in 1648 to 45,000 at its peak in 1678. This was, of course, very expensive, and as we have seen, imposing new taxes on subjects required the consent of their political representatives. In German lands, those representatives met in bodies known as *Landtags*, and each of the Elector's territories had its own, made up of representatives from the towns and the nobility. In exchange for the *Landtags'* approval of a one-time taxation grant to expand the army, Frederick William promised to respect their political powers. Once he had his grant, however, he simply ignored his commitments, and continued to collect the taxes without consent.

He was able to do this not only because he had the army to use as a tool for repression, but because he had solicited the support of the nobles, known as Junkers, at the expense of the urban middle class and peasants.[21] The exclusive rights of Junkers alone to own land and to evict peasants was affirmed, and all peasants were presumed to be serfs unless they could produce written proof of their free status.

The army was virtually the only institution common to all of the Elector's territories, and in time it became the core of Brandenburg–Prussia. Its chief administrative body, the General War Commissariat, increasingly took over administrative functions throughout Brandenburg–Prussia, supervising the assessment and collection of taxes, overseeing economic and fiscal reform, and eventually appropriating most of the functions of city governments. In many ways, Brandenburg-Prussia was an army with a state rather than a state with an army. In addition, as we will see in Chapter 7, Frederick William proved to be an adept player in the convoluted diplomacy of the time. He used his army to play an important role in the wars provoked by Louis XIV, sometimes on the side of the Sun King and sometimes against him, and during the Dutch War (1672–8) he changed sides no fewer than three times.

The reputation of the Great Elector's successor, his son Frederick III (1688–1713), has suffered by comparison with that of his father. Devoted to the pomp and ceremony of court life, Frederick III made it his primary goal to attain a royal title that would reflect his dynasty's new prominence and power. After years of striving, he convinced Holy Roman Emperor Leopold I to grant him the title "King in Prussia," and in 1701 that title was confirmed in an elaborate coronation ceremony (there would be no "king *of* Prussia" until 1772). King Frederick I has often been criticized for his vast spending on trappings such as titles and palaces and for his costly pursuit of a royal title. However, his age valued ritual and symbol much more than ours does, and it may be that in order to be taken seriously by other rulers, he needed not only to behave like a king, but to be one.

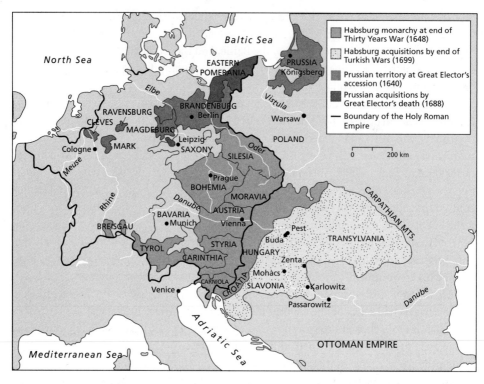

Map 6.2 Brandenburg–Prussia and the Habsburg monarchy in the seventeenth century

By the early eighteenth century, a distinct version of royal absolutism had emerged in Brandenburg–Prussia, based on the cooperation of the nobility, the exclusion of the small and weak middle class from the political process, and the enserfment of peasants. The army not only defended the state, it defined it, and was the institution in which the king and nobles worked together.

THE HABSBURG MONARCHY

Since the reign of Charles V, the Holy Roman Emperors of the Habsburg dynasty had sought to restore real meaning and power to the imperial title in Germany, but those ambitions had been decisively defeated by the Peace of Westphalia in 1648. Henceforth the Habsburg dynasty would focus its attention on the three basic components of its own patrimonial lands, which were separate in terms of politics, law, institutions, and ethnicity. In the Austrian lands, which they ruled as archdukes, their power had been consolidated and enhanced by the Thirty Years war, and likewise with Bohemia, which they ruled as kings. In repressing the Bohemian revolt that led to the Thirty Years War, the Habsburgs made the previously elective kingship hereditary in their dynasty, and abolished the extensive political power of the nobles. Furthermore, rebellious Protestant Bohemian nobles had been dispossessed of their land and replaced by reliable Catholics: just 82 aristocrats controlled 62 per cent of the peasants in Bohemia.

The final and most complex piece of the three Habsburg territories was Hungary. Since 1526, Hungarian nobles had consistently elected a Habsburg king, but there was no guarantee that they would continue to do so. They possessed the *jus resistendi*: a positive constitutional right of rebellion against any violation of their rights and privileges. In addition, the fact that the Ottoman Empire now controlled two-thirds of the historic Hungarian kingdom gave the nobles political leverage that they could use against the Habsburg Kings who ruled the remainder (now known as "Royal Hungary"). Indeed, many Hungarian nobles preferred Ottoman to Habsburg rule, since the Ottomans were content to leave local affairs in the hands of the nobles, as long as the latter paid the required taxes and did not stir up trouble. In addition, many Hungarian nobles were Protestant, and the Ottomans allowed them to practise their religion in relative freedom, while the Habsburgs had become militant champions of the reformed Tridentine Catholic Church. Habsburg rulers wanted to apply the same solutions to Hungary that they had to Bohemia (as one imperial adviser put it, "to put the Hungarians into Czech trousers"),[22] but were prevented from doing so by the ever-present Ottoman threat, against which they needed the support of the Hungarian nobles.

This situation would change dramatically in the later seventeenth century. By 1699 the armies of Emperor Leopold I (r. 1658–1705) had defeated the Ottomans and brought all of Hungary under Habsburg rule (see Chapter 7). Without the Ottoman threat, Hungarian nobles found their political position weakened; thus Leopold was able to have the *jus resistendi* abolished and the Hungarian throne made hereditary in his dynasty. Religious toleration was formally maintained, but in practice was very narrowly defined. Land in the newly conquered areas of Hungary was granted to loyal Catholics, further cementing the rule of the Catholic Habsburgs. While Hungarian nobles retained their control over their estates and their serfs, they were completely excluded from the imperial government.

Absolutism in the Habsburg monarchy was more cooperative than in Brandenburg–Prussia, in that more power was left in the hands of nobles and local elites. This was a strength in that it gave the leading members of the empire both a stake in its integrity and a sense of belonging to a larger enterprise, one defined by its dynastic allegiance and its devotion to reformed Catholicism. (The empire would become even more diverse after 1714, when it would incorporate the southern Netherlands and large parts of Italy, previously ruled by the Emperors' Spanish Habsburg cousins.) But its weaknesses would become apparent in the course of the eighteenth and nineteenth centuries. In the secular Age of Enlightenment, could a vast and diverse empire continue to be united by devotion to a single set of religious principles and practices? Could loyalty to a dynasty survive the lack of a clear male succession, as would happen in the eighteenth century? Could a disjointed and multi-ethnic empire maintain its integrity in the face of rising nationalism in the nineteenth century? The fact that the Habsburg empire survived as a Great Power until 1918 is a testament to the strengths of Habsburg rule.

In most ways, the Habsburg monarchy violates our notions of what a state should be. It was, in fact, the antithesis of a national state, with multiple languages and nationalities and no real unifying features apart from allegiance to a single religion and ruling dynasty. From the vantage point of the twenty-first century, however, it may make more sense than it did a century ago. Can we see in the Habsburg Empire a template for the European Union itself—a union of states and peoples in which commitment to national self-determination is less important than commitment to a common set of principles?

RUSSIA

Until at least the sixteenth century, Russia was as exotic to Europeans as Persia or Siam. At that time it had no access to the Baltic and was extremely difficult to reach overland, and it was further isolated from Europe by its Eastern Orthodox religion. Believing their land to be the home of the true faith, many Russians considered Europeans to be infidels or heretics, and feared that contact with them would incur the wrath of the Almighty.

After the first Russian state, based in the city of Kiev, had been destroyed by the Mongols in the thirteenth century, it was succeeded by a series of regional states whose rulers owed vague allegiance and annual tribute to the Mongol khans. "Russia" was thus a geographic and cultural construct rather than a political one. By the later fifteenth century, however, one Russian state had not only absorbed most of the others, but also established its independence from the Mongols or, as they became known, Tatars. This was the Grand Duchy of Moscow, or Muscovy. By the 1470s Grand Duke Ivan III (r. 1462–1505) was referring to as himself as Tsar (derived from "caesar") or emperor of all Russians. Since large numbers of Orthodox Russians lived in the Polish-Lithuanian commonwealth, this declaration marked the beginning of a long conflict with Poland, which took additional impetus from the fact that Poland stood between Russia and the Baltic Sea ports that would give the latter easier access to western Europe. Throughout the sixteenth century, Russia would wage war against Poland and Sweden in a largely unsuccessful effort to gain a Baltic foothold.

The reign of Ivan IV, or Ivan the Terrible (r. 1533–84) almost undid the achievements of his predecessors. Fear and hatred of the *boyars* (hereditary nobility) led him to launch a violent campaign against them. Then in the 1560s, he fundamentally disrupted the political system by dividing Russia into two parts. One was to be administered by a *boyar* council or *Duma*, while the other, the *oprichnina*, became the Tsar's personal property, within which the inhabitants' land tenure was only conditional, at the pleasure of the Tsar. Ivan's enemies and opponents of the *oprichnina* were savagely repressed. This policy made effective government impossible, and although it was abolished in 1572, the damage to the country's political and social stability was enormous.

Ivan himself had killed his eldest son in a fit of rage, and a younger son had died in an accident. Thus on his death the throne passed to his feeble-minded middle son, Feodor (r. 1584–98). After his death without heirs, the early seventeenth century was marked by a disputed succession and a series of civil and foreign wars, and domestic rebellions, but this

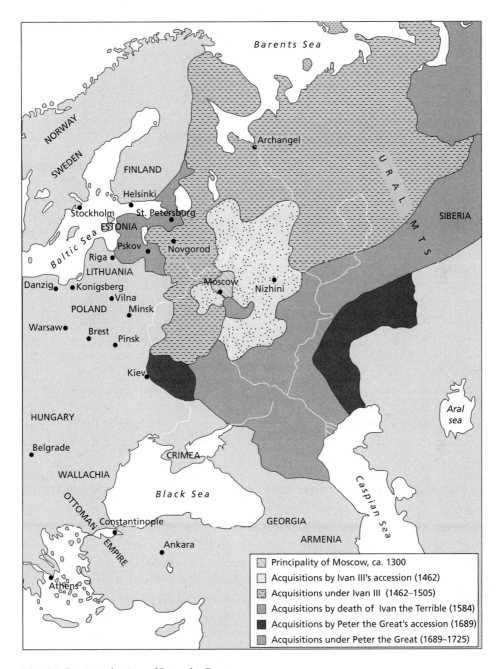

Map 6.3 Russia at the time of Peter the Great

"Time of Troubles" came to an end in 1618, when an assembly of nobles chose a new Tsar in the person of Michael Romanov (r. 1618–45), whose dynasty would remain in power until the Russian Revolution of 1917.

During this period, ties between Russia and Europe had been slowly but steadily increasing. In the sixteenth century English sailors and merchants had established a trade route through the port of Archangel on the far northern White Sea, but more direct communication to the west was hampered by the dominant presence of Poland and Sweden in the Baltic. Both Michael and his son Alexei (r. 1645–76) sought foreign expertise in military and technical matters, and by the middle of the seventeenth century Moscow had a substantial foreign population. Contact with Europe would accelerate under Alexei's son Peter I (Peter the Great; r. 1682–1725).

Born in 1672, Peter was just four when his father died and his older half-brother became Tsar. On the latter's death in 1682 Peter and another half-brother, the blind and mentally challenged Ivan, became co-rulers but the latter (who would die in 1696) was Tsar in name only, and during Peter's childhood, his older half-sister Sophia served as regent. In the meantime Peter was more or less exiled to a village outside Moscow, where he indulged his insatiable curiosity, learning about boats and sailing, weapons, and military technology of all sorts. As he grew to manhood he spent a great deal of time in the "German Quarter" where much of Moscow's foreign population lived, becoming convinced of Russia's backwardness and the necessity of modernization through the adoption of European culture and technology.

In 1689 Peter and his supporters overthrew Sophia and he began to implement his vision of a new Russia. In 1695 he began building a navy to fight the Ottomans in the Black Sea and the Swedes in the Baltic (see Chapter 7), and the following year he set out on the first of two extended trips to western Europe, during which he exposed his entourage to European culture and technology and engaged hundreds of foreign craftsmen to work in Russia. In 1703, on land conquered from Sweden in the Great Northern War (1700–21), he began building a new capital city. Designed in the grand western style, St. Petersburg was consciously intended to stand in contrast to the traditionally Russian (and, to Peter, primitive) Moscow, far to the south and east in the Russian interior. To further his military goals, his government encouraged the establishment of industrial enterprises, including iron mines and foundries for cannon, sawmills for shipbuilding, textile mills for uniforms and sails, and so on. To train administrators and officers, he founded a series of academies, and coerced Russian nobles into sending their sons to the west for schooling.

The absolutism of Peter the Great was more explicitly based on cooperation between ruler and nobles than that of either Brandenburg–Prussia or the Habsburg monarchy. In addition to strengthening nobles' control over their serfs and estates, Peter did away with the conditional land tenure instituted by Ivan the Terrible. In exchange, Russian nobles were explicitly obliged to serve the state in either the armed forces or the government. To ensure active participation, Peter instituted a Table of Ranks with fourteen gradations and required that all nobles, regardless of their hereditary status, start at the bottom and earn promotion through a combination of seniority and merit.

The complex legacy of Peter's reign is significant not only for Russia but for Europe as a whole, as it definitively tied Russia into European civilization. There can be no doubt that Peter turned Russia into a European power alongside France, England, the Habsburg monarchy, and Brandenburg–Prussia. However, his efforts to drag his "backward" country into the modern European world were less successful. A portion of the Russian elite was indeed westernized, but many more traditional Russians felt that their leaders had abandoned the old ways. This perception was reinforced by Peter's treatment of the Russian Orthodox Church: not only did he abolish the position of Patriarch (its head) and turn the church into a department of the government, but he and his cronies took childish pleasure in shocking the pious. Already disappointed in the heir to the throne, his son Alexei, Peter was well aware that traditionalists would take advantage of the younger man's weakness to undo all the reforms that Peter himself had achieved. Relations between the two became so strained that Alexei fled to the Holy Roman Empire. Lured back by promises of clemency, he was convicted of treason and tortured to reveal his accomplices. Alexei died in prison before his father had to decide whether to have him executed.

The political system that Peter built was more "absolute" than even the France of Louis XIV. Yet it could not function effectively without a motivated and energetic ruler such as Peter himself: with less inspired leadership, as would be the case through much of the eighteenth century, there was significant drift and lack of direction. Moreover, although Alexei's "treason" led Peter to declare that the Tsar had the right to name his own successor, he never took that step himself. For much of the eighteenth century, therefore, infighting over the succession further destabilized the system, at least until the reign of Catherine the Great (1762–96).

There is an even deeper paradox at the heart of Peter's legacy. He did successfully turn Russia to the west, but in a sense this was possible only because Russia was not like Europe. What made Peter's accomplishments, from victory in war (see Chapter 7) to reform of the administration and economy, to the building of St. Petersburg, possible was the subjugation of the vast mass of Russians who were serfs. In fact, by reinforcing the nobles' power over their serfs, Peter deepened the fundamental differences between Russia and the west. He made Russia more like Europe by making it less like Europe. The evolutionary process of Russia's integration into Europe was already underway when Peter came to power, and it would likely have accelerated over time—but he replaced it with revolutionary change, and in so doing made modernization more wrenching and divisive than it might otherwise have been.

Chapter Conclusion

In this chapter we have examined the evolution of European states in the seventeenth century in response to the crisis of the religious wars outlined in Chapter 4. Not only did the long-term processes of centralization or state-building continue, but there was an increasing emphasis on the ruler's authority within an increasingly powerful central government. The primary motor of the evolution toward absolutism was the need to pay the costs of waging war. To assess and collect the taxes owed, state power was extended and the rights and privileges of the society of orders were curtailed. When those affected fought back, confrontations such as the Fronde in France and the English Revolution were the result. Although the measures taken to overcome this resistance were ad hoc and improvised, and there was no "master plan," they nevertheless had the effect of concentrating power in the hands of rulers and governments.

Some rulers were relatively successful in reducing the restrictions on their power posed by the society of orders. In no case, however, were they eliminated completely. Even the most absolute regime represents a compromise between the ruler and national or local elites. In a few places, rulers were not so successful in overcoming those restrictions, resulting in limited monarchy. While in England the outcome was an effective partnership of ruler and elites, conducted through the vehicle of Parliament, in Poland the balance of power was so heavily weighted in the nobles' favour that effective government was impossible. Different regimes sat at different points along a spectrum.

Over the course of the seventeenth century, the administrative and intellectual foundations of the modern state continued to evolve under the auspices of the dynastic European monarchies. Historians have sometimes exaggerated the novelty of this evolution, especially when viewed from the vantage point of national states as they would emerge in the nineteenth century. Nevertheless, the political ideal of Christendom was long gone by 1700. What was coming into being to replace it was a world of sovereign states that owed no allegiance to anything outside themselves. The next chapter will look at the relations among those states.

Questions for Critical Thought

1. Why do you think the issue of absolute monarchy has provoked so much debate among historians? Might historians have been misled by knowing what was to come? Explain.
2. What do the various political disturbances of the mid-seventeenth century (the Fronde, the English Civil War, the revolts in Catalonia and Portugal, and political instability elsewhere) have in common?
3. How did political change in the seventeenth century both uphold and undermine the privileges of the society of orders?

Weblinks

The Putney Debates:
www.csulb.edu/~ssayeghc/tudorstuart/putneydebates.htm

Versailles 3D:
www.versailles3d.com/en/

Further Reading

Davies, Norman. *God's Playground: A History of Poland.* Vol. I. *The Origins to 1795,* 2nd ed. New York: Columbia University Press, 2005. The most complete and authoritative history in English.

Elliott, J.H. *Richelieu and Olivares*. Cambridge: Cambridge University Press, 1984. A fascinating and illuminating comparison of the lives and careers of the two greatest statesmen of the early seventeenth century.

Goubert, Pierre. *Louis XIV and Twenty Million Frenchmen*. Trans. Anne Carter. New York: Pantheon, 1970. By a leading French social historian of the Annales school.

Harris, Tim. *Revolution: The Great Crisis of the British Monarchy, 1685–1720*. London: Penguin, 2006. The best recent interpretation of the Glorious Revolution.

Hill, Christopher. *The World Turned Upside Down: Radical Ideas during the English Revolution*. Harmondsworth: Penguin, 1972. A classic study of radical religious and political movements in seventeenth-century England.

Hughes, Lindsey. *Peter the Great: A Biography*. New Haven: Yale University Press, 2002. An excellent political biography and overview of the reign.

Ingrao, Charles. *The Habsburg Monarchy, 1618–1815*. Cambridge: Cambridge University Press. An accessible and comprehensive overview of a most complex state.

Israel, Jonathan. *The Dutch Republic: Its Rise, Greatness, and Fall, 1477–1806*. Oxford: Oxford University Press, 1995. A massive work that covers not only the Dutch Revolt in the sixteenth century, but the Golden Age of the seventeenth, and includes treatments of political, economic, social, cultural, and intellectual history.

Knecht, Robert J. *Richelieu*. London: Longman, 2000. A recent and accessible account by a leading historian of France.

Lynch, John. *The Hispanic World in Crisis and Change, 1598–1700*. Oxford: Blackwell, 1992. A masterful synthesis by one of the leading authorities.

Moote, A. Lloyd. *Louis XIII, the Just*. Berkeley and Los Angeles: University of California Press, 1989. The authoritative biography in English.

Rabb, Theodore K. *The Struggle for Stability in Early Modern Europe*. Oxford: Oxford University Press, 1975. A nuanced assessment of the "general crisis" of the seventeenth century.

Ranum, Orest. *The Fronde: a French Revolution*. New York: Norton, 1993. The most recent and comprehensive overview by one of the eminent historians of seventeenth-century France.

Roberts, Michael. *Gustavus Adolphus and the Rise of Sweden*. London: English Universities Press, 1973. By the leading English-language historian of Sweden.

Upton, A.F. *Charles XI and Swedish Absolutism*. Cambridge: Cambridge University Press, 1998. A detailed examination of political change in Sweden in the later seventeenth century.

Wolf, John B. *Louis XIV*. New York: Norton, 1968. Still the standard biography in English.

Woolrych, Austin. *Britain in Revolution, 1625–1660*. Oxford: Oxford University Press, 2002. A masterful and detailed narrative from the accession of Charles I to the Restoration.

Notes

1. Perry Anderson, *Lineages of the Absolutist State* (London: Verso, 1974), p. 32.
2. Alexis de Tocqueville (1805–59) was a French politician, philosopher, and historian. In *The Old Regime and the Revolution* (1856), he firmly cemented in the popular mind (a) the picture of the *ancien régime* as autocratic and despotic, and (b) the idea that although it made the French Revolution necessary, it also served the evolution of the modern French state.

3. Henry had previously been married to Marguerite de Valois, the sister of three French kings (Francis II, Charles IX, and Henry III). It was their wedding in 1572 that became the occasion for the St. Bartholomew's Massacres of 1572. Never close, they separated in 1582, and their marriage (which had produced no children) was finally annulled in 1599. Henry then married Marie de Medici (a niece of the Grand Duke of Tuscany).

4. *The Political Testament of Cardinal Richelieu*, trans. Henry Bertram Hill (Madison: University of Wisconsin Press, 1965), p. 11.

5. Cited in John B. Wolf, *Louis XIV* (New York: Norton, 1968), p. 185.

6. In the royal chapel at Versailles, the king and his family sat in a balcony, and the chairs on the main floor were arranged to face the balcony rather than the altar at the front of the chapel.

7. W.H. Lewis, *The Splendid Century: Life in the France of Louis XIV* (New York: Doubleday, 1957).

8. Cited in David Harris Willson, *King James VI and I* (London: Jonathan Cape, 1963), pp. 206–7.

9. So called because the room where it met had a dark blue ceiling painted with stars.

10. Since this event, no monarch has entered the House of Commons; thus the speech from the throne is always delivered in the House of Lords. Similarly in Canada, the governor-general (the monarch's representative) delivers the throne speech in the Senate, and never enters the lower House.

11. Cited in Christopher Hill, *God's Englishman: Oliver Cromwell and the English Revolution* (New York: Harper, 1970), p. 103.

12. In fact, Cromwell was offered the crown several times, but consistently refused it on principle.

13. One of Charles's illegitimate sons, the Duke of Monmouth, launched a rebellion that was quickly snuffed out and cost him his life.

14. This last request was a red herring; the legitimacy of the heir was the only legitimate ground on which to oppose his eligibility to inherit the throne.

15. James had done no such thing; he maintained until his dying day (in 1701) that he was the rightful King of England. So did his son, James Francis Edward (1688–1766), who came to be known as the "Old Pretender," and his son, Charles Edward (1720–88), the "Young Pretender," or "Bonnie Prince Charlie."

16. J.H. Elliott, *The Count-Duke of Oliveras, The Statesman in an Age of Decline* (New Haven: Yale University Press, 1986), pp. 196–7.

17. The Arminians were also known as the Remonstrants, because they remonstrated against (i.e., objected to) official efforts to enforce strict Calvinism. Their Calvinist opponents objected to their objection, and thus became known as "Counter-Remonstrants" or "Gomarists" after one of their leaders, Franciscus Gomarus (1563–1641).

18. Unlike England, the Dutch Republic was not a "monarchy" per se, since the Princes of Orange would not become kings until the nineteenth century. Nevertheless, the general principle holds.

19. A.F. Upton, *Charles XI and Swedish Absolutism* (Cambridge: Cambridge University Press, 1998), p. 147.

20. Ernst Ekman, "The Danish Royal Law of 1665," *Journal of Modern History* 29, 2 (1957), p. 106.

21. The name is derived from the German *jung herr*, "young lord," and came to be applied generically to the nobility of Eastern Germany. Junkers were stereotypically violent and crude, delighting in warfare and hunting. Like many stereotypes, this one had just enough truth to it to become a stereotype in the first place.

22. Cited in Charles W. Ingrao, *The Habsburg Monarchy, 1618–1815*, 2nd ed. (Cambridge: Cambridge University Press, 2000), p. 69.

7

Diplomacy and Warfare in the Age of Absolutism

Patterns of international relations in the later seventeenth century may seem familiar to those acquainted with later periods of history: sovereign governments and their armed forces vying for control of land, people, and resources. But this resemblance should not lead us to assume that international relations were conducted according to modern norms. This was a period of significant transition in the ways states and rulers related to one another. As we have seen, rulers increasingly governed their states as sovereign entities, without allegiance or accountability to any outside authority, and states interacted as sovereign entities, but none of them yet had a theoretical foundation for international relations. What we see is a mixture of theories and practices, some that hearken back to earlier times and others that anticipate the future.

In the Middle Ages, when rulers still paid at least lip service to the ideal of Christendom, relations among rulers were supposed to embody peace, justice, and Christian brotherhood. In theory, the rulers of Christendom were members of a single family, bound together by their common allegiance to a Christian empire. In practice, however, relations among rulers were conducted primarily on the basis of dynastic rights and feudal relations. Thus in the Hundred Years War Edward III of England claimed the throne of France through his mother's dynastic connection to the French royal house, and (as we saw in the Introduction) relations between the two kingdoms were complicated by the fact that in his continental territories (Aquitaine, Anjou, Touraine, Maine) the King of England was a vassal of the King of France. This is not to say that strategic considerations, or land, or resources did not play a role in international relations. Nevertheless, rulers often pursued dynastic claims that made little sense from a purely strategic or economic viewpoint; the attempt by the French King Charles VII to claim the Kingdom of Naples in 1494 is a classic example. Even when an action did make strategic sense, a ruler might feel compelled to justify it on the grounds of feudal and/or dynastic relationships. Relations among rulers were also regulated by various conventions that did not always go together easily: for example, a warrior ethic emphasizing pride and courage, a code of chivalry centred on elaborate forms of courtesy and deference, and religious values such as peace and mercy.

In the sixteenth century religious divisions were added to the mix of elements influencing international relations. By 1648, when the Peace of Westphalia was signed, religion was no longer a primary motor, but it continued to play a role as a pretext or an irritant. For example, England and France shared a common maritime and commercial foe in the Dutch Republic, but their official religions kept them from joining forces, even as many English and Dutch Protestants sought to make common cause against the Catholic French, especially after the revocation of the Edict of Nantes in 1685. And while the feudal entanglements of the Middle Ages had faded into irrelevance as causes of war by the later seventeenth century, they could still be deployed as pretexts (as Louis XIV would do in 1688, when his invasion of Germany sparked the War of the League of Augsburg). Nor did any ruler yet conduct foreign policy on the basis of what was good for an abstract entity called France, or England, or Spain, let alone for an entity such as Brandenburg–Prussia or the Habsburg Monarchy. This is not to say that such considerations were completely absent; however, they were still understood as the interests of the ruling dynasty, rather than of the nation. Louis XIV, who is supposed to have said "I am the state," probably never spoke those exact words, but he certainly could have. He made no distinction between what was good for his Bourbon dynasty and what was good for the Kingdom of France, which was not necessarily the same thing as the French nation.

If relations among rulers were no longer governed by the ideals of Christendom, what did govern them? In a world composed of sovereign rulers and states, was there any principle that could bring order to the chaos that might ensue in the absence of a higher authority? In 1588 an Italian Jesuit named Giovanni Botero published a book entitled *On Reason of State* (*Della Ragion di Stato*). Like Machiavelli before him, he focused on the maintenance of power, although he disagreed with the Florentine's apparent advocacy of amorality in the interests of power. Although Botero never intended it to be used in this way, "reason of state" became justification for any action that served to maintain or expand the ruler's power. In domestic politics, such thinking allowed a minister such as Richelieu to justify virtually anything. As one of Louis XIII's admirers put it, "necessity excuses and justifies everything."[1] In relations between states, such thinking undermined efforts to establish norms of conduct, and it continues to undermine them today.

The Dutch lawyer and humanist Hugo Grotius (1583–1645), in *On the Laws of War and Peace* (1625), saw all sovereign rulers as equal. He also argued that the laws governing rulers and subjects alike are derived from nature rather than God, and would exist even if God did not (as a consequence he is often considered the founder of natural law theory). Although these natural laws bind rulers to pursue peace, there are circumstances that justify war, such as self-defence. There are also natural laws that govern the conduct of all wars, even those without a just cause. Likewise, the German Lutheran Samuel Pufendorf (1632–94), in *Of the Law of Nature and of Nations* (1672), argued that peace is the natural state of humanity, but that human sinfulness renders it fragile. With the assumption that rulers were equal in their sovereignty, and that they would inevitably pursue their own interests, there was now nothing left of the political aspect of Christendom, even in theory.

In the later seventeenth century the principal international concern in western Europe was a series of wars provoked by the ambition of Louis XIV of France. In northern Europe it was the challenge posed to Sweden's control of the Baltic by the increasingly powerful Russia of Peter the Great. Meanwhile, in central and southeastern Europe, the Ottomans were being driven out of Hungary by the forces of the Habsburg Emperor Leopold I, and from the Black Sea region by the Russians. The warfare and diplomacy of this period reflect the entanglement of numerous factors: dynastic ties, feudal relations, religion, and increasingly, calculation of national interest.

The Wars of Louis XIV in Western Europe

From the beginning of his personal reign in 1661 until his death in 1715, diplomacy and warfare in western Europe revolved around the ambitions of Louis XIV. His aggression overshadowed other tensions and rivalries, and caused erstwhile rivals to put aside their own quarrels to defeat him.

An indication of Louis's concern for his *gloire* was the fact that in 1661, shortly after the Peace of the Pyrenees had made France's ascendancy over Spain official, he ordered his ambassadors to assume precedence at all diplomatic functions. In London, this decree sparked a street brawl between the retinues of the rival ambassadors. Louis threatened Spain with war, leading Philip IV of Spain (his father-in-law) to back down and agree that French ambassadors should be received first everywhere except in Vienna, at the court of his Habsburg cousins. *Gloire*, like gold, was a finite commodity, and for Louis to acquire more, he had to take it away from someone else. By the same token, other rulers were well aware that Louis's ambitions threatened their own *gloire*.

After Louis's concern for his *gloire*, the most salient factor in international relations in the later seventeenth century was the question of the Spanish Succession. As we have seen, Charles II was destined to be the last Habsburg King of Spain. Even if Spain was no longer the dominant power in Europe, it still had a vast empire, including territories in the Netherlands, Italy, and the New World, and the ruler who gained possession of them could be catapulted to a position of European hegemony. Knowing that Charles could die at any time, every ruler in Europe was anxious either to acquire a piece of the empire for himself or at least to deny a share to his rivals. Of course none of Charles's subjects, noble or otherwise, in Spain or anywhere else, would have any part in determining who would succeed him. The outcome would be decided by dynastic inheritance; but generations of marriage alliances meant that there were no fewer than ten potential claimants. The strongest candidates were Emperor Leopold I, of the Austrian branch of the Habsburgs, and Louis XIV of the Bourbon dynasty, both of whom were directly related to the Spanish Habsburgs through both their mothers and their wives.

THE WAR OF DEVOLUTION, 1667–1668

Louis XIV fought his first major war against Spain in 1667–8. It is known as the War of Devolution for reasons that demonstrate the importance of dynastic relations. As a result

HISTORICAL DEBATE

Louis XIV's Foreign Policy

Students of Louis XIV's foreign policy have identified a variety of principles as the driving forces behind it. François Mignet (1796–1884), focusing on the dynastic rivalry between the Bourbons and Habsburgs, believed that its ultimate goal was to secure the Spanish succession for the Bourbons.

> One may say that the Spanish succession was the pivot on which turned almost the entire reign of Louis XIV. . . .
>
> For the century and a half that the two houses that governed France and Spain confronted each other, . . . there was a fierce struggle between them, suspended by moments of repose. The year 1659 had been one of these intermittent periods: the Peace of the Pyrenees and the marriage of Maria Theresa and Louis XIV had pacified the two countries and reconciled the two families; but . . . [t]he marriage of Louis XIV and the Infanta Maria-Theresa would shortly serve to renew the war: it would furnish the subject matter for the last act of a drama that had been played out between the two houses for such a long time. . . .
>
> François A. Mignet, *Négociations relative à la succession d'Espagne sous Louis XIV* (Paris: 1835), vol. 1, pp. lii–liii, trans. Mark Konnert.

Albert Sorel (1842–1906) was among the giants of nineteenth-century French historiography. An ardent patriot, he believed that throughout the Middle Ages, French rulers had aspired to restore the "natural boundaries" that defined ancient Gaul: the Alps, the Pyrenees, the Mediterranean, and the Atlantic. In his view, the tragedy of Louis XIV was that he neglected this tradition for the sake of his own ambition.

> The policy of the Capetians [the royal dynasty from 987 to 1328] . . . had two principal objects: internally to create a nation which should be homogeneous and a state which should be coherent, and externally to ensure, by securing good frontiers, the independence of the nation and the strength of the state.
>
> The policy of the French state was determined by geography. . . . It was based on a fact—the empire of Charlemagne . . . (pp. 276–7).
>
> . . . . The rights of succession to the great emperor [Charlemagne] were sought for in the very beginnings of his empire. The search was pushed back to ancient Gaul. Caesar . . . was quoted as a witness to the origins of the nation. . . . The writings of Strabo [Greek geographer, c. 64 BCE–c. 24 CE] were translated into Latin. . . . Gaul, it said, was bounded by the Pyrenees, the Alps and the Rhine; these are the "natural frontiers" and geography knows no others . . . (pp. 291–2).

In the Latin Testament of Richelieu there is the famous sentence: "The aim of my ministry has been to give back to Gaul the frontiers destined by nature, to give the Gauls a Gallic king, to identify France with Gaul, and to re-establish the new Gaul wherever the old one had been." The authenticity of his *Testamentum Politicum* has been challenged . . . [but] the essential thing is that its compiler, whoever he was, inter-preted the thought of the Cardinal this way . . . (pp. 311–2)

Louis XIV unhappily was not content with the satisfactory and practical "common wars" of his predecessors. He also had his "grand design" and "war of magnificence." Indeed, this was his dominant idea. [Pursuing the Spanish succession] all but ruined the work of Richelieu. Louis XIV misused his inheritance externally as he did within France, and because of the same inordinate ambition and desire for absolute rule (p. 320).

Albert Sorel, *Europe and the French Revolution: The Political Traditions of the Old Regime*, ed. and trans. Alfred Cobban and J.W. Hunt (London: Collins, 1969).

Gaston Zeller (1890–1960) was one of the leading historians of early modern French diplomacy. He refuted Sorel's theory regarding France's "natural frontiers" and instead related Louis's for-eign policy to his own personality:

He [Louis XIV] desired war not to achieve a predetermined goal, to make conquests or to humble a too-powerful adversary, but because war furnished the opportunity to earn the praises that history showers on great commanders. He who proudly claimed responsibility only to God, in reality lived in a constant and confining dependence on public opinion. . . . Where did it come from, this need to shine, to dazzle, to eclipse all others, to perform great deeds, to accomplish "unique feats?" . . . . The quest for "*gloire*" was, at least in the first part of the reign, the supreme goal. . . .

Gaston Zeller, "Politique extérieure et diplomatie sous Louis XIV", *Revue d'histoire moderne*, 6, 32 (1931), pp. 128–9, trans. Mark Konnert.

In his classic biography of Louis XIV, the American historian John B. Wolf returned to the question of frontiers:

. . . Mid-seventeenth-century statesmen . . . had no idea of "natural" or "national" frontiers, but they did think of "defensible" ones. In the 1630s and again in the 1650s foreign armies threatened to swarm on to Paris as they had done in the sixteenth century; Richelieu, and after him Mazarin, wished to gain control of the "gates" that these foreigners might use. . . . It would be absurd to assume that preoccupation with the "gates" of his kingdom was the sole axis of Louis' policy, but it is equally false to fail to recognize his concern.

John B. Wolf, *Louis XIV* (New York: W.W. Norton, 1968), p. 189.

of the 1659 Treaty of the Pyrenees, Louis XIV had married the Spanish princess Maria Theresa, who was the daughter of King Philip IV and the older half-sister of Charles II. In return for her dowry, Maria Theresa renounced all her claims to Spanish possessions. However, the amount of money involved was so massive that it had to be paid in instalments, and the full amount still had not been paid by the time Philip IV died in 1665. This gave Louis and his diplomats a pretext to argue that his wife's renunciation of her succession rights was inoperative, and therefore that, according to the laws that governed succession in the Spanish Netherlands, important parts of those territories ought to "devolve" upon" (be inherited by) her rather than her brother Charles.

The French army that invaded the Spanish Netherlands in the spring of 1667 encountered almost no opposition, as Spain was still recovering from its long struggle to recover the territory it lost following the Portuguese revolt of 1640. At the same time, another French army occupied the Franche-Comté region of Burgundy. England and the Dutch Republic were then fighting the second Anglo-Dutch War, but their shared alarm at the prospect that France might gain control of the English Channel quickly led them to make peace. Then, with Sweden, they formed a Triple Alliance and used the threat of war to impose a settlement on Louis XIV. Under the Treaty of Aix-la-Chapelle (1668) France returned Franche-Comté to Spain, but kept some strategic territories along the border of the Spanish Netherlands, including the important city of Lille. In this way Louis became eligible for at least a portion of the Spanish empire when Charles II eventually died.

Even while the war was underway, Louis and Leopold I had signed a secret treaty partitioning the Spanish empire between them. Its very secrecy worked against it, however, as every ruler in Europe had some interest in the disposition of the Spanish empire, and any agreement required a general consensus.

Although the Dutch and the French had traditionally had cordial relations, based on their common hostility to Spain, Louis felt betrayed by the republic's participation in the Triple Alliance. Urged on by both Colbert and le Tellier (who for once set their rivalry aside), Louis decided to punish the Dutch. In preparation, France bribed Sweden to abandon the Triple Alliance and threaten potential allies of the Dutch in northern Germany, in particular the Great Elector of Brandenburg, in order to keep them at home. In addition, France concluded the Treaty of Dover with England, committing the two countries to a joint war against their mutual enemy.

THE DUTCH WAR, 1672–1678

In the spring of 1672, a French army of 120,000 invaded the Dutch Republic, quickly capturing the important cities of Utrecht and Arnhem. The government of Johan de Witt offered huge concessions, but Louis contemptuously rejected them. It seemed possible that he might seize not only the Spanish Netherlands, but the whole of the Dutch Republic as well. The way to Amsterdam seemed open, but Louis ordered a halt so that his army would not outrun its supplies, and the Dutch used the respite to open the dikes, a desperate measure that flooded the countryside and reduced the country to a collection of island towns surrounded by water. This halted the French advance and allowed the Dutch to regroup their forces.

Among the consequences of the invasion were the overthrow of the regents and the ascendancy of William III, Prince of Orange (see Chapter 6). Working tirelessly to isolate France, he gained the support not only of Emperor Leopold I but, in a stunning reversal, of Spain, which now declared war on France in alliance with the Dutch. In 1674 Charles II of England similarly abandoned the alliance with France formed in the Treaty of Dover. Peace negotiations began in 1676, but were not concluded until 1678. Under the Peace of Nijmegen, Louis acquired several more towns and fortresses along the boundary of the Spanish Netherlands, and as well as Franche-Comté from Spain. But this marked the zenith of Louis XIV's foreign policy and the point at which it began to fail. Although he would wage two more long and costly wars, France would gain very little more in the way of territory. Furthermore, his aggression against the Dutch led rulers across Europe to suspect that he intended to dominate Europe, with the result that a number of long-time rivals eventually put aside their own quarrels in order to prevent French hegemony in Europe.

THE WAR OF THE LEAGUE OF AUGSBURG, 1689–1698

Having strengthened his northeastern frontier with the Spanish Netherlands, Louis now turned his sights directly to the east. The complex dynastic and feudal ties of the borderlands between France and Germany gave France many potential pretexts for meddling in German affairs, and (as we noted in Chapter 4) the fact that France was a guarantor of the Peace of Westphalia meant that it could easily fabricate an excuse to intervene in German territory. Several special "courts of reunion" (*Chambres de réunion*) were set up to investigate French claims on territory in the borderlands, but in reality their function was to justify military seizure and annexation. Any territory or district that had ever been attached to or dependent on any territory ruled by the King of France was fair game. Then, once that territory had been seized, any territory that had ever been attached to or dependent on it was eligible for seizure. In this way France took over most of both Alsace and the Duchy of Luxembourg, among other territories. And in 1681 Louis annexed the entirely German city of Strasbourg, even though he had no legal claim whatever to it.

Louis initially faced little opposition. Emperor Leopold I, theoretically the defender of the Holy Roman Empire, was preoccupied with the threat posed by the Ottomans, while William III of Orange struggled to activate the cumbersome political machinery of the Dutch Republic, and Charles II of England was reluctant to call Parliament to grant the necessary tax revenue (see Chapter 6). By 1686, however, Louis's aggression had caused even the normally fractious German princes to put aside their quarrels and form a common front against France. The rulers of Saxony, the Palatinate, and Bavaria, along with Emperor Leopold and the kings of both Spain and Sweden, formed the League of Augsburg to defend the territorial settlements of Westphalia and Nijmegen.

The Nine Years War, or War of the League of Augsburg, began in 1688, when Louis invaded Germany in an effort to have his candidate installed as Archbishop of Cologne,

VOICES

Louis XIV and Colbert Justify the Dutch War

In his *Mémoires*, written for the edification of his son, Louis XIV reflected on the causes of the Dutch War:

> . . . one may . . . impute the source and the origin of the present war between France and the United Provinces to their ingratitude, their bad faith, and their insupportable vanity. Everyone knows that this people owe the establishment of their free republic to the powerful protection that my predecessors have granted them over the past century, be it against the House of Austria, their former sovereign or against the Empire or England. . . . I had in vain solicited Spain, after the death of the Most Catholic King [Philip IV, in 1665] to render justice to the queen [Maria Theresa, Louis's wife] regarding her legitimate claims to the Netherlands. Overwhelmed by continual refusals, I took up arms and made war in those provinces to redeem the claims of this princess and to restore to her the states that belonged to her. God, the protector of justice, blessed and advanced my arms; all knelt before me, and hardly had I appeared when the majority of the best places of the Low Countries put themselves under my obedience. As my affairs prospered, neither England nor the Empire opposed me. . . . I found in my way only my former good and faithful friends the Dutch, who, rather than being interested in my good fortune, which was the foundation of their state, wished to impose their laws upon me and oblige me to make peace, even daring to threaten me in the event that I should refuse to accept their mediation. I admit that their insolence roused me to anger and that I was prepared, at the risk of my conquests in the Spanish Netherlands, to turn all my strength against this haughty and ungrateful nation, but having neither the troops nor the allies required for this, I dissimulated; I concluded an honorable peace, but resolved to punish this wickedness at another time.

Camille Rousset, *Histoire de Louvois et de son administration politique et militaire* (Paris: 1872), vol. 1, pp. 321–2, trans. Mark Konnert.

In keeping with his mercantilist assumptions, Colbert had long desired to enrich France's industry and commerce by weakening those of the Dutch Republic. Thus when Louis decided to punish the Dutch for their "betrayal," these concerns pushed France towards war with the Dutch. In the first excerpt below, Colbert writes to the French ambassador to the Dutch Republic in 1670. In the second, from July 1672, when French armies appeared to be marching triumphantly towards Amsterdam, Colbert outlines his vision of a postwar commercial order.

Paris, October 24, 1670

To M. de Pomponne, ambassador in the Hague

I found the reports contained in the letter you took the trouble to write to me on the 16th of this month very noteworthy; but, as the commerce and manufactures of Holland may not diminish without passing to some other country, and perhaps the measures and assistance that the King has ordained to re-establish them [i.e., commerce and manufactures] in his kingdom may contribute to attracting them in part, to the profit of his subjects, I pray you to work to discover if these reports on these subjects are trustworthy. . . . We have perhaps nothing as important and so necessary for the general welfare of the State, if at the same time that we see the growth of our commerce and manufactures within the kingdom, we are once again assured, if these views are trustworthy, of the effective diminution of the commerce and manufactures of the States of Holland, which have been accustomed to having everything.

I do not know what might be the cause of the rumours of a rupture [between France and Holland] if not that the conscience of States of Holland is reproaching them greatly for their ingratitude towards the King.

Propositions on the advantages that might be gained from the States of Holland for increasing the commerce of the kingdom. July 8, 1672:

If the King defeats the provinces that compose the United Provinces of the Netherlands, their commerce becoming the commerce of His Majesty's subjects, there is nothing greater to be desired. And if His Majesty, in considering what would be most advantageous for both his new and old subjects, estimates for the good of his service to share the advantages of this commerce, to remove a part of that of Holland in order to pass it into French hands, it would be easy to find expedients by which the new subjects would be obliged to submit.

But if His Majesty restores the States [i.e., the United Provinces or Dutch Republic] to the sovereignty that they have not been able to defend, and if he wishes to content himself with imposing upon them conditions that benefit his own subjects, it is necessary to consider that the Dutch have six main commerces from which His Majesty might derive great advantages for his subjects. . . .

If His Majesty were to impose upon them all or part of these conditions, his revenues would increase in proportion to the advantages that his subjects would receive from them. . . . [and] due to the abundance of money which would be found in the kingdom, the people would be able to pay higher taxes.

Pierre Clément (ed.), *Instructions et mémoires de Colbert* (Paris: 1833), vol. 2, part 2, pp. 571, 658–60, trans. Mark Konnert.

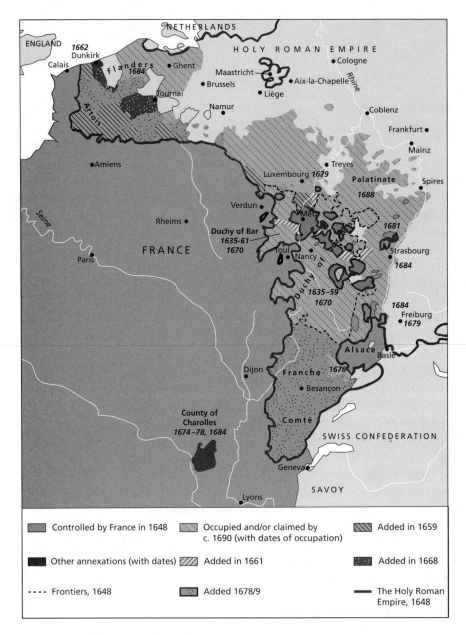

Map 7.1 Territorial acquisitions of Louis XIV

one of the most important ecclesiastical territories in Germany. He clearly hoped to present his enemies with a *fait accompli*, but he miscalculated badly. His opponents were galvanized into action when the French army ransacked the Palatinate. Louis assumed that James II and his supporters would resist the invasion of England by William of Orange, and that the attention of both England and the Dutch Republic would therefore be focused on that conflict (see Chapter 6). Instead, as we have seen, James panicked and fled, with the result that Louis's most intractable opponent became King of England and was able to direct both England's navy and its financial might against France.

At first the war went quite well for France, which took a number of important territories in the Netherlands and northwestern Germany. But eventually English money and naval power began to take effect, and a series of poor harvests led to widespread famine and destitution in France. By 1697 all sides were exhausted, and since the long awaited death of Charles II of Spain seemed imminent, Louis agreed to make peace in order to concentrate on the Spanish Succession. Under the Treaty of Ryswick he surrendered almost all the gains he had made since the 1678 Treaty of Nijmegen, except for Strasbourg, and recognized William III as King of England. To discourage any future French aggression, the treaty also allowed the Dutch to build a series of fortresses in the Spanish Netherlands.

THE WAR OF THE SPANISH SUCCESSION, 1702–1713

The question of the Spanish Succession was now front and centre on the international scene. The secret treaty between Louis XIV and Leopold I had never had any realistic chance of gaining acceptance among other leaders, and now that Leopold had taken most of Hungary back from the Ottomans, he was in a much stronger position in relation to Louis. Thus in 1698 France, England, and the Dutch Republic signed another partition treaty, and this one did achieve the desired consensus. Spain itself, along with its American colonies, the Spanish Netherlands, and Sardinia were to be inherited by Leopold's grandson Joseph Ferdinand of Bavaria, then still a young boy; Milan would go to Archduke Charles, a younger son of Leopold; and the rest (primarily Naples, Sicily, and several other small Italian territories) to Louis XIV's eldest son, Louis, the "Grand Dauphin." This division might have worked, since it preserved a general balance between Europe's two most powerful rulers. But the Spanish objected strenuously to the division of their empire by outsiders. Thus, later that year, Charles II wrote a will that left all his possessions to Joseph Ferdinand. In 1699, however, the young prince died, and the process of negotiation had to start all over again.

In June 1700, therefore, England, France, and the Dutch Republic negotiated another partition treaty, which assigned Spain, its American colonies, and the Spanish Netherlands to Archduke Charles, and Naples, Sicily, and Lorraine—an independent duchy within the Holy Roman Empire, situated on France's eastern frontier—to the son of Louis XIV. (The Duke of Lorraine was to be bribed to abandon his duchy in exchange for the much richer territory of Milan.) However, Leopold opposed this settlement, as he wanted to retain Habsburg control of northern Italy, and once again the Spanish government and nobles objected to a plan that divided their empire without their consent. Thus Charles II rewrote his will yet again, this time leaving his entire empire to one of Louis XIV's younger grandsons, Philip of Anjou. The reasoning behind this plan was twofold: while Philip's grandfather would be able to help him defend the empire's integrity, the fact that he was a younger grandson minimized the risk that he would eventually inherit the French throne as well and then subordinate the interests of his Spanish subjects to those of the French.

When Charles II did finally die, in November 1700, Louis XIV had to decide whether to abide by the treaty signed with the English and Dutch only months earlier, or accept the terms of Charles II's will, by which his grandson Philip would inherit the entire Spanish empire. He chose the latter course, and in the spring of 1701 his grandson, now King Philip V of Spain, arrived in Madrid. Although annoyed, the signatories of the partition treaty might have been persuaded to accept this resolution. However, Louis then proceeded to have the Parlement of Paris affirm the traditional order of succession to the French throne, ensuring that Philip could one day inherit the French crown as well. He then had his grandson name him regent for the Spanish Netherlands, and ordered the Dutch to evacuate the border fortresses that they had been granted in the Treaty of Ryswick. War was now inevitable, for no other European ruler could tolerate the possibility that France and Spain might one day be united under a single ruler. All the mistrust and suspicion of Louis that had built up over the previous decades now came to the fore.

The War of Spanish Succession began in 1702 and would drag on until 1713; it was a bloody and exhausting struggle for all sides, but especially for France, coming on the heels of the War of the League of Augsburg. Philip V proved to be a popular and effective ruler, supplying the long-needed political will to reform Spanish society and government (see Chapter 10). Thus when an allied Anglo-Dutch force invaded the peninsula in 1702, it attracted little support from the Spanish. At the same time, the eruption of a Huguenot revolt in the Cévennes mountains of south-central France required an army to suppress it, reducing the forces available to fight the king's foreign enemies. Worn down by a series of military defeats and poor harvests, Louis offered to return all his conquests and withdraw French armies from Spain in return for peace. But the allies did not trust him. Sensing that he was on the ropes, they demanded that Louis agree to help them drive his grandson Philip from the Spanish throne if he should refuse to leave it. Louis refused, and the war continued.

By 1711, however, all the combatants were running out of steam. On Leopold's death in 1705 he had been succeeded by his eldest son. But Joseph I himself died in 1711, leaving the title of Holy Roman Emperor to his younger brother, Charles VI (r. 1711–40). Although the English and Dutch were no more willing to see the entire Spanish empire fall into the new Emperor's lap than they were to see the same man rule both France and Spain, the Dutch were feeling the strain of decades of war, and in England, a change in government ministers brought to power a group that favoured peace over continuing war. Meanwhile, France was near the brink of collapse. Military defeat, domestic revolt, and a series of personal tragedies had caused Louis to wonder if God were punishing him for his hubris. His eldest son, the Grand Dauphin, died in 1711. The following year, his eldest grandson, the Duke of Burgundy, died of measles, along with his wife, of whom Louis was very fond, and the elder of their two surviving sons.

Philip V of Spain opened the way for peace in 1713 when he voluntarily relinquished any claim to the French throne for himself and his heirs. In 1713 and 1714 the various combatants signed a series of treaties known collectively as the Peace of Utrecht. Together, they parcelled out the Spanish empire in such a way that no one power could threaten to dominate in the way that France had under Louis XIV, or that Spain had for a century before that. Philip V was confirmed in his rule of Spain and its overseas colonies, while Holy Roman Emperor Charles VI gained Milan, Naples, Sardinia, and the southern Netherlands, henceforth known as the Austrian Netherlands. France kept Alsace and Strasbourg, Franche-Comté, and the gains it had previously made along its northeastern frontier with the (now) Austrian Netherlands. England gained not only the fortress of Gibraltar on the southern tip of Spain (a sore point in relations between the two countries even today) and a privileged position in the Spanish colonial trade—including the *asiento*, an exclusive contract to supply African slaves to Spanish colonies in the Americas—but several French territories in the New World: Newfoundland, Acadia, and St. Kitts. Indeed, the Peace of Utrecht was the first such document to treat colonial possessions as something other than an afterthought. In the decades to come, colonial strategy and conflicts would assume ever-greater importance in European diplomacy and warfare (see Chapter 11).

Louis XIV died in September 1715. Of the 54 years since his personal reign began in 1661, France had been at war for more than half. Shortly before his death, he is said to have told his five-year-old great-grandson (who would succeed him as Louis XV): "I have loved war too much."

Habsburgs and Ottomans

In the later seventeenth century, a series of Habsburg rulers shifted their focus from Germany to their own patrimonial lands. Over a period of decades, their armies pushed the Muslim forces of the Ottoman Empire out of Hungary, clearing the way for the Habsburgs to take control of the restive Hungarian nobility.

The Ottoman Empire stands alongside the Spanish Habsburg empire, the Mughal Empire in India, and the Qing dynasty in China as one of the great powers of the early modern world. For all its European possessions, the Ottoman Empire was fundamentally non-European in its history, its political and social systems, and, of course, its religion.

The Ottomans were ethnic Turks from central Asia who had settled in Anatolia (modern Turkey) in the thirteenth century. By the early fifteenth century, Ottoman armies had already conquered large parts of southeastern Europe, and when they took the Byzantine capital of Constantinople in 1453, they extinguished the last remnant of the Roman Empire. In the course of the sixteenth century the Ottomans conquered Egypt and North Africa, as well as the Arabian peninsula and the Muslim holy places of Mecca and Medina. Conquest of Mesopotamia and Yemen would establish an Ottoman naval and commercial presence in the Indian Ocean. Under Sultan Suleiman the Magnificent (1520–66), the Ottoman Empire reached its greatest extent. In 1526 at the Battle of Mohàcs, Ottoman armies defeated and killed in battle King Louis II of Hungary and Bohemia. Although the Hungarian nobles elected Emperor Charles V's brother Ferdinand as their new king, two-thirds of the kingdom was under Ottoman occupation. Twice—in 1529 and 1532—Ottoman armies marched up the Danube valley and besieged the imperial capital of Vienna. Further conquests around the Black Sea, in the region of what are now Romania, Moldova, Ukraine, Georgia, and Armenia, would eventually lead to conflict with Russia (see below).

As we have seen, Turkish naval power not only dominated the eastern Mediterranean but threatened commerce and ports as far to the west as Spain. Although the threat to the western Mediterranean receded after the Battle of Lepanto (off southwestern Greece) in 1571, where a combined Spanish, Venetian, and Papal fleet inflicted a decisive defeat on the Ottoman navy, pirates owing allegiance to the Ottomans continued to raid shipping and ports as far west as Spain.

Following the death of Suleiman the Magnificent in 1566, the Ottoman state entered a period of weakness and decline, but the decline was arrested, at least temporarily, with the accession in 1632 of Murad IV, who reconquered Baghdad and Iraq from the Persians in 1638–9. The recovery continued with the appointment of Mehmed Köprülü as grand vizier in 1656. With dictatorial powers and ruthless efficiency he reformed the administration and fiscal system, allowing the empire to resume its expansion. His major success in this respect was the subjection of Transylvania. Since the 1540s, this portion of the historic Kingdom of Hungary had been an autonomous principality under the general authority and protection of the Ottoman Empire. In the 1650s, however, the increasingly independent actions of Prince George Ràkòzi II alarmed the Ottomans, and in 1658 they invaded. By 1660 Transylvania had been incorporated directly into the empire. Even the grand vizier's death in 1661 did not interrupt the Ottoman revival, as his son Ahmed Köprülü continued his father's policies, albeit with less brutality. Ottoman troops continued to press westward into Royal Hungary until 1664, when they were defeated at St. Gotthard on the Austrian border by a Habsburg army that they outnumbered two to one. Habsburg forces did not follow up on this victory, however, as the Emperor was concerned about the ambitions of Louis XIV and did not want to be caught unprepared for the death of Charles II of Spain. The Treaty of Vasvar (1664) bought the Habsburgs peace in the east, but it came at a high price. Leopold surrendered several border fortresses, recognized the Ottomans' control of Transylvania, and paid a large annual tribute to the Sultan, in return for a truce of twenty years.

Hungarian nobles felt that Leopold had sacrificed their interests to those of the Habsburg dynasty in the west, but a plot to overthrow Habsburg rule of Royal Hungary led to increased repression. Nobles were taxed, Protestants persecuted, and the government was handed to foreigners. A Protestant Hungarian nobleman named Imre Thököly led a rebellion against Habsburg rule, invoking the *jus resistendi*. The Ottoman government recognized him as king of an independent Hungary. Ahmed Körpülü had died in 1676 and was replaced as grand vizier by his brother-in-law Kara Mustafa, who in 1683 launched an invasion up the Danube and once again laid siege to Vienna.

Vastly outnumbered, Leopold and his court fled west to Passau, from where he directed military operations and enlisted allies. For two months the Ottoman army besieged the Habsburg capital, with brutal cruelty on both sides. Leopold found support not only among the German princes, but from King John Sobieski of Poland (r. 1674–96), who feared that Poland was next on the Ottoman agenda. In September 1683, on the Kahlenberg heights in the Viennese suburbs, an allied force under Sobieski defeated the larger

Turkish army, which then retreated down the Danube in disarray. This ended the Ottoman threat to central Europe. Sobieski was hailed as a hero, and at the church service celebrating Vienna's delivery, the theme of the sermon was a verse from the Gospel of John, referring to John the Baptist: "There was a man sent from God whose name was John."

Leopold might not have followed up on his victory at St. Gotthard twenty years earlier, but this time he stayed in the field, pushing the Ottoman armies south and east down the Danube valley. Now the pope and Peter the Great of Russia joined the victorious alliance, and by 1687 they had evicted the Ottomans from virtually all of Hungary and Transylvania. These were the victories that, as we saw in Chapter 6, allowed Leopold to impose Habsburg absolutism on the Hungarian nobles. Only the looming Spanish succession prompted him to make peace with the Ottomans in the Treaty of Karlowitz (1699), ratifying Habsburg conquests in Hungary since 1683. The Ottoman retreat continued through the early eighteenth century, and in 1718 the Treaty of Passarowitz added more territory—the Banat (a territory now shared by Romania, Serbia, and Hungary) and portions of Serbia and Wallachia—to the Habsburg holdings. Although the Ottoman Empire continued to hold most of the Balkans and Greece, it was now in decline, and in the nineteenth century its remaining European lands would be carved up by European powers and eventually become independent states.

Russia, Sweden, and the Great Northern War

Peter the Great of Russia had undertaken his ambitious reform program (see Chapter 6) for military purposes above all, and was not slow to put his forces into action. In 1695 he joined the Habsburg alliance that had lifted the siege of Vienna, and his army laid siege to the Ottoman fortress of Azov on the Black Sea, at the mouth of the Don River. Gaining access to warm-water ports was part of Peter's long-term campaign to increase Russia's contact with the west. But the Ottomans were able to supply the fortress from the water, and the Russians, lacking a navy, were powerless to prevent it. The following year, with his usual energy and enthusiasm, Peter had a fleet built on the River Don and floated to the Black Sea, which he then used to conquer Azov. Although he had hoped to play a leading role in a grand alliance against the Ottomans, this plan was forestalled by the Treaty of Karlowitz in 1699, and the preoccupation of other rulers with the Spanish Succession.

In 1700, therefore, Peter joined an alliance with King Augustus II of Poland (r. 1697–1706, 1709–33) and Frederick IV of Denmark (r. 1699–1730) directed against Sweden's new king, Charles XII (r. 1697–1718) in hopes of dismembering his Baltic empire. Sweden had emerged from the Thirty Years War as the dominant power in the Baltic and northern Europe, but now its supremacy was challenged not only by Poland and Denmark, its traditional rivals, but by the rising power of Russia. Although the three allies thought that the youthful Charles XII (just fourteen when he became king in 1697) would prove an easy target, he proved to be an extraordinarily able and courageous commander. He also benefited from the fact that his father, Charles XI (r. 1660–97), had left him an exceptionally efficient army and navy. Launched in early 1700 when the allies invaded Swedish territory in northern Germany,

Livonia, and Ingria, the Great Northern War would continue until 1721. Charles quickly turned the tables on his attackers, besieging Copenhagen and forcing the Danish king to sign a humiliating treaty. Meanwhile, the Russians had laid siege to the town of Narva in Swedish Ingria, and Charles now rushed from Denmark to confront them. In November a Swedish force outnumbered 40,000 to 6,000 inflicted a humiliating defeat on the Russians. Assuming that Russia was now effectively out of the war, he then turned to Poland, and by 1702 had occupied Warsaw. By 1704 Charles had driven Augustus off the Polish throne and replaced him as king with the more amenable Polish nobleman Stanislas Leszcynski (r. 1704–9, 1733–6). But Augustus, who was also Elector of Saxony, continued to fight, and was supported by many Polish nobles. Thus Charles XII invaded Saxony and forced Augustus both to withdraw from the war and to recognize Leszcynski as King of Poland.

Having defeated Denmark and Poland, Charles now turned his attention back to Peter and Russia. In early 1708 Charles led his army in an attack on Russia from Poland, whose ultimate goal was Moscow. By this time, however, Russia had recovered from the defeat at Narva, and Peter's efforts to reform the Russian army had begun to pay off. Anticipating the strategy that their descendants would use against Napoleon in the nineteenth century and against the Nazis in the twentieth, the Russians drew the Swedes into the vast Russian interior, destroying supplies as they went. This forced the Swedes to turn south into the Ukraine to find supplies for the winter. There Charles also hoped to enlist the support of

Map 7.2 Europe in 1721, after the treaties of Utrecht and Nystad

the Ukrainian Cossacks against their common Russian enemy, but the extreme winter of 1708–9 took a heavy toll on his forces. When fighting resumed in the spring, he attacked the fortress of Poltava, which lay between him and Moscow, but there he suffered a crushing defeat: 7000 Swedes were killed and another 2000 taken prisoner. Charles and the remnants of his army escaped to the south, where they were given refuge by the Ottoman sultan.

Although the outcome of the Great Northern War was effectively decided in 1709 at Poltava, it dragged on until 1721. During Charles's absence in the Ottoman Empire, his enemies rejoined the war. Augustus reclaimed the Polish throne and Denmark invaded southern Sweden. By the time Charles returned to Sweden, all his military gains had been reversed, and he died in 1718. Under a series of treaties made in 1720–21, Denmark absorbed the disputed neighbouring territory of Holstein but gave up its claim to its former provinces in southern Sweden, and most of Sweden's northern German territories passed to Hanover and Brandenburg–Prussia, which had joined the anti-Swedish alliance. The 1721 Treaty of Nystad between Russia and Sweden confirmed the former's ascendancy in northern Europe. Peter the Great gained for Russia the former Swedish territories of Estonia, Livonia, eastern Karelia, and Ingria, where the construction of St. Petersburg was already well advanced.

Chapter Conclusion

The peace settlements of Utrecht, Karlowitz, and Nystad ushered in a new era in European diplomacy. Since the French invasion of Italy in 1494, preventing the acquisition of hegemonic power, first by the Habsburg empire in various manifestations, and later by France under Louis XIV, had been among the implicit goals of the other European rulers, but there was no explicit or conscious commitment to maintaining a balance of power as a governing principle of international relations. In practice each ruler was still interested primarily maximizing his own interests, regardless of the consequences for the overall distribution of power. After those treaties, however, at least until the 1790s and the wars unleashed by the French Revolution, relations between European rulers would reflect a much more deliberate commitment to preventing any one power from attempting to achieve dominance in the way that Louis XIV had. As we will see in Chapter 10, five powers would dominate eighteenth-century warfare and diplomacy: France, Great Britain, Brandenburg–Prussia, the Habsburg monarchy, and Russia. Spain, Sweden, Denmark, and the Dutch Republic would play smaller, yet often important roles, while Poland would lapse into impotence and eventually be swallowed up by its neighbours, and the Ottoman Empire would continue to decline in power and shrink in size.

Until the end of the seventeenth century, European diplomacy had been played out on three major stages: western Europe, where France, Spain, England, and the Dutch Republic were the main contenders; northern Europe, where Sweden, Poland, Denmark, and now Russia and Brandenburg-Prussia vied for control of the Baltic and its lucrative grain trade; and the southeast, where the Habsburg monarchy and Russia to a lesser extent confronted the Ottoman Empire. These arenas, while not hermetically sealed off from each other, were largely independent. By the early eighteenth century, however, European diplomacy was much more integrated: what happened in one arena inevitably affected the balance of power in the entire system.

At the same time a clearer distinction was emerging between the interests of ruling dynasties and those of the states they ruled. Rulers and ministers increasingly justified their actions and policies by reference to the interests of an impersonal state that they just happened to rule. The state, which had been developing under the auspices of personal and hereditary monarchy, with its increasingly sophisticated machinery and bureaucracy, was beginning to emerge as an entity in itself, with its own interests and logic. The state was still imperfectly aligned with the "nation," however, even in France, and the alignment in the Habsburg monarchy was considerably worse.

Once religious differences were no longer the primary drivers of diplomacy and warfare, and with the increasing separation between the interests of the state and those of the ruling dynasty, international relations became more calculating and rational. The impersonal and abstract state was an entity whose interests were much more susceptible to cost–benefit analysis than the triumph of the True Faith or the *gloire* of Louis XIV. Although rulers and ministers continued to clothe their interests in the language of dynastic claims, this was increasingly window dressing rather than the motor of international relations. At the same time that armed forces were becoming increasingly disciplined and effective tools, as well as more deadly on the battlefield, warfare became more limited, both in its aims and in its impact on civilian populations.

Questions for Critical Thought

1. How did relations between states in the seventeenth century differ from those of today? In what ways are they similar?
2. How did the decline of religious passion affect international relations in the later seventeenth century?
3. How important was the "nation" in international affairs?
4. How might a more explicit and conscious commitment to a balance of power as the key component of international relations change the ways in which rulers and states conducted their relations?

Further Reading

The works on individual states listed at the end of Chapter 6 are all relevant to the present chapter as well. In addition, the following books focus specifically on the warfare and diplomacy of the period.

Ekberg, C.J. *The Failure of Louis XIV's Dutch War*. Chapel Hill: University of North Carolina Press, 1979. Focuses on the impact of the war on France and Louis XIV's foreign policy.

Goffman, Daniel. *The Ottoman Empire and Early Modern Europe*. Cambridge: Cambridge University Press, 2002. Emphasizes the enduring ties between the Ottoman Empire and Christian Europe.

Jones, J.R. *Britain and Europe in the Seventeenth Century*. New York: Norton, 1966. A brief overview of Britain's arrival on the European stage as a great power.

Lynn, John A. *The Wars of Louis XIV*. London: Longman, 1999. A comprehensive treatment of the Sun King's wars and diplomacy.

Oakley, Stewart P. *War and Peace in the Baltic, 1560–1790*. London: Routledge, 1992. Useful on the Great Northern War and Russia's rise in northern Europe.

Setton, Kenneth M. *Venice, Austria and the Turks in the Seventeenth Century*. Philadelphia: American Philosophical Society, 1992.

Sonnino, Paul. *Louis XIV and the Origins of the Dutch War*. Cambridge: Cambridge University Press, 1988. A detailed account of the origins and aims of the Dutch War.

Note

1. Cited in Mark Greengrass, *Christendom Destroyed: Europe 1517–1648* (London: Viking, 2014), p. 533. More recently, Richard Nixon—the US president who was forced to resign over the Watergate scandal and cover-up—expressed a similar view: "When the President does it, that means it's not illegal."

8

Economy and Society Transformed:
The Eighteenth Century

By the end of the eighteenth century, Europe was a very different place than it had been even fifty years earlier. The most dramatic markers of change were the two events that heralded the arrival of the modern world: the French Revolution, which transformed the exercise of political power, and the Industrial Revolution, which transformed the patterns of subsistence and daily life that had governed the lives of the vast majority of people since the development of agriculture eight to ten thousand years earlier.

Yet whereas we know what would happen by the end of the eighteenth century, the people who lived through those changes did not. And this puts historians in the difficult position of trying to do two different things at once: to understand the past on its own terms and to analyze how the past became the present. The general tendency has been to focus on the developments leading to the seismic shifts that eventually occurred. But this focus can prevent us from noticing significant continuities, and in so doing lead us to conclusion that what did happen was inevitable. As one historian has put it, "the beginning of historical wisdom about the eighteenth century . . . is to forget the French Revolution."[1] The same could be said of the Industrial Revolution. Although the usual approach is to view the eighteenth century through the lens of the changes to come, the chapters that follow will try to look at the events of the period less from the perspective of what was to follow and more from the perspective of what had come before. We will attempt to be as true as possible to the reality of the past, while drawing attention to the subterranean changes that, although they seem obvious in hindsight, were probably not apparent at the time.

Breaking the Demographic Mould

Over the course of the eighteenth century, the demographic and social patterns established in the wake of the Black Death began to break down. This eventually resulted in significant population growth, especially in the later 1700s, and, in conjunction with the related changes taking place in agriculture and industry, it altered the basic nature of European society. These changes were no less real for being incremental, regionally variable, and largely unperceived by the people who lived through them.

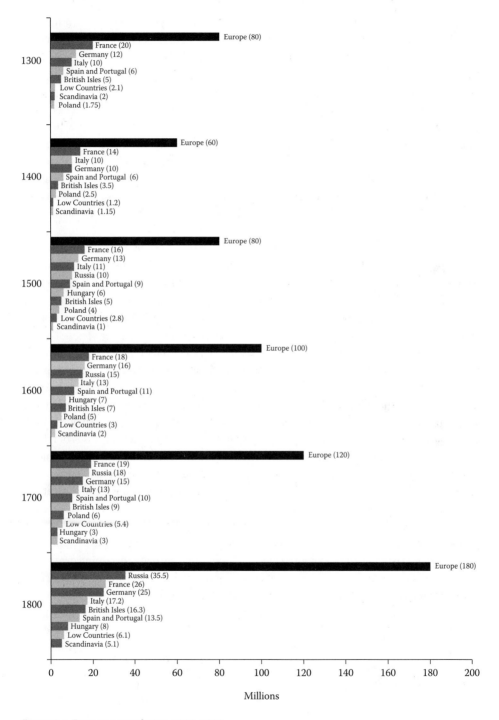

Figure 8.1 European population, 1300–1800

Between 1700 and 1740 the European population grew from roughly 120 million to 140 million. By this time the population had recovered from the demographic setbacks of the seventeenth century, such as the Thirty Years War. As in the period following the Black Death, the cycle had come full circle: subsistence crises, epidemic disease, and widespread warfare had stalled and even reversed the population growth of the sixteenth century. Just as in the earlier period, the decline had contained within it the seeds of the next expansion. Now, however, in the mid-eighteenth century, something quite unprecedented happened: not only did the population keep growing, but the rate of expansion accelerated. The growth rate in the latter half of the eighteenth century was roughly double that of the first half. By the end of the century the population of Europe had reached some 180 to 190 million people. Furthermore, the growth continued, not only in Europe, but throughout the world. This was the beginning of the worldwide trend that by the early twenty-first century would see the population of the planet surpass 7 billion.

There were significant regional variations, but the overall trend is unmistakable. The population of England and Wales grew from about 9 million in 1700 to approximately 16 million in 1800. France, always the most populous country in western Europe, grew from 19 million to 26 million. Spain grew from 7.5 million to 11.5 million, and Italy from 13 million to over 17 million. Prussia and Sweden likely doubled their inhabitants, while Hungary and Russia may have tripled theirs.

What lay behind this unprecedented demographic expansion? There is no single answer, but research has identified a number of contributing factors. As we saw in Chapter 1, population levels were determined by a delicate balance between birth rates and death rates. In the absence of artificial contraception and modern medical care, age of marriage was virtually the only variable under human control. Historical demographers have established that the average age at first marriage is quite sensitive to economic conditions. Periods of relative prosperity allowed couples to marry and set up their own households sooner than in times of economic stagnation. This enabled them to begin reproducing a year or two earlier than their parents' generation did. This was certainly the case in England, where the average age at first marriage declined steadily throughout the eighteenth century. Although the picture is less clear elsewhere, in large parts of continental Europe, a series of good harvests in the 1730s produced a "baby boom" of sorts, which contributed to population growth later in the century.

Although rising birth rates contributed to demographic growth, declining death rates probably had a greater impact, especially declining rates of infant mortality. Small changes in infant mortality had a significant cumulative effect, as the growing numbers of babies who survived in each generation grew up to produce more babies of their own who survived. A study of the French parish of Auneuil demonstrates this impact. For the first third of the eighteenth century, infant mortality was what it had always been: about half of the babies born would die before reaching adulthood. After 1750, almost 60 per cent of babies survived to adulthood; in relative terms, this is a huge difference. Likewise in England: in the village of Colyton, the proportion of children dying before age 15 declined from 30 to 25 per cent between 1700 and 1750.

Why did death rates decline? Once again, we have no single answer. There was a marked decline in the toll taken by epidemic disease, but except in the case of smallpox deaths it was not due to any great advance in medical knowledge. The most notable change was in the bubonic plague. Endemic since the Black Death of the fourteenth century, it now virtually disappeared from western Europe, although there were periodic outbreaks in eastern Europe and the Ottoman Empire. Political changes played a role here. As governments assumed greater power, large cities were able to enforce sanitation measures that probably contributed to the decline of the plague. Urban planning measures, including sewer construction, street widening, and changes in building materials (from wood and thatched roofs to brick, stone, and tile) provided fewer habitats suitable for rats. Stricter quarantine measures were also enforced, especially on ships and travellers from areas where plague was still a problem. Nevertheless, medical authorities were just as ignorant of the plague's causes in 1800 as they had been in 1400.

Other diseases did continue to take a heavy toll: dysentery, typhoid, typhus, tuberculosis, influenza, and malaria. But even here, there may have been some small regional improvements. For example, the draining of swamps for farmland in some areas reduced the breeding grounds for mosquitoes, which helped to reduce malaria on a local scale. Although smallpox remained the most feared killer, especially of the young, by the end of the century the process of controlling its spread would have begun.

It was well known that those who survived smallpox acquired immunity to the disease. In several widely separated parts of the world—the Ottoman Empire, West Africa, and possibly China—people experimented with exposing patients to a (hopefully) mild form of the disease in order to confer immunity. The patient would be scratched with an implement that had been exposed to the pus in the pustules of a smallpox victim. Although this procedure, known as inoculation, could work, it was unpredictable, as doses were difficult to calibrate, and on occasion the disease would spread beyond its intended target. That the practice became known in western Europe in the early eighteenth century was largely due to the advocacy of Lady Mary Wortley Montagu (1689–1762), the wife of the English ambassador to the Ottoman Empire. A smallpox survivor herself, she had both her children inoculated, and her example helped to persuade the Prince and Princess of Wales (later King George II of England and Queen Caroline) to do the same for their children. But the practice continued to arouse fear, as a number of people who tried it did not survive, among them the well-known New England preacher and theologian Jonathan Edwards (1703–58).

By the 1790s, however, it had long been observed that milkmaids were largely immune to smallpox, and a number of physicians theorized that this was the result of exposure to the related but less harmful disease of cowpox. Thus the English physician Edward Jenner (1749–1823) developed and popularized the process that we know as vaccination, where the patient was deliberately exposed to cowpox in order to confer immunity to smallpox. Although this innovation came too late to explain the demographic expansion of the eighteenth century, it surely contributed to the population explosion that the globe has experienced since then. In Canada smallpox vaccination was deemed no longer necessary for the general population in 1972, and in 1979 the World Health Organization declared that the smallpox virus had been eradicated, although several samples are preserved (under very heavy security) in laboratories around the world.

Changes in the nature of warfare also contributed to the decline in death rates and hence to demographic expansion. By the later seventeenth century armies were becoming more disciplined and professional as governments improved their command structures and brought armies in the field under greater central control. Free agent contractors such as Wallenstein, whose business was war, were relegated to the past. Increasingly, soldiers were housed in barracks rather than billeted with local residents, and were fed and supplied through quartermaster corps rather than direct levies on civilians. Discipline was enforced through brutal codes of military justice, and pay became more regular. All these changes reduced the occasions for conflict between soldiers and civilians; in a sense, the military became more closely integrated into society and less of a parasitical burden on it. At the same time, religion had ceased to be a driving force in warfare and diplomacy, and relations among European states had come to focus primarily on preserving a balance of power. As a consequence, wars were fought for more limited and attainable goals, amenable to rational calculation and cost–benefit analysis. As armies became larger and better equipped, and their training more professional, they also became even more expensive. Rulers and their generals, having invested massive resources in their armed forces, became increasingly cautious about risking those investments in battle. Much eighteenth-century warfare thus consisted of elaborate manoeuvring to gain a tactical advantage over the enemy that would force him to withdraw rather than risk battle from a disadvantageous position. In this way, even as armies became more deadly on the battlefield, their disastrous impact on civilian populations was reduced.

All these factors—lower age of marriage, decreasing infant mortality, control of some epidemic diseases, and changes in armies and warfare—played a role in expanding population growth. The most important factors of all, however, were improvements in the quantity, quality, and variety of food available to many people. Some of this had to do with the development of infrastructure, as improvements in road and canal systems made it easier to transport food where it was needed. Governments removed many of the internal tariffs and tolls that had hindered trade within their borders and asserted greater control over currency, weights, and measures, all of which simplified commerce. There is also some evidence of better climatic conditions after the "little ice age" of the seventeenth century. Most importantly, however, the eighteenth century saw profound changes in European agriculture (see below).

There is also some evidence of changing patterns of family life in the eighteenth century, although it is subject to varying interpretations. As was discussed in Chapter 1, rates of illegitimate birth had traditionally been relatively low—not more than about 5 per cent. This pattern appears to have begun changing in the mid-eighteenth century. It was now not uncommon for between 10 and 20 per cent of all births to be illegitimate. In Paris, for example, fully one-quarter of babies born in the later eighteenth century appear to have been illegitimate. It is likely that the growth of rural industry (see below) allowed many young people to escape the constraints imposed by a limited supply of land. Having an alternative source of income meant they no longer had to wait for land to be freed up (most often by the death of a father) in order to establish a household, and this permitted them to marry younger. There is some evidence to suggest that marriage was becoming a more personal and emotional matter, and less a matter of calculation. With the loosening of the bonds of the village community, and the increasing importance placed on romantic attachment, there is also evidence that many young women engaged in sex on the promise of marriage, only to be disappointed. In other words, pregnancy no longer led automatically to marriage.

One consequence was an expansion in the foundling hospitals that cared for abandoned children. These institutions were not new, but the eighteenth century saw dramatic increases both in their numbers and in the numbers of children they housed. Growing government concern with social welfare, often in response to Enlightenment thought (see Chapter 9), contributed to the expansion of foundling hospitals, and therefore was in part responsible for the rise in the numbers of children entrusted to the state, some of whom were abandoned because their impoverished parents could no longer support them. It is also evident, however, that rising rates of illegitimacy were the primary reason for this phenomenon.

Among elite families—that is, the upper ranks of the bourgeoisie and the nobility—there is evidence of changing attitudes towards love, marriage, family, and child-rearing. Many of these changes were no doubt linked to the Enlightenment emphasis on individual reason and liberty, but it is once more difficult to distinguish cause and effect. As we saw in Chapter 1, the choice of marriage partners was usually determined by social and economic considerations, although we cannot say that romantic love never played a role. Now, however, there is evidence that increasing importance was placed on romantic love as the primary basis for choice of a spouse, at least among those who could afford to discount economic concerns. This was reflected in the fiction that was then emerging as a new literary genre: love was a major theme in novels such as *Pamela; or, Virtue Rewarded* (1740), by Samuel Richardson (1689–1761). There is also evidence that emotional ties and companionship began to play a more important role in elite marriages than they had in the past, although it is difficult to separate ideals and reality. Were spouses truly more affectionate, or was the new emphasis on the expression of love a matter of conforming to new social norms? In any case, it seems clear the ideal of family life was changing, and that many people were trying to live up to the new ideal.

These changes were also expressed in house construction, at least among the well-to-do. There was an increased emphasis on privacy for the master and mistress of the family, with separate sleeping quarters and rooms designed for different functions. In the past, even in royal palaces, one room simply opened onto the next, and one might have to walk through several intervening rooms to get to one's destination, but now houses were built with corridors. Even among the most aristocratic families, there was an increased desire for privacy and intimacy. The noble household with dozens of liveried servants was increasingly a thing of the past.

As we saw in Chapter 1, most parents in the early modern period loved their children deeply, but that love was expressed differently than it is today. Over the eighteenth century, we can see the emergence of the modern conception of childhood, possibly because the decline in child mortality allowed parents to make greater emotional investments in individual children. There is indeed some demographic evidence of intentional family planning, mostly through *coitus interruptus*, although primitive condoms were becoming increasingly common. Although there had previously been a conception of childhood as a discrete phase of life, the nature of that conception began to change. There was less emphasis on the taint of original sin and the need to tame the wilful and sinful child. Following Locke's theory that that the mind begins as a *tabula rasa* and requires careful nurture to develop the ability to reason, more attention was paid to education. Whereas in the past children were believed to need strict discipline, including corporal punishment, to train them to obey human and divine authority, Enlightenment writers developed the notion that children are pure and innocent until they are corrupted by exposure to the evils of the world.

In addition to a general expansion of education, a consumer market developed that was dedicated to products for children. Toy shops began to appear in prosperous urban areas, and there was a growing demand for children's games and books. Among elite women, the use of wet nurses began to decline, and breastfeeding became increasingly popular as a way of promoting the mother–child bond. The most noteworthy example may be Marie Antoinette, Queen of France from 1774 to 1792, who for a time breastfed her own daughter.

At first these innovations were limited to members of the elite, who could afford them and were aware of Enlightenment ideals. For the vast majority in both towns and countryside, family life remained unchanged. In fact, the use of wet nurses became more common among working women, whose labour was increasingly essential to family survival.

Marie Antoinette breastfeeding her daughter.

An Agricultural Revolution

As with the other "revolutions" that reshaped European civilization in the eighteenth century, what historians have labelled the Agricultural Revolution is most apparent in historical hindsight. The developments that comprised this revolution were incremental and regionally disparate. Nevertheless, in the course of the eighteenth century European agriculture was fundamentally transformed. In a society where the vast majority of people were still farmers and land was still the primary form of wealth, such dramatic changes inevitably brought broader economic and social changes with them.

As we saw in Chapter 1, these changes began in the Middle Ages and continued throughout the sixteenth and seventeenth centuries, although they were spread very unevenly. The most important change was the commercialization of agriculture, in which food was increasingly produced for sale rather than subsistence. Although this shift began centuries earlier, it was not until the eighteenth century that its cumulative impact transformed European agriculture.

Part of this transformation involved the introduction of new crops. Although the potato, native to the Andes of South America, had been known since in Europe since the sixteenth century, it was not planted on any scale until rising grain prices in the 1700s provided an incentive. Potatoes had many advantages over grain: not only could they be grown in poorer soil, but they were less susceptible to rain, drought, frost, or hail, and were more nutritious; in addition, an acre planted with potatoes could feed two or three times as many people as an acre planted with grain, and if potatoes were used as animal fodder, people could enrich their diets with more meat and dairy products. Potato cultivation was promoted by many governments with great success. Potato cultivation was well established in Germany, Switzerland, and the Netherlands by 1800, and in Ireland it has been estimated that 80 per cent of people's calories came from potatoes by that date. What was not appreciated was the danger inherent in relying on a single crop. In the 1840s, the famine caused by the potato blight would result in the death of more a million Irish people and the emigration of another 250,000.

Maize, which North Americans know as corn, was first domesticated in Mesoamerica and by the time of Columbus's voyages was a dietary staple throughout the Americas. It was taken to Spain at an early date, but was not widely cultivated until the eighteenth century, and even then was considered suitable only for feeding animals or the poor. Yet as a human food source corn had many of the same advantages over Old World grain crops that potatoes did. It can grow in areas that are too dry for rice but too wet for wheat. Its output per unit of land is twice as high as wheat, and it has a shorter growing season. It is also relatively high in carbohydrates, sugars, and fat, all of which were desperately needed in a population that struggled to maintain an adequate caloric intake.

The basic problem with European agriculture was that it was inefficient and unproductive. Although there were regional variations, the return on each seed of grain sown seldom exceeded 6:1; that is, for every seed sown, six would be reaped at the harvest. Some would of course have to be set aside for the next season's planting, while some went to pay taxes, tithes, and manorial fees of various sorts. Of course, the family had to be fed, often leaving little or nothing for sale on the market. (By way of comparison, modern grain farmers routinely expect yields of 40:1.) By 1800, yields in England and the Netherlands had reached 10:1, but in other areas they remained stagnant. In much of central and western Europe, the power of landlords and manorial traditions worked against innovation, while in eastern Europe, landlords simply coerced more labour from their serfs to increase production.

Cereal grains such as wheat and rye are good sources of food energy, but growing them depletes the soil of nutrients, particularly nitrogen. There were solutions to this problem, but they all came with significant costs. For example, livestock manure could be used as fertilizer, but raising animals required pasture, which reduced the land available for crops, and the food value of the meat and dairy products they provided in no way compensated for the loss of the grain crops that would otherwise have been grown there. Another solution was crop rotation. Typically, village lands were divided into three sections, only two of which would be sown with crops in any given year. The third section would be left to lie fallow (idle), to let the soil recover nitrogen from the air. Some regions even left half the land unplanted each year. Of course, this meant that one-third or even half of the land was not producing food at any given time.

The key to growing more food lay in bringing more of this fallow land into production on a regular basis. A number of innovations, discovered by observation, made this possible. Certain crops, such as legumes (peas and beans, for example) actually drew nitrogen from the air and restored it to the soil; so did clover (used for grazing). It was also discovered that certain crops, such as turnips, depleted the soil of different nutrients, and so could be integrated into the rotation cycle without harming the soil. In what came to be known as "convertible husbandry," a given field would alternate between crop production and pasture. This served the dual purpose of fertilizing land for crops while feeding animals, and thus keeping it in the food production system. In these ways, in many areas the fallow stage could be greatly reduced, or even eliminated.

In many low-lying areas, especially in the Netherlands and England, land was drained and reclaimed for agriculture. New World crops such as potatoes and corn were integrated into the rotation cycle by the end of the eighteenth century. The introduction of industrial cash crops such as linen, hops, hemp, and tobacco meant that more people could be supported on smaller plots of land. Increasingly, faster and more efficient horses replaced oxen in ploughing, and the spread of friction-reducing iron ploughs (rather than wood) resulted in greater efficiency as well. Scythes replaced sickles, enabling much more efficient reaping. The seed drill, developed in England by Jethro Tull (1674–1740), was a horse-drawn machine that planted seeds in neat rows and at the correct depth, resulting in much less waste than broadcasting seed by hand. Greater productivity allowed for more experimentation with selective breeding of plants and animals, resulting in even greater increases in productivity.

These innovations were most concentrated in the Low Countries, especially the Dutch Republic, whose dominance of the Baltic grain trade allowed its farmers to concentrate on growing crops for profit rather than subsistence. The fact that this region was highly urbanized also encouraged commercial production, while its networks of rivers and canals facilitated transportation and reduced costs. In the course of the seventeenth and eighteenth centuries, many of these practices would be adopted in England as well.

Elsewhere, however, these innovations were not widely adopted until the nineteenth century, mainly because of political and economic conditions. In most of Europe, where feudal and manorial restrictions on village life were stronger than in the Netherlands and England, landlords typically resisted such changes. Because taxes and tithes were often assessed as proportions of specific crops rather than as a cash amount, allowing new crops would frequently diminish landlords' revenues. For example, if a peasant was obliged to pay his lord one-tenth of his wheat crop, but grew less wheat and more turnips or potatoes, the peasant would keep more of the land's produce for himself. Where peasants' tenure was insecure and farmland could be seized by the lord, either at will, as in much of eastern Europe, or on the death of the current tenant, there was little incentive to invest labour and money in improving productivity. Similarly, farmers in Spain were discouraged from improving their land when nobles who raised sheep for their wool were entitled to move their flocks between grazing pastures across farmland, without regard for the damage to crops and soil. Manorial restrictions on land ownership made it difficult to buy and sell land, and inefficient banking and credit mechanisms that helped to freeze landholding patterns also discouraged flexibility and innovation. In much of western Europe, royal and municipal governments used their political power to legislate reduced prices for grain purchases from the surrounding countryside, in order to guarantee affordable prices for urban populations. This too dissuaded many farmers from investing in new practices.

The communal nature of traditional village agriculture also worked against innovation. As we saw in Chapter 1, few peasant families owned any land outright, and their lands were typically scattered in strips throughout the village fields, in no logical sequence. This made it difficult, if not impossible, for one farmer to innovate without affecting his neighbours. Agriculture was a communal undertaking, bound by village traditions and the consensus of the community. The fact that a failed experiment could put the survival of one's family at risk was another deterrent to innovation.

In the Dutch Republic and England, where central governments had reduced the political power of the nobility over the years, landlords' rights over village communities and the restrictions of communal farming were less stringent than elsewhere in Europe. Although Dutch farmers were well ahead of their English counterparts, having adopted some innovations as early as the sixteenth century, many of their practices were introduced to England by Charles Townshend (1674–1738), who served as ambassador to the Dutch Republic from 1708 to 1711. In particular, he advocated a four-field rotation system that incorporated grains, legumes, and turnips. Having introduced this system on his own lands, he became such an enthusiastic promoter that he earned the nickname "Turnip Townshend."

In the rest of western Europe, a few progressive landlords adopted new techniques around the same time, but they were not applied on a broad scale until after the reforms of the revolutionary era had swept away noble privileges and manorial restrictions. Innovation took even longer to reach eastern Europe, where noble landowners who wanted to improve productivity could simply coerce more labour from their serfs.

The benefits of agricultural innovation were far-reaching. New crops and greater productivity improved nutrition and health, which in turn contributed to demographic growth; better nourishment for pregnant women and young children was particularly important in reducing infant and child mortality. Selective breeding of animals resulted in more meat and dairy products, as well as more manure for fertilizer. Once farm families were able to produce more food than they needed for sustenance, they could sell their surpluses and earn discretionary income that allowed them to purchase more manufactured goods. This in turn increased employment, and a higher standard of living among workers contributed to further population growth. What we see in the eighteenth century is the creation of a virtuous cycle, with increases in agricultural productivity having multiplier effects throughout the economy and society as a whole.

Agriculture in the Netherlands had been largely commercial in nature since the later Middle Ages, and noble landowners there had fewer legal privileges than their counterparts in most other places. As a consequence, the process of innovation was led by independent farmers, and caused little wrenching change. Elsewhere, however, changes in agriculture came with significant costs. The major casualties were the communal village system of agriculture, and those peasant farmers who scraped by on its margins. Even in England, where manorial restrictions and the legal privileges of the nobility had been eroded by the "rise of the gentry" and the burgeoning power of Parliament, agriculture was still largely conducted on a communal village basis.

Because English landlords could not rely on seigneurial dues, as landlords in western Europe did, or on serf labour, as was common farther east, they had a greater need to make their estates profitable. To that end, as we saw in Chapter 1, many landlords in the sixteenth and seventeenth centuries resorted to enclosure: the consolidation of the scattered strips that made up each family's holdings into one contiguous bloc enclosed by a hedge, a fence, or a ditch. Peasants who had written proof of their tenancy ("freeholders") could not easily be evicted, and some even benefited from the consolidation of their land. By contrast, "copyholders," whose tenancy was merely customary, could lose both their land and their livelihood. Since the main reason for enclosure had been to raise sheep for the wool trade, in many cases the practice also had the effect of removing land from food cultivation. For these reasons, governments generally opposed enclosure, but of course many of the landlords involved had significant political influence. Between 1500 and 1650, therefore, perhaps 10 per cent of the arable land in England was enclosed.

This percentage would rise dramatically in the eighteenth century. The innovations in agriculture discussed above, together with a growing urban population, made enclosure even more attractive to landlords, and not only in order to raise sheep or grow commercial crops themselves: they could also charge tenant farmers much higher rents for enclosed land. At the same time, the ascendancy of Parliament gave landowners greater political influence. Between 1750 and 1850, more than 4000 Acts of Enclosure were passed, enclosing some 2,400,000 hectares (6 million acres) of land; that is, about 25 per cent of the arable land in England, including between 800,000 and 1,200,000 hectares (2 million to 3 million acres) of common land. Even in the first half of the eighteenth century, before this avalanche of legislation began, perhaps half that amount had already been enclosed by "common agreement" among landowners (no doubt significant pressure was exerted on the recalcitrant).

Clearly, those who suffered most from enclosure were the copyholders who were expropriated. Freeholders were entitled to the same amount of land they had held before enclosure: the only difference was that now it was consolidated in a single field rather than scattered through many. However, the disappearance of the common lands was a substantial loss. Although a proportion of the former commons was added to each freeholder's enclosed field, its value was insignificant compared to the value of access to a large piece of common land where, in the past, every family could graze an animal, pick berries, or gather firewood. In addition, freeholders were required to pay the costs of enclosure—surveying, construction of fences, digging of ditches, and so on—and those who could not afford them would be forced to sell.

Historians are still debating the impact and significance of the enclosure movement. It used to be thought that dispossessed peasants drifted to the cities in search of work, and that the availability of their labour was one of the factors that helped to start the Industrial Revolution. But many now question this hypothesis. For one thing, cities were always a magnet for some rural people, and there is little to indicate that rural-to-urban migration increased disproportionately in the eighteenth century. For another, large-scale factory employment did not become common until the early nineteenth century, decades after enclosure began to increase significantly. Furthermore, although many lost their land, their labour was still needed on land owned by others. Indeed, the practices introduced by the Agricultural Revolution likely required more, and more intensive, labour than the traditional system. More intensive farming, with more rotation, required more digging, ploughing, fertilizing, and weeding, and without new machinery, all this had to be done by hand. Greater productivity required more labour at the harvest, and more livestock required more labour to milk the cows, churn the butter, shear the sheep, and so on.

Nor did enclosure result in the immediate extinction of small-scale farmers, although both their numbers and their share of the land declined. A farmer with less than 10 hectares (25 acres) would find it hard to compete with the larger, more specialized farms whose proprietors frequently had access to more of the capital needed to improve their land. Over the ensuing years and decades, therefore, many small farmers were forced to sell to their larger competitors.

If enclosure did not drive hordes of dispossessed peasants into the cities, at least not immediately, it certainly did expand the class of landless agrarian labourers—a rural proletariat—whose survival depended on finding paid work on someone else's land. Together, enclosure and dramatic population growth produced a perceptible increase in rural poverty in the later eighteenth century. In all likelihood it was this that led future factory workers to move to the rapidly expanding industrial cities such as Birmingham

VOICES

The Impact of Enclosure

Today the characteristic English countryside scene of rolling green fields surrounded by pictur-esque stone walls or hedges may seem timeless, but in fact it is the relatively recent product of the enclosure movement of the eighteenth and nineteenth centuries. Enclosure was controversial at the time. While advocates of agricultural innovation praised its benefits, many Romantic poets la-mented the loss of the harmony and social integration they associated with the village community.

Arthur Young (1741–1820) was a celebrated English writer on agriculture, economics, and politics who wrote in praise of enclosure in his book *Political Arithmetic: Containing Observa-tions on the Present State of Great Britain and the Principles of Her Policy in the Encouragement of Agriculture* (1774).

> Respecting open-field lands, the quantity of labour in them is not comparable to that of enclosures; for, not to speak of the great numbers of men that in enclosed countries are constantly employed in winter in hedging and ditching, what comparison can there be between the open-field system of one half or one third of the lands being in fallow, receiving only three ploughings, and the same portion now tilled four, five, or six times by midsummer, then sown with turnips, those hand-hoed twice, and then drawn by hand and carted to stalls, or else hurdled out in portions for fatting sheep! What a scar-city of employment in one case, what a variety in the other! . . . I should also remind the reader of other systems of management . . . every article of which is an increase of labour. Then he should remember the vast tracts of country uncultivated in the last century which have been enclosed and converted into new farms, a much greater tract in eighty years than these writers dream of: all this is the effect of enclosures, and con-sequently they also have yielded a great increase of employment.
>
> . . . Thus the land yields a greater neat produce in food for mankind—the landlord doubles his income which enables him to employ so many more manufacturers and artisans—the farmer increases his income, by means of which he also does the same—the hides and wool are a creation of so much employment for other manufacturers. How anyone from such a system can deduce the melancholy prospects of depopulation, famine, and distress is to me amazing.
>
> G.E. Mingay (ed.), *Arthur Young and His Times* (London: Macmillan, 1975), pp. 104–5.

Oliver Goldsmith (1728–74) was an Anglo-Irish poet, novelist, and playwright. Here are two excerpts from his long poem *The Deserted Village* (1770), a lament for an idyllic way life that has been destroyed by the forces of greed and commerce.

Sweet smiling village, loveliest of the lawn,
Thy sports are fled, and all thy charms withdrawn;
Amidst thy bowers the tyrant's hand is seen,
And desolation saddens all thy green:
One only master grasps the whole domain,
And half a tillage stints thy smiling plain . . .

Ill fares the land, to hastening ills a prey,
Where wealth accumulates, and men decay:
Princes and lords may flourish, or may fade;
A breath can make them, as a breath has made;
But a bold peasantry, their country's pride,
When once destroyed, can never be supplied.

The reactions of those most immediately affected by enclosures are more difficult to assess, as they left few written records. There were of course protests and even riots against enclosure, but they were generally recorded (and condemned) by those promoting it. Occasionally, however, we get glimpses of popular perceptions, as in this anonymous letter from 1799 addressed to one "Oliver Cromwell" of Cheshunt Park (clearly not the Lord Protector discussed in Chapter 6). The spelling and grammar are haphazard, but there is no mistaking the petitioners' passionate opposition to the enclosure of their common land.

Whe right these lines to you who are the Combin'd of the Parish of Cheshunt in the Defence of our Parrish rights which you unlawfully are about to disinherit us of . . .
    Resolutions is maid by the aforesaid Combin'd that if you intend of inclosing Our Commond Commond [sic] fields Lammas Meads Marshes &c Whe Resolve . . . before that bloudy and unlawful act is finished to have your hearts bloud if you proceede in the aforesaid bloudy act Whe like horse leaches will cry give, give until whe have spilt the bloud of every one that wishes to rob the Inosent unborn. It shall not be in your power to say I am safe from the hands of my Enemy for Whe like birds of pray will prively lie in wait to spil the bloud of the aforesaid Charicters whose names and places of abode are as prutrified sores in our Nostrils. Whe declair that thou shalt not say I am safe when thou goest to thy bed for beware that thou liftest not thine eyes up in the most mist of flames. . . .

Quoted in E.P. Thompson, *The Making of the English Working Class* (Harmondsworth: Penguin, 1963), p. 240.

and Manchester. They were not driven off the land by enclosure as much as they were drawn to industrial factory work by the hope (often forlorn) of escaping poverty and finding a better life for themselves and their families.

Industry

In 1700 an experienced farmer would have had a fairly good idea of the way agriculture would change in the course of the century, at least in the Netherlands and England. In the case of industry, however, it would have taken a clairvoyant to foresee the changes to come by 1800. Most discussions of industry in the eighteenth century focus on the origins of the Industrial Revolution that would transform the world in the course of the nineteenth and twentieth centuries. With hindsight, those developments are fairly clear, but we should not think that they were evident at the time, much less that they were the product of forethought or deliberation.

As we saw in Chapter 1, industrial development before the eighteenth century was hampered by the lack of a large, socially diverse market to purchase output, a scarcity of capital investment, and primitive fuel and power. All these circumstances would begin to change in the course of the eighteenth century, although the full impact of those changes would not be felt until the nineteenth century.

In early modern Europe there were three types of manufacturing. Most peasant households produced their own textiles, furniture, and simple tools and equipment. Goods that could not be made at home were produced by skilled craftsmen in shops regulated by the privileged guild monopolies. Finally, there was rural or cottage industry—also known as the "putting-out system"—in which entrepreneurs avoided the restrictions of the urban guilds by "putting out" the materials needed for production to peasant households and having them do the work (see Chapter 1). Over the course of the eighteenth century, both household and craft manufacturing were increasingly eclipsed by rural industry. Historians seeking the origins of the Industrial Revolution have naturally focused on this phenomenon, which is often referred to as "proto-industry." This term, however, has been criticized as anachronistic, since to identify something as "proto" is to take for granted the existence of the thing that has yet to develop, as if its development were inevitable.

There is no doubt that the growth of rural industry was connected to demographic expansion and the Agricultural Revolution, although it is difficult to distinguish between causes and effects. Did a growing population promote the growth of rural industry by providing both demand and a labour force? Or did the growth of rural industry contribute to population growth by providing both employment opportunities and greater incentive for agricultural innovation to meet growing demand? No doubt both, but the interactions were complex and influenced by many other factors. For a time, population growth, especially in the cities, may have provided a spur to greater production. But as the population grew and the price of food rose, people may have had less disposable income to spend on manufactured goods.

Industrial growth prior to the Industrial Revolution was also the product of deliberate government policies, although these varied widely by state, region, and industry. As we have seen, mercantilist thinking dictated that states should become as self-sufficient as possible in manufactured goods, and to that end, governments imposed tariffs on imported versions of goods that could be produced locally. At the same time they established and subsidized domestic industries, usually by granting them special privileges such as monopolies or protection from foreign competition. In many cases, these policies benefited uncompetitive enterprises producing high-cost and often outmoded goods, and thus misdirected capital away from more productive investments. Thus in France Jean-Baptiste Colbert granted privileges to manufacturers of luxury goods such as tapestries, fine glassware, and porcelain, and in so doing "succeeded chiefly in endowing his country with uncompetitive, high-cost industries, many of which did not survive the end of his patronage."[2] Similarly, the products of the porcelain works established by King Frederick the Great of Prussia (r. 1740–86) in Berlin were of very high quality, but could not be profitably sold. To dispose of the surplus production, the government decreed that Jews seeking the required permission to marry pay a predetermined sum to the factory, which would then foist the unsellable merchandise on them. In this way the great Jewish philosopher and writer Moses Mendelsohn (1729–86), grandfather of the composer Felix Mendelsohn, became the proud owner of twenty porcelain apes.[3]

Not all such enterprises were failures, however. The Saint-Gobain glassworks in France began in 1665 with 230 workers, grew to 1500 by 1700, and is still in operation today. The silk and velvet works established in Berlin by Frederick the Great had 460 looms in 1767, 835 in 1771, and 1,750 in 1778.[4] Despite the failures, then, such policies did expand industry beyond what purely market forces could have accomplished. Whether such industries, or indeed other more important or productive ones, might have grown more spontaneously without state sponsorship is an open question.

At the same time, in many places other long-established privileges were being rescinded. Since most manufacturing activity was organized in guilds, they bore the brunt of these efforts, but they were not alone. The great Scottish philosopher Adam Smith (1723–90) objected to guilds on the grounds that their power to restrict trade and monopolize markets interfered with the natural laws governing economic activity (see Chapter 9). Other sorts of privilege also came under attack, such as the rights of some towns to impose duties on goods in transit, or to purchase grain from the surrounding countryside at a fixed price. What most governments opposed, however, were privileges that they had not granted, and that were inconsistent with their perceptions of the state's interests.

Thus as states developed more sophisticated fiscal systems and bureaucracies, they were able to erode and in some cases even abolish such privileges and monopolies. According to the French economist who became finance minister to Louis XVI, Anne Robert Jacques Turgot (1727–81), guilds "retarded the progress of . . . crafts, through the innumerable difficulties encountered by inventors with whom different corporations [i.e., guilds] dispute the right to exploit their discoveries,"[5] and their "arbitrary and selfish rules . . . ensure an incalculable reduction of commercial and industrial activity."[6] In 1776 he abolished guilds, but the reaction was so hostile that six months later he was forced to repeal the edict. Guilds would remain strong in most of western Europe until the reforms of the Revolutionary era swept aside all such corporate privileges.

The Dutch economic historian Jan de Vries has proposed that the Industrial Revolution was preceded by a change in economic behaviour that he calls an "industrious revolution," in which we can see the origins of the modern consumer society. In the past, when peasant families made most of the things they needed themselves, there was very little that they needed to purchase, and once a particular need had been filled, they were inclined to choose leisure over further acquisition. No doubt this behaviour was due in part to the scarcity of goods available and in part to the lack of disposable income; but it was also a traditional habit of mind. In the eighteenth century, however, we begin to see evidence of both a rise in the consumption of manufactured goods and a decrease in the time devoted to leisure activities. In other words, people became were willing to work longer and harder—to become more "industrious"—in order to purchase the increasingly varied consumer goods produced by rural industry, including not only fabrics and clothing, but items such as metalware, pottery, and toys for their children. They themselves thus became both producers and consumers of a more elaborate material culture. Like so much else, this shift appears to have begun in the Netherlands and England and spread through the rest of Europe in the course of the nineteenth and even the twentieth century.

In addition, new goods and services provided more outlets for spending and consumption, many of which came either from European colonies or from commerce with non-Europeans. The increasing availability of sugar, coffee, tea, chocolate, and tobacco created new patterns of consumption. People began to spend money not only on those commodities themselves but on a host of related goods and services, such as cups, mugs, and teapots; pipes and snuffboxes; and coffeehouses.

Similar changes become apparent if we look at alcoholic beverages. Traditionally, most people drank whatever was produced locally (often at home): typically beer and ale in the north, and wine in warmer climates. For the elites, of course, there was a well-established trade in premium wines from Bordeaux and Burgundy, sweet or fortified wines such as sherry from Spain, port from Portugal, and Malmsey from the Portuguese island of Madeira. Mirroring the developments discussed above, production for sale on the market increasingly displaced household production. The growth of the sugar industry in the New World led to the introduction of a new drink called rum, and many wine-producing areas began to produce and market distilled wines such as brandy (the English word is a corruption of the French *vin brulé*, "burned wine," referring to the distillation process). Technical improvements in distillation lowered the price of grain spirits such as whisky, vodka, and gin, and allowed them to compete in the marketplace, especially among poorer people. The government of England subsidized the production of gin (originally a Dutch product) as a way of using surplus grain and supporting its price in the interests of large farmers. As a result gin consumption exploded in the eighteenth century, and by 1740 England was producing six times as much gin as beer. Many critics saw in gin the root of diverse

William Hogarth, "Beer Street" and "Gin Lane." William Hogarth (1697–1764) was an English satirist, social critic, painter, and cartoonist. In the agitation that led to the passage of the Gin Act in 1751, he published the parallel editorial cartoons "Beer Street" and "Gin Lane." In the former, the inhabitants, nourished by wholesome English ale, are well-fed and prosperous, and the arts and culture flourish. In the latter, crime and vice abound. An inebriated women lets her child fall to its death, while the cadaverous man has presumably chosen gin over food.

social evils, and in 1751 its consumption was legally restricted to licensed establishments, although enforcement was difficult and illegal sales and production continued.

It may seem strange today, but in general governments tried to discourage the consumption of new products through sumptuary legislation. For one thing, this was a temperamentally conservative era in which people almost instinctively mistrusted change and novelty. In addition, governments were concerned that ordinary people spending their money on frivolities would decrease the amount available to be taxed. Governments and social elites were also concerned to preserve social distinctions through attempting to restrict the access of ordinary people to goods traditionally accessible only to the aristocracy.

Textiles remained by far the most important industry throughout the eighteenth century, and it is in textile production that we see the beginnings of the fundamental transformation that would come to be known as the Industrial Revolution. Since the sixteenth century, rural industry or the "putting-out" system had been expanding at the expense of the urban guild-based system. Although this trend intensified in the eighteenth century, rural industry remained essentially traditional in nature, and there is no reason to think that, on its own, its expansion would have led to an Industrial Revolution.

By far the most important textiles were woollens, which were produced in a range of styles and qualities to suit every taste and budget. Although silk manufacturing had begun in Europe as early as the fifteenth century, silk was a luxury, and the market for it was very small compared to the market for more pedestrian fabrics such as linen (made from flax in various places, including Ireland, Spain, Brittany, and Scotland). Before the eighteenth century, cotton too was a luxury commodity, but by the later 1600s inexpensive calicoes from India were becoming available, and the demand for them became so great that many governments attempted to restrict their importation in order to protect domestic textile industries and (in keeping with mercantilist orthodoxy) prevent their trade imbalances with Asia from increasing.

By the 1770s, however, Britain's American colonies were producing raw cotton in substantial quantities, and technical innovations were making domestic production more feasible. Thus Britain lifted its restrictions, and demand for cotton exploded. English imports of raw cotton reached 4.2 million pounds in 1772 and 41.8 million in 1800 as new methods of manufacturing began to take hold. Nor was the cotton industry confined to England: by 1790 more than 170 places in France were also manufacturing cotton fabrics, and cotton looms were appearing through much of Europe. At first the thread had to be imported from India, as Europeans had difficulty producing thread strong enough to stand up to the weaving process, but technical innovation (see below) eventually improved its quality and further reduced the cost of the final product. In fact, it was in English cotton manufacturing that the Industrial Revolution began.

Many factors help to explain why the revolution happened first in England. For example, unlike states such as France and Spain, England was a unified market, without internal tolls and tariffs to hinder trade and increase its expense and difficulty. In the course of the sixteenth and seventeenth centuries, it had also made significant investments in canals and roads. The growth of overseas and colonial trade (see below) was undoubtedly also a factor: although historians disagree on the exact nature of its contribution, the profits from overseas trade certainly made capital available for investment. In addition, England had an efficient vehicle for allocating it. The Bank of England had been founded in 1694 to manage government debt, but it soon branched out into accepting deposits and lending money to companies as well to government. England also had bountiful deposits of coal and iron, both of which would be essential to the growth of industry. Other areas were no less favoured, however. Privileged groups such as nobles and guilds had less power in England than in many other places, but this was equally true of the Netherlands, which also enjoyed the benefits associated with the Agricultural Revolution, including the population growth that both expanded the market for industrial goods and increased the numbers of workers available to produce them. In short, England had little or nothing that other countries did not. Vague as it may be, perhaps the key to its success was that it brought all the above factors together in a way that was unique.

In any event, it was in England that a series of inventions and technical innovations led to the birth of modern industry, in which production was concentrated in large factories and carried out by workers with no ties to the world of agriculture. Two things stand out about this innovation. First is the rapid acceleration of its pace: whereas the century from 1660 to 1760 saw 210 new patents granted in England, the next twenty-nine years saw 976. Second is the fact that these inventions were not the product of scientific research and development by government-sponsored institutes, but of humble tinkerers and craftsmen. The process was not planned, but incremental and haphazard, and although we focus on the "successful" inventions and innovations, there were surely many more that ended up on the scrap heap.

In 1733 John Kay (1704–79), the son of a yeoman farmer, patented the flying shuttle. Now, instead of moving the shuttle back and forth by hand, the weaver could "throw" it across the loom and let it bounce back, greatly reducing the time and effort involved. It would not be widely adopted for several decades, however, because the spinners who made the thread could not keep up with the increase in the weavers' efficiency. This problem would be solved by the invention of several other devices. In 1764 a carpenter and weaver named James Hargreaves (1720–78) patented the spinning jenny, which allowed one person to operate several spinning wheels at once. Three years later, Richard Arkwright (1732–92), a former barber, patented the water frame, which automated the spinning process and, because it was powered by water, required the construction of one of the first factories designed expressly to accommodate machinery as well as workers. In 1779 a spinner named Samuel Crompton invented the spinning mule, which combined the multiple spindles of the spinning jenny with the water power of the water frame. The mule and its subsequent improvements permitted the spinning of thinner and stronger thread that could stand up to a mechanized loom. In 1785 Edmund Cartwright patented the first successful power loom, although there had been earlier versions. Since all this machinery was powered by water, the factories that used it had to be located near adequate supplies of flowing water. The county of Lancashire in northwestern England proved to be ideal, and quickly became the centre of the textile industry. As a consequence, the town of Manchester grew from 17,000 inhabitants in 1760 to 180,000 in 1830.

Even so, water power was both finite and unreliable (rivers freeze in the winter, flood in the spring, and become too slow in the summer). Thus by the end of the eighteenth century, some factories were beginning to use steam power instead. Although an early steam engine had been invented by Thomas Newcomen (1663–1729), it could not be used to power industrial machinery until it was refined in the 1760s by James Watt (1736–1819), who greatly improved the engine's efficiency and added a system of valves that allowed reciprocating motion. Steam power would not be widely applied to industrial machinery, even in England, until the early nineteenth century, but the essential pieces were all in place by the late 1700s.

Since steam power itself required fuel, the wide availability of coal in England was another key factor in the country's industrial success. Coal also came to play an important role in the production of industrial machinery, which required a steady and affordable supply of steel. Before the eighteenth century, the fuel of choice for refining iron had been charcoal, but as forests were cleared it became more expensive. Because charcoal was also fragile and difficult to transport, iron forges had to be located in or near the forests that supplied it, and this in turn hindered large-scale investment in refineries and forges, which would have to be dismantled and moved when the local supply of charcoal was exhausted. Coal was unsuitable for this purpose as its combustion imparted impurities to the iron that weakened the final product. In the early eighteenth century, the English ironworker Abraham Darby (1678–1717) came up with a method of smelting iron ore using coke, a by-product of the burning of coal that could be used to refine iron without compromising the integrity of the metal. The use of coke also permitted blast furnaces that produced the much higher temperatures required to produce steel. Previously, production of steel—an alloy of iron and carbon—had required high-grade iron ore, which had been available primarily in Sweden. Now, however, steel could be produced with English iron ore. The puddling and rolling process, developed in the 1780s by Henry Cort (1741–1800) further improved the strength and quality of refined iron, to the point where it could be more extensively used in industrial machinery. As it was more cost-effective to transport iron ore than coal, the blast furnaces and steel mills came to be located in regions rich in coal deposits, including Staffordshire, Yorkshire, South Wales, and parts of Scotland.

By the end of the eighteenth century, a new economy was beginning to take shape in Britain, based on the mass production of goods for an international and even a global market. Industrial production not only reduced the price of manufactured goods but in many cases improved the quality to the point that the rural industry could not compete. In the nineteenth century the British industrial model would spread to continental Europe, first to the Netherlands and France, and then on to Germany, Italy, and beyond. More than anything else, it was the productive potential of European industry that made possible the European global domination of the nineteenth and early twentieth centuries. We see also the origins here of the inter-related and self-sustaining growth characteristic of industrial economies: industrialization of textiles required metal for machinery and steam engines, which required iron, coal, and steel, which required mines, refineries, and factories to produce the machinery, as well as the infrastructure to transport raw materials and support production, such as housing for managers and workers, shops, and so on.

The explosive growth of industrial production also had far-reaching social effects. It was in this period that mass urbanization began, and burgeoning industrial cities such as Manchester and Birmingham struggled to supply adequate housing, water, and social services for the thousands of new residents that their factories required. At the same time, the privileged orders whose prestige and power had been based on their control of land found their political and socials positions increasingly challenged by the growing numbers of middle- and working–class people who made their living from industrial production instead. In 1800, of course, these fundamental transformations were still largely in the future. Most industrial production still proceeded along traditional rural industry lines, and the vast majority of Europeans who continued to make their living from farming had no idea of the vast changes that were about to transform their world.

Commerce and Finance

Even in the eighteenth century it seemed obvious that the expansion of overseas trade played a crucial role in the rise of industry: through the capital that trade generated, the captive markets it generated, and the access to raw materials it provided. These connections were also consistent with the mercantilist emphasis on the importance of trade. Add the fact that it was Great Britain that led the way in both overseas commerce and industry, and the links between overseas trade and the beginnings of industrialization seem ironclad.

On the other hand, it is possible that this view confuses correlation with cause, or even reverses cause and effect. Did the growth of overseas trade stimulate industrial development in Britain, or did the output of British industry facilitate overseas expansion? Questions of this kind are difficult to answer, even today, but the weight of the evidence currently suggests that industrialization was more a cause of Britain's domination of overseas trade than a result of it. Colonial empires probably represented a net drain on the resources of European governments, including Britain's, and although certain segments of society made enormous profits from colonial trade—the owners of sugar plantations and slave ships, for example—there is little concrete evidence that they invested those profits in industrial enterprises rather than land, government bonds, or conspicuous consumption.

In fact, the more compelling link between trade and economic development is to be found in the much less glamorous world of local and regional transactions. As we saw in Chapter 1, trade on any scale beyond the local was traditionally hindered by primitive transportation infrastructure. It has been estimated that the price of coal in England doubled as soon the transport distance exceeded five miles (8.5 km) by road, and only twenty to thirty miles (32 to 48 km) by water. Countries such as Britain, France, Spain, Portugal, and the Scandinavian kingdoms had the benefit of long coastlines that facilitated transport by sea, but even they had trouble moving goods much beyond the coastal ports.

In order for farmers to risk shipping their produce any distance, they had to be confident that it would reach the market safely. Likewise, industrial entrepreneurs needed to be assured of access to their markets, and they also needed reliable supplies of raw materials. Over the course of the eighteenth century, several developments dramatically reduced the cost of transportation and commercial transactions. As with so much else, the Netherlands, Britain, and France led the way: in general, the rest of Europe would not follow suit until the nineteenth century.

In the past, one problem was the fact that roads and rivers did not have individual owners who could charge for their use and thus benefit from improving them. In the eighteenth century, however, the growth of state power in France allowed the royal government to take on the responsibility for road improvements. The budget of the administrative body in charge more than quadrupled between 1700 and 1770, and more than 40,000 kilometres of roads were built. The travel time between Paris and Lyon was cut in half, from ten days to five. The British government took a different approach, passing legislation that permitted entrepreneurs to build turnpikes (toll roads). In this way the time required to travel from London to Birmingham was reduced from two days in 1740 to nine hours in 1780.

The situation was similar when it came to water transport. The Netherlands had long benefited from an extensive network of navigable rivers supplemented by canals, and both Britain and France set out to do the same. Whereas in France this was largely a state-sponsored effort, in England it was led by private investors. By 1760 England's navigable waterways had doubled to about 2300 kilometres, and the years after 1760 saw a canal-building boom. As in the railway boom of the next century, however, many of the new canals proved uneconomical and their investors lost their money.

Man-made hindrances such as tariffs, tolls, and the privileges of towns and guilds compounded the natural obstacles to trade. Britain and the Netherlands had eliminated those privileges in the sixteenth and seventeenth centuries, but in most of the rest of Europe they would persist until after the French Revolution. In Germany, for example, many towns and guilds had the legal right to compel farmers and manufacturers to sell all their goods to urban merchants, and to force the sale of goods in transit to local merchants, who would then re-export them. In France, even as the government was building roads and canals to facilitate trade, it re-organized internal tariffs into a system known as the "Five Great Farms," and then sold the right to collect these tariffs to private businessmen whose interests as "farmers of the royal customs" worked against the liberalization of internal trade.

In the eighteenth century, newer forms of commercial organization were developed and expanded. In the past, merchants had operated either as individuals or in limited partnerships that seldom outlasted a particular voyage or venture, and although the sixteenth and seventeenth centuries had seen the formation of many larger enterprises modelled on the Dutch East India Company, even these attempted to operate in the traditional way, as privileged monopolies. In much of Europe, both agriculture and industry continued to be monopolized by privileged corporations in the eighteenth century. In Britain and the Netherlands, however, weaker guild structures meant that producers and merchants were less constrained by privileged groups. As a consequence, it is in those countries that we see an economic landscape developing that looks familiar to modern eyes: one in which individuals and companies compete with one another for customers and market share.

Continuing improvements in banking and credit also facilitated trade. Bankers and merchants had long been issuing letters of credit for large transactions in place of heavy and vulnerable coinage. In the course of the eighteenth century, a new level of sophistication was attained, whereby banks became clearinghouses for commercial debts in exchange for a small commission. In this way, merchants could realize profits and redeploy their capital more quickly and effectively. While most people still relied on gold and silver coins for everyday transactions, technical improvements in coinage and increased state power to prevent fraud and counterfeiting helped to grease the wheels of commerce.

With the establishment of the first stock exchanges, first in Amsterdam, then in London and elsewhere, it became possible to buy and sell shares in companies, and this gave merchants and entrepreneurs a way of raising investment capital. But there were no regulations to prevent fraud and abuse. In 1716 John Law (1671–1729), a Scottish financier and economist residing in France, established the General Private Bank (*Banque Générale Privée*), which was to become France's first central bank. Although it was privately owned, its major assets consisted of government loans. Law and the bank (with the implied backing of the government) then set up the Mississippi Company as a monopoly in control of French trade in the New World territory of Louisiana (much larger than the current US state of the same name; on paper it encompassed the entire basin drained by the Mississippi River). In 1720 Philippe d'Orléans, the Regent of France, appointed a Law Controller-General of Finances, lending royal approval both to the bank and to the Mississippi Company. Since shares could be bought on credit, they became the object of widespread speculation, and many people went heavily into debt in order acquire them. Share prices rose from 25 to 1000, then to 5000, and even 15,000 *livres*. As in other bubbles, before and since, once shares began to decline in value in 1720, people rushed to sell them and the price plummeted. Many people suffered huge losses, the French economy was thrown into chaos, and Law was forced to flee France; he died in poverty in 1729.

A similar bubble inflated and burst in England. The South Sea Company was formed in 1711 as a private joint-stock company with the ostensible purpose of trading in South America. Although its assets were largely fictional, it had the backing of the government, and it became the object of widespread speculation. Originally sold for £100, the price of shares reached a peak of £1000 before the bubble burst in 1720. Investigations revealing insider trading, manipulation, and outright fraud shook public confidence in both the government and financial system.

Orders and Classes

Over the course of the eighteenth century, the growth of state power, demographic expansion, and the changes in agriculture and industry combined to transform the social structure of Europe from one based on orders or estates to one based more on socio-economic class. As we saw in Chapter 1, this transition had begun in the early modern period, but it now reached a "tipping point" where subterranean changes became irreversible. As with the Industrial Revolution, historians have sometimes read too much into these changes, ignoring the significant continuities that remained in place. This attitude is reflected in the use of the term *ancien régime* ("former regime") to refer to eighteenth-century society.[7] In order to characterize something as "former," it must already have been replaced by something new. The term was coined after the French Revolution to describe a vanished world of noble privilege and hierarchical social relations. From that post-revolutionary perspective, revolution becomes the inevitable outcome of this transformation, whereby something "new and improved" replaced something old and decrepit.

Even if this transformation did not make revolution inevitable, its consequences were nevertheless far-reaching and profound. Like the agricultural and industrial changes discussed above, the social changes were most obvious in northwestern Europe: Britain, France, the Netherlands, and western Germany. They were somewhat less noticeable in Italy and Spain, and to the east of central Germany they would not be felt until well into the nineteenth century.

Throughout the sixteenth and seventeenth centuries, European society and government had been dominated by a hereditary nobility. By the eighteenth century, although nobles continued to play a role in European society far out of proportion to their overall numbers, the nature of that role had changed. They were now only a part—albeit the most important and obvious part—of an aristocratic elite whose membership was no longer defined primarily by family and heredity (although these continued to be important), but by wealth, culture, and lifestyle.

As we have seen in previous chapters, the political power of nobles was challenged by rulers throughout the sixteenth and seventeenth centuries. By the eighteenth century, the great noble who could challenge the ruler by mobilizing his provincial power base was a thing of the past in western Europe. Ambitious nobles still schemed for political power, of course, but now they did so primarily in the context of the ruler's regime, whether at court, in the bureaucracy, or in the armed forces. The growth of state power had finally succeeded in "taming" the nobility by tying nobles' political interests to those of the state. No longer did powerful nobles dream of reversing the movement towards political centralization and establishing a kind of noble republic with a figurehead king. The crucial point was passed somewhere around the middle of the seventeenth century. As we saw in Chapter 6, absolute monarchy in its various forms was in some ways a cooperative venture between the ruler and elites that allowed them to dominate society and government by parcelling out the spoils of power. Nobles continued to dominate European governments throughout the eighteenth century, but from the inside.

State-building also affected the composition of the nobility in that it undermined nobles' power of patronage. Although historians of early modern Europe have often exaggerated the expansion and effectiveness of state bureaucracies, it is true that by the eighteenth century the civil services of most European states were larger and more effective than ever before. As a consequence, rulers no longer had to rely on powerful nobles and their networks of clients among the lesser provincial nobility and urban elites to govern the realm. This development deprived many lesser nobles of important sources of influence and income, and, combined with economic changes, made it difficult for them to maintain their status. There is a good deal of evidence that nobles declined as a proportion of the overall population. In France, for example, in the mid-1400s nobles made up about 1 per cent of the population, but this figure had declined to 0.52 per cent by the time of the French Revolution in 1789. In Castile, nobles comprised about 10 per cent of the population in 1600, but in Spain as a whole their proportion had declined to 3.8 per cent by 1787.[8] There is also some evidence that the middle ranks of the nobility became somewhat wealthier, while the wealth of both the upper and lower ranks declined in relative terms. In a telling example of the alliance of state power and noble privilege, many rulers launched investigations of the nobility aimed at removing from its ranks those whose claims were suspect, or who had not "lived nobly." From the ruler's point of view, this served the purpose of curtailing tax exemptions, while from that of the "true" nobles who made the cut, it served to enhance their status by reducing their numbers. One hand washed the other.

Since the Middle Ages, land had been the primary form of noble wealth, and the centrality of land to noble identity and noble fortunes continued throughout the early modern period. At the same time, other forms of wealth and income were becoming more important. Pensions and grants from the king, employment in the civil service and, especially, the armed forces, and income from investments all supplemented income from landed estates. Rulers had for some time encouraged nobles to take a more active role in commerce and industry—for example, by moving to loosen the rules concerning *dérogeance*, or loss of noble status—and although some continued to refuse "demeaning" occupations, many complied. Indeed, many nobles turned out to be highly "entrepreneurial," whether in mining, commerce, agriculture, finance, or real estate. The fact that, in the eighteenth century, there was little to distinguish nobles from the wealthy bourgeoisie was a strong sign that the society based on orders was being replaced by one based on socio-economic classes.

Land ownership continued to be important to most nobles, and a country estate was an essential acquisition for those seeking to rise from the upper ranks of the bourgeoisie into the nobility. In the eighteenth century, however, more and more nobles began to loosen their ties to their estates. Those who could afford to support two homes built elaborate townhouses to live in, and increasingly the country estate was a source of income rather than identity. When the English traveller Arthur Young travelled through France just prior to the French Revolution, he was astonished to find so few nobles in the countryside: "The country [is] deserted, or if a gentleman is in it, you find him in some wretched hole, to save money which is lavished with profusion in the luxuries of a capital."[9]

Changes in agriculture were also reflected in changes in the nobility. Nobles historically were not merely landowners but also lords: that is, their possession of the land came with certain powers over the peasants who farmed it. The ubiquity of this arrangement was reflected in the aphorism, "No land without a lord." In western Europe, as we have seen, most personal obligations had faded away, but farther east peasants were becoming less free. The spread of capitalist agriculture—the production of food to be sold for profit in the growing cities—turned nobles from lords into proprietors who increasingly made their income not from the customary fees and dues paid by peasants, many of which were eroded by inflation, but from rents paid by tenants, or from the crops grown on their estates, which in many cases were managed by employees on their behalf. These developments were encouraged by government policy: since rulers were keen to limit lords' powers over their peasants, noble powers of justice and taxation were increasingly whittled away by royal judges and tax collectors.

Meanwhile, the concept of nobility itself was changing. As rulers enhanced their powers, they sought to reduce both the nobility's independence and its violence; Louis XIII's attempt to outlaw duelling (Chapter 6) was just one example. The values of the feudal warriors who considered themselves to be the king's natural partners in government were increasingly inappropriate for a world centred on the ruler's court.

For one thing, members of the nobility, female as well as male, were increasingly educated. As late as the sixteenth century, it was not uncommon even for prominent noblemen to be completely illiterate, and to consider formal education and literacy as proper only to servile pencil-pushers, not men of power and action like themselves. This began to change as early as the Renaissance: in Castiglione's *The Courtier*, for example, the true gentleman was expected to be as accomplished in poetry as in swordsmanship. By the eighteenth century, a nobleman who expected to advance at court or in the government had to be well acquainted with literature and the arts in order to contribute to polite conversation.

At the same time, and for many of the same reasons, nobles' personal habits were undergoing what the German sociologist Norbert Elias (1897–1990) called the "civilizing process." The great humanist Erasmus had counselled that it was not polite to start a conversation with someone who was urinating or defecating, and Henry III of France was killed in 1589 (see Chapter 4) by an assassin he received while sitting on the toilet. Increasingly, now, however, nobles were taught that bodily functions should be carried out in private, that one should use a handkerchief, not the tablecloth or one's sleeve, to blow one's nose, and use a fork rather than a knife or one's fingers to eat. The expression of strong emotion was also discouraged as unbecoming to members of the social elite. It was no accident that the word "courtesy" was derived from the word "court": increasingly, the model for personal behaviour was that of the royal court.

By the later eighteenth century many nobles were downplaying the hereditary nature of their place in society and seeing their nobility, and the status and power that went with it, as the consequence of their education, refinement, and good taste. They saw themselves as part—albeit the most important part—of an aristocratic social elite that transcended the boundaries of hereditary nobility. In his 1759 novel *Candide*, the great Enlightenment writer Voltaire (1694–1778), a member of the wealthy bourgeoisie, ridiculed the provincial German Baron of Thunder-ten-Tronckh, who

> was one of the most influential noblemen in Westphalia, for his house had a door and several windows and his hall was actually draped with tapestry. Every dog in the courtyard was pressed into service when he went hunting, and his grooms acted as whips. The village curate was his private chaplain. They all called him Your Lordship, and laughed at his jokes.[10]

Such contempt served to marginalize poor nobles who were unable or unwilling to join the refined elite. But it cut both ways: if social superiority was a matter of education, taste, and refinement, then it was accessible to anyone with the means and ability to attain it, regardless of family background. This, in fact, was part of Voltaire's point. In this way, the evolution of noble culture undermined the notion of nobility itself. Increasingly, in the eighteenth century, the operative concept was not that of the hereditary noble, but that of the gentleman, who might or might not be of noble blood.

English society provided a kind of model for this transition, in that its titled nobility, the peerage, was limited to about 200 families and enforced through strict primogeniture. Only the eldest son inherited the noble title and the bulk of the land and property. Younger sons and their descendants formed the gentry, who were the functional equivalent of the lower nobility on the continent, but lacked noble status and privileges. Often knighted and therefore distinguished by the honorific "Sir," they formed the local elite of England. As we saw above, it was because they could not rely on manorial dues that they led the way in the Agricultural Revolution. Because they could not rely on noble status to distinguish themselves from the common herd, they were quite open to concepts of "gentlemanliness" that depended on taste and refinement.

One way that members of this aristocratic elite distinguished themselves from their social inferiors was through participation in the burgeoning market for consumer goods. The changes in industry, finance, and commerce discussed above combined to give wealthy elites the opportunity to display their wealth and taste through the acquisition of luxury goods. Food and drink became increasingly refined among the elite, and fashions in clothing changed frequently. The fact that luxury goods were available to anyone who could afford them, regardless of ancestry, further eroded the idea that hereditary nobles were innately superior.

The fact that (unlike "noble") "middle class" was never a legal designation makes it difficult to be precise about numbers, let alone wealth. Still, the evidence available suggests that throughout western Europe the middle class was growing in number and in wealth in the eighteenth century. In England between 1688 and 1803, the urban middle class rose from about 9 per cent of the population to around 15 per cent, and its share of national income doubled, from 20 to 40 per cent. The French bourgeoisie likely doubled in size between 1660 and 1789, along with its share of the national wealth. Historically, the nobility of the Dutch Republic had never been very large or strong, and the importance of cities and commerce meant that the middle class had been prominent for a long time; it was the bourgeois society *par excellence*. Although trade and industry did not boom in Mediterranean Europe as they did in the maritime northwest, Italy and Spain too had significant middle classes. Farther east, as we have seen, the middle classes were smaller in size, less wealthy, and less important: in Hungary they made up no more than 2 per cent of the population, and in Russia only about 2.5 per cent (half as much as the nobility).[11]

The myth of the "rising bourgeoisie" has been used to explain almost everything in European history since the Middle Ages. (A "myth" in this sense is not necessarily false: however, it is an all-purpose explanation, invoked so frequently that it assumes the aura of truth regardless of actual facts.) As we have seen, the bourgeoisie had been rising for centuries in the sense that its wealthy and socially ambitious members of the middle classes had been attaining noble status: for those people, "middle class" status was a transitional phase, not a goal in itself.

One influential interpretation of the French Revolution even attributes it to the bourgeoisie's seizure of the political power and social position that it felt entitled to by its growing wealth. However, this view seems to owe more to the fact that the wealthy middle class came to dominate European society in the 1800s than it does to the eighteenth-century evidence. Although in hindsight we can certainly detect signs of the rise of the bourgeoisie in France—as elsewhere in western Europe—in the 1700s, they would have been very difficult to see at the time. Similarly, even if traces of an embryonic middle-class consciousness were beginning to emerge by the end of the eighteenth century, the continuities outweighed the changes.

Most ambitious bourgeois continued to aspire to noble status, although it was now becoming harder to attain. This was in part because nobles always resisted increases in their numbers, as these tended to cheapen their status, but more importantly because the demand was outstripping the supply. There were simply too many wealthy bourgeois to be accommodated in the ranks of the nobility. In France, for example, the price of a venal office in the royal government—the usual vehicle of social mobility—rose dramatically, as did the price of the land required to "live nobly," as a result of overall demographic growth and, especially, the growth of the middle class.

Fortunately, the distinction between noble and commoner was becoming less important, as nobles and wealthy bourgeois alike increasingly formed a single aristocratic elite. In the words of a leading historian of pre-Revolutionary and Revolutionary France:

> Nobles and bourgeois became less and less distinguishable from one another. Increasingly, nobility came to seem merely a special set of privileges that certain men of property happened to have, but these privileges decreasingly marked off a coherent class or social group. In this sense the importance of the traditional orders of society certainly was on the wane. The noble order, which had once constituted France's unchallenged social elite, had been replaced, or rather absorbed by what it seems perfectly fair to call a class.[12]

If this was the case, then how are we to explain the anti-noble sentiment that would erupt during the French Revolution? There are at least two plausible explanations. First, the archaic voting procedures of the Estates-General, summoned to meet in 1789 for the first time since 1615, reflected an outmoded social scheme. King Louis XVI (r. 1774–91), in decreeing that each estate—the clergy, the nobles, and the Third Estate (theoretically everyone else, but in practice the urban middle class)—would have one vote, anachronistically restored social distinctions that were in process of fading away. Second, the men elected to represent the Third Estate in 1789 were not the wealthy and powerful bourgeois who were increasingly forming an aristocratic elite alongside the nobility. They were what we might call the professional middle class: lesser civil servants, teachers, physicians, and, above all, lawyers, who were increasingly coming to doubt that their efforts would ever be rewarded in the traditional ways.

Demographic and economic changes also affected the "lower orders," and by the end of the eighteenth century both urban and rural "poor" were behaving more like socio-economic classes. In the countryside, the process of social stratification continued and even intensified. A lucky few were able to take advantage of their opportunities, and formed a rural middle class of prosperous tenant farmers for whom agriculture was a profitable business. Most, of course, were not so fortunate. Demographic expansion, especially in the latter half of the century, reduced the landholdings of many peasants to the point that they could no longer support their families, and many lost their rights to any land at all. There-fore they had to supplement their income with other sorts of employment. Many worked lands owned or leased by others, either as hired labour or as sharecroppers. Many derived or supplemented their income through employment in rural industry. Many drifted into cities looking for work, and some resorted to begging and/or crime. Just as population growth was driving up the price of grain, and hence bread, these people were losing access to the land, resulting in greater poverty. What we see here are the origins of an industrial working class or proletariat: a class of people with no source of livelihood apart from the wages they are paid for their labour. When industrial factories began to appear, first in Britain and then, over the course of the nineteenth century, on the continent, it was these people and their children who found employment there.

The picture in the towns was somewhat different, in part because social and economic structures were less fluid than in the countryside, and the rights and prerogatives of the privileged orders were more deeply embedded in urban institutions, particularly in the guild structures that dominated urban economic, social, and political life. The privileged orders in the towns found themselves threatened from above and below. On the one hand, as we have seen, governments in the eighteenth century increasingly tried to reduce the power of guilds to restrict trade and manufacturing, either in the name of liberalizing the economy or in order to grant monopolistic privileges to some other preferred group. On the other hand, the power of the urban ruling class was also threatened from below. As we saw in Chapter 1, journeymen were increasingly on the outside looking in, prevented from becoming master craftsmen themselves by guild masters seeking to protect their own privileged positions. Journeymen of various trades would often band together in in-formal (and often illegal) organizations in order to advance and protect their interests. It was no accident that when industrial workers began to form unions in the nineteenth century, they looked a great deal like these journeymen's associations.

As the rural poor flocked into cities, they joined the ranks of the un- or under-employed poor, the beggars, and the criminals. Utterly dependent on buying food, espe-cially the bread that was the mainstay of their diet, they were a destabilizing element that frequently provoked fear and loathing among the propertied elite. It was this fear and loathing that led to what Foucault called the "great confinement" (Chapter 1), in which the poor, the mad, the sick, and, increasingly, the non-white and non-European were "othered" and shut away in institutions such as hospitals, workhouses, and asylums. In keeping with the developing "scientific" thought of the Enlightenment (Chapter 9), they would then be healed, improved, or corrected through discipline, surveillance, and regulation (see Chapter 1).

Chapter Conclusion

By the end of the eighteenth century, European society had changed dramatically, as had the European economy. Most of the changes had begun by the sixteenth century, if not earlier, but it was in the eighteenth that their cumulative impact became obvious. Although some of them must have been apparent to the people who lived through them, others were probably not. Many people remarked on the growth of rural industry, for instance; and the urban guild members who fought its expansion were clearly aware of the threat it posed to their own privileged positions. But rural industry was still very traditional in nature, and it would have been very difficult to anticipate the sweeping changes about to be brought by the Industrial Revolution.

Some of the changes in the world of agriculture and the countryside would have been more apparent than others, and more so in some regions than others. Peasants, whose shrinking landholdings compelled them to work on someone else's lands in order to feed their families, were certainly aware that their circumstances had changed. And those dispossessed by enclosure frequently demonstrated their displeasure. Yet other changes may not have been so obvious: for example, the general increase in the quantity and variety of food available. These changes too began in earlier centuries, and would not affect most of Europe until the nineteenth century, but a crucial point was passed in the eighteenth.

We may well imagine that people were not very conscious of changes in demographic patterns, as these were incremental and cumulative rather than conscious and dramatic. It is difficult to say how aware ordinary people would have been of the changes that were altering the most basic facts of their lives: birth, marriage, and death. If one or two more of their offspring survived the perils of childhood, would they attribute it to divine blessing, or luck, or fate? In the absence of accurate censuses, even people who were aware that the population was growing could not have known the scale of the growth. Governments typically did all they could to encourage population growth, as it was seen as essential to the prosperity and security of the kingdom. Of the very few who considered the negative consequences, the most important was the English clergyman and political economist Thomas Malthus (1766–1834). In his *Essay on the Principle of Population* (1798), he observed that while agricultural production increases only arithmetically (1, 2, 3, 4), population increases exponentially (2, 4, 16, 256), and that population growth would eventually outstrip growth in the supply of food. Any effort to relieve the misery of the poor was doomed to failure, since it would only encourage them to have more children and make the inevitable correction that much more traumatic. Epidemics, wars, and natural disasters, as unfortunate as they might have been, were ultimately necessary and even beneficial in that that they served to correct the balance between population and the supply of food.

It is yet another measure of how much things had changed in the course of the eighteenth century that his dire predictions were not fulfilled, for Malthus based his observations on the past and did not recognize the fundamental changes going on around him. In a sense, he was driving while watching the rear-view mirror.

Contemporaries were struck by the growing numbers of the poor, especially those responsible for aiding, controlling, or punishing them. This, of course, was not new. As far back as the 1500s, secular authorities had begun providing poor relief, but this effort took on a different character in the eighteenth century, when Enlightenment thinkers (see Chapter 9) encouraged the application of "scientific" methods to social issues. This has been characterized by some as an "enlightened" and humane approach to the less fortunate members of society, and by others as a way of punishing those who did not conform to the prevailing social norms.

Questions for Critical Thought

1. Suppose you had been born in 1690, somewhere in western Europe, and lived until 1790. What changes in your life and world would have been most apparent to you? How might your observations have differed, depending on your social status and occupation?
2. How did the changing economy affect European nobles?
3. Why did population expand so dramatically in the eighteenth century, and what challenges did this expansion pose?
4. How does our knowing what would happen in the future affect our understanding of eighteenth-century Europe?

Weblinks

Enclosures in Berkshire:
www.berkshireenclosure.org.uk/research_reading_map.asp

Michel Foucault:
www.michel-foucault.com/index.html

Further Reading

De Vries, Jan. *European Urbanisation, 1400–1800*. Cambridge MA: Harvard University Press, 1984. The authoritative study.

Dewald, Jonathan. *The European Nobility, 1400–1800*. Cambridge: Cambridge University Press, 1996. A comprehensive treatment of the nobility in the early modern period.

DuPlessis, Robert S. *Transitions to Capitalism in Early Modern Europe*. Cambridge: Cambridge University Press, 1997. A comprehensive analysis of the growing importance of the market in agriculture and industry. Valuable suggested readings.

Foucault, Michel. *Madness and Civilization: A History of Insanity in the Age of Reason*, trans. Richard Howard. New York: New American Library, 1965. Introduces the concept of the "great confinement," which he would develop further in *Discipline and Punish: The Birth of the Prison* (1976).

Hufton, Olwen. *The Poor of Eighteenth-Century France*. Oxford: Clarendon Press, 1974. A classic study of the growing underclass.

Ogilvie, Sheilagh. *Institutions and European Trade: Merchant Guilds, 1000–1800*. Cambridge: Cambridge University Press, 2011. A wide-ranging analysis of privilege, commerce, and economics.

Ogilvie, Sheilagh, and Cerman, Markus (eds.). *European Proto-Industrialisation*. Cambridge: Cambridge University Press, 1996. A valuable collection of essays on the current state of the debate on proto-industrialization.

Overton, Mark. *Agricultural Revolution in England: The Transformation of the Agrarian Economy, 1500–1850*. Cambridge: Cambridge University Press, 1996. The best recent survey of the entire early modern period and beyond.

Notes

1. Derek Beales, "Religion and Culture," in T.C.W. Blanning, *The Eighteenth Century* (Oxford: Oxford University Press, 2000), p. 131.
2. Jan de Vries, *The Economy of Europe in an Age of Crisis, 1600–1750* (Cambridge: Cambridge University Press, 1976), p. 90.
3. Robert S. DuPlessis, *Transitions to Capitalism in Early Modern Europe* (Cambridge: Cambridge University Press, 1997), p. 205.
4. DuPlessis, p. 205.
5. Quoted in Sheilagh Ogilvie, "The European Economy in the Eighteenth Century," in T.C.W. Blanning (ed.), *The Eighteenth Century* (Oxford: Oxford University Press, 2000), p. 113.
6. Quoted in DuPlessis, p. 240.
7. The French term *ancien régime* is usually translated as "old regime," but "former" more accurately reflects the sense of the word in French.
8. Jonathan Dewald, *The European Nobility, 1400–1800* (Cambridge: Cambridge University Press, 1996), pp. 22–5.
9. Quoted in Dewald, p. 49.
10. Voltaire, *Candide*, trans. John Butt (London: Penguin, 1947), p. 19.
11. William Doyle, *The Old European Order, 1660–1800*, 2nd ed. (Oxford: Oxford University Press, 1992), p. 144.
12. William Doyle, *The Ancien Regime*, 2nd ed. (Houndmills: Palgrave, 2001), p. 25.

9

Culture and Religion in the Age
of the Enlightenment

When it comes to cultural and intellectual history, the eighteenth century is generally thought of as the "Age of the Enlightenment." This is not inaccurate, for the intellectual and cultural movement of the Enlightenment was certainly prominent. But it can be misleading, since eighteenth-century cultural and intellectual life was not limited to the Enlightenment. In particular, if we look at the eighteenth century only through lens of the Enlightenment, we will significantly underestimate the continuing importance of traditional religion, whether Catholic or Protestant, in the lives of most Europeans, especially in the first half of the century.

The Enlightenment

As with the Renaissance, the Enlightenment as most educated people today imagine it is somewhat different from the Enlightenment perceived by historians, let alone to those who were part of it. For many, including the participants, the Enlightenment—even more than the Renaissance—inaugurated the modern era. The shackles of past ignorance were gleefully discarded, rationality was glorified, rights were proclaimed, and liberty was established. Indeed, many of the values that that are most prized today were championed by enlightened thinkers and writers. At the same time, a postmodern view of the Enlightenment has emerged according to which its emphasis on "reason," human perfectibility, and universal values, was responsible for many of the horrors of the modern age, including western imperialism, totalitarianism, and genocide. Thus western ideals of rationality, tolerance, and progress can be interpreted as alien impositions on cultures that had their own different standards:

> Against [the Enlightenment] postmodernists argued that different cultures should be left to determine their own ends, and refused to discriminate morally or politically between them. At best the Enlightenment had been one of those

cultures, peculiar to eighteenth-century Europe; it was a terrible mistake ever to have accepted its claims to universal significance.[1]

Many of the values that we take for granted in the "modern" world were completely foreign to the eighteenth century, among them democracy, gender and racial equality, and universal education. Without ignoring its contributions to our world, then, we must look at the Enlightenment as a historical movement and period that in a number of ways was very different from what many today understand it to have been.

Recent historical writing on the Enlightenment has also emphasized its diverse and sometimes even contradictory elements. The Enlightenment appears not as a monolithic whole, but as a bundle of ideas and trends that in many cases coexist uneasily if at all. If that view is accurate, are we justified even in thinking that there was such a thing as "the Enlightenment"? The answer is surely yes, if only because many people at the time identified themselves as "enlightened," whatever they might have meant by that term. Even more crucially, although they might not have come up with the same answers, or even the same questions, the thinkers of the Enlightenment proceeded according to similar general principles and assumptions.

What were those general principles and assumptions? In the very broadest terms, the Enlightenment *was* the application of "scientific" methodology to problems of human relations and human society.[2] By the early eighteenth century, European elites had generally accepted Newton's proposition that the physical universe was governed by regular, predictable, and rational laws. If that was the case, then surely human affairs were governed by similar laws. According to Antoine-Nicolas de Caritat, Marquis de Condorcet (1743–94):

> the sole foundation for belief in the natural sciences is this idea, that the general laws directing the phenomena of the universe, known or unknown, are necessary and constant. Why should this principle be any less true for the development of the intellectual and moral faculties of man than for the other operations of nature?[3]

This was the overriding goal of the Enlightenment: to discover those laws and use them as the template for reform of society and its institutions. There could be significant, even vehement disagreement about what the laws were, or how to change institutions to conform to them, but there was general agreement about the ultimate goal.

Thus "nature" was one key concept of the Enlightenment. Another was "reason": "objective thinking, without passion, prejudice or superstition, and without reference to non-verifiable statements such as those of religious revelation."[4] Not only were both the physical and human realms governed by uniform laws; those laws were also accessible to the human mind through the application of reason. Every human practice and institution was to be tested for conformity to two standards: nature and reason. If it failed either of these tests, then there was no excuse for keeping it. In this way religious revelation, tradition, and custom were all excluded as sources of legitimation for institutions or practices.

The Enlightenment was a European movement, and many enlightened thinkers could be found in England, Scotland, Spain, Germany, and Italy; important variations of enlightened thought could also be found in different regions. Yet France, specifically Paris, was its unquestioned centre. Many leading figures of the Enlightenment either were French or spent significant periods of time in France. And many, if not most, major enlightened works were written in French, which had replaced Latin as the international language of culture and literature.

The quintessential Enlightenment figure was the philosophe. Although the obvious translation is "philosopher," the connotations of that term do not do justice to the philosophe's role. The philosophe was no ivory-tower intellectual, shut away in his study contemplating ultimate questions from afar. He (almost all the philosophes were men) was deeply engaged with society, concerned not only to point out what was unnatural or irrational, but to change society. Writers and thinkers of the Enlightenment thought of themselves as an international community, a "Republic of Letters," united not by nationality or ethnicity or political allegiance, but by a common set of values.

The philosophe was also a social creature who sought to reach as broad an audience as possible, not only to critique and instruct, but also to entertain. In Paris and elsewhere, enlightened themes were discussed and debated in informal discussion groups known as *salons*, often meeting at the home of a socially prominent woman who invited the guests, chose the topics for discussion, and moderated the proceedings. Some salons, such as those of Madame Geoffrin and Madame du Deffand in Paris, were regular events. Coffeehouses and taverns also served as meeting places, and local worthies across Europe formed academies devoted to discussion and debate; two English examples were the Manchester Literary and Philosophical Society and the Birmingham-based Lunar Society. It was just such an academy, in the French city of Dijon, that sponsored the essay contest through which a young Genevan writer named Jean-Jacques Rousseau was first thrust into the spotlight.

Increasing literacy and access to education opened the world of ideas to a broader range of people. Newspapers and magazines appeared with increasing frequency, and the first lending libraries made books available even to those who could not afford to buy them. All these things were part of what the German sociologist Jürgen Habermas has called the "public sphere": an arena outside the traditional spaces of churches, royal courts, and universities, where ideas were germinated, discussed, and disseminated. The essence of the public sphere is that is beyond the control of any single person or institution. Knowledge itself was becoming a commodity exchanged in a marketplace.

Part and parcel of the development of the public sphere was increasing public access to cultural performances. In the past, concerts, operas, and plays had been performed almost exclusively for select audiences, such as the royal court, or noble patrons and their guests. Although public theatres were not unknown in the seventeenth century—Shakespeare's Globe is the pre-eminent example—in the eighteenth their number and popularity grew dramatically. Now that their livelihoods depended more on ticket sales than aristocratic patronage, playwrights began to dispense with the classical subjects and forms expected by noble audiences and construct their work around "ordinary" people and situations.

Three notable examples were the plays by Pierre-Augustin de Beaumarchais (1732–99) in which the Spanish valet Figaro regularly outwitted the hapless aristocrats who employed him. *The Barber of Seville*, *The Marriage of Figaro*, and *The Guilty Mother* were all tremendously popular despite official disapproval and occasional censorship.

In music we see the same trends. The German composer Georg Friedrich Handel (1685–1759) was probably the first musician to make a handsome living by composing and conducting for a paying public. Franz Josef Haydn (1732–1809) gained the patronage of the fabulously wealthy Hungarian noble Prince Esterhazy. Yet he also composed and conducted for the public, successfully straddling both worlds. So did Wolfgang Amadeus Mozart (1756–91), who benefited from the patronage of the Archbishop of Salzburg and Holy Roman Emperor Joseph II, but also composed music and operas for the ticket-buying public, most notably *The Magic Flute* (1791).

Yet another aspect of this Enlightenment sociability was the fraternal organization known as the Freemasons. Although it began as the guild of stonemasons, its humble origins were eventually eclipsed by its gentlemanly membership. Emphasizing enlightened values such as rationality, civility, and tolerance, it became fashionable in England, France, Germany, Italy, the Low Countries, and Spain, although its insistence on secrecy regarding its rituals made it a target for suppression, especially in Catholic countries. Even today, Freemasonry is sometimes seen as a radical and subversive cult.

As with any such diffuse movement, it is impossible to be precise about many aspects of the Enlightenment. Enlightened thinkers often differed vehemently with one another. In a sense, the Enlightenment was a moving target, always shifting and developing, often in paradoxical ways. Nevertheless, if we are not too dogmatic about it, we can think of the Enlightenment in three broad phases, although elements of all three phases overlapped and were even concurrent in some cases. In the first phase, enlightened ideas were new, radical, and even dangerous; we will look at this opening stage largely through the careers of its two giants: Voltaire and Montesquieu. In the second phase, enlightened ideas became more broadly acceptable among social elites; we will follow the progress of their spread through the publishing history of the single greatest work of the Enlightenment, the *Encyclopaedia* (1751–72). The third phase comprised a number of different elements. Once enlightened ideas had been widely accepted in some segments of elite society, some thinkers responded by "pushing the envelope," pursuing those ideas to radical conclusions that even they knew would be unacceptable to the vast majority. Others specialized in discrete areas of research and thought. For example, whereas Voltaire had been a polymath, writing on subjects that ranged from politics and religion to science and philosophy, later writers zeroed in on specific areas: economics (Adam Smith, François Quesnay and the physiocrats), criminology (Cesare Beccaria), history (Giambatista Vico, Edward Gibbon), or psychology (Etienne de Condillac). Yet another thread was a reaction against enlightened thought. The Enlightenment had always had its critics, and only a portion of the educated elite was ever devoted to its ideals. In the latter half of the century, however, the critics became more vocal and more numerous. Chief among them was the black sheep of the enlightened family, Jean-Jacques Rousseau.

THE EARLY ENLIGHTENMENT: VOLTAIRE AND MONTESQUIEU

Voltaire was the pen-name of François-Marie Arouet (1694–1778), arguably the Enlightenment's most widely read and influential philosophe. Born into the highest level of the Parisian bourgeoisie, he received the best education money could buy. As a young playwright, poet, and man-about-town, he cut a dashing figure, but his satirical pen got him in trouble when a young nobleman he had insulted sent his servants to beat him up. (As a noble, it was beneath his dignity to challenge the commoner Voltaire himself.) When Voltaire sued for damages, the nobleman used his influence to have him imprisoned in the Bastille without a trial. Voltaire suggested exile to England as an alternative to prison, and he was allowed to leave the kingdom.

The three years he spent in England were critical to the development of Voltaire's own thought, and to the Enlightenment itself. Looking at England through rose-coloured glasses, Voltaire perceived it to be a model society. While France laboured under an absolute monarchy, the English Parliament restrained despotism. In England the path to wealth and influence was open to talented commoners like himself, whereas in France society and government alike were dominated by ignorant and selfish nobles. Free of the religious fanaticism promoted by the monopolistic Catholic Church, England appeared to Voltaire as a haven of religious toleration. Only England could have produced Isaac Newton and John Locke, the geniuses who to Voltaire seemed the apostles of a new age. Several years after returning to France, he published his views on English society, government, and religion in his *Philosophical Letters* (1733), also known as *Letters on the English Nation*.

Throughout his long career, Voltaire wrote and published broadly. While continuing to write plays and poetry, now largely forgotten, he also produced a number of historical works, including *The Age of Louis XIV* (1751), in which he praised the Sun King's cultural achievements and subjugation of the nobility, *The History of the Russian Empire under Peter the Great* (1759–63), and *Essays on the Manners and Spirit of Nations* (1756). In the latter, a comparative universal history outlining the progress of civilization, he explicitly rejected traditional Christian historiography. *Elements of the Philosophy of Newton* (1745) made Newton's physics and cosmology more accessible to educated laypeople.

Voltaire also wrote novels, the most famous of which is *Candide, or Optimism* (1759). In 1755 a disastrous earthquake had struck Lisbon, with tremendous loss of life and property, leading Voltaire to ponder why a supposedly loving and omnipotent deity would permit such a tragedy. His particular target was the optimistic philosophy of the great German mathematician and philosopher Gottfried Leibniz (1646–1716), who had used a logical method derived from Descartes to theorize that, although the world is not perfect, it is the best of all the possible worlds that a beneficent God could have created. The title character, Candide, is a naïve and innocent young man who goes on a series of adventures accompanied by his tutor Pangloss, who in the face of horror and tragedy perseveres in his philosophy of "metaphysico-theologo-cosmonigology," and responds to every setback with the phrase "All is for the best in the best of all possible worlds."

A dedicated critic of organized religion, especially Christianity, Voltaire took as his motto the phrase *écrasez l'infâme*—"crush the infamous thing"—by which he meant intolerance, bigotry, superstition, and fanaticism. To his mind, all these vices were exemplified in Christianity, above all in the Catholic Church. Voltaire did believe in a Supreme Being; as he famously wrote, "If God did not exist, it would be necessary to invent him." But he rejected the idea that the deity concerned himself with human affairs. (We will explore this view, which would become known as Deism, below.) Voltaire's conviction that organized religion was an instrument of oppression was borne out in the Calas affair of 1761–5. Jean Calas was a Protestant merchant in the southern city of Toulouse. When his son committed suicide in 1761, the family said that he had been murdered by an intruder, in order to avoid the opprobrium that suicide carried. But Catholic religious and judicial authorities insisted that Calas had murdered his son to prevent him from converting to Catholicism. He was put on trial, and against overwhelming evidence was convicted of murder. Despite horrific torture, he refused to confess and was ultimately executed in 1762. When Voltaire became aware of the case, he made it a *cause célèbre*, leading a campaign to have the sentence overturned and Calas exonerated. In 1763, in his *Treatise on Tolerance on the Occasion of the Death of Jean Calas*, he condemned Catholic fanaticism and argued for universal religious toleration. In 1764, largely because of Voltaire's efforts, the sentence was annulled, and in 1765 Calas was posthumously exonerated of all charges.

Voltaire became a wealthy and influential man, probably one of the first to support himself entirely by writing, together with judicious investment. Named royal historiographer in 1745, he was elected to the prestigious Académie Française the following year. Nevertheless, in 1758 he bought a country estate at Ferney in Switzerland, just beyond the reach of French censors and judges, and continued to exercise his influence from there for the next two decades, only returning to Paris shortly before his death in 1778.

The other giant of the early Enlightenment was Charles-Louis de Secondat, Baron de Montesquieu (1689–1755). A member of the high nobility who would become a judge in the Parlement of Bordeaux, he first came to public attention with his novel *Persian Letters* in 1721. Capitalizing on the popularity of travel literature, it was, like *Gulliver's Travels*, a kind of fictional travel literature, though a very different kind. It consists of a series of letters by two Persian travellers to France. Although Montesquieu had no real knowledge of Persia, his travellers' observations regarding the barbarism and superstition of European society suggest that their homeland is a model of tolerant rationality by comparison.

Like Voltaire, Montesquieu was favourably impressed by the fact that, in England, the monarch's power was restrained by the parliament. Unlike Voltaire, who described French nobles as self-interested and ignorant, Montesquieu believed that they too, like the English parliamentarians, performed the valuable function of restraining royal despotism. These views are expressed in his greatest work, *The Spirit of the Laws* (1748), which many have considered the founding work of political science. In it he argued that no one system of government was equally suitable for all times and nations. Rather, a host of factors, including climate, geography, history, and racial characteristics, determined what was appropriate in any particular situation. Republicanism was best suited to small states in cool climates, whereas despotism was appropriate for large tropical empires. In moderate climates, such as France and most of western Europe, monarchy was the preferred option. What distinguished monarchy from despotism was that in the former the power of the ruler was restrained by intermediate groups such as the nobles. In France, according to Montesquieu, nobles exercised this restraint primarily through parlements such as that of Bordeaux, in which he himself was a judge. Their wealth meant that nobles were above motivation by material gain, and because they were not elected, they could not be influenced by the mob or temporary fads. It was Montesquieu who introduced the concept of checks and balances to political discourse—a principle that would be enshrined in the US constitution, with its separation of legislative, executive, and judicial powers.

DIDEROT AND THE *ENCYCLOPÉDIE*

In 1745 a Paris publisher approached a young writer with a proposition to translate into French a two-volume encyclopaedia published in England in 1728. The writer in questions was Denis Diderot (1713–84), who had already attracted notice as a rising star in the Republic of Letters, even though he (in contrast to Voltaire and Montesquieu) was the son of a provincial artisan. Diderot persuaded the publisher to embark on an ambitious new project instead: a multi-volume work that would sum up all current knowledge according to the latest enlightened ideas. As his co-editor he recruited Jean le Rond d'Alembert (1717–83), a prominent mathematician and philosopher who, as a nobleman, was much better connected than the relatively humble Diderot. It was d'Alembert who in 1750 wrote the prospectus for the forthcoming work, which was sold by subscription. Over the next twenty years, twenty-eight volumes would be published (seventeen of text, eleven of illustrations), the cumulative effort of 140 contributors, among them most of the leading figures of the Enlightenment: Voltaire, Montesquieu, Rousseau, and Diderot himself.

Subtitled "A Classified Dictionary of the Sciences, Arts, and Trades," the *Encyclopédie* was intended not as a neutral collection of knowledge but, as Diderot himself wrote in the entry entitled "Encyclopédie," "to change the general way of thinking": that is, to change society along enlightened lines. Its 60,000 articles dealt not only with religion, government, and philosophy but with science, industry, and the trades, exemplifying Bacon's belief that scientific progress would lead to increased human happiness. Many of its almost 3000 engravings were elaborate illustrations of scientific and technical processes.

The publication history of the *Encyclopédie* itself reflects the progress of Enlightenment thought through Europe's literate elites. The seven volumes published between 1751 and 1756, with the permission of the royal censor, scandalized the conservative and devout. The Bishop of Montauban railed: "Up till now, Hell has vomited its venom, so to speak, drop by drop. Today there are torrents of errors and impieties. . . . " And the attorney general declared that the purpose of the project was "to propagate materialism, to destroy religion, to inspire a spirit of independence, and to nourish the corruption of morals." Devout Catholics were outraged by d'Alembert's entry on Geneva, which

Technical processes in the *Encyclopédie*. The *Encyclopédie* contained thousands of engraved illustrations of technical and industrial processes, including these images depicting cutlery- and glass-making.

praised the supposedly rational approach to religion of the city's Calvinist clergy. In January 1757 an assassination attempt on Louis XV resulted in a general backlash against anything new and "radical," and in 1759 the Parlement of Paris ordered the suppression of the *Encyclopédie*. Discouraged, d'Alembert quit the project, but over the next decade Diderot worked tirelessly to complete it while the sympathetic royal censor turned a

Frontispiece of the *Encyclopédie*. The frontispiece of the *Encyclopédie* (1772) illustrates the intentions behind the work. Diderot described it as follows: "Beneath an Ionic Temple, the Sanctuary of Truth, one sees Truth enveloped in a veil and radiating light which parts the clouds and disperses them. To the right, Reason and Philosophy are busy, one in raising the veil from Truth, the other in tearing it away. At her feet, Theology, on her knees, receives the light from on high. In following this chain of figures, one finds on the same side Memory, Ancient and Modern History; History records the pomp and ceremony, and Time serves as its support. Below them are grouped Geometry, Astronomy, and Physics. The figures below this group represent Optics, Botany, Chemistry, and Agriculture. At the bottom are several Arts and Professions which derive from the Sciences. At the left of Truth one sees Imagination, who positions herself to adorn and crown Truth. Below Imagination, the artist has placed the different genres of Poetry: Epic, Dramatic, Satire, and Pastoral. After that come the other Arts of Imitation: Music, Painting, Sculpture, and Architecture."

© Lebrecht Music and Arts Photo Library / Alamy Stock Photo

blind eye. Publication resumed in the 1760s, and the last volume of illustrations appeared in 1772.

There is nothing like controversy to encourage sales, and the *Encyclopédie* became an eighteenth-century bestseller. Sold by subscription, the original edition of 4000 copies was quickly fulfilled, despite its high price: 1500 *livres*, at a time when the average French worker's household lived on roughly 200 *livres* a year. Less expensive editions would eventually be published at about one-sixth of the original price, putting it well within the reach of the middle class. Although the vast majority of subscriptions came from within France, copies were sold across Europe, in England, Spain, Germany, Italy, and even Russia.

ENLIGHTENED THEMES

To do justice to the scope of enlightened thought would take volumes. Nevertheless, in this section we will briefly highlight some of its most important themes, their sources, and their development over the course of the eighteenth century.

Historical debate

The Secularism of the Enlightenment

To many of the thinkers who made the Enlightenment, the critique of organized religion was its central feature. The philosopher Immanuel Kant called the Enlightenment "the escape of men from their self-caused immaturity—chiefly in matters of religion." Here are excerpts from two historical works, which although they are not diametrically opposed, do argue for different interpretations.

> We are accustomed to think of the eighteenth century as essentially modern in its temper. Certainly, the Philosophes themselves made a great point of having renounced the superstition and hocus-pocus of medieval Christian thought, and we have usually been willing to take them at their word. Surely, we say, the eighteenth century was the pre-eminently the age of reason, surely the Philosophes were a skeptical lot, atheists in effect if not by profession, addicted to science and the scientific method, always out to crush the infamous, valiant defenders of liberty, equality, fraternity, freedom of speech, and what you will. All very true. And yet I think the Philosophes were nearer the Middle Ages, less emancipated from the preconceptions of medieval Christian thought, than they quite realized or we have commonly supposed. . . .
>
> . . . They had put off the fear of God, but maintained a respectful attitude towards the deity. They ridiculed the idea that the universe had been created in six days, but still believed it to be a beautifully articulated machine designed by the Supreme Being according to a rational plan. . . . The Garden of Eden was for them a myth, no doubt, but they looked enviously back to the golden age of Roman virtue, or across the water to the unspoiled innocence of an Arcadian civilization that flourished in Pennsylvania. They renounced the authority of the church and Bible, but exhibited a naïve faith in the authority of nature and reason. They scorned metaphysics, but were proud to be called philosophers. They dismantled heaven, somewhat prematurely it seems, since they retained their faith in the immortality of the soul. They courageously discussed atheism, but not before the servants. They defended toleration valiantly, but could with difficulty tolerate priests. They denied that miracles ever happened, but believed in the perfectibility of the human race. . . . In spite of their rationalism and their humane sympathies, in

Religion

Any discussion of major Enlightenment themes must give a prominent place to the critique of established and organized religion. The foundations of that critique had been laid over generations, in response to the revulsion against dogmatic absolutism produced by spite of their aversion to hocus-pocus and enthusiasm and dim perspectives, in spite of their eager skepticism, their engaging cynicism, their brave youthful blasphemies and talk of hanging the last king in the entrails of the last priest—in spite of all of it, there is more of Christian philosophy in the writings of the Philosophes than has yet been dreamt of in our histories.

Carl L. Becker, *The Heavenly City of the Eighteenth-Century Philosophers* (New Haven: Yale University Press, 1932), pp. 29–31.

The philosophes' claim to distance from their Christian world has rarely been fully honoured. Instead the philosophes have been sarcastically commended for "merely" secularizing religious ideas and caricatured as medieval clerks in modern dress, ungrateful and forgetful heirs of the Christian tradition who combated the pious wish for salvation in the name of a secular salvation disguised as progress; who denied the immortality of the soul only to substitute the immortality of reputation; who laughed at religious idolatry but had their own saints—Bacon, Newton, and Locke; who excommunicated their heretics—Rousseau; and even made pilgrimages—to Ferney.

Such analogies are seductive and even telling: they draw attention to origins the philosophes did not like to remember. There was some point after all in the derisive observation that the Enlightenment was a derivative, vulgarized restatement of Christian values: the new philosophy a secularized faith, optimism a secularized hope, humanitarianism a secularized charity. . . .

But from the vantage point of each camp the same set of facts takes on two very important shapes. What Christians saw, with some justice, as an act of imitation, the philosophes saw, with greater justice, as an act of repudiation, or at best, of exploitation. . . . For even when the philosophes openly sought a secular equivalent for a Christian idea, they were engaged in a revolutionary activity: it makes a difference whether a man is terrified of hell or concerned for his posthumous reputation, makes God or a historical figure into a father figure, admires a universe that allows the invasions of Providence or one that persists in unalterable, lawful regularity. The origins of ideas may be a clue to their function, they do not determine it. Christianity made a substantial contribution to the philosophes' education, but of the definition of the Enlightenment it forms no part.

Peter Gay, *The Enlightenment: An Interpretation*, vol. 1: *The Rise of Modern Paganism* (New York: Knopf, 1966), pp. 322–3.

decades of religious warfare, and the alienation that many educated people felt in the face of the churches' hostility to scientific discoveries, exemplified by the Catholic Church's condemnation of Galileo. In the minds of many, Newton's cosmology posited a universe of rational laws that seemed to leave little place for the God of Christianity. (As we saw in

Chapter 5, this interpretation would have horrified Newton, but that was how his work was understood.)

Beyond this general *zeitgeist*, there were several thinkers who laid the groundwork for the Enlightenment attack on Christianity, some of them more intentionally than others. Richard Simon (1638–1712) was a French priest who applied historical and philological techniques to the Bible. His intent was not to question the divine inspiration of Scripture, but to buttress its authority by making certain obscure passages and events more comprehensible. Nevertheless, his *Critical History of the Old Testament* (1679) showed the Old Testament to be a much rewritten compilation that had changed over time. Even though he had obtained official permission to publish it, the book became so controversial that it was eventually condemned and placed on the Index of Forbidden Books. Undeterred, Simon in 1689 published *Critical History of the New Testament*, which was greeted with similar hostility.

The attacks on biblical authority offered by Pierre Bayle (1647–1706) were more deliberate. A Huguenot refugee from France who settled in the Dutch Republic, he was often inconsistent and contradictory in his own beliefs. His chief work, inspired in part by Descartes's principle that nothing should escape rational scrutiny, was one of the earliest attempts at an encyclopedia: entitled *Historical and Critical Dictionary* (1697), it was a wide-ranging and frequently devastating critique of conventional wisdom. In particular, Bayle saw the Bible as a collection of inconsistent myths and fables, the exposure of which he took to render much of current Christianity untenable in a rational age.

In this climate, it is not surprising that some thinkers tried to render Christianity more "rational." John Locke made an important contribution to this effort in *The Reasonableness of Christianity* (1695), arguing that the application of reason to the faith strengthened rather than weakened it, and that reason applied to nature led inevitably to Christian belief. Once faith had been subjected to reason, however, it was impossible to prevent others from reaching different conclusions. In his 1696 work *Christianity Not Mysterious*, John Toland (1670–1722) argued against belief in anything inconsistent with human reason, including biblical miracles.

Clearly, then, the Deism of the Enlightenment was not without precedents. Most philosophes retained a belief in a Supreme Being who, having created a universe governed by universal mathematical laws accessible to human reason, no longer played an active role in it. The most common analogy cast God as a watchmaker: the existence of a watch presupposes the existence of a watchmaker, but once the watch it has been made, it will continue to function without any attention from its maker.

If the same was true of the world, the implication was clear: organized religion and dogmatic theology were untenable. If all churches and organized religions were mistaken, then there was no conceivable basis for intolerance or persecution. Belief in miracles and the supernatural was ridiculed as childish superstition, as were religious practices such as sacraments, pilgrimages, and veneration of relics.

All organized religion was fair game, but the principal targets were Christianity and, above all, the Catholic Church, which most of the philosophes considered to be the incarnation of Voltaire's *infâme*, the stronghold of superstition, fanaticism, intolerance, and bigotry. Even so, outright professions of atheism were relatively rare in the eighteenth century. Not only must there be a Supreme Being, who created the universe and endowed it with rational universal laws, but belief in a Supreme Being and an afterlife was essential to preserve moral order in society.

If God no longer played any active role in human affairs, if Christ was a moral teacher rather than the Son of God sent to redeem mankind, if all churches and religions were instruments of superstition and oppression, what constituted proper religious observance? Here again we may turn to Voltaire:

> To worship God: to leave to every man freedom to serve Him according to his own ideas: to love one's neighbours; enlighten them, if one can; pity them, if they are in error: to regard as immaterial, questions which would never have given trouble if no importance had been attached to them: this is my religion, which is worth all your systems and all your symbols.[5]

Expressions of atheism did become slightly more common in the later Enlightenment. The Swiss philosophe Paul-Henri Thiry, Baron d'Holbach (1723–89) was a prominent contributor to the *Encyclopédie* who sponsored a salon frequented by many leading Enlightenment thinkers. In his chief work, *The System of Nature*, published under a pseudonym in 1770, he argued explicitly for a materialistic view of the universe that left no room for a deity. Scholars disagree on the precise position of the Scottish philosopher David Hume (1711–76), but he clearly left open the possibility that God might not exist, or that if He did, His existence was unprovable from either nature or reason. Atheists remained a distinct minority, however, and the audience for their works was very small. As Holbach put it, "Atheism, like philosophy and every profound and abstract science, is . . . by no means suited to the common people, nor even to the majority."[6]

Politics

In matters of politics and government, enlightened thinkers were more united in what they rejected than in what they accepted. What they rejected was hereditary divine-right monarchy as it had developed over the previous centuries. Here too, important foundations had been laid in earlier years. Most important was the emerging concept of the contractual origin of political power. As we have seen, Thomas Hobbes in *Leviathan* had located the origins of political power in an agreement among the people to endow the sovereign with complete authority. Once that agreement had been reached, however, subjects had no right of resistance or redress. The contract was among the people, not between sovereign and people, and therefore the sovereign could not be bound by a contract to which he was not a party. Besides, if people did resist the sovereign, they would return to the state of nature, which Hobbes described as worse than the worst tyranny.

Locke addressed Hobbes's views in his *Two Treatises of Civil Government*. Although published in 1689 as a retroactive legitimation of the Glorious Revolution of 1688, it had been written earlier and in fact had little to do with contemporary political events. Locke used Hobbes's basic approach of deducing the purpose and nature of political power from its origins. But he started from different premises and reached very different conclusions. In Locke's more optimistic view, society preceded government, and the state of nature was not the "war of all against all" that Hobbes had posited. Rather, Locke held that people were generally inclined to respect one another's natural rights to life, liberty, and property. These rights were still subject to invasion by others, however, and their enjoyment could be rendered more certain and secure through the introduction of civil government: "The great and chief end . . . of men's uniting into commonwealths and putting themselves under government, is the preservation of their property." If the government is no longer fulfilling its purpose, or is indeed actively violating it, it may legitimately be resisted and overthrown in defence of natural rights. Here was a statement of universal rights independent of time or place: not the rights of "freeborn Englishmen," but of men everywhere and at all times. The emphasis on property must be underlined here, for while all had the rights of life and liberty, only men of property were entitled to political rights.

By and large, enlightened thinkers believed that ordinary people, peasants and workers, had no political rights, and they mistrusted democracy, which they equated with "mob rule." One of the very few thinkers who ascribed political rights to ordinary people was Jean-Jacques Rousseau (see below). Even fewer advocated political rights for women. What ordinary people did have a right to was good government, government according to enlightened principles that increased progress and human happiness. To paraphrase Abraham Lincoln, they advocated government for the people, but not by the people.

Where enlightened thinkers were less than united was on the question of how to achieve these aims. As we have seen, Montesquieu held the protection of liberty against despotism to be paramount, and stressed a constitutional order that embodied checks and balances against such abuses. Voltaire, on the other hand, while admiring and idealizing the British system, held that French nobles were too self-interested and ignorant to play the lofty role that Montesquieu had assigned them. Thus he (and others) urged rulers to use their power to implement enlightened reforms. This was the kernel of the enlightened despotism, or enlightened absolutism, that we will look at in the next chapter.

Enlightened political thinkers believed the "system" of hereditary divine right monarchies that dominated Europe in the early modern period to be hopelessly archaic and irrational. States, even monarchies, required written constitutions that reflected the natural laws of politics. Large and complex states such as France or England contained too many vested interests for this to be possible in the near term. (Indeed, writing a constitution for France would turn out to be one of the major goals—and difficulties—of the French Revolution.) Constitutions were written, however, for a number of smaller and newer states. The most obvious example was the constitution of the newly independent United States, which clearly reflected Montesquieu's emphasis on the necessity of checks and balances to prevent despotic abuses of power. In 1755 the Mediterranean island of Corsica had recently established its independence from the Italian city of Genoa. Several years later, the leader of the rebels, himself heavily influenced by Montesquieu, asked for

Rousseau's assistance in drawing up a constitution, based on the principles of his recently published *Social Contract*. Accordingly, in 1765 Rousseau drafted the work known as *Constitutional Project for Corsica* (1765); but he never finished it, as the French conquest of the island in 1769 made the effort moot. A similar request from a Polish statesman would result in Rousseau's *Considerations on the Government of Poland* (1772). Even some rulers believed in the importance of written constitutions: Grand Duke Leopold of Tuscany (1765–90) proposed a written constitution for that state, although it was never put into effect (see Chapter 10).

Economics

As enlightened thought developed and broadened, thinkers turned their attention to more specific aspects of human society; indeed, the Enlightenment saw the birth of the social sciences (note the terminology) as discrete areas of inquiry. Among those areas was economics or, as it was known then, political economy. As we have seen, economic thinking at the time was dominated by the assumptions ("philosophy" is too grand a term) that came to be called mercantilism. In the 1770s, however, a group of French thinkers known as the physiocrats would subject these and other pillars of the economic order to the Enlightenment tests of reason and conformity to natural laws.

The physiocrats advocated economic and fiscal reform. Their leading figure was François Quesnay (1694–1774), who contributed a number of entries to the *Encyclopédie*, and whose most important economic work was the *Tableau économique* of 1758. The physiocrats believed that, in the final analysis, the only true sources of wealth were land and agriculture: industry was sterile in that it processed the products of the land but created nothing new in itself, while trade and commerce simply shuffled existing goods around. Land therefore had to be made as productive as possible through fundamental agricultural reform. Small peasant holdings restricted by traditional and feudal obligations should be replaced by large consolidated landholdings, as was happening in England (see Chapter 8), and grain should be allowed to find its "natural" price, free of government regulation. In the long run, they argued, grain production would increase, prices would fall, and everyone would benefit from an efficient market economy. They also advised fundamental fiscal reform, proposing that France's confusing, contradictory, inefficient, and inequitable mishmash of existing taxes be replaced by a single tax on all land, with no exemptions whatever. Of course, lower prices "in the long run" are no comfort to people who need to eat every day, and the peasants who stood to be stripped of their lands were not the only ones who opposed the physiocrats' program: so did workers whose survival depended on reasonably priced bread; and the privileged orders, the church and nobility, who were determined to protect their tax exemptions. The physiocrat Anne Robert Jacques Turgot, who was appointed finance minister in 1774, sought to implement many physiocratic policies, most notably freeing the trade in grain. As we will see in Chapter 10, however, widespread resistance and bread riots (the "Flour War") would lead to his dismissal and the reversal of his reforms.

Central to the ideology of the physiocrats was the belief that economic activity was governed by natural laws, and that those laws should be left to operate unhindered. This concept, which the physiocrats called *laissez-faire* ("let it be," or "leave it alone") was given its fullest eighteenth-century expression by Adam Smith (1723–90) in his *Inquiry into the Nature and Causes of the Wealth of Nations* (1776), more commonly known as *The Wealth of Nations*. A friend and contemporary of his fellow Scot David Hume, Smith was a moral philosopher who focused his attention on economics after travelling in France and meeting Quesnay and other physiocrats.

Smith adopted the *laissez-faire* concept, but otherwise disagreed with many physiocratic ideas. In his view, the true source of wealth was labour, and therefore he argued that industry and commerce were also able to contribute to the general wealth of nations. In order to do so, however, they needed to be free of any laws and regulations that violated the "natural laws" of economics. Smith believed that each individual, in pursuing his own enlightened self-interest, unintentionally contributed to the greater good of all. Thus any regulation that interfered with individuals' pursuits was in the end counterproductive. Sharply critical of mercantilistic laws and policies designed to direct economic activity in the interests of the state, Smith believed that more wealth would be created if those regulations were abolished and individuals were free to conduct their economic lives as they saw fit:

> It is only for the sake of profit that any man employs a capital [invests his money] in the support of industry. . . . By directing that industry in such a manner as its produce may be of the greatest value, he intends only his own gain. [But] he is in this, as in many other cases, led by an invisible hand to promote an end which was no part of his intention. By pursuing his own interest he frequently promotes that of the society more effectually than when he really intends to promote it (Book 4, Chapter 2).

On a global scale, then, different countries would produce the goods and services to which they were most suited, and trade those goods and services with others for those things they did not produce themselves. Smith was a pioneer in the concept of comparative advantage. Although in some places *The Wealth of Nations* proved remarkably prescient—there is a famous section on the advantages of the division of labour—Smith had little direct knowledge of the changes that were even then beginning to transform British industry (see Chapter 8).

Today *The Wealth of Nations* is often misread as a defence of capitalism unrestrained by any regulation whatever. To the contrary, Smith argued that merchants and employers continually tended towards monopoly—that is, restraint of economic freedom—and therefore that vigorous regulations were needed to prevent such conspiracies.

History, Human Nature, and Society
Adam Smith's optimistic faith that individuals' pursuit of their own enlightened self-interest would naturally bring about progress for all was a hallmark of mainstream

Enlightenment thought. Indeed, the notion of Enlightenment is inherently progressive. The idea that knowledge was the product of sensory perceptions processed by rational minds (derived in large part from Locke's *Essay Concerning Human Understanding*; see Chapter 5) was an article of faith for most of the philosophes. Empiricism was at the heart of the enlightened quest to formulate natural laws regarding human society, as the physiocrats and Adam Smith had done for economics, and as Montesquieu had done for politics and government. Other thinkers took up parallel quests in other facets of human society. As in the case of religion, however, the more radical thinkers began to undermine the very notions on which the Enlightenment had been based.

If progress was inherent in the very concept of enlightenment, then this progress should also be apparent in facts of history. Indeed, the Enlightenment marked a transformation in the understanding of the past. Now history could be written not only to record the deeds of "great men," to extoll the glories of the past, or to illumine the workings of divine providence, but to shed light on the darkness of the past, to reveal the progress achieved thus far, and by implication to project this historical progress into the future.

Voltaire, as we have seen, wrote a number of historical works whose general theme might be described as the progress of reason and civilization over barbarism, but the most famous historical work of the Enlightenment was probably *The Decline and Fall of the Roman Empire*, a massive six-volume study by the Englishman Edward Gibbon (1737–94). Gibbon famously attributed the fall of the western empire to the influence of "barbarism and religion," arguing that Christianity undermined Roman civic virtue by debasing the value of life in this world.

The notion of history as the story of progress was given its fullest expression by the Marquis of Condorcet (1743–94), whose *Sketch for a Historical Picture of the Progress of the Human Spirit* would be published posthumously in 1795. (Arrested for counter-revolutionary activities during the Reign of Terror, he died in prison in 1794.) Condorcet argued that human society in the eighteenth century, having progressed through a number of historical phases, was now poised on the brink of even further advances. He proposed to demonstrate

> that nature has set no term to the perfection of human faculties; the perfectibility of man is truly infinite; that the progress of this perfectibility, from now onwards independent of any power that might wish to halt it, has no other limit than the duration of the globe upon which nature has cast us. This progress will doubtless vary in speed, but it will never be reversed. . . . [7]

Condorcet was also more radical than the majority of philosophes in calling for the abolition of slavery, political rights for ordinary people, and greater equality for women (see "Voices" below).

A very different approach to history was taken by an obscure Neapolitan professor named Giambattista Vico (1668–1744), who in 1725 published *The New Science*. A devout Catholic, Vico saw in history more than the opportunity to beat Christianity over the head: in his view, history offered knowledge of humanity as it was made by people themselves. History was progressive, but not in the sense intended by Voltaire or Condor-cet. Each past age had its own ways of thinking and expression, and the writing of history required a sensitive and nuanced approach. Rather than condemn myths as superstitious hokum, Vico believed that they could be used to help reconstruct the past:

> The story of the past, instead of being an educative manual, in which reason struggled with ignorance and superstition . . . was an account whose meaning lay within itself, in which any period was as significant as any other.[8]

Vico's work was not widely read or appreciated until the nineteenth century, as it did not conform to the Enlightenment's historical themes of progression out of darkness and a fixed and rational human nature.

The Italian nobleman Cesare Beccaria (1738–94) did for criminology and penol-ogy what Smith had done for economics in establishing the "natural" laws that ought to govern punishment. In his very influential work *On Crimes and Punishments* (1764), he argued for a secular and utilitarian approach. Punishment should not be understood as the divine penalty for sin, but as a means for society to defend itself. Thus punishment should be designed to correct criminal behaviour rather than, as was usually the case, to deter others by inflicting savage punishments in revenge for what were often quite minor crimes. He also argued against both judicial torture and capital punishment. His work was widely read, and its principles were eventually incorporated into legal codes in around the world.

The confidence embodied by Smith, Condorcet, and others began to fray as some thinkers started to push enlightened ideas to the point that they seemed to undercut the basis of the Enlightenment itself. For example, Julien la Mettrie (1709–51) was a physician who, like Holbach, embraced atheism and a purely materialistic worldview. From his per-spective, the human mind is simply a mechanism for processing the information provided by the senses. In *L'Homme machine* (1747) he argued that it was futile to search for mean-ing beyond the physical world:

> Who knows if the reason for the existence of man is not his existence itself. Perhaps chance has thrown him down at a given point on the earth's surface, without our being able to know how or why. . . . We know nothing about nature: causes hidden within nature itself many have produced everything.[9]

In a similar vein, Etienne Bonnot de Condillac (1714–80) in *Treatise on Sensations* (1754), a founding work of modern psychology and anthropology, maintained that reason and "human nature" themselves were the product of sensation and experience, and that know-ledge of the physical world was contingent, limited to appearances:

> Ideas in no way allow us to know beings as they actually are; they merely depict them in terms of their relationship with us, and this alone is enough to prove

the vanity of the efforts of those philosophers who pretend to penetrate into the nature of things.[10]

For his part, Claude Adrien Helvétius (1715–71) in *On the Mind* (1758) proposed that humans had no inborn sense of morality. Extending Locke's concepts of sensation and knowledge, he argued that, since people seek to pursue pleasure and avoid pain, morality was materialist and utilitarian in nature. His work was heavily criticized by other philosophes, including Voltaire and Diderot, and was condemned by both the Catholic Church and the Parlement of Paris as heretical.

REACTION AND ROUSSEAU

Although the eighteenth century is widely considered "the Age of the Enlightenment" or "the Age of Reason," it is important to recognize that not all thinkers believed reason to be the cure for what ailed humanity. Among the skeptics was Jonathan Swift (1667–1745), the author of *Gulliver's Travels* (1726). Although the account of Gulliver's voyage to Lilliput in Part I, with its scathing critique of European political and religious conflicts, seems fully in line with Enlightenment principles, later sections suggest a more critical perspective. In Part III, for example, Gulliver visits the flying island of Laputa, whose inhabitants are engrossed in preposterous scientific experiments with no practical application, including extracting sunbeams from cucumbers and processing excrement in order to reconstitute the original food of which it was composed. And in Part IV Swift demonstrates the impossibility of relying on reason alone. Gulliver is marooned on an island inhabited by two species: the Yahoos, who are human in form but uncivilized and savage, devoid of reason, and the Houyhnhnms, the completely rational horses that rule over the Yahoos. Gulliver, repulsed by the Yahoos, joins a Houyhnhnm's household, where he learns to admire their rational nature. Yet in the end, even though he has some semblance of reason, he is exiled from the island as a savage Yahoo. Thus he returns to England, only to find that he now sees his own family as Yahoos; repulsed by them, he prefers to converse with his horses.

The most penetrating critique of the Enlightenment came from one who had been counted among its ranks: Jean-Jacques Rousseau (1712–78). He was born in Protestant Geneva, the son of a watchmaker. But his mother died a few days later, and his father, having remarried, moved away, virtually abandoning the young Rousseau to a series of foster households. Largely self-educated, he lacked the confidence and social polish of someone like Voltaire.

After moving to Paris in 1742, he became friendly with Diderot. He would contribute many entries to the *Encyclopédie*, several of them on music, in which he had a lifelong interest. But it was the essay he wrote for the contest in the provincial city of Dijon that first brought him to public attention. In his winning answer to the question "Has the restoration of the arts and sciences contributed to the purification of morals?" Rousseau went against the grain of the Enlightenment, arguing that mankind had never been happier and more moral than in its natural state. In his essay, published in 1750 as *A Discourse on the Moral Effects of the Arts and Sciences*, he asserted that progress and civilization in the form of property, government, and social conventions had corrupted humans by alienating them from their natural goodness and purity.

Although Rousseau's writings could be maddeningly inconsistent and even contradictory, this was his central idea. He did not believe that society could fully recapture its lost innocence; yet the appropriate reforms could move them closer to that state. During his lifetime, Rousseau was best known for two novels: *Julie, or the New Heloïse* (1761) and *Emile, or On Education* (1762). The heroine of the former is an aristocratic young woman who has a love affair with her older tutor, St. Preux. She eventually breaks off the affair and marries Wolmar, a wealthy friend of her father, becoming an exemplary wife and mother. St. Preux is eventually hired by Wolmar to tutor his and Julie's children. In the end, Julie sacrifices her own life to save one of her children, thereby atoning for her youthful indiscretion. Told in the form of tear-jerking letters, it attracted a large and passionate following. One adoring reader wrote to Rousseau:

> I dare not tell you the effect it made on me. No, I was past weeping. A sharp pain convulsed me. My heart was crushed. Julie dying was no longer an unknown person. I believed I was her sister, her friend, her Claire. My seizure became so strong that if I had not put the book away I would have been as ill as all those who attended that virtuous woman in her last moments.[11]

In *Emile, or On Education* (1762) Rousseau explored the question of how to educate children without corrupting their natural instincts. The first four sections follow Emile's progress from boyhood through adolescence as he learns from a tutor who stresses experience over books and sees education as development of the moral self. In the fifth, addressing the education of Emile's future wife, Sophie, Rousseau condemned the use of wet nurses and strongly advocated that women breastfeed their own children. But he believed that the women's education should be strictly limited to preparing them to be wives and mothers (see "Voices," below). One of the book's most famous passages is "The Confession of Faith of a Savoyard Vicar," later published separately, in which Rousseau set out his vision of a naturalistic deist religion. Objections to this section led to public burnings of the book in both Paris and Geneva.

Although today Rousseau is best known for his political writings, they attracted relatively little attention during his life. In the *Discourse on the Origins of Inequality Among Men* (1754) he maintained that inequality among men, who in their natural state were equal and good, originated in private property:

> The first man, who after enclosing a piece of ground, took it into his head to say this is mine, and found people simple enough to believe him, was the real founder of civil society. How many crimes, how many wars, how many murders, how many misfortunes and horrors, would that man have saved the

human species, who pulling up the stakes or filling in the ditches should have cried to his fellows: Beware of listening to this impostor; you are lost, if you forget that the fruits of the earth belong equally to us all, and the earth itself to nobody.[12]

Without a doubt, Rousseau's most influential work is *The Social Contract* (1762), in which he explored the nature and purpose of government. Beginning with the famous words "Man is born free, yet we see him everywhere in chains," he set out his vision of an ideal political order, one in which no man would be subject to another except by his own consent. In contrast to Hobbes and Locke, according to whom people cede some (Locke) or all (Hobbes) of their natural liberty to a sovereign external to themselves, Rousseau argued that people cede their natural liberty as individuals to the community as a whole, which alone is sovereign. In other words, every man is both a subject and a ruler, inasmuch as he himself is part of the community to which he has given up his natural liberty as an individual. If his private desires conflict with his desires as a member of the community, the "general will," true freedom consists in putting the general will ahead of the private. A famous passage makes the jarring claim that the individual can be forced to be free:

> In order then that the social compact may not be a vain formulary, it tacitly includes this engagement, which alone can give force to the others, that whoever refuses to obey the general will shall be constrained to do so by the whole body; which means nothing else than that he will be forced to be free; for such is the condition which, uniting every citizen to his native land, guarantees him from all personal dependence, a condition that ensures the control and working of the political machine. . . . [13]

Rousseau was under no illusion that his system could be implemented in eighteenth-century Europe. It was an ideal towards which to strive, but was achievable only in a small republic such as his home town of Geneva, to whose citizens the work was dedicated. It nevertheless represented a new vision of politics in which the fundamental values are morality, civic virtue, and patriotism rather than hierarchy and obedience. *The Social Contract* was largely ignored during Rousseau's lifetime, but its language of general will and civic virtue would be taken up by the revolutionaries of 1789. Thus, paradoxically, Rousseau has been seen as a champion both of liberty and of totalitarianism.

Rousseau's emphasis on the natural goodness of man and the corruption of civilization put him at odds with many philosophes. Voltaire called *Emile* a "hodgepodge of a silly wet nurse in four volumes. . . . He [Rousseau] says as many hurtful things against the philosophes as against Jesus Christ, but the philosophes will be more indulgent than the priests." Nevertheless, he did appreciate the "Confession of Faith of a Savoyard Vicar": "forty pages against Christianity, among the boldest ever known . . . it is regrettable that

VOICES

Enlightenment and Gender

In general, Enlightenment thinking on gender was in line with that of virtually all the religious, scientific, political, and medical authorities who believed that women were inferior to men. As Rousseau put it in *Emile* (1762):

> In the union of the sexes each contributes equally to the common aim, but not in the same way.... One ought to be active and strong, the other passive and weak. One must necessarily will and be able; it suffices that the other put up little resistance.
>
> There is no parity between the two sexes in regard to the consequences of sex. The male is male only at certain moments. The female is female her whole life....
>
> The strictness of the relative duties of the two sexes is not and cannot be the same. When woman complains on this score about unjust man-made inequality, she is wrong. This inequality is not a human institution—or at least, it is the work not of prejudice but of reason.
>
> All the faculties common to the two sexes are not equally distributed between them; but taken together, they balance out. Woman is worth more as a woman and less as a man. Wherever she makes use of her rights, she has the advantage. Wherever she wants to usurp ours, she remains beneath us.

Jean-Jacques Rousseau, *Emile, or On Education*, trans. Allan Bloom (New York: Basic Books, 1979), pp. 358, 361, 363–4.

Among the few dissenting voices was Condorcet. He was hardly a feminist; he believed that women "might not be able to contribute to scientific progress by discoveries ... of the first order, which require prolonged study and extraordinary force of mind." Nevertheless, he directly opposed Rousseau's essentialist views on the nature of women:

> This exclusion [of women from political rights] must be an act of tyranny, unless it can be proved that the natural rights of women are not absolutely the same as those of men, or that women are not capable of exercising these rights.
>
> Now the rights of men result simply from the fact that they are sentient beings, capable of acquiring moral ideas and of reasoning concerning these ideas. Women, having these same qualities, must necessarily possess equal rights. Either no individual has any true rights, or all have the same....
>
> It would be difficult to prove that women are incapable of exercising the rights of citizenship. Why should individuals exposed to pregnancy and other passing indispositions be unable to exercise rights which no one had dreamed of withholding from persons who have the gout all winter or catch cold quickly? ...
>
> It has been said that women ... obey their feelings rather than their conscience. This observation ... proves nothing. It is not nature, but education, and social existence,

that causes this difference. . . . The things with which they are occupied with and upon which they act are precisely those which are regulated by natural propriety and sentiment. It is therefore unjust to allege, as an excuse for continuing to refuse women the enjoyment of their natural rights, grounds which only have a kind of reality because women do not exercise these rights.

If reasons such as these were admitted against women, it would also be necessary to deprive of the rights of citizenship that portion of the people who, because they are occupied in constant labor, can neither acquire knowledge nor exercise their reason. . . . The various aristocracies have had nothing but similar pretexts as their foundation or excuse. . . .

From "On the Admission of Women to the Rights of Citizenship" in Keith M. Baker (ed.), *Condorcet: Selected Writings* (Indianapolis: Bobbs-Merrill, 1976), pp. 100, 102.

Among the causes of the progress of the human mind that are of the utmost importance to the general happiness, we must number the complete annihilation of the prejudices that have brought about an inequality of rights between men and women, an inequality fatal even to the party in whose favour it works. It is vain for us to look for a justification of this principle in any differences of physical organization, intellect, or moral sensibility between men and women. This inequality has its origin solely in an abuse of strength. . . .

From "Sketch for a Historical Picture of the Progress of the Human Mind," in Keith M. Baker (ed.), *Condorcet: Selected Writings* (Indianapolis: Bobbs-Merrill, 1976), p. 274.

The Enlightenment has typically been portrayed as a male phenomenon, to which women contributed primarily as hostesses of salons. Towards the end of the century, however, more and more women made their own contributions, none more profoundly than Mary Wollstonecraft (1759–97). When the revolutionary government denied women full political participation, she responded with *A Vindication of the Rights of Woman* (1792):

[Is it] not inconsistent and unjust to subjugate women . . .? Who made man the exclusive judge, if woman partake with him the gift of reason? . . .

To account for, and excuse the tyranny of man, many ingenious arguments have been brought forward to prove, that the two sexes, in the acquirement of virtue, ought to aim at attaining a very different character: or, to speak explicitly, women are not allowed to have sufficient strength of mind to acquire what really deserves the name of virtue. Yet it should seem, allowing them to have souls, that there is but one way appointed by Providence to lead *mankind* to either virtue or happiness. . . .

[Rousseau's] character of Sophia is, undoubtedly a captivating one, thought it appears to me grossly unnatural; however, it is not the superstructure, but the foundation of her character, the principles on which her education was built, that I mean to attack. . . .

Mary Wollstonecraft, *A Vindication of the Rights of Woman*, 2nd ed., ed. Carol H. Poston (New York: W.W. Norton, 1988), pp. 4–5, 19, 24.

they should have been written by a knave." On reading *The Discourse on the Origins of Inequality* Voltaire famously wrote to its author:

> I have received, sir, your new book against the human species, and I thank you for it . . . no one has ever been so witty as you are in trying to turn us into brutes: to read your book make one long to go on all fours. Since, however, it is now some sixty years since I gave up the practice, I feel that it is unfortunately impossible for me to resume it.[14]

Rousseau was an influential voice against the Enlightenment's optimistic faith in reason alone. His insistence on the importance of emotion and untaught feeling would be reflected in the emerging Romantic movement in the arts and literature. His belief in the goodness of mankind in its natural state, the "noble savage," was a counterweight to the assumption that Europeans were inherently superior to other civilizations (see Chapter 11). His convictions regarding the innocence of children and the importance of education as emotional and moral development would also have a significant impact on family life, counteracting the traditional view of children as willful sinners in need of strict discipline.

SCIENCE IN THE ENLIGHTENMENT

As we have noted, there are strong links between the Scientific Revolution of the seventeenth century and the Enlightenment of the eighteenth; the very core of the enlightened project was the application of scientific and rational analysis to human society and institutions. In the most general sense, scientific ways of thinking displaced theology, at least among a portion of the literate elite; a number of the philosophes took a strong interest in science; much of the *Encyclopédie* was devoted to science and technology; and membership in scientific academies was *de rigueur* in certain circles.

The voyages of discovery, beginning in the fifteenth and sixteenth century and continuing into the eighteenth (see Chapters 5 and 11), revealed the existence of countless plants and animals previously unknown to Europeans. Growing knowledge of the globe led many people to collect specimens themselves and attempt to classify them. Among them was the Swedish botanist and physician Carl Linnaeus (1707–78), who devised the taxonomic system—still used today—according to which plants and animals are identified by class, order, genus, species, and variety. He saw in the world of living organisms a parallel to Newton's universe: a harmonious and complete system created by a benevolent God, governed by immutable universal laws. His system of taxonomy was therefore seen as revealing the real relationships between creatures, uncovering the mind of God in the realm of the living as Newton had for the heavens.

Linnaeus's views were challenged by Georges-Louis Buffon (1707–88), whose massive *Natural History of the Earth* was published in thirty-six volumes between 1749 and 1788. Unlike Linnaeus, Buffon believed that nature did indeed have a history, that species were not immutable but had changed over time, and that any taxonomic system was simply a human convenience, and could not reveal fundamental truths about nature. An early forerunner of Darwin, he believed that all beings had evolved from similar origins over a much longer time period than had previously been imagined. One of Buffon's disciples was Jean-Baptiste Lamarck (1744–1829), who proposed that organisms evolved as individuals adapted to local conditions and then passed on to their offspring the characteristics they acquired through adaptation.

Chemistry too saw significant developments in the eighteenth century. As we saw in Chapter 5, Newton had taken a keen interest in "alchemy." The German physician Georg Ernest Stahl (1659–1734) had theorized that combustion and other chemical processes were the result of the exchange of an omnipresent substance called phlogiston. Thus wood burned when heated because, in Aristotelian terms, the element fire was part of its composition. As it burned, it gave off phlogiston into the surrounding air. The wood stopped burning when the surrounding air was saturated with phlogiston and could absorb no more. The English dissenting theologian and clergyman Joseph Priestley (1733–1804) was able to show that the air we breathe was not a single substance, but was made up of several components ("gases" to us, "airs" in the eighteenth century). Through experimentation, he discovered that one of these "airs" supported more intense combustion for a longer period of time. This "dephlogisticated air" (which we call oxygen) improved combustion because it allowed the burning substance to expel more phlogiston more quickly.

The French chemist Antoine Lavoisier (1743–94) turned phlogiston theory on its head. Discovering that combustion increased weight, even though the expulsion of phlogiston should have decreased it, he established that something in the surrounding air was absorbed. He also discovered that "oxygen" (he coined the word) was responsible for other chemical processes as well, such as the one we call the oxidation of metals. Dephlogisticated air was not simply regular air with the phlogiston removed, but rather an active agent in itself, capable of combining with other substances to form new substances. He called irreducible substances such as oxygen "elements," and in so doing established modern chemistry.

Churches and Religion in the Eighteenth Century

To think of the eighteenth century exclusively as the "Age of Reason" or "Enlightenment" would be to ignore not only the vast majority of Europeans—Catholic and Protestant—who held traditional religious views, but the importance of several movements of religious revival that ran directly contrary to Enlightenment secularism.

As we saw in Chapter 4, by the latter half of the 1600s religion was no longer a primary consideration in relations between rulers and states. Yet almost all governments continued to insist on the importance of uniformity not only of religious practice, but of belief, and the churches did their best to ensure the orthodoxy of their followers. This was the concept of confessionalization, introduced in Chapter 3. Yet apart from the solidly Catholic lands of Italy, Portugal, and Spain, and the solidly Lutheran Scandinavian states, there were very few countries without dissenting religious minorities. In France, despite the revocation of the Edict of Nantes in 1685, there remained a substantial Huguenot minority. In addition, although Jansenism had been officially suppressed in the early 1700s, it retained the support of some segments among the elite, and continued to be a troublesome religious and political issue throughout the eighteenth century (see Chapter 10). In Germany, although the north was generally Protestant and the south Catholic, the fortunes of war and dynastic inheritance meant that boundaries were frequently redrawn, and as a result there was hardly a region without a religious minority. Although in many ways the Habsburg lands had become the centre of Counter-Reformation spirituality, Bohemia, Moravia, Hungary, Transylvania, and even Austria itself all had Protestant minorities. Habsburg victories against the Ottomans ensured that Habsburg territories were becoming more religiously diverse, rather than less. Although officially Calvinist, the Dutch Republic was home to substantial numbers of Catholics, Mennonites, and Jews, all of whom were allowed to practise their faiths in private. In England, membership in the official Church of England was required in order to run for Parliament, to serve as an officer in the armed forces, to attend university, or to hold a government job. In general, however, Protestant Dissenters or Nonconformists were allowed to worship freely; and although Catholicism was officially proscribed, active persecution of Catholics was rare.

Towards the end of the eighteenth century, signs of genuine religious toleration, as opposed to grudging coexistence, became more common. No doubt this trend reflected the influence of Enlightenment thought, which found a receptive audience among educated elites and even some rulers, the "enlightened despots" (see Chapter 10). Rulers also began to realize that it was in their interest to promote tolerance, since tempering the influence of their official churches could enhance their own power, and that integrating religious minorities into the society and economy would increase productivity and add to their revenues. Frederick the Great of Prussia (1740–86), the nominally Calvinist ruler of a largely Lutheran population, allowed greater toleration of Catholics, and for the most part left Jewish populations alone, though without granting them official toleration. Holy Roman Emperor Joseph II (r. 1780–90) in 1781 decreed official toleration for Lutheran, Calvinist, and Orthodox populations in the heavily Catholic Habsburg lands, and later extended the policy to Jews as well, despite significant opposition to the move. In France, the 1787 Edict of Toleration ended legal discrimination against the Huguenots. And in England, although Catholics would not achieve full legal toleration until 1829, legal restrictions were increasingly ignored after the failed Jacobite rebellion of 1745, despite periodic outbursts of popular antagonism such as the Gordon Riots of 1780 (see Chapter 10).

While the Catholic Counter-Reformation is usually thought of as a sixteenth-century phenomenon, some have argued that its reforms did not filter down to the masses of Catholic Europe until the eighteenth century. Millions of lay Catholics continued to join and support lay confraternities (now firmly subordinated to priestly authority) dedicated to pious activities such as pilgrimages, charitable works, education, and maintenance of churches. A particular form of Catholic devotion, the Sacred Heart of Jesus, gained a new popularity in the eighteenth century: more than 1000 confraternities were established in France and Italy alone between 1694 and 1769. Pilgrimage sites became more popular than ever, and many new ones were established, most of them devoted either to Eucharistic devotion (adoration of the consecrated host as the body of Christ) or to the Virgin Mary; the shrine of Mariazell in Austria alone attracted hundreds of thousands of pilgrims every year. In Catholic Europe, the numbers of clergy reached all-time highs in the eighteenth century; France had more than 8000 monastic houses, and the Habsburg lands 2500.

Assessing the spirituality of lay people is more difficult than counting monasteries, but here too most of the evidence suggests that traditional practice and belief remained strong among lay Catholics, at least until relatively late in the century. Participation in the sacraments of baptism, confession, marriage, and extreme unction was nearly universal. Although it is impossible to know exactly how people understood the sacraments, the expansion of general literacy as well as religious education would suggest that knowledge of the faith was greater than ever before. The Council of Trent had decreed that, at a minimum, all Catholics must confess and receive Mass annually at Easter; in the eighteenth century, attendance at Easter Mass reached 95 per cent in many parishes.

Even so, there is some evidence that change was under way later in the eighteenth century. In a very influential study, the French historian Michel Vovelle examined wills written in the southern region of Provence.[15] In the first half of the eighteenth century, more than 80 per cent of wills made elaborate provisions for requiem masses and devotional candles, as well as funeral processions and so on. But after about 1760, such provisions declined dramatically in both urban and rural settings. What this means is open to debate. According to some historians, including Vovelle, it points to a process of "dechristianization" on the eve of the French Revolution, especially among literate urbanites. According to others, it is more reflective of a shift in Catholic piety, away from exuberant external displays and towards a more interior and reflective religion. If this was the case, it could be seen as a sign of the influence of Jansenist principles, despite the official suppression of the movement itself. A similar trend can be seen in the work of Luigi Antonio Muratori (1672–1750), an Italian priest and scholar whose treatise *On the Well-Ordered Devotion of Christians* (1747) called for a simpler and less flamboyant popular religion. The Church as a whole had become too wealthy and worldly; monks and nuns were too numerous and idle, parish priests should be better trained (and paid), and people should be encouraged to read the scriptures for themselves. In addition, Muratori argued that the Jesuits exercised too much influence on the Church. These roughly "Jansenist" views have been taken by some historians to constitute a veritable "Catholic Enlightenment," elements of which were influential in Italy, the Habsburg lands, and southern Germany.

The Jesuits did play an extremely important role in the Tridentine Catholic Church. Active as missionaries around the world, they were the dominant force in Catholic education, not only in secondary schools but in in many universities. The fact that many rulers had Jesuits as their religious advisers or confessors earned them a reputation for power-mongering, and their ability to find a moral justification for virtually any course of action attracted accusations of ethical casuistry. Many devout Catholics who saw the Jesuits as morally lax blamed the influence of the rational ideals of the Enlightenment.

Jesuit missionary activities also attracted criticism. In South America, Spanish and Portuguese colonizers objected to Jesuits' efforts to protect indigenous people from exploitation and allow converts to practise Christianity without adopting European culture or customs. In the eyes of their enemies, the Jesuits' accommodation of indigenous customs compromised the essential truth of Christianity. In 1752, when a territory formerly under Spanish control was about to be traded to a much more oppressive Portuguese regime, Jesuit missionaries led the local people to what is now Paraguay, where together they established a kind of self-governing state. (This was the historical background to the 1986 film *The Mission* with Robert De Niro and Jeremy Irons.)

Jesuit missions in China also attracted criticism. Like many Europeans, Jesuits were impressed by Chinese culture and philosophy, elements of which dovetailed with both Christian and classical ethics. In the previous century the Jesuit Matteo Ricci (1552–1610) had accommodated several elements of Chinese culture, wearing traditional Chinese robes, for example, and allowing converts to continue the custom of ancestor veneration on the grounds that it was a cultural rather than a religious tradition. In the eyes of rival missionary orders, however, such "pagan" practices could not be tolerated, and they asked Rome to intervene. Over the course of the seventeenth century, the papacy issued some rulings in favour of both parties, but in the early eighteenth century it definitively condemned the so-called "Chinese Rites," leading China to retaliate by banning Christianity and persecuting converts.

In the latter part of the century the Jesuits' enemies prevailed. They were expelled from Portugal in 1759, from France in 1764, and from Spain and Naples three years later. Also in 1767, the government of the otherwise extremely devout Habsburg Empress Maria Theresa (r. 1740–80) confiscated the Society's property to fund a public school system (see Chapter 10). Finally, in 1773, under pressure from numerous Catholic rulers Pope Clement XIV suppressed the Society altogether, although it would be re-established in 1814.

Protestantism too experienced significant changes with the rise of reform movements within the established denominations, including Pietism and the Moravian Brethren in Germany and Methodism in England. As diverse as these movements were, they shared several common roots: dissatisfaction with sterile theological debates in the established churches, a sense that the latter were neglecting the spiritual welfare of ordinary people, and a reaction against the tendency, in official circles, to accommodate the rationalizing spirit of the Enlightenment.

By 1700 the established Lutheran churches of the north German states had been effectively incorporated into state structures, becoming at once more worldly and more interested in formal theology than in morality and inner spirituality. The "father" of Pietism was Philipp Jakob Spener (1635–1705), a German Lutheran pastor whose critique of those tendencies led Elector Frederick III (later King Frederick I) of Brandenburg-Prussia to offer him a position at the newly founded University of Halle. As the Calvinist ruler of a largely Lutheran population, Frederick hoped that Pietism, by combining a Calvinist emphasis on personal piety and morality with the Lutheran theology of salvation through faith alone, might offer a way of strengthening the relationship between ruler and people. Among the most influential figures at the University of Halle was August Hermann Francke (1663–1727), who sent Spener's works to Lutheran pastors throughout Brandenburg–Prussia and actively solicited support from members of the elite. To promote the development of inner spirituality, Francke and the Pietists encouraged the formation of small study and prayer groups, and established schools, orphanages, a printing press, and a library. Although foreign missions had been rare among Protestants, Pietist missionaries were soon working throughout central Europe and in North America. When Frederick William I (r. 1713–40) succeeded his father, he continued to support Pietism, requiring that all Lutheran pastors spend two years at the University of Halle.

Pietism did not have the same impact elsewhere in Germany, where the rulers did not welcome critiques of luxury and conspicuous consumption. Lutheran clergy discriminated against Pietists, and in states such as Saxony, Pietist clergy were purged, their schools closed, and their study groups forbidden.

Nevertheless, Pietism found a convert in Count Nicolaus von Zinzendorf (1700–60), who opened his estates in Saxony to a group of Moravian Brethren (spiritual descendants of the Hussites) after they were expelled from their homes in what is now the Czech Republic. They established a new model community at Herrnhut, where they practised a strict personal morality and sought mystical and spiritual union with Christ. Expelled from Saxony in 1736, Zinzendorf went on to establish Moravian communities across Europe, as well as in England and the New World. The towns of Bethlehem and Nazareth, Pennsylvania, and Salem, North Carolina, were all founded as Moravian communities. Zinzendorf and the Moravians were also heavily involved in missions in such far-flung areas as Greenland, the West Indies, Labrador, South America, and Egypt. As many as half of all the Protestant missionaries active in the eighteenth century may have been Moravians.

Among those influenced by the Moravians was a young Englishman named John Wesley (1703–91), the founder of Methodism. As students at Oxford he and his brother Charles (1707–88) had formed a "Holy Club" to study scripture and pray, and although he was ordained as a minister in the Church of England, he came to believe that the institution had become too closely attached to the elite of English society. The Wesleys took a different path, visiting prisons and caring for the poor and sick. In 1735 Wesley was invited to go to Savannah, Georgia, as a missionary, and during the voyage there he met a group of Moravian missionaries whose faith and morality made a deep impression on him. Embittered by his lack of success in Georgia, on his return to England he sought out the Moravians. In 1738, while attending a Moravian service, he experienced a personal connection with Christ: "I felt my heart strangely warmed. I felt I did trust in Christ, Christ alone for salvation, and an assurance was given me that He had taken away my sins, even mine, and saved me from the law of sin and death." The feeling of certainty and emotional assurance he experienced in that moment of conversion was in a sense a reaction against an official church that emphasized the rationality of religion. It was also distinct from the Calvinist emphasis on predestination, in that Wesley believed that salvation was freely available to all.

John Wesley never intended to break from the Church of England; what he sought was a spiritual revival that would renew it. He and his followers, initially called "methodists" pejoratively, travelled throughout England preaching to large crowds, especially in the growing industrial and mining towns that were underserved by the official church. Congregational hymn singing was an integral part of Methodist worship, and Charles Wesley composed the words to more than six thousand hymns, many of which are still widely used in Christian worship. Although Wesley intended his movement to complement the official church, the religious establishment refused both to ordain Methodist ministers and to admit Methodists to communion. By the time of John Wesley's death in 1791, the Methodists had formed their own church, which would become one of the largest Protestant denominations in the world. Although he was politically conservative, and emphasized moral regeneration and personal morality more than social activism,

John and Charles Wesley preaching in Cornwall. An open-air sermon, with both men and women of different social classes. Note the man overcome with emotion at the lower left.

Following Wesley's own conversion experience, Methodists stressed an inner conviction and assurance of salvation, at a time when the official Church of England, along with Locke, Toland, and others, emphasized "reasonableness." Charles Wesley, who underwent a similar conversion, emphasized the same theme in many hymns:

> And can it be that I should gain
> an interest in the Savior's blood!
> Died he for me? who caused his pain!
> For me? who him to death pursued?
> Amazing love! How can it be
> that thou, my God, shouldst die for me?
>
> Long my imprisoned spirit lay,
> fast bound in sin and nature's night;
> thine eye diffused a quickening ray;
> I woke, the dungeon flamed with light;
> my chains fell off, my heart was free,
> I rose, went forth, and followed thee.
>
> No condemnation now I dread;
> Jesus, and all in him, is mine;
> alive in him, my living Head,
> and clothed in righteousness divine,
> bold I approach th' eternal throne,
> and claim the crown, through Christ my own.

John Wesley strongly supported the movement to abolish the slave trade, and Methodists would become deeply involved in social reform movements for causes such as universal education, temperance, and prison reform.

George Whitefield (1714–70) was a friend and early associate of the Wesleys who later broke with them over theological differences but gained fame as an itinerant evangelist in the American colonies. Preaching to thousands at open-air revival meetings, he was a major figure in the North American movement known as the "Great Awakening."

The eighteenth century also saw significant changes in the lives of European Jews. In 1782 Joseph II granted official toleration to the Jews in the Habsburg lands (see Chapter 10); and in 1784 they were granted permission to reside anywhere in France. As individuals, however, Jews elsewhere continued to face discrimination, especially in Poland and Russia. The Enlightenment was a double-edged sword in this respect, for even though its critique of bigotry and intolerance seemed to support greater toleration for all faiths, philosophes such as Voltaire, Diderot, and Holbach often singled out Judaism as the embodiment of all that they detested about organized religion.

A number of the well-educated and relatively prosperous Jews of western Europe, particularly in Germany, responded to Enlightenment thought by promoting a specifically Jewish Enlightenment known as the *Haskalah*. A leading figure in this movement was Moses Mendelssohn (1729–86). Having trained as a rabbi, he was a scholar of the Talmud (the Jewish religious and legal code), but also studied widely in Christian and secular philosophy, and was acquainted with both the philosopher Immanuel Kant and the dramatist Gotthold Ephraim Lessing (1729–81), whose play *Nathan the Wise* (1779) was one of the first positive portrayals of Judaism in European literature. Eventually settling in Berlin under the protection of Frederick the Great, Mendelssohn was a powerful defender of Judaism who emphasized its essential rationality as a moral code and its consonance with enlightened ideals. Nevertheless, while encouraging his people to embrace their religion, he also urged them to participate fully in European society and culture.

As in the Protestant churches, at the same time that this rational emphasis was developing in Judaism, a more mystical, exuberant, and emotional counterpart was emerging in the form of the Hasidic movement. Founded in Ukraine by Rabbi Israel ben Eliezer (1700–60), also known as the Baal Shem Tov ("master of the good name"; Besht for short), Hasidism (from the Hebrew for "loving kindness") quickly attracted adherents throughout eastern Europe. Hasidic worship included joyous singing and dancing promoting a trance-like state in which worshippers could commune with the Holy.

Education, Literacy, and Literature

We saw in Chapter 1 that literacy began to increase in the sixteenth century. It was not until later in the eighteenth century, however, that some of the more dramatic consequences became evident.

Determining historical rates of literacy is tricky. Historians usually compare the numbers of people who were able to sign their names on documents against those who made a mark such as an "x," but this method has a number of potential pitfalls. In early modern Europe, reading was generally taught before writing, so there must have been many people who could read to some degree but could not sign their names. Conversely, some people were probably able to painstakingly reproduce a signature without being able to read. Women were undoubtedly less literate than men, but since they would have had fewer occasions to sign their names, the gender gap in literacy is hard to determine. Even so, the overall trend is unmistakable: by the end of the eighteenth century, more Europeans were literate than ever before.

In general, Protestants were more literate than Catholics, men than women, and city-dwellers than country folk. By the 1750s approximately 65 per cent of Scottish men could read, up from 25 per cent a century earlier. In England literacy among men doubled over the same period, from 30 to 60 per cent, and women's literacy rate reached 35 per cent. Overall rates were lower in France, but increased by similar factors. Between the late seventeenth and late eighteenth centuries, male literacy rates rose from 29 to 47 per cent, and female from 14 to 27 per cent. In Paris on the eve of the French Revolution, roughly 80 per cent of men could read, as could 40 per cent of women. Sweden had the highest rates of literacy in Europe prior to 1800, probably approaching 100 per cent.[16]

As one would expect, literacy rates varied by occupation and social class. In Germany and England almost all male landowners were literate, but the rate fell to about half among domestic servants, and to less than one-third among peasants. Highly skilled workers such as goldsmiths and metal workers were more literate than their less skilled counterparts.

How did literacy spread? Clearly, significant resources must have gone into education, but the nature of those resources and the patterns of education varied dramatically. By the sixteenth century, most towns of any size in western Europe would have had a school for the sons of the elite; in France these were called *collèges* and in Germany *gymnasia*. Some were run by city governments, others by private individuals or foundations. In preparation for university, boys would learn Latin and perhaps a smattering of Greek, and become familiar with the canon of classical and Christian literature. It was through these schools that humanism became the common currency among urban elites.

The Reformations gave additional impetus to education. Protestant reformers like Luther believed that individual Christians should be able to read and study the Bible for themselves. Virtually every Protestant state in Germany ordered the establishment of primary schools to teach the basics of literacy and Christian piety, although implementation of those orders took time. In 1686 the Swedish Royal Law not only subordinated the Lutheran Church to the royal government, but required parents to teach their children to read. As a result, literacy rates in Sweden were the highest in Europe.

Although, contrary to popular belief, the Roman Catholic Church did not forbid individual Bible reading, it did not promote the practice as Protestant churches did. The Jesuits placed a very strong emphasis on education, and in Catholic jurisdictions they not only established many new schools but took over many existing ones. By 1556 the order was already running thirty-three schools in seven countries. Other religious orders were also active in both boys' and girls' education.

Outside the cities, the picture is less clear. Local pastors and priests were expected to conduct catechism classes, and some also endeavoured to teach basic literacy. Independent schoolmasters and teachers also ran schools, but they depended on tuition payments from parents who in many cases relied on their children's labour to help support the family, and therefore were reluctant to let them devote time and energy to schooling, let alone to pay for it.

In the course of the eighteenth century many countries sought to broaden access to education. This effort was largely driven by the political philosophy known as cameralism (see Chapter 10), which advocated regulation of all aspects of society in order to increase productivity and thereby enhance both general prosperity and government revenue. King Frederick William I of Prussia (r. 1713–40) decreed that all children should attend school, although enforcement was not universal. In the Habsburg territories, where education had been essentially a Jesuit monopoly, the suppression of the order in 1773 led to greater government involvement. In 1775 Empress Maria Theresa issued a General School Ordinance that provided government subsidies for a school in every community, with compulsory attendance for children and teachers appointed by the government in order to guarantee Catholic orthodoxy. Again, though, implementation and enforcement proved difficult, and a 1781 census of Bohemia and Austria indicated that less than a third of eligible children were actually enrolled. In fact, universal primary education was not achieved anywhere in Europe before the nineteenth century.

A sharp increase in printed material in the eighteenth century was no doubt due in part to the increase in literacy. Much of this material took the form of flimsy, inexpensive books known in English as chapbooks and in France as *livres bleus*. The latter name referred to a collection called the *Bibliothèque bleue*, published in the city of Troyes, which had cheap blue paper covers and were sold by itinerant peddlers. Most of the texts were of traditional kind: works of religious devotion, adventure tales of knights in shining armour, and practical works such as almanacs. There were also the precursors of newspapers and magazines: commentaries on current events, many of which, like modern supermarket tabloids, specialized in scandal. Even though most countries except for England imposed censorship on the publishing industry, such works were printed and sold illegally. Historian Robert Darnton estimates that this underground trade accounted for 50 per cent of all the titles and 20 per cent of all the books sold in later eighteenth-century France.

According to some historians, people in the eighteenth century not only read more, but began to read differently. In the past, when books were more expensive, people tended to read the same few books over and over (especially the Bible), but now books became another consumer commodity. One of the chief manifestations of this "reading revolution" was the huge growth in popularity of novels. Book-length works of fiction in prose had not been unknown, but their numbers and variety reached new heights in the eighteenth century. Among the most popular were Daniel Defoe's *Robinson Crusoe* (1719), a realistic account of a castaway's life on a desert island; Samuel Richardson's sentimental, moralizing tales *Pamela* (1740) and *Clarissa* (1753); and Henry Fielding's *Tom Jones* (1749), the humorous, sometimes bawdy story of a likeable rogue. One French bestseller was Rousseau's *Julie*; another was Louis-Sébastien Mercier's *The Year 2440* (1770), a utopian critique of his own time set far in the future.

If the early modern centuries were a time of dramatic growth in education at the popular level, for universities it was largely a period of stagnation. As was the case with humanism in the Renaissance period, both the Scientific Revolution and the Enlightenment took place largely outside the universities—in some ways even in opposition to them. While in England and France universities became the preserve of the idle rich, in Scandinavia and the Protestant areas of Germany they were devoted primarily to the training of theologians and pastors, and in Italy, Spain, and Catholic Germany they were dominated by teaching orders, especially the Jesuits. Yet there were some important exceptions. In the Protestant states of Brandenburg–Prussia and Hanover, the universities of Halle and Göttingen were founded in 1694 and 1734 respectively to train civil servants for the emerging cameralist state, and their curricula emphasized agriculture, forestry, and mining, in addition to law and history. In Scotland too, the universities of Glasgow and Edinburgh managed to escape the stultifying blanket of tradition. Glasgow in particular was the home of some of the Scottish Enlightenment's brightest lights, including David Hume and Adam Smith.

Chapter Conclusion

The eighteenth century clearly played a central role in the formation of the modern western world. While literate elites increasingly looked to science rather than religion to make sense of the universe and humanity's place in it, some Christians sought to accommodate their faith to reason, while others reacted against this tendency by emphasizing inner spirituality and personal morality. By the end of the eighteenth century, however, European society was unmistakably more secular and less religious than at the beginning.

The extent to which enlightened ideas penetrated the broader society is unclear. Evidence that these ideas were debated in taverns and coffeehouses is not hard to find. But there is also ample evidence that the overwhelming majority of ordinary people remained highly traditional in their culture and beliefs.

Increasing educational opportunities and literacy certainly opened up the possibility for enlightened ideas to spread beyond the elite members of society. Massive investments in education were motivated in part by rulers' desire to enhance the productive capacity of their subjects, and thereby increase their own revenues, and in part by the desire to produce better Christians, who would also be more obedient subjects. What was not foreseen was that once people have learned to read, there is no longer any way to control what they read—or what they write. In this sense, the expansion of education may have backfired. Similarly, the expansion of the public sphere created an arena for the expression of public opinion that by definition was beyond the control of political or religious authorities.

However they might have differed regarding politics and government, the philosophes generally agreed that the purpose of government was the good of the governed rather than that of the governing class. Men (and women too, according to some) had universal rights, independent of time and place, which governments were put into place to safeguard. Although this concept was not entirely novel in the 1700s, by the latter part of the century it would dominate political discourse, helping to foment both the American and French Revolutions.

Much the same may be said of the Enlightenment view of progress. Firmly rooted in the Scientific Revolution that had begun to reveal the workings of the physical world, enlightened thinkers sought to apply scientific methods to the problems of humanity. Of course, the very notion of Enlightenment—the light of the present dispelling the darkness of the past—is inherently progressive. Stated most plainly by Condorcet, it would soon become an article of faith among educated Europeans that things not only can get better with time, but that they normally do. If we can now see some of the problems that came with that progress, this by no means diminishes the impact that the Enlightenment had in its time, and that it continues to have in ours.

Questions for Critical Thought

1. What aspects of the established order did the Enlightenment threaten most acutely?
2. Were the philosophes realistic in their ambitions to reform society? What parts of their "program" seem most and least realistic?
3. Do you see any tensions or contradictions in the enlightened thought?
4. What were the long-term consequences of increasing literacy among ordinary people?
5. Which elements of the Enlightenment seem most relevant to today? Which seem least relevant?

Weblinks

Fordham University, Enlightenment:
http://legacy.fordham.edu/halsall/mod/modsbook10.asp

Encyclopedia of Diderot and d'Alembert Collaborative Translation Project:
http://quod.lib.umich.edu/d/did/

Further Reading

Burke, Peter. *Popular Culture in Early Modern Europe.* London: Temple Smith, 1978. The essential study of the changing culture of ordinary people.

Darnton, Robert. *The Great Cat Massacre and Other Episodes in French Cultural History.* New York: Basic Books, 1984. A series of classic essays.

Edelstein, Dan. *The Enlightenment: A Genealogy.* Chicago: University of Chicago Press, 2010. Re-examines the roots of the Enlightenment as a way of restoring its historical context in order to understand what it meant in the eighteenth century.

Habermas, Jürgen. *The Structural Transformation of the Public Sphere.* Trans. Thomas Burger. Cambridge Mass.: MIT Press, 1991. The classic work.

Hempton, David. *Methodism: Empire of the Spirit.* New Haven: Yale University Press, 2006. The best study of John Wesley and his movement.

Munck, Thomas. *The Enlightenment: A Comparative Social History, 1721–1794.* London: Arnold, 2000. Examines the impact of the Enlightenment outside the intellectual elite.

Outram, Dorinda. *The Enlightenment,* 3rd ed. Cambridge: Cambridge University Press, 2013. The best brief overview, with an excellent annotated bibliography.

Ward, W.R. *Christianity under the Ancien Régime, 1648–1789.* Cambridge: Cambridge University Press, 1999. Focuses on beliefs and practices rather than institutions.

Notes

1. John Robertson, *The Case for the Enlightenment: Scotland and Naples 1680–1760* (Cambridge: Cambridge University Press, 2005), pp. 1–2.
2. I enclose "scientific" in quotation marks, because it was not until the nineteenth century that "science" came to be used in our sense of the word: that is, as a distinct form of inquiry governed by its own methods. The early modern term for what we call "science" was "natural philosophy": the branch of philosophy that dealt with the natural world.
3. Keith M. Baker (ed.), *Condorcet: Selected Writings* (Indianapolis: Bobbs-Merrill, 1976), p. 258.
4. Dorinda Outram, *The Enlightenment,* 3rd ed. (Cambridge: Cambridge University Press, 2013), p. 100.
5. S.G. Tallentyre, *Voltaire in His Letters: Being a Selection from His Correspondence* (London: G.P. Putnam's Sons, 1919), p. 258.
6. Cited in Norman Hampson, *The Enlightenment: An Evaluation of Its Assumptions, Attitudes and Values* (London: Penguin, 1968), p. 160.

7. Keith M. Baker (ed.), *Condorcet: Selected Writings* (Indianapolis: Bobbs–Merrill, 1976), p. 211.
8. Hampson, p. 236.
9. Quoted in Hampson, p. 93.
10. Quoted in Outram, p. 104
11. Robert Darnton, *The Great Cat Massacre and Other Episodes in French Cultural History* (New York: Viking, 1984), p. 243.
12. Jean-Jacques Rousseau, *The Social Contract and Discourse on the Origin of Inequality*, ed. Lester G. Crocker (New York: Pocket Books, 1967), pp. 211–12.
13. Rousseau, *The Social Contract*, p. 22.
14. Quoted in Ben Ray Redmond (ed.), *The Portable Voltaire* (Harmondsworth: Penguin, 1949), p. 493.
15. Michel Vovelle, *Piété baroque et déchristianisation en Provence au XVIIIe siècle* (Paris: Seuil, 1978).
16. Thomas Munck, *The Enlightenment: A Comparative Social History* (London: Arnold, 2000), p. 48.

10

The Eighteenth-Century State System

In the realm of politics and government, as in those of the economy, society, culture, and religion, the eighteenth century saw significant transformations. In 1700 the *ancien régime* seemed as solid as ever: the vast majority of Europeans were ruled by absolute monarchs of various descriptions, supported by the privileged orders of the aristocracy and the church. Yet by 1800 a revolutionary tide that had begun in France—the epitome of absolute monarchy a mere seventy-five years earlier—had swept the old order away. With hindsight we can identify the origins of this tectonic shift, but they were almost completely invisible to contemporaries, who had no reason to suspect that the future would differ much from the past. Although the factors that led to these changes achieved a kind of critical mass in the course of the eighteenth century, their origins lay in earlier times.

In thinking about eighteenth-century European states, therefore, we confront a paradox. From the perspective of the seventeenth century, the European states of the eighteenth certainly appear much more stable and orderly. This is true whether we look at their internal politics or at their relations with each other. Yet by the end of that century the French Revolution would have not only overthrown the oldest and seemingly most stable monarchy in Europe, but challenged the monarchical order throughout Europe and launched the two decades of ideologically driven conflict known as the revolutionary and Napoleonic wars. Historians have therefore been drawn like moths to the bright lights of the revolution and, instead of looking at the eighteenth century on its own terms, have tended to treat it as merely a prologue. Seen in the light of its fate, the *ancien régime* appears pre-ordained for destruction and revolution becomes inevitable. This chapter will attempt to highlight the continuities without ignoring the roots of the dramatic changes to come.

Over the course of the century, several important themes emerge. One is the continued development of the modern sovereign state under the auspices of hereditary monarchy. As we saw in Chapter 7, European states were already behaving as sovereign entities in their relations with one another. Internally, however, it was still hard to distinguish between the ruler and the state. That began to change in the 1700s, as the state came to be seen as something separate from the ruler and dynasty, with interests and values of its own. Whereas Louis XIV is said to have declared himself the embodiment of the state—"*L'État, c'est moi*" ("I am the state")—Frederick the Great of Prussia (r. 1740–86) declared, "The ruler is the first servant of the state." While divine-right monarchy was still the order of the day, subjects and rulers alike increasingly thought of the ruler's power in terms of its practical utility, in many cases under the influence of enlightened ideas. When Frederick said that his crown was simply a hat that let in the rain, he was deliberately setting aside the traditional basis of monarchical power and replacing it with the concept of service to the state, utility, and public welfare. The eighteenth century thus saw an uncoupling of the state and its development from hereditary monarchy.

Another major theme that emerged in the eighteenth century was the continuing expansion of the bureaucracy's reach into the lives of the state's subjects. This was the product of several factors, among them the increasingly intense competition among eighteenth-century states. The fact that this competition was now global in scale necessitated not only the extraction of more tax revenue from subjects, but the rationalization and streamlining of the state, in order to make it as efficient as possible in its use of resources. The dominant economic assumptions of mercantilism, combined with the expansion of bureaucracies, also led to greater involvement of governments in their subjects' lives. So too did the concern for religious and moral reform and the continuing quest for religious uniformity. As we will see below, many of these themes dovetailed with the prescriptions of "enlightened despotism," but rulers did not need to be devoted to enlightened principles in order to adopt them in the interests of strengthening the state. The result was what one historian has called "the well-ordered police state" (in this context "police state" refers not to dictatorship, but to "administration in the broadest sense, that is, institutional means . . . to secure peaceful and orderly existence for the population").[1]

Paradoxically, another major theme was growing consciousness of individual rights. In early modern Europe, rights had belonged for the most part to groups rather than individuals; this was the essence of the society of orders. Now, however, under influence of the Enlightenment, rights were increasingly attributed to individuals. This was especially notable in the realm of law, as ruler after ruler sought to streamline and rationalize a chaotic hodgepodge of legal codes and practices. This process would reach its zenith towards the end of the century with the American Declaration of Independence (1776) and the French Revolutionary Declaration of the Rights of Man and the Citizen (1789)—though of course almost nobody considered equal rights for women.

Another important theme was the growth of political consciousness among ordinary people. The spread of literacy combined with growing middle-class wealth and leisure to spur the development of political awareness. This awareness was both encouraged and expanded by new forms of communication and sociability. Newspapers and magazines proliferated, especially in Great Britain and the Dutch Republic. Elsewhere, not even government censorship could completely stem the hunger for political news and commentary. Although such publications were usually beyond the means of workers and peasants, the word spread to the poorer and often less literate parts of society via coffeehouses, taverns, and reading rooms. Public opinion was becoming a potent political force, and governments were not above appealing to or manipulating it in pursuit of their goals, often with unforeseen and unwanted consequences.

Enlightened Despotism

A recurrent subject of debate in the historiography of eighteenth-century politics and government has been the concept known variously as enlightened despotism or enlightened absolutism (see Debate, below).[2] At the heart of this concept is the idea that a number of European rulers in the later eighteenth century used their power to enact reforms inspired by Enlightenment thought.

One reason the concept of enlightened despotism has endured is that Enlightenment thought did inspire some rulers to undertake reforms. Yet, as we will see in this chapter, in many instances enlightened ideals were sacrificed to political needs. Historians who dismiss the concept see enlightened thought as mere window dressing for rulers' efforts to enhance either their own power or that of the states they ruled. Despite their enlightened pretensions, for example, neither Frederick the Great of Prussia nor Catherine the Great of Russia would abolish serfdom in their lands. Despite enlightened lip-service to international peace and harmony, Frederick would without provocation seize the province of Silesia from the Habsburg monarchy. And when the opportunity presented itself, both Frederick and Catherine would join forces with Holy Roman Emperor Joseph II (often held up as the epitome of the enlightened ruler) to cynically dismember the Kingdom of Poland and take the parts they wanted. When enlightened principles clashed with *raison d'état*, the latter usually won.

Yet that is not the whole story. Catherine the Great's efforts to stop the persecution of non-Catholics in Poland, however futile, did nothing to increase her power. Likewise, Joseph II instituted toleration of Protestants and Jews despite public opposition that rendered his other goals more difficult to attain. If their reforms fall short of our ideals, we must keep in mind the practicalities of eighteenth-century government, as well as the advances these reforms represented over the past. The fact that no eighteenth-century state allowed full religious liberty or freedom of the press should not blind us to the important reforms that were accomplished. In short, Enlightenment ideals did contribute to reform in the eighteenth-century state.

Another important source of reform was the political approach known as cameralism, which originated in Prussia under Frederick William I (see below). Derived from the Latin for "chamber," the term referred to the centralization of policy-making in the royal chambers—that is, in the hands of the king and his ministers. An extension of seventeenth-century mercantilism, cameralism involved regulating not only the economy but all aspects of society in the interests of the state. Thus education and agrarian reform were encouraged because improvements in nutrition and literacy would make the workforce more prosperous and productive, hence capable of paying more in the way of tax revenue. Religious toleration was encouraged in the interest of strengthening the state, as was continued subordination of church to state, an extension of the confessionalization process that had begun during the Reformations. Although the goals of the cameralists overlapped in part with those of the Enlightenment, their ultimate purpose was to advance the interests of the state rather than the individual.

The tension between the two is apparent in the concept of enlightened despotism. To understand the latter, it is crucial to be aware of the relevant contexts, one of which was the long-term development of European states outlined in previous chapters. From this angle, many "enlightened" reforms were not new, but continuations of longstanding trends: for example, the widespread efforts to codify and rationalize patchwork legal systems, or to reduce privileges such as tax exemptions. In addition, the eighteenth century was a period of intense international competition among European states, now waged increasingly on a global basis. In such a cut-throat diplomatic and military context, the advantage did not necessarily lie with the rulers who had the greatest resources at their disposal, but with those who were able to make the most efficient use of their resources. Rulers therefore sought to streamline and rationalize their states and governments, to harness their subjects and economies, to make the most efficient use possible of their resources. It just so happened that many of the reforms associated with enlightened despotism also served the purposes of strengthening and streamlining the state.

If it is difficult to draw direct connections between enlightened thinkers and specific reforms, it is impossible to come up with a definitive list of all the reforms that enlightened monarchs sought to enact. Nevertheless, there were a number of common elements in the program of enlightened despotism. Guiding them all was the basic assumption that, just as the physical universe was governed by natural laws, so was human society (including government and politics), and that the goal was to bring government into alignment with those laws. There was thus a tendency, not limited to enlightened despots, towards written constitutions, rather than the customary ones that were the norm. The most notable example was the US constitution with its exemplification of checks and balances.

In practice, these elements could mean a number of things. As was mentioned above, there was a general attitude that the ruler existed to serve the state rather than the reverse. Grand Duke Leopold of Tuscany (r. 1765–90; later Holy Roman Emperor Leopold II, 1790–2), the brother of Emperor Joseph II, declared that "a ruler, even a hereditary ruler, is only a delegate, a servant of the people whose cares and troubles he must make his own."[3] In line with the secular tone of the Enlightenment, religious toleration was an essential component, as was reducing the power and privileges of traditional churches. This was especially true in Catholic lands, as in the minds of those influenced by the enlightened thought, the Catholic Church stood for all they condemned: superstition, intolerance, and fanaticism. Most European states were illogical hodgepodges of different legal systems and legal codes, mostly customary in nature. Such arrangements not only perpetuated practices that many considered backward or barbaric, such as torture, but were also irrational in that subjects of the same ruler could be subject to wildly different legal codes and procedures. Why should some regions, groups, or institutions be exempt from contributing to the general welfare based on some archaic precedent? Part of the simplification and

HISTORICAL DEBATE

Enlightened Despotism

For the nineteenth and much of the twentieth century, European historians generally agreed that enlightened despotism was an incontrovertible fact of European history, like the Protestant Reformation or the French Revolution. Since the 1960s, the value of the concept has been subject to increasing scrutiny and doubt. Nevertheless, as H.M Scott has noted, no matter how often its obituary is written, the concept "obstinately refuse[s] to die."[4]

> . . . [T]he new thought entered as a profoundly subversive element into the conception of state and society. According to the traditional concept, the rights which the state recognized were based upon a grant from on high, from the sovereign. They were privileges bestowed, not rights belonging to the individual as such and . . . based on his nature as a human being. Enlightened thought proclaimed the unalterable value of such rights, which were to be recognized by all as the foundation of the state. . . .
>
> Enlightened despotism was thus a theory which contained the seeds of future political development, but which in the dynastic climate of the eighteenth century became a new impulse toward the further development of absolutism. . . . It drew upon the initial premise that sovereignty had its origin from the people . . . and concluded that its end was the benefit of the people . . .
>
> The sovereign could be compared to a proprietor who managed his belongings; his own interests lay in administering it in the best manner. Absolutism guaranteed good government because the prince had every profit from governing well, every loss from governing badly.
>
> But this presupposed one condition: that the sovereign know his proper interests, that he be conscious of his limitations, that he be, in a word, "enlightened." The basic order of society rested upon certain natural principles. . . . An enlightened ruler would be one who based his actions upon such principles . . . and was aware of the true laws of nature and reason.
>
> Thus absolutism, which appeared at the start of the century to have exhausted its possibilities of development, recovered its impetus and vigour. . . . The Enlightenment by renewing the fundamental conception of state and society cleared the path of obstacles. . . . With the Enlightenment the state completed its definitive renunciation of the middle ages. Like a river which sweeps all before it, absolutism followed its course and in a few years crowned the work pursued through centuries of conflict.

Franco Valsecchi, *Storia D'Italia*, vol. 7 (Milan: A. Mondadori, 1959), quoted in Roger Wines (ed.), *Enlightened Despotism: Reform or Reaction?* (Boston: D.C. Heath, 1967), pp. 6–10. Republished with permission of Wadsworth; permission conveyed through Copyright Clearance Center, Inc.

. . . [I]f Frederick the Great is described as an enlightened despot, on what grounds is the title refused to Frederick William I, the principal founding father of Prussian absolutism, whose social and political ideas and methods of government were accepted by Frederick the Great in most essentials? Similarly, if Catherine the Great is included among the enlightened despots, should not Peter the Great be included also? Was not Napoleon the last of the enlightened despots, or should this title be accorded to Napoleon III? One writer even goes so far as to wonder whether it should not be accorded to Bismarck.

If the term can be applied as widely as this it plainly has no value as a historical concept. . . . Even so, however, the difficulty of defining it remains, for obviously no definition of it is possible unless it can first be established what the essential principles of the Enlightenment were and which of them a government had to accept before it could quality for the title of enlightened. . . .

In fact, however, there is no agreement about which were the essential changes in government and society that enlightened thinking demanded; for the body of thought that goes by the name Enlightenment contained, particularly in France, a number of ideas (notably liberty and equality however defined) that were mutually exclusive in the circumstances of the eighteenth century, and have indeed commonly proved to be so in later centuries.

There seems, in fact, to be no limit to the number of times one can classify and reclassify the rulers of eighteenth-century Europe in accordance with their attitude to an intellectual movement which embraced many mutually incompatible opinions and about whose essential characteristics there is wide disagreement.

The truth of the matter would seem to be that though in the second half of the eighteenth century the enlightened assumptions about life and government . . . were fashionable among the ruling classes in most European countries, not only the strength of the desire for change, but the particular enlightened principles on which attention was focussed varied greatly from one state or area to another.

. . . [The concept of enlightened despotism has] now outlived its usefulness as a tool for investigating the period of transition between "feudalism" . . . and the nineteenth-century societies that were based on freedom of property and enterprise, and on equality before the law.

C.B.A Behrens, "Enlightened Despotism," *Historical Journal*, 18 (1975), pp. 401–8.

rationalization of political society was the curtailment of the legal and particularly the fiscal privileges of guilds, nobles, provinces, and established churches.

There are three "textbook" examples of enlightened despotism: Frederick the Great of Prussia (r. 1740–86), Holy Roman Emperor Joseph II (r. 1780–90), and Catherine the Great of Russia (r. 1762–97). These will be discussed below when we turn our attention to their respective states. First, however, we will look at a number of rulers and ministers of less powerful states who also implemented enlightened reforms. In some ways, these are better examples of the species, in that they were less constrained by international politics than were the rulers of great powers.

In Spain, Philip V (r. 1700–46) provided the royal energy and direction that the last Habsburg kings had lacked. He introduced an administrative system modelled on Louis XIV's in France, and managed to reduce the regional independence that had characterized Habsburg Spain. In the complex diplomacy of the eighteenth century, Spain even managed to recover some of the territory it had lost in 1713–14 under the Peace of Utrecht: in the 1730s, Naples and Sicily were returned to Spain and combined into a single kingdom under the rule of Philip's younger son Charles. Political and administrative reform continued under Ferdinand VI (r. 1746–59) and his minister, the Marquis of Ensenada. On his death, his younger brother Charles, King of Naples and Sicily, became Charles III of Spain (r. 1759–88).

Charles had already embarked on a program of reform in Naples and Sicily that encompassed many enlightened ideals, including decreasing the wealth and influence of the Church. Under his rule Naples became the leading centre of the Enlightenment in southern Europe, and when he became King of Spain in 1759, he set out to implement similar reforms there. Although personally very devout, he reduced the power of the papacy in his kingdom, marginalized the Spanish Inquisition, and expelled the Jesuits, who had been the primary agents of papal power in Spain. Colleges and universities, which had been heavily influenced by the Jesuits, were secularized, and a new network of secondary schools was established. He also secularized charitable institutions, deregulated the grain market, began to implement agrarian reforms, limited guild privileges, and curtailed the fiscal privileges of the nobles as well as the Church.

In Portugal, the Marquis de Pombal (1699–1782) served as prime minster throughout the reign of King José I (r. 1750–77). A virtual dictator, he did a great deal to reform and strengthen the Portuguese state, much of it consistent with enlightened principles. He removed restrictions on the "New Christians" whose ancestors had converted from Islam and Judaism, curtailed the power of the Church and the Inquisition, and made Portugal the first European state to expel the Society of Jesus. Since the latter had provided most of the country's teachers, a state-sponsored system of secondary schools was then established and the University of Coimbra reformed. In addition, Pombal abolished slavery in Portugal (though not in its Brazilian colony, where the sugar industry relied on slaves); reformed and rationalized government administration; and used mercantilistic measures to encourage trade and industry. In Pombal's Portugal, however, the motivation for reform was the desire to strengthen the state rather than commitment to enlightened ideals. Even the expulsion of the Jesuits was motivated by suspicion of their influence and wealth, and the purpose of the educational reforms was to provide administrators for the government rather than for the benefit of ordinary people. Enlightenment ideas were of interest only to the extent that they could enhance the wealth and power of the state and Pombal himself.

In Denmark, Johann Struensee (1737–72) rose to prominence at the court as the personal physician to the mentally ill King Christian VII (r. 1766–1808) and the lover of his wife, Queen Caroline Matilda (their scandalous relationship inspired the film *A Royal Affair*). His wide-ranging reform program reflected a deep commitment to enlightened ideals, including freedom of the press, abolition of torture, and prohibition of the slave trade in Denmark's overseas colonies. Within a few years, however, his arrogant refusal to compromise, not to mention his affair with the queen, provoked a palace coup that ended in Struensee's arrest and execution in 1772. More cautious reforms were eventually implemented in the 1780s and 1790s, when A.P. Bernstorff (1735–97) used his influence as foreign minister to institute a number of educational, economic, and agrarian reforms, including the abolition of serfdom in 1788.

Like Spain, Sweden had declined from its seventeenth-century great power status, having lost its dominant role in northern Europe to Russia and Prussia. After the death of Charles XII in 1718, his sister Queen Ulrike Eleonore (r. 1718–21) capitulated to noble demands and undid the Declaration of Sovereignty of 1693, with its assertion of royal absolutism (see Chapter 6). In 1720 she abdicated in favour of her husband, who became King Frederick I (r. 1720–51). He had no interest in ruling, however, and as a consequence the government of Sweden once again became a noble monopoly. This was the so-called "Age of Liberty," although the liberty was clearly only for nobles.

In 1772 King Gustav III of Sweden (r. 1771–92) took advantage of divisions among the nobles to restore strong royal rule. Educated in the principles of the Enlightenment, he had personally corresponded with leading figures of the French Enlightenment. As king, he not only introduced physiocratic economic reforms, but abolished torture and instituted limited but real toleration of non-Lutheran Christians and Jews. He aroused significant opposition among the nobles, however, and was assassinated in 1792.

Grand Duke Leopold of Tuscany (r. 1765–90), later Holy Roman Emperor Leopold II (1790–2), was deeply influenced by Enlightenment thought. He proposed a written constitution that would have severely limited the power of the ruler in favour of local and regional assemblies, although it was never put into effect. In line with the principles of the physiocrats, he abolished guilds and freed the grain trade. In addition, he introduced a new criminal code that eradicated torture and the death penalty, reduced the power of the papacy in his territory, and abolished the Inquisition.

BRANDENBURG–PRUSSIA

King Frederick II of Prussia (r. 1740–86), commonly known as Frederick the Great, has often been held up as the prototype of enlightened despotism. As was noted in the Debate box, however, this characterization is only partially justified. Although Frederick was profoundly influenced by Enlightenment thought, the general thrust of his policies was entirely in keeping with those of his father, Frederick William I.

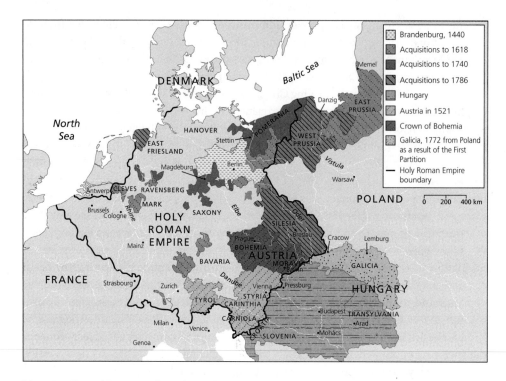

Map 10.1 Central Europe in the eighteenth century

As we saw in Chapter 6, the territories we are calling Brandenburg–Prussia rose to prominence in the later seventeenth century, largely through the leadership of Frederick William, the Great Elector (1640–88). His son and successor preserved this achievement and (as we saw in Chapter 6) added the prestige of a royal title as King Frederick I in Prussia (1688–1713). Devoted to culture and the arts, Frederick I strove to make Berlin, the small town that was his capital, a centre of European culture. But he was also devoted to pomp and ceremony, spending vast sums on his coronation in 1701, and modelling his court on the Versailles of Louis XIV.

Frederick's successor, King Frederick William I (r. 1713–40) was a very different kind of man and ruler. He gave his father a magnificent funeral, but then set out to remake everything in his own image. All the money that his father had spent on luxuries was redirected to the military. Henceforth the royal family would dine on wood and pewter rather than china and silver. Palace interiors were whitewashed and gardens transformed into parade grounds. The royal stables were reduced from 600 horses to 120, and courtiers were instructed to travel by foot where possible. The royal court was drastically restructured as the new king established a new pecking order in which the field marshal took overall precedence. Anything that did not serve to increase the state's power was discarded.

A miser in everything else, Frederick William was prepared to spend unlimited money on his army, which doubled in size from 40,000 in 1713 to 80,000 in 1740, and consumed more than two-thirds of the government's revenue. Yet despite his devotion to the army (or perhaps because of it), he was extremely reluctant to use it in battle. Moreover, priding himself on his plainspoken nature, he wanted nothing to do with the slippery complexities of diplomacy.

Frederick William expected his subjects to obey him exactly as soldiers obeyed their commanders. From the army to the economy, from religion to the law, there was no detail too small to escape the king's attention. In his own words: "I must be served with life and limb, with house and wealth, with honour and conscience, everything must be committed except eternal salvation—that belongs to God, but all else is mine."[5]

Frederick William steered the development of the state apparatus in directions that concentrated power in his hands, bypassing the traditional system of councils and relying instead on a small group of advisers who met in his chambers; as was noted above, this was the origin of cameralism. In 1723 he streamlined what was already a relatively efficient bureaucratic structure by creating the General Directory of Revenues, War, and Domains to serve as the supreme administrative body for all his scattered lands. It assessed and collected taxes, supplied the army, and handled the significant revenues from the estates owned directly by the ruling Hohenzollern dynasty, which made up about half of East Prussia and roughly a quarter of the land in king's other territories. Although venality of office was not unknown, most bureaucrats served at the king's pleasure, and as a result the Prussian bureaucracy gained a reputation for efficiency and professionalism—qualities that were essential if poor and underpopulated Prussia were to play a significant role in Europe as a whole. As we saw in Chapter 6, Prussian absolutism was based on the cooperation of the Junker nobility, and it was the army above all that was the arena for this cooperation. Although Frederick William did open up some opportunities for talented non-nobles in the bureaucracy, the officer corps of the army remained the preserve of the nobility.

Frederick William's relationship with his eldest son, Frederick, born in 1712, was deeply troubled. Determined to mould his heir into a clone of himself, he gave the boy a company of 130 cadets to drill at the age of six, and frequently subjected him to both physical and psychological abuse, beating him even for falling off a horse, or wearing gloves in cold weather.

But Frederick was as different from Frederick William as the latter had been from his own father. An avid reader, he defied his father by surreptitiously acquiring a library of several thousand volumes, including works by Descartes, Bayle, Locke, and Voltaire. He wrote bad poetry in French, became an accomplished amateur flutist and composer, and at sixteen began signing his name as "Frédéric, le philosophe." All this only enraged Frederick William into greater abuse.

So untenable did the prince's situation become that in 1730 he attempted to flee the kingdom with his best friend, a fellow army officer, but their plan was exposed and both young men were imprisoned. The friend was sentenced to death, and Frederick was compelled to witness his beheading (he fainted). Nevertheless, his father's methods did eventually have the desired effect, for three years later, when his father demanded that he marry a Protestant cousin of the future Habsburg Empress Maria Theresa (see below), he complied. But the couple never had any children, and she would be exiled from the court as soon as he became king. Although it has often been speculated that Frederick was homosexual, there is no ironclad evidence either way. What is certain is that he had no interest in perpetuating the Hohenzollern dynasty as distinct from the Prussian state.

On the death of Frederick William in 1740, Frederick continued in the direction his father had set, but in addition took a number of actions that reflected his enlightened convictions. One of his first acts was to recall the philosopher Christian Wolff, a leading figure in the German Enlightenment who had been expelled from the country for impiety in 1723 on the orders of Frederick William. Frederick also revived the Berlin Academy of Sciences, which his father had marginalized to the point of obscurity. He corresponded with several of the philosophes, and Voltaire himself lived as a guest at the royal court in Potsdam for several years, before the two men had a falling out.

In religion, Frederick rejected traditional Christianity in favour of Deism, but made no attempt to interfere with the beliefs of his subjects. Indeed, Prussia had a long tradition of relative tolerance in matters of religion: while the Hohenzollern dynasty was traditionally Calvinist, its subjects were overwhelmingly Lutheran, and the Great Elector had welcomed Huguenot refugees from France. After seizing Silesia (see below), Frederick would extend his policy of toleration to the Catholics who made up a substantial part of its population. Jews were not granted full equality, but were left undisturbed to govern their own affairs. Although this policy may fall short of current ideals, Prussia was still the most religiously tolerant state in Europe.

Frederick also continued his father's pursuit of legal reform, but in an enlightened direction. At the beginning of his reign, he abolished torture and greatly reduced the scope of capital punishment at a time when even supposedly "liberal" England was increasing it. Civil law too was rationalized and standardized, gaining Frederick the praise of ordinary people and enlightened opinion-makers alike. As we saw earlier, he was deeply committed to the idea that the ruler existed to serve the state: rulers were obliged to govern in the best interests of their subjects. However, this did not mean that subjects had any role to play in policy-making, much less a right to resist the government. In economic matters Frederick was a traditional mercantilist, seemingly out of step with the physiocrats' advocacy of laissez-faire. Emphasizing the accumulation of gold and silver bullion, protectionism, monopolies, a tightly regulated grain trade, state direction, and self-sufficiency, his economic policies would not have looked out of place in the time of Colbert. In 1740, in one of the most important events of the reign, ignoring treaty commitments and without provocation, he seized the populous and prosperous Habsburg province of Silesia, where rural industry was flourishing. By 1750 Silesia accounted for virtually half of Prussia's exports.

In his views of society as well, Frederick remained wedded to the past. Whereas his father had at least made some room in the bureaucracy for talented members of the bourgeoisie, Frederick enhanced the nobility's stranglehold on important positions, both in the civil service and in the army. He decreed that no noble land could be sold to non-nobles without his written permission, and did not continue his father's practice of buying noble estates to add to the royal domain. Although he recognized that serfdom had no place in an enlightened age, his hands were tied by the power of the nobles, who would not cooperate with the state unless they retained control over their estates and serfs. On Crown lands, he did reduce the compulsory labour services owed by the serfs and in some cases replaced labour services with payments in produce. He also confirmed the hereditary nature of peasant holdings. When he encouraged similar measures on private estates, however, the hostile reactions of the noble owners forced him to back away. On the other hand, although they were serfs, Prussian peasants were not badly off in material terms. On average, they paid roughly 30 per cent of their output to the state; the figure in France was comparable, and French peasants usually owed an equal amount to their landlords as well. In a land where labour was scarce, it would not have been in any landowner's interest to oppress his peasants too heavily. If there were no relatively wealthy peasant farmers in Prussia, as there were in countries like France, there was also no problem with widespread rural poverty and vagrancy. Unlike Russia (see below), eighteenth-century Prussia never experienced any widespread peasant unrest.

Frederick William I had required that all children attend school, but his son did little to encourage education for peasants, even as he bolstered universities as training grounds for bureaucrats. In Frederick's view, peasants should have enough education to do their jobs—to farm the land, pay their taxes, and make little soldiers for the army—but not so much as to give them ideas above their station. Was Frederick the Great an enlightened ruler? Yes, within the limits dictated by the interests of the state. Where he could implement enlightened policies without harming the state, as in the case of religious toleration and legal reform, he did. The fact that these reforms also benefited the state did not mean they were unenlightened. Where a reform would have weakened the state, however, as in the case of eliminating serfdom, he drew back. He was clearly committed to the arrangement under which the nobles would serve the Prussian state and army as long as they remained in control of their estates and serfs. There was no large and prosperous middle class whose support might have enabled him to challenge noble supremacy. But there is no evidence that he wanted to; in fact, the evidence points in the opposite direction.

If Frederick the Great was not as enlightened as we might like him to have been, he was certainly enlightened enough for Immanuel Kant, perhaps the leading philosopher of the eighteenth century, and a professor at the Prussian University of Königsberg:

> If we are asked, "Do we now live in an enlightened age?" the answer is "No, but we do live in an age of enlightenment. As things now stand, much is lacking which prevents men from being . . . capable of using their own reason in religious matters. . . . But, on the other hand, we have clear indications that the field has now been opened wherein men may freely deal with these things and that the obstacles to general enlightenment . . . are gradually being reduced. In this respect, this is the age of enlightenment, or the century of Frederick.[6]

THE HABSBURG MONARCHY

The reign of the Habsburg Holy Roman Emperor Joseph II (r. 1780–90) offers a useful counter-example to that of Frederick the Great. In his efforts to reform the Habsburg monarchy along enlightened lines, he neglected political realities. As a consequence, he died a disappointed man, and most of his reforms had to be overturned by his successor.

Here again, context is crucial. In the seventeenth century, Habsburg rulers had abandoned their efforts to restore power and meaning to the title of Holy Roman Emperor in Germany. Although they would continue to hold the title (with one exception) until the dissolution of the Empire in 1806, it had little real political significance. The Habsburg monarchy was based on a series of parallel compromises between the nobles of its various components that allowed them a good deal of local power and autonomy over their estates and serfs even as they lent their support to the ruling dynasty. The basic principle was the same as in Prussia, but the precise circumstances varied, and in the Habsburg monarchy the army was not the only venue for cooperation. In addition, the monarchs and their ministers were committed to Tridentine Catholicism as a source of unity in a state that lacked linguistic, cultural, or ethnic unity. In the course of the eighteenth century, both these elements—loyalty to the dynasty and commitment to the Catholic Church—would be profoundly challenged by the secularism of the Enlightenment and the lack of a male heir. The reforms attempted by Joseph II would put both of these sources of unity in jeopardy.

Leopold I had been succeeded on the throne by his eldest son Joseph I (r. 1705–11), who continued the War of the Spanish Succession and successfully appeased the Hungarian nobles into acquiescence. When he died without a male heir, he was succeeded by his brother Charles VI (r. 1711–40), who also would have only daughters, the eldest of whom was Maria Theresa (b. 1717). This posed a serious problem, since a woman could not be elected Holy Roman Emperor, the various components of the monarchy might refuse to accept a female ruler, and foreign powers might use the pretext of a woman ruler to break up the monarchy. Female rule, therefore posed a very real threat to the dynasty.

To counter this threat, in 1713 Charles VI issued a proclamation known as the Pragmatic Sanction, which declared that the Habsburg territories could not be divided even if the throne passed to a woman. As a piece of paper, however, it was worthless unless the various states of the monarchy and other European rulers agreed to it. Charles therefore spent the bulk of his reign attempting to guarantee its acceptance. In the 1720s he persuaded all his various lands to ratify it, and over the coming years most European rulers, including Frederick William I of Prussia, also agreed to recognize the integrity of the monarchy and the possibility of a female succession. When Maria Theresa succeeded her father in 1740, however, Frederick the Great, the new king of Prussia, violated the agreement made by his father and, as we have seen, invaded her province of Silesia, launching the War of Austrian Succession (1740–8; see below). Weakened by internal strain and foreign war, Maria Theresa had to acquiesce, but recovering Silesia would become one of her chief goals.

The other complication was that Maria Theresa, or whichever of Charles's daughters or nieces might succeed him, could not be elected Holy Roman Emperor. Although politically empty, the title still carried a great deal of prestige and remained important to the dynasty. Eventually, Maria Theresa managed to arrange the election of her husband,

Francis Stephen, to the imperial throne. Raised at the Habsburg court in preparation for the marriage, he had become Duke of Lorraine in 1729, but in 1737 he ceded the duchy to France in exchange for France's acceptance of the Pragmatic Sanction and was made Grand Duke of Tuscany instead. On his election as Emperor in 1745, he became formal co-regent with his wife in her hereditary lands, although Maria Theresa was clearly the principal partner in their political relationship.

Not only did the Habsburg monarchy survive the challenges of female rule, internal dissent, and foreign war, but in some ways it was strengthened by meeting them. In Maria Theresa and her son, Joseph II, we see the two faces of enlightened despotism: one intent on strengthening the state regardless of enlightened principles, and the other intent on implementing those principles regardless of the interests of the state. If Maria Theresa and the Habsburg monarchy were to survive in a highly competitive international environment, the machinery of the state needed to be streamlined, updated, and rationalized. So, although very much a devout traditional Catholic, Maria Theresa did in fact implement many reforms that might be considered part of the program of enlightened despotism.

Those reforms were impelled by the need to strengthen the state and, in the short term, to recover Silesia. They were relatively successful in Austria and Bohemia, strongly resisted in Hungary, and not even attempted in Italy and the Netherlands. Although a devout Catholic, she prohibited further growth of Church lands and took some steps to tax Church wealth and placed a moratorium on the growth of monasteries and convents. Although she did not contemplate freeing the serfs, she did promote a scheme under which serfs could provide cash payments in lieu of obligatory labour services and domain lands (those under the lord's direct management) could be divided and leased to peasants.

It was therefore ironic that her son Joseph II—who, unlike his mother, did believe in the ideals of the Enlightenment—was so much less successful, largely because the sincerity of his beliefs led him to discount political practicalities. On the death of his father in 1765, Joseph was elected Holy Roman Emperor and named co-ruler with his mother in the hereditary Habsburg lands. For the next fifteen years, the two ruled together, but when his mother died in 1780, Joseph finally felt free to impose the wide-ranging reforms he had always envisioned. Unlike his mother, however, Joseph took a doctrinaire approach, and refused to compromise with messy political realities. In terms of administration, he proposed a sweeping rationalization and harmonization of the patchwork Habsburg monarchy. Austria, Bohemia, Hungary, and the other central European lands were to be governed as a single unit with German as its official language. In Italy (where Tuscany was ruled by Joseph's brother Leopold; see above), the governance of Milan was to be streamlined and rationalized. The Austrian Netherlands were to see the end of old provincial distinctions and abolition of both the representative estates and the privileges of the wealthy urban ruling classes, including the guilds.

Joseph believed that serfdom was an irrational medieval relic, inefficient in its use of labour (since serfs had no incentive to become more productive) and detrimental to the state (in that serfs were unable to contribute their fair share to its maintenance). In 1781 he freed peasants from all personal restrictions; henceforth they would be able to move to a different estate if they had met all their obligations to their former lord, to marry without their lord's consent, and to leave the land altogether and take up a trade.

In 1784 he announced a plan to enact a uniform land tax, with no privileged exemptions, and to require lords to pay serfs for their labour services; this, together with the previous abolition of personal servitude, amounted to the abolition of serfdom. But noble resistance delayed implementation and enforcement was haphazard. Moreover, because emancipation was not accompanied by land redistribution, at least not right away, peasants continued to depend on their former lords for the land they needed to feed themselves and their families.

Although Joseph was personally devout, he did not share the effusive Counter-Reformation piety of his mother and the Habsburg dynasty in general. Seeking to purge religious life of "superstition," he abolished numerous religious holidays, forbade many pilgrimages, simplified church ritual, and decreed that new churches must be built in a plain and severe style rather than the flamboyant Rococo style favoured by his predecessors. He also went further than his mother had in extending state control over the Church. The power of the pope in his lands was circumscribed, many monasteries were closed and their lands confiscated, and those that remained were forbidden to acknowledge the authority of Rome. The money raised from the sale of the confiscated lands was to be used for

Joseph II plowing a field. Joseph was concerned with agrarian reform, and saw freeing the serfs as a way of liberating their labour and making it more productive. Here he is shown in 1769 plowing the field of a Bohemian farmer.

charity and to provide more parish priests. In 1781 the Patent of Toleration granted complete religious freedom and civil equality to Lutheran, Calvinist, and Orthodox Christians, and was later extended to cover Jews as well. In keeping with enlightened principles, Joseph relaxed government censorship, greatly reduced the number of titles on the Index of Forbidden Books in his lands, and encouraged the publication of works advocating social and economic reform.

For all his good intentions, however, most of Joseph's reforms met with fierce opposition. It is not hard to see why the privileged—nobles, Church, guilds—resisted change (noble opposition forced the postponement of his land tax until after his death). Nor is it difficult to appreciate the provincial and regional opposition that his centralization plans provoked, especially in Hungary and the Netherlands (one Dutch group, led by the lawyer Jean François Vonck, went so far as to oppose monarchy itself and advocate broader political participation), but also in the central hereditary lands of Austria, Bohemia, and Moravia. Yet even those who, in Joseph's view, had the most to gain from his reforms in many cases opposed them. Devout Catholics of all social classes resented the loss of their traditional religious rituals, his attacks on the power of the Church, and his toleration of Protestants and Jews. And while peasants might have been grateful for their emancipation, it meant little without land ownership. Finding that a freer press only encouraged opposition, Joseph reimposed censorship in 1789.

By the time of his death the following year, Joseph was bitter and disillusioned. He had tried to do everything all at once and was high-handed in his approach, refusing to consult or compromise, believing that the rationality of his agenda was self-evident and that anyone who opposed him was either vicious or stupid. Although his brother Leopold, as Grand Duke of Tuscany, had adopted enlightened policies himself, on his succession as Emperor he was forced to reverse most of his brother's reforms in order to restore stability amidst the turmoil unleashed by the French Revolution.

RUSSIA

We saw in Chapter 6 how, despite Peter the Great's superficial westernization of Russia society—symbolized by the transfer of political power from Moscow to St. Petersburg—the great mass of Russians who were serfs remained devoted to their traditional ways. Indeed, even as Russia became more western, it became less western, as the restrictions of serfdom were increased throughout the seventeenth and eighteenth centuries.

In addition, although Peter had succeeded in concentrating power in the hands of the Emperor and converting nobles into state servants, the political system was not stable. Because of his conflict with his son Alexei, which ended in Alexei's death, Peter had claimed the right to name his own successor, but he never exercised it.[7] The consequence was several decades of plotting and intrigue on the part of would-be rulers and their supporters. On Peter's death, his widow reigned as Catherine I from 1725 to 1727, and when she died and the throne passed to Alexei's son, who became Emperor Peter II. A boy of twelve, he was controlled by a series of unscrupulous and greedy nobles,

VOICES

From Catherine the Great's *Instruction*

Written by Catherine herself, the *Instruction* (*Nakaz*) for the Legislative Commission echoed enlightened thinkers such as Montesquieu, Diderot, and Beccaria, as well as the German cameralists. Voltaire himself called it "the finest monument of the age."[8]

9. The ruler of Russia is autocratic: for no other power, other than that concentrated in his person, can operate with the effectiveness required by such a vast state.

13. What is the object of autocratic government? Not to deprive men of their natural freedom, but to guide their actions towards the greatest good.

14. Therefore the government which can best accomplish this end, while placing the least restriction on natural freedom, is that which corresponds most closely to the aspirations which reasonable persons may be supposed to hold, and corresponds to the aim to which men invariably aspire in the formation of civil society.

33. The laws must protect as far as possible the security of each individual citizen.

34. The equality of all citizens consists in their all being subject to the same laws.

240. It is far better to prevent crimes than to punish them.

and died of smallpox in 1730. And so the drift continued. The Supreme Privy Council installed Peter the Great's niece Anna (r. 1730–40) on the throne, thinking that she too would be easily dominated. But she had ruled the duchy of Courland (in modern Latvia) for almost twenty years, and though she swore to observe various restrictions on her power as Empress, she soon broke her promise and ruled as an autocrat until her death in 1740. She was succeeded by her infant grand-nephew, who became Emperor Ivan VI at the age of eight weeks. Within a year, however, Ivan and his supporters were overthrown in a bloodless coup led by soldiers of the Imperial Guard, in favour of Elizabeth, a daughter of Peter the Great.

Elizabeth reigned from 1741 until her death in 1762 and finally brought some stability to Russian government. Indeed, many of the reforms later carried out by Catherine the Great had their roots in Elizabeth's reign, including significant reforms to criminal law, the fiscal system, local administration, the military, and the economy. Although Russia had continued to participate in European diplomacy since the death of Peter the Great, it

241. The prevention of crime is the object and aim of a good system of laws, which is none other than the art of leading men to the greatest good . . .

252. Since Natural Law commands us to strive as much as we can for the welfare of all men, we are bound to relieve the position of those under our sway, as far as common sense permits.

253. Consequently we are bound to avoid reducing men to a state of slavery unless absolute necessity requires it, and if we do so, it is not for our own gain, but for the benefit of the State.

263. However, it is also necessary to remove the causes which have often led to revolts of serfs against their masters; for unless we recognize these causes, it is impossible to prevent such occurrences by law, even though the tranquillity of both parties depends on this.

294. There can be no industry or well-established trade where agriculture is abandoned or neglected.

295. Agriculture cannot flourish where the peasant has nothing of his own.

296. This is based on a very simple principle, namely that everyone takes more care of his own property than of someone else's, and takes no trouble at all over something of which he may risk being deprived by another.

A. Lentin (ed.), *Enlightened Absolutism (1760–1790): A Documentary Sourcebook* (Newcastle-upon-Tyne: Avero, 1985), pp. 34, 37, 75, 114.

had not been a central actor. Under Elizabeth, however, it played important roles in both the War of Austrian Succession (1740–8) and the Seven Years War (1756–63).

Since Elizabeth had never married, on her death in 1762 the throne passed to her nephew, a German prince who became Peter III. Frequently drunk and prone to fits of rage, he cared nothing for Russia, but was a fanatic admirer of Frederick the Great, and therefore proceeded at once to pull Russia out of the anti-Prussian alliance of the Seven Years War (see below). His punishment was not long in coming: after barely six months on the throne, he was overthrown in a coup orchestrated by his estranged wife Catherine and her lover Grigori Orlov, with the backing of many influential nobles as well as the Guards regiments stationed in St. Petersburg. Peter was eventually murdered in prison, if not with Catherine's direct knowledge, then with her tacit permission.

Catherine was by birth a German princess from a small northern state. Born Sophie of Anhalt-Zerbst in 1729, she had been married to Peter, the heir to the Russian throne, in 1745, in keeping with Peter the Great's policy of establishing dynastic relations between his family and the ruling houses of Europe. Although Anhalt-Zerbst was politically insignificant, Peter's aunt, Empress Elizabeth, had approved of the match because Sophie's family had close ties to both Prussia and Sweden. On converting to the Russian Orthodox Church, Sophie had taken the name Catherine (Ekaterina in Russian) in honour of Peter the Great's Empress, who was Elizabeth's mother. An energetic, attractive, and appealing woman, she wanted nothing to do with her husband, and took many lovers throughout her life.

Catherine had been well-educated for a princess of her time, and over the years she gained a reputation in western Europe as the epitome of the enlightened ruler. She owned a copy of the *Encyclopédie*, and corresponded with a number of prominent philosophes, among them Voltaire and Diderot (the latter even visited her in St. Petersburg in 1773).

In the first decade of her reign, Catherine undertook a number of reforms designed to help Russia become a truly European society. She encouraged the establishment of schools, provided subsidies for Russian writers and publishers, and not only convened a Legislative Commission to begin the reform process, but provided the terms of reference for it in a document called *The Instruction* (*Nakaz*). Made up of delegates elected to represent the various elements of society (excluding the serfs), the Commission met in Moscow in 1767–8, but it accomplished little before war with the Ottomans put a hold on its proceedings. Although the *Nakaz* seemed to call for reform of serfdom, for example (see Voices box), noble delegates resisted any effort in that direction.

Russia's vast expanse and still sparse population, combined with primitive infrastructure and communications, made it extremely difficult for Moscow to exercise effective control in remote regions. Peter the Great had never come up with an effective system of local government, despite prolonged experimentation, and as a result local government essentially remained in the hands of landlords, with very little central supervision. Meanwhile, Russia had been expanding not only through conquest, but through settlement and migration as Russian peasants, many escaping serfdom, settled in underpopulated areas to the south and the east, including the region that is now Ukraine. Here they often mingled with various groups of Cossacks—self-governing communities, renowned for their horsemanship, who often fought alongside Russians against the Turks, but just as often battled Russia itself in defence of their freedom. If any Russian ruler were to fully incorporate these lands, then serfdom would have to be imposed on them and the independence of the Cossacks curtailed. But how this could be done in the absence of even rudimentary instruments of local administration remained a mystery.

A watershed in Catherine's reign was the Pugachev Rebellion of 1773–4. Emilian Pugachev (1742–75) was a Cossack soldier who had deserted from the Russian army and returned home to lead the Cossack resistance against Russian authority. Continuing long-standing Russian policy, Catherine's government had been seeking to extend its control over the Cossack communities in the south and east of the country, between the Black and Caspian Seas, and impose Russian-style serfdom on the escaped serfs and free peasants who had settled in the area. Claiming to be Tsar Peter III, Pugachev attracted a large following of Cossacks, discontented peasants, and restive members of ethnic minorities.

He established a popular government and issued decrees freeing serfs and granting religious toleration and freedom from conscription. For a time, he and his ragtag army of up to 30,000 evaded the Russian forces sent to suppress them, invading noble estates, destroying records, and brutally massacring nobles and their families. In the end, though, Pugachev was betrayed by some of his fellow Cossacks and turned over to the imperial army. He was taken back to Moscow in an iron cage, tortured, and executed, although Catherine did reduce the punishments of other rebels, and eventually decreed a general pardon.

Pugachev's rebellion prompted Catherine to reorganize and strengthen local administration. Russia was divided into fifty districts, each run by a centrally appointed governor with extensive powers. Catherine made sure that the governors were men that she trusted to execute her will. Local nobles were given important roles as agents of the central government, but subordinate to the governors' authority. At the same time, the rebellion demonstrated to Catherine the necessity of strengthening nobles' control over their serfs. She abandoned any thought of improving the serfs' lot, much less of their eventual or gradual emancipation. The 1785 Charter of the Nobility not only gave nobles more power over their serfs, but freed them both from the obligation of state service and from all taxation.

Catherine the Great once more presents us with the paradox of enlightened despotism. Although personally she was among the most enlightened of European rulers, events and the interests of the state drove her in a different direction. Despite her enlightened views, the need to strengthen central control drove her to enhance the privileges of the nobility at the expense of the serfs.

FRANCE

How was it that France, the exemplar of royal absolutism under Louis XIV, less than seventy-five years after his death became the first country to overthrow its monarchy? The kingdom did have many problems, but they were likely not unsolvable, and a succession of ministers had proposed and even begun to enact substantial reforms. Two of the biggest problems, however, were at the centre of the political system: neither Louis XV (r. 1715–74) nor his grandson Louis XVI (r. 1774–92) was up to the task that heredity had assigned him. Lacking the confidence and perseverance required to make unpopular changes, both were inclined to agree with the last person they had talked to. They were not stupid or vicious, but because they were ineffectual, the court and government became hotbeds of intrigue as the factions surrounding ambitious nobles and ministers schemed to maximize their influence.

A second major problem was the antiquated, inefficient, and corrupt taxation system. Everyone paid a dizzying array of sales taxes and, in times of war, a primitive income tax of 10 per cent called the tenth or *dixième*, but the most important direct tax was the *taille*, which was paid only by the less wealthy members of French society: nobles and the Church were mostly exempt from it, as were many towns and wealthy bourgeois. A third major problem was the lack of a central bank to facilitate government borrowing in the way that the Bank of England did (after the unfortunate experience of the Mississippi bubble, discussed in Chapter 8, the Central Bank of France would not be established until 1800). As a consequence the French government had to borrow either from individuals or from syndicates of financiers who in many cases had made their fortunes collecting indirect taxes, and thus in effect lent the government its own tax revenue at inflated interest rates. Without a central bank, the government and its creditors were in a sense financial hostages to each other: government default would mean ruin for the creditors, and since the latter were relatively few, financial difficulty for any of them might leave the government in a very difficult situation. Among the measures taken to reform the fiscal system was the imposition, in 1749, of a permanent 5 per cent tax called the *vingtième* (twentieth) on all of French society; however, the Church protested so bitterly that it was finally exempted.

The latter point highlights another major challenge faced by the government: the entrenched interests of the society of orders. The achievement of seventeenth-century French rulers had been to tame the society of orders without overturning it, to make it apparent to the privileged orders that they had more to gain by going along with the monarch than by confrontation and conflict. Without a determined monarch to drive the message home, through either persuasion or coercion, the privileged orders seized the opportunity to turn the royal government into the agent of their self-preservation. Nowhere is this more apparent than with the Parlements, the highest courts of law in the kingdom. The Parlement of Paris was clearly the most important, but it had provincial counterparts with more restricted jurisdictions. Staffed by judges who had bought their positions, and in so doing acquired noble status, they stood at the apex of the venal bureaucracy. Their chief political lever was their control of the registration without which royal edicts could not legally be enforced. They had traditionally had the right to "remonstrate" (to object) when, for example, the proposed law conflicted with another law or violated precedent in some way. In most cases these remonstrances were a matter of fine-tuning legislation or cleaning up the legal language, but on occasion the judges objected to a proposed law on principle and would refuse registration until their objections had been satisfied. The king, as the ultimate source of justice, could compel registration by physically attending the court in a special ceremony known as a *lit de justice*.[9] But this required a determined king, since to choose this option would be to admit that that he was acting against the advice of his most important judges.

Louis XIV had severely weakened the Parlements' power to obstruct royal policy by requiring them to register a royal decree before remonstrating against it. But when Louis XV came to the throne he was a boy of five, and his regent—his great-uncle, Philippe, Duke of Orléans (1674–1723)—had reversed that measure in an effort to gain the Parlements' support. For the rest of the century, therefore, the privileged orders were able to use the Parlements to frustrate any reform plans that might have diminished their wealth, status, or power.

When Orléans died, Louis XV was still just thirteen, but he was legally an adult, and he chose to make his childhood tutor, Cardinal André-Hercule de Fleury (1653–1743), his principal minister. Already in his seventies, Fleury would effectively govern France until his death at the age of 89. He brought some order to government finances, with the result that the budget even showed a small surplus in the 1730s, and he was relatively cautious in foreign affairs: the only conflict in which France became involved during his tenure was the relatively brief War of the Polish Succession (1733–8). It was also under Fleury that the project of expanding the road system began.

The most significant controversy of this period concerned Jansenism. As we saw in Chapter 6, the bull *Unigenitus* (1713) had decisively condemned key Jansenist tenets, but had also inadvertently condemned some teachings formerly accepted as legitimate Catholic doctrine. Thus while some priests maintained that adherence to the bull was essential to salvation, others argued to the contrary. Moreover, the bull appeared to violate the "Gallican liberties" of the Catholic Church in France. Fleury, who had no objection to the contents of the bull, embarked on a campaign to marginalize the Jansenists and in 1730 proposed making *Unigenitus* a law of both Church and State. The Parlement of Paris objected vigorously, forcing Fleury to resort to a *lit de justice*. Although the law was then duly registered, he had incurred significant bitterness for very little gain: in the end, widespread opposition forced the government to suspend enforcement of the law, and the issue was put on the back burner.

After the cardinal's death in 1743, Louis decided to rule without a first minister, and it was at this point that the court became a hotbed of factional scheming. In 1749, when, as we have seen, he gave in to the Church and exempted it from the *vingtième* tax, the message was clear: the king could be manipulated by whoever screamed the loudest. At the same time, the cautious truce between the Jansenists and their opponents was ruptured when the Archbishop of Paris decreed that the sacraments would be administered only to those who could produce a note verifying that they had confessed to an "authorized" priest—that is, one who subscribed to *Unigenitus*. Both Jansenists and the judges of the Parlement were outraged. A number of prominent judges were Jansenists themselves, but they were not the only ones to object to this heavy-handed edict. The Parlement heard appeals of decisions denying the sacraments, only to have those cases removed from their jurisdiction to the royal council. The Parlement drew up a list of "grand remonstrances" that both denounced the denial of sacraments and asserted the Parlement's role as upholder of the customary constitution: "When there is a conflict between the king's absolute power and the good of his service, the court respects the latter, rather than the former, not to disobey but in order to discharge its obligations."[10]

In 1768 René de Maupeou (1714–92) became Chancellor, and he soon launched an all-out assault on the Parlement. In November 1770 he picked a fight with the judges when he presented legislation that reaffirmed the *vingtième* and forbade the judges to remonstrate before registration. This was enforced through a *lit de justice* in December, and in January 1771 the judges of the Parlement of Paris and three provincial Parlements were arrested and sent into internal exile. Those Parlements were replaced by new courts in which venality of office was abolished, the jurisdiction of the Parlement of Paris was reduced, and although the new judges would still have the power to remonstrate, they would be required to register the legislation first. This "Maupeou Revolution" was widely deplored.

Venal officeholders, nobles, and members of the upper bourgeoisie protested against "tyranny," as did readers of Montesquieu, for whom the Parlements represented their defence against despotism. Voltaire, on the other hand, believed the reforms were necessary in order to reduce privilege and rationalize the state. Increasingly, the Parlements and their supporters claimed to be defending not just their historic privileges, but the rights of the nation and its citizens, and the judges began to phrase their remonstrances in the contractual language used by political philosophers such as Locke and Rousseau. Despite the outcry, the king supported his chancellor, who over the next few years achieved substantial legal and fiscal reform.

When Louis XV died unexpectedly in 1774, his twenty-year-old grandson became King Louis XVI (1774–92). The inexperienced and impressionable king was persuaded to restore the Parlements that Maupeou had replaced, undoing his constitutional revolution. Fiscal reform continued to be the most pressing need, but, as in the past, the power of the Parlements, factional intrigues, and the king's indecisiveness all worked against it. In addition, the king's wife, the Habsburg princess Marie Antoinette, became a lightning rod for dissent.

In 1774, as we have seen, Anne Robert Jacques Turgot was appointed finance minister. An experienced administrator, he was full of reform ideas, many suggested by the physiocrats. He tried to free the trade in grain from various restrictions and actually abolished the guilds, if only temporarily. His reforms aroused serious opposition, including a series of bread riots known as the "Flour War," and he was forced to rescind many of them. He also attempted to circumvent the Parlements by instituting a series of regional consultative assemblies made up of men of property, regardless of their legal status. He made many enemies, among them the Queen, and was dismissed in 1776.

Turgot was succeeded by the Swiss Protestant banker Jacques Necker (1732–1804) who brought to the post a reputation for financial wizardry. But his efforts to centralize the budgeting process in his hands aroused the opposition of his rival ministers. Forbidden by the king to raise taxes, he resorted to loans to finance the government's debt, which was now increasing faster than ever as a result of France's support for the American colonists in their rebellion against King George III. He made even more enemies when, in 1781, he made the government's financial statement public for the first time—a move that his rivals saw as a power play to enhance his own position, an appeal to public opinion that violated royal discretion. Necker's goal was to demonstrate to the king's creditors, actual and potential, that the government's finances were basically sound, but he understated both the annual deficit and the portion of the government's revenues that went to servicing the debt, which by this time was approximately 50 per cent. Just as Turgot had proposed, Necker too tried to introduce regional assemblies that would lend his proposals popular legitimacy. Although Necker's enemies forced his resignation in 1783, his misrepresentation of government finances made it difficult, if not impossible, for his successors to enact meaningful reform.

For the next six years, until the outbreak of the Revolution in 1789, there was no firm hand guiding the government, and its financial situation continued to worsen. In 1786 yet another finance minister, Charles de Calonne, informed the king that government faced imminent bankruptcy and proposed yet another reform program, much of which echoed Turgot's: a new tax on land to replace the *vingtième*, with no exemptions, administered by a series of regional bodies without reference to social status; the abolition of internal customs barriers, and the reform of indirect taxation. Knowing that his plans would face opposition from the Parlements, Calonne persuaded the king to convene an extraordinary body known as the Assembly of Notables to approve the plan and lend it the legitimacy of public support. But he failed to pack the Assembly with supporters: thus it not only rejected his plans but accused him of "despotism" and the royal government of fiscal incompetence. Some of the Notables had been willing to give up their privileges and exemptions, but felt that such radical changes required more public input and representation than they could supply. They argued that only the Estates-General, which had not been summoned since 1614, could break the logjam.

Calonne had no choice but to resign. The new finance minister, Loménie de Brienne, had been one of Calonne's chief antagonists in the Assembly of Notables. Now, however, confronted with the reality of impending bankruptcy, he too attempted a wide-ranging reform package. When the Parlement refused to register it, Brienne imitated Maupeou and in May 1788 exiled the Parlement. Provincial Parlements protested and refused to register the reforms, while general public outrage at this perceived act of "tyranny" was reflected in outbreaks of violence in some provincial towns. In November, Louis XVI relented and recalled the Parlement of Paris, having previously agreed to a meeting of the Estates-General to be held in Versailles the following May.

In one sense, the privileged orders of France got their wish: they succeeded in obstructing a series of reform agendas that would have curtailed their fiscal privileges. Although the nobles were at the forefront of this resistance, particularly the noble judges of the Parlements, they were supported by the institutional Church and its privileged hierarchy, as well as many bourgeois who, after all, wanted what the nobles already had. To defend their privileged status, however, they summoned forces that would soon escape their control. Having called for a meeting of the Estates-General, they fully expected to dominate the assembly; no one could foresee that it would set in motion the chain of events that led ultimately to the abolition of the monarchy itself. They had used the language of the "nation," natural rights, contractual government, and resistance to despotism to appeal to popular opinion, without recognizing that those ideas could just as easily be used to justify the abolition of their own superior status and privileges.

Many of the reforms proposed by Maupeou, Turgot, Necker, and Calonne reflected the program of enlightened despotism, in particular those intended to reduce privilege and rationalize the state apparatus, especially the fiscal system. Had they succeeded, it is at least conceivable that the Revolution could have been avoided; but they did not. One reason for this lack of success was that neither Louis XV nor Louis XVI was single-minded or confident enough to defy the wishes of large segments of the privileged elite. Another, and perhaps more important, reason they failed was that France—unlike Russia, Prussia, and the Habsburg lands—had a politically aware public that was large enough to back up the privileged elites in their resistance. What would evolve into the French Revolution began when this public realized that its interests were not the same as those of the elites who forced the Estates-General on a reluctant king. At the time, however, this development could not be foreseen.

GREAT BRITAIN

By 1700 the government of England had evolved into a stable and mutually beneficial partnership of the monarchy and the parliamentary representatives of the upper classes. Although the Glorious Revolution of 1688–9 had demonstrated that Parliament was the dominant partner, the monarch had not been reduced to a figurehead: the ruler still possessed significant powers in the realms of foreign affairs, the military, and the choice of advisers and ministers. It was Parliament, however, that granted the funds that allowed the ruler to exercise those powers, and over the course of the eighteenth century it came to be accepted that the ministers chosen by the monarch had to have the support of a majority in Parliament.

The Act of Settlement of 1701 had guaranteed that the throne of England would pass to a Protestant on the death of Queen Anne, but concern remained that Scotland might recognize the claim of the exiled Stuarts. To prevent this, in 1701 the Act of Union had brought England and Scotland together to form the single united kingdom of Great Britain. On the queen's death in 1714, therefore, the German Elector of Hanover became King George I (r. 1714–27).

The new king might not have been the dimwitted dullard portrayed by his enemies, but he was not personally popular. He never learned to speak more than a few words in English, and was more concerned with Hanover and Germany than with Britain. Thus he was content to leave the government of Britain in the hands of the Whig politicians who had pushed the Act of Settlement through Parliament while he concentrated on diplomatic affairs. Whig domination was also furthered by the fact that among the Tories were a number of Jacobites (supporters of the claims to the throne of the exiled James II and his descendants). One Jacobite uprising took place in 1715, and in 1745 supporters of "Bonnie Prince Charlie" would mount another.

George II (r. 1727–60) came to the throne on the death of his father, and although he did learn to speak heavily accented English, he was still more concerned with events on the continent than with England. It was during his reign that parliamentary government assumed a recognizable form. The most significant figure in this respect was Sir Robert Walpole, who is widely considered Britain's first Prime Minister in the sense that his power depended on maintaining not only the favour of the king, but the support of a majority in Parliament.

It must be emphasized that Parliament in the eighteenth century was not a democratic institution. The hereditary upper house, the House of Lords, was in many ways still the dominant chamber, and even the House of Commons did not represent the "people" in any real sense. Less than 5 per cent of the population were entitled to vote, and demographic changes over the generations meant that many ridings had so few voters that it was easy to intimidate, manipulate, or bribe them. The most notorious of these "rotten boroughs" was Old Sarum, which had no inhabitants at all: thus its Member of Parliament was elected by landowners who lived elsewhere. There were also "pocket boroughs" whose members were chosen by at most a handful of landowners, and sometimes just one. The Duke of Newcastle controlled seven such seats, which he would simply bestow on relatives, friends, or supporters. Although the numbers of voters did vary from town to town, in roughly three-quarters of the ridings, MPs were elected by fewer than five hundred voters, and even where the franchise was relatively broad, the fact that the ballot was not secret made it easy for a local strongman to use bribery or intimidation to determine how they were cast.

Walpole was the dominant figure in British politics from 1721 until 1741, maintaining the confidence of both George I and George II as well as his fellow Whigs. The practices he used to keep his MPs' support are considered corrupt and anti-democratic today but were perfectly acceptable at the time. Voters would be bribed or intimidated to elect Walpole's chosen candidates, and to persuade the MPs elected in this way to support the government they or their relatives were given cushy government jobs with salaries but practically no responsibilities. His power, and the dominance of the Whigs, depended on not rocking the boat; one of his remarks on this subject has become a common aphorism: "Let sleeping dogs lie." As long as the Tories were tainted by the Jacobites within their ranks, they had no hope of challenging the Whigs. But party boundaries were still fluid and imprecise in any case. In fact, the real division in English politics in the eighteenth century was not so much between Whigs and Tories as between "court" and "country." The "country" faction included both Tories and disaffected Whigs, and its members cast themselves as the opponents of the corrupt oligarchs who enjoyed the spoils of power and neglected the general welfare. This point of view found eloquent expression in *The Idea of a Patriot King* (1740) by Henry St. John, Viscount Bolingbroke (1678–1751). A government minister under Anne, he turned to political theory after his Jacobite sympathies ruined his political career. According to Bolingbroke, the government had been corrupted by lust for power and gain, and the general welfare of the kingdom therefore depended on loyal subjects who would speak truth to power. It was in this period that the concept of the "loyal opposition"—one that could oppose the government of the day and still be loyal to king and country—began to take shape.

The British political system was emphatically not democratic by modern standards. Nevertheless, it was able to provide for more and broader public input than was possible in France, where, as we have seen, reformers struggled to establish a forum that could give their plans legitimacy. Although Englishmen never tired of contrasting their "liberty" with the "despotism" of France, it was precisely because Britain's political system incorporated its leading subjects that its government was much more effective than that of France. We see this most clearly in the area of government finances. In Britain as in France, the wars of the eighteenth century led the government to incur mountains of debt. Expenditures on the army and navy regularly consumed more than half of the government's budget. Britain was able to manage this financial burden in part because its nobles were not exempt from taxation. More importantly, in the eighteenth century Britain began to rely more on excise or sales taxes on consumer goods than on income or land taxes. By the middle of the century, the revenue from excise taxes provided more than half of government revenue, while income and land taxes contribute only about one-fifth. The government therefore benefited greatly from the rise in consumerism discussed in Chapter 8, as more and more goods came to be bought in the marketplace rather than produced at home. But because these taxes were collected at the retail level, they did not arouse nearly the opposition that other forms of taxation did. In fact, British subjects paid approximately one-quarter of their annual per capita income in taxes—roughly twice as much as their counterparts in supposedly despotic France.

Not only was the British government able to raise large amounts of tax revenue, but it was efficient and effective in its collection and administration of them. This too was in large part attributable to the fact that the social and economic elites who paid a large proportion of the taxes were intimately involved in the system. Expenditures were closely monitored by the Treasury Board, and the system of excise taxes was supervised by a Board of Commissioners that presided over an increasingly professional staff.

The effectiveness of the fiscal system allowed the government to borrow money much more efficiently than the French government. The Bank of England gave individual investors a mechanism to buy government debt, and because the creditor base was so large and diffuse, the risk of default was not nearly as concentrated as in France. The predictable and regular flow of revenue assured lenders of the government's creditworthiness, and therefore it was able to borrow at lower interest rates. So even though the British government borrowed huge amounts of money, this practice did not have the dire consequences that it did in France.

After Walpole's resignation in 1741, various factions within his party competed for primacy. As is often the case when one party has held power for a long time, divisions developed over the spoils of power, rather than any particular principles. Among the disaffected "country" Whigs was William Pitt the Elder (1708–78). One of Walpole's most vociferous critics, he believed that Britain should take a much stronger stance in overseas colonial conflicts, and when the Seven Years War broke out, he became Prime Minister, assembling a coalition of like-minded Whigs and Tories.

Pitt was erratic and domineering, however, and he was quickly dismissed when George III became king in 1760. The grandson of George II, he was the first of the Hanoverian dynasty to be born in England, and he spoke English as his mother tongue; in fact, he never visited Hanover. Inspired by Bolingbroke's ideal of the "patriot king," he was determined to do away with factionalism and recover the powers that his two predecessors had allowed the Whigs to usurp. He appointed as his Prime Minister his former tutor, the Scottish Earl of Bute, who purged the ministry of the old-guard Whigs who had dominated for so long, and relied instead on Tories and disaffected Whigs. Since Bute's position clearly depended on the favour of the king rather than a majority in Parliament, many Whigs suspected that the king was attempting to circumvent Parliament and establish a "tyranny." When government ministers used the same tactics to build support in

Parliament that the Whigs had used for decades, they were denounced for "corruption" and "despotism."

One notable aspect of British politics in the later eighteenth century was the growth in political awareness and participation outside the traditional governing classes. Expanding literacy and the proliferation of newspapers and magazines brought politics to a much broader audience than ever before. Even if they were not able to vote, ordinary people became increasingly involved in the political issues of the day. We can see this in the career of John Wilkes (1725–97). The son of a London distiller, he entered the House of Commons in 1757 as a supporter of William Pitt. When George III dismissed Pitt and appointed Bute in his

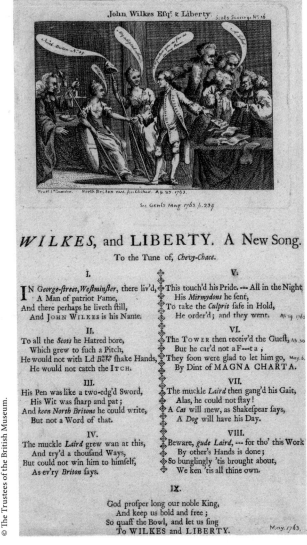

Wilkes and Liberty: A New Song. The lyrics of a popular song dedicated to John Wilkes, with an illustration in which Liberty introduces Wilkes to Britannia as "My adopted son." Britannia welcomes him, and he declares "I'll protect you as far as in my power." The cap on Liberty's spear is labelled "North Briton No. 45," a reference to Wilkes's notorious publication.

place, Wilkes established a weekly newsletter called *The North Briton*, in which he regularly attacked the new Prime Minister. Then in the notorious issue number 45 he went after the king personally. George III ordered his arrest, but Wilkes was protected by his parliamentary immunity as an MP. His enemies then discovered a raunchy poem he had written years earlier, and to avoid arrest for pornography, he fled to exile in France. Found guilty in absentia, he was declared an outlaw and expelled from Parliament, but in 1768 he returned to England and was elected to represent the London riding of Middlesex, where the franchise was relatively broad. When Parliament refused to recognize his election, Wilkes and his supporters encouraged widespread popular protest. Wilkes's notoriously ugly face and the phrase "Wilkes and Liberty," inspired the popular political campaign, complete with posters, pamphlets, songs, and commemorative plates and mugs. Twice more Wilkes was elected for Middlesex, and twice more Parliament refused to let him take his seat. He was also elected sheriff and then Lord Mayor of London, but was never allowed to take up either position.

Another vehicle for extra-parliamentary politics was the petition. In 1774 the Society for the Protection of the Bill of Rights gathered 38,000 signatures on a petition demanding not only that Wilkes be allowed to take his seat in Parliament, but also substantial electoral reform. The fact that it was supported by a faction of Whigs looking to embarrass the government of the day indicates that politics was no longer the exclusive preserve of aristocratic cliques and their supporters. In 1780, 44,000 people signed a petition opposing greater toleration for Catholics, and after 1788 a number of anti-slavery petitions attracted as many as 100,000 signatures.

Demonstrations and riots also gave voice to the concerns of ordinary people. In 1768 a pro-Wilkes demonstration in London attracted 20,000 people. Fearing disorder, the government called in the army to suppress it, at the cost of twelve lives. And in 1780 an anti-Catholic campaign led by Lord George Gordon sparked a week of riots in London. Though we may see such events as popular politics, to the authorities of the day they looked like mob rule. In fact, in the 1780s the threat of violent revolution seemed more acute in England than in France.

The most important development of George III's reign was undoubtedly the loss of the thirteen colonies in North America. The roots of the American Revolution are in some senses similar to those of the French Revolution, which it would help to inspire. During the Seven Years War, Britain had successfully defended its American colonies against the French and their indigenous allies, but at very great cost. By the end of the war in 1763, the government's debt had swollen to 137 million pounds, and the annual interest on it was 5 million pounds—this in an era when the government's total annual revenue came to only about 8 million pounds. At the same time, the American colonies had exploded in terms of both population and prosperity. The population of New York doubled between 1750 and 1770, while that of North Carolina grew six-fold. The value of American exports to Britain doubled in the same period, and by 1760 more than one-quarter of Britain's overseas trade was with its American colonies. From the government's perspective, it only made sense that its prosperous colonies should contribute more to their own defence and assume their share of responsibility for the nation's debts.

In 1764 a Sugar Act taxed American imports of sugar from the Caribbean; in 1765 the Stamp Act taxed colonial newspapers, legal documents, and licences; and in 1766 the Declaratory Act asserted Parliament's right to impose taxation in the colonies as it saw fit, just as it did in Britain. Many colonists resisted these measures, and as in Britain, growing popular political participation was seen as a threat to the established order. The same desire for popular political participation that drove the "Wilkes and Liberty" movement was also apparent in the colonies, and for a time Whig opposition to George III's "tyranny" and American resistance to taxation ran in parallel channels. On both sides of the Atlantic, the government responded with repression—forcible, if need be—of popular political demonstrations. In Boston in 1770 a demonstration against the billeting of troops in private homes led soldiers to fire upon the crowd, killing five. In 1773, when the Tea Act imposed new duties on tea imports, the result was the "Boston Tea Party," in which colonists disguised as indigenous people destroyed a cargo of tea in the harbour before it could be unloaded and taxed. The government responded in 1774 with the Coercive or (as the colonists called them) the Intolerable Acts. The port of Boston was closed, the Massachusetts colonial assembly dissolved, and the colony placed under direct military rule.

By 1775 the thirteen colonies had begun to coordinate their resistance, and in 1776 they declared their independence. They argued that the government's efforts to tax them were illegitimate because they had not consented to them—"no taxation without representation." George III and his ministers took the position that Parliament had consented to these measures, and that most taxpayers even in Britain did not have the vote: rather, they—like the colonists—were represented "virtually." Inspired by Locke's contractual conception of government, and the opposition discourse that contrasted the simplicity and virtue of the "country" with the corruption and tyranny of the "court," the colonists used the language of universal human rights (the "Rights of Man," in eighteenth-century terms) to justify their rebellion and independence.

In the end, of course, British attempts at military repression failed, and in 1783, with the aid of France and Spain, the Americans established their own republican state, the United States of America. The consequences of the American Revolution were enormous, if not immediately apparent. As was noted above, the debt that France incurred by assisting the Americans helped to push its government to the brink of fiscal catastrophe. A number of French soldiers fought alongside the Americans against their joint British enemy, among them the Marquis de Lafayette (1757–1830), who would later play a key role in the French Revolution. For such liberal-minded Europeans, the new republic represented the potential of popular liberty and virtue, in line with enlightened thought about the contractual nature of government and resistance to despotism. In Britain, there were renewed calls for political reform. In 1783 William Pitt the Younger (1759–1806), the son of the elder Pitt, became Prime Minister at the age of twenty-four and attempted the reform of Parliament, but was largely unsuccessful, resulting in greater discontent. By now the king was suffering from prolonged bouts of mental illness, possibly linked to porphyria (a genetic disorder prevalent in his extended family). When people at the time considered the possibility of violent revolution, therefore, they thought first of seething Britain rather than seemingly placid France.

Although in some ways the American Revolution was a kind of dress rehearsal for the coming French Revolution, there were significant differences: most notably, the fact that the pillars of the old order in Europe—monarchy, aristocracy, and church—were weaker in America. As a consequence, when revolution did reach Europe in 1789, the confrontation between revolutionary ideals and the old order was bound to be more violent and bitter than it had been in the New World.

One similarity between the American and French Revolutions was that both originated in resistance to governmental efforts to reform an outmoded fiscal structure in order to bolster state power. Just as France was seeking to curtail the unearned fiscal privileges of the aristocracy, so Britain was seeking to extract what it considered a fair share of expenses from a privileged region. In some ways, George III and his ministers were attempting to implement some of the agenda of enlightened despotism, although they were motivated solely by the interests of the state, without the additional spur of enlightened ideals. As in France, those affected negatively by reforms were numerous and powerful enough to resist and ultimately defeat them. From the perspective of European history, what is significant about the American Revolution is that enlightened discourse about human rights was invoked to defeat enlightened discourse about political reform. This paradoxical situation highlights the contradiction at the very heart of the notion of enlightened despotism.

THE DUTCH REPUBLIC

The Dutch Republic in the eighteenth century may well serve as a case study in the transformation of politics. After dominating European commerce and finance for a century, Dutch merchants found their pre-eminence in decline. Generations of warfare had saddled the Republic with enormous debts, and many of the regent class were content to live as rentiers, investing in the debt of their own and other governments. The relative decline of Dutch commerce and manufacturing, combined with agricultural stagnation, led to widespread poverty among the working and peasant classes.

The political structure of the Republic was incapable of counteracting these trends. Since 1702, when William III had died without heirs, the position of *stadtholder* had been left vacant, and the political pendulum had swung back in favour of the regent class. The putative national government, the States-General, resembled a debating chamber more than a national legislature, and that was fine with the regent oligarchy: political power continued to lie with the provinces and cities, which the regents controlled. During the War of the Austrian Succession, the French conquest of much of the neighbouring Austrian Netherlands had caused a panic, highlighting as did the lack of central leadership and the absence of a commanding military presence in the office of captain-general, traditionally held by the *stadtholder*. With the support of a broad segment of the population, the position of *stadtholder* was restored in the person of William IV, Prince of Orange (1711–51), a distant relative of William III.

William IV came to power amid hopes that he would be able to reform the archaic political structure and break the stranglehold of the regents on the political and economic life of the country. But it soon became apparent that he was satisfied merely to replace the power of the regents with his own. On his death in 1751, his three-year-old son became William V, with the regents once again in control until he reached the age of majority in 1766. Even then, however, William remained largely ineffective.

Meanwhile, the political ground was shifting under the feet of both the *stadtholder* and the regents. As in England and elsewhere, political consciousness was growing among ordinary people—merchants, craftsmen, and farmers—and fusing with Enlightenment rhetoric about the rights of man. In the Dutch Republic, the result took the form of a Patriot movement; or rather, multiple Patriot movements, reflecting the diversity of the Republic's towns and provinces. What they shared was the perception that Orangists and regents alike were corrupt and self-interested, concerned only with preserving their privileges and rehashing old battles. Patriot activists called for an effective national government regulated by a written constitution that gave voice to sober men of property like themselves.

This three-way conflict reached a crisis as a result of the American Revolution. The Prince of Orange had close ties with the British royal family, and Orangists generally favoured the British side. The regents generally favoured neutrality (traditionally better for commerce), but many merchants were quite happy to supply the American rebels, while Patriots saw in the struggle of the American colonists a mirror image of their own desire for political rights. Accordingly, Britain declared war on the Republic in 1780 and quickly seized not only its West Indian colonies but much of the Dutch merchant fleet.

This catastrophe inflamed political debate in the Dutch Republic, as Patriot ideology now merged with a militant anti-British nationalism. A draft constitution was proposed in 1785 that echoed the US Declaration of Independence. Patriot groups formed their own citizen militias to battle Orangists, and by the late 1780s a civil war was developing. After Patriots seized control of Utrecht, Amsterdam, and The Hague, the States of Holland tried to defuse the tension by depriving William V of the title of captain-general and refusing to supply troops for his army. As preparations began for elections to a national assembly, the prospect of an entirely new political order for the Dutch Republic began to take shape.

William V seemed disinclined to fight for his power, but his wife was not. A sister of Frederick the Great, in 1787 she prevailed on him to invade and restore order. When Prussian forces restored William V to power, many leading Patriots fled to France, where they were soon caught up in the ferment of the French Revolution.

Diplomacy and War in the Eighteenth Century

The Peace of Utrecht—the treaties that ended the War of the Spanish Succession in 1713–14—had inaugurated a new era in European diplomacy, one that would last until the outbreak of the wars provoked by the French Revolution in 1792. No longer would the foreign policy of European states be driven by religion, or by concern for the *gloire* of the ruler. In keeping with the internal development of European states, diplomats and rulers were now more conscious of the interests of the state as an abstract entity. The goal of diplomacy and warfare was increasingly to expand the territory or resources of the state. At the same time, statesmen were conscious of the need to maintain a balance of power that would prevent any one state from dominating the system as Habsburg Spain had, or France under Louis XIV. State alliances would now be determined by national interest, unencumbered by dynastic ties or religious considerations. In this way the eighteenth century came to be characterized by uncertain, shifting alliances as rulers and foreign ministers constantly reassessed their positions and interests. Diplomacy took on a much more calculating and ruthless character, and war became a more focused and deliberate means of extending state power—what the Prussian military theorist Carl von Clausewitz (1780–1831) would call "the continuation of politics by other means."

Although war became more deadly on the battlefield, it generally became less disastrous for civilian populations. The reasons for going to war in the eighteenth century included territorial expansion, unclear or disputed succession, and conflicts involving colonies or control of the sea. It was in this period that overseas and colonial concerns, which had been considered relatively unimportant, became determining factors in relations among European states.

Although alliances frequently shifted, one constant was the enduring conflict between Great Britain and France. Britain was always wary of efforts by France to expand its influence in the Netherlands, as French control of the Channel and North Sea coasts inevitably threatened British commerce. France, for its part, was continually looking for ways to diminish British trade. Their rivalry extended not only westward to the Caribbean and North America, but eastward to India.

Another constant was the rivalry between Prussia and the Habsburg monarchy for pre-eminence in Germany. Although Frederick William I had been sufficiently old-fashioned to concede primacy in Germany to the Habsburgs, this was not the case with Frederick the Great, who considered the Holy Roman Empire to be an irrelevant anachronism, and who, unlike his cautious father, was willing to use his army in battle.

Russia's only consistent rivalry was with the fading Ottoman Empire, whose lands around the Black Sea it coveted. There were irritations in Russian relations with both the Habsburgs and Prussia, but different Russian rulers at different times were willing to work with either and in some cases both, as was the case with successive partitions of Poland.

For several decades after the protracted period of war examined in Chapter 7, Europe had remained relatively peaceful. Britain and France were exhausted by their long struggle, and both Walpole and Fleury were more interested in domestic stability than territorial conquest. Frederick William I of Prussia was content to keep building his army without using it; Habsburg rulers were focused on ensuring recognition of the Pragmatic Sanction; and Russia was preoccupied by the instability of its political leadership.

The first major conflict to disrupt this period of stability was the War of the Polish Succession (1733–7), which illustrated many of the general themes noted above. What sparked the war was concern among various rulers that allowing one of their rivals to determine the disputed succession would add unduly to his strength and thus threaten the balance of power. Since the outbreak of the Great Northern War in 1700, two adversaries had claimed the Polish throne: Augustus II, who was also the Elector of Saxony, and the Polish nobleman Stanislas Leszcynski. Augustus had been elected king by the Polish nobles in 1697, but Charles XII of Sweden had ousted him and installed Leszcynski in his place in 1704. The fortunes of war restored Augustus to the throne in 1709. An involved and active king, Augustus attempted, with some success, to enhance the still very limited powers of the Polish monarchy, and to make the crown hereditary in his family. But Leszcynski had not renounced his claim. Having settled in France, where his daughter Marie married the young Louis XV in 1725, Leszcynski had French backing for his claim to the Polish throne.

When Augustus II died in 1733, the Polish *Sejm* elected Leszcynski to succeed him despite the objections of Russia's Empress Anna and the Habsburg Emperor Charles VI, both of whom recognized Augustus's son as king. Since France and Spain (both ruled by kings of the Bourbon dynasty) were backing Leszcynski, Britain lined up with Austria and Russia. Most of the fighting took place outside Poland, primarily in western Germany and in Italy. A preliminary peace was negotiated in 1735 and formally ratified in the Treaty of Vienna of 1738. Augustus II's son was recognized as King Augustus III of Poland (r. 1743–63) as well as Elector of Saxony. To compensate Leszcynski for his renunciation of the Polish throne, he was made Duke of Lorraine, replacing (as we saw earlier) Francis Stephen, who became Grand Duke of Tuscany. Charles III of Spain, who had long wanted to restore Spanish power in Italy, gained Sicily and Naples, which had been given to the Habsburgs in the Peace of Utrecht.

The War of the Austrian Succession (1740–8) was much more serious. Even though his father had accepted the Pragmatic Sanction, agreeing to recognize the right of a female to inherit all the Habsburg lands, when Frederick the Great became King of Prussia in 1740, he took advantage of the presumed weakness of Maria Theresa to seize the prosperous Habsburg province of Silesia on the barest of pretexts. The Elector of Bavaria soon followed suit, invading Bohemia and enlisting France to support his claim to the throne of Austria. Then France went on to strike its own blow against its historic foe by conquering much of the Austrian Netherlands. Unexpectedly, however, Maria Theresa was able to rally Hungary to her side, and in alliance with Britain eventually turned the tables on her enemies.

But the War of the Austrian Succession was not limited to Europe. Since 1739 Britain had been fighting Bourbon Spain (a French ally) in the largely maritime and colonial conflict known as the War of Jenkins' Ear.[11] Now on opposite sides of the conflict in Europe, Britain and France took the opportunity to go after one another's colonial possessions, often with the assistance of indigenous allies. In North America each harassed the other's settlements, and in 1745 the British succeeded in taking the French stronghold of

Louisbourg, on Cape Breton Island. Meanwhile in India, where the French and English East India Companies allied themselves with rival Indian rulers, the British tried and failed to take the French fortress of Pondichéry, while the French succeeded in taking the British stronghold of Madras.

In 1748 the war was formally ended by the Treaty of Aix-la-Chapelle, which restored the pre-war status quo almost entirely: the exception was Silesia, which Prussia kept. Otherwise Maria Theresa retained control of the Habsburg territories. France gave back its conquests in the Austrian Netherlands and recovered Cape Breton, including Louisbourg, from the English, while the English East India Company recovered Madras from the French. The treaty also ended the conflict between Britain and Spain, with Britain retaining its trading position in the Spanish empire in the New World, including the profitable *asiento*, the contract for supplying Spanish colonies with African slaves.

In reality, however, the Treaty of Aix-la-Chapelle marked no more than a hiatus in hostilities. British and French forces continued to fight in North America and India, while in Europe Maria Theresa was determined to recover Silesia and punish Frederick the Great. Thus in 1756 she and her foreign minister, Count Kaunitz, engineered the so-called "Diplomatic Revolution." Reversing centuries of hostility, France and the Habsburg monarchy now formed an alliance against Prussia, in which Russia and Sweden joined them, while Britain allied itself with Prussia, although its small standing army was preoccupied with colonial matters and all it could offer was financial support.

The Seven Years War began in 1756 when Frederick the Great, facing a hostile alliance, invaded Saxony in a pre-emptive strike. He decisively defeated a French and Habsburg army in 1757, but Russia invaded from the east, taking the Prussian provinces of Pomerania and Brandenburg, and even occupying Berlin for a time. Sorely pressed on all sides, Frederick managed to preserve his lands only through the brilliant campaigning that won him and his army their illustrious reputations. His opponents lost an important advantage with the death of Empress Elizabeth of Russia in 1762 and the accession of Peter III (see above), who was a great admirer of Frederick and therefore signed a separate peace (the Treaty of St. Petersburg, 1762) that permitted the latter to concentrate his attention on France and the Habsburgs. The Treaty of Hubertusburg in in February 1763 once again restored the pre-war status quo in Europe, leaving Silesia permanently under Prussian rule.

Notwithstanding the Treaty of Aix-la-Chapelle, hostilities between France and Britain overseas had never entirely stopped. In the Ohio valley a network of French forts stood in the way of westward migration from the British colonies on the coast, and in 1754 a British force under a young officer named George Washington attempted to take one of them (Fort Duquesne, now Pittsburgh). But the French and their indigenous allies prevailed; this was the beginning of the conflict that in US history is known as the French and Indian War. Similarly in India, the French and English East India Companies, together with their respective Indian allies, had never really stopped fighting. In both cases, the beginning of the Seven Years War was the pretext for full-scale conflict. In many ways, the Seven Years War, or at least the French–British component of it, was the first global conflict.

At first the French made some impressive gains, seizing Calcutta in India and the Mediterranean island of Minorca. But when dissatisfaction with the war effort brought William Pitt the Elder to power in Britain in 1758 (see above), he soon took the battle to the French. In 1758 British forces demolished the fortress of Louisbourg, and in October 1759 Quebec fell to General James Wolfe in the Battle of the Plains of Abraham. A British naval victory at Quiberon Bay, off the Atlantic coast of France, the following month secured Britain's command of the Atlantic, and thereafter the French were unable to reinforce their outposts in the New World. The fall of Montreal in 1760 opened the entire St. Lawrence valley to the British, who also conquered the Caribbean sugar islands of Guadeloupe (1759) and Martinique (1762).

In India too, British forces were able to turn the tables on the French. A British force under Robert Clive recaptured Calcutta and in 1757 at the Battle of Plassey defeated a large army of Indian rulers allied with the French. After the capital of French India, Pondichéry, fell to the British in 1761, the French presence there was no longer significant.

The Treaty of Paris (1763) more or less ratified Britain's supremacy overseas. Although France regained Guadeloupe and Martinique, the British kept Cape Breton Island, Quebec, and virtually all the French territories east of the Mississippi River.[12] Most of the French were content to let go of Canada, which Voltaire dismissed as "a few acres of snow" (*quelques arpents de neige*), as long as they could keep the lucrative sugar colonies of Martinique and Guadeloupe. Britain also gained the colony of Florida from France's ally Spain, although Spain was granted the French lands west of the Mississippi

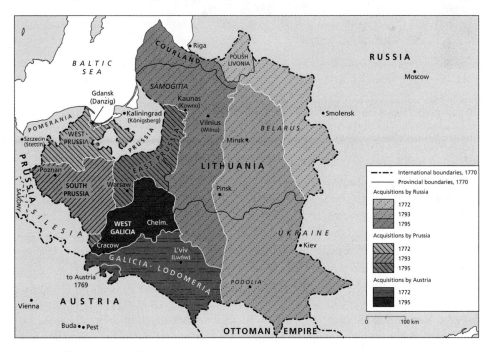

Map 10.2 The partitions of Poland

Le Gâteau des Rois (The Cake of Kings), 1773. A French satire on the first division of Poland. Second from the left, King Stanislaus of Poland struggles to keep his crown on his head as Catherine the Great, Joseph II, and Frederick the Great all gaze away from the map as if repulsed by what they are doing. Above, an angel uses two trumpets to herald their double achievement in maintaining peace while accomplishing their material aims.

in compensation. Although France would pursue its quarrel with Britain in the American Revolutionary War, with disastrous consequences for the French monarchy, the Seven Years War was the last major conflict in Europe before the outbreak of the Revolutionary Wars in 1792.

Russia had played only a tangential role in the War of Austrian Succession, but was much more involved in the Seven Years War. Its primary concern was expansion to the south and east, which brought it into conflict not only with various Cossack tribes, as we have seen, but also with the Ottoman Empire. A war with the Ottomans in 1735–9, in which Russia fought alongside the Habsburgs, gained it possession of the Black Sea fortress of Azov. Some thirty years later, a second Russo-Turkish conflict (1768–74) ended in the Treaty of Kuchuk Kainarji, which declared the Russian Emperor to be the protector of the Sultan's Orthodox Christian subjects and ceded the Crimean peninsula to Russian control. Now Russia had a springboard for further encroachment into Ottoman territory.

At the same time, Russia joined with Prussia and the Habsburg monarchy to scheme against Poland in a way that exemplified the new diplomatic realities. Augustus III, who was also Elector of Saxony, was more interested in the latter than in Poland, which resumed the slide towards political incoherence and internal anarchy that his father had temporarily halted. On his death in 1763, Catherine the Great of Russia and Frederick the Great of Prussia used their influence among Polish nobles to have them elect the Polish nobleman Stanislas Poniatowski (1732–98) as king, thinking that he would be easy to control. But he proved to be an effective and activist ruler, and therefore alienated many nobles who were accustomed to running the show, such as it was. In 1768, when a rebellion of Russian Orthodox Christians in eastern Poland raised the spectre of Russian intervention, Stanislas enlisted Britain and Prussia as allies, hoping to prevent a Russian invasion. But in a cynical move that demonstrated the triumph of *raison d'état* and the transitory nature of alliances, Prussia joined with the Habsburgs and Russia in negotiating a treaty among themselves that sliced off portions of Poland to their own benefit. Under military threat, and in reaction against Stanislas's reforms, the Polish *Sejm* agreed to the plan. Prussia gained the territory of West Prussia, which now linked Brandenburg and East Prussia. Russia gained a collection of Polish provinces in the northeast, while the Habsburgs obtained the province of Galicia in the south. At a stroke Poland lost 30 per cent of its territory and 50 per cent of its population. In losing West Prussia to Frederick the Great, Poland lost its most important access to Baltic Sea and control of more than 80 per cent of its foreign trade. Fatally weakened, Poland would be partitioned twice more (in 1793 and in 1795) by its rapacious neighbours, after which it would disappear from the map until 1918.

Chapter Conclusion

The concept of enlightened despotism, or enlightened absolutism, has come up many times in this chapter. As we have seen, not all the reforms undertaken in the eighteenth century, even by "enlightened" monarchs, can be seen in that light. And even supposedly "unenlightened" monarchs (Maria Theresa, Frederick William I) undertook some reforms that could be considered part of the enlightened "program," such as codification of laws and reductions of fiscal privilege. The most successful enlightened despots were the ones who put the state's interests first, like Frederick the Great, who implemented reforms only as far as they benefited the state, or at least did not harm it. Those who lost sight of the state's interests, like Joseph II, would not only forfeit their reforms, but put their states' survival in question.

Enlightened despotism was a possibility only where political and social structures favoured it. In politically complex societies such as England and France, with strong middle classes and lower classes that were increasingly aware of political issues, concerted opposition from the Parlements (France) and Parliament (England) made the "enlightened" reduction of privilege extremely difficult. The societies of central and eastern Europe were simpler, with smaller, less powerful middle classes and larger, mostly unfree peasant populations under the control of noble landlords. Without a large and wealthy middle class for support, rulers there could not attack noble political power in the way that Louis XIV had. If rulers could work out a modus vivendi with their nobles, however, reform was a possibility, as long as they did nothing to violate the agreement. This was the achievement of Frederick the Great and the Achilles heel of Joseph II.

One incentive for rulers to implement reforms, whether or not they were motivated by enlightened ideals, was the opportunity to streamline the apparatus of the state and make it more efficient. This consideration assumed particular importance in the international environment of the eighteenth century, in which rulers and states needed every advantage they could get in their competition with other states.

As was mentioned at the beginning of this chapter, one of most important developments of the eighteenth century was the emergence of the impersonal state from the shadow of hereditary monarchy, under whose auspices it had been developing since the late Middle Ages. Even rulers increasingly thought of themselves as custodians rather than owner-proprietors, couching their actions in the language of "the Rights of Man," "the general good," or "the greatest happiness of the people." What they did not foresee was the danger that this ultimately posed not only to their power, but to monarchy itself. In France, however, this language was appropriated by privileged groups such as the nobility and the Parlements, in defence of their privileges against a "despotic" king and his ministers. That they were playing with fire was evident only after the fact, when the edifice of monarchy had burned to the ground.

Questions for Critical Thought

1. Which "enlightened" reforms of the eighteenth century foreshadowed modern political structures and conceptions? Which did not?
2. Is "enlightened despotism" a useful concept in thinking about the evolution of the state and politics?
3. A key feature of eighteenth-century political history was the decoupling of an abstract state from hereditary dynastic monarchy. How was this manifested and what were its consequences?
4. What aspects of politics and government did not change in the course of the eighteenth century?

Weblinks

"Frederick the Great and the Enigma of Prussia" (BBC documentary):
www.youtube.com/watch?v=nuI2zPyouiA

"League of Gentlemen: Officers of the 17th and 18th Centuries," by John A. Lynn (a leading military historian of early modern Europe):
www.historynet.com/league-of-gentlemen-officers-of-the-17th-and-18th-centuries.htm

Further Reading

Blanning, T.C.W., ed. *The Eighteenth Century*. Oxford: Oxford University Press, 2000. An important collection of essays by leading scholars.

Colley, Linda. Britons: *Forging the Nation, 1707–1837*, rev. ed. New Haven: Yale University Press, 2009. The best recent examination of eighteenth-century Britain.

Doyle, William. *The Ancien Regime*, 2nd ed. Houndmills: Palgrave, 2001. A brief and accessible analysis of pre-revolutionary France.

Hufton, Olwen. *Europe: Privilege and Protest, 1730*, 2nd ed. Oxford: Blackwell, 2000. Especially strong on the transformation of politics. Excludes Britain.

Raeff, Marc. *The Well-Ordered Police State: Social and Institutional Change through Law in the Germanies and Russia, 1600–1800*. New Haven: Yale University Press, 1983. A pioneering study of expanding state control and cameralism.

Scott, H.M., ed. *Enlightened Absolutism: Reform and Reformers in Later Eighteenth-Century Europe*. Ann Arbor: University of Michigan Press, 1990. An instructive and important collection of essays on enlightened despotism.

Woloch, Isser, and Brown, Gregory S. *Eighteenth-Century Europe: Tradition and Progress, 1715–1789*, 2nd ed. New York: Norton, 2012. A comprehensive survey with an extensive bibliography.

Notes

1. Marc Raeff, *The Well-Ordered Police State: Social and Institutional Change through Law in the Germanies and Russia, 1600–1800* (New Haven: Yale University Press, 1983), p. 5.
2. The two terms are used virtually interchangeably. In English, "enlightened despotism" has been the dominant term, although in many ways it is less satisfactory than "enlightened absolutism" because of its connotations of dictatorship and tyranny.
3. Eberhard Weis, "Enlightenment and Absolutism in the Holy Roman Empire: Thoughts on Enlightened Absolutism in Germany," *Journal of Modern History*, 58 (1986), Supplement, p. 197.
4. H.M. Scott, *Enlightened Absolutism: Reform and Reformers in Later Eighteenth-Century Europe* (Ann Arbor: University of Michigan Press, 1990), p. 1.
5. Quoted in Gerhard Ritter, *Frederick the Great: A Historical Profile*, trans. Peter Paret (Berkeley: University of California Press, 1970), p. 19.
6. Quoted in Roger Wines (ed.), *Enlightened Despotism: Reform or Reaction?* (Boston: D.C. Heath, 1967), p. 16.
7. Peter preferred "Emperor" to the historic title "Tsar." Until the Russian Revolution of 1917, therefore, all Russian rulers were technically emperors, although "tsar" continued in common usage.
8. John T. Alexander, *Catherine the Great: Life and Legend* (Oxford: Oxford University Press, 1989), p. 101.
9. Literally, "bed of justice," referring to the canopied litter in which the king entered the Parlement's chamber.
10. Quoted in Olwen Hufton, *Europe: Privilege and Protest, 1730–1789* (Oxford: Blackwell, 2000), p. 224.
11. In 1731 a Spanish ship had seized a British ship suspected of smuggling in the Caribbean, and in the fighting the ear of the British captain (Jenkins) was severed. The ear was supposedly used as a prop in Parliament during an inflammatory speech demanding war with Spain.
12. France did retain fishing rights in Newfoundland, as well as the small islands of St-Pierre and Miquelon in the Gulf of St. Lawrence, which remain French possessions today.

11

Europe in the World, 1650–1800

In the Middle Ages Europe was a relatively isolated region at the far western end of the Eurasian landmass, both poorer and less advanced than the Middle East, India, and China. In the late fifteenth century European explorers, sailors, and merchants began to "discover" the rest of the globe, establishing contact with Asia and decimating indigenous populations in the New World. By the mid-seventeenth century Europe was quickly catching up to the older and wealthier societies to the east: the Turkish Ottoman Empire, which dominated the eastern Mediterranean and Middle East; the Mughal empire, which ruled much of the Indian subcontinent; and China, where the Manchu Qing dynasty had recently replaced the xenophobic and isolationist Ming dynasty. By the end of the eighteenth century Europe was poised on the brink of an unprecedented global dominance that would last throughout the nineteenth century and into the twentieth. What factors allowed Europe not only to catch up with older and wealthier civilizations, but in short order to surpass them? What effects did this process have on European states and societies? How did Europe's achievement of dominance affect the global balance? These questions are the subject of this chapter.

Colonial Empires in the New World

By the middle of the seventeenth century, only Spain and Portugal had established durable colonial empires in the New World. The English settlements in North America, concentrated in Virginia and New England, were still small, the French settlements in Acadia and Quebec were even smaller, and the future was precarious for all of them. A century later, things were very different. In the Caribbean, both England and France had established plantation societies devoted to sugar production: England had Jamaica and Barbados, and France St. Domingue (modern Haiti), Martinique, and Guadeloupe. In addition, the Dutch had commercial entrepôts on Curaçao and St. Eustatius, and even Denmark had acquired several islands (now part of the US Virgin Islands). On the east coast of North America a string of English settlements stretched from Georgia to Maine. And to the north, renewed French interest in overseas affairs, driven largely by Louis XIV's finance minister, Jean-Baptiste Colbert (Chapter 6), had brought new life to the settlements of New France. With the growth of their empires in the New World, colonial rivalries moved out of the background to become the driving force in relations between European states.

The motivation for these developments was the vast wealth that could be generated by exploiting the resources of the Americas. The riches went far beyond the gold and silver available in places like Mexico and Peru, although these were very important; indeed, after a significant slump in the seventeenth century, silver production in the Spanish empire tripled over the course of the eighteenth. By 1700, the New World, Europe, and Africa were closely linked in a triangular trade pattern: basic commodities such as sugar, fur, timber, indigo, tobacco, and precious metals were shipped from the New World to Europe; manufactured goods from Europe such as textiles, metal wares, firearms, and rum (made with sugar produced in the New World) were shipped to Africa, and people from Africa were shipped to the New World to provide the slave labour on which the plantation system depended. The

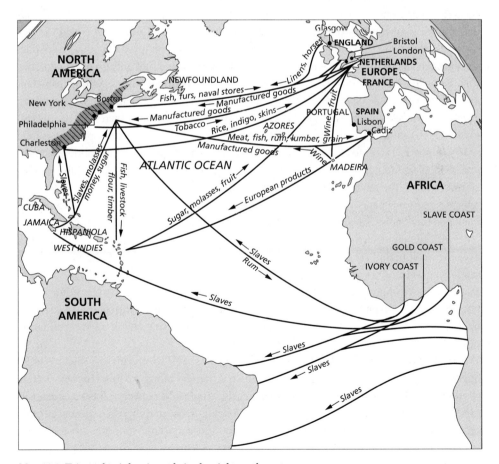

Map 11.1 Triangular Atlantic trade in the eighteenth century

most important plantations were the sugar-producing operations of Brazil and the West Indies, but other crops that depended on slave labour included tobacco, indigo, rice, and eventually cotton and coffee. These staples were then shipped back to Europe for processing, domestic sale, and export to other countries. In addition, Spanish, French, and English colonies produced primary commodities such as fish, grain, furs, and timber, which could be sold not only in Europe but in the Caribbean, which did not grow enough food to feed either its few European colonists or its vast numbers of African slaves. In the latter case, molasses would be shipped back to North America to be processed into rum, both for internal consumption and for export. Clearly, the economic relationship between the Old World and the New had evolved beyond simple resource extraction and exploitation of precious metals.

As far as European rulers and governments were concerned, colonies existed for the benefit of their mother countries, all of which attempted to extend their own governance structures to their overseas possessions. Thus royal viceroys or governors were appointed to represent the monarch, administrative structures were put in place that followed European models, and colonial commerce was restricted in accordance with the interests of the mother country. Until very late in the eighteenth century, for example, inhabitants of Spanish America were forbidden to trade with any ship that did not operate out of the port of Càdiz, which held the monopoly on trade with the colonies. The English Navigation Acts required that English colonies sell their products only to England or other English colonies, and that only English or colonial ships be used to carry goods. When growing colonies tired of importing everything from their mother countries and began to establish their own manufacturing facilities, the metropolitan governments tried to minimize the threat to their own manufacturers by restricting the sale of colonial manufactured goods to the colonies that produced them. But these provisions were nearly impossible to enforce, especially in Spanish America, where industrial development was primitive and English, French, or Dutch merchants could supply goods of higher quality at lower prices. The restrictions were easier for inhabitants of English colonies to accept, as they realized some benefit from the mother country in the form of English capital for investment and the English naval strength that safeguarded their settlements and commerce.

Until the eighteenth century, European powers had not exercised very tight control over their colonial possessions. As we saw in Chapter 10, however, the Enlightenment era saw a general trend towards the rationalization of state operations. Thus Britain sought to make its increasingly prosperous American colonies contribute more to the home country, which had been paying for their defence. By this time, however, the colonies had developed a sense of their own identity, and they rebelled at what they saw as the subordination of their interests to those of the mother country.

Similar considerations led Spain and Portugal as well to rationalize their colonial operations, with the result that most of Spanish America, along with Portuguese Brazil, would likewise become independent in the early nineteenth century. The situation was different for the plantation colonies of the Caribbean. Because they relied almost entirely on their mother countries for political, military, and economic support, most of them would not become independent until the twentieth century.

By 1800, Spanish America had a total population of approximately 14.5 million people, concentrated in the valleys of Mexico and Peru. While the countryside was inhabited primarily by indigenous and *mestizo* (mixed) subsistence farmers, urban populations were largely *mestizo* and Creole (people of Spanish ancestry born in the New World). Spain also had territories in the Caribbean, including Cuba, Puerto Rico, and the

Map 11.2 European colonial empires in the New World

eastern half of the island of Hispaniola (the modern Dominican Republic), but the sugar cane they grew was only a minor component of the agricultural production that, with silver, was the main source of wealth in Spanish America. Thus for a long time the islands were of interest to Spain mainly as bases for the ships that controlled access to the Gulf of Mexico. Officially, trade to and from Spanish America was a government monopoly operated through the port of Càdiz.[1] In fact, however, smuggling was widespread, and illegal trade flourished with British, French, and Dutch merchants.

In theory Spain claimed all of the Americas except for Brazil (assigned to Portugal by the 1494 Treaty of Tordesillas). However, vast parts of the territory were obviously not under Spanish control, including the English and French colonies in North America; the vast expanses of land to the west where indigenous peoples had their own cultures, economies, and political structures; the Dutch colony of Suriname; and the French outpost of Cayenne (now French Guiana). Nevertheless, the area under Spanish control did expand as Spanish soldiers, settlers, and missionaries established outposts in what are now Argentina, Uruguay, Texas, New Mexico, and California.

We saw in Chapter 10 how Charles III, having introduced a variety of reforms in Naples and Sicily, did the same when he inherited the Spanish throne. In addition, he took steps to address the corruption and lax administration in Spain's overseas colonies that he believed were preventing them from realizing their potential. The wealth and privileges of the Catholic Church were reduced and the Jesuits expelled; intendants were appointed to oversee colonial administration; and additional troops were sent, both to protect against foreign incursions and to suppress indigenous uprisings. At the same time, to reduce the grievances leading to uprisings, the laws governing indigenous labour were reformed, and the practice of *repartimiento*—forcing workers to buy goods at artificially high prices— was prohibited. Nevertheless, the fact that most of the new positions were filled by Spaniards from Spain (*peninsulares*) rather than Creoles was an irritant to many of the latter, who resented what they saw as meddling by a far-off power that knew nothing of their world and their concerns. After the death of Charles III in 1788, Spain would undergo a period of inept royal leadership, foreign invasion, and civil war, during which its colonies would follow the example of the British colonists and declare their independence.

By the later sixteenth century, Brazil had become Portugal's most lucrative overseas territory, and the destination for significant numbers of settlers. Sugar plantations worked by African slaves quickly became the major suppliers of sugar to Europe and beyond, with the result that by 1580 Brazil had roughly 20,000 Portuguese residents and 14,000 African slaves. Their long experience along the coast of West Africa put the Portuguese in a good position to acquire slaves for Brazilian sugar plantations, and they established a number of fortresses and trading posts along the West African coast where slaves were kept before they were sold and forced onto ships for the horrific "middle passage" to the New World.

The dynastic union of Portugal and Spain from 1580 to 1640 exposed the former's overseas possessions to the enemies of Spain. Two French incursions during this period were short-lived, but from 1630 to 1654 the Dutch West India Company controlled much of Brazil's northeastern coast. The restoration of Portugal's independence in 1640 permitted it to take more concerted action, and in 1661 the Dutch signed a treaty formally abandoning their claims to Brazil.

In addition to sugar, Brazil produced timber, tobacco, and leather, and together these products made Brazil Portugal's most important source of revenue; in fact, Brazil was substantially wealthier than Portugal itself. The discovery of significant gold deposits in the late seventeenth century attracted roughly a million people to the area, of whom probably 600,000 came from Portugal itself. Brazil's non-indigenous population continued to expand from perhaps 100,000 in 1600 to 300,000 in 1700 and more than 3,000,000 in 1800—equivalent to the population of the mother country—of whom as many as one-third were African slaves. By the later eighteenth century, settlers had established a Portuguese presence throughout most of what is now Brazil.

Meanwhile, Portugal's efforts to strengthen its administration of the colony intensified when gold shipments dropped precipitously after the middle of the century. The Marquis of Pombal (see Chapter 10) established commercial monopolies to circumvent the British traders who had established a dominant position in Portuguese colonial commerce. Taxes were raised, the influence of the Church was curtailed, and in order to increase the population, Pombal eliminated legal distinctions between Portuguese and indigenous people and promoted intermarriage, although these measures likely had little impact. Although the Brazilian elite remained closely tied to Portugal, these measures provoked considerable discontent among less privileged settlers, some of whom planned an uprising for independence in the southern province of Minas Gerais in 1789. It failed, however, and Brazil would not become independent from Portugal until 1822, during the great age of Latin American revolutions for independence.

The Dutch were represented in the New World by a trading company modelled after the East India Company, and it was this West India Company that established sugar plantations worked by African slaves in northeastern Brazil (discussed above), as well as on a handful of islands known as the Netherlands Antilles. In the same 1667 treaty that ceded New Amsterdam (present-day New York) to England, Dutch possession of Suriname on the northeastern coast of South America was recognized. Nevertheless, the position of the Dutch in the New World was marginal compared to that of their competitors, and their own dominant position in the East Indian trade.

To the north, English settlements had been established in New England and Virginia by the early seventeenth century. The settlements of Massachusetts Bay (now Boston), Plymouth, Rhode Island, and Connecticut were founded largely by Puritans escaping government harassment in England (see Chapter 6); the Jamestown settlement in Virginia was begun by a chartered company, but in 1624 was taken over by the Crown; and Maryland was founded by a royal grant in the 1630s as a refuge for English Catholics. By 1650 the total English population of North America was still no more than about 50,000, and their future quite insecure. Over the next few decades, however, their numbers increased. The English conquered New Amsterdam in 1664 and renamed it New York. Charleston in what is now South Carolina, established in 1670, was settled primarily by planters and slaves from Barbados. Pennsylvania was founded in 1681 by a grant of King Charles II to the Quaker leader William Penn (1684–1718).

As the Spanish had done in their colonial empire, English colonists established the political institutions familiar to them. In addition to a governor, appointed in England, each colony had an assembly, which frequently obstructed the governor's agenda. While the nature and scope of the franchise differed from one colony to another, the assemblies generally had the power—like Parliament itself—to authorize the collection of tax revenue on an annual basis. As in England, clashes between the executive and the local representatives were frequent, especially over money, and governors often had difficulty bending colonial assemblies to their will.

The British North American colonies grew dramatically in the eighteenth century, both demographically and economically. By the 1770s their overall population had reached 2.5 million—roughly one-third the size of Great Britain itself. The colonies became increasingly integrated into the British economy, as markets for British manufactured goods, suppliers of agricultural products not grown in Britain (such as tobacco), sources of wealth for lending or investment, and sources of food for the plantations on the Caribbean islands. With the expanding population came the desire for more land, and the colonies quickly spread inland from the coastal plains. But they were hemmed in first by the Appalachian mountains and then, in the Ohio valley, by the presence of the French and their indigenous allies (see below). As we saw in Chapter 10, the resulting tensions were among the factors that led to the Seven Years War. Following the 1763 Treaty of Paris, in which France ceded its North American colonies to Britain, the 1774 Quebec Act incorporated the French territory of Louisiana (which then included the Ohio valley and the Mississippi basin) into Quebec, rather than opening it to settlement from the older British colonies. Colonial resentment of this measure, along with efforts to tighten central control over the colonies, helped to spur the independence movement that led to the formation of the United States. In essence, the American Revolution was a creole rebellion by prosperous and populous colonies that saw their interests subordinated to the economic, political, and diplomatic interests of the mother country. Their resentment combined with the natural rights political discourse of the Enlightenment to produce a potent movement that not only achieved independence for the United States, but helped to inspire independence movements in Spanish and Portuguese America as well.

Earlier French attempts to establish colonies in North America had foundered in the face of harsh conditions and hostility from some indigenous groups. Although Samuel de Champlain (1574–1635) had established settlements in Acadia (1605) and Quebec (1608), they languished until the later seventeenth century. French explorers did, however, penetrate the interior of the continent via the St. Lawrence River and Great Lakes. Jean Nicolet (1598–1642) explored Lake Michigan and what is now Wisconsin. Together, the Jesuit priest Jacques Marquette (1637–75) and Louis Jolliet (1645–1700) explored the northern reaches of the Mississippi River in the 1670s. René-Robert de la Salle (1641–87) travelled the whole length of the river and claimed the entire territory for King Louis XIV, calling it Louisiana. He established a short-lived settlement on the gulf coast of what is now Texas and a series of forts from Louisiana to the Great Lakes and the St. Lawrence valley.

French colonies in North America received a fresh impetus during the reign of Louis XIV, when Colbert took over the settlements that had failed to thrive under the private ownership of the Company of New France and put them under direct royal control. The administrative system of France was imposed in the New World, complete with a military governor and civilian intendant. Concerted efforts were made to attract colonists to the St. Lawrence valley and Quebec in particular (Acadia, in modern New Brunswick and Nova Scotia, was an afterthought). To provide wives for the soldiers and colonists, almost all of whom were men, the Crown sent some 800 young women, known as *filles du roi* ("daughters of the king"), between 1663 and 1673, providing them with dowries as well as free passage. Although the numbers of colonists did begin to grow, they probably never exceeded 100,000 even in the eighteenth century—a small fraction of the population of the English colonies to the south—and they remained heavily dependent on the mother country for survival.

As we saw in Chapter 10, hostilities between France and England extended across the Atlantic in the eighteenth century. After changing hands several times in the seventeenth century, Acadia was ceded to Britain in the Peace of Utrecht in 1714. In exchange, the French retained Cape Breton Island, where they built the fortress of Louisbourg to protect the approaches to the St. Lawrence. During the War of the Austrian Succession (1740–8) French and British forces clashed in the Ohio valley, and the English captured Louisbourg, which was returned to France in the 1748 Treaty of Aix-la-Chapelle, prompting the English to establish a fortress at Halifax in 1749. Six years later, in 1755, Britain expelled some 10,000 French Acadians and confiscated their lands. Some settled on Cape Breton Island and in what are now New Brunswick and Prince Edward Island. Some "returned" either to France or to its colonies in the Caribbean, and others made their way to Louisiana, where their descendants would come to be known as Cajuns.

The Seven Years War (1756–63) has been called the first great war for empire. Population growth and land hunger led the British colonists to push westwards beyond the Appalachian mountains where they encountered French fortresses and native allies of the French. Although the French held their own against the British in the Ohio valley, events elsewhere sealed their fate. In 1758 British forces once again captured Louisbourg, and this time destroyed the fortress. In 1759 Quebec fell to the British general James Wolfe. In the 1763 Treaty of Paris, France regained Martinique and Guadeloupe, which the British had taken during the war, in exchange for its North American possessions east of the Mississippi to the British. France's North American territories west of the Mississippi, as well as the city of New Orleans, were ceded to Spain.

Ties between New France and the mother country had remained too close during the eighteenth century for its people to develop the kind of independent identity that the British and Spanish colonists did. After the fall of Quebec the British allowed the people of New France to retain their Catholic religion and distinctive legal and social structures and traditions. The vastly greater numbers of British colonists to the south represented a continuing threat to the people of New France, and for this reason they focused their energy on preserving their French culture and Catholic faith.

Trading Empires in Asia

If Europeans in the New World focused on building colonial empires, in Asia a number of large and powerful empires were already in place. Therefore European activity centred almost exclusively on trade, and for the most part Europe's presence was limited to fortified trading posts in the regions of Indian Ocean and East Asia. In exchange for their permission to trade, local rulers received valuable revenue and, increasingly, access to European technology and expertise, primarily military.

The Portuguese had been the first Europeans to establish a permanent presence in the Indian Ocean and Asia, but in the course of the seventeenth century they were eclipsed by the Dutch East India Company (VOC). The VOC took over Portuguese establishments in India, Sri Lanka, and Malacca (in modern Malaysia), which commanded the vital straits between Sumatra and the Malay peninsula. But it was above all a trading company, and it positively discouraged the acquisition of territory except where necessary for commercial purposes. The only Dutch territorial possession of any consequence in the east was Batavia (now Jakarta) and the surrounding territory on the island of Java. For several centuries what Europeans had wanted from Asia was spices, but since there were very few European goods that Asian traders desired, the spice trade necessitated a significant outflow of bullion, especially silver (it has been estimated that one-third of the silver mined in the New World ended up in Asia). This would remain an issue until the nineteenth century, when industrialization made it possible for mass-produced manufactured goods to dominate Asian markets.

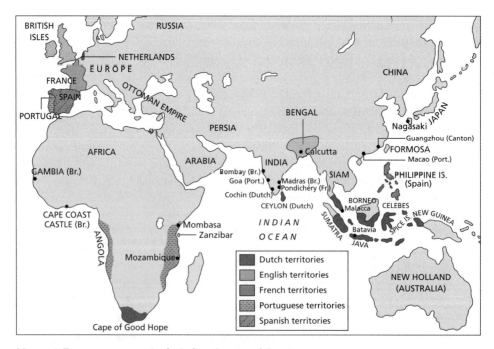

Map 11.3 European presence in the Indian Ocean and East Asia

By 1700, decades of war had weakened the Dutch Republic vis–à-vis its English and French competitors, and the dominance of the VOC was beginning to wane. Although it did promote the cultivation of coffee in Java, otherwise it remained overwhelmingly focused on the spice trade, and neglected to gain a foothold in other increasingly popular Asian products, such as tea from China and Japan, silk, porcelain, lacquer ware, and brightly coloured cotton calicoes from India. Although the company remained profitable for a long time, it was clearly behind the curve in Asian trade, and it was dissolved in 1799.

The English East India Company (EEIC) operated somewhat differently than the VOC. Kept out of the spice trade by the latter in the seventeenth century, it turned its attention to the Indian subcontinent instead. At the time, most of India was ruled by the powerful Mughals: Muslims of Mongol–Turkish descent who had arrived as conquerors in the sixteenth century but left in place local political, economic, and social systems in exchange for taxes and tribute. After the death of the ruthlessly effective emperor Aurangzeb (1658–1707), under whom the Mughal empire reached its maximum extent, regional rulers began to reassert their authority.

Before the mid-eighteenth century, the EEIC operated in much the same way in India as the Dutch company did in the East Indies, as merchants rather than as agents of empire. Granted permission to trade in Bombay (Mumbai) and several other ports, by 1700, the company had established important fortified trading posts in Madras (Chennai) and Calcutta (Kolkata), on India's east coast. At the same time, its focus shifted from the spice trade to other commodities, primarily cotton, tea, and, eventually, opium for export to China.

By the middle of the eighteenth century, however, the decline of the Mughal empire led both the EEIC and its rival, the French East India Company, to form alliances with local rulers. By the end of the Seven Years War the British had effectively expelled the French from India and the EEIC had taken on a new role as an agent of British power. Though still a private company, it was effectively in control of large parts of India, including the large and prosperous state of Bengal, where it made its headquarters at Calcutta (Kolkata).

The impact of European traders, sailors, and soldiers was less significant in China and Japan, where strong central governments made it much more difficult for Europeans to exploit internal divisions. European trade in China required the explicit permission of the emperor, and was limited to a handful of southern Chinese ports, most notably Guangzhou (Canton). In addition, since Europe produced nothing that the Chinese wanted to buy, for a long time Europeans had to pay for Chinese goods with silver. This situation did not change until the British began smuggling vast quantities of Indian opium—banned by the emperor in 1729—into China. In the nineteenth century, Britain would fight two wars in China to guarantee that opium could be freely exported to China. Japan was even more resistant to European contact than China. The Portuguese had established trading relations with Japan in the sixteenth century, and Portuguese missionaries, most notably St. Francis Xavier, had gained considerable numbers of converts there. In 1614, however, a new shogun (military dictator) inaugurated a new age in Japanese history by outlawing Christianity, persecuting Japanese Christians, and severely restricting Japan's contact with the outside world. From 1640 to 1868, foreign trade would be limited to a lone Dutch outpost on an island in Nagasaki harbour.

The New Age of Exploration

In the course of the eighteenth century, European sailors also explored regions of the globe that until then had been largely unknown. Among those regions was the Pacific Ocean. Every year since 1565, a Spanish treasure fleet had sailed west from Acapulco to Manila, bearing gold and silver to exchange for Asian imports. And a number of sailors had followed Magellan in circumnavigating the globe (Francis Drake even explored the west coast of North America as far north as modern San Francisco), but their voyages had no lasting impact. In the seventeenth century it was widely assumed that a southern counterpart to the large, inhabited continents of the northern hemisphere must exist somewhere in the south Pacific, and several attempts were made to find it. In the course of searching for this mythical *terra australis*, the Dutch captain Abel Tasman circumnavigated Australia, landed in New Zealand, and explored many islands in the southwest Pacific, including New Guinea. But his employers, the VOC, were interested only in trade opportunities, and the lands he explored seemed too poor and inhospitable to be worth exploiting.

By the later eighteenth century, the motives for overseas exploration had expanded beyond the desire for land and resources to include strategic considerations. France hoped to restore the prestige it had lost with its defeats in North America and India; Spain was concerned to protect its tenuous hold on the Pacific coast of the Americas; and Britain, faced with declining prosperity in the West Indies and emerging troubles in North America, saw the Pacific as a sort of back door to the riches of East Asia. At the same time, the quest for scientific knowledge began to play an increasingly significant role.

In 1766 Louis-Antoine de Bougainville (1729–1811) was commissioned by Louis XV of France to circumnavigate the globe. Accompanied by a team of civilian scientists, including a botanist, a cartographer, an astronomer, and a historian, he visited a number of islands, including Tahiti, which he claimed for France. Returning in 1779, in 1771 he published a very popular account of his voyage, in which he portrayed the Tahitians as innocent "noble savages," living in a paradise on earth.

Twenty years later, Jean-François de Galaup, Count of Lapérouse (1741–88), a naval officer and veteran of the Seven Years War, was commissioned by the French government to complete the explorations of Captain James Cook (below) and map previously uncharted areas. Setting out in 1785, he spent four years exploring the Pacific, visiting Easter Island, the Hawaiian Islands, California, Alaska, the Kamchatka Peninsula, Korea, and Australia. Although all members of the expedition were lost some time after March 1789, probably in the Solomon Islands, Lapérouse had already sent some letters and observations back to France, and from them an account of his voyage was published.

By far the most prominent and prolific explorer of the Pacific was the English captain James Cook (1728–79). An experienced sailor in the British merchant fleet, he served in the Seven Years War, and during the siege of Quebec mapped much of the St. Lawrence River and the island of Newfoundland. His navigational and cartographic skills led to a commission on behalf of the Royal Society to sail into the Pacific and observe the transit of Venus across the sun. On this first voyage (1768–71) Cook's ship *Endeavour* sailed around Cape Horn into the Pacific and then westwards to Tahiti. He then mapped the two islands of New Zealand, proving that they were not, as had been theorized, a peninsula of the long-sought southern continent. In April 1770 he landed on the southeastern coast of Australia at the place he would name Botany Bay (Britain would establish its first Australian penal colony there in 1788) and first encountered the aboriginal people of Australia. From there he sailed north, nearly sinking the *Endeavour* on the Great Barrier Reef, and then continued through the Torres Strait that divides New Guinea and Australia, across the Indian Ocean and around the Cape of Good Hope back to Britain.

In 1772 Cook was charged on behalf of the Royal Society to explore farther south for the hypothetical *terra australis*. Because of the prevailing winds in these latitudes (the "roaring forties") he sailed from west to east around the Cape of Good Hope and across the Indian Ocean. He crossed the Antarctic Circle at several points, but never encountered the Antarctic mainland. He concluded that there must be land to the south, on the basis of the fresh-water ice he saw, but that it would be desolate and uninhabitable. Cook's observations and records on this voyage proved beyond doubt that the *terra australis* was a myth.

Returning to England a hero, Cook was given a lucrative but undemanding job in semi-retirement. He was also elected to the Royal Society, which awarded him a medal for completing his latest circumnavigation without losing a single man to scurvy. Although no one in Cook's day knew that scurvy is caused by lack of vitamin C, it was correctly associated with the lack of fresh food, so Cook was adamant that his men should have as much fresh food as was possible, and he experimented with preventives, including sauerkraut and citrus juice.[2]

Cook came out of his comfortable semi-retirement in 1776 to undertake another search for the fabled Northwest Passage, but this time from the Pacific rather than the Atlantic. Earlier expeditions by John Davis (1550–1605), Henry Hudson (d. 1611), and William Baffin (d. 1622) had concluded that there was an ocean above the North American continent, but that it was choked by ice for much of the year. After revisiting New Zealand and Tahiti, Cook became the first European to set foot on the Hawaiian Islands, which he named the Sandwich Islands. He then explored the west coast of North America from California north. After landing in what is now Oregon, he sailed past the Strait of Juan de Fuca, not realizing that what we know as Vancouver Island was in fact an island, and went ashore at Nootka Sound, where he traded with the local people. He then continued north along the coast of British Columbia and Alaska, through the Bering Strait and into the Arctic Ocean, but was then stymied by sea ice and concluded that the Northwest Passage, if it did exist, was impassable.[3] On the return voyage, in February 1779, he once again landed in Hawaii, this time on the "big island" of Hawaii itself, and was killed in an altercation with the local people that has given rise to a spirited debate among historians and anthropologists (see "Debate," below). His ships and crew would eventually return to Britain the following year.

Spain's exploration of the Pacific under the reforming monarch Charles III (see above and Chapter 10) was intended to strengthen its claim to the entire west coast of North America. Alessandro Malaspina (1754–1810) was an Italian nobleman who became an officer in the Spanish navy. Having sailed around the world between 1786 and 1788, in 1789 he was put in charge of a scientific expedition to the north Pacific. After sailing up the west coast of South and North America as far as Alaska, Malaspina, like Cook, concluded that there was no navigable Northwest Passage to be found. Like Cook as well, he landed at Nootka Sound, where he established friendly relations with the indigenous people. In addition, he mapped much of Vancouver Island and the surrounding islands. In 1792, a subordinate of Malaspina's named Dionisio Galiano (1760–1805) encountered a British expedition under Captain George Vancouver (1757–98), who had sailed with Cook and was now also mapping the Pacific Northwest. Although Spain's ambitions clashed with those of Britain, the two captains negotiated an agreement that acknowledged Britain's rights and interests in the area.[4]

Russia too was a presence in the Pacific. Peter the Great had enlisted the Dane Vitus Bering (1681–1741) to explore and map the unknown territory between Russia and North America. In 1725 he travelled overland across Siberia to the Kamchatka peninsula, where his party built two ships. He then sailed through the strait that now bears his name,

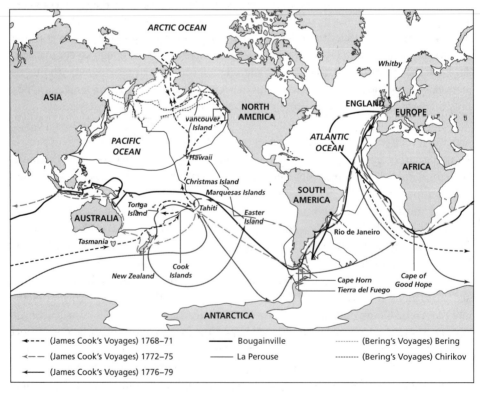

Map 11.4 Pacific explorations in the eighteenth century

establishing that Asia and North America were indeed separate landmasses, and that there was access from the Pacific to the Arctic Ocean. But he was not able to sight Alaska, and the advancing ice forced him to turn back. Embarking on a second and larger expedition in 1741, he sailed across the Bering Sea to Alaska, and explored the Aleutian Islands, but poor weather and illness forced the expedition to go ashore on an uninhabited island, where Bering died in 1741. In the 1740s, when Russian fur traders began to venture across the Bering Sea in search of pelts from seals, sea lions, and especially sea otters, they began to establish trading and hunting posts on land. Eventually, Russian settlements would be established on Kodiak Island and at Sitka. In the early nineteenth century, Russian trading posts would be established as far south as California, as well as in the Hawaiian Islands. But the distances involved were too great for the Russian outposts to be profitable, and in the end they would be abandoned to Britain and the United States.

Race, Slavery, and Empire

As we saw in Chapter 5, the discovery of new peoples provoked a variety of reactions among Europeans. Some, like las Casas, argued for their common humanity as children of God, while others perceived an essential inferiority that justified their exploitation and even their enslavement. These issues became particularly pressing in the eighteenth century, when encounters with unknown lands and peoples coincided with the Enlightenment's exploration of the nature of humanity and its relationship to the natural world. Enlightenment views on the varieties of humanity and their interaction were diverse, ambiguous, and even contradictory, sometimes even within the thought of the same person.

Inevitably, greater knowledge of other peoples and societies led to awareness that European attitudes, culture, and religion were neither universal nor unique. Since the first voyages of discovery in the fifteenth century, Christian Europeans had seen themselves as necessarily superior to non-Christian peoples, and this attitude was still standard in the eighteenth century. At the same time, one thread of enlightened thought set advanced, scientific European thought in contrast to the presumed ignorance and superstition of non-Europeans. In this way, the Christian–heathen dichotomy was reinforced by a civilized–savage one.

Another thread of enlightened thought led to a different analysis, however. Many Europeans were impressed by the rationality and tolerance they saw (or thought they saw) in India or China and compared it favourably with the intolerance and bigotry they condemned in European society. Still another thread is evident in Rousseau's conception of the "noble savage." When travellers like Bougainville wrote idyllic accounts of life in the south Pacific, they provided grist to the mill of those who condemned the unnatural, artificial character of "civilized" life. Even if a given non-European society did not fit the "noble savage" stereotype as well as the Tahitians did, the dire consequences for it of European interference provided ample material for critics of European societies.

The notion of "race" itself was ambiguous and contested. Sometimes the term was used as a marker of social distinction, as in references to a noble "race" whose superiority

HISTORICAL DEBATE

The Death of Captain Cook

The circumstances of Cook's death have been the subject of an extremely bitter academic debate. In the 1980s the cultural anthropologist Marshall Sahlins asserted that on his original landfall in January, Cook was received by the Hawaiians as the god Lono, the deity associated with fertility, peace, and games, because his arrival had coincided with a festival during which Lono was believed to arrive from the sea on a boat. After exploring the islands for a month, the expedition stopped again to repair a mast. When a small boat was stolen, Cook went ashore with several marines to force the return of the boat by taking a chief named Kalani'opu'u hostage, and it was then that he was killed. According to Sahlins, it was because the season of Lono had now passed that the prelogical, mystical, and "mythological" mental universe of the Hawaiians required the ritual death of his avatar.

In 1992, the Sri Lankan anthropologist Gananath Obeyesekere objected that none of Cook's crew mentioned that he had been taken for a deity (the earliest reference to the idea dates from the 1820s), and questioned Sahlins' claim that Cook's arrival coincided with the festival of Lono. Above all, however, he felt that Sahlins infantilized the Hawaiians by claiming that they mistook someone who was obviously not Hawaiian for one of their gods.

Sahlins responded that Obeyesekere erred in assuming that western "bourgeois" rationality was a universal standard; that the Hawaiians interpreted Cook's actions in terms of their own culturally constructed reality; and that, ironically, Obeyesekere had been culturally colonized by the rationality of western imperialists, which itself was a cultural construct. Below are excerpts from both sides of the debate, beginning with Obeyesekere's summary of Sahlins' position:

> When the great navigator and "discoverer" of Polynesia James Cook landed on the shores of Hawai'i . . . during the festival of Makahiki, he was greeted as the returning god Lono. This is fact; and it is incorporated into practically every history of Hawai'i. . . . I question this "fact," which I show was created in the European imagination of the eighteenth century and after. . . . To put it bluntly, I doubt that the natives created their European god; the Europeans created it for them. This "European god" is a myth of conquest, imperialism, and civilization—a triad that cannot be easily separated. . . .
>
> When Sahlins expounded his thesis . . . at Princeton University in 1983, I was completely taken aback at his assertion that when Cook arrived in Hawai'i the natives believed that he was their god Lono and called him Lono. Why so? Naturally my mind went back to my Sri Lankan and South Asian experience. I could not think of any parallel example in the long history of contact between foreigners and Sri Lankans or, for that matter, Indians. . . .
>
> . . . I do not object to mythic thought per se but to the assumption of lack of rational reflection implicit in the premise of prelogical, mystic, or mythic thought.

Furthermore, prelogicality and mysticality are, in the Western myth model, associated with "feeling," and feeling is opposed to thought. Thus, if natives think mystically, prelogically, or like children, they must, it is assumed, lack mature abilities.

Gananath Obeyesekere, *The Apotheosis of Captain Cook: European Mythmaking in the Pacific* (Princeton: Princeton University Press, 1997), pp. 3, 8, 15.

Presuming that as a native Sri Lankan he has a privileged insight into how Hawaiians thought, Obeyesekere . . . claims that for a long time now Western scholars have deceived themselves and others with the conceit that indigenous peoples, as victims of magical thinking and their own traditions, could do nothing but welcome their European "discoverers" as gods. . . . He says that [my writings on Cook] add new dimensions to the European myth of the indigenous people's irrationality.

. . . why should the reactions of South Asian peoples to European colonials—South Asians, who have been dealing with diverse and exotic foreigners for millennia—why should they be the basis for knowing Polynesians who, for just as long, had been isolated from any such experience? The underlying thesis is crudely ahistorical, a not-too-implicit notion that all natives so-called (by Europeans) are alike, most notably in their common cause for resentment.

. . . What guides my response is a concern to show that commonsense bourgeois realism, when taken as a historiographic conceit, is a kind of symbolic violence done to other times and other customs. I want to suggest that one cannot do good history, not even contemporary history, without regard for ideas, actions, and ontologies that are not and never were our own. Different cultures, different rationalities.

. . . The only difference between Obeyesekere's position and the garden variety of European imperialist ideology is . . . that he reverses their values. He would give the "natives" all that "rationality" Western people take to be the highest form of thought, while endowing the Europeans, including the outsider-anthropologists, with the kind of the mindless repetition of myth they have always despised—that is, as "native." Which is also to say that this self-proclaimed defence of "preliterate people who cannot speak for themselves" is imperialist hegemony masquerading as subaltern resistance.

The ultimate victims, then, are Hawaiian people. Western empirical good sense replaces their own view of things, leaving them with a fictional history and a pidgin ethnography. . . . Hawaiian people appear on stage as dupes of European ideology. Deprived thus of their agency and culture, their history reduced to a classic meaninglessness: they lived and suffered—and then they died.

Marshall Sahlins, *How "Natives" Think: About Captain Cook, for Example* (Chicago: University of Chicago Press, 1995), pp. 1, 4–5, 14, 197–8. Republished with permission of University of Chicago Press; permission conveyed through Copyright Clearance Center, Inc.

VOICES

Enlightenment and Empire

Bougainville's description of Tahiti inspired Diderot to write a fictional "Supplement" to it in the form of several dialogues, three of which are excerpted below. In the first, a Tahitian elder bids farewell to the visitors. The second recounts a conversation between a French priest and his Tahitian host Orou. In the third, two friends, A and B, discuss the lessons of Bougainville's voyage.

"Weep, unhappy Tahitians! Weep—not for the going but for the coming of those wicked and ambitious men. . . . There will come a day when they return, in one hand the scrap of wood you see hanging at this man's girdle [a crucifix], in the other the steel you see at that man's side, to bind you in chains. . . ."

Then, turning to Bougainville, he added: "And you, you leader of brigands . . . We are innocent, we are happy, and you can only harm our happiness. We follow the pure instinct of nature, and you have tried to erase its trace from our souls. Here, all things belong to all men, and you have preached some strange distinction between *thine* and *mine*. . . .

. . . Orou! You understand these men's language; explain to us . . . the words written on that strip of metal: *This country belongs to us.* This country yours! Why? . . . If one day a Tahitian were to land on your shores and carve on one of your stones . . . , 'This country belongs to Tahiti,' what would you think? . . . We have no wish to exchange what you call our ignorance for your useless knowledge. Everything that is good for us, and that we need, we already possess . . . (pp. 67–8).

Here the worthy chaplain complains of the shortness of his stay in Tahiti and thus the difficulty of getting to know the customs of its people—a people wise enough to have opted for mediocrity [that is, moderation], favoured enough by its climate to enjoy untroubled hours of ease, active enough to provide for all its basic needs, and indolent enough for its innocence, its tranquillity, and its happiness to be in no danger from the great leap forward of mind. . . . Labour and the fruits of labour were in common. The word *property* was very little used; the passion of love, being reduced to a simple physical appetite, produced none of the turmoil that it does with us . . . (p. 102).

A. How brief our legal codes would be, if we strictly adhered in them to the code of nature. How many vices and errors Man would be spared!

B. Shall I tell you in brief the history of almost all our woe? . . . Once there was a natural man: inside that man there was installed an artificial man, and within the cave a civil war began which lasted the whole of his life. Sometimes the natural man gains the upper hand, sometimes he is worsted by the moral and artificial man; an in either case the poor monster is plagued, torn, tormented, and stretched on the rack (p. 108).

Denis Diderot, *This is Not a Story and Other Stories*, trans. P.N. Furbank (Columbia: University of Missouri Press, 1991).

In 1770 Guillaume Thomas François Raynal (1713–96) published a hugely popular account of European overseas expansion. Although he condemned the evils of imperialism and slavery in general, he was especially critical of Spanish conduct in the New World, and frequently contrasted the wholesome lives of indigenous people with the rapacious conduct of their conquerors.

Nothing in the history of mankind in general and of the peoples in Europe in particular has been so significant as the discovery of the New World and the route to India by the Cape of Good Hope. These events marked the beginning of a revolution in the commerce and the power of nations, and in the way of life, the industry and the government of all peoples. It was from this moment on that the inhabitants of the most far-flung lands were brought closer together by new relationships and new needs. The productions of equatorial climes began to be consumed in polar regions; the manufactures of the North were transported to the South; the fabrics of the Orient became prized luxuries in the West; and everywhere, men exchanged their opinions, their laws, their customs, their sicknesses, their remedies, their virtues and their vices.

It was in the month of October, 1492, that . . . Columbus landed on one of the Bahama islands . . . taking possession of it in the name of Queen Isabella. No-one in Europe at that time imagined that there might be some injustice in seizing a country which was not inhabited by Christians. . . .

[The natives] displayed trust and gaiety; they brought fruit with them, and they carried the Spaniards on their shoulders to help them ashore. . . . the sailors sent ashore by Columbus to explore were fêted everywhere they went. . . .

Tell me, reader, do you see here civilized people arriving among savages, or savages received by civilized people? What does it matter that they were naked, that they lived in huts . . . , that they had neither a code of laws, nor a system of civil or criminal justice, provided that they were gentle, humane and beneficent, provided that they had the virtues which characterize man? . . . let us forget, if we can, or rather let us remember, that first moment of discovery, that first encounter between the two worlds, which makes us find our own so hateful.

Peter Jimack (ed.), *A History of the Two Indies: A Translated Selection of Writings from Raynal's Histoire philosophique et politique des établissements des Européens dans les Deux Indes* (Aldershot: Ashgate, 2006), pp. 1, 77.

was innate, a matter of heredity or "blood." Sometimes it was used to distinguish nationalities, as in "the Spanish race," or "the German race." It was also used in the context of religion: "the Jewish race," or "the Mohammedan race." Encounters with very different peoples and societies caused Europeans to rethink and qualify their notions of race, without arriving at any consistent view.

In keeping with the Enlightenment belief that discovering the "natural" laws governing society would facilitate reform, some thinkers turned their gaze on humans and sought to establish their place in the natural order. The French natural historian Buffon (Chapter 9) argued that all humans came from a single origin (monogenesis), and that physical differences such as skin colour, hair, and stature were attributable to different environments. Linnaeus, on the other hand, argued for multiple origins (polygenesis): initially identifying four varieties of humans—white Europeans, red Amerindians, black Africans, and brown Asians—he later added pygmies, wild men, and giants as separate categories, without coherently explaining their relationship with the first four types. Enlightenment thinking about race combined with Christian theology in some interesting and not always consistent ways. The Church, of course, upheld the monogenetic view that all humans had descended from Adam and Eve, and considered black people to be descendants of Noah's son Ham, who was cursed by his father. Among those who rejected biblical authority, however, some maintained that the races were fundamentally different in origin and nature. While Linnaeus wondered whether pygmies qualified as human beings, others believed that orangutans ought to be considered human, because they used tools and seemed to communicate. No consensus was reached regarding how different varieties of humans related to each other and to the natural world as a whole.

Practically speaking, theories about race had little impact in colonial societies, where the superiority of Europeans was simply assumed. Government policy usually tried to keep different "races" separate from each other. But this policy was difficult to enforce as long as the vast majority of European settlers were men. After a few generations, therefore, the Spanish and Portuguese American populations were a widely varied mixture of European, indigenous, and African ancestry, and the conflation of "race" with social and legal status led to a dizzying array of classification schemes. Although relationships between European women and non-European men were generally forbidden (and could be savagely punished), sexual relations between European men and "native" women were often accepted.

Relationships between European men and indigenous women were relatively rare in the British North American colonies, partly because more white women immigrated and partly because there were fewer indigenous people in the areas where the first colonies were located. Once slavery was established in the southern colonies, however, the sexual exploitation of African women by white men became increasingly common. In the Indian Ocean and Asia, Europeans were in a fundamentally different position, since as a rule European governments did not expect to establish colonies there. Few European women were willing to make the long and dangerous journey to live in climates that exposed them to various tropical diseases. In the port cities of the east there were substantial populations of mixed European and Asian descent. Nevertheless, the Dutch East India Company at times encouraged its employees to marry indigenous women as a way of forming ties that might facilitate trade, and building a population that was Dutch in character if not in ethnicity. Likewise, the English East India Company, at least in the seventeenth century, promoted intermarriage between its employees and Indian women.

It is impossible to consider the subjects of race and empire without returning to the issue of slavery. As we saw in Chapter 5, slavery was integral to the mining of precious metals in Peru, the cultivation of sugar in Brazil and the West Indies, and eventually the production of commodities such as indigo (used in dyes), coffee, tobacco, cacao, and cotton. European traders established fortified trading posts on the west coast of Africa, where they would purchase slaves from African or Arab merchants. Indeed, the profits made through the slave trade underpinned a number of powerful west African states in the early modern period. Slaving was by no means a vice unique to Europeans: the slave trade in Africa and the Indian Ocean was long-established and extensive. But European demand increased the numbers of people enslaved many times over. African slavery was essential to the operation of the Atlantic economy as it developed in the seventeenth and eighteenth centuries. By the later eighteenth century, the slaves exported from west Africa by the British alone were likely worth ten times the value of all other African exports combined. All European countries with a maritime presence were active participants: Britain, France, Portugal, Spain, the Dutch Republic, even Denmark and Sweden. British traders were especially prominent, for not only did they transport slaves to British colonies in the West Indies and North America, but in 1713 the Spanish government granted them the coveted *asiento*: the contract (previously held by Portuguese and then French merchants) as the sole suppliers of slaves to Spanish colonies in the New World.

It has been estimated that, between 1450 and 1800, 7.5 million African slaves were forcibly transported to the New World, three-quarters of them in the eighteenth century. Since up to 25 per cent of slaves died during the voyage from diseases contracted in the cramped and unsanitary conditions, it is likely that the total number of Africans enslaved reached 10 million. In the eighteenth century, approximately 400,000 slaves landed in British North America, 1 million in Spanish colonies, more than 1 million in the West Indies, and perhaps 3 million in Brazil. The demand for slaves in the mines and the sugar plantations was virtually inexhaustible, as their numbers were constantly being reduced by disease, extreme heat, and dangerous labour conditions. In the British West Indies in 1780, there were approximately 350,000 slaves, although well over 1 million had been imported since the mid-seventeenth century. In North America, however, the slave population was basically self-reproducing, probably because the climate was more temperate, and the labour less dangerous and exhausting. In addition, as North America was farther removed from the most important slave markets, owners there generally had to pay more for their slaves: thus it made economic sense to treat them somewhat less harshly and encourage natural reproduction.

The transfer of wealth from the Americas to Europe, made possible largely by African slavery, played an important role in Europe's transformation at the end of the eighteenth century and its rise to global dominance in the nineteenth and twentieth. It is difficult to distinguish cause and effect and to delineate the connections very precisely, as we will see below. Nevertheless, slaves clearly generated an enormous amount of wealth, both for plantation owners and for those involved in their transport and sale. Ports such as Bristol, Liverpool, Nantes, and Bordeaux profited immensely from the slave trade and its spinoff effects. The slave trade provided employment not only for the crews who sailed the ships, but for those who built and supplied the vessels, made the ropes, sails, and metal fittings, and so on. Financial services such as insurance and banking also prospered, as did all the businesses that supplied goods and services to those who made their fortunes in human trafficking.

In Europe the impact of slavery went beyond the purely economic. In early modern European society, "us versus them" prejudice had traditionally focused on religion: Christian versus Muslim, Christian versus Jew, and eventually Protestant versus Catholic. Although there had been slaves in Europe, they were never very numerous, were limited mostly to port cities in the Mediterranean, and for the most part were not African. The exponential growth of slavery in the Americas, however, and the fact that these slaves were almost exclusively black Africans, meant that black skin came to denote servility and inferiority.

Enlightenment views of slavery were as diverse, ambiguous, and conflicted as they were regarding race. One might assume that an intellectual and cultural movement ostensibly devoted to progress and liberty would be repulsed by the exploitation of human beings. And it is certainly not hard to find enlightened thinkers who expressed opposition to slavery, including Montesquieu, although he and most others fell short of advocating outright abolition. At the same time, Enlightenment thinkers who embraced secularism may have inadvertently helped to justify slavery by rejecting the idea that possession of a soul was the essential characteristic of humanity. Likewise, the impulse to study and classify mankind as an object of natural history may have helped to justify and perpetuate slavery. If there were in fact different species of man, as many natural historians believed, was it not reasonable to assume that some species were inferior and "natural slaves?" Aristotle himself had thought that slavery was the "natural" state for some peoples. Not all Enlightenment thinking about conformity to nature and natural laws was progressive.

Nor did religion offer any clear-cut guidance. The Bible seems to assume that slavery is a natural and inevitable feature of human society. Both supporters and opponents of slavery were able to find biblical justification for their positions, supporters pointing to the supposed "curse of Ham" and opponents embracing the spiritual equality emphasized in the New Testament.

Nevertheless, by the end of the eighteenth century, anti-slavery sentiment in Europe was clearly on the increase. In Britain, the Society for Effecting the Abolition of the Slave Trade was a mass movement that gathered thousands of signatures on petitions. One of its leading members was William Wilberforce (1759–1833), an independent MP who repeatedly introduced abolitionist legislation in Parliament. In 1807 Parliament finally abolished the slave trade in the British Empire, although slavery itself would not be abolished until 1833. In Britain and its North American colonies, much of the impetus for the abolition of slavery came from minority religious groups such as the Methodists, Moravians, and Quakers, but "mainstream" churches either remained on the sidelines or supported slavery. This was as true of Protestant churches in Britain and its colonies, the Dutch Republic and elsewhere as it was of the Catholic Church in France, Spain, and Portugal and their colonies.

In France, the efforts of Wilberforce and others helped to inspire the *Société des Amis des Noirs* (Society of the Friends of Black People), but its supporters were limited to a small elite that included Condorcet and the chemist Lavoisier. In 1794 the revolutionary government emancipated all slaves without explicitly banning the slave trade. The decision may have reflected revolutionary devotion to the principles of "liberty, equality, and fraternity," but it was also driven by an immense slave revolt in the French West Indian colony of St. Domingue (modern Haiti) that had begun in 1791. It was hardly the first slave revolt in the Americas; a number of revolts had even led to the formation of autonomous slave republics, some of which had entered into treaty relations with European powers. But the revolt in Haiti was far larger in scale, and under the brilliant leadership of Toussaint Louverture (1743–1803)—a former slave who had been freed in 1776—it effectively succeeded in establishing an independent country. In 1802 Napoleon Bonaparte revoked the emancipation decree and sent troops to Haiti that captured Louverture and deported him to France, where he died in prison the following year. But within a few months they had been defeated, and in January 1804 Haiti officially became the second republic in the Americas.

Empire, Industry, and the Beginnings of European Global Domination

By 1800 Europe was beginning to outpace the older and more populous civilizations of south and east Asia in terms of economic growth and development, and for next two centuries it would dominate the world both economically and politically. Many people have tried to explain how a relatively poor and backward outpost on the western fringe of the Eurasian landmass became the dominant power in the world. No doubt the Industrial Revolution played a key role; but even if that is true, we still need to ask why the Industrial Revolution took place in Europe (beginning in Britain), rather than some other part of the world that was equally wealthy and sophisticated, and even more populous. Kenneth Pomeranz points out that Japan, southeastern China, and India (in particular Bengal) all had highly developed proto-industries that compared favourably with Europe's in the eighteenth century.[5] In short, there was nothing in Europe's DNA that on its own can explain the "great divergence" of the nineteenth century. Some have argued that factors such as scientific innovation, property laws, and the "Protestant" work ethic set Europe apart from the rest of the world. Others have maintained that that the key lies in external rather than internal factors: specifically, in the exploitation of the wealth and resources of the Americas.

The sociologist Immanuel Wallerstein examines this question from a modified Marxist perspective in *The Modern World-System* (four volumes, 1974–2011). He argues that from the end of the Middle Ages on, Europe developed a number of characteristics and institutions that facilitated the growth of capitalism and would eventually bring about the Industrial Revolution, among them a relatively free labour pool, productive urban populations, and government policies that encouraged investment and long-distance trade. From the sixteenth century on, those factors allowed the countries of western Europe (the "core" region) to exploit the labour and resources of other regions (the "periphery"): primarily eastern Europe, the Americas, and eventually parts of Asia and Africa. Together, the core and periphery (along with a "semi-periphery" in southern Europe) constituted a "world-system" in which the unfree labour of the periphery generated the surplus that both made the Industrial Revolution possible and necessitated the continued exploitation of unfree labour in the periphery. Wallerstein's explanation thus combines external factors (the availability of labour and resources in the periphery) and internal factors (the socio-economic developments that allowed the core to establish its dominance in the first place).

Not everyone has agreed with Wallerstein's analysis, however. Some critics point out that the bulk of investment in industrial enterprises came from domestic sources, and that most of the profits from colonial sources were either spent on estates and conspicuous consumption, or invested in safe vehicles such as government debt. A slightly different perspective has been proposed by Pomeranz in *The Great Divergence: China, Europe, and the Making of the World Economy* (2000). Although he agrees with Wallerstein that the New World is the key to the puzzle, he argues that the elements that the New World supplied were not surplus value or capital to be invested, but raw materials and precious metals. Slavery was a crucial part of the process, as it reduced the cost of exploiting these resources. So too was the demographic decimation of indigenous populations, since it meant that a greater proportion of New World resources could be exploited to the benefit of Europeans. In short, a surplus of land in the Americas and the use of slave labour to exploit it freed up the land and labour in Europe that made the Industrial Revolution possible:

> Western Europeans' innovations in organizing for exploration and durable conquest and in creating institutions that combined entrepreneurship with intense coercion—plus favourable global conjunctions shaped by everything from Amerindians' vulnerability to smallpox to the massive supplies of New World silver . . . —gave them much of their edge. This, in turn, gave western Europeans a privileged position from which to endure the last century of the "biological old regime," with its multiple ecological challenges, and even continue expanding industries (from textiles to brewing to iron) that made great demands on the products of the land.[6]

Focusing on India rather than China, the historian Prasannan Parthasarathi agrees with Pomeranz on a number of points. Europe's "Great Divergence" cannot be explained by factors internal to Europe alone, since parts of India and China were equally advanced both economically and technologically. Britain's (and later Europe's) "great leap forward" is to be explained not by what they had that no one else did, but by two things that they lacked.

The first was Indian cotton: the world's most valuable manufactured product in the eighteenth century, and an essential trade good for those seeking to buy slaves in West Africa (in the early 1700s cotton accounted for roughly half of British exports to that region). Since Britain produced little that could be directly exchanged for Indian cotton cloth, the latter had to be purchased with gold and silver, much of which was mined in the New World. Mercantilist government policies drove the innovations required to establish a domestic cotton industry that could challenge India's, and those innovations would transform industry and the economy in the nineteenth century.

The second thing that Europe lacked was an unlimited supply of the wood that had been essential both for fuel and for building materials. The fact that, by the eighteenth century, deforestation had caused prices to rise significantly meant that the cotton mills of Lancashire had to be fuelled by coal, the exploitation of which spawned a host of related industrial developments, from the steam engine to railways to metallurgy. It was not that India or China lacked things that Europe had, but rather that India and China lacked the same incentive to innovate that Britain and Europe had:

> Neither of these pressures—shortages of wood and competition from global trade—was found in eighteenth-century India. From this perspective, British advances in cotton and coal were solutions to problems that did not exist in the Indian subcontinent. Only one, ecological problems due to deforestation and dwindling supplies of wood, operated in large parts of China. . . . In China, as in India, British technological breakthroughs in cotton and coal, while revolutionary, did not address major needs. Therefore, the British path of change was either unnecessary or inadequate for the pressing social, political and economic needs of the advanced parts of Asia in the eighteenth century.[7]

Chapter Conclusion

By the mid-1600s Europe was comparable to the Ottoman Empire, China, and India in terms of technology as well as economic and political development. By 1800, European colonies in the New World were so well-established and prosperous that they had begun to differentiate themselves from their respective mother countries. What was not yet apparent was that political subordination of the colonies to the metropoles would not be necessary for the continued growth and prosperity of either. Britain and the new US republic, for example, would establish close, mutually beneficial cultural and economic relations within a century of the latter's rebellion. The Americas would continue to be important to the European economy as sources of raw materials and markets for finished goods, but political subordination in the form of colonial rule was not required.

In 1650 European sailors and traders required the permission of local rulers to operate in the Indian Ocean and Asia. By 1800 European governments and trading companies had established a dominant position and were governing large areas either directly, as in the case of the English East India Company, or indirectly through indigenous figureheads.

In the nineteenth century, the British would use their economic muscle, and especially in the opium trade, to gain ascendancy over China. Clearly, the balance of power had shifted in favour of the Europeans.

By 1650 European sailors, merchants, and explorers were familiar with the lands and peoples of the Atlantic and Indian Ocean regions, but much of the globe was still *terra incognita*, including most of the Pacific region, the interior and the west coast of the Americas, and Australia and New Zealand. By 1800 these blank spaces on the map were well on the way to being filled in. Here too Europeans would establish their political, cultural, and economic dominance through mass immigration in the nineteenth and twentieth centuries, creating what Alfred Crosby called "Neo-Europes" in temperate zones: Canada, the United States, Australia, New Zealand, and Argentina, among others.[8]

Why this happened has been the subject of debate among historians, sociologists, and economists, among others. Some have argued that European civilization had unique features—science, capitalism, financial practices, democracy, or property rights, for example—that, alone or in combination, led to its global dominance. Others have argued that various parts of the world had at least some of these features, and perhaps others that Europeans did not; and that Europe was not distinct enough to explain the scale of the divergence. Moreover, many of the factors that supposedly distinguished Europe from other regions, such as democracy, were not present when the foundations of its dominance were being laid, and it is difficult to point to any scientific advances that contributed to European expansion before the nineteenth century.

What is certain is that Europe's global domination was made possible by a massive transfer of wealth from the New World to the Old, and that much of this wealth was achieved at the cost of great human suffering. Although some of this misery, including the decimation of indigenous populations by Old World pathogens, may have been unforeseen, the centuries-long enslavement of millions of Africans was no accident.

To most eighteenth-century Europeans, this expansion must have looked like progress, spreading the blessings of Christianity, civilization, and commerce to a benighted and backward world. Even at the time, however, some questioned the triumphalist narrative, and the civilization of Europe itself was profoundly influenced by Europeans' encounters with other cultures. For better or for worse, the European global hegemony that took shape in the early modern centuries, together with the more recent reactions to it, continues to define the contours of the world we all live in today.

Questions for Critical Thought

1. Why were supposedly "liberal" thinkers of the Enlightenment so contradictory, ambiguous, and conflicted on the subjects of race and slavery?
2. What sorts of impacts did the discovery of new lands and new peoples have on European society in the eighteenth century? Were they different from the impacts of earlier discoveries?

3. Was it inevitable that European colonies in the New World would become independent? What factors made independence more or less likely?
4. What accounts for Europe's global domination in the nineteenth and twentieth centuries? What role(s) did colonial empires and their resources play? How important was slavery to this process?

Weblinks

The Trans-Atlantic Slave Trade Database:
http://slavevoyages.org

Captain Cook Society:
http://www.captaincooksociety.com/

Further Reading

Cañizares-Esguerra, Jorge. *How to Write the History of the New World: Histories, Epistemologies, and Identities in the Eighteenth-Century Atlantic World*. Stanford: Stanford University Press, 2001. A fascinating study of the development of Creole identity.

Chaudhuri, K.N. *The Trading World of Asia and the English East India Company, 1660–1760*. Cambridge: Cambridge University Press, 1978. The definitive treatment of the impact of the East India Company and its place in Asian trade.

Davis, Ralph. *The Rise of the Atlantic Economies*. Ithaca: Cornell University Press, 1973. A classic survey.

Elliott, J.H. *Empires of the Atlantic World: Britain and Spain in America, 1492–1830*. New Haven: Yale University Press, 2006. An instructive comparison of British and Spanish experiences in the New World.

Ferguson, Niall. *Civilization: The West and the Rest*. London: Allen Lane, 2011. Argues that the Europe's rise to global domination can be attributed to its development of six "killer apps:" competition, science, democracy, medicine, consumerism, and the work ethic.

Hannaford, Ivan. *Race: The History of an Idea in the West*. Baltimore: Johns Hopkins University Press, 1996. A good starting point for the development of ideas about race.

Muthu, Sankar. *Enlightenment against Empire*. Princeton: Princeton University Press, 2003. An examination of Enlightenment thought questioning the value and legitimacy of empire.

Pagden, Anthony. *Lords of All the World: Ideologies of Empire in Spain, Britain, and France, c. 1500–c. 1800*. Baltimore: Johns Hopkins University Press, 1995. Explores different and evolving conceptions of colonial empires.

Parry, J.H. *Trade and Dominion: The European Overseas Empires in the Eighteenth Century*. London: Weidenfeld and Nicolson, 1971. A comprehensive overview, organized thematically.

Thomas, Hugh. *The Slave Trade: The Story of the Atlantic Slave Trade, 1440–1870*. New York: Simon and Schuster, 1997. A massive and detailed account.

Wallerstein, Immanuel. *World-Systems Analysis: An Introduction*. Durham: Duke University Press, 2004. A concise overview of world-systems analysis, although light on historical content.

Notes

1. Previously the port of Seville had housed the government monopoly on trade, but the river Guadalquivir began to silt up badly in the seventeenth century, and trade was transferred to the port of Càdiz, nearer the mouth of the river.
2. This is the origin of the slang term "limey" for English people.
3. The Norwegian explorer Roald Amundsen became the first to complete the Northwest Passage entirely by ship, sailing from east to west between 1903 and 1906. The first ship to complete the voyage in one season was the RCMP schooner St. Roch, which sailed from west to east in 1944. In recent years, climate change and advances in shipbuilding have opened the possibility of commercial transit.
4. The two expeditions met near the present-day city of Vancouver. In recognition of the peaceful resolution of the encounter, the body of water was named English Bay, while the shoreline to the south was named Spanish Banks, names that are still in use today.
5. Kenneth Pomeranz, *The Great Divergence: China, Europe, and the Making of the Modern World Economy* (Princeton: Princeton University Press, 2000).
6. Pomeranz, *The Great Divergence*, p. 285.
7. Prasannan Parthasarathi, *Why Europe Grew Rich and Asia Did Not: Global Economic Divergence, 1600–1850* (Cambridge: Cambridge University Press, 2011), p. 203.
8. Alfred W. Crosby, *Ecological Imperialism: The Biological Expansion of Europe, 900–1900* (Cambridge: Cambridge University Press, 1986), pp. 2–3, 6–7, 146–9, 302–8.

Epilogue

On May 5, 1789, amid the regal splendour of the palace of Versailles, King Louis XVI of France opened the first meeting of the Estates-General since 1615. Although no one knew it at the time, this was the beginning of French Revolution. We saw in Chapter 10 how, in their efforts to buttress their privileges, nobles and clergy had unwittingly given voice to forces that soon escaped their control. Within a matter of weeks, the delegates of the Third Estate declared themselves to constitute a National Assembly representing not a single order of French society, but the nation itself. Their goal was to establish a limited monarchy of the kind they believed to exist on the other side of the English Channel, one in which the monarch would govern in partnership not just with the nobles and clergy, as in the past, but with the broader elite made up of men of property and substance like themselves. Ordinary peasants and workers soon discovered that they too could influence the course of events, whether through passive resistance or through active participation in the political process.

Over the next twenty years, the sequence of events unleashed at Versailles would put an end to the political world of early modern Europe. In hindsight, the forces that brought about this political upheaval can be seen emerging with increasing clarity throughout the eighteenth century. At the same time, equally profound, if less dramatic, changes in other areas had been slowly, unevenly transforming economic and social life: innovations in agriculture, a new demographic regime, the beginnings of the Industrial Revolution, expanding education and literacy, a new mental universe dominated by science rather than theology, and Europe's growing global dominance. Having originated centuries earlier, these aspects of the modern world had gradually taken shape over the course of the early modern era.

It has been a central argument of this book that a crucial point was passed somewhere around the middle of the seventeenth century. We began with the notion of Christendom: the ideal that dominated medieval thinking about religion, government, and culture. Yet by 1650 there was virtually nothing left of it. Renaissance humanism had driven a wedge between the mental universe of the medieval scholastics and that of the increasingly literate urban elite, while the Reformations had shattered the religious unity of Christendom. Through it all, what would eventually emerge as the modern state began to take shape. Indeed, the passion and violence unleashed by religious division played a central role in the ongoing development of the state. Attempting to remedy the deficiencies in the scientific paradigms inherited from ancient Greece, by 1700 European mathematicians and scientists had discarded them completely, dealing another blow to the religious authority of the established churches.

At the same time, Europe had been developing from a relatively poor backwater at the end of the Middle Ages to the point where, by 1800, it was beginning to assert its dominance over much older and traditionally much wealthier civilizations in the Middle

East and Asia. This dominance was due in large part to the unleashing of unimagined productive capacity in the Industrial Revolution, which over the course of the nineteenth century would spread quickly throughout Europe from its origins in Britain. What made the Industrial Revolution itself possible was the massive transfer of wealth from the New World to the Old, beginning in the late fifteenth century. Although the precise mechanics of the process are still subject to debate, what cannot be debated is that this wealth was achieved at the cost of great human misery in the form of slavery. Although the age of European global domination has now passed, the world we live in today continues to be shaped by its legacies, both positive and negative.

The emergence of the modern state was one of three "big ideas" with which this book began. Starting in the late Middle Ages, and continuing through the sixteenth and seventeenth centuries, the state shook off the claims to universal power of both the medieval emperors and the universal Church, as well as the incipient anarchy of feudalism. In the course of the eighteenth century, even rulers in many cases came to distinguish the state from themselves, as an abstract entity with interests and a logic of its own. In this context, the French Revolution was the state's declaration of independence from monarchy, and the beginning of its association with the nation—an association that would flourish in the nineteenth and twentieth centuries.

The second "big idea" was the development of modern notions of individualism. With the Renaissance, the individual began to acquire a value and dignity that went beyond his or her possession of an immortal soul. The Protestant concept of the "priesthood of all believers" put individual Christians in a direct and unmediated relationship with God, and although this was not the intention of the reformers who developed it, eventually contributed to the notion that the lives of all people were of equal value. Eventually, conflicts between rulers and subjects in the sixteenth and seventeenth centuries would lead to the articulation of human rights that even monarchs would not be permitted to abrogate. In the course of the Enlightenment, these rights were increasingly seen as universal, as "Rights of Man," not contingent on time and place in the way that, for example, the "rights of free-born Englishmen" had been. In the course of the French Revolution, these rights would be recognized in the Declaration of the Rights of Man and the Citizen, and some revolutionary thinkers would even extend them to women. By modern standards, of course, these rights were extremely limited. It would be a long time before political rights were extended to all men, let alone to women. And although the idea that indigenous people around the world and the millions of Africans held in slavery also had rights was beginning to take hold, its supporters were still in the minority at the end of the eighteenth century.

Finally, the third "big idea" that came into being in early modern Europe was the notion of progress. Throughout the Middle Ages, the Renaissance, and the Reformations, if people thought of progress at all, what they imagined was a return to some lost ideal: the Garden of Eden, the Roman Empire, or perhaps the early church. The passage of time brought decay rather than improvement, and the best one could hope for was to go back to an earlier time. Although the Scientific Revolution at first provoked doubt and uncertainty, eventually it became clear that that the knowledge of the ancients had in fact been surpassed. Enlightenment thinkers' application of "scientific" thought to human society and human nature persuaded people like Condorcet that human perfectibility was not only possible but inevitable, and in the nineteenth century progress would come to be considered a universal law, like Newton's law of gravity.

One can believe that on the whole these developments were generally positive without being blind to their negative aspects and consequences. The power of the modern state dedicated to the protection and expansion of human rights has brought great benefits to many, many people. On the other hand, when the power of the state is perverted and used to enforce a particular view of a nation or ideology (as in Nazi Germany, or the Soviet Union under Stalin, or Cambodia under the Khmer Rouge), the rights of the individual can be suppressed rather than protected and enhanced by it. This possibility was inherent in Rousseau's idea of the "General Will," and became reality when the moderate reforms of the French Revolution gave way to the "Reign of Terror." Likewise, the assumption that progress is more or less automatic, seemingly borne out by previously unimaginable scientific and technological advances, has brought tremendous benefits to great numbers of people. On the other hand, we have had to come to grips with the darker side of this progress, from pollution and environmental degradation to climate change and the possibility of nuclear annihilation.

Throughout this book, I have tried to balance the historian's tasks: to understand the past on its own terms, without reference to later norms and standards; but at the same time to point out how elements of the present originated in the past, and how we got here from there. If we in the twenty-first century are better able to perceive both the good and the bad (by our standards) in early modern Europe, this ability does not reflect any intellectual or moral superiority on our part: it is simply the product of historical and cultural perspective.

Index